THE RECORDS OF THE FEDERAL CONVENTION OF 1787

Volume II

THE RECORDS
OF THE
FEDERAL CONVENTION
OF 1787

EDITED BY

MAX FARRAND

REVISED EDITION IN FOUR VOLUMES

VOLUME II

NEW HAVEN AND LONDON · YALE UNIVERSITY PRESS

Second printing, 1974.

International standard book number: 0–300–0448–6 (cloth)
0–300–081–2 (paper)

Printed in the United States of America by
The Murray Printing Co.,
Forge Village, Massachusetts.

Published in Great Britain, Europe, and Africa by
Yale University Press, Ltd., London.
Distributed in Latin America by Kaiman & Polon, Inc., New York City; in Australasia and Southeast Asia by John Wiley & Sons Australasia Pty. Ltd., Sydney; in India by UBS Publishers' Distributors Pvt., Ltd., Delhi; in Japan by John Weatherhill, Inc., Tokyo.

SATURDAY, JULY 14, 1787.

JOURNAL

Saturday July 14. 1787.

It was moved and seconded to agree to the following proposition, namely.

That to secure the liberties of the States already confederated, the number of representatives in the first branch from the States which shall hereafter be established, shall never exceed the representatives from such of the thirteen United States as shall accede to this Confederation.

On the question to agree to the proposition

it passed in the negative [Ayes — 4; noes — 5; divided — 1.]

It was moved and seconded to reconsider the two propositions reported from the grand Committee, and agreed by the House to stand part of the report — entered on the Journal of the 6. instant

It was moved and seconded to postpone the second clause of the report from the grand Committee, entered on the Journals of the 6 instant, in order to take up the following. namely

That the second branch of the Legislature shall have Thirty six Members of which number

New Hampshire shall have	2.
Massachusetts	4
Rhode Island	1
Connecticut	3
New York	3
New Jersey	2
Pennsylvania	4
Delaware	1
Maryland	3
Virginia	5

No Carolina 3
So Carolina 3
Georgia .... 2.

On the question to postpone, it passed in the negative. [Ayes—4; noes—6.][1]

and then the House adjourned till Monday

DETAIL OF AYES AND NOES

	New Hampshire	Massachusetts	Rhode Island	Connecticut	New York	New Jersey	Pennsylvania	Delaware	Maryland	Virginia	North Carolina	South Carolina	Georgia	Questions	Ayes	Noes	Divided
[154]		aye		aye		no	dd	aye	aye	no	no	no	no	That the number of representatives in ye first branch from the States hereafter to be established shall not exceed the representatives from the States already confederated	4	5	1
[155]		no		no		no	aye	no	aye	aye	no	aye	no	To postpone the 2d clause of the report from the grand Committee of the 6. instant in order to take up the substitute offd by Mr Pinckney	4	6	

MADISON

Saturday. July 14. in Convention

Mr. L. Martin called for the question on the whole report, including the parts relating to the origination of money bills, and the equality of votes in the 2d. branch.

Mr. Gerry. wished before the question should be put, that the attention of the House might be turned to the dangers apprehended from Western States. He was for admitting them

[1] Vote 155, Detail of Ayes and Noes, which notes that this substitute was offered "by Mr. Pinkney".

on liberal terms, but not for putting ourselves into their hands. They will if they acquire power like all men, abuse it. They will oppress commerce, and drain our wealth into the Western Country. To guard agst. these consequences, he thought it necessary to limit the number of new States to be admitted into the Union, in such a manner, that they should never be able to outnumber the Atlantic States.[2] He accordingly moved "that in order to secure the ⟨liberties of the⟩ States already confederated, the ⟨number of⟩ Representatives in the 1st. branch ⟨of the States which shall hereafter be established⟩ shall never exceed in number, the Representatives from such of the States ⟨as shall accede to this confederation.⟩ [3]

Mr. King. seconded the motion.

Mr. Sherman, thought there was no probability that the number of future States would exceed that of the Existing States. If the event should ever happen, it was too remote to be taken into consideration at this time. Besides We are providing for our posterity, for our children & our grand Children, who would be as likely to be citizens of new Western States, as of the old States. On this consideration alone, we ought to make no such discrimination as was proposed by the motion.

Mr. Gerry. If some of our children should remove, others will stay behind, and he thought it incumbent on us to provide for their interests. There was a rage for emigration from the Eastern States to the Western Country and he did not wish those remaining behind to be at the mercy of the Emigrants. Besides foreigners are resorting to that Country, and it is uncertain what turn things may take there. — On the question for agreeing to the Motion of Mr. Gerry, ⟨it passed in the negative.⟩

Mas. ay. Cont. ay. N. J. no Pa. divd. Del: ay. Md. ay. Va. no. N. C. no. S. C. no. Geo. no. [Ayes — 4; noes — 5; divided — 1.]

Mr. Rutlidge proposed to reconsider the ⟨two propositions touching the originating of⟩ money bills ⟨in the first⟩ & the equality of votes in the second branch.

---

[2] See Appendix A, CCCXXXII. [3] Revised from *Journal*.

Mr. Sherman was for the question on the whole at once. It was he said a conciliatory plan, it had been considered in all its parts, a great deal of time had been spent on it, and if any part should now be altered, it would be necessary to go over the whole ground again.

Mr. L. Martin urged the question on the whole. He did not like many parts of it. He did not like having two branches, nor the inequality of votes in the 1st. branch. He was willing however to make trial of the plan, rather than do nothing.[4]

Mr. Wilson traced the progress of the Report through its several stages, remarking yt when on the question concerning an equality of votes, the House was divided, our Constituents had they voted as their representatives did, would have stood as $\frac{2}{3}$ agst. the equality, and $\frac{1}{3}$ only in favor of it. This fact would ere long be known, and it will appear that this fundamental point has been carried by $\frac{1}{3}$ agst. $\frac{2}{3}$. What hopes will our Constituents entertain when they find that the essential principles of justice have been violated in the outset of the Governmt. As to the privilege of originating money bills, it was not considered by any as of much moment, and by many as improper in itself. He hoped both clauses wd. be reconsidered. The equality of votes was a point of such critical importance, that every opportunity ought to be allowed, for discussing and collecting the mind of the Convention on it.

Mr. L. Martin denies that there were $\frac{2}{3}$ agst. the equality of votes. The States that please to call themselves large, are the weekest in the Union. Look at Masts. Look at Virga. Are they efficient States? He was for letting a separation take place if they desired it. He had rather there should be two Confederacies, than one founded on any other principle than an equality of votes in the 2d branch at least.

Mr Wilson was not surprised that those who say that a minority does more than the majority should say that that minority is stronger than the majority. He supposed the next assertion will be that they are richer also, though he hardly

[4] See Appendix A, CXCII.

expected it would be persisted in when the States shall be called on for taxes & troops —

Mr. Gerry also animadverted on Mr. L. Martins remarks on the weakness of Masts. He favored the reconsideration with a view not of destroying the equality of votes; but of providing that the States should vote per capita. which he said would prevent the delays & inconveniences that had been experienced in Congs. and would give a national aspect & Spirit to the management of business. He did not approve of a reconsideration of the clause relating to money bills. It was of great consequence. It was the corner stone of the accomodation. If any member of the Convention had the exclusive privilege of making propositions, would any one say that it would give him no advantage over other members. The Report was not altogether to his mind. But he would agree to it as it stood rather than throw it out altogether.

The reconsideration being tacitly agreed to

Mr. Pinkney moved that instead of an equality of votes the States should be represented in the 2d branch as follows: N. H. by. 2. members. Mas 4. R. I. 1. Cont. 3. N. Y. 3. N. J. 2. Pa. 4. Del 1. Md. 3. Virga. 5. N. C. 3. S. C. 3. Geo. 2. making in the whole 36.[5]

Mr. Wilson seconds the motion

Mr. Dayton. The smaller States can never give up their equality. For himself he would in no event yield that security for their rights.

Mr. Sherman urged the equality of votes not so much as a security for the small States; as for the State Govts. which could not be preserved unless they were represented & had a negative in the Genl. Government. He had no objection to the members in the 2d b. voting per capita, as had been suggested by (Mr. Gerry)

Mr — ⟨Madison⟩ concurred in the motion ⟨of Mr. Pinkney⟩ as a reasonable compromise.

Mr. Gerry said he should like the motion, but could see no hope of success. An accomodation must take place, and

[5] See Appendix A, CLVIII (7), CCXXXVIII.

it was apparent from what had been seen that it could not do so on the ground of the motion. He was utterly against a partial confederacy, leaving other States to accede or not accede; as had been intimated.

Mr. King said it was always with regret that he differed from his colleagues, but it was his duty to differ from (Mr Gerry) on this occasion. He considered the proposed Government as substantially and formally, a General and National Government over the people of America. There never will be a case in which it will act as a federal Government on the States and not on the individual Citizens. And is it not a clear principle that in a free Govt. those who are to be the objects of a Govt. ought to influence the operations of it? What reason can be assigned why the same rule of representation sd. not prevail in the 2d. branch as in the 1st.? He could conceive none. On the contrary, every view of the subject that presented itself, seemed to require it. Two objections had been raised agst. it, drawn 1. from the terms of the existing compact. 2. from a supposed danger to the smaller States. — As to the first objection he thought it inapplicable. According to the existing confederation, the rule by which the public burdens is to be apportioned is *fixed*, and must be pursued. In the proposed Govermt. it cannot be fixed, because indirect taxation is to be substituted. The Legislature therefore will have full discretion to impose taxes in such modes & proportions as they may judge expedient. As to the 2d. objection, he thought it of as little weight. The Genl. Governt. can never wish to intrude on the State Governts. There could be no temptation. None had been pointed out. In order to prevent the interference of measures which seemed most likely to happen, he would have no objection to throwing all the State debts into the federal debt, making one aggregate debt of about 70,000,000, of dollars, and leaving it to be discharged by the Genl. Govt. — According to the idea of securing the State Govts. there ought to be three distinct legislative branches. The 2d. was admitted to be necessary, and was actually meant, to check the 1st. branch, to give more wisdom, system, & stability to the Govt. and ought

clearly as it was to operate on the people to be proportioned to them. For the third purpose of securing the States, there ought then to be a 3d. branch, representing the States as such and guarding by equal votes their rights & dignities. He would not pretend to be as thoroughly acquainted with his immediate Constituents as his colleagues, but it was his firm belief that Masts. would never be prevailed on to yield to an equality of votes. In N. York (he was sorry to be obliged to say any thing relative to that State in the absence of its representatives, but the occasion required it), in N. York he had seen that the most powerful argument used by the considerate opponents to the grant of the Impost to Congress, was pointed agst. the viccious constitution of Congs. with regard to representation & suffrage. He was sure that no Govt. could last that was not founded on just principles. He preferred the doing of nothing, to an allowance of an equal vote to all the States. It would be better he thought to submit to a little more confusion & convulsion, than to submit to such an evil. It was difficult to say what the views of different Gentlemen might be. Perhaps there might be some who thought no Governmt. co-extensive with the U. States could be established with a hope of its answering the purpose. Perhaps there might be other fixed opinions incompatible with the object we were pursuing. If there were, he thought it but candid that Gentlemen would speak out that we might understand one another.

Mr. Strong. The Convention had been much divided in opinion. In order to avoid the consequences of it, an accomodation had been proposed. A Committee had been appointed; and though some of the members of it were averse to an equality of votes, a Report has been made in favor of it. It is agreed on all hands that Congress are nearly at an end. If no Accommodation takes place, the Union itself must soon be dissolved. It has been suggested that if ⟨we⟩ can not come to any general agreement the principal States may form & recommend a scheme of Government. But will the small States in that case ever accede it. Is it probable that the large States themselves will under such circumstances embrace

and ratify it. He thought the small States had made a considerable concession in the article of money bills, and that ⟨they⟩ might naturally expect some concessions on the other side. From this view of the matter he was compelled to give his vote for the Report taken all together.

Mr ⟨Madison⟩ expressed his apprehensions that if the proper foundation of Governmt was destroyed, by substituting an equality in place of a proportional Representation, no ⟨proper⟩ superstructure would be raised.[6] If the small States really wish for a Government armed with the powers necessary to secure their liberties, and to enforce obedience on the larger members as well as on themselves he could not help thinking them extremely mistaken in their means. He reminded them of the consequences of laying the existing confederation on improper principles. All the principal parties to its compilation, joined immediately in mutilating & fettering the Governmt. in such a manner that it has disappointed every hope placed on it. He appealed to the doctrine & arguments used by themselves on ⟨a former occasion.⟩ It had been very properly observed by (Mr. Patterson) that Representation was an expedient by which the meeting of the people themselves was rendered unnecessary; and that the representatives ought therefore to bear a proportion to the votes which their constituents if convened, would respectively have. Was not this remark as applicable to one branch of the Representation as to the other? But it had been said that the Governt. would ⟨in its operation⟩ be partly federal, partly national; that altho' in the latter respect the Representatives of the people ought to be in proportion to the people: yet in the former it ought to be according to the number of States. If there was any ⟨solidity⟩[7] in this distinction he was ready to abide by it, if there was none it ought to be abandoned. In all cases where the Genl. Governt. is to act on the people, let the people be represented and the votes be proportional. In all cases where the Governt. is to act on the States as such, in like manner as Congs. now act

[6] Crossed out "that would either fulfill the public wishes, or a credit to the Convention".

[7] Crossed out "force or ability".

on them, let the States be represented & the votes be equal. This was the true ground of compromise if there was any ground at all. But he denied that there was any ground. He called for a single instance in which the Genl. Govt. was not to operate on the people individually. The practicability of making laws, with coercive sanctions, for the States as political bodies, had been exploded on all hands. He observed that the people of the large States would in some way or other secure to themselves a weight proportioned to the importance accruing from their superior numbers. If they could not effect it by a proportional representation in the Govt. they would probably accede to no Govt. which did not in great measure depend for its efficacy on their voluntary cooperation; in which case they would indirectly secure their object. The existing confederacy proved that where the acts of the Genl. Govt. were to be executed by the particular Govts the latter had a weight in proportion to their importance No one would say that either in Congs. or out of Congs. Delaware had equal weight with Pensylva. If the latter was to supply ten times as much money as the former, and no compulsion could be used, it was of ten times more importance, that she should furnish voluntarily the supply.[8] In the Dutch Confederacy the votes of the Provinces were equal. But Holland, which supplies about half the money, governed the whole republic. He enumerated the objections agst an equality of votes in the 2d. branch, notwithstanding the proportional representation in the first. 1. the minority could negative the will of the majority of the people. 2. they could extort measures by making them a condition of their assent to other necessary measures. 3. they could obtrude measures on the majority by virtue of the peculiar powers which would be vested in the Senate. 4. the evil instead of being cured by time, would increase with every new State that should be admitted, as they must all be admitted on the principle of equality. 5. the perpetuity it would give to the ⟨preponderance of the⟩ Northn. agst. the Southn. Scale was a serious consideration. It

[8] See Appendix A, CLVIII (38).

seemed now to be pretty well understood that the real difference of interests lay, not between the large & small but between the N. & Southn. States. The institution of slavery & its consequences formed the line of discrimination. There were 5 States on the South, 8 on the Northn. side of this line. Should a proportl. representation take place it was true, the N. side would still outnumber the other: but not in the same degree, at this time; and every day would tend towards an equilibrium.

Mr. Wilson would add a few words only. If equality in the 2d. branch was an error that time would correct, he should be less anxious to exclude it being sensible that perfection was unattainable in any plan: but being a fundamental and a perpetual error, it ought by all means to be avoided. A vice in the Representation, like an error in the first concoction, must be followed by disease, convulsions, and finally death itself. The justice of the general principle of proportional representation has not in argument at least been yet contradicted. But it is said that a departure from it so far as to give the States an equal vote in one branch of the Legislature is essentail to their preservation. He had considered this position maturely, but could not see its application. That the States ought to be preserved he admitted. But does it follow that an equality of votes is necessary for the purpose? Is there any reason to suppose that if their preservation should depend more on the large than on the small States, the security of the States agst. the Genl. Government would be diminished? Are the large States less attached to their existence, more likely to commit suicide, than the small? An equal vote then is not necessary as far as he can conceive: and is liable, among other objections to this insuperable one: The great fault of the existing Confederacy is its inactivity. It has never been a complaint agst. Congs. that they governed overmuch. The complaint has been that they have governed too little. To remedy this defect we were sent here. Shall we effect the cure by establishing an equality of votes, as is proposed? no; this very equality carries us directly to Congress: to the system which it is our duty to rectify. The small States cannot indeed act, by virtue of this equality, but they may controul

the Govt. as they have done in Congs. This very measure is here prosecuted by a minority of the people of America. Is then the object of the Convention likely to be accomplished in this way? Will not our Constituents say? we sent you to form an efficient Govt and you have given us one more complex indeed, but having all the weakness of the former Govērnt. He was anxious for uniting all the States under one Govērnt. He knew there were some respectable men who preferred three confederacies, united by offensive & defensive alliances. Many things may be plausibly said, some things may be justly said, in favor of such a project. He could not however concur in it himself; but he thought nothing so pernicious as bad first principles.

Mr. Elseworth asked two questions one of Mr. Wilson, whether he had ever seen a good measure fail in Congs. for want of a majority of States in its favor? He had himself never known such an instance: the other of Mr. ⟨Madison⟩ whether a negative lodged with a majority of the States even the smallest, could be more dangerous than the qualified negative proposed to be lodged in a single Executive Magistrate, who must be taken from some one State?

Mr. Sherman, signified that his expectation was that the Genl. Legislature would in some cases act on the *federal principle*, of requiring quotas. But he thought it ought to be empowered to carry their own plans into execution, if the States should fail to supply their respective quotas.

On the question for agreeing to Mr Pinkney's motion for allowing N. H. 2. Mas. 4. &c — ⟨it passed in the negative⟩

Mas. no. Mr. King ay. Mr. Ghorum absent. Cont. no. N. J. no. Pa. ay. Del. no. Md. ay. Va. ay. N. C. no. S. C. ay Geo. no. [Ayes — 4; noes — 6.]

Adjourned,

KING

Memorandum

July 15. 87

About twelve days since the convention appointed a Grand Comee. consisting of Gerry, Elsworth, Yates, Patterson, Franklin, Bedford, Martin, Mason, Davie, Rutledge & Baldwin to adjust the Representation in the two Brs. of the Legislature of the US — They reported yt. every 40,000 Inhabs. taken agreeably to the Resolution of Cong. of ye. 18 Ap. 1783 shd. send one member to the first Br of the Legislatr. yt. this Br. shd. originate exclusively money Bills, & also originate ye. appropiations of money — and that in ye Senate or upper Br. each state shd. have one vote & no more — the Representation as to the first Br. was twice recommitted altho not to the same committee, finally it was agreed yt. Taxation of the direct sort & Representation shd. be in direct proportion with each other — that the first Br. shd. consist of 65 memb: viz. N H. 3: M. 8: R I. 1: C. 5: NY. 6: N J. 4: P. 8: D. 1: M. 6: V. 10: NC. 5: SC. 5: G. 3: and that the origination of money Bills and the Appropriations of money shd. belong in the first instance to yt. Br. but yt. in the Senate or 2d. Br. each State shd. have an equal Vote — in this situation of the Report it was moved by S. Car. that in the formation of the 2d. Br. instead of an equality of Votes among the States, that N H shd. have 2: M. 4: R I. 1: C. 3. N Y 3. N J. 2. P 4. D 1. M 3. V 5. N C. 3. S C. 3 G 2. Total 36 —
on the question to agree to this apportionment, instead of the equality (Mr. Gorham being absent) Mass. Con. N Jer. Del. N Car & Georg. No —
Penn. Mar. Virg. & S Car. Ay —
This Question was taken and to my mortification by the Vote of Mass lost on the 14th. July — [9]

[9] [Endorsed:] 15 July | Senate. shall the States be | Equal in the number of Senators, | inequality lost by vote | of Mass —

MONDAY, JULY 16, 1787.

JOURNAL

Monday July 16. 1787.

The question being taken on the whole of the report from the grand Committee as amended
it passed in the affirmative [Ayes — 5; noes—4; divided—1.]
and is as follows, namely,

Resolved — That in the original formation of the Legislature of the United States the first Branch thereof shall consist of Sixty five members — of which number

New Hampshire shall send	Three
Massachusetts	Eight
Rhode Island	One
Connecticut	Five
New York	Six
New Jersey	four
Pennsylvania	Eight
Delaware	One
Maryland	Six
Virginia	Ten
North Carolina	Five
South Carolina	Five
Georgia	Three.

But as the present situation of the States may probably alter in the number of their inhabitants the Legislature of the United States shall be authorized from time to time to apportion the number of representatives: and in case any of the States shall hereafter be divided, or enlarged by addition of territory, or any two or more States united, or any New States created within the limits of the United States the Legislature of the United States shall possess authority to regulate the

number of representatives: in any of the foregoing cases upon the principle of their number of inhabitants, according to the provisions hereafter mentioned, namely,

Provided always that representation ought to be proportioned according to direct Taxation; and in order to ascertain the alteration in the direct Taxation, which may be required from time to time by the changes in the relative circumstances of the States — Resolved that a Census be taken within six years from the first Meeting of the Legislature of the United States, and once within the term of every Ten years afterwards of all the inhabitants of the United States in the manner and according to the ratio recommended by Congress in their resolution of April 18. 1783 — and that the Legislature of the United States shall proportion the direct Taxation accordingly.

Resolved That all Bills for raising or appropriating money, and for fixing the salaries of the Officers of the Government of the United States shall originate in the first Branch of the Legislature of the United States, and shall not be altered or amended by the second Branch — and that no money shall be drawn from the Public Treasury but in pursuance of appropriations to be originated by the first Branch.

Resolved That in the second Branch of the Legislature of the United States each State shall have an equal vote.

It was moved and seconded to agree to the first clause of the sixth resolution reported from the Committee of the whole House namely

"That the national Legislature ought to possess the legisla-
"tive rights vested in Congress by the confederation"

which passed unanimously in the affirmative

It was moved and seconded to commit the second clause of the Sixth resolution reported from the Committee of the whole House

which passed in the negative [Ayes — 5; noes — 5.]

[To adjourn Ayes — 5; noes — 5.
To adjourn Ayes — 7; noes — 2; divided — 1.][1]

[1] Votes 158, 159, Detail of Ayes and Noes.

And then the House adjourned till to-morrow at 11 o'Clock A. M.

DETAIL OF AYES AND NOES

	New Hampshire	Massachusetts	Rhode Island	Connecticut	New York	New Jersey	Pennsylvania	Delaware	Maryland	Virginia	North Carolina	South Carolina	Georgia	Questions	Ayes	Noes	Divided
[156]		dd		aye		aye	no	aye	aye	no	aye	no	no	To agree to the whole of the report from the grand Committee	5	4	1
[157]		no		aye		no	no	no	aye	aye	no	aye	aye	To commit the second Clause of the 6. resolution from the Committee of the whole House.	5	5	
[158]		no		no		aye	aye	no	aye	aye	aye	no	no	To adjourn	5	5	
[159]		aye		no		aye	aye	no	aye	aye	aye	aye	dd	To adjourn	7	2	1

MADISON

Monday, July 16. In Convention

On the question for agreeing to the whole ⟨Report as amended &⟩[2] including the equality of votes in the 2d. branch. ⟨it passed in the Affirmative⟩

Mas. divided Mr. Gerry, Mr. Strong. ay. Mr. King Mr. Ghorum no. Cont. ay. N. J. ay. Pena. no. Del. ay. Md. ay. Va. no. N. C. ay. Mr. Spaight no S. C. no. Geo. no. [Ayes — 5; noes — 4; divided — 1.] ⟨(Here enter the whole in the words entered in the Journal July 16)⟩

⟨The whole, thus passed is in the words following[3] viz "Resolved that in the original formation of the Legislature of "the U. S. the first branch thereof shall consist of sixty-five mem-"bers, of which number N. Hampshire shall send 3. Massts. 8. "Rh. I. 1. Connt. 5. N. Y. 6. N. J. 4. Pena. 8. Del. 1. Maryd. 6. "Virga. 10. N. C. 5. S. C. 5. Geo. 3. — But as the present situa-"tion of the States may probably alter in the number of their "inhabitants, the Legislature of the U. S. shall be authorized

[2] Revised from *Journal*.

[3] Copied from *Journal*.

"from time to time to apportion the number of Reps.; and in "case any of the States shall hereafter be divided, or en-"larged by, addition of territory, or any two or more States "united, or any new States created within the limits of the "U. S. the Legislature of the U. S. shall possess authority "to regulate the number of Reps, in any of the foregoing "cases, upon the principle of their number of inhabitants, "according to the provisions hereafter mentioned, namely — "provided always that representation ought to be proportioned "according to direct taxation; and in order to ascertain the "alteration in the direct taxation, which may be required from "time to time by the changes in the relative circumstances "of the States *P* Resolved that a Census be taken within six "years from the 1st. meeting of the Legislature of the U. S. "and once within the term of every 10 years afterwards of all the "inhabitants of the U. S. in the manner and according to the "ratio recommended by Congress in their Resolution of April "18. 1783. and that the Legislature of the U. S. shall propor-"tion the direct taxation accordingly *P* Resolved, that all "bills for raising or appropriating money, and for fixing the "salaries of officers of the Govt. of the U. S. shall originate "in the first branch of the Legislature of the U. S. and shall not "be altered or amended in 2d. branch: and that no money "shall be drawn from the public Treasury, but in pursuance of "appropriations to be originated in the 1st — branch. *P* Re-"solvd. that in the 2d. branch of the Legislature of the U. S. "each State shall have an equal vote"⟩ [4]

The 6th. Resol: in the Report from the Come. of the whole House, which had been postponed in order to consider the 7 & 8th. Resol'ns; was now resumed. see the Resoln: ⟨The 1s. member⟩ "That the Natl. Legislature ought to ⟨pos-

[4] On this compromise, see Appendix A, LXV*a*, CXXV, CXLVI*a*, CLVI, CLVIII (26–27), CLXVI, CLXX, CLXXVII, CLXXVIII, CLXXXVIII, CXCI, CXCIII, CCI, CCXVI, CCXIX, CCXXV, CCXXX, CCLXII, CCLXIV, CCLXVII, CCLXXIV, CCC, CCCIII, CCCV, CCCXIII, CCCXIX, CCCXXVI, CCCXXXVI, CCCLXIII, CCCLXXI, CCCLXXII, CCCLXXXIII, CCCC. Upon the general compromising spirit of the Convention, see Appendix A, XXXII, XXXVIII, LXXXV, CXIII, CXXVI*a*, CXXXVII, CXL, CXLII, CLXXXVI, CC, CC*a*, CCXVII, CCXXIV, CCXXXII, CCLXXXII, CCLXXXIX, CCCII, CCCXLI.

sess⟩[5] the Legislative Rights vested in Congs. by the Confederation." ⟨was⟩ Agreed to nem. Con.
⟨The next⟩ "And moreover to legislate in all cases to which the separate States are incompetent; or in which the harmony of the U. S. may be interrupted by the exercise of individual legislation," ⟨being⟩ read for a question

Mr. Butler calls for some explanation of the extent of this power; particularly of the word *incompetent.* The vagueness of the terms rendered it impossible for any precise judgment to be formed.

Mr. Ghorum. The vagueness of the terms constitutes the propriety of them. We are now establishing general principles, to be extended hereafter into details which will be precise & explicit.

Mr. Rutlidge, urged the objection started by Mr. Butler and moved that the clause should be committed to the end that a specification of the powers comprised in the general terms, might be reported.

On the question for a commitment, ⟨the States were equally divided⟩

Mas. no. Cont. ay. N. J. no. Pa. no. Del. no. Md. ay. Va. ay. N. C. no. S. C. ay. Geo. ay: So it was lost. [Ayes — 5; noes — 5.]

Mr. Randolph. The vote of this morning (involving an equality of suffrage in 2d. branch) had embarrassed the business extremely. All the powers given in the Report from the Come. of the whole, were founded on the supposition that a Proportional representation was to prevail in both branches of the Legislature — When he came here this morning his purpose was to have offered some propositions that might if possible have united a great majority of votes, and particularly might provide agst. the danger suspected on the part of the smaller States, by enumerating the cases in which it might lie, and allowing an equality of votes in such cases.* But finding from the preceding vote that they persist in demand-

* ⟨See the paper in appendix communicated by Mr. R. to J. M., July 10.⟩[6]

[5] Revised from *Journal.*

[6] See Appendix A, LVIII.

ing an equal vote in all cases, that they have succeeded in obtaining it, and that N. York if present would probably be on the same side, he could not but think we were unprepared to discuss this subject further. It will probably be in vain to come to any final decision with a bare majority on either side For these reasons he wished the Convention might adjourn, that the large States might consider the steps proper to be taken in the present solemn crisis of the business, and that the small States might also deliberate on the means of conciliation.

Mr. Patterson, thought with Mr. R. that it was high time for the Convention to adjourn that the rule of secrecy ought to be rescinded, and that our Constituents should be consulted. No conciliation could be admissible on the part of the smaller States on any other ground than that of an equality of votes in the 2d. branch. If Mr Randolph would reduce to form his motion for an adjournment sine die, he would second it with all his heart.

Genl. Pinkney wished to know of Mr R. whether he meant an adjournment sine die, or only an adjournment for the day. If the former was meant, it differed much from his idea He could not think of going to S. Carolina, and returning again to this place. Besides it was chimerical to suppose that the States if consulted would ever accord separately, and beforehand.

Mr. Randolph, had never entertained an idea of an adjournment sine die; & was sorry that his meaning had been so readily & strangely misinterpreted. He had in view merely an adjournment till tomorrow in order that some conciliatory experiment might if possible be devised, and that in case the smaller States should continue to hold back, the larger might then take such measures, he would not say what, as might be necessary.

Mr. Patterson seconded the adjournment till tomorrow, as an opportunity seemed to be wished by the larger States to deliberate further on conciliatory expedients.

On the question for adjourning till tomorrow, ⟨the States were equally divided.⟩

Mas. no. Cont. no. N. J. ay. Pa. ay. Del. no. Md. ay. Va. ay. N. C. ay. S. C. no. Geo. no. So it was lost. [Ayes — 5; noes — 5.]

Mr. Broome thought it his duty to declare his opinion agst. an adjournment sine die, as had been urged by Mr. Patterson. Such a measure he thought would be fatal. Something must be done by the Convention tho' it should be by a bare majority.

Mr. Gerry observed that Masts. was opposed to an adjournment, because they saw no new ground of compromise. But as it seemed to be the opinion of so many States that a trial shd be made, the State would now concur in the adjournmt.

Mr. Rutlidge could see no need of an adjournt. because he could see no chance of a compromise. The little States were fixt. They had repeatedly & solemnly declared themselves to be so. All that the large States then had to do, was to decide whether they would yield or not. For his part he conceived that altho' we could not do what we thought best, in itself, we ought to do something. Had we not better keep the Govt. up a little longer, hoping that another Convention will supply our omissions, than abandon every thing to hazard. Our Constituents will be very little satisfied with us if we take the latter course.

Mr. Randolph & Mr. King renewed the motion to adjourn till tomorrow.

On the question Mas. ay. Cont. no. N. J. ay. Pa. ay. Del. no. Md. ay. Va. ay. N. C. ay. S. C. ay. Geo. divd. [Ayes — 7; noes — 2; divided — 1.]

Adjourned[7]

On the morning following before the hour of the Convention a number of the members from the larger States, by common agreement met for the purpose of consulting on the proper steps to be taken in consequence of the vote in favor of an equal Representation in the 2d. branch, and the apparent inflexibility of the smaller States on that point — Several members from the latter States also attended. The time was

[7] See further Appendix A, LXIII.

wasted in vague conversation on the subject, without any specific proposition or agreement. It appeared indeed that the opinions of the members who disliked the equality of votes differed so much as to the importance of that point, and as to the policy of risking ⟨a failure of⟩ a⟨ny⟩ general act of the Convention by inflexibly opposing it. Several of them supposing that no good Governnt could or would be built on that foundation, and that as a division of the Convention into two opinions was unavoidable it would be better that the side comprising the principal States, and a majority of the people of America, should propose a scheme of Govt. to the States, than that a scheme should be proposed on the other side, would have concurred in a firm opposition to the smaller States, and in a separate recommendation, if eventually necessary. Others seemed inclined to yield to the smaller States, and to concur in such an Act however imperfect & exceptionable, as might be agreed on by the Convention as a body, tho' decided by a bare majority of States and by a minority of the people of the U. States. It is probable that the result of this consultation satisfied the smaller States that they had nothing to apprehend from a Union of the larger, in any plan whatever agst. the equality of votes in the 2d. branch.[8]

[8] See Appendix A, CXXXVII, CCCLXXI.

TUESDAY, JULY 17, 1787.

JOURNAL

Tuesday July 17. 1787.

It was moved and seconded to postpone the considn of the second clause of the Sixth resolution reported from the Committee of the whole House in order to take up the following

"To make laws binding on the People of the United States "in all cases which may concern the common interests of "the Union: but not to interfere with the government of the "individual States in any matters of internal police which "respect the government of such States only, and wherein "the general welfare of the United States is not concerned."

which passed in the negative [Ayes — 2; noes — 8.] [1]

It was moved and seconded to alter the second clause of the 6th resolution so as to read as follows, namely

"and moreover to legislate in all cases for the general interests of the Union, and also in those to which the States are separately incompetent, or in which the harmony of the United States may be interrupted by the exercise of individual legislation

which passed in the affirmative [Ayes — 6; noes — 4.] [2]

[To agree to the second clause of the 6. resolution as amended. Ayes — 8; noes — 2.] [3]

On the question to agree to the following clause of the sixth resolution reported from the Committee of the whole House, namely,

"to negative all laws passed by the several States contra-"vening in the opinion of the national legislature, the articles

---

[1] Vote 160, Detail of Ayes and Noes, which notes that the motion was "offered by Mr. Sherman".

[2] Vote 161, Detail of Ayes and Noes, which notes that the amendment was "offered by Mr. Bedford".

[3] Vote 162, Detail of Ayes and Noes.

"of union, or any treaties subsisting under the authority of "the Union"

it passed in the negative [Ayes — 3; noes — 7.]

It was moved and seconded to agree to the following resolution namely.

Resolved that the legislative acts of the United States made by virtue and in pursuance of the articles of Union and all Treaties made and ratified under the authority of the United States shall be the supreme law of the respective States as far as those acts or Treaties shall relate to the said States, or their Citizens and Inhabitants — and that the Judiciaries of the several States shall be bound thereby in their decisions, any thing in the respective laws of the individual States to the contrary notwithstanding

which passed unanimously in the affirmative

On the question to agree to the first clause of the 9th resolution reported from the Committee of the whole House namely "That a national Executive be instituted to consist of a Single Person"

it passed unanimously in the affirmative [Ayes — 10; noes — 0.]

It was moved and seconded to strike the words

"national legislature" out of the second clause of the 9th resolution, reported from the Committee of the whole House and to insert the words

"the Citizens of the United States"

which passed in the negative [Ayes — 1; noes — 9.]

It was moved and seconded to alter the second clause of the 9th resolution reported from the Committee of the whole House so as to read

"To be chosen by Electors to be appointed by the several Legislatures of the individual States"

which passed in the negative [Ayes — 2; noes — 8.]

It was moved and seconded to agree to the following clause namely

"to be chosen by the national Legislature

which passed unan: in the affirmative. [Ayes — 10; noes — 0.]

It was moved and seconded to postpone the consideration of the following clause

for the term of seven years"

which was unanimously agreed to

On the question to agree to the following clause namely

"with power to carry into effect the national laws"

it passed unanimously in ye affirmative

On the question to agree to the following clause namely

"to appoint to offices in cases not otherwise provided for"

it passed unanimously in the affirmative

It was moved and seconded to strike out the following words namely

"to be ineligible a second time"

which passed in the affirmative [Ayes — 6; noes — 4.]

It was moved and seconded to strike out the words "seven years" and to insert the words "good behaviour."

which passed in the negative. [Ayes — 4; noes — 6.]

It was moved and seconded to strike out the words

"seven years"

which passed in the negative [Ayes — 4; noes — 6.][4]

And then the House adjourned till to-morrow at 11 o'Clock A. M.

---

[4] Vote 170, Detail of Ayes and Noes. Immediately following this, the printed *Journal* (pp. 185–6) inserted from Detail of Ayes and Noes (Votes 171–173):—

"It was moved and seconded to reconsider the vote to strike out the words, 'to be ineligible a second time'."

"Passed unanimously (eight states) in the affirmative.

"It was moved and seconded to reconsider immediately.

"Passed in the affirmative. . . . [Ayes — 6; Noes — 2.]

"It was moved and seconded to reconsider the clause to-morrow.

"Passed unanimously in the affirmative."

This is probably an error. There is nothing in the Journal or Detail of Ayes and Noes which would assign these questions to July 17 rather than to July 18. Madison did not originally record any of these questions on July 17, but Madison does record two of them on July 18. That only eight states voted corresponds to the attendance on July 18 rather than July 17. The "to-morrow" on which the question was reconsidered was July 19. These questions, therefore, doubtless belong to the records of July 18.

Detail of Ayes and Noes

	New Hampshire	Massachusetts	Rhode Island	Connecticut	New York	New Jersey	Pennsylvania	Delaware	Maryland	Virginia	North Carolina	South Carolina	Georgia	Questions	Ayes	Noes	Divided
[160]		no		aye		no	no	no	aye	no	no	no	no	To postpone the 2 clause of ye 6th resolution, to take up a motion offered by Mr Sherman	2	8	
[161]		aye		no		aye	aye	aye	aye	no	aye	no	no	To agree to the amendment offered to the 6th.resolution by Mr Bedford	6	4	
[Beginning sixth loose sheet]																	
[162]		aye		aye		aye	aye	aye	aye	aye	aye	no	no	To agree to the second clause of the 6. resolution as amended.	8	2	
[163]		aye		no		no	no	no	no	aye	aye	no	no	To agree to the last clause of the 6 resolution as reported from the Committee of the whole House.	3	7	
[164]		aye		aye		aye	aye	aye	aye	aye	aye	aye	aye	The National Executive to consist of a Single Person unanimous	10		
[165]		no		no		no	aye	no	no	no	no	no	no	That the National Executive be chosen by the Citizens of the United States.	1	9	
[166]		no		no		no	no	aye	aye	no	no	no	no	That the national Executive be chosen by Electors to be appointed by the individual Legislatures	2	8	
[167]		aye		aye		aye	aye	aye	aye	aye	aye	aye	aye	That the national Executive be chosen by the Legislature of the United States	10		
[168]		aye		aye		aye	aye	no	aye	no	no	no	aye	To strike out the words "to be ineligible a second time"	6	4	
[169]		no		no		aye	aye	aye	no	aye	no	no	no	To strike out the words "seven years" and insert the words "good behaviour"	4	6	
[170]		aye		no		no	aye	aye	no	no	aye	no	no	To strike out the words "seven years"	4	6	

MADISON

Tuesday July 17. in Convention

Mr. Governr. Morris moved to reconsider the whole Resolution agreed to yesterday concerning the constitution of the 2 branches of the Legislature. His object was to bring the House to a consideration in the abstract of the powers necessary to be vested in the general Government. It had been said, Let us know how the Govt. is to be modelled, and then we can determine what powers can be properly given to it. He thought the most eligible course was, first to determine on the necessary powers, and then so to modify the Governt. as that it might be justly & properly enabled to administer them. He feared if we proceded to a consideration of the powers, whilst the vote of yesterday including an equality of the States in the 2d. branch, remained in force, a reference to it, either mental or expressed, would mix itself with the merits of every question concerning the powers. — this motion was not seconded. (It was probably approved by several members, who either despaired of success, or were apprehensive that the attempt would inflame the jealousies of the smaller States.)

The 6th. Resoln. in the Report of the Come. of the whole relating to the powers, which had been postponed in order to consider the 7 & 8th. relating to the Constitution of the, Natl. Legislature, was now resumed —

Mr. Sherman observed that it would be difficult to draw the line between the powers of the Genl. Legislatures, and those to be left with the States; that he did not like the definition contained in the Resolution, and proposed in place of the words "of individual legislation" line 4 inclusive, to insert "to make laws binding on the people of the ⟨United⟩ States in all cases ⟨which may concern the common interests of the Union⟩; but not to interfere with ⟨the Government of the individual States in any matters of internal police which respect the Govt. of such States only, and wherein the General⟩ welfare of the U. States is not concerned." [5]

[5] Revised from *Journal.*

Mr. Wilson 2ded. the amendment as better expressing the general principle.

Mr Govr Morris opposed it. The internal police, as it would be called & understood by the States ought to be infringed in many cases, as in the case of paper money & other tricks by which Citizens of other States may be affected.

Mr. Sherman, in explanation of his ideas read an enumeration of powers, including the power of levying taxes on trade, but not the power of *direct taxation.*

Mr. Govr. Morris remarked the omission, and inferred that for the deficencies of taxes on consumption, it must have been the meaning of Mr. Sherman, that the Genl. Govt. should recur to quotas & requisitions, which are subversive of the idea of Govt.

Mr. Sherman acknowledged that his enumeration did not include direct taxation. Some provision he supposed must be made for supplying the deficiency of other taxation, but he had not formed any.[6]

On Question on Mr. Sherman's motion,[7] ⟨it passed in the negative⟩

Mas. no. Cont. ay. N. J. no. Pa. no. Del. no. Md. ay. Va. no. N. C. no. S. C. no. Geo. no. [Ayes — 2; noes — 8.]

Mr. Bedford moved that the ⟨2d. member of Resolution 6.⟩ be so altered as to read "⟨and moreover⟩ to legislate in all cases for the general interests of the Union, and also in those to which the States are separately incompetent," ⟨or in which the harmony of the U. States may be interrupted by the exercise of individual Legislation".⟩ [8]

Mr. Govr. Morris 2ds. ⟨the motion.⟩

Mr. Randolph. This is a formidable idea indeed. It involves the power of violating all the laws and constitutions of the States, and of intermeddling with their police. The last member of the sentence is ⟨also⟩ superfluous, being included in the first.

[6] See Appendix A, CXXIII.

[7] Madison originally recorded but struck out that the question was "for postponing in order to take on" Sherman's motion.

[8] Revised from *Journal.*

Mr. Bedford. It is not more extensive or formidable than the clause as it stands: *no State* being *separately* competent to legislate for the *general interest* of the Union.

On question for agreeing to Mr. Bedford's motion. ⟨it passed in the affirmative.⟩

Mas. ay. Cont. no. N. J. ay. Pa. ay. Del. ay. Md. ay. Va. no. N. C. ay. S. C. no. Geo. no. [Ayes — 6; noes — 4.]

On the sentence as amended, ⟨it passed in the affirmative.⟩

Mas. ay. Cont. ay. N. J. ay. Pa. ay. Del. ay. Md. ay. Va. ay. N. C. ay. S. C. no. Geo. no. [Ayes — 8; noes — 2.]

⟨The next. —⟩ "To negative all laws passed by the several States ⟨contravening in the opinion of the Nat: Legislature the articles of Union, or any treaties subsisting under the authority of ye Union"⟩ [9]

Mr. Govr. Morris opposed this power as likely to be terrible to the States, and not necessary, if sufficient Legislative authority should be given to the Genl. Government.

Mr. Sherman thought it unnecessary, as the Courts of the States would not consider as valid any law contravening the Authority of the Union, and which the legislature would wish to be negatived.

Mr. L. Martin considered the power as improper & inadmissable. Shall all the laws of the States be sent up to the Genl. Legislature before they shall be permitted to operate?

Mr. ⟨Madison,⟩ considered the negative on the laws of the States as essential to the efficacy & security of the Genl. Govt. The necessity of a general Govt. proceeds from the propensity of the States to pursue their particular interests in opposition to the general interest. This propensity will continue to disturb the system, unless effectually controuled. Nothing short of a negative on their laws will controul it. They can pass laws which will accomplish their injurious objects before they can be repealed by the Genl Legislre. or be set aside by the National Tribunals. Confidence can ⟨not⟩ be put in the State Tribunals as guardians of the National authority and interests. In all the States these are more or less

---

[9] Revised from *Journal*.

dependt. on the Legislatures. In Georgia[10] they are appointed annually by the Legislature. In R. Island the Judges who refused to execute an unconstitutional law were displaced, and others substituted, by the Legislature who would be willing instruments of the wicked & arbitrary plans of their masters. A power of negativing the improper laws of the States is at once the most mild & certain means of preserving the harmony of the system. Its utility is sufficiently displayed in the British System. Nothing could maintain the harmony & subordination of the various parts of the empire, but the prerogative by which the Crown, stifles in the birth every Act of every part tending to discord or encroachment. It is true the prerogative is sometines misapplied thro' ignorance or a partiality to one particular part of ye. empire: but we have not the same reason to fear such misapplications in our System. As to the sending all laws up to the Natl. Legisl: that might be rendered unnecessary by some emanation of the power into the States, so far at least, as to give a temporary effect to laws of immediate necessity.

Mr. Govr. Morris was more & more opposed to the negative. The proposal of it would disgust all the States. A law that ought to be negatived will be set aside in the Judiciary departmt. and if that security should fail; may be repealed by a Nationl. law.

Mr. Sherman. Such a power involves a wrong principle, to wit, that a law of a State contrary to the articles of the Union, would if not negatived, be valid & operative.

Mr. Pinkney urged the necessity of the Negative.

On the question for agreeing to the power of negativing laws of States &c." ⟨it passed in the negative.⟩

Mas. ay. Ct. no. N. J. no. Pa. no. Del. no. Md. no. Va. ay. N. C. ay. S. C. no. Geo. no. [Ayes — 3; noes — 7.][11]

⟨Mr. Luther Martin moved the following resolution "that the Legislative acts of the U. S. made by virtue & in pursuance of the articles of Union, and all treaties made & ratified under the authority of the U. S. shall be the supreme law of

[10] "Rh. Isd. &" twice struck out.

[11] See Appendix A, CXXXVII.

the respective States, as far as those acts or treaties shall relate to the said States, or their Citizens and inhabitants — & that the Judiciaries of the several States shall be bound thereby in their decisions, any thing in the respective laws of the individual States to the contrary notwithstanding" which was agreed to nem: con:.⟩ [12]

9th. Resol: "that Natl. Executive consist of a single person." Agd. to nem. con.

"To be chosen by the National Legisl:"

Mr. Governr. Morris was pointedly agst. his being so chosen. He will be the mere creature of the Legisl: if appointed & impeachable by that body. He ought to be elected by the people at large, by the freeholders of the Country. That difficulties attend this mode, he admits. But they have been found superable in N. Y. &. in Cont. and would he believed be found so, in the case of an Executive for the U. States. If the people should elect, they will never fail to prefer some man of distinguished character, or services; some man, if he might so speak, of continental reputation. If the Legislature elect, it will be the work of intrigue, of cabal, and of faction: it will be like the election of a pope by a conclave of cardinals; real merit will rarely be the title to the appointment. ⟨He moved to strike out "National Legislature" & insert "citizens of U. S"⟩

Mr. Sherman thought that the sense of the Nation would be better expressed by the Legislature, than by the people at large. The latter will never be sufficiently informed of characters, and besides will never give a majority of votes to any one man. They will generally vote for some man in their own State, and the largest State will have the best chance for the appointment. If the choice be made by the Legislre. A majority of voices may be made necessary to constitute an election.

Mr. Wilson. two arguments have been urged agst. an

[12] Taken from *Journal.* Madison had originally recorded only the substance. For Martin's explanation of this resolution, see Appendix A, CLXXXIX, CXCII, also CXXXVII, CLXIII, CCLXXII, CCCLXXXVIII, CCCXCI, CCCXCVIII. See further, above June 8, note 3, and below August 23.

election of the Executive Magistrate by the people. 1 the example of Poland where an Election of the supreme Magistrate is attended with the most dangerous commotions. The cases he observed were totally dissimilar. The Polish nobles have resources & dependents which enable them to appear in force, and to threaten the Republic as well as each other. In the next place the electors all assemble in one place: which would not be the case with us. The 2d. argt. is that a *majority* of the people would never concur. It might be answered that the concurrence of a majority of people is not a necessary principle of election, nor required as such in any of the States. But allowing the objection all its force, it may be obviated by the expedient used in Masts. where the Legislature by majority of voices, decide in case a majority of people do not concur in favor of one of the candidates. This would restrain the choice to a good nomination at least, and prevent in a great degree intrigue & cabal. A particular objection with him agst. an absolute election by the Legislre. was that the Exec: in that case would be too dependent to stand the mediator between the intrigues & sinister views of the Representatives and the general liberties & interests of the people.

Mr. Pinkney did not expect this question would again have been brought forward; An Election by the people being liable to the most obvious & striking objections. They will be led by a few active & designing men. The most populous States by combining in favor of the same individual will be able to carry their points. The Natl. Legislature being most immediately interested in the laws made by themselves, will be most attentive to the choice of a fit man to carry them properly into execution.

Mr. Govr. Morris. It is said that in case of an election by the people the populous States will combine & elect whom they please. Just the reverse. The people of such States cannot combine. If their be any combination it must be among their representatives in the Legislature. It is said the people will be led by a few designing men. This might happen in a small district. It can never happen throughout the continent. In the election of a Govr. of N. York, it some-

times is the case in particular spots, that the activity & intrigues of little partizans are successful, but the general voice of the State is never influenced by such artifices. It is said the multitude will be uninformed. It is true they would be uninformed of what passed in the Legislative Conclave, if the election were to be made there; but they will not be uninformed of those great & illustrious characters which have merited their esteem & confidence. If the Executive be chosen by the Natl. Legislature, he will not be independent on it; and if not independent, usurpation & tyranny on the part of the Legislature will be the consequence. This was the case in England in the last Century. It has been the case in Holland, where their Senates have engrossed all power. It has been the case every where. He was surprised that an election by the people at large should ever have been likened to the polish election of the first Magistrate. An election by the Legislature will bear a real likeness to the election by the Diet of Poland. The great must be the electors in both cases, and the corruption & cabal wch are known to characterize the one would soon find their way into the other. Appointments made by numerous bodies, are always worse than those made by single responsible individuals, or by the people at large.

Col. Mason. It is curious to remark the different language held at different times. At one moment we are told that the Legislature is entitled to thorough confidence, and to indefinite power. At another, that it will be governed by intrigue & corruption, and cannot be trusted at all. But not to dwell on this inconsistency he would observe that a Government which is to last ought at least to be practicable. Would this be the case if the proposed election should be left to the people at large. He conceived it would be as unnatural to refer the choice of a proper character for chief Magistrate to the people, as it would, to refer a trial of colours to a blind man. The extent of the Country renders it impossible that the people can have the requisite capacity to judge of the respective pretensions of the Candidates. ——

Mr Wilson. could not see the contrariety stated (by Col. Mason) The Legislre. might deserve confidence in some

respects, and distrust in others. In acts which were to affect them & yr. Constituents precisely alike confidence was due. In others jealousy was warranted. The appointment to great offices, where the Legislre. might feel many motives, not common to the public confidence was surely misplaced. This branch of business it was notorious, was most corruptly managed of any that had been committed to legislative bodies.

Mr. Williamson, conceived that there was the same difference between an election in this case, by the people and by the legislature, as between an appt. by lot, and by choice. There are at present distinguished characters, who are known perhaps to almost every man. This will not always be the case. The people will be sure to vote for some man in their own State, and the largest State will be sure to succede. This will not be Virga. however. Her slaves will have no suffrage. As the Salary of the Executive will be fixed, and he will not be eligible a 2d. time, there will not be such a dependence on the Legislature as has been imagined.

Question on an election by the people instead of the Legislature; ⟨which passed in the negative.⟩

Mas. no. Cont. no. N. J. no. Pa. ay. Del. no. Md. no. Va. no. N. C. no. S. C. no. Geo. no. [Ayes — 1; noes — 9.]

Mr. L. Martin moved that the Executive be chosen by Electors appointed by the ⟨several⟩ Legislature⟨s of the individual States.⟩ [13]

Mr. Broome 2ds. On the Question, ⟨it passed in the negative.⟩

Mas. no. Cont. no. N. J. no. Pa. no. Del. ay. Md. ay. Va. no. N. C. no. S. C. no. Geo. no. [Ayes — 2; noes — 8.]

On the question on the words "to be chosen by the Nationl. Legislature" ⟨it passed unanimously in the affirmative.⟩ [14]

"For the term of seven years" — postponed nem. con. on motion of Mr. Houston & Gov. Morris.

"to carry into execution the nationl. laws" — agreed to nem. con.

[13] Madison originally recorded this motion, that the electors were to be appointed by the "Natl Legislature." It was revised from *Journal*.

[14] Madison originally recorded the vote in detail — ten states, each "ay".

"to appoint to offices in cases not otherwise provided for". — agreed to nem. con.

"to be ineligible a second time" — Mr. Houston moved to strike out this clause.

Mr. Sherman 2ds. the motion.

Mr. Govr. Morris espoused the motion. The ineligibility proposed by the clause as it stood tended to destroy the great motive to good behavior, the hope of being rewarded by a re-appointment. It was saying to him, make hay while the sun shines.

On the question for striking out as moved by Mr. Houston, ⟨it passed in the affirmative.⟩

Mas. ay. Cont. ay. N. J. ay. Pa. ay. Del. no. Md. ay. Va. no. N. C. no. S. C. no. Geo. ay. [Ayes — 6; noes — 4.]

"For the term of 7 years" resumed

Mr. Broom was for a shorter term since the Executive Magistrate was now to be re-eligible. Had he remained ineligible a 2d. time, he should have preferred a longer term.

Docr. McClurg moved * to strike out 7 years, and insert "during good behavior". By striking out the words, declaring him not re-eligible, he was put into a situation that would keep him dependent for ever on the Legislature; and he conceived the independence of the Executive to be equally essential with that of the Judiciary department.

Mr. Govr. Morris 2ded. the motion. He expressed great pleasure in hearing it. This was the way to get a good Government. His fear that so valuable an ingredient would not be attained had led him to take the part he had done. He was indifferent how the Executive should be chosen, provided he held his place by this tenure.

Mr. Broome highly approved the motion. It obviated all his difficulties.

Mr. Sherman considered such a tenure as by no means safe or admissible. As the Executive Magistrate is now re-eligible, he will be on good behavior as far as will be necessary.

* ⟨The probable object of this motion was merely to enforce the argument against the re-eligibility of the Executive Magistrate, by holding out a tenure during good behaviour as the alternative for keeping him independent of the Legislature.⟩

If he behaves well he will be continued; if otherwise, displaced on a succeeding election.

Mr. Madison. * If it be essential to the preservation of liberty that the Legisl: Execut: & Judiciary powers be separate, it is essential to a maintenance of the separation, that they should be independent of each other. The Executive could not be independent of the Legislure, if dependent on the pleasure of that branch for a re-appointment. Why was it determined that the Judges should not hold their places by such a tenure? Because they might be tempted to cultivate the Legislature, by an undue complaisance, and thus render the Legislature the virtual expositor, as well the maker of the laws. In like manner a dependence of the Executive on the Legislature, would render it the Executor as well as the maker of laws; & then according to the observation of Montesquieu, tyrannical laws may be made that they may be executed in a tyrannical manner. There was an analogy between the Executive & Judiciary departments in several respects. The latter executed the laws in certain cases as the former did in others. The former expounded & applied them for certain purposes, as the latter did for others. The difference between them seemed to consist chiefly in two circumstances—1. the collective interest & security were much more in the power belonging to the Executive than to the Judiciary department. 2. in the administration of the former much greater latitude is left to opinion and discretion than in the administration of the latter. But if the 2d. consideration proves that it will be more difficult to establish a rule sufficiently precise for trying the Execut: than the Judges, & forms an objection to the same tenure of office, both considerations prove that it might be more dangerous to suffer a Union between the Executive & Legisl: powers, than between the Judiciary & Legislative

* ⟨The view here taken of the subject was meant to aid in parrying the animadversions likely to fall on the motion of Dr. McClurg, for whom J. M. had a particular regard.[15] The Docr. though possessing talents of the highest order, was modest & unaccustomed to exert them in public debate.⟩

[15] Crossed out "and whose appointment to the Convention he had actively promoted."

powers. He conceived it to be absolutely necessary to a well constituted Republic that the two first shd. be kept distinct & independent of each other. Whether the plan proposed by the motion was a proper one was another question, as it depended on the practicability of instituting a tribunal for impeachmts. as certain & as adequate in the one case as in the other. On the other hand, respect for the mover entitled his proposition to a fair hearing & discussion, until a less objectionable expedient should be applied for guarding agst. a dangerous union of the Legislative & Executive departments.

Col. Mason. This motion was made some time ago, & negatived by a very large majority. He trusted that it wd. be again negatived. It wd. be impossible to define the misbehaviour in such a manner as to subject it to a proper trial; and perhaps still more impossible to compel so high an offender holding his office by such a tenure to submit to a trial. He considered an Executive during good behavior as a softer name only for an Executive for life. And that the next would be an easy step to hereditary Monarchy. If the motion should finally succeed, he might himself live to see such a Revolution. If he did not it was probable his children or grandchildren would. He trusted there were few men in that House who wished for it. No state he was sure had so far revolted from Republican principles as to have the least bias in its favor.

Mr. Madison, was not apprehensive of being thought to favor any step towards monarchy. The real object with him was to prevent its introduction. Experience had proved a tendency in our governments to throw all power into the Legislative vortex. The Executives of the States are in general little more than Cyphers; the legislatures omnipotent. If no effectual check be devised for restraining the instability & encroachments of the latter, a revolution of some kind or other would be inevitable. The preservation of Republican Govt. therefore required some expedient for the purpose, but required evidently at the same time that in devising it, the genuine principles of that form should be kept in view.

Mr. Govr. Morris was as little a friend to monarchy as any gentleman. He concurred in the opinion that the way to

keep out monarchial Govt. was to establish such a Repub. Govt. as wd. make the people happy and prevent a desire of change.

Docr. McClurg was not so much afraid of the shadow of monarchy as to be unwilling to approach it; nor so wedded to Republican Govt. as not to be sensible of the tyrannies that had been & may be exercised under that form. It was an essential object with him to make the Executive independent of the Legislature; and the only mode left for effecting it, after the vote destroying his ineligibility a second time, was to appoint him during good behavior.

On the question for inserting "during good behavior" in place of 7 years (⟨with a⟩ re-eligibility) ⟨it passed in the negative.⟩ [16]

Mas. no. Ct. no. N. J. ay. Pa. ay. Del. ay. Md. no. Va. ay. N. C. no. S. C. no. Geo. no.* [Ayes — 4; noes — 6.]

On the motion "to strike out seven years" ⟨it passed in the negative.⟩

Mas. ay. Ct. no. N. J. no. Pa. ay. Del. ay. Md. no. Va. no. N. C. ay. S. C. no. Geo. no.† [Ayes—4; noes—6.]

⟨It was now unanimously agreed that the vote which had struck out the words "to be ineligible a second time" should be reconsidered tomorrow.⟩[17]

Adjd.[18]

* –This vote is not to be considered as any certain index of opinion, as a number in the affirmative probably had it chiefly in view to alarm those attached to a dependence of the Executive on the Legislature, & thereby facilitate some final arrangement of a contrary tendency. ⟨The avowed friends of an Excutive, "during good behaviour" were not more than three or four nor is it certain they would finally have adhered to such a tenure. An independence of the three great departments of of each other, as far as possible, and the responsibility of all to the will of the community seemed to be generally admitted as the true basis of a well constructed government.⟩

† There was no debate on this motion the apparent object of many in the affirmative was to secure the reeligibility by shortening the term, and of many in the negative to embarrass the plan of referring the appointment & dependence of the Eexcutive to the Legislature.

[16] See Appendix A, CCLXX, CCXCV.

[17] Taken from *Journal* which is in error, see above note 4.

[18] See further Appendix A, LXIV.

WEDNESDAY, JULY 18, 1787.

JOURNAL

Wednesday July 18. 1787.

[To reconsider the clause which makes the Executive reeligible Ayes — 8; noes — o.

To reconsider immediately Ayes — 6; noes — 2.

To reconsider the clause to-morrow Ayes — 8; noes —o.][1]

It was moved and seconded to postpone the consideration of the following clause in the 9th resolution reported from the Committee of the whole House namely

for the term of seven years"

which passed unanimously in ye affirmative

It was moved and seconded to postpone the consideration of the remaining clause of the 9th and the 10th resolution in order to take up the 11th resolution.

which passed in the affirmative [Ayes — 4; noes — 3; divided — 1.]

On the question to agree to the following clause of the 11th resolution namely

"That a national Judiciary be established"

it passed unanimously in the affirmative

On the question to agree to the following clause of the 11th resolution namely

"To consist of One supreme Tribunal

it passed unanimously in the affirmative

It was moved and seconded to strike out the words

"second branch of the national Legislature" and to insert the words "national executive" in the 11. resolution

which passed in the negative. [Ayes — 2; noes — 6.]

---

[1] Votes 171–173, Detail of Ayes and Noes. It required a unanimous vote to reconsider immediately. Upon the assignment of these questions to this day, see July 17 note 4.

It was moved and seconded to alter the 3rd cause of the 11th resolution so as to read as follows, namely,

The Judges of which shall be nominated and appointed by the Executive by and with the advice and consent of the second Branch of the Legislature of the United States — and every such nomination shall be made at least days prior to such appointment

which passed in the negative [Ayes — 4; noes — 4.]

It was moved and seconded to alter the 3rd clause of the 11th resolution so as to read as follows namely

That the Judges shall be nominated by the Executive and such nomination shall become an appointment if not disagreed to within days by two thirds of the second branch of the Legislature.

It was moved and seconded to postpone the consideration of the last amendment

which was unanimously agreed to

On the question to agree to the following clause of the 11th resolution namely "to hold their Offices during good behaviour"

it passed unanimously in the affirmative

On the question to agree to the following clause of the eleventh resolution namely

"to receive, punctually, at stated times a fixed compensa-
"tion for their services"

it passed unanimously in the affirmative

It was moved and seconded to strike the words

"Encrease or" out of the eleventh resolution

which passed in the affirmative [Ayes—6; noes—2.]

On the question to agree to the clause as amended namely
"to receive, punctually, at stated times, a fixed compensation
"for their services in which no diminution shall be made so
"as to affect the Persons actually in Office at the time of such
"diminution"

it passed unanimously in the affirmative

On the question to agree to the 12th resolution namely

"That the national Legislature be empowered to appoint
"inferior Tribunals"

it passed unanimously in the affirmative [Ayes—9; noes—0.]

It was moved and seconded to strike the words

"impeachments of national Officers" out of the 13th resolution

which passed unanimously in the affirmative

It was moved and seconded to alter the 13th resolution so as to read as follows namely

That the jurisdiction of the national Judiciary shall extend to cases arising under laws passed by the general Legislature, and to such other questions as involve the National peace and harmony

which passed unanimously in the affirmative

On the question to agree to the 14 resolution namely

Resolved That provision ought to be made for the admission of States lawfully arising within the limits of the United States, whether from a voluntary junction of government and territory, or otherwise with the consent of a number of voices in the national Legislature less than the whole.

it passed unanimously in the affirmative

On the question to agree to the first clause of the 15th resolution reported from the Committee of the whole House

it passed in the negative [Ayes — 2; noes — 7.]

On the question to agree to the last clause of the 15th resolution

it passed unanimously in the negative

It was moved and seconded to alter the sixteenth resolution so as to read as follows namely

That a republican form of Government shall be guaranteed to each State — and that each State shall be protected against foreign and domestic violence

which passed in the affirmative

[To agree to the 16th resolution as amended Ayes — 9; noes — 0.] [2]

And then the House adjourned till to-morrow at 11 o'Clock A. M.

[2] Vote 180, Detail of Ayes and Noes.

DETAIL OF AYES AND NOES

	New Hampshire	Massachusetts	Rhode Island	Connecticut	New York	New Jersey	Pennsylvania	Delaware	Maryland	Virginia	North Carolina	South Carolina	Georgia	Questions	Ayes	Noes	Divided
[171]		aye		aye			aye	aye	aye	aye	aye	aye		To reconsider the clause which makes the Executive reeligible	8		
[172]		aye		aye			no	aye	aye	no	aye	aye		To reconsider immediately	6	2	
[173]		aye		aye			aye	aye	aye	aye	aye	aye		To reconsider the clause to-morrow	8		
[174]		aye		aye			no	aye	aye	no	dd	no		To postpone the considn of the remaining clauses of the 9 resolution, and the 10 resolution to take up ye 11th	4	3	1
[175]		aye		no			aye	no	no	no	no	no		That the Judges shall be appointed by the National Executive	2	6	
[176]		aye		no			aye	no	aye	aye	no	no		That the Judges shall be nominated and appointed by the Executive by & wt the advice and consent of ye 2 branch	4	4	
[177]		aye		aye			aye	aye	aye	no	no	aye		To strike out the words "encrease or"	6	2	
[178]		aye		aye			aye	aye	aye	aye	aye	aye	aye	That the National Legislature be empowered to appoint inferior Tribunals	9		
[179]		no		no			no	no	no	aye	aye	no	no	To agree to the first clause of the 15 resolution	2	7	
[180]		aye		aye			aye	aye	aye	aye	aye	aye	aye	To agree to the 16th resolution as amended	9		

MADISON

Wednesday July 18. in Convention

On motion of Mr. L. Martin ⟨to fix tomorrow⟩ for reconsidering the vote concerning "eligibility of Exective. a 2d time" ⟨it passed in the affirmative.⟩ [3]

Mas. ay. Cont. ay. N. J. absent. Pa. ay. Del. ay. Md. ay.

[3] Revised from *Journal*, where questions and votes are given in greater detail.

Va. ay. N. C. ay. S. C ay. Geo absent. [Ayes — 8; noes — 0; absent — 2.]

The residue of Resol. 9. concerning the Executive was postpd. till tomorrow.[4]

Resol. 10. that Executive shl. have a right to negative legislative acts not afterwards passed by $\frac{2}{3}$ of each branch. Agreed to nem. con.[5]

Resol. 11. "that a Natl. Judiciary be estabd. to consist of one supreme tribunal." agd. to nem. con.

"The Judges of which to be appointd. by the 2d. branch of the Natl. Legislature."

Mr. Ghorum, wd. prefer an appointment by the 2d branch to an appointmt. by the whole Legislature; but he thought even that branch too numerous, and too little personally responsible, to ensure a good choice. He suggested that the Judges be appointed by the Execuve. with the advice & consent of the 2d branch, in the mode prescribed by the constitution of Masts. This mode had been long practised in that country, & was found to answer perfectly well.

Mr. Wilson, still wd. prefer an an appointmt. by the Executive; but if that could not be attained, wd. prefer in the next place, the mode suggested by Mr. Ghorum. He thought it his duty however to move in the first instance "that the Judges be appointed by the Executive." Mr. Govr. Morris 2ded. the motion.

Mr. L. Martin was strenuous for an appt. by the 2d. branch. Being taken from all the States it wd. be best informed of characters & most capable of making a fit choice.

Mr. Sherman concurred in the observations of Mr. Martin, adding that the Judges ought to be diffused, which would be more likely to be attended to by the 2d. branch, than by the Executive.

Mr Mason. The mode of appointing the Judges may

---

[4] Madison originally added "nem con." but apparently in view of Vote 174 printed in *Journal* struck this out.

[5] Madison is evidently wrong in stating that Resolution 10 was "agreed to nem. con." According to the Journal it was *postponed*. It was passed July 21 (see *Records* of that date).

depend in some degree on the mode of trying impeachments, of the Executive. If the Judges were to form a tribunal for that purpose, they surely ought not to be appointed by the Executive. There were insuperable objections besides agst. referring the appointment to the Executive. He mentioned as one, that as the seat of Govt. must be in some one State, and the Executive would remain in office for a considerable time, for 4, 5, or 6 years at least he would insensibly form local & personal attachments within the particular State that would deprive equal merit elsewhere, of an equal chance of promotion.

Mr. Ghorum. As the Executive will be responsible in point of character at least, for a judicious and faithful discharge of his trust, he will be careful to look through all the States for proper characters. — The Senators will be as likely to form their attachments at the seat of Govt where they reside, as the Executive. If they can not get the man of the particular State to which they may respectively belong, they will be indifferent to the rest. Public bodies feel no personal responsibly and give full play to intrigue & cabal. Rh. Island is a full illustration of the insensibility to character produced by a participation of numbers, in dishonorable measures, and of the length to which a public body may carry wickedness & cabal.

Mr. Govr. Morris supposed it would be improper for an impeachmt. of the Executive to be tried before the Judges. The latter would in such case be drawn into intrigues with the Legislature and an impartial trial would be frustrated. As they wd. be much about the seat of Govt they might even be previously consulted & arrangements might be made for a prosecution of the Executive. He thought therefore that no argument could be drawn from the probability of such a plan of impeachments agst. the motion before the House.

Mr. M⟨adison⟩, suggested that the Judges might be appointed by the Executives with the concurrence of ⟨$\frac{1}{3}$ at least⟩ [6] of the 2d. branch. This would unite the advantage of respon-

[6] Madison originally recorded this as "$^2/_3$".

sibility in the Executive with the security afforded in the 2d. branch agst. any incautious or corrupt nomination by the Executive.

Mr. Sherman, was clearly for an election by the Senate. It would be composed of men nearly equal to the Executive, and would of course have on the whole more wisdom. They would bring into their deliberations a more diffusive knowledge of characters. It would be less easy for candidates to intrigue with them, than with the Executive Magistrate. For these reasons he thought there would be a better security for a proper choice in the Senate than in the Executive.

Mr. Randolph. It is true that when the appt. of the Judges was vested in the 2d. branch an equality of votes had not been given to it. Yet he had rather leave the appointmt. there than give it to the Executive. He thought the advantage of personal responsibility might be gained in the Senate by requiring the respective votes of the members to be entered on the Journal. He thought too that the hope of ⟨receiving⟩ appts. would be more diffusive if they depended on the Senate, the members of which wd. be diffusively known, than if they depended on a single man who could not be personally known to a very great extent; and consequently that opposition to the System, would be so far weakened

Mr. Bedford thought there were solid reasons agst. leaving the appointment to the Executive. He must trust more to information than the Senate. It would put it in his power to gain over the larger States, by gratifying them with a preference of their Citizens. The responsibility of the Executive so much talked of was chimerical. He could not be punished for mistakes.

Mr. Ghorum remarked that the Senate could have no better information than the Executive They must like him, trust to information from the members belonging to the particular State where the Candidate resided. The Executive would certainly be more answerable for a good appointment, as the whole blame of a bad one would fall on him alone. He did not mean that he would be answerable under any other penalty than that of public censure, which with honorable minds was a sufficient one.

On the question for referring the appointment of the Judges to the Executive, ⟨instead of the 2d. branch⟩ [7]

Mas. ay. Cont. no. Pa. ay. Del. no. Md. no Va. no. N. C. no. S. C. no — ⟨Geo. absent.⟩ [Ayes — 2; noes — 6; absent — 1.]

Mr. Ghorum moved "that the Judges be ⟨nominated and appointed⟩ by the Executive, by & with the advice & consent of the 2d branch ⟨& every such nomination shall be made at least days prior to such appointment"⟩ [7]. This mode he said had been ratified by the experience of 140 years in Massachussts. If the appt. should be left to either branch of the Legislature, it will be a mere piece of jobbing.

Mr. Govr. Morris 2ded. & supported the motion.

Mr. Sherman thought it less objectionable than an absolute appointment by the Executive; but disliked it as too much fettering the Senate.

Question on Mr. Ghorum's motion

Mas. ay. Con. no. Pa ay. Del. no. Md. ay. Va. ay. N. C. no. S. C. no. Geo. ⟨absent.⟩ [Ayes — 4; noes — 4; absent — 1.]

⟨Mr.⟩ Mr⟨adison⟩ moved that the Judges should be nominated by the Executive, & such nomination should become an appointment ⟨if not⟩[8] disagreed to within days by ⅔ of the 2d. branch. Mr. Govr. ⟨Morris⟩ 2ded. the motion. By common consent the consideration of it was postponed till tomorrow.

"⟨To hold their offices during good behavior" & "to receive fixed salaries" agreed to nem: con:⟩ [9]

"In which (salaries of Judges) no increase or diminution shall be made, ⟨so as to affect the persons at the time in office.")

Mr. Govr. Morris moved to strike out " or increase". He thought the Legislature ought to be at liberty to increase salaries as circumstances might require, and that this would not create any improper dependence in the Judges.

Docr. Franklin ⟨was in favor of the motion⟩, Money may not

---

[7] Revised from *Journal*.

[8] Revised from *Journal*, originally Madison recorded "unless".

[9] Taken from *Journal*.

only become plentier, but the business of the department may increase as the Country becomes more populous.

Mr. ⟨Madison.⟩ The dependence will be less if the *increase alone* should be permitted, but it will be improper even so far to permit a dependence Whenever an increase is wished by the Judges, or may be in agitation in the legislature, an undue complaisance in the former may be felt towards the latter. If at such a crisis there should be in Court suits to which leading members of the Legislature may be parties, the Judges will be in a situation which ought not to suffered, if it can be prevented. The variations in the value of money, may be guarded agst. by taking for a standard wheat or some other thing of permanent value. The increase of business will be provided for by an increase of the number who are to do it. An increase of salaries may be easily so contrived as not to effect persons in office.[10]

Mr. Govr. Morris. The value of money may not only alter but the State of Society may alter. In this event the same quantity of wheat, the same value would not be the same compensation. The Amount of salaries must always be regulated by the manners & the style of living in a Country. The increase of business can not be provided for in the supreme tribunal in the way that has been mentioned. All the business of a certain description whether more or less must be done in that single tribunal — Additional labor alone in the Judges can provide for additional business. Additional compensation therefore ought not to be prohibited.

On the question for striking out "or increase" [11]

Mas. ay. Cont. ay. Pa. ay. Del. ay. Md. ay. Va. no. N. C. no. S. C. ay. Geo. ⟨absent⟩ [Ayes — 6; noes — 2; absent — 1.] ⟨The whole clause as amended was then agreed to nem: con:⟩[12]

12. Resol: "that Natl. ⟨Legislature⟩ be empowered to appoint inferior tribunals"

Mr. Butler could see no necessity for such tribunals. The State Tribunals might do the business.

Mr. L. Martin concurred. They will create jealousies &

[10] Stricken out "and [illegible words] plea during the life of Judges."

[11] See Appendix A, CCXV. [12] Taken from *Journal*.

oppositions in the State tribunals, with the jurisdiction of which they will interfere.

Mr. Ghorum. There are in the States already ⟨federal⟩ Courts with jurisdiction for trial of piracies &c. committed on the Seas. no complaints have been made by the States or the Courts of the States. Inferior tribunals are essential to render the authority of the Natl. Legislature effectual

Mr. Randolph observed that the Courts of the States can not be trusted with the administration of the National laws. The objects of jurisdiction are such as will often place the General & local policy at variance.

Mr. Govr. Morris urged also the necessity of such a provision

Mr. Sherman was willing to give the power to the Legislature but wished them to make use of the State Tribunals whenever it could be done. with safety to the general interest.

Col. Mason thought many circumstances might arise not now to be foreseen, which might render such a power absolutely necessary.[13]

On question for agreeing to 12. Resol: ⟨empowering the National Legislature to appoint⟩[14] "inferior tribunals". Agd. to nem. con.

13. Resol: ⟨"Impeachments of national officers" were struck out "on motion for the purpose.⟩[14] "The jurisdiction of Natl. Judiciary". Several criticisms having been made on the definition; it was proposed by Mr ⟨Madison⟩ so to alter as to read thus — "that the jurisdiction shall extend to all cases arising under the Natl. laws: And to such other questions as may involve the Natl. peace & harmony." which was agreed to nem. con.

Resol. 14. ⟨providing for the admission of new States⟩[14] Agreed to nem. con.

Resol. 15. that provision ought to be made for the continuance of Congs. &c. & for the completion of their engagements."

Mr. Govr. Morris thought the assumption of their engage-

[13] See also Appendix A, CLVIII (50).

[14] Taken from *Journal.*

ments might as well be omitted; and that Congs. ought not to be continued till all the States should adopt the reform; since it may become expedient to give effect to it whenever a certain number of States shall adopt it.

Mr. ⟨Madison⟩ the clause can mean nothing more than that provision ought to be made for preventing an interregnum; which must exist in the interval between the adoption of the New Govt. and the commencement of its operation, if the old Govt. should cease on the first of these events.

Mr. Wilson did not entirely approve of the manner in which the clause relating to the engagements of Congs. was expressed; but he thought some provision on the subject would be proper in order to prevent any suspicion that the obligations of the Confederacy might be dissolved along with the Governt. under which they were contracted.

On the question on the 1st part–relating to continuance of Congs."

Mass. no-Cont. no. Pa. no. Del-no. Md. no. Va. ay. N. C. ay. S. C. *ay. Geo. no. [Ayes — 3; noes — 6.]

The 2d. part as to completion of their engagements. disagd. to. nem. con.

Resol. 16. "That a Republican Constitution & its existing laws ought to be guaranteid to each State by the U. States."

Mr. Govr. Morris — thought the Resol: very objectionable. He should be very unwilling that such laws as exist in R. Island should be guaranteid.

Mr. Wilson. The object is merely to secure the States agst. dangerous commotions, insurrections and rebellions.

Col. Mason. If the Genl Govt. should have no right to suppress rebellions agst. particular States, it will be in a bad situation indeed. As Rebellions agst. itself originate in & agst. individual States, it must remain a passive Spectator of its own subversion.

Mr. Randolph. The Resoln. has 2. Objects. 1. to secure Republican Government. 2. to suppress domestic commotions. He urged the necessity of both these provisions.

Mr. ⟨Madison⟩ moved to substitute "that the Constitutional

* ⟨In the printed Journal, S. Carolina — no.⟩

authority of the States shall be guarantied to them respectively agst. domestic as well as foreign violence."

Docr. McClurg seconded the motion.

Mr. Houston was afraid of perpetuating the existing Constitutions of the States. That of Georgia was a very bad one, and he hoped would be revised & amended. It may also be difficult for the Genl. Govt. to decide between contending parties each of which claim the sanction of the Constitution.

Mr. L. Martin was for leaving the States to suppress Rebellions themselves.

Mr. Ghorum thought it strange that a Rebellion should be known to exist in the Empire, and the Genl. Govt. shd. be restrained from interposing to subdue it, At this rate an enterprising Citizen might erect the standard of Monarchy in a particular State, might gather together partizans from all quarters, might extend his views from State to State, and threaten to establish a tyranny over the whole & the Genl. Govt. be compelled to remain an inactive witness of its own destruction. With regard to different parties in a State; as long as they confine their disputes to words they will be harmless to the Genl. Govt. & to each other. If they appeal to the sword it will then be necessary for the Genl. Govt., however difficult it may be to decide on the merits of their contest, to interpose & put an end to it.

Mr. Carrol. Some such provision is essential. Every State ought to wish for it. It has been doubted whether it is a casus federis at present. And no room ought to be left for such a doubt hereafter.

Mr. Randolph moved to add as amendt. to the motion; "and that no State be at liberty to form any other than a Republican Govt." Mr. ⟨Madison⟩ seconded the motion

Mr. Rutlidge thought it unnecessary to insert any guarantee. No doubt could be entertained but that Congs. had the authority if they had the means to co-operate with any State in subduing a rebellion. It was & would be involved in the nature of the thing.

Mr. Wilson moved as a better expression of the idea, "that a Republican ⟨form of Governmt. shall⟩ be guarantied

to each State & that each State shall be protected agst. foreign & domestic violence.[15]

This seeming to be well received, Mr. ⟨Madison⟩ & Mr. Randolph withdrew their propositions & on the Question for agreeing to Mr. Wilson's motion it passed nem. con.

Adjd.[16]

[15] Revised from *Journal*.

[16] See Appendix A, LXV.

THURSDAY, JULY 19, 1787.

JOURNAL

Thursday July 19. 1787.

It was moved and seconded to reconsider the several clauses of the 9th resolution which respect the appointment, duration, and eligibility of the National Executive.

and unanimously agreed to reconsider immediately [Ayes — 10; noes — 0.] [1]

It was moved and seconded to agree to the following proposition,[2] namely,

"to be chosen by Electors appointed for that purpose by the Legislatures of the States, in the following proportion

One person from each State whose numbers, according to the ratio fixed in the resolution, shall not exceed 100,000 — *Two* from each of the others, whose numbers shall not exceed 300,000 — and *Three* from each of the rest.

On the question to agree to the following clause namely

"To be chosen by electors appointed for that purpose by the Legislatures of the States"

it passed in the affirmative. [Ayes —6; noes — 3; divided — 1. Ayes — 8; noes — 2.] [3]

It was agreed to postpone the consideration of the remainder of the proposition.

It was moved and seconded to agree to the following clause, namely,

"for the term of seven years"

---

[1] Vote 181, Detail of Ayes and Noes. Vote there given is Ayes, 9; noes, 1; but "No Caroa withdraw their negative."

[2] Vote 187, Detail of Ayes and Noes (July 20) shows that this proposition was "Mr. Ellsworth's".

[3] Votes 182 and 183, Detail of Ayes and Noes, showing question was divided.

which passed in the negative [Ayes — 3; noes — 5; divided — 2.][4]

On the question to agree to the following clause namely "for the term of six years"

it passed in the affirmative [Ayes — 9; noes — 1.][5]

On the question to restore the words "to be ineligible a second time"

it passed in the negative. [Ayes — 2; noes — 8].[6]

And then the House adjourned till to-morrow at 11 o'Clock A. M.

Detail of Ayes and Noes

	New Hampshire	Massachusetts	Rhode Island	Connecticut	New York	New Jersey	Pennsylvania	Delaware	Maryland	Virginia	North Carolina	South Carolina	Georgia	Questions	Ayes	Noes	Divided
[181]		aye		aye		aye	aye	aye	aye	aye	no	aye	aye	To reconsider all the clauses of the 9th resolution except the first. — No Caroa withdraw their negative.	9	1	
[182]		dd		aye		aye	aye	aye	aye	aye	no	no	no	"To be chosen by electors appointed for that purpose"	6	3	1
[183]		aye		aye		aye	aye	aye	aye	no	aye	no	aye	"by the Legislatures of the States"	8	2	
[184]		no		no		no	no	no	no	no	aye	aye	no	To restore the words "to be ineligible a second time"	2	8	
[185]		dd		no		aye	no	no	no	no	dd	aye	aye	for "seven years"	3	5	2
[186]		aye		aye		aye	aye	no	aye	aye	aye	aye	aye	for "six years"	9	1	

MADISON

Thursday, July. 19. in Convention.

On reconsideration of the vote rendering the Executive re-eligible a 2d. time,

4 Vote 185, Detail of Ayes and Noes.

5 Vote 186, Detail of Ayes and Noes.

6 Vote 184, Detail of Ayes and Noes. The order of these votes in Detail of Ayes and Noes is confirmed by Madison.

Mr. Martin moved to reinstate the words "to be ineligible a 2d. time".

Mr. Governeur Morris. It is necessary to take into one view all that relates to the establishment of the Executive; on the due formation of which must depend the efficacy & utility of the Union among the present and future States. It has been a maxim in political Science that Republican Government is not adapted to a large extent of Country, because the energy of the Executive Magistracy can not reach the extreme parts of it. Our Country is an extensive one. We must either then renounce the blessings of the Union, or provide an Executive with sufficient vigor to pervade every part of it. This subject was of so much importance that he hoped to be indulged in an extensive view of it. One great object of the Executive is to controul the Legislature. The Legislature will continually seek to aggrandize & perpetuate themselves; and will seize those critical moments produced by war, invasion or convulsion for that purpose. It is necessary then that the Executive Magistrate should be the guardian of the people, even of the lower classes, agst. Legislative tyranny, against the Great & the wealthy who in the course of things will necessarily compose — the Legislative body. Wealth tends to corrupt the mind & to nourish its love of power, and to stimulate it to oppression. History proves this to be the spirit of the opulent. The check provided in the 2d. branch was not meant as a check on Legislative usurpations of power, but on the abuse of lawful powers, on the propensity in the 1st. branch to legislate too much to run into projects of paper money & similar expedients. It is no check on Legislative tyranny. On the contrary it may favor it, and if the 1st. branch can be seduced may find the means of success. The Executive therefore ought to be so constituted as to be the great protector of the Mass of the people. — It is the duty of the Executive to appoint the officers & to command the forces of the Republic: to appoint 1. ministerial officers for the administration of public affairs. 2. Officers for the dispensation of Justice — Who will be the best Judges whether these appointments be well made? The people at

large, who will know, will see, will feel the effects of them— Again who can judge so well of the discharge of military duties for the protection & security of the people, as the people themselves who are to be protected & secured? He finds too that the Executive is not to be re-eligible. What effect will this have? 1. it will destroy the great incitement to merit public esteem by taking away the hope of being rewarded with a reappointment. It may give a dangerous turn to one of the strongest passions in the human breast. The love of fame is the great spring to noble & illustrious actions. Shut the Civil road to Glory & he may be compelled to seek it by the sword. 2. It will tempt him to make the most of the Short space of time allotted him, to accumulate wealth and provide for his friends. 3. It will produce violations of the very constitution it is meant to secure. In moments of pressing danger the tried abilities and established character of a favorite Magistrate will prevail over respect for the forms of the Constitution. The Executive is also to be impeachable. This is a dangerous part of the plan. It will hold him in such dependence that he will be no check on the Legislature, will not be a firm guardian of the people and of the public interest. He will be the tool of a faction, of some leading demagogue in the Legislature. These then are the faults of the Executive establishment as now proposed. Can no better establishmt. be devised? If he is to be the Guardian of the people let him be appointed by the people? If he is to be a check on the Legislature let him not be impeachable. Let him be of short duration, that he may with propriety be re-eligible.—It has been said that the candidates for this office will not be known to the people. If they be known to the Legislature, they must have such a notoriety and eminence of Character, that they cannot possibly be unknown to the people at large. It cannot be possible that a man shall have sufficiently distinguished himself to merit this high trust without having his character proclaimed by fame throughout the Empire. As to the danger from an unimpeachable magistrate he could not regard it as formidable. There must be certain great officers of State; a minister of finance, of war, of foreign affairs &c.

These he presumes will exercise their functions in subordination to the Executive, and will be amenable by impeachment to the public Justice. Without these ministers the Executive can do nothing of consequence. He suggested a biennial election of the Executive at the time of electing the 1st. branch, and the Executive to hold over, so as to prevent any interregnum in the Administration. An election by the people at large throughout so great an extent of country could not be influenced, by those little combinations and those momentary lies which often decide popular elections within a narrow sphere. It will probably, be objected that the election will be influenced by the members of the Legislature; particularly of the 1st. branch, and that it will be nearly the same thing with an election by the Legislature itself. It could not be denied that such an influence would exist. But it might be answered that as the Legislature or the candidates for it would be divided, the enmity of one part would counteract the friendship of another; that if the administration of the Executive were good, it would be unpopular to oppose his re-election, if bad it ought to be opposed & a reappointmt. prevented; and lastly that in every view this indirect dependence on the favor of the Legislature could not be so mischievous as a direct dependence for his appointment. He saw no alternative for making the Executive independent of the Legislature but either to give him his office for life, or make him eligible by the people. — Again, it might be objected that two years would be too short a duration. But he believes that as long as he should behave himself well, he would be continued in his place. The extent of the Country would secure his re-election agst the factions & discontents of particular States. It deserved consideration also that such an ingredient in the plan would render it extremely palatable to the people. These were the general ideas which occurred to him on the subject, and which led him to wish & move that the ⟨whole constitution of the Executive⟩ might undergo reconsideration.

Mr. Randolph urged the motion of Mr. L. Martin for restoring the words making the Executive ineligible a 2d. time. If he ought to be independent, he should not be left under a

temptation to court a re-appointment. If he should be re-appointable by the Legislature, he will be no check on it. His revisionary power will be of no avail. He had always thought & contended as he still did that the danger apprehended by the little States was chimerical, but those who thought otherwise ought to be peculiarly anxious for the motion. If the Executive be appointed, as has been determined, by the Legislature, he will probably be appointed either by joint ballot of both houses, or be nominated by the 1st. and appointed by the 2d. branch. In either case the large States will preponderate. If he is to court the same influence for his re-appointment, will he ⟨not⟩ make his revisionary power. and all the other functions of his administration subservient to the views of the large States. Besides — is there not great reason to apprehend that in case he should be re-eligible, a false complaisance in the Legislature might lead them to continue an unfit man in office in preference to a fit one. It has been said that a constitutional bar to reappointment will inspire unconstitutional endeavours to perpetuate himself. It may be answered that his endeavous can have no effect unless the people be corrupt to such a degree as to render all precautions hopeless: to which may be added that this argument supposes him to be more powerful & dangerous, than other arguments which have been used, admit, and consequently calls for stronger fetters on his authority. He thought an election by the Legislature with an incapacity to be elected a second time would be more acceptable to the people that the plan suggested by Mr. Govr. Morris.[7]

Mr. King. did not like the ineligibility. He thought there was great force in the remark of Mr. Sherman, that he who has proved himself to be most fit for an Office, ought not to be excluded by the constitution from holding it. He would therefore prefer any other reasonable plan that could be substituted. He was much disposed to think that in such cases the people at large would chuse wisely. There was indeed some difficulty arising from the improbability of a general

[7] See further Appendix A, CCXII.

concurrence of the people in favor of any one man. On the whole he was of opinion that an appointment by electors chosen by the people for the purpose, would be liable to fewest objections.

Mr. Patterson's ideas nearly coincided he said with those of Mr. King. He proposed that the Executive should be appointed by Electors to be chosen by the States in a ratio that would allow one elector to the smallest and three to the largest States.

Mr. Wilson. It seems to be the unanimous sense that the Executive should not be appointed by the Legislature, unless he be rendered in-eligible a 2d. time: he perceived with pleasure that the idea was gaining ground, of an election mediately or immediately by the people.

Mr. ⟨Madison⟩ If it be a fundamental principle of free Govt. that the Legislative, Executive & Judiciary powers should be *separately* exercised; it is equally so that they be *independently* exercised. There is the same & perhaps greater reason why the Executive shd. be independent of the Legislature, than why the Judiciary should: A coalition of the two former powers would be more immediately & certainly dangerous to public liberty. It is essential then that the appointment of the Executive should either be drawn from some source, or held by some tenure, that will give him a free agency with regard to the Legislature. This could not be if he was to be appointable from time to time by the Legislature. It was not clear that an appointment in the 1st. instance ⟨even⟩ with an ineligibility afterwards would not establish an improper connection between the two departments. Certain it was that the appointment would be attended with intrigues and contentions that ought not to be unnecessarily admitted. He was disposed for these reasons to refer the appointment to some other Source. The people at large was in his opinion the fittest in itself.[8] It would be as likely as any that could be devised to produce an Executive Magistrate of distinguished Character. The people generally could only know & vote for

[8] Crossed out: "It was the source from which the Legislature He was persuaded".

some Citizen whose merits had rendered him an object of general attention & esteem. There was one difficulty however of a serious nature attending an immediate choice by the people. The right of suffrage was much more diffusive in the Northern than[9] the Southern States; and the latter could have no influence in the election on the score of the Negroes. The substitution of electors obviated this difficulty and seemed on the whole to be liable to the fewest objections.

Mr. Gerry. If the Executive is to be be elected by the Legislature he certainly ought not to be re-eligible. This would make him absolutely dependent. He was agst. a popular election. The people are uninformed, and would be misled by a few designing men. He urged the expediency of an appointment of the Executive by Electors to be chosen by the State Executives. The people of the States will then choose the 1st. branch: The legislatures of the States the 2nd. branch of the National Legislature, and the Executives of the States, the National Executive — This he thought would form a strong attachnt. in the States to the National System. The popular mode of electing the chief Magistrate would certainly be the worst of all. If he should be so elected & should do his duty, he will be turned out for it like Govr Bowdoin in Massts & President Sullivan in N. Hamshire.

On the question on Mr Govr. Morris motion to reconsider generally the Constitution of the Executive —

Mas. ay. Ct. ay. N. J. ay. & all the others ay.

Mr. Elseworth moved to strike out the appointmt. by the Natl. Legislature, and insert "to be chosen by electors appointed by the Legislatures of the States in the following ratio; towit—one for each State not exceeding 200,000[10] inhabts. two for each above yt. number & not exceeding 300,000. and, three for each State exceeding 300,000. — Mr. Broome 2ded. the motion

Mr Rutlidge was opposed to all the modes except the appointmt. by the Natl. Legislature. He will be sufficiently independent, if he be not re-eligible

[9] Crossed out "Eastern &".

[10] Journal gives this 100,000.

Mr. Gerry preferred the motion of Mr. Elseworth to an appointmt. by the Natl. Legislature, or by the people; tho' not to an appt. by the State Executives. He moved that the electors proposed by Mr. E. should be 25 in number, and allotted in the following proportion. to N. H. 1. to Mas. 3. to R. I. 1. to. Cont. 2-to N. Y. 2-N. J. 2. Pa. 3. Del. 1. Md. 2. Va. 3. N. C. 2. S. C. 2. Geo. 1.

The question as moved by Mr. Elseworth being divided, on the 1st. part shall ye. Natl. Executive be appointed by Electors?

Mas-divd. Cont. ay. N. J. ay. Pa. ay. Del. ay. Md. ay. Va. ay- N. C. no. S. C. no. Geo. no. [Ayes — 6; noes — 3; divided — 1.]

On 2d. part shall the Electors be chosen by State Legislatures?

Mas. ay. Cont. ay. N. J. ay. Pa. ay. Del. ay. Md. ay. Va. no. N. C. ay. S. C. no. Geo. ay. [Ayes — 8; noes — 2.]

The part relating to the ratio in which the States sd. chuse electors was postponed nem. con.

Mr. L. Martin moved that the Executive be ineligible a 2d. time.

Mr. Williamson 2ds. the motion. He had no great confidence in the Electors to be chosen for the special purpose. They would not be the most respectable citizens; but persons not occupied in the high offices of Govt. They would be liable to undue influence, which might the more readily be practiced as some of them will probably be in appointment 6 or 8 months before the object of it comes on.

Mr. Elseworth supposed any persons might be appointed Electors, excepting solely, members of the Natl. Legislature.

On the question shall he be ineligible a 2d. time?

Mas. no. Ct. no. N. J. no. Pa. no. Del. no. Md. no. Va. no. N. C. ay. S. C. ay. Geo. no. [Ayes — 2; noes — 8.]

On the question shall the Executive continue for 7 years? ⟨It passed in the negative⟩ Mas. divd. Cont. ay.* N — J. no.* Pa. no. Del. no. Md. no. Va. no. N. C. divd. S. C. ay. Geo. ay. [Ayes — 3; noes — 5; divided — 2.]

* ⟨In the printed Journal Cont. no. N. Jersey ay⟩

Mr. King was afraid we shd. shorten the term too much.

Mr. Govr Morris was for a short term, in order to avoid impeachts. which wd. be otherwise necessary.

Mr. Butler was agst. a frequency of the elections. Geo & S. C. were too distant to send electors often.

Mr. Elseworth was for 6 years. If the elections be too frequent, the Executive will not be firm eno'. There must be duties which will make him unpopular for the moment. There will be *outs* as well as *ins*. His administration therefore will be attacked and misrepresented.

Mr. Williamson was for 6 years. The expence will be considerable & ought not to be unnecessarily repeated. If the Elections are too frequent, the best men will not undertake the service and those of an inferior character will be liable to be corrupted.

On question for 6 years?

Mas. ay. Cont. ay. N. J. ay. Pa. ay. Del. no. Md. ay. Va. ay. N. C. ay. S. C. ay. Geo. ay. [Ayes — 9; noes — 1.]

Adjourned

FRIDAY, JULY 20, 1787.

JOURNAL

Friday July 20. 1787.

It was moved and seconded to postpone the consideration of the clause, respecting the number of Electors, entered on the Journal yesterday in order to take up the following namely,

Resolved that for the first election of the supreme Executive the proportion of Electors shall be as follows, namely

New Hampshire	1	Delaware	1
Massachusetts	3	Maryland	2
Rhode Island	1	Virginia	3
Connecticut	2	North Carolina	2
New York	2	South Carolina	2
New Jersey	2	Georgia	1
Pennsylvania	3		

in all 25. Electors.

On the question to postpone

it passed in the affirmative [Ayes—6; noes—4.][1]

It was moved and seconded to refer the last motion to a Committee

which passed in the negative. [Ayes—3; noes—7.][2]

It was moved and seconded to add one Elector to the States of New Hampshire and Georgia.

which passed in the affirmative. [Ayes—6; noes—4.]

The last motion having been misunderstood, it was moved and seconded that it be put again — and on the question to give an additional Elector to each of the States of New Hampshire and Georgia

[1] Vote 187, Detail of Ayes and Noes, which notes that the proposition was "Mr Gerry's".

[2] Vote 188, Detail of Ayes and Noes. *Cf.* Madison's report of these proceedings.

it passed in the negative. [Ayes — 3; noes — 7.]
On the question to agree to the above resolution respecting the first election of the supreme Executive

it passed in the affirmative. [Ayes — 6; noes — 4.]
It was moved and seconded to agree to the following resolution
Resolved That the Electors respectively shall not be Members of the National Legislature, or Officers of the Union, or eligible to the office of supreme Magistrate

which passed in the affirmative.
It was moved and seconded to agree to the following clause of the 9th resolution reported from the Committee of the whole House namely

"To be removable on impeachment and conviction of malpractice or neglect of duty"
It was moved and seconded to postpone the consideration of the last motion

which passed in the negative. [Ayes — 2; noes — 8.]
It was moved and seconded to agree to the clause

which passed in the affirmative [Ayes — 8; noes — 2.]
It was moved and seconded to agree to the following clause namely

"to receive a fixed compensation for the devotion of his time to public service"

which passed unan: in the affirmative [Ayes — 10; noes — 0.]
It was moved and seconded to agree to the following clause, namely

"to be paid out of the national Treasury"

which passed unan: in the affirmative [Ayes — 10; noes — 0.][3]

---

[3] Vote 194, Detail of Ayes and Noes.

In the Detail of Ayes and Noes at this point the secretary of the Convention did something which was quite misleading: He wrote the question in the blank of 195, but recorded the votes in the space below, *i. e.*, in 196. When the first question was taken on August 16, he was evidently unprepared and recorded the vote in the first available blank which happened to be that of 195, and wrote the question "14 sect. of the 6 article" after the question the vote of which had been recorded. This accounts for New Hampshire's vote, and Madison notes that Massachusetts was absent when this vote was taken on August 16. When John Quincy Adams prepared the printed

DETAIL OF AYES AND NOES

	New Hampshire	Massachusetts	Rhode Island	Connecticut	New York	New Jersey	Pennsylvania	Delaware	Maryland	Virginia	North Carolina	South Carolina	Georgia	Questions	Ayes	Noes	Divided
[187]		aye		no		no	aye	no	no	aye	aye	aye	aye	To postpone Mr Ellsworth's motion for electing the Executive to take up Mr Gerry's	6	4	
[188]		no		no		aye	no	aye	aye	no	no	no	no	To refer Mr Gerry's motion to a Committee of detail	3	7	
[189]		no		aye		aye	aye	no	no	aye	no	aye	aye	To add One Elector to the States of Georgia and New Hampshire	6	4	
[190]		no		aye		no	no	no	no	no	no	aye	aye	The last motion repeated	3	7	
[191]		aye		aye		no	aye	no	no	aye	aye	aye	no	To agree to the proposition for the first election of the Supreme Executive, offered by Mr Gerry.	6	4	
[192]		aye		no		no	no	no	no	no	no	aye	no	To postpone the consideration of the clause which respects the impeachment of the Executive	2	8	
[193]		no		aye		aye	aye	aye	aye	aye	aye	no	aye	To agree to the clause respecting the impeachmt of the Executive.	8	2	
[194]		aye		aye		aye	aye	aye	aye	aye	aye	aye	aye	To receive a fixed compensation for the devotion of his time to Public service. unanimous	10		
[195]	aye[3]			aye		no	aye	aye	aye	aye	aye	aye	aye	To be paid out of the national Treasury unanimous 14 sect. of the 6 article	9	1	
[196]		aye		aye		aye	aye	aye	aye	aye	aye	aye	aye				
[197]		aye		no		aye	aye	aye	aye	aye	no	aye	aye	To adjourn			

[End of sixth loose sheet]

[To adjourn Ayes — 8; noes — 2.][4]
and then the House adjourned till to-morrow at 11 o'Clock A. M.

MADISON

Friday July 20 — in Convention

The ⟨postponed⟩ Ratio of Electors for appointing the Executive; to wit 1 for each State whose inhabitants do not exceed 100,000,[5] &c. being taken up.

ˣMr. ⟨Madison⟩ observed that this would make in time all or nearly all the the States equal. Since there were few that would not in time contain the number of inhabitants entitling them to 3 Electors; that this ratio ought either to be made temporary, or so varied as that it would adjust itself to the growing population of the States.

Mr. Gerry moved that in the *1st. instance* the Electors should be allotted to the States in the following ratio: to N. H. 1. Mas. 3. R. I. 1. Cont. 2. N. Y. 2. N. J. 2. Pa. 3. Del. 1. Md. 2. Va. 3. N. C. 2. S. C. 2. Geo. 1.[6]

On the question to postpone in order to take up this motion of Mr. Gerry. ⟨It passed in the affirmative.⟩

Mas. ay. Cont. no. N. J. no. Pa. ay. Del. no. Md. no. Va. ay. N. C. ay. S. C. ay. Geo. ay. [Ayes — 6; noes — 4.]

Mr. Elseworth moved that 2 Electors be allotted to N. H. Some rule ought to be pursued; and N. H. has more than 100,000 inhabitants. He thought it would be proper also to allot 2. to Georgia.

Mr. Broom & Mr. Martin moved to postpone Mr. Gerry's allotment of Electors, leaving a fit ratio to be reported by

Journal he failed to solve this difficulty. He accordingly ignored Vote 196, and ascribed the vote of August 16 to the first question in the blank of 195. He ascribed the vote of New Hampshire to Massachusetts and recorded the total as "Yeas, 9; nay, 1," in spite of the fact that the Journal specifically stated that the question was "passed unan: in the affirmative." Madison was misled by this, see below.

[4] Vote 197, Detail of Ayes and Noes.

[5] 100,000 is not as Madison reported this on July 19, but accords with the Journal.

[6] Madison reports this same motion made July 19, but perhaps not seconded and now repeated.

the Committee to be appointed for detailing the Resolutions.

On this motion.

Mas-no. Ct. no. N. J. ay. Pa. no. Del. ay. Md. ay. Va. no. N. C. no. S. C. no. Geo. no. [Ayes — 3; noes — 7.]

Mr. Houston 2ded. the motion of Mr. Elseworth to add another Elector to N. H. & Georgia. On the Question:

Mas. no. Ct ay. N. J. no. Pa. no. Del. no. Md no. Va. no. N. C. no. S. C.-ay-Geo-ay. [Ayes — 3; noes — 7.] [7]

Mr. Williamson moved as an amendment to Mr. Gerry's allotment of Electors in the 1st. instance that in future elections of the Natl. Executive, the number of Electors to be appointed by the several States shall be regulated by their respective numbers of Representatives in the 1st. branch pursuing as nearly as may be the present proportions.

On question on Mr. Gerry's ratio of Electors

Mas. ay. Ct ay. N. J. no. Pa. ay. Del. no. Md. no. Va. ay-N. C. ay. S. C. ay. Geo. no. [Ayes — 6; noes — 4.]

"to be removeable on impeachment and conviction ⟨for⟩ malpractice or neglect of duty". See Resol: 9:

Mr. Pinkney & Mr Govr. Morris moved to strike out this part of the Resolution. Mr P. observd. he ⟨ought not to⟩ be impeachable whilst in office

Mr. Davie. If he be not impeachable whilst in office, he will spare no efforts or means whatever to get himself re-elected. He considered this as an essential security for the good behaviour of the Executive.[8]

Mr Wilson concurred in the necessity of making the Executive impeachable whilst in office.

Mr. Govr. Morris. He can do no criminal act without Coadjutors who may be punished. In case he should be re-elected, that will be sufficient proof of his innocence. Besides who is to impeach? Is the impeachment to suspend his functions. If it is not the mischief will go on. If it is the impeachment will be nearly equivalent to a displacement,

[7] Madison's account of these proceedings differs from the Journal, but the result is the same.

[8] Crossed out: "To punish him when".

and will render the Executive dependent on those who are to impeach

Col. Mason. No point is of more importance than that the right of impeachment should be continued. Shall any man be above Justice? Above all shall that man be above it, who can commit the most extensive injustice? When great crimes were committed he was for punishing the principal as well as the Coadjutors. There had been much debate & difficulty as to the mode of chusing the Executive. He approved of that which had been adopted at first, namely of referring the appointment to the Natl. Legislature. One objection agst. Electors was the danger of their being corrupted by the Candidates: & this furnished a peculiar reason in favor of impeachments whilst in office. Shall the man who has practised corruption & by that means procured his appointment in the first instance, be suffered to escape punishment, by repeating his guilt?

Docr. Franklin was for retaining the clause as favorable to the executive. History furnishes one example only of a first Magistrate being formally brought to public Justice. Every body cried out agst this as unconstitutional. What was the practice before this in cases where the chief Magistrate rendered himself obnoxious? Why recourse was had to assassination in wch. he was not only deprived of his life but of the opportunity of vindicating his character. It wd. be the best way therefore to provide in the Constitution for the regular punishment of the Executive when his misconduct should deserve it, and for his honorable acquittal when he should be unjustly accused.

Mr. Govr Morris admits corruption & some few other offences to be such as ought to be impeachable; but thought the cases ought to be enumerated & defined:

Mr. ⟨Madison⟩ — thought it indispensable that some provision should be made for defending the Community agst the incapacity, negligence or perfidy of the chief Magistrate. The limitation of the period of his service, was not a sufficient security. He might lose his capacity after his appointment. He might pervert his administration into a scheme of pecula-

tion or oppression. He might betray his trust to foreign powers. The case of the Executive Magistracy was very distinguishable, from that of the Legislative or of any other public body, holding offices of limited duration. It could not be presumed that all or even a majority of the members of an Assembly would either lose their capacity for discharging, or be bribed to betray, their trust. Besides the restraints of their personal integrity & honor, the difficulty of acting in concert for purposes of corruption was a security to the public. And if one or a few members only should be seduced, the soundness of the remaining members, would maintain the integrity and fidelity of the body. In the case of the Executive Magistracy which was to be administered by a single man, loss of capacity or corruption was more within the compass of probable events, and either of them might be fatal to the Republic.

Mr. Pinkney did not see the necessity of impeachments. He was sure they ought not to issue from the Legislature who would in that case hold them as a rod over the Executive and by that means effectually destroy his independence. His revisionary power in particular would be rendered altogether insignificant.

Mr. Gerry urged the necessity of impeachments. A good magistrate will not fear them. A bad one ought to be kept in fear of them. He hoped the maxim would never be adopted here that the chief Magistrate could do ⟨no⟩ wrong.

Mr. King expressed his apprehensions that an extreme caution in favor of liberty might enervate the Government we were forming. He wished the House to recur to the primitive axiom that the three great departments of Govts. should be separate & independent: that the Executive & Judiciary should be so as well as the Legislative: that the Executive should be so equally with the Judiciary. Would this be the case if the Executive should be impeachable? It had been said that the Judiciary would be impeachable. But it should have been remembered at the same time that the Judiciary hold their places [9] not for a limited time, but during good

[9] Crossed out: "for life".

behaviour. It is necessary therefore that a forum should be established for trying misbehaviour. Was the Executive to hold his place during good behaviour? [10] — The Executive was to hold his place for a limited term like the members of the Legislature; Like them particularly the Senate whose members would continue in appointmt the same term of 6 years. he would periodically be tried for his behaviour by his electors, who would continue or discontinue him in trust according to the manner in which he had discharged it. Like them therefore, he ought to be subject to no intermediate trial, by impeachment. He ought not to be impeachable unless he hold his office during good behavior, a tenure which would be most agreeable to him; provided an independent and effectual forum could be devised; But under no circumstances ought he to be impeachable by the Legislature. This would be destructive of his independence and of the principles of the Constitution. He relied on the vigor of the Executive as a great security for the public liberties.

Mr. Randolph. The propriety of impeachments was a favorite principle with him; Guilt wherever found ought to be punished. The Executive will have great opportunitys of abusing his power; particularly in time of war when the military force, and in some respects the public money will be in his hands. Should no regular punishment be provided, it will be irregularly inflicted by tumults & insurrections. He is aware of the necessity of proceeding with a cautious hand, and of excluding as much as possible the influence of the Legislature from the business. He suggested for consideration an idea which had fallen (from Col Hamilton) of composing a forum out of the Judges belonging to the States: and even of requiring some preliminary inquest whether just grounds of impeachment existed.

Doctr. Franklin mentioned the case of the Prince of Orange during the late war. An agreement was made between France & Holland; by which their two fleets were to unite at a certain time & place. The Du⟨t⟩ch fleet did not appear. Every body

[10] Crossed out: "He wished this were the case. But it was not."

began to wonder at it. At length it was suspected that the Statholder was at the bottom of the matter. This suspicion prevailed more & more. Yet as he could not be impeached and no regular examination took place, he remained in his office, and strengtheing his own party, as the party opposed to him became formidable, he gave birth to the most violent animosities & contentions. Had he been impeachable, a regular & peaceable inquiry would have taken place and he would if guilty have been duly punished, if innocent restored to the confidence of the public.

Mr. King remarked that the case of the Statholder was not applicable. He held his place for life, and was not periodically elected. In the former case impeachments are proper to secure good behaviour. In the latter they are unnecessary; the periodical responsibility [11] to the electors [12] being an equivalent security.

Mr Wilson observed that if the idea were to be pursued, the Senators who are to hold their places during the same term with the Executive. ought to be subject to impeachment & removal.

Mr. Pinkney apprehended that some gentlemen reasoned on a supposition that the Executive was to have powers which would not be committed to him: ⟨He presumed⟩ that his powers would be so circumscribed as to render impeachments unnecessary.

Mr. Govr. Morris,'s opinion had been changed by the arguments used in the discussion. He was now sensible of the necessity of impeachments, if the Executive was to continue for any time in office. Our Executive was not like a Magistrate having a life interest, much less like one having an hereditary interest in his office. He may be bribed by a greater interest to betray his trust; and no one would say that we ought to expose ourselves to the danger of seeing the first Magistrate in foreign pay without being able to guard agst it by displacing him. One would think the King of England well secured agst bribery. He has as it were a fee

[11] Crossed out "trial".

[12] Crossed out "rendering them unnecessary".

simple in the whole Kingdom. Yet Charles II was bribed by Louis XIV. The Executive ought therefore to be impeachable for treachery; Corrupting his electors, and incapacity were other causes of impeachment. For the latter he should be punished not as a man, but as an officer, and punished only by degradation from his office. This Magistrate is not the King but the prime-Minister. The people are the King. When we make him amenable to Justice however we should take care to provide some mode that will not make him dependent on the Legislature.

⟨It was moved & 2ded. to postpone the question of impeachments which was negatived. Mas. & S. Carolina only being ay.⟩[13]

On ye. Question, Shall the Executive be removeable on impeachments?

Mas. no. Ct. ay. N. J. ay. Pa. ay. Del. ay. Md. ay. Va. ay. N. C. ay. S. C. no. Geo-ay- [Ayes — 8; noes — 2.]

"Executive to receive fixed compensation, Agreed to nem. con-

"⟨to be paid out of the National Treasury" agreed to, N. Jersey only in the negative.⟩[14]

Mr. Gerry & Govr. Morris moved 'that the Electors of the Executive shall not be members of the Natl. Legislature, nor officers of the U. States, nor shall the Electors themselves be eligible to the ⟨supreme⟩ Magistracy."[15] Agreed to nem. con.

Docr. McClurg asked whether it would not be necessary, before a Committee for detailing the Constitution should be appointed, to determine on the means by which the Executive. is to carry the laws into effect, and to resist combinations agst. them. Is he to have a military force for the purpose, or to have the command of the Militia, the only existing force that can be applied to that use? As the Resolutions now

[13] Taken from *Journal.*

[14] Madison originally had added to preceding question "to be paid out of the Natl treasury" and had recorded the whole as agreed to unanimously. He was misled by *Journal* into making the changes incorporated in the text. See above note 3.

[15] This motion by Gerry and Morris is placed earlier in the Journal.

Stand the Committee will have no determinate directions on this great point.

Mr. Wilson thought that some additional directions to the Committee wd. be necessary.

Mr. King. The Committee are to provide for the end. Their discretionary power to provide for the means is involved according to an established axiom.

Adjourned

SATURDAY, JULY 21, 1787.

JOURNAL

Saturday July 21. 1787.

It was moved and seconded to add the following clause to the resolution respecting the Electors of the supreme Executive, namely

"Who shall be paid out of the national Treasury for the "devotion of their time to the public service"

which passed unanimously in the affirmative. [Ayes—9; noes — 0.][1]

It was moved and seconded to add after the words "national Executive" in the 10th resolution the words "together with the supreme national Judiciary."

which passed in the negative [Ayes — 3; noes — 4; divided — 2.][2]

It was moved and seconded to agree to the 10th resolution, as reported from the Committee of the whole House, namely

Resolved that the national Executive shall have a right to negative any legislative act, which shall not be afterwards passed unless by two third parts of each Branch of the national Legislature.

which passed unanimously in the affirmative [Ayes — 9; noes — 0.]

On the question to agree to the following amendment of the 3rd clause of the 11th resolution, namely

"That the Judges shall be nominated by the Executive,

---

[1] Vote 63, Detail of Ayes and Noes, see above, *Records* of June 15.

The secretary was evidently unprepared when this first question was taken, and recorded it in a convenient blank space which happened to be at the bottom of the 2d loose sheet of the Detail of Ayes and Noes.

[2] Vote 198, Detail of Ayes and Noes.

"and such nomination shall become an appointment if not "disagreed to by the second Branch of the Legislature"

it passed in the negative [Ayes — 3; noes — 6.]

On the question to agree to the following clause of the 11th resolution, as reported from the Committee of the whole House, namely

"The Judges of which shall be appointed by the second "Branch of the national Legislature"

it passed in the affirmative [Ayes — 6; noes — 3.]

[To adjourn Ayes — 1; noes — 8.] [3]

And then the House adjourned till Monday next at 11 o'clock A. M.

Detail of Ayes and Noes

[Beginning of seventh loose sheet]

	New Hampshire	Massachusetts	Rhode Island	Connecticut	New York	New Jersey	Pennsylvania	Delaware	Maryland	Virginia	North Carolina	South Carolina	Georgia	Questions	Ayes	Noes	Divided
[198]		no		aye			dd	no	aye	aye	no	no	dd	To join the supreme Judiciary with the Executive in the negative	3	4	2
[199]		aye		aye			aye	aye	aye	aye	aye	aye	aye	That the supreme Executive shall possess a revisionary negative	9		
[200]		aye		no			aye	no	no	aye	no	no	no	To agree to the nomination of the Judges by the Executive which shall become an appointment unless disagreed to by the second Branch of ye Legislature	3	6	
[201]		no		aye			no	aye	aye	no	aye	aye	aye	The Judges shall be appointed by the second Branch of the Legislature	6	3	
[202]		no		no			aye	no	no	no	no	no	no	To adjourn	1	8	

[3] Vote 202, Detail of Ayes and Noes. There is no reason for ascribing this question to this place in the proceedings, except for its position in the Detail of Ayes and Noes.

MADISON

Saturday July 21 in Convention

Mr. Williamson moved that the Electors of the Executive should be paid out of the National Treasury for the Service to be performed by them". Justice required this: as it was a national service they were to render. The motion was agreed to nem.— con.

Mr. Wilson moved as an amendment to Resoln: 10. that the ⟨supreme⟩ Natl Judiciary should be associated with the Executive in the Revisionary power". This proposition had been before made, and failed; but he was so confirmed by reflection in the opinion of its utility, that he thought it incumbent on him to make another effort: The Judiciary ought to have an opportunity of remonstrating agst projected encroachments on the people as well as on themselves. It had been said that the Judges, as expositors of the Laws would have an opportunity of defending their constitutional rights. There was weight in this observation; but this power of the Judges did not go far enough. Laws may be unjust, may be unwise, may be dangerous, may be destructive; and yet not be so unconstitutional as to justify the Judges in refusing to give them effect. Let them have a share in the Revisionary power, and they will have an opportunity of taking notice of these characters of a law, and of counteracting, by the weight of their opinions the improper views of the Legislature. — Mr ⟨Madison⟩ 2ded. the motion

Mr Ghorum did not see the advantage of employing the Judges in this way. As Judges they are not to be presumed to possess any peculiar knowledge of the mere policy of public measures. Nor can it be necessary as a security for their constitutional rights. The Judges in England have no such additional provision for their defence, yet their jurisdiction is not invaded. He thought it would be best to let the Executive alone be responsible, and at most to authorize him to call on Judges for their opinions,

Mr. Elseworth approved heartily of the motion. The aid of

the Judges will give more wisdom & firmness to the Executive. They will possess a systematic and accurate knowledge of the Laws, which the Executive can not be expected always to possess. The law of Nations also will frequently come into question. Of this the Judges alone will have competent information.

Mr. ⟨Madison⟩ — considered the object of the motion as of great importance to the meditated Constitution. It would be useful to the Judiciary departmt. by giving it an additional opportunity of defending itself agst: Legislative encroachments; It would be useful to the Executive, by inspiring additional confidence & firmness in exerting the revisionary power: It would be useful to the Legislature by the valuable assistance it would give in preserving a consistency, conciseness, perspicuity & technical propriety in the laws, qualities peculiarly necessary; & yet shamefully wanting in our republican Codes. It would moreover be useful to the Community at large as an additional check agst. a pursuit of those unwise & unjust measures which constituted so great a portion of our calamities. If any solid objection could be urged agst. the motion, it must be on the supposition that it tended to give too much strength either to the Executive or Judiciary. He did not think there was the least ground for this apprehension. It was much more to be apprehended that notwithstanding this co-operation of the two departments, the Legislature would still be an overmatch for them. Experience in all the States had evinced a powerful tendency in the Legislature to absorb all power into its vortex. This was the real source of danger to the American Constitutions; & suggested the necessity of giving every defensive authority to the other departments that was consistent with republican principles.

Mr. Mason said he had always been a friend to this provision. It would give a confidence to the Executive, which he would not otherwise have, and without which the Revisionary power would be of little avail.

Mr. Gerry did not expect to see this point which had undergone full discussion, again revived. The object he conceived

of the Revisionary power was merely to secure the Executive department agst. legislative encroachment. The Executive therefore who will best know and be ready to defend his rights ought alone to have the defence of them. The motion was liable to strong objections. It was combining & mixing together the Legislative & the other departments. It was establishing an improper coalition between the Executive & Judiciary departments. It was making Statesmen of the Judges; and setting them up as the guardians of the Rights of the people. He relied for his part on the Representatives of the people as the guardians of their Rights & interests. It was making the Expositors of the Laws, the Legislators which ought never to be done. A better expedient for correcting the laws, would be to appoint as had been done in Pena. a person or persons of proper skill, to draw bills for the Legislature.

Mr. Strong thought with Mr. Gerry that the power of making ought to be kept distinct from that of expounding, the laws. No maxim was better established. The Judges in exercising the function of expositors might be influenced by the part they had taken, in framing the laws.

Mr. Govr. Morris. Some check being necessary on the Legislature, the question is in what hands it should be lodged. On one side it was contended that the Executive alone ought to exercise it. He did not think that an Executive appointed for 6 years, and impeachable whilst in office, wd. be a very effectual check. On the other side it was urged that he ought to be reinforced by the Judiciary department. Agst. this it was objected that Expositors of laws ought to have no hand in making them, and arguments in favor of this had been drawn from England. What weight was due to them might be easily determined by an attention to facts. The truth was that the Judges in England had a great share in ye Legislation. They are consulted in difficult & doubtful cases. They may be & some of them are members of the Legislature. They are or may be members of the privy Council, and can there advise the Executive as they will do with us if the motion succeeds. The influence the English Judges may have in the latter capacity in strengthening the Executive check

can not be ascertained, as the King by his influence in a manner dictates the laws. There is one difference in the two Cases however which disconcerts all reasoning from the British to our proposed Constitution. The British Executive has so great an interest in his prerogatives and such powerful means of defending them that he will never yield any part of them. The interest of our Executive is so inconsiderable & so transitory, and his means of defending it so feeble, that there is the justest ground to fear his want of firmness in resisting incroachments. He was extremely apprehensive that the auxiliary firmness & weight of the Judiciary would not supply the deficiency. He concurred in thinking the public liberty in greater danger from Legislative usurpations than from any other source. It had been said that the Legislature ought to be relied on as the proper Guardians of liberty. The answer was short and conclusive. Either bad laws will be pushed or not. On the latter supposition no check will be wanted. On the former a strong check will be necessary: And this is the proper supposition. Emissions of paper money, largesses to the people — a remission of debts and similar measures, will at sometimes be popular, and will be pushed for that reason At other times such measures will coincide with the interests of the Legislature themselves, & that will be a reason not less cogent for pushing them. It might be thought that the people will not be deluded and misled in the latter case. But experience teaches another lesson. The press is indeed a great means of diminishing the evil, yet it is found to be unable to prevent it altogether.

Mr. L. Martin. considered the association of the Judges with the Executive as a dangerous innovation; as well as one which, could not produce the particular advantage expected from it. A knowledge of mankind, and of Legislative affairs cannot be presumed to belong in a higher deger degree to the Judges than to the Legislature. And as to the Constitutionality of laws, that point will come before the Judges in their proper official character. In this character they have a negative on the laws. Join them with the Executive in the Revision and they will have a double negative. It is neces-

sary that the Supreme Judiciary should have the confidence of the people. This will soon be lost, if they are employed in the task of remonstrating agst. popular measures of the Legislature. Besides in what mode & proportion are they to vote in the Council of Revision?

⟨Mr.⟩ M⟨adison⟩ could not discover in the proposed association of the Judges with the Executive in the Revisionary check on the Legislature any violation of the maxim which requires the great departments of power to be kept separate & distinct. On the contrary he thought it an auxiliary precaution in favor of the maxim. If a Constitutional discrimination of the departments on paper were a sufficient security to each agst. encroachments of the others, all further provisions would indeed be superfluous. But experience had taught us a distrust of that security; and that it is necessary to introduce such a balance of powers and interests, as will guarantee the provisions on paper. Instead therefore of contenting ourselves with laying down the Theory in the Constitution that each department ought to be separate & distinct, it was proposed to add a defensive power to each which should maintain the Theory in practice. In so doing we did not blend the departments together. We erected effectual barriers for keeping them separate. The most regular example of this theory was in the British Constitution. Yet it was not only the practice there to admit the Judges to a seat in the legislature, and in the Executive Councils, and to submit to their previous examination all laws of a certain description, but it was a part of their Constitution that the Executive might negative any law whatever; a part of *their* Constitution which had been universally regarded as calculated for the preservation of the whole. The objection agst. a union of the Judiciary & Executive branches in the revision of the laws, had either no foundation or was not carried far enough. If such a Union was an improper mixture of powers, or such a Judiciary check on the laws, was inconsistent with the Theory of a free Constitution, it was equally so to admit the Executive to any participation in the making of laws; and the revisionary plan ought to be discarded altogether.

Col Mason Observed that the defence of the Executive was not the sole object of the Revisionary power. He expected even greater advantages from it. Notwithstanding the precautions taken in the Constitution of the Legislature, it would so much resemble that of the individual States, that it must be expected frequently to pass unjust and pernicious laws. This restraining power was therefore essentially necessary. It would have the effect not only of hindering the final passage of such laws; but would discourage demagogues from attempting to get them passed. It had been said (by Mr. L. Martin) that if the Judges were joined in this check on the laws, they would have a double negative, since in their expository capacity of Judges they would have one negative. He would reply that in this capacity they could impede in one case only, the operation of laws. They could declare an unconstitutional law void. But with regard to every law however unjust oppressive or pernicious, which did not come plainly under this description, they would be under the necessity as Judges to give it a free course. He wished the further use to be made of the Judges, of giving aid in preventing every improper law. Their aid will be the more valuable as they are in the habit and practice of considering laws in their true principles, and in all their consequences.

Mr. Wilson. The separation of the departments does not require that they should have separate objects but that they should act separately tho' on the same objects. It is necessary that the two branches of the Legislature should be separate and distinct, yet they are both to act precisely on the same object

Mr. Gerry had rather give the Executive an absolute negative for its own defence than thus to blend together the Judiciary & Executive departments. It will bind them together in an offensive and defensive alliance agst. the Legislature, and render the latter unwilling to enter into a contest with them.

Mr. Govr. Morris was surprised that any defensive provision for securing the effectual separation of the departments should be considered as an improper mixture of them. Sup-

pose that the three powers, were to be vested in three persons, by compact among themselves; that one was to have the power of making — another of executing, and a third of judging, the laws. Would it not be very natural for the two latter after having settled the partition on paper, to observe, and would not candor oblige the former to admit, that as a security agst. legislative acts of the former which might easily be so framed as to undermine the powers of the two others, the two others ought to be armed with a veto for their own defence, or at least to have an opportunity of stating their objections agst. acts of encroachment? And would any one pretend that such a right tended to blend & confound powers that ought to be separately exercised?[4] As well might it be said that If three neighbours had three distinct farms, a right in each to defend his farm agst. his neighbours, tended to blend the farms together.

Mr. Ghorum. All agree that a check on the Legislature is necessary. But there are two objections agst. admitting the Judges to share in it which no observations on the other side seem to obviate. the 1st. is that the Judges ought to carry into the exposition of the laws no prepossessions with regard to them. 2d. that as the Judges will outnumber the Executive, the revisionary check would be thrown entirely out of the Executive hands, and instead of enabling him to defend himself, would enable the Judges to sacrifice him.

Mr. Wilson. The proposition is certainly ⟨not⟩ liable to all the objections which have been urged agst. it. According to (Mr. Gerry) it will unite the Executive & Judiciary in an offensive & defensive alliance agst. the Legislature. According to Mr. Ghorum it will lead to a subversion of the Executive by the Judiciary influence. To the first gentleman the answer was obvious; that the joint weight of the two departments was necessary to balance the single weight of the Legislature. To the 1st. objection stated by the other Gentleman it might be answered that supposing the prepossion to mix

[4] Crossed out: "Every man must see that such a right had a tendency shortly to bring Take another illustration".

itself with the exposition, the evil would be overbalanced by the advantages promised by the expedient. To the 2d. objection, that such a rule of voting might be provided in the detail as would guard agst. it.

Mr. Rutlidge thought the Judges of all men the most unfit to be concerned in the revisionary Council. The Judges ought never to give their opinion on a law till it comes before them. He thought it equally unnecessary. The Executive could advise with the officers of State, as of war, finance &c. and avail himself of their information and opinions.

On Question on Mr. Wilson's motion for joining the Judiciary in the Revision of laws[5] ⟨it passed in the negative⟩ —

Mas. no. Cont. ay. N. J. not present. Pa. divd. Del. no. Md. ay. Va. ay. N. C. no. S. C. no. Geo. divd. [Ayes — 3; noes — 4; divided — 2.]

⟨Resol: 10 giving the Ex. a qualified veto⟩ without the amendmt. was then agd. to nem. con.

The motion made by Mr. ⟨Madison⟩ July 18. & then postponed, "that the Judges shd. be nominated by the Executive & such nominations become appointments unless disagreed to by ⅔ of the 2d. branch of the Legislature," was now resumed.

Mr. Madison stated as his reasons for the motion. 1 that it secured the responsibility of the Executive who would in general be more capable & likely to select fit characters than the Legislature, or even the 2d. b. of it, who might hide their selfish motives under the number concerned in the appointment- 2 that in case of any flagrant partiality or error, in the nomination, it might be fairly presumed that ⅔ of the 2d. branch would join in putting a negative on it. 3. that as the 2d. b. was very differently constituted when the appointment of the Judges was formerly referred to it, and was now to be composed of equal votes from all the States, the principle of compromise which had prevailed in other instances required in this that their shd. be a concurrence of two authorities, in one of which the people, in the other the states, should be

[5] See further Appendix A, CCLXXXVII, CCCXXI.

represented. The Executive Magistrate wd be considered as a national officer, acting for and equally sympathising with every part of the U. States. If the 2d. branch alone should have this power, the Judges might be appointed by a minority of the people, tho' by a majority, of the States, which could not be justified on any principle as their proceedings were to relate to the people, rather than to the States: and as it would moreover throw the appointments entirely into the hands of ye Nthern States, a perpetual ground of jealousy & discontent would be furnished to the Southern States.

Mr. Pinkney was for placing the appointmt. in the 2d. b. exclusively. The Executive will possess neither the requisite knowledge of characters, nor confidence of the people for so high a trust.

Mr. Randolph wd. have preferred the mode of appointmt. proposed formerly by Mr Ghorum, as adopted in the Constitution of Massts. but thought the motion depending so great an improvement of the clause as it stands, that he anxiously wished it success. He laid great stress on the responsibility of the Executive as a security for fit appointments. Appointments by the Legislatures have generally resulted from cabal, from personal regard, or some other consideration than a title derived from the proper qualifications. The same inconveniencies will proportionally prevail if the appointments be be referred to either branch of the Legislature or to any other authority administered by a number of individuals.

Mr. Elseworth would prefer a negative in the Executive on a nomination by the 2d. branch, the negative to be overruled by a concurrence of ⅔ of the 2d. b. to the mode proposed by the motion; but preferred an absolute appointment by the 2d. branch to either. The Executive will be regarded by the people with a jealous eye. Every power for augmenting unnecessarily his influence will be disliked. As he will be stationary it was not to be supposed he could have a better knowledge of characters. He will be more open to caresses & intrigues than the Senate. The right to supersede his nomination will be ideal only. A nomination under such circumstances will be equivalent to an appointment.

Mr. Govr. Morris supported the motion. 1. The States in their corporate capacity will frequently have an interest staked on the determination of the Judges. As in the Senate the States are to vote the Judges ought not to be appointed by the Senate. Next to the impropriety of being Judge in one's own cause, is the appointment of the Judge. 2. It had been said the Executive would be uninformed of characters. The reverse was ye truth. The Senate will be so. They must take the character of candidates from the flattering pictures drawn by their friends. The Executive in the necessary intercourse with every part of the U. S. required by the nature of his administration, will or may have the best possible information. 3. It had been said that a jealousy would be entertained of the Executive. If the Executive can be safely trusted with the command of the army, there can not surely be any reasonable ground of Jealousy in the present case. He added that if the Objections agst. an appointment of the Executive by the Legislature, had the weight that had been allowed there must be some weight in the objection to an appointment of the Judges by the Legislature or by any part of it.

Mr. Gerry. The appointment of the Judges like every other part of the Constitution shd. be so modeled as to give satisfaction both to the people and to the States. The mode under consideration will give satisfaction to neither. He could not conceive that the Executive could be as well informed of characters throughout the Union, as the Senate. It appeared to him also a strong objection that $\frac{2}{3}$ of the Senate were required to reject a nomination of the Executive. The Senate would be constituted in the same manner as Congress. And the appointments of Congress have been generally good.

Mr. ⟨Madison⟩, observed that he was not anxious that $\frac{2}{3}$ should be necessary to disagree to a nomination. He had given this form to his motion chiefly to vary it the more clearly from one which had just been rejected. He was content to obviate the objection last made, and accordingly so varied the motion as to let a majority reject.

Col. Mason found it his duty to differ from his colleagues

in their opinions & reasonings on this subject. Notwithstanding the form of the proposition by which the appointment seemed to be divided between the Executive & Senate, the appointment was substantially vested in the former alone. The false complaisance which usually prevails in such cases will prevent a disagreement to the first nominations. He considered the appointment by the Executive as a dangerous prerogative. It might even give him an influence over the Judiciary department itself. He did not think the difference of interest between the Northern and Southern ⟨States⟩ could be properly brought into this argument. It would operate & require some precautions in the case of regulating navigation, commerce & imposts; but he could not see that it had any connection with the Judiciary department.

On the question, the motion now being "that the executive should nominate, & such nominations should become appointments unless disagreed to by the Senate"

Mas. ay. Ct. no. Pa. ay. Del. no. Md. no. Va. ay. N. C. no. S. C. no. Geo. no. [Ayes — 3; noes — 6.]

On question for agreeing to the clause as it stands by which the Judges are to be appointed by 2d. branch

Mas. no. Ct. ay. Pa. no. Del. ay. Md. ay. Va. no. N. C. ay. S. C. ay. Geo. ay. [Ayes — 6; noes — 3.]

Adjourned[6]

---

[6] See further Appendix A, LXVI, LXVII.

MONDAY, JULY 23, 1787.

JOURNAL

Monday July 23rd. 1787.

The honorable John Langdon and Nicholas Gillman Esquires, Deputies from the State of New Hampshire, attended and took their seats

The following credentials were produced and read —

(Here insert the credentials of the Deputies of the State of New Hamr[1]

On the question to agree to the 17th resolution, as reported from the Committee of the whole House, namely

"That provision ought to be made for the amendment of "the articles of union, whensoever it shall seem necessary"

it passed unanimously in the affirmative.

It was moved and seconded to add after the word "States" in the 18 resolution, the words "and of the national government"

which passed in the affirmative

On the question to agree to the 18th resolution as amended namely

"That the legislative, Executive, and Judiciary Powers "within the several States, and of the national Government, "ought to be bound by oath to support the articles of union"

It passed unanimously in the affirmative

It was moved and seconded to strike the following words out of the 19th resolution reported from the Committee of the whole House namely

"to an Assembly or assemblies of representatives, recom- "mended by the several Legislatures, to be expressly chosen "by the people to consider and decide thereon"

which passed in the negative. [Ayes — 3; noes — 7.]

---

[1] See Appendix B.

On the question to agree to the 19th resolution as reported from the Committee of the whole House, namely

Resolved that the amendments which shall be offered to the confederation by the Convention ought at a proper time or times after the approbation of Congress to be submitted to an assembly or assemblies of representatives, recommended by the several Legislatures, to be expressly chosen by the People to consider and decide thereon

it passed in the affirmative [Ayes — 9; noes — 1.]

Ir was moved and seconded to agree to the following resolution, namely

Resolved that the representation in the second Branch of the Legislature of the United States consist of Members from each State, who shall vote per capita.

It was moved and seconded to fill up the blank with the word "Three"

which passed in the negative. [Ayes — 1; noes — 9.]

It was moved and seconded to fill up the blank with the number "Two"

which was unanimously agreed to [Ayes — 10; noes — 0.]

On the question to agree to the resolution as filled up —

it passed in the affirmative. [Ayes — 9; noes — 1.]

It was moved and seconded to reconsider that clause of the resolution respecting the appointment of the supreme Executive.

which passed in the affirmative [Ayes — 7; noes — 3.]

and to-morrow was assigned for the reconsideration. [Ayes — 8; noes — 2.]

[To adjourn. Ayes — 0; noes — 10.][2]

It was moved and seconded that the proceedings of the Convention for the establishment of a national government, except what respects the Supreme Executive, be referred to a Committee for the purpose of reporting a Constitution conformably to the Proceedings aforesaid — which passed unanimously in the affirmative [Ayes — 10; noes — 0.]

---

[2] Vote 210, Detail of Ayes and Noes, which gives an obviously wrong summary of the vote.

DETAIL OF AYES AND NOES

	New Hampshire	Massachusetts	Rhode Island	Connecticut	New York	New Jersey	Pennsylvania	Delaware	Maryland	Virginia	North Carolina	South Carolina	Georgia	Questions	Ayes	Noes	Divided
[203]	no	no		aye			no	aye	aye	no	no	no	no	To strike out the words "an assembly or assemblies of representatives recommended by the sevl Legislatures to be expressly chosen by the People to consider and decide thereon" in the last resolution	3	7	
[204]	aye	aye		aye			aye	no	aye	aye	aye	aye	aye	To agree to the last resolution	9	1	
[205]	no	no		no			aye	no	no	no	no	no	no	To fill up the blank in the resolution respecting the number of representatives in ye 2 branch wh "three.	1	9	
[206]	aye	aye		aye			aye	aye	aye	aye	aye	aye	aye	To fill up the blank with the word "Two" unanimous			
[207]	aye	aye		aye			aye	aye	no	aye	aye	aye	aye	To agree to the resolution respecting the number of representatives in the 2nd branch and the manner of voting	9	1	
[208]	aye	aye		aye			no	aye	no	no	aye	aye	aye	To reconsider the clause respecting the appointment of the supreme Executive.	7	3	
[209]	aye	aye		no			no	aye	aye	aye	aye	aye	aye	To reconsider the clause respecting the Executive to-morrow	8	2	
[210]	no	no		no			no	no	no	no	no	no	no	To adjourn.	10		
[211]	aye	aye		aye			aye	aye	aye	aye	aye	aye	aye	To agree to refer the Proceedings of the Convention to a Commitee			
[212]	no	no		no			no	aye	no	no	no	no	no	That the Committee consist of a Member from each State	1	9	
[213]	aye	aye		aye			no	no	aye	no	no	aye	no	That the Committee consist of Seven	5	5	
[214]	aye	aye		aye			aye	aye	aye	aye	aye	aye	aye	That the Committee consist of five, unanimous	10		

On the question that the Committee consist of a Member from each State

it passed in the negative [Ayes — 1; noes — 9.]

On the question that the Committee consist of Seven

it passed in the negative [Ayes — 5; noes — 5.]

On the question that the Committee consist of five

it passed unanimously in the affirmative. [Ayes — 10; noes — 0.]

To-morrow assigned for appointing the Committee. and then the house adjourned till to-morrow at 11 o'clock.

MADISON

Monday. July. 23. in Convention.

⟨Mr. John Langdon & Mr. Nicholas Gilman from N. Hampshire took their seats.⟩[3]

Resoln: 17. that provision ought to be made for future amendments of the articles of Union. Agreed to nem con.

Resoln. 18. "requiring the Legis: Execut: & Judy. of the States to be bound by oath to support the articles of Union". taken into consideration.

Mr. Williamson suggests that a reciprocal oath should be required from the National officers, to support the Governments of the States.

Mr. Gerry moved to insert as an amendmt. that the oath of the Officers of the National Government also should extend to the support of the Natl. Govt. which was agreed to nem. con.

Mr. Wilson said he was never fond of oaths, considering them as a left handed security only. A good Govt. did not need them. and a bad one could not or ought not to be supported. He was afraid they might too much trammel the the Members of the Existing Govt in case future alterations should be necessary; and prove an obstacle to Resol: 17. just agd. to.[4]

Mr. Ghorum did not know that oaths would be of much

[3] Taken from *Journal*. [4] See Appendix A, CXCII.

use; but could see no inconsistency between them and the 17. Resol: or any regular amendt. of the Constitution. The oath could only require fidelity to the existing Constitution. A constitutional alteration of the Constitution, could never be regarded as a breach of the Constitution, or of any oath to support it.

Mr Gerry thought with Mr. Ghorum there could be no shadow of inconsistency in the case. Nor could he see any other harm that could result from the Resolution. On the other side he thought one good effect would be produced by it. Hitherto the officers of ⟨the two⟩ Governments had considered them as distinct from, not as parts of the-General System, & had in all cases of interference given a preference to the State Govts. The proposed oaths will cure that error. —

The Resoln. (18). was agreed to nem. con. —

Resol: 19. referring the new Constitution to Assemblies to be chosen by the people for the express purpose of ratifying it" was next taken into consideration.

Mr. Elseworth moved that it be referred to the Legislatures of the States for ratification. Mr. Patterson 2ded. the motion.

Col. Mason considered a reference of the plan to the authority of the people as one of the most important and essential of the Resolutions. The Legislatures have no power to ratify it. They are the mere creatures of the State Constitutions, and cannot be greater than their creators. And he knew of no power in any of the Constitutions, he knew there was no power in some of them, that could be competent to this object. Whither then must we resort? To the people with whom all power remains that has not been given up in the Constitutions derived from them. It was of great moment he observed that this doctrine should be cherished as the basis of free Government. Another strong reason was that admitting the Legislatures to have a competent authcrity, it would be wrong to refer the plan to them, because succeeding Legislatures having equal authority could undo the acts of their predecessors; and the National Govt. would stand in each State on the weak and tottering foundation of an Act of Assembly. There was a remaining consideration of some weight.

In some of the States the Govts. were ⟨not⟩ derived from the clear & undisputed authority of the people. This was the case in Virginia. Some of the best & wisest citizens considered the Constitution as established by an assumed authority. A National Constitution derived from such a source would be exposed to the severest criticisms.

Mr Randolph. One idea has pervaded all ⟨our⟩ proceedings, to wit, that opposition as well from the States as from individuals, will be made to the System to be proposed. Will it not then be highly imprudent, to furnish any unnecessary pretext by the mode of ratifying it. Added to other objections agst. a ratification by Legislative authority only, it may be remarked that there have been instances in which the authority of the Common law has been set up in particular States agst. that of the Confederation which has had no higher sanction than Legislative ratification. — Whose opposition will be most likely to be excited agst. the System? That of the local demogagues who will be degraded by it from the importance they now hold. These will spare no efforts to impede that progress in the popular mind which will be necessary to the adoption of the plan, and which every member will find to have taken place in his own, if he will compare his present opinions with those brought with him into the Convention. It is of great importance therefore that the consideration of this subject should be transferred from the Legislatures where this class of men, have their full influence to a field in which their efforts can be less mischievous. It is moreover worthy of consideration that some of the States are averse to any change in their Constitution, and will not take the requisite steps, unless expressly called upon to refer the question to the people.

Mr. Gerry. The arguments of Col. Mason & Mr. Randolph prove too much, they prove an unconstitutionality in the present federal ⟨system⟩ & even in some of the State Govts. Inferences drawn from such a source must be inadmissable. Both the State Govts. & the federal Govt. have been too long acquiesced in, to be now shaken. He considered the Confederation to be paramount to any State Constitution. The

last article of it authorizing alterations must consequently be so as well as the others, and everything done in pursuance of the article must have the same high authority with the article. — Great confusion he was confident would result from a recurrence to the people. They would never agree on any thing. He could not see any ground to suppose that the people will do what their rulers will not. The rulers will either conform to, or influence the sense of the people.

Mr. Ghorum was agst. referring the plan to the Legislatures. 1. Men chosen by the people for the particular purpose, will discuss the subject more candidly than members of the Legislature who are to lose the power which is to be given up to the Genl. Govt. 2. Some of the Legislatures are composed of several branches. It will consequently be more difficult in these cases to get the plan through the Legislatures, than thro' a Convention. 3. in the States many of the ablest men are excluded from the Legislatures, but may be elected into a Convention. Among these may be ranked many of the Clergy who are generally friends to good Government. Their services were found to be valuable in the formation & establishment of the Constitution of Massachts. 4. the Legislatures will be interrupted with a variety of little business. by artfully pressing which, designing men will find means to delay from year to year, if not to frustrate altogether the national system. 5 — If the last art: of the Confederation is to be pursued the unanimous concurrence of the States will be necessary. But will any one say. that all the States are to suffer themselves to be ruined, if Rho. Island should persist in her opposition to general measures. Some other States might also tread in her steps. The present advantage which N. York seems to be so much attached to, of taxing her neighbours ⟨by the regulation of her trade⟩, makes it very probable, that she will be of the number. It would therefore deserve serious consideration whether provision ought not to be made for giving effect to the System without waiting for the unanimous concurrence of the States.

Mr. Elseworth. If there be any Legislatures who should find themselves incompetent to the ratification, he should be

content to let them advise with their constituents and pursue such a mode as wd be competent. He thought more was to be expected from the Legislatures than from the people. The prevailing wish of the people in the Eastern States is to get rid of the public debt; and the idea of strengthening the Natl. Govt. carries with it that of strengthening the public debt. It was said by Col. Mason 1. that the Legislatures have no authority in this case. 2. that their successors having equal authority could rescind their acts. As to the 2d. point he could not admit it to be well founded. An Act to which the States by their Legislatures, make themselves parties, becomes a compact from which no one of the parties can recede of itself. As to the 1st. point, he observed that a new sett of ideas seemed to have crept in since the articles of Confederation were established. Conventions of the people, or with power derived expressly from the people, were not then thought of. The Legislatures were considered as competent. Their ratification has been acquiesced in without complaint. To whom have Congs. applied on subsequent occasions for further powers? To the Legislatures; not to the people. The fact is that we exist at present, and we need not enquire how, as a federal Society, united by a charter one article of which is that alterations therein may be made by the Legislative authority of the States. It has been said that if the confederation is to be observed, the States must *unanimously* concur in the proposed innovations. He would answer that if such were the urgency & necessity of our situation as to warrant a new compact among a part of the States, founded on the consent of the people; the same pleas would be equally valid in favor of a partial compact, founded on the consent of the Legislatures.

Mr. Williamson thought the Resoln. (19) so expressed as that it might be submitted either to the Legislatures or to Conventions recommended by the Legislatures. He observed that some Legislatures were evidently unauthorized to ratify the system. He thought too that Conventions were to be preferred as more likely to be composed of the ablest men in the States.

Mr. Govr. Morris considered the inference of Mr. Elseworth from the plea of necessity as applied to the establishment of a new System on ye. consent of the people of a part of the States, in favor of a like establishnt. on the consent of a part of the Legislatures as a non sequitur. If the Confederation is to be pursued no alteration can be made without the unanimous consent of the Legislatures: Legislative alterations not conformable to the federal compact, would clearly not be valid. The Judges would consider them as null & void. Whereas in case of an appeal to the people of the U. S., the supreme authority, the federal compact may be altered by a *majority of them*; in like manner as the Constitution of a particular State may be altered by a majority of the people of the State. The amendmt. moved by Mr. Elseworth erroneously supposes that we are proceeding on the basis of the Confederation. This Convention is unknown to the Confederation.

Mr. King thought with Mr. Elseworth that the Legislatures had a competent authority, the acquiescence of the people of America in the Confederation, being equivalent to a formal ratification by the people. He thought with Mr. E— also that the plea of necessity was as valid in the one case as in the other. At the same time he preferred a reference to the authority of the people expressly delegated to Conventions, as the most certain means of obviating all disputes & doubts concerning the legitimacy of the new Constitution; as well as the most likely means of drawing forth the best men in the States to decide on it. He remarked that among other objections made in the State of N. York to granting powers to Congs. one had been that such powers as would operate within the State, could not be reconciled to the Constitution; and therefore were not grantible by the Legislative authority. He considered it as of some consequence also to get rid of the scruples which some members of the States Legislatures might derive from their oaths to support & maintain the existing Constitutions.

Mr. ⟨Madison⟩ thought it clear that the Legislatures were incompetent to the proposed changes. These changes would make essential inroads on the State Constitutions, and it would be a novel & dangerous doctrine that a Legislature

could change the constitution under which it held its existence. There might indeed be some Constitutions within the Union, which had given, a power to the Legislature to concur in alterations of the federal Compact. But there were certainly some which had not; and in the case of these, a ratification must of necessity be obtained from the people. He considered the difference between a system founded on the Legislatures only, and one founded on the people, to be the true difference between a *league* or *treaty*, and a *Constitution*. The former in point of *moral obligation* might be as inviolable as the latter. In point of *political operation*, there were two important distinctions in favor of the latter. 1. A law violating a treaty ratified by a preexisting law, might be respected by the Judges as a law, though an unwise or perfidious one. A law violating a constitution established by the people themselves, would be considered by the Judges as null & void. 2. The doctrine laid down by the law of Nations in the case of treaties is that a breach of any one article by any of the parties, frees the other parties from their engagements. In the case of a union of people under one Constitution, the nature of the pact has always been understood to exclude such an interpretation. Comparing the two modes in point of expediency he thought all the considerations which recommended this Convention in preference to Congress for proposing the reform were in favor of State Conventions in preference to the Legislatures for examining and adopting it.

On question on Mr Elseworth's motion to refer the plan to the Legislatures of the States

N. H. no. Mas. no. Ct. ay. Pa. no- Del. ay- Md. ay. Va. no. N- C- no. S. C- no. Geo. no. [Ayes — 3; noes — 7.]

Mr. Govr. Morris moved that the reference of the plan be made to one general Convention, chosen & authorized by the people to consider, *amend*, & establish the same.—Not seconded.

On question for agreeing to Resolution 19, touching the mode of Ratification ⟨as reported from the Committee of the Whole; viz, to refer the Constn. after the approbation of Congs. to assemblies chosen by the people:⟩[5]

---

[5] Revised from *Journal*.

N. H. ay. Mas- ay. Ct. ay. Pa. ay. Del. no. Md. ay. Va. ay. N. C. ay. S. C. ay. Geo. ay. [Ayes — 9; noes — 1.]

Mr. Govr. Morris & Mr. King moved that the representation in the second branch consist of   members from each State, who shall vote per capita.[6]

Mr Elseworth said he had alway approved of voting in that mode.

Mr. Govr. Morris moved to fill the *blank* with *three*. He wished the Senate to be a pretty numerous body. If two members only should be allowed to each State, and a majority be made a quorum the power would be lodged in 14 members, which was too small a number for such a trust.

Mr Ghorum preferred two to three members for the blank. A small number was most convenient for deciding on peace & war &c. which he expected would be vested in the 2d. branch. The number of States will also increase. Kentucky, Vermont, the province of Mayne & Franklin will probably soon be added to the present number. He presumed also that some of the largest States would be divided. The strenghth of the general Govt. will lie not in the largeness, but in the smallness of the States.

Col. Mason thought *3* from each State including new States would make the 2d. branch too numerous. Besides other objections, the additional expence ought always to form one, where it was not absolutely necessary.

Mr. Williamson. If the number be too great, the distant States will not be on an equal footing with the nearer States. The latter can more easily send & support their ablest Citizens. He approved of the voting per capita.

On the question for filling the blank with "*three*"

N. H. no. Mas. no. Cont. no. Pa. ay. Del. no. Va. no. N. C. no. S. C. no. Geo. no. [Ayes — 1; noes — 8.] [7]

On question for filling it with "two." Agreed to nem- con,

Mr. L Martin was opposed to voting per Capita, as departing from the idea of the *States* being represented in the 2d. branch.

[6] See Appendix A, CLXX, CLXXI.

[7] Journal includes Maryland in the negative.

Mr. Carroll, was not struck with any particular objection agst. the mode; but he did not wish so hastily to make so material an innovation.

On the question on the whole motion viz. the 2d. b. to consist of 2 members from each State and to vote per capita."

N. H. ay. Mas. ay. Ct. ay. Pa. ay. Del. ay. Md. no. Va. ay. N. C. ay. S. C. ay. Geo. ay. [Ayes — 9; noes — 1.]

Mr. Houston & Mr. Spaight moved "that the appointment of the Executive by Electors chosen by the Legislatures of the States, be reconsidered." Mr. Houston urged the extreme inconveniency & the considerable expense, of drawing together men from all the States for the single purpose of electing the Chief Magistrate.

On the question which was put without any debate

N. H. ay. Mas. ay. Ct. ay. Pa. no. Del — ay. Md. no. Virga. no. N. C. ay. S. C. ay. Geo. ay. [Ayes — 7; noes — 3.]

Ordered that to morrow be assigned for the reconsideration. ⟨Cont & Pena. no — all the rest ay —⟩[8]

Mr. Gerry moved that the proceedings of the Convention for the establishment of a Natl. Govt. (except the part relating to the Executive), be referred to a Committee to prepare & report a Constitution conformable thereto.

Genl. Pinkney reminded the Convention that if the Committee should fail to insert some security to the Southern States agst. an emancipation of slaves, and taxes on exports,[9] he shd. be bound by duty to his State to vote agst. their Report. — The appt. of a Come. as moved by Mr. Gerry. Agd. to nem. con.[10]

Shall the Come. consist of 10 members" ⟨one from each State prest.⟩.[11] — All the States were *no.* except Delaware. *ay.*

Shall it consist of 7. members.

N. H. ay Mas. ay. Ct. ay. Pa. no. Del. no. Md. ay. Va.

---

[8] Taken from *Journal.*

[9] Upon these questions see further August 21, note 15; August 22, note 2; and August 25, note 7.

[10] The idea of a Committee of Detail seems to have been generally accepted previous to this date. It is referred to in debate and in correspondence, and later no secret is made of it. See Appendix A, LXVI, LXIX, LXXIII, LXXV.

[11] Revised from *Journal.*

no. N. C. no. S. C. ay. Geo. no. [Ayes — 5; noes — 5.] The question being lost ⟨by an equal division of Votes.⟩

It was agreed nem — con — that the Commttee consist of 5 members, ⟨to be appointed tomorrow.⟩[12]

Adjourned

PATERSON[13]

1. The Constitutionality of
the Measure.
Reasons.

1. The people the Source of Power. Union —

2. The Legr. of To-Morrow may repeal the Act of the Legr. of To-Day. So as to Convention —

3. Some of the Constns. not well or authoritatively founded — Acquiesence.

Expediency.
2 Branches in some of the States —
Judges, etc excluded —
The very Men that will oppose — Rh. Island —

The Debt will go with the Govt. — this a prevailing Idea—

The Legr. has no Right to alter the Constn. or the Confedn. —

Not acting under the Confedn. Nothing but a Compact resting upon the 13 States.

Congress over again.

A Violation of the Compact by one of the Parties, leaves the rest at Large, and exonerated from the Agreemt.

[12] Taken from *Journal.*

[13] These notes seem to cover the debates of July 23. Down to the first blank line, *i. e.*, through the word "Acquiesence", the notes refer to the speech of Mason. "Expediency" may refer to Randolph's speech. Down to the next blank line, *i. e.*, from "Expediency" through "Rh. Island", the notes refer to the speech of Gorham. The next line, beginning with "The Debt" and ending with "Idea", refers to Ellsworth's remarks. The rest of these notes probably refer to Madison's speech.

The above assignment is based upon Professor McLaughlin's notes in *American Historical Review*, January, 1904, IX, p. 339.

TUESDAY, JULY 24, 1787.

JOURNAL

Tuesday July 24th 1787.

It was moved and seconded to strike the following words out of the resolution respecting the supreme Executive namely "by electors appointed for that purpose by the Leg-"islatures of the States" and to insert the words

"by the national Legislature"

which passed in the affirmative. [Ayes — 7; noes — 4.]

It was moved and seconded to strike out the word "six" and to insert the word "fifteen."

It was moved and seconded to postpone the consideration of the resolution respecting the Executive

which passed in the negative [Ayes — 4; noes — 6; divided — 1.]

It was moved and seconded to agree to the following resolution namely.

Resolved that the supreme Executive shall be chosen every years

by Electors to be taken by lot from the national Legislature; the Electors to proceed immediately to the choice of the Executive, and not to separate until it be made

The question of Order being taken on the last Motion — it was determined that the motion is in order. [Ayes — 7; noes — 4.][1]

On the question to postpone the consideration of the resolution, it passed unanimously in the affirmative

The House then produced to ballot for the Committee of detail when the honorable Mr Rutledge, Mr Randolph, Mr Gorham, Mr Elsworth, and Mr Wilson were chosen —

[1] Vote 217, Detail of Ayes and Noes, which notes that the motion under consideration was "Mr. Wilson's".

It was moved and seconded to discharge the Committee of the whole House from acting on the propositions submitted to the Convention by the honorable Mr C. Pinckney — and that the said propositions be referred to the Committee to whom the Proceedings of the Convention are referred

which passed unanim: in the affirmative

It was moved and seconded to take the like order on the propositions submitted to the Convention by the honorable Mr Paterson

which passed unan: in the affirmative

and the the House adjourned till to-morrow at 11 o'Clock A. M.

DETAIL OF AYES AND NOES

	New Hampshire	Massachusetts	Rhode Island	Connecticut	New York	New Jersey	Pennsylvania	Delaware	Maryland	Virginia	North Carolina	South Carolina	Georgia	Questions	Ayes	Noes	Divided
[215]	aye	aye		no		aye	no	aye	no	no	aye	aye	aye	To strike out the words "by Electors &ca and to insert the words "by the national Legislature"	7	4	
[216]	no	no		aye		no	aye	dd	aye	aye	no	no	no	To postpone the resolution respecting the Executive	4	6	1
[217]	aye	aye		no		aye	aye	aye	aye	aye	no	no	no	whether Mr Wilson's motion respecting the election of the Executive be in order.	7	4	

[GERRY'S MOTION] [2]

That ye Legislatures of ye several States shall ballot in ye in ye following proportions for ye supreme Executive, & a Majority of votes shall determine the Election, but in case there shall not be a Majority, the four persons having ye

[2] This document in Gerry's handwriting on a scrap of paper is among the Secretary's papers in the Department of State. The names of the states and the numbers opposite them are on the back of the paper.

highest votes shall be candidates for ye office, & out of these the first Branch shall elect two, & the second Branch shall determine which of ye two so elected shall be chief Magistrate

N H	1
Mass	3
R I	1
Con	2
N Y	2
N J	2
P —	3
D	1
M	2
V	3
N C	2
S C	2
G —	1
	25

[Wilson's Motion] [3]

The Executive shall be chosen every years by Electors to be taken by lot from the national legislature — the electors to proceed immediately to the choice of the Executive and not to separate until it be made —

Suppose the whole to consist of 90 —

65
25
―
90

then put in 90 balls — of which as many as the proposed number of electors shall be gilded — those who draw these balls to be Electors

MADISON

Tuesday July 24. in Convention

The appointment of the Executive by Electors reconsidered.

Mr. Houston moved that he be appointed by the "Natl. Legislature. ⟨instead of "Electors appointed by the State Legislatures" according to the last decision of the mode⟩ [4] He dwelt chiefly on the improbability, that capable men would undertake the service of Electors from the more distant States.

Mr. Spaight seconded the motion.

[3] This document on a scrap of paper is among the Secretary's papers. The first paragraph is on one side of the paper, the rest on the other side. A line is drawn through the "65" and "25".

[4] Revised from *Journal.*

Mr. Gerry opposed it. He thought there was no ground to apprehend the danger urged by Mr. Houston. The election of the Executive Magistrate will be considered as of vast importance and will excite great earnestness. The best men, the Governours of the States will not hold it derogatory from their character to be the electors. If the motion should be agreed to, it will be necessary to make the Executive ineligible a 2d. time, in order to render him independent of the Legislature; which was an idea extremely repugnant to his way of thinking.

Mr. Strong supposed that there would be no necessity, if the Executive should be appointed by the Legislature, to make him ineligible a 2d. time; as new elections of the Legislature will have intervened; and he will not depend for his 2d. appointment on the same sett of men as his first was recd. from. It had been suggested that *gratitude* for his past appointment wd. produce the same effect as dependence for his future appointment. He thought very differently. Besides this objection would lie agst. the Electors who would be objects of gratitude as well as the Legislature. It was of great importance not to make the Govt. too complex which would be the case if a new sett of men like the Electors should be introduced into it. He thought also that the first characters in the States would not feel sufficient motives to undertake the office of Electors.

Mr. Williamson was for going back to the original ground; to elect the Executive for 7 years and render him ineligible a 2d. time. The proposed Electors would certainly not be men of the 1st. nor even of the 2d. grade in the States. These would all prefer a seat either in the Senate or the other branch of the Legislature. He did not like the Unity in the Executive. He had wished the Executive power to be lodged in three men taken from three districts into which the States should be divided. As the Executive is to have a kind of veto on the laws, and there is an essential difference of interests between the N. & S. States, particularly in the carrying trade, the power will be dangerous, if the Executive is to be taken from part of the Union, to the part from which he is

not taken. The case is different here from what it is in England; where there is a sameness of interest throughout the Kingdom. Another objection agst. a single Magistrate is that he will be an elective King, and will feel the spirit of one. He will spare no pains to keep himself in for life, and will then lay a train for the succession of his children. It was pretty certain he thought that we should at some time or other have a King; but he wished no precaution to be omitted that might postpone the event as long as possible. — Ineligibility a 2d. time appeared to him to be the best precaution. With this precaution he had no objection to a longer term than 7 years. He would go as far as 10 or 12 years.

Mr. Gerry moved that the Legislatures of the States should vote by ballot for the Executive in the same proportions as it had been proposed they should chuse electors; and that in case a majority of the votes should ⟨not⟩ center on the same person, the 1st. branch of the Natl. Legislature should chuse two out of the 4 candidates having most votes, and out of these two, the 2d. branch should chuse the Executive.[5]

Mr. King seconded the motion — and on the Question to postpone in order to take it into consideration, The *noes* were so predominant that the States were not counted.

Question on Mr. Houston's motion that the Executive be appd. by Nal. Legislature

N. H. ay. Mas. ay. Ct. no. N. J. ay. Pa. no. Del. ay. Md. no. Va. no. N. C. ay. S. C. ay. Geo. ay. [Ayes — 7; noes — 4.]

Mr. L. Martin & Mr. Gerry moved to reinstate the ineligibility of the Executive a 2d. time.[6]

Mr. Elseworth. With many this appears a natural consequence of his being elected by the Legislature. It was not the case with him. The Executive he thought should be reelected if his conduct proved him worthy of it. And he will be more likely to render him⟨self⟩ worthy of it if he be rewardable with it. The most eminent characters also will be more willing to accept the trust under this condition, than if they foresee a necessary degradation at a fixt period.

---

[5] See above, Journal, "Gerry's Motion".

[6] See Appendix A, CXCI.

Mr. Gerry. That the Executive shd. be independent of the Legislature is a clear point. The longer the duration of his appointment the more will his dependence be diminished — It will be better then for him to continue 10, 15, or even 20 — years and be ineligible afterwards.

Mr. King was for making him re-eligible. This is too great an advantage to be given up for the small effect it will have on his dependence, if impeachments are to lie. He considered these as rendering the tenure during pleasure.

Mr. L. Martin, suspending his motion as to the ineligibility, moved "that the appointmt. of the Executive shall continue for Eleven years.

Mr Gerry suggested fifteen years.

Mr. King twenty years. This is the medium life of princes.*

Mr. Davie Eight years

Mr. Wilson. The difficulties & perplexities into which the House is thrown proceed from the election by the Legislature which he was sorry had been reinstated. The inconveniency of this mode was such that he would agree to almost any length of time in order to get rid of the dependence which must result from it. He was persuaded that the longest term would not be equivalent to a proper mode of election, unless indeed it should be during good behaviour. It seemed to be supposed that at a certain advance of life, a continuance in office would cease to be agreeable to to the officer, as well as desireable to the public. Experience had shewn in a variety of instances that both a capacity & inclination for public service existed — in very advanced stages. He mentioned the instance of a Doge of Venice who was elected after he was 80 years of age. The popes have generally been elected at very advanced periods, and yet in no case had a more steady or a better concerted policy been pursued than in the Court of Rome. If the Executive should come into office at 35. years of age, which he presumes may happen & his continuance should be fixt at 15 years. at the age of 50. in the very prime of life, and with all the aid of experience, he must be

*⟨This might possibly be meant as a caricature of the previous motions in order to defeat the object of them.⟩

cast aside like a useless hulk. What an irreparable loss would the British Jurisprudence have sustained, had the age of 50. been fixt there as the ultimate limit of capacity or readiness to serve the public. The great luminary (Ld. Mansfield) held his seat for thirty years after his arrival at that age. Notwithstanding what had been done he could not but hope that a better mode of election would yet be adopted; and one that would be more agreeable to the general sense of the House. That time might be given for further deliberation he wd. move that the present question be postponed till to-morrow.

Mr Broom seconded the motion to postpone.

Mr. Gerry. We seem to be entirely at a loss on this head. He would suggest whether it would not be advisable to refer the clause relating to the Executive to the Committee of detail to be appointed. Perhaps they will be able to hit on something that may unite the various opinions which have been thrown out.

Mr. Wilson. As the great difficulty seems to spring from the mode of election, he wd. suggest a mode which had not been mentioned. It was that the Executive be elected for 6 years by a small number, not more than 15 of the Natl Legislature, to be drawn from it, not by ballot, but by lot and who should retire immediately and make the election ⟨without separating⟩.[7] By this mode intrigue would be avoided in the first instance, and the dependence would be diminished. This was not he said a digested idea and might be liable to strong objections.

Mr. Govr. Morris. Of all possible modes of appointment that by the Legislature is the worst. If the Legislature is to appoint, and to impeach or to influence the impeachment, the Executive will be the mere creature of it. He had been opposed to the impeachment, but was now convinced that impeachments must be provided for, if the appt. was to be of any duration. No man wd. say, that an Executive known to be in the pay of an Enemy, should not be removable in

[7] Taken from *Journal.*

some way or other. He had been charged heretofore (by Col. Mason) with inconsistency in pleading for confidence in the Legislature on some occasions, & urging a distrust on others. The charge was not well founded. The Legislature is worthy of unbounded confidence in some respects, and liable to equal distrust in others. When their interest coincides precisely with that of their Constituents, as happens in many of their Acts, no abuse of trust is to be apprehended. When a strong personal interest happens to be opposed to the general interest, the Legislature can not be too much distrusted. In all public bodies there are two parties. The Executive will necessarily be more connected with one than with the other. There will be a personal interest therefore in one of the parties to oppose as well as in the other to support him. Much had been said of the intrigues that will be practiced by the Executive to get into office. Nothing had been said on the other side of the intrigues to get him out of office. Some leader of party will always covet his seat, will perplex his administration, will cabal with the Legislature, till he succeeds in supplanting him. This was the way in which the King of England was got out, he meant the real King, the Minister. This was the way in which Pitt (Ld. Chatham) forced himself into place. Fox was for pushing the matter still farther. If he had carried his India bill, which he was very near doing, he would have made the Minister, the King in form almost as well as in substance. Our President will be the British Minister, yet we are about to make him appointable by the Legislature. Something had been said of the danger of Monarchy — If a good government should not now be formed, if a good organization of the Execuve should not be provided, he doubted whether we should not have something worse than a limited Monarchy. In order to get rid of the dependence of the Executive on the Legislature, the expedient of making him ineligible a 2d. time had been devised. This was as much as to say we shd. give him the benefit of experience, and then deprive ourselves of the use of it. But make him ineligible a 2d. time-and prolong his duration even to 15-years, will he by any wonderful interposition of providence at that period

cease to be a man? No he will be unwilling to quit his exaltation, the road to his object thro' the Constitution will be shut; he will be in possession of the sword, a civil war will ensue, and the Commander of the victorious army on which ever side, will be the despot of America. This consideration renders him particularly anxious that the Executive should be properly constituted. The vice here would not, as in some other parts of the system be curable- It is ⟨the⟩ most difficult of all rightly to balance the Executive. Make him too weak: The Legislature will usurp his powers: Make him too strong. He will usurp on the Legislature. He preferred a short period, a re-eligibility, but a different mode of election. A long period would prevent an adoption of the plan: it ought to do so. He shd. himself be afraid to trust it. He was not prepared to decide on Mr. Wilson's mode of election just hinted by him. He thought it deserved consideration. It would be better that chance sd. decide than intrigue.

⟨On A question to postpone the consideration of the Resolution on the subject of the Executive⟩[8]

N. H. no. Mas. no. Ct. ay. N. J. no. Pa. ay. Del. divd. Md. ay. Va. ay. N. C. no. S. C. no. Geo. no. [Ayes — 4; noes — 6; divided — 1.]

Mr. Wilson ⟨then⟩ moved[9] that the Executive be chosen every years by Electors to be taken by lot from the Natl Legislature who shall proceed immediately to the choice of the Executive ⟨and not separate until it be made⟩"[10]

Mr. Carrol 2ds. the motion

Mr Gerry. this is committing too much to chance. If the lot should fall on a sett of unworthy men, an unworthy Executive must be saddled on the Country. He thought it had been demonstrated that no possible mode of electing by the Legislature could be a good one.

Mr. King — The lot might fall on a majority from the same State which wd. ensure the election of a man from that State.

[8] Madison originally confused Wilson's motion to postpone with his suggestion of choosing electors by lot. Later he struck this out and substituted from *Journal* the wording of the text.

[9] See above, Journal, "Wilson's Motion".

[10] Taken from *Journal.*

We ought to be governed by reason, not by chance. As no body seemed to be satisfied, he wished the matter to be postponed

Mr. Wilson did not move this as the best mode. His opinion remained unshaken that we ought to resort to the people for the election. He seconded the postponement.

Mr. Govr. Morris observed that the chances were almost infinite agst. a majority of electors from the same State.

⟨On a question whether the last motion was in order, it was determined in the affirmative; 7. ays. 4 noes.⟩ [11]

On the question of postponemt. it was agreed to nem. con.

Mr Carrol took occasion to observe that he considered the clause declaring that direct taxation on the States should be in proportion to representation, previous to the obtaining an actual census, as very objectionable, and that he reserved to himself the right of opposing it, if the Report of the Committee of detail should leave it in the plan.

Mr. Govr. Morris hoped the Committee would strike out the whole of the clause proportioning direct taxation to representation. He had only meant it as a* bridge to assist us over a certain gulph; having passed the gulph the bridge may be removed. He thought the principle laid down with so much strictness, liable to strong objections

On a ballot for a Committee to report a Constitution conformable to the Resolutions passed by the Convention, the members chosen were

Mr. Rutlidge, Mr Randolph, Mr. Ghorum, Mr. Elseworth, Mr. Wilson — [12]

⟨On motion to discharge the Come. of the whole from the propositions submitted to the Convention by Mr. C. Pinkney as the basis of a constitution, and to refer them to the Committee of detail just appointed. it was agd. to nem. con.

A like motion then made & agreed to nem: con: with respect to the propositions of Mr Patterson

Adjourned.⟩ [11]

*The object was to lessen the eagerness on one side, & the opposition on the other, to the share of Representation claimed by the S. ⟨Sothern⟩ States on account of the Negroes.

[11] Taken from *Journal*.

[12] See Appendix A, CCXCIII.

WEDNESDAY, JULY 25, 1787.

JOURNAL

Wednesday July 25. 1787.

It was moved and seconded to agree to the following amendment to the resolution respecting the election of the supreme Executive namely

"except when the Magistrate last chosen shall have con-
"tinued in office the whole term for which he was chosen, and
"be reeligible in which case the choice shall be by Electors
"appointed for that purpose by the several Legislatures"

it passed in the negative [Ayes — 4; noes — 7.][1]

It was moved and seconded to agree to the following amendment to the resolution respecting the supreme Executive, namely

"Provided that no person shall be capable of holding
"the said office for more than six years in any term of twelve"

It was moved and seconded to postpone the consideration of the last amendment

which passed in the negative. [Ayes — 5; noes — 6.][2]

On the question to agree to the amendment

it passed in the negative [Ayes — 5; noes — 6.]

[That the members of the Committee be furnished with copies of the proceedings Ayes — 10; noes — 1.[3]

That the members of the House take copies of the resolutions which have been agreed to Ayes — 5; noes — 6.[4]]

It was moved and seconded to refer the resolution respecting

---

[1] Vote 218, Detail of Ayes and Noes, which states that the amendment was "Mr Elsworth's".

[2] Vote 219, Detail of Ayes and Noes, which states that the amendment was "Mr Pinckney's".

[3] Vote 221, Details of Ayes and Noes.

[4] Vote 222, Detail of Ayes and Noes. Motion was made by Luther Martin, see Appendix A, CLVIII (27).

the Executive (except that clause which provides that it consist of a single Person) to the Committee of detail.

Before a determination was taken on the last motion [To adjourn Ayes — 9; noes — 2.][5] The House adjourned till to-morrow at 11 o'Clock A. M.

DETAIL OF AYES AND NOES

	New Hampshire	Massachusetts	Rhode Island	Connecticut	New York	New Jersey	Pennsylvania	Delaware	Maryland	Virginia	North Carolina	South Carolina	Georgia	Questions	Ayes	Noes	Divided
[218]	aye	no		aye		no	aye	no	aye	no	no	no	no	To agree to Mr Elsworth's amendment in the election of the Executive.	4	7	
[219]	no	no		aye		aye	aye	no	aye	aye	no	no	no	To postpone Mr Pinckney's amendment	5	6	
[220]	aye	aye		no		no	no	no	no	no	aye	aye	aye	To agree to Mr Pinckney's amendment	5	6	
[221]	aye	aye		aye		aye	aye	aye	aye	aye	aye	no	aye	That the Members of the Committee be furnished with copies of the proceedings	10	1	
[222]	no	no		aye		aye	no	aye	no	aye	aye	no	no	That the Members of the House take copies of the resolutions which have been agreed to	5	6	
[223]	no	aye		no		aye	aye	aye	aye	aye	aye	aye	aye	To adjourn			

MADISON

Wednesday July 25. In Convention

Clause relating to the Executive again under consideration

Mr. Elseworth moved "that the Executive be appointed by the Legislature," except when ⟨the magistrate last chosen shall⟩ have ⟨continued in office the whole term for which he was chosen, & be reeligible, in which case the choice shall be⟩ by -Electors appointed by the Legislatures of the States ⟨for that

[5] Vote 223 Detail of Ayes and Noes.

purpose.")〉[6] By this means a deserving Magistrate may be reelected without making him dependent on the Legislature.

Mr. Gerry repeated his remark that an election at all by the Natl. Legislature was radically and incurably wrong; and moved[7] that the Executive be appointed by the Governours & Presidents of the States, with advice of their Councils, and when there are no Councils by Electors chosen by the Legislatures. The executives to vote in the following proportions: 〈viz —〉

Mr. 〈Madison.〉 There are objections agst. every mode that has been, or perhaps can be proposed. The election must be made either by some existing authority under the Natil. or State Constitutions — or by some special authority derived from the people — or by the people themselves. — The two Existing authorities under the Natl. Constitution wd be the Legislative & Judiciary. The latter he presumed was out of the question. The former was in his Judgment liable to insuperable objections. Besides the general influence of that mode on the independence of the Executive, 1. the election of the Chief Magistrate would agitate & divide the legislature so much that the public interest would materially suffer by it. Public bodies are always apt to be thrown into contentions, but into more violent ones by such occasions than by any others. 2. the candidate would intrigue with the Legislature, would derive his appointment from the predominant faction, and be apt to render his administration subservient to its views. 3. The Ministers of foreign powers would have and make use of, the opportunity to to mix their intrigues & influence with the Election. Limited as the powers of the Executive are, it will be an object of great moment with the great rival powers of Europe who have American possessions, to have at the head of our Governmt. a man attached to their respective politics & interests. No pains, nor perhaps expence, will be spared, to gain from the Legislature an appointmt. favorable to their wishes. Germany & Poland are witnesses of this danger. In the former, the election of the Head of the

---

[6] Revised from *Journal.*

[7] Crossed out "renewed his motion".

Empire, till it became in a manner hereditary, interested all Europe, and was much influenced[8] by foreign interference — In the latter, altho' the elective Magistrate has very little real power, his election has at all times produced the most eager interference of forign princes, and has in fact at length slid entirely into foreign hands. The existing authorities in the States are the Legislative, Executive & Judiciary. The appointment of the Natl Executive by the first was objectionable in many points ⟨of view⟩, some of which had been already mentioned. He would mention one which of itself would decide his opinion. The Legislatures of the States had betrayed a strong propensity to a variety of pernicious measures.[9] One object of the Natl. Legislre. was to controul this propensity. One object of the Natl. Executive, so far as it would have a negative on the laws, was to controul the Natl. Legislature, so far as it might be infected with a similar propensity. Refer the appointmt of the Natl. Executive to the State Legislatures, and this controuling purpose may be defeated. The Legislatures can & will act with some kind of regular plan, and will promote the appointmt. of a man who will not oppose himself to a favorite object. Should a majority of the Legislatures at the time of election have the same object, or different objects of the same kind, the Natl Executive, would be rendered subservient to them. — An appointment by the State Executives, was liable among other objections to this insuperable one, that being standing bodies, they could & would be courted, and intrigued with by the Candidates, by their partizans, and by the Ministers of foreign powers. The State Judiciarys had not & he presumed wd. not be proposed as a proper source of appointment. The Option before us then lay between an appointment by Electors chosen by the people — and an immediate appointment by the people. He thought the former mode free from many of the objections which had been urged agst. it, and greatly preferable to an appointment by the Natl. Legislature. As the electors would be chosen for the occasion, would meet at once, & proceed immediately

[8] Crossed out "to say the least".

[9] Crossed out "petty acts".

to an appointment, there would be very little opportunity for cabal, or corruption,. As a further precaution, it might be required that they should meet at some place, distinct from the seat of Govt. and even that no person within a certain distance of the place at the time shd. be eligible. This mode however had been rejected so recently & by so great a majority that it probably would not be proposed anew. The remaining mode was an election by the people or rather by the ⟨qualified part of them.⟩[10] at large. With all its imperfections he liked this best. He would not repeat either the general argumts. for or the objections agst this mode. He would only take notice of two difficulties which he admitted to have weight. The first arose from the disposition in the people to prefer a Citizen of their own State, and the disadvantage this wd. throw on the smaller States. Great as this objection might be he did not think it equal to such as lay agst. every other mode which had been proposed. He thought too that some expedient might be hit upon that would obviate it. The second difficulty arose from the disproportion of ⟨qualified voters⟩[10] in the N. & S. States, and the disadvantages which this mode would throw on the latter. The answer to this objection was 1. that this disproportion would be continually decreasing under the influence of the Republican laws introduced in the S. States, and the more rapid increase of their population. 2. That local local considerations must give way to the general interest. As an individual from the S. States he was willing to make the sacrifice.

Mr. Elseworth. The objection drawn from the different sizes of the States, is unanswerable. The Citizens of the largest States would invariably prefer the Candidate within the State; and the largest States wd. invariably have the man.

Question on Mr. Elseworth's motion as above.

N. H. ay. Mas. no. Ct. ay. N. J. no. Pa. ay. Del. no-Md. ay. Va no. N- C. no. S. C. no. Geo. no. [Ayes — 4; noes — 7.]

Mr. Pinkney moved that the election by the Legislature

[10] Crossed out "freeholders".

be qualified with a proviso that no person be eligible for more than 6 years in any twelve years. He thought this would have all the advantage & at the same time avoid in some degree the inconveniency, of an absolute ineligibility a 2d. time.

Col. Mason approved the idea. It had the sanction of experience in the instance of Congs. and some of the Executives of the States. It rendered the Executive as effectually independent, as an ineligibility after his first election, and opened the way at the same time for the advantage of his future services. He preferred on the whole the election by the Natl. Legislature: Tho' Candor obliged him to admit, that there was great danger of foreign influence, as had been suggested. This was the most serious objection with him that had been urged.

Mr Butler. The two great evils to be avoided are cabal at home, & influence from abroad. It will be difficult to avoid either if the Election be made by the Natl Legislature. On the other hand, the Govt. should not be made so complex & unwieldy as to disgust the States. This would be the case, if the election shd. be referred to the people. He liked best an election by Electors chosen by the Legislatures of the States. He was agst. a re-eligibility at all events. He was also agst. a ratio of votes in the States. An equality should prevail in this case. The reasons for departing from it do not hold in the case of the Executive as in that of the Legislature.

Mr. Gerry approved of Mr Pinkney's motion as lessening the evil.

Mr Govr. Morris was agst. a rotation in every case. It formed a political School, in wch. we were always governed by the scholars, and not by the Masters — The evils to be guarded agst in this case are. 1. the undue influence of the Legislature. 2. instability of Councils. 3. misconduct in office. To guard agst. the first, we run into the second evil. we adopt a rotation which produces instability of Councils. To avoid Sylla we fall into Charibdis. A change of men is ever followed by a change of measures We see this fully exemplified in the vicissitudes among ourselves, particularly in

the State of Pena. The selfsufficiency of a victorious party scorns to tread in the paths of their predecessors. Rehoboam will not imitate Solomon. 2. the Rotation in office will not prevent intrigue and dependence on the Legislature. The man in office will look forward to the period at which he will become re-eligible. The distance of the period, the improbability of such a protraction of his life will be no obstacle. Such is the nature of man, formed by his benevolent author no doubt for wise ends, that altho' he knows his existence to be limited to a span, he takes his measures as if he were to live forever. But taking another supposition, the inefficacy of the expedient will be manifest. If the magistrate does not look forward to his re-election to the Executive, he will be pretty sure to keep in view the opportunity of his going into the Legislature itself. He will have little objection then to an extension of power on a theatre where he expects to act a distinguished part; and will be very unwilling to take any step that may endanger his popularity with the Legislature, on his influence over which the figure he is to make will depend. 3. To avoid the third evil, impeachments will be essential, and hence an additional reason agst an election by the Legislature. He considered an election by the people as the best, by the Legislature as the worst, mode. Putting both these aside, he could not but favor the idea of Mr. Wilson, of introducing a mixture of lot. It will diminish, if not destroy both cabal & dependence.

Mr. Williamson was sensible that strong objections lay agst an election of the Executive by the Legislature, and that it opened a door for foreign influence. The principal objection agst. an election by the people seemed to be, the disadvantage under which it would place the smaller States. He suggested as a cure for this difficulty, that each man should vote for 3 candidates. One of these he observed would be probably of his own State, the other 2. of some other States; and as probably of a small as a large one.

Mr. Govr. Morris liked the idea, suggesting as an amendment that each man should vote for two persons one of whom at least should not be of his own State.

Mr ⟨Madison⟩ also thought something valuable might be made of the suggestion with the proposed amendment of it. The second best man[11] in this case would probably be the first, in fact. The only objection which occurred was that each Citizen after havg. given his vote for his favorite fellow Citizen wd. throw away his second on some obscure Citizen of another State, in order to ensure the object of his first choice. But it could hardly be supposed that the Citizens of many States would be so sanguine of having their favorite elected, as not to give their second vote with sincerity to the next object of their choice. It[12] might moreover be provided in favor of the smaller States that the Executive should not be eligible more than   times in   years from the same State.

Mr. Gerry — A popular election in this case is radically vicious. The ignorance of the people would put it in the power of some one set of men dispersed through the Union & acting in Concert to delude them into any appointment. He observed that such a Society of men existed in the Order of the Cincinnati. They were respectable, United, and influencial. They will in fact elect the chief Magistrate in every instance, if the election be referred to the people. — His respect for the characters composing this Society could not blind him to the danger & impropriety of throwing such a power into their hands.

Mr. Dickenson. As far as he could judge from the discussion which had taken place during his attendance, insuperable objections lay agst an election of the Executive by the Natl. Legislature; as also by the Legislatures or Executives of the States — He had long leaned towards an election by the people which he regarded as the best and purest source. Objections he was aware lay agst this mode, but not so great he thought as agst the other modes. The greatest difficulty in the opinion of the House seemed to arise from the partiality of the States to their respective Citizens. But, might not this very partiality be turned to a useful purpose. Let

[11] Crossed out: "in the partial Judgment of each Citizen towards his immediate fellow Citizen".

[12] Crossed out: "As a further safeguard".

the people of each State chuse its best Citizen. The people will know the most eminent characters of their own States, and the people of different States will feel an emulation in selecting those of which they will have the greatest reason to be proud — Out of the thirteen names thus selected, an Executive Magistrate may be chosen either by the Natl Legislature, or by Electors appointed by it.

On a Question which was moved for postponing Mr. Pinkney's motion, in order to make way for some such proposition as had been hinted by Mr. Williamson & others. ⟨it passed in the negative.⟩

N. H. no. Mas. no. Ct. ay. N. J. ay. Pa. ay. Del. no. Md. ay. Va ay. N. C. no. S. C. no. Geo. no. [Ayes — 5; noes — 6.]

On Mr. Pinkney's motion that no person shall serve in the Executive more than 6 years in 12. years, ⟨it passed in the negative.⟩

N. H. ay. Mas. ay. Ct. no. N. J. no. Pa. no. Del. no. Md. no. Va. no. N. C. ay. S. C. ay. Geo. ay [Ayes — 5; noes — 6.]

⟨On a motion that the members of the Committee be furnished with copies of the proceedings it was so determined; S. Carolina alone being in the negative —

It was then moved[13] that the members of the House might take copies of the Resolions which had been agreed to; which passed in the negative.

N. H. no — Mas. no. Con — ay. N. J. ay. Pa. no — Del. ay. Maryd. no. V — ay. N—C. ay. S. C. no — Geo. no —⟩[14] [Ayes — 5; noes — 6.]

Mr. Gerry & Mr Butler moved to refer the ⟨resolution⟩ relating to the Executive ⟨(except the clause making it consist of a single person)⟩ to the Committee of detail[15]

Mr. Wilson hoped that so important a branch of the System wd. not be committed untill a general principle shd. be fixed by a vote of the House.

Mr Langdon was for the Committment. — Adjd.[16]

---

[13] This motion was made by Luther Martin, see Appendix A, CLVIII (27).

[14] Taken from *Journal*.

[15] Revised from *Journal*.

[16] See further Appendix A, LXVIII, LXIX.

THURSDAY, JULY 26, 1787.

JOURNAL

Thursday July 26. 1787.

It was moved and seconded to amend the third clause of the resolution respecting the national executive so as to read as follows, namely

"for the term of seven years to be ineligible a second "time"

which passed in the affirmative [Ayes — 7; noes — 3.]

On the question to agree to the whole resolution respecting the supreme Executive namely.

Resolved That a national Executive be instituted

to consist of a Single Person

to be chosen by the national Legislature

for the term of seven years

to be ineligible a second time

with power to carry into execution the national Laws

to appoint to Offices in cases not otherwise provided for.

to be removable on impeachment and conviction of malpractice or neglect of duty.

to receive a fixed compensation for the devotion of his time to public service

to be paid out of the public Treasury.

it passed in the affirmative. [Ayes — 6; noes — 3; divided — 1.]

It was moved and seconded to agree to the following Resolution namely.

Resolved That it be an instruction to the Committee to whom were referred the proceedings of the Convention for the establishment of a national government, to receive a clause or clauses, requiring certain qualifications of landed prop-

erty and citizenship in the United States for the Executive, the Judiciary, and the Members of both branches of the Legislature of the United States; and for disqualifying all such persons as are indebted to, or have unsettled accounts with the United States from being Members of either Branch of the national Legislature.

It was moved and seconded to strike out the word "landed"

it passed in the affirmative [Ayes — 10; noes — 1.]

On the question to agree to the clause respecting the qualification as amended

it passed in the affirmative [Ayes — 8; noes — 3.]

It was moved and seconded to add the words "and Pensioners of the Government of the United States" to the clause of disqualification

which passed in the negative. [Ayes —3; noes — 7; divided — 1.]

It was moved and seconded to strike out the following words, namely

"or have unsettled accounts with"

which passed in the affirmative. [Ayes — 9; noes — 2.]

On the question to agree to the clause of disqualification as amended

it passed in the negative [Ayes — 2; noes — 9.]

It was moved and seconded to agree to the following resolution namely

Resolved that it be an instruction to the Committee to whom were referred the proceedings of the Convention for the establishment of a national Government, to receive a clause or clauses for preventing the seat of the national Government being in the same City or Town with the seat of the Government of any State, longer than until the necessary public Buildings can be erected.

It was moved and seconded to postpone the consideration of the last resolution.

It was moved and seconded to refer such proceedings of the Convention, as have been agreed on since Monday last, to the Committee of detail

which passed unanimously in ye affirmative

[To adjourn till monday August Ayes — 11; noes — 0.][1] and then the House adjourned till monday Augt 6th

Detail of Ayes and Noes

	New Hampshire	Massachusetts	Rhode Island	Connecticut	New York	New Jersey	Pennsylvania	Delaware	Maryland	Virginia	North Carolina	South Carolina	Georgia	Questions	Ayes	Noes	Divided
[224]	aye			no		aye	no	no	aye	aye	aye	aye	aye	for the term of "seven years" "to be ineligible a second time." (supreme Executive)	7	3	
[225]	aye			aye		aye	no	no	no	dd	aye	aye	aye	To agree to the whole resolution respecting the supreme Executive	6	3	1
[226]	aye	aye		aye		aye	aye	aye	no	aye	aye	aye	aye	To strike out the word "landed" in the qualification	10	1	
[227]	aye	aye		no		aye	no	no	aye	aye	aye	aye	aye	To agree to the clause of qualification	8	3	
[228]	no	aye		no		no	no	no	aye	no	dd	no	aye	To agree to the amendment for disqualification officers under the government and Pensioners.	3	7	1
[229]	aye	aye		aye		no	aye	aye	aye	aye	aye	aye	no	To strike out the words or have unsettled accounts with	9	2	
[230]	no	no		no		no	no	no	no	no	aye	no	aye	To agree to the clause of disqualification	2	9	
[231]	aye	aye		aye		aye	aye	aye	aye	aye	aye	aye	aye	To adjourn till monday August			

End of seventh loose sheet]

MADISON

Thursday July. 2⟨6⟩ in Convention

Col. Mason. In every Stage of the Question relative to the Executive, the difficulty of the subject and the diversity of the opinions concerning it have appeared. Nor have any of the modes of constituting that department been satisfac-

[1] Vote 231, Detail of Ayes and Noes.

tory. 1. It has been proposed that the election should be made by the people at large; that is that an act which ought to be performed by those who know most of Eminent characters, & qualifications, should be performed by those who know least. 2 that the election should be made by the Legislatures of the States. 3. by the Executives of the States. Agst these modes also strong objections have been urged. 4. It has been proposed that the election should be made by Electors chosen by the people for that purpose. This was at first agreed to: But on further consideration has been rejected. 5. Since which, the mode of Mr Williamson, requiring each freeholder to vote for several candidates has been proposed. This seemed like many other propositions, to carry a plausible face, but on closer inspection is liable to fatal objections. A popular election ⟨in any form⟩, as Mr. Gerry has observed, would throw the appointment into the hands of the Cincinnati, a Society for the members of which he had a great respect; but which he never wished to have a preponderating influence in the Govt. 6. Another expedient was proposed by Mr. Dickenson, which is liable to so palpable & material an inconvenience that he had little ⟨doubt⟩ of its being by this time rejected by himself. It would exclude every man who happened not to be popular within his own State; tho' the causes of his local unpopularity might be of such a nature as to recommend him to the States at large. 7. Among other expedients, a lottery has been introduced. But as the tickets do not appear to be in much demand, it will probably, not be carried on, and nothing therefore need be said on that subject. After reviewing all these various modes, he was led to conclude– that an election by the Natl Legislature as originally proposed, was the best. If it was liable to objections, it was liable to fewer than any other. He conceived at the same time that a second election ought to be absolutely prohibited. Having for his primary object, for the pole star of his political conduct, the preservation of the rights of the people, he held it as an essential point, as the very palladium of Civil liberty, that the great officers of State, and particularly the Executive should at fixed periods return

to that mass from which they were at first taken, in order that they may feel & respect those rights & interests, Which are again to be personally valuable to them. He concluded with moving that the constitution of the Executive as reported by the Come. of the whole be re-instated, viz. "that the Executive be appointed for seven years, & be ineligible a 2d. time,"

Mr. Davie seconded the motion

Docr. Franklin. It seems to have been imagined by some that the returning to the mass of the people was degrading the magistrate. This he thought was contrary to republican principles. In free Governments the rulers are the servants, and the people their superiors & sovereigns. For the former therefore to return among the latter was not to *degrade* but to *promote* them– and it would be imposing an unreasonable burden on them, to keep them always in a State of servitude, and not allow them to become again one of the Masters.

Question on Col. Masons motion as above; ⟨which passed in the affirmative⟩

N. H. ay. Masts. not on floor. Ct. no. N. J. ay. Pa. no. Del. no. Md. ay. Va. ay. N. C. ay. S. C. ay. Geo. ay. [Ayes — 7; noes — 3; absent — 1.]

Mr. Govr. Morris was now agst. the whole paragraph. In answer to Col. Mason's position that a periodical return of the great officers of the State into the mass of the people, was the palladium of Civil liberty he wd. observe that on the same principle the Judiciary ought to be periodically degraded; certain it was that the Legislature ought on every principle– yet no one had proposed. or conceived that the members of it should not be re-eligible. In answer to Docr. Franklin, that a return into the mass of the people would be a promotion. instead of a degradation, he had no doubt that our Executive like most others would have too much patriotism to shrink from the burden of his office, and too much modesty not to be willing to decline the promotion.

⟨On the question on the whole resolution as amended in the words following [2] — "that a National Executive be

[2] Madison originally recorded, "Question on the whole clause including Col. Mason's amendment". Later he substituted from *Journal* the words of the text.

instituted — to consist of a single person — to be chosen by the Natl. legislature — for the term of seven years — to be ineligible a 2d. time — with power to carry into execution the natl. laws — to appoint to offices in cases not otherwise provided for — to be removeable on impeachment & conviction of mal-practice or neglect of duty — to receive a fixt compensation for the devotion of his time to the public service, to be paid out of the Natl. Treasury" — it passed in the affirmative[3]⟩

N. H. ay. Mas. not on floor. Ct. ay. N. J. ay. Pa. no. Del. no. Md. no. Va. divd. Mr. B. ⟨Blair⟩ & Col. M. ⟨Mason⟩ ay. Genl. W. ⟨Washington⟩ & Mr M — ⟨Madison⟩ no. Mr. Randolph happened to be out of the House. N– C– ay. S. C. ay. Geo. ay. [Ayes — 6; noes — 3; divided — 1; absent — 1.]

Mr Mason moved "that the Committee of detail be instructed to receive a clause requiring certain qualifications of landed property & citizenship ⟨of the U. States⟩ in members of the Legislature,[4] and disqualifying persons having unsettled Accts. with or being indebted to the U. S. ⟨from being members of the Natl. Legislature"⟩[5] — He observed that persons of the latter descriptions had frequently got into the State Legislatures, in order to promote laws that might shelter their delinquencies; and that this evil had crept into Congs. if Report was to be regarded.

Mr Pinckney seconded the motion

Mr Govr. Morris. If qualifications are proper, he wd. prefer them in the electors rather than the elected. As to debtors of the U. S. they are but few. As to persons having unsettled accounts he believed them to be pretty many. He thought however that such a discrimination would be both odious & useless. and in many instances unjust & cruel. The delay of settlemt. had been more the fault of the public than of the individuals. What will be done with those patriotic Citizens who have lent money, or services or property to their Country, without having been yet able to obtain a liquidation of their claims? Are they to be excluded?

[3] For further discussion of this subject, see references under September 6, note 23.

[4] Crossed out: "Executive & Judiciary".

[5] Revised from *Journal*.

Mr. Ghorum was for leaving to the Legislature, the providing agst such abuses as had been mentioned.

Col. Mason mentioned the parliamentary qualifications adopted in the Reign of Queen Anne, which he said had met with universal approbation

Mr. ⟨Madison⟩ had witnessed[6] the zeal of men having accts. with the public, to get into the Legislatures for sinister purposes. He thought however that if any precaution were to be taken for excluding them, the one proposed by Col. M⟨ason⟩ ought to be new modelled. It might be well to limit[7] the exclusion to persons who had recd money from the public, and had not accounted for it.

Mr Govr. Morris—It was a precept of great antiquity as well as of high authority that we should not be righteous overmuch. He thought we ought to be equally on our guard agst. being wise over much. The proposed regulation would enable the Govent. to exclude particular persons from office as long as they pleased He mentioned the case of the Commander in chief's presenting his account for secret services, which he said was so moderate that every one was astonished at it; and so simple that no doubt could arise on it. Yet had the Auditor been disposed to delay the settlement, how easily might he have affected it, and how cruel wd. it be in such a case to keep a distinguished & meritorious Citizen under a temporary disability & disfranchisement. He mentioned this case merely to illustrate the objectionable nature of the proposition. He was opposed to such minutious regulations in a Constitution. The parliamentary qualifications quoted by Col. Mason, had been disregarded in practice; and was but a scheme of the landed agst the monied interest.

Mr Pinckney & Genl. Pinckney moved to insert by way of amendmt. the words Judiciary & Executive so as to extend the qualifications to those departments which was agreed to nem con

Mr. Gerry thought the inconveniency of excluding a few worthy individuals who might be public debtors or have unsettled accts ought not to be put in the Scale agst the public

[6] Crossed out "the evil mentioned by Col. Mason".

[7] Crossed out "to avoid objections by limiting".

advantages of the regulation, and that the motion did not go far enough.

Mr. King observed that there might be great danger in requiring landed property as a qualification since it would exclude the monied interest, whose aids may be essential in particular emergencies to the public safety.[8]

Mr. Dickenson. was agst. any recital of qualifications in the Constitution. It was impossible to make a compleat one, and a partial one would by implication tie up the hands of the Legislature from supplying the omissions, The best defence lay in the freeholders who were to elect the Legislature. Whilst this Source should remain pure, the public interest would be safe. If it ever should be corrupt, no little expedients would repel the danger. He doubted the policy of interweaving into a Republican constitution a veneration for wealth. He had always understood that a veneration for poverty & virtue, were the objects of republican encouragement. It seemed improper that any man of merit should be subjected to disabilities in a Republic where merit was understood to form the great title to public trust, honors & rewards.

Mr Gerry if property be one object of Government, provisions for securing it can not be improper.

Mr. ⟨Madison⟩ moved to strike out the word *landed*, before the word, "qualifications". If the proposition sd. be agreed to he wished the Committee to be at liberty to report the best criterion they could devise. Landed possessions were no certain evidence of real wealth. Many enjoyed them to a great extent who were more in debt than they were worth. The unjust laws of the States had proceeded more from this class of men, than any others. It had often happened that men who had acquired landed property on credit, got into the Legislatures with a view of promoting an unjust protection agst. their Creditors. In the next place, if a small quantity of land should be made the standard. it would be no security. —if a large one, it would exclude the proper representatives of those classes of Citizens who were not landholders. It

[8] See Appendix A, CLXXII.

was politic as well as just that the interests & rights of every class should be duly represented & understood in the public Councils. It was a provision every where established that the Country should be divided into districts & representatives taken from each, in order that the Legislative Assembly might equally understand & sympathise, with the rights of the people in every part of the Community. It was not less proper that every class of Citizens should have an opportunity of making their rights be felt & understood in the public Councils. The three principle classes into which our citizens were divisible, were the landed the commercial, & the manufacturing. The 2d. & 3rd. class, bear as yet a small proportion to the first. The proportion however will daily increase. We see in the populous Countries in Europe now, what we shall be hereafter. These classes understand much less of each others interests & affairs, than men of the same class inhabiting different districts. It is particularly requisite therefore that the interests of one or two of them should not be left entirely to the care, or the impartiality of the third. This must be the case if landed qualifications should be required; few of the mercantile, and scarcely any of the manufacturing class, chusing whilst they continue in business to turn any part of their Stock into landed property. For these reasons he wished if it were possible that some other criterion than the mere possession of land should be devised. He concurred with Mr. Govr. Morris in thinking that qualifications in the Electors would be much more effectual than in the elected. The former would discriminate between real & ostensible property in the latter; But he was aware of ⟨the difficulty of⟩ forming any uniform standard that would suit the different circumstances & opinions prevailing in the different States.

Mr. Govr Morris 2ded. the motion.

On the Question for striking out "landed"

N. H. ay. Mas. ay. Ct. ay N. J. ay. Pa. ay. Del. ay. Md. no Va. ay. N. C. ay. S. C. ay. Geo. ay. [Ayes — 10; noes — 1.]

On Question on 1st. part of Col. Masons proposition as to qualification of property & citizenship" ⟨as so amended⟩ [9]

[9] Taken from *Journal*.

N. H. ay. Masts. ay. Ct. no. N. J. ay. Pa. no. Del. no. Md. ay. Va. ay. N. C. ay. S. C. ay. Geo. ay. [Ayes — 8; noes — 3.]

"The 2d. part, for disqualifying debtors, and persons having unsettled accounts", being under consideration

Mr. Carrol moved to strike out "having unsettled accounts"

Mr. Ghorum seconded the motion; observing that it would put the commercial & manufacturing part of the people on a worse footing than others as they would be most likely to have dealings with the public.

Mr. L– Martin. if these words should be struck out, and the remaining words concerning debtors retained, it will be the interest of the latter class to keep their accounts unsettled as long as possible.

Mr. Wilson was for striking them out. They put too much power in the hands of the Auditors, who might combine with rivals in delaying settlements in order to prolong the disqualifications of particular men. We should consider that we are providing a Constitution for future generations, and not merely for the peculiar circumstances of the moment. The time has been, and will again be when the public safety may depend on the voluntary aids of individuals which will necessarily open accts. with the public, and when such accts. will be a characteristic of patriotism. Besides a partial enumeration of cases will disable the Legislature from disqualifying odious & dangerous characters.

Mr. Langdon was for striking out the whole clause for the reasons given by Mr Wilson. So many Exclusions he thought too would render the system unacceptable to the people.

Mr. Gerry. If the argumts. used to day were to prevail, we might have a Legislature composed of public debtors, pensioners, placemen & contractors. He thought the proposed qualifications would be pleasing to the people. They will be considered as a security agst unnecessary or undue burdens being imposed on them ⟨He moved to add "pensioners" to the disqualified characters which was negatived.

N. H. no Mas. ay. Con. no. N. J. no. Pa. no. Del no Maryd.

ay. Va. no. N. C. divided. S. C. no. Geo. ay.⟩[10] [Ayes — 3; noes — 7; divided — 1.]

Mr. Govr. Morris The last clause, relating to public debtors will exclude every importing merchant. Revenue will be drawn it is foreseen as much as possible, from trade. Duties of course will be bonded. and the Merchts. will remain debtors to the public. He repeated that it had not been so much the fault of individuals as of the public that transactions between them had not been more generally liquidated & adjusted. At all events to draw from our short & scanty experience rules that are to operate through succeeding ages, does not savour much of real wisdom.

On question for striking out "persons having unsettled accounts with the U. States."

N. H. ay. Mas. ay. Ct. ay. N. J. no. Pa. ay. Del. ay. Md. ay. Va. ay. N. C. ay. S. C. ay. Geo. no. [Ayes — 9; noes — 2.]

Mr. Elseworth was for disagreeing to the remainder of the clause disqualifying public debtors; and for leaving to the wisdom of the Legislature and the virtue of the Citizens, the task of providing agst. such evils. Is the smallest as well largest debtor to be excluded? Then every arrear of taxes will disqualify. Besides how is it to be known to the people when they elect who are or are not public debtors. The exclusion of pensioners & placemen in Engd is founded on a consideration not existing here. As persons of that sort are dependent on the Crown, they tend to increase its influence.

Mr. Pinkney sd. he was at first a friend to the proposition, for the sake of the clause relating to qualifications of property; but he disliked the exclusion of public debtors; it went too far. It wd. exclude persons who had purchased confiscated property or should purchase Western territory of the public, and might be some obstacle to the sale of the latter.

On the question for agreeing to the clause disqualifying public debtors

N. H. no. Mas– no. Ct. no. N–J. no. Pa. no. Del. no. Md. no. Va. no. N. C. ay. S. C. no. Geo. ay. [Ayes — 2; noes — 9.]

[10] Undoubtedly taken from *Journal*, although there is no clue there that the motion was made by Gerry.

Col. Mason. observed that it would be proper, as he thought, that some provision should be made in the Constitution agst. choosing for the seat of the Genl. Govt. the City or place at which the seat of any State Govt. might be fixt. There were 2 objections agst. having them at the same place, which without mentioning others, required some precaution on the subject. The 1st. was that it tended to produce disputes concerning jurisdiction — The 2d. & principal one was that the intermixture of the two Legislatures tended to give a provincial tincture to ye Natl. deliberations. He moved that the Come. be instructed to receive a clause to prevent the seat of the Natl. Govt. being ⟨in the same City or town with⟩ the seat of ⟨the Govt. of⟩ any State ⟨longer⟩ than untill the necessary public buildings could be erected.[11]

Mr. Alex. Martin 2ded. the motion.

Mr. Govr. Morris did not dislike the idea, but was apprehensive that such a clause might make enemies of Philda. & N. York which had expectations of becoming the Seat of the Genl. Govt.

Mr. Langdon approved the idea also: but suggisted the case of a State moving its seat of Govt. to the natl. seat after the erection of the public buildings

Mr. Ghorum. the precaution may be evaded by the Natl. Legislre. by delaying to erect the public buildings

Mr. Gerry conceived it to be the genel. sense of America, that neither the Seat of a State Govt. nor any large commercial City should be the seat of the Genl. Govt.

Mr. Williamson liked the idea, but knowing how much the passions of men were agitated by this matter, was apprehensive of turning them agst. the system. He apprehended also that an evasion might be practiced in the way hinted by Mr. Ghorum.

Mr. Pinkney thought the seat of a State Govt. ought to be avoided; but that a large town or its vicinity would be proper for the seat of the Genl. Govt.

Col. Mason did not mean to press the motion at this time,

[11] Revised from *Journal.*

nor to excite any hostile passions agst. the system. He was content to withdraw the motion for the present.

Mr. Butler was for fixing ⟨by the Constitution⟩ the place, & a central one, ⟨for the seat of the Natl Govt⟩

The ⟨proceedings since monday last were referred unanimously to the⟩[12] Come. of detail, ⟨and the Convention then unamously⟩[13] Adjourned till Monday. Augst. 6. that ⟨the⟩ Come. of detail ⟨might⟩ have time to prepare & report the Constitution:[14]

⟨The whole proceedings as referred are as follow: (here copy them from the Journal p. 207.

With the above resolutions were referred the propositions offered by Mr. C. Pinckney on the 29th of May. & by Mr. Patterson on the 15th. of June.⟩[13]

[12] Madison originally noted that "The Resolution constituting the executive as amended, was referred". Later he struck that out and substituted from *Journal* the wording of the text.

[13] Taken from *Journal*.

[14] The appointment of a committee, its members and general purpose, and the adjournment of the Convention until August 6, were reported in the local newspapers. See further Appendix A, LXX–LXXVII.

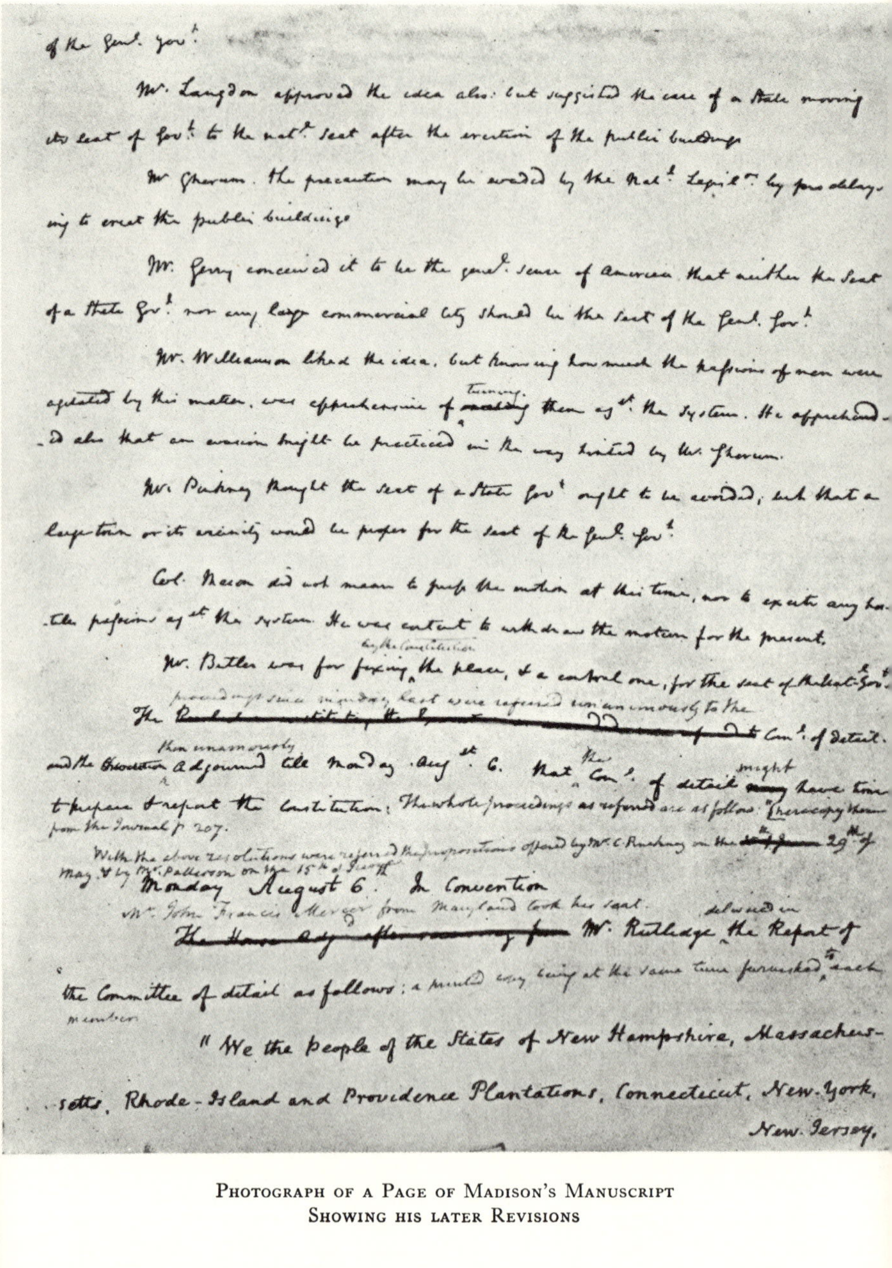

of the Genl. Govt.

Mr. Langdon approved the idea also: but suggested the case of a State moving its seat of Govt. to the natl. seat after the erection of the public buildings

Mr. Ghorum. the precaution may be evaded by the Natl. Legislre. by postponing to erect the public buildings

Mr. Gerry conceived it to be the genl. sense of America, that neither the Seat of a State Govt. nor any large commercial City should be the seat of the Genl. Govt.

Mr. Williamson liked the idea, but knowing how much the passions of men were agitated by this matter, was apprehensive of turning them agst. the System. He apprehended also that an evasion might be practised in the way hinted by Mr. Ghorum.

Mr. Pinkney thought the seat of a State Govt. ought to be avoided; but that a large town or its vicinity would be proper for the seat of the Genl. Govt.

Col. Mason did not mean to press the motion at this time, nor to excite any hostile passions agst. the system. He was content to withdraw the motion for the present.

Mr. Butler was for fixing by the Constitution the place, & a central one, for the seat of the Natl. Govt.

The proceedings since Monday last were referred unanimously to the Comte. of detail, and the Convention then unanimously Adjourned till Monday Augst. 6. that the Comte. of detail might have time to prepare & report the Constitution: The whole proceedings as referred are as follows: [here copy them from the Journal p. 207.

With the above resolutions were referred the propositions offered by Mr. C. Pinckney on the 29th. of May, & by Mr. Patterson on the 15th. of June.

Monday August 6. In Convention

Mr. John Francis Mercer from Maryland took his seat.

Mr. Rutledge delivered in the Report of the Committee of detail as follows; a printed copy being at the same time furnished to each member.

"We the people of the States of New Hampshire, Massachusetts, Rhode-Island and Providence Plantations, Connecticut, New-York, New-Jersey,

Photograph of a Page of Madison's Manuscript
Showing his later Revisions

COMMITTEE OF DETAIL

[Among the Wilson Papers in the Library of the Historical Society of Pennsylvania are found a number of documents evidently relating to the work of the Committee of Detail. With a few additions from other sources, it is possible to present a nearly complete series of documents representing the various stages of the work of the Committee. All documents obtainable are here given.]

I [1]

[PROCEEDINGS OF THE CONVENTION, JUNE 19 — JULY 23.]

1. Resolved That the Government of the United States ought to consist of a Supreme Legislative, Judiciary and Executive
2. Resolved That the Legislature of the United States ought to consist of two Branches
3. Resolved That the Members of the first Branch of the Legislature of the United States ought to be elected by the People of the several States — for the Term of two Years — to be of the Age of twenty five Years at least — to be ineligible to and incapable of holding any Office under the Authority of the United States (except those peculiarly belonging to the Functions of the first Branch) during the Time of Service of the first Branch
4. Resolved That the Members of the second Branch of the Legislature of the United States ought to be chosen by the Individual Legislatures — to be of the Age of thirty Years at least — to hold their Offices for the Term of six Years; one third to go out biennially — to receive a Compen-

[1] This document, found among the Wilson Papers, evidently represents the proceedings referred to the Committee of Detail by the resolution of July 23. On the first page is an estimate of representation based upon state requisitions; see *Records* of June 9, note 24.

sation for the Devotion of their Time to the public Service — to be ineligible to and incapable of holding any Office under the Authority of the United States (except those peculiarly belonging to the Functions of the second Branch) during the Term for which they are elected, and for one Year thereafter.

5\. Resolved. That each Branch ought to possess the Right of originating Acts.

6\. Resolved That the Right of Suffrage in the first Branch of the Legislature of the United States ought not to be according to the Rules established in the Articles of Confederation but according to some equitable Ratio of Representation

7\. Resolved That in the original Formation of the Legislature of the United States the first Branch thereof shall consist of sixty five Members of which Number New Hampshire shall send *three* — Massachusetts *eight* — Rhode Island *one* — Connecticut *five* — New. York *six* — New-Jersey *four* — Pennsylvania *eight* — Delaware *one* — Maryland *six* — Virginia *ten* — North. Carolina *five* — South Carolina *five* — Georgia *three*.

But as the present Situation of the States may probably alter in the Number of their Inhabitants, the Legislature of the United States shall be authorised from Time to Time to apportion the Number of Representatives; and in Case any of the States shall hereafter be divided, or enlarged by Addition of Territory, or any two or more States united, or any new States created within the Limits of the United States, the Legislature of the United States shall possess Authority to regulate the Number of Representatives in any of the foregoing Cases, upon the Principle of the Number of their Inhabitants, according to the Provisions herein after mentioned namely — Provided always that Representation ought to

be proportioned according to direct Taxation: And in order to ascertain the Alteration in the direct Taxation, which may be required from Time to Time, by the Changes in the relative Circumstances of the States —

Resolved that a Census be taken, within six years from the first Meeting of the Legislature of the United States, and once within the Term of every ten Years afterwards, of all the Inhabitants of the United States in the Manner and according to the Ratio recommended by Congress in their Resolution of April 18th. 1783 — And that the Legislature of the United States shall proportion the direct Taxation accordingly.

Resolved that all Bills for raising or Appropriating Money, and for fixing the Salaries of the Officers of the Government of the United States shall originate in the first Branch of the Legislature of the United States, and shall not be altered or amended by the second Branch; and that no money shall be drawn from the public Treasury but in Pursuance of Appropriations to be originated by the first Branch

Resolved that from the first Meeting of the Legislature of the United States until a Census shall be taken, all Monies for supplying the public Treasury by direct Taxation shall be raised from the several States according to the Number of their Representatives respectively in the first Branch

8. Resolved That in the second Branch of the Legislature of the United States each State shall have an equal Vote.

Resolved That the Legislature of the United States ought to possess the legislative Rights vested in Congress by the Confederation; and moreover to legislate in all Cases for the general Interests of the Union, and also in those Cases to which the States are separately incompetent, or in which the Harmony of the United States may be inter-

COMMITTEE OF DETAIL, I

rupted by the Exercise of individual Legislation.

Resolved That the legislative Acts of the United States made by Virtue and in Pursuance of the Articles of Union, and all Treaties made and ratified under the Authority of the United States shall be the supreme Law of the respective States so far as those Acts or Treaties shall relate to the said States, or their Citizens and Inhabitants; and that the Judicatures of the several States shall be bound thereby in their Decisions, any thing in the respective Laws of the individual States to the contrary notwithstanding.

Resolved That a national Executive be instituted to consist of a single Person — to be chosen for the Term of six Years — with Power to carry into Execution the national Laws — to appoint to Offices in Cases not otherwise provided for — to be removeable on Impeachment and Conviction of mal Practice or Neglect of Duty — to receive a fixed Compensation for the Devotion of his Time to public Service — to be paid out of the public Treasury.

Resolved That the national Executive shall have a Right to negative any legislative Act, which shall not be afterwards passed, unless by two third Parts of each Branch of the national Legislative.

Resolved That a national Judiciary be established to consist of one Supreme Tribunal — the Judges of which shall be appointed by the second Branch of the national Legislature — to hold their Offices during good Behaviour — to receive punctually at stated Times a fixed Compensation for their Services, in which no Diminution shall be made so as to affect the Persons actually in Office at the Time of such Diminution

Resolved That the Jurisdiction of the national Judiciary shall extend to Cases arising under the Laws

passed by the general Legislature, and to such other Questions as involve the national Peace and Harmony.

Resolved That the national Legislature be empowered to appoint inferior Tribunals.

Resolved That Provision ought to be made for the Admission of States lawfully arising within the Limits of the United States, whether from a voluntary Junction of Government and Territory, or otherwise, with the Consent of a number of Voices in the national Legislature less than the whole.

Resolved That a Republican Form of Government shall be guarantied to each State; and that each State shall be protected against foreign and domestic Violence.

Resolved That Provision ought to be made for the Amendment of the Articles of Union, whensoever it shall seem necessary.

Resolved That the legislative, executive and judiciary Powers, within the several States, and of the national Government, ought to be bound by Oath to support the Articles of Union.

Resolved That the Amendments which shall be offered to the Confederation by the Convention ought at a proper Time or Times, after the Approbation of Congress, to be submited to an Assembly or Assemblies of Representatives, recommended by the several Legislatures, to be expressly chosen by the People to consider and decide thereon.

Resolved That the Representation in the second Branch of the Legislature of the United States consist of two Members from each State, who shall vote *per capita.*

II[2]

[PROCEEDINGS OF THE CONVENTION, JULY 24–JULY 26.]

Resolved That a National Executive be instituted
to consist of a Single Person
to be chosen by the National Legislature
for the Term of seven years
to be ineligible a second time
with power to carry into execution the national Laws
to appoint to Offices in cases not otherwise provided for
to be removable on impeachment and conviction of malpractice or neglect of duty
to receive a fixed compensation for the devotion of his time to public service
to be paid out of the public Treasury.

Resolved That it be an instruction to the Committee to whom were referred the proceedings of the Convention for the establishment of a national government, to receive a clause or clauses, requiring certain qualifications of property and citizenship in the United States for the Executive, the Judiciary, and the Members of both branches of the Legislature of the United States.

III[3]

1. A Confederation between the free and independent States of N. H. &c. is hereby solemnly made uniting them together under one general superintending Government for their common Benefit and for their Defense and Security against all Designs and Leagues that may be injurious to their Interests and against all Forc[e][4] and Attacks offered to or made upon them or any of them

---

[2] Compiled from the *Records* to supplement I.

[3] This document, found among the Wilson Papers, is evidently an outline of the Pinckney Plan. See Appendix D. The New Jersey Plan was also referred to the Committee of Detail.

[4] Or "Foes".

2 The Stile

3 Mutual Intercourse — Community of Privileges — Surrender of Criminals — Faith to Proceedings &c.

4 Two Branches of the Legislature — Senate — House of Delegates — together the U. S. in Congress assembled

H. D. to consist of one Member for every thousand Inhabitants $\frac{3}{5}$ of Blacks included

Senate to be elected from four Districts — to serve by Rotation of four Years — to be elected by the H. D. either from among themselves or the People at large

5 The Senate and H. D. shall by joint Ballot annually chuse the Presidt. U. S. from among themselves or the People at large. — In the Presidt. the executive Authority of the U. S. shall be vested. — His Powers and Duties — He shall have a Right to advise with the Heads of the different Departments as his Council

6 Council of Revision, consisting of the Presidt. S. for for. Affairs, S. of War, Heads of the Departments of Treasury and Admiralty or any two of them togr wt the Presidt.

7 The Members of S. & H. D. shall each have one Vote, and shall be paid out of the common Treasury.

8 The Time of the Election of the Members of the H. D. and of the Meeting of U. S. in C. assembled.

9 No State to make Treaties -- lay interfering Duties — keep a naval or land Force (Militia excepted to be disciplined &c according to the Regulations of the U. S.

10. Each State retains its Rights not expressly delegated — But no Bill of the Legislature of any State shall become a law till it shall have been laid before S. &. H. D. in C. assembled and received their Approbation.

11. The exclusive Power of S & H. D. in C. Assembled

12. The S. & H. D. in C. ass. shall have the exclusive Power of regulating Trade and levying Imposts — Each State may lay Embargoes in Time of Scarcity

13 ——— of establishing Post-Offices

14. S. & H. D. in C. ass. shall be the last Resort on Appeal in Disputes between two or more States; which Authority shall be exercised in the following Manner &c

15. S. & H. D. in C. ass. shall institute Offices and appoint Officers for the Departments of for. Affairs, War, Treasury and Admiralty ——

They shall have the exclusive Power of declaring what shall be Treason & Misp. of Treason agt. U. S. — and of instituting a federal judicial Court, to which an Appeal shall be allowed from the judicial Courts of the several States in all Causes wherein Questions shall arise on the Construction of Treaties made by U. S. — or on the Law of Nations — or on the Regulations of U. S. concerning Trade & Revenue — or wherein U. S. shall be a Party — The Court shall consist of Judges to be appointed during good Behaviour — S. & H. D. in C. ass shall have the exclusive Right of instituting in each State a Court of Admiralty, and appointing the Judges &c of the same for all maritime Causes which may arise therein respectively.

16. S & H. D. in C. ass. shall have the exclusive Right of coining Money — regulating its Alloy & Value — fixing the Standard of Weights and Measures throughout U. S.

17. Points in which the Assent of more than a bare Majority shall be necessary.

18 Impeachments shall be by the H. D. before the Senate and the judges of the federeal judicial Court.

19. S. & H. D. in C. ass. shall regulate the Militia thro' the U. S.

20. Means of enforcing and compelling the Payment of the Quota of each State.

21. Manner and Conditions of admiting new States.

22. Power of dividing annexing and consolidating States, on the Consent and Petition of such States.

23. The assent of the Legislature of States shall be sufficient to invest future additional Powers in U. S. in C. ass. and shall bind the whole Confederacy.

24. The Articles of Confederation shall be inviolably observed,ˣ and the Union shall be perpetual; ˣunless altered as before directed[5]

[5] The crosses are evidently intended to indicate that the last two clauses should be reversed.

25 The said States of N. H. &c guarantee mutually each other and their Rights against all other Powers and against all Rebellions &c.

IV [6]

In the draught of a fundamental constitution, two things deserve attention:

1. To insert essential principles only, lest the operations of government should be clogged by rendering those provisions permanent and unalterable, which ought to be accomodated to times and events. and
2. To use simple and precise language, and general propositions, according to the example of the (several) constitutions of the several states. (For the construction of a constitution of necessarrily differs from that of law)

1. A preamble seems proper not for the purpose of designating the ends of government and human polities — This (business, if not fitter for the schools, is at least sufficiently executed display of theory, howsoever proper in the first formation of state governments, (seems) *is* unfit here; since we are not working on the natural rights of men not yet gathered into society, but upon those rights, modified by society, and (supporting) *interwoven with* what we call (states) the rights of states — Nor yet is it proper for the purpose of mutually pledging the faith of the parties for the observance of the articles — This may be done more solemnly at the close of the

---

[6] This document from the George Mason Papers was reproduced in photographic facsimile by William M. Meigs, in the *Growth of the Constitution* (Philadelphia: J. B. Lippincott Company, 1899). It is reprinted here by the courtesy of Mr. Meigs and the Lippincott Company. It is in the handwriting of Edmund Randolph with emendations by John Rutledge. In the text here given those portions in parentheses were crossed out in the original, italics represent changes made in Randolph's handwriting, and the emendations in Rutledge's handwriting are enclosed in angle brackets ⟨ ⟩.

For a transcription of this document from the original MS, see Volume IV.

draught, as in the confederation — But the object of our preamble ought to be briefly to (represent) declare, that the present foederal government is insufficient to the general happiness, that the conviction of this fact gave birth to this convention; and that the only effectual (means) ⟨mode⟩ which they (could) ⟨can⟩ devise, for curing this insufficiency, is the establishment of a supreme legislative executive and judiciary — (In this manner we may discharge the first resolution. We may then proceed to establish)[6a] Let it be next declared, that the following are the constitution and fundamentals of government for the United States[6b] — After this introduction, let us proceed to the

2. First resolution — This resolution involves three particulars

1. the style of the United States, which may continue as it now is.
2 a declaration that (an) ⟨a⟩ supreme (execu) legislative executive and judiciary shall be established; and
3 a declaration, that these departments shall be distinct, (except) and independent of each other, except in specified cases.

In the next place, treat of the legislative, judiciary and executive in their order, and afterwards, of the miscellaneous subjects, as they occur, bringing together all the resolutions, belonging to the same point, howsoever they may be scattered about *and leaving to the last the steps necessary to introduce the government* — (Tak) The following plan is therefore submitted

I The Legislative

1. shall consist of two branches: viz:
   a) a house of delegates; and
   b) a senate;
2. which together shall be called "the legislature of the "United States of America".

3 a) The house of delegates

1. (shall never be greater in number than

To effect this, pursue a rule, similar to that

[6a] Marginal note crossed out: "1st resolution".

[6b] Marginal note crossed out: "2d resolution".

prescribed in the 16th. article of the New-York constitution.)

2. Each state shall send delegates, according to the ratio, recommended by congress

3. to ascertain this point, let a census be taken *in due time* as the national legislature shall direct; within six years from the first meeting of the legislature; and

once in every term of ten years thereafter

4. the census being taken and returned, the legislature shall apportion the representation:

5. The qualifications of (a) delegates shall be the age of twenty five years at least. and citizenship:[7] (and any person possessing these qualifications may be elected except)

6. Their duration in office shall be for two years.

7. The elections shall be *biennially* held on the same day through the *same* state(s): except in case of accidents, and where an adjournment to the succeeding day may be necessary.

8. The place shall be fixed by the (national) legislatures from time to time, or on their default by the national legislature.

9. So shall the presiding officer

10. (Votes shall be given by ballot, unless ⅔ of the national legislature shall choose to vary the mode.)

11. The qualification of electors shall be the same (throughout the states; viz.) *with that in the particular states unless the legislature shall hereafter direct some uniform qualification to prevail through the states.*

(citizenship:
manhood
sanity of mind

[7] Marginal note crossed out: "qu: if a certain term of residence and a certain quantity of landed property ought not to be made by the convention further qualifications."

COMMITTEE OF DETAIL, IV

previous residence for one year, or possession of real property within the state for the whole of one year, or inrolment in the militia for the whole of a years.)[8]

(12. All persons who are may be elected)

12. A majority shall be a quorum for business; but a smaller number may be authorized by the house to call for and punish nonattending members, and to adjourn for any time not exceeding one week

13. (quaere. how far the right of expulsion may be proper.) The house of delegates shall have power over its own members.

14. The delegates shall be privileged from arrest[9] (or assault) *personal restraint* during their attendance, for so long a time before
and after,
as may be necessary, for travelling to and from the legislature (and they shall have no other privilege whatsoever.)

(15. Their wages shall be)

16 They shall be ineligible to *and incapable of holding* offices under the authority of the united states, during the term of service of the house of delegates.

17. Vacancies *by death disability or resignation* shall be supplied by a writ from the (*speaker or any other person, appointed by the house.*) *governor of the state, wherein they shall happen.*

18. The house shall have power to make rules for its own government.

19 The house shall not adjourn without the concurrence of the senate for more than one week, nor without such concurrence to any other place, than the one at which they are sitting.

[8] Marginal note crossed out: "These qualifications are not justified by the resolutions."

[9] "arrest" underscored in the original.

4 b) The Senate —

(1. shall consist of members; each possessing a vote)

2. *the legislature of* Each state shall (send) *appoint* two (members) senators using their discretion as to the time and manner of choosing them.

3. the qualification of (a) senators shall be
   the age of 25 years at least:
   citizenship in the united states:
   and property to the amount of

4. (Their duration in office shall)
   They shall be elected for six years and immediately after the first election they shall be divided by lot *as near as may be* into (four) *three* classes, (six in each class,) and numbered 1, 2, 3: and the seats of the members of the first class shall be vacated at the expiration of the (first) second year, of the second class at the expiration of the fourth and of the third class at the end of the sixth year, and so on continually, that a third part of the senate may be biennially chosen.

5. A majority shall be a quorum for business. but a smaller number may be authorized to call for and punish non attending members and to adjourn (for any time not exceeding one week) ⟨from day to day⟩.

6. Each senator shall have one vote

(6) *7*. The senate shall have power over its own members.

(7) *8*. The senators shall be privileged from arrest [10] *personal restraint* during their attendance,
   and for so long a time before
   and so long after,
   as may be necessary for travelling to and from the legislature
   (and they shall have no other privileges whatsoever.)

(8) *9*. The senators shall be ineligible to and incapable

[10] "arrest" underscored in the original.

COMMITTEE OF DETAIL, IV

of holding any office under the authority of the united states,

during the term for which they are elected, and for one year thereafter,

(except in the instance of those offices, which may be instituted for the better conducting of the business of the senate, while in session)

(10. Vacancies)

(10. The wages of the senators shall be paid out of the (nat) treasury of the united states.:

those wages for the first six years shall be dollars per diem —

at the beginning of (the) every sixth year after the first, the supreme judiciary shall cause a special jury of the most respectable merchants and farmers to be summoned to declare what shall have been the averaged value of wheat during the last six years, in the state, where the legislature may be sitting: And for the six subsequent years, the senators shall receive per diem the averaged value of bushels of wheat.)

11. The (house) *Senate* shall have power to make rules for its own government

12. The Senate shall not adjourn without the concurrence of the house of delegates for more than (one week) ⟨3 days⟩, nor without such concurrence to any place other than that at which they are sitting.

The following are

1 the legislative powers; *with certain exceptions; and under certain restrictions*

(2 with certain exceptions and)

(3 under certain restrictions)

agrd. 1. To raise money by taxation, unlimited as to sum, *for the (future) past (or) ⟨&⟩ future debts and necessities of the union* and to establish rules for collection

Exception(s)

agrd. No Taxes on exports. — Restrictions 1. direct

taxation proportioned to representation 2. No (headpost) capitation-tax which does not apply to all inhabitants under the above limitation (& to be levied uniform) 3. no (other) *indirect* tax which is not common to all 4. (Delinquencies shall be be distress — [illegible words]) 5. To regulate commerce ⟨both foreign & domestic⟩

2. ⟨no State to lay a duty on imports —⟩

Exceptions

1. no Duty on exports.

2. no prohibition on (such) ⟨ye⟩ Importations of ⟨such⟩ inhabitants ⟨or People as the sevl. States think proper to admit⟩

3. no duties by way of such prohibition.

Restrictions

1. A navigation act shall not be passed, but with the consent of (eleven states in) ⟨⅔d. of the Members present of⟩ the senate and (10 in) ⟨the like No. of⟩ the house of representatives.

(2. Nor shall any other regulation — and this rule shall prevail, whensoever the subject shall occur in any act.)

(3. the lawful territory To make treaties of commerce
(qu: as to senate) Under the foregoing restrictions)

4. (To make treaties of peace or alliance
(qu: as to senate) under the foregoing restrictions, and without the surrender of territory for an equivalent,
and in no case, unless a superior title.)

5. To make war⟨: (and)⟩ raise armies. ⟨& equip Fleets.⟩

6. To provide tribunals and punishment for mere offences against the law of nations.

⟨Indian Affairs⟩[11]

7. To declare the law of piracy, felonies and captures on the high seas, and captures on land.

⟨to regulate Weights & Measures⟩[11]

---

[11] Marginal note.

8. To appoint tribunals, inferior to the supreme judiciary.

9. To adjust upon the plan heretofore used *all* disputes between the States ⟨respecting Territory & Jurisdn⟩

10. To (regulate) ⟨The exclusive right of⟩ coining ⟨money (Paper prohibit) no State to be perd. in future to emit Paper Bills of Credit witht. the App: of the Natl. Legisle nor to make any (Article) Thing but Specie a Tender in paymt of debts⟩[11a]

11. To regulate naturalization

12. (To draw forth the) ⟨make Laws for calling forth the Aid of the⟩ militia, (or any part, or to authorize the Executive to embody them) ⟨to execute the Laws of the Union to repel Invasion to inforce Treaties suppress internal Comns.⟩

13. To establish post-offices

14. To subdue a rebellion in any particular state, on the application of the legislature thereof.

⟨of declaring the Crime & Punishmt of Counterfeitg it⟩[11a]

15. To enact articles of war.

16. To regulate the force permitted to be kept in each state.

(17. To send embassadors)

⟨Power to borrow Money–
To appoint a Treasurer by (joint) ballot.⟩[11a]

18. To declare it to be treason to levy war against or adhere to the enemies of the U. S.

19. (To organize the government in those things, which)

⟨Insert the 11 Article⟩

(All laws of a particular state, repugnant hereto, shall be void, and in the decision thereon, which shall be vested in the supreme judiciary, all incidents without which the general principles cannot be satisfied shall be considered, as involved in the general principle.)

⟨That Trials for Criml. Offences be in the State where the Offe was comd — by Jury — and a right to make all Laws necessary to carry the foregoing Powers into Execu —⟩

2. The powers belonging peculiarly to the representatives are those concerning money-bills

3. The powers destined for the senate peculiarly, are

COMMITTEE OF DETAIL, IV

1. To make treaties of commerce
2. to make ⟨Treaties of⟩ peace ⟨& Alliance⟩
3. to appoint the judiciary
4. ⟨to send Embassadors⟩

4. The executive ⟨Governor of the united People & States of America.⟩[11a]
1. shall consist of a single person.
2. who shall (hold) be elected by the Legislature ⟨by (joint) Ballot (& in) each Ho. havg a Negative on the other⟩
3. and *shall* hold his office for the term of (six) *seven* years
4. and shall be ineligible thereafter.
5. His powers shall be
    1. to carry into execution the national laws.
    2. to (command and superintend the militia,) ⟨to be Commander in Chief of the Land & Naval Forces of the Union & of the Militia of the sevl. states⟩[11a]
    (3. to direct their discipline)
    (4. to direct the executives of the states to call them or any part for the support of the national government)
    5. to appoint to offices not otherwise provided for. ⟨by the constitution⟩
    ⟨shall propose to the Legisle. from Time to Time by Speech or Messg such Meas as concern this Union⟩[11a]
    6. to be removeable on impeachment,
        made by the house of representatives
    and (on) conviction
        (of malpractice
        or neglect of duty;)
        before the supreme judiciary[12]
⟨of Treason Bribery or Corruption.⟩

[11a] Marginal note.

[12] Madison ascribes this provision to the constitution of Virginia, see Appendix A, CCCXCII.

COMMITTEE OF DETAIL, IV

7. to receive a fixed compensation for
the devotion of his time to public service
the quantum of which shall be settled
by the national legislature
to be paid out of the national
treasury ⟨no Increase or decrease during
the Term of Service of the Executive⟩[12a]

8. (and) to have a qualified negative on legislative acts so as to require repassing by ⅔

9. and shall swear fidelity to the union, (as the legislature shall direct.) ⟨by taking an oath of office⟩

10. receiving embassadors *11. commissioning officers.* *12. convene legislature* ⟨The Presidt of ye Senate to succeed to the Executive in Case of (death) Vacancy untill the Meeting of the Legisle The power of pardoning vested in the Executive (which) his pardon shall not however, be pleadable to an Impeachmt.⟩[12a]

5. The Judiciary

1. shall consist of one supreme tribunal
2. the judges whereof shall be appointed by the senate
3. and of such inferior tribunals, as the legislature may (appoint) ⟨establish⟩

(4. the judges of which shall be also appointed by the senate —)

5 all the judges shall hold their offices during good behaviour;

6. and shall receive punctually,
at stated times
a (fixed) compensation for their services,
to be settled by the legislature
in which no diminution shall be made, so as to affect the persons actually in office at the time of such diminution.
and shall swear fidelity to the union.

7. The jurisdiction of the supreme tribunal shall extend
1 to all cases, arising under laws passed by the general ⟨Legislature⟩

COMMITTEE OF DETAIL, IV

2. to impeachments of officers, and
3. to *such* other cases, as the national legislature may assign, as involving the national peace and harmony,
in the collection of the revenue
in disputes between citizens of different states
⟨in disputes between a State & a Citizen or Citizens of another State⟩[12a]
in disputes between different states; and
in disputes, in which subjects or citizens of other countries are concerned
⟨& in Cases of Admiralty Jurisdn⟩

But this supreme jurisdiction shall be appellate only, except in ⟨Cases of Impeachmt. & (in)⟩ those instances, in which the legislature shall make it original. and the legislature shall organize it

8. The whole or a part of the jurisdiction aforesaid according to the discretion of the legislature may be assigned to the inferior tribunals, as original tribunals.

Miscellaneous provisions

1 New states soliciting admission into the Union
(1. must be within the present limits of the united states)
2. must lawfully arise, that is
(a– in the territory of the united states, with the assent of the legislature)
(b– within the limits of a particular state, by the consent of a major part of the people of that state.)

⟨States lawfully arising & if within the Limits of any of the prest. States by Consent of the Legisle. of those States.⟩[12a]

3. shall be admitted only on the suffrage of ⟨$\frac{2}{3}$ds⟩ in the house of representatives and ⟨the like No in the⟩ Senate

[12a] Marginal note.

4. & shall be admitted on the same terms with the original states (but the number of states or votes required on particular measures shall be readjusted —)

5. provided always, that the legislature may use their discretion in (refusing) *admitting* or rejecting, and may make any condition concerning the (old) debt of the union ⟨at that Time.⟩

(6. provided also, that the western states are intitled to admission on the terms specified in the act of congress of)

2. The guarantee is

1. to prevent the establishment of any government, not republican

(2) ⟨3.⟩ to protect each state against internal commotion: and

(3) ⟨2.⟩ against external invasion.

4. But this guarantee shall not operate ⟨in the last Case⟩ without an application from the legislature of a state.

5.

3. The legislative executive and judiciaries of the states shall swear fidelity to the union, as the national legislature shall direct.

4. The ratification of the reform is — After the approbation of congress — to be made

by a special convention ⟨in each State⟩
recommended by the assembly
to be chosen for the express purpose
of considering and approving or rejecting it in toto:
and this recommendation may be used from time to time

5. (An alteration may be effected in the articles of union, on the application of two thirds *nine* ⟨$\frac{2}{3}$d⟩ of the state legislatures ⟨by a Convn.⟩) ⟨on appln. of $\frac{2}{3}$ds of the State Legislatures to the Natl. Leg. they call a Convn. to revise or alter ye Articles of Union⟩

COMMITTEE OF DETAIL, IV

(6. The plighting of faith ought to be in solemn terms)
Addenda

1. The assent of the (major part of the people) ⟨Conventions⟩ of states shall give (birth) operation to this constitution
2. Each assenting state shall notify its assent to congress: who shall publish a day for its commencement, not exceeding *After such publication, or with* the (failure thereof), *assent of the major part of the assenting states* after the expiration of days *from the giving of the assent of the ninth state,*
    1. each legislature shall direct the choice of representatives, *according to the seventh article* and provide for their support:
    2. each legislature shall also choose senators; and provide for their support
    3. they shall meet at ⟨the Place &⟩ on the day assigned by congress, (or as the major part of the assenting states shall agree, on any other day.)
    4. They shall as soon as may be after meeting elect the executive: and proceed to execute this constitution.

The object of an address is to satisfy the people of the propriety of the proposed reform.

To this end the following plan seems worthy of adoption

1. To state the general objects of a confederation.
2. To shew by general, but pointed observations, in what (particulars) respects, our confederation has fallen short of those objects.
3. The powers, necessary to be given, will then follow as a consequence of the defects
4. A question next arises, whether these powers can *with propriety* be vested in congress. The answer is, that they cannot
5. *But* As some states may possibly meditate partial confederations, it would be fit now to refute this opinion briefly.
6. It follows then, that a government of the whole on

COMMITTEE OF DETAIL, V

national principles, with respect to taxation &c is most eligible.

7. This would lead to a short exposition of the leading particulars in the constitution.

8. This done, conclude in a suitable manner.

This is the shortest scheme, which can be adopted. For it would be strange to ask (for) new powers, without assigning some reason—it matters not how general soever—which may apply to all of them Besides we ought to furnish the advocates of the plan in the country with some general topics. Now I conceive, that these heads do not more, than comprehend the necessary points.

V[13]

already confederated united and known (known) by the Stile of the United States of America"

We The People of the States of New-Hampshire &C do (agree upon,) ordain declare and establish the following (Frame of Government as the) Frame of Govt as the Constitution (of the "United States of America" according to which we and our Posterity shall be governed under the Name and Stile of the "United States of America") of the said United States

I

in a general Assembly to consist of two separate and distinct Bodies of Men, the one to be called the House of Representatives, of the People

The legislative Power of the United States shall be vested in two (Branches a Senate and a House of Representatives;) each of which Bodies shall

[13] Document V in Wilson's handwriting was found among the Wilson Papers. It appears to be the beginning of a draft with an outline of the continuation. Parts in parentheses were crossed out in the original.

COMMITTEE OF DETAIL, V

of the United States the other the Senate of the United States.

have a Negative on the other

2.

The Members of the House of Representatives shall be chosen biennially by the People of the United States in the following Manner. Every Freeman of the Age of twenty one Years (having a freehold Estate within the United States) who has (having) resided in the United States for the Space of one whole Year immediately preceding the Day of Election, and has a Freehold Estate in at least fifty Acres of Land

The Continuation of the Scheme

1. To treat of the Powers of the legislative[13a]
2. To except from those Powers certain specified Cases
3 To render in certain Cases a greater Number than a Majority necessary
4. To assign to H. Repr — any Powers peculiarly belonging to it
5 To assign, in same Manner, Powers which may, with Propriety be vested in it.
6 To treat of the Executive
7 of the Judiciary

Miscellaneous Resolutions

1. Admission of new States
2. The Guaranty to each State
3. The Obligation to support the Art. of Union
4. The Manner of Ratification

[13a] Or "legislature".

5. The Manner of Alteration.
6. The plighting of mutual Faith

to be added

1. How many States will be necessary to assent to this Plan

2. What Day shall be appointed for the States to give an Answer

3. Qu. whether any Thing should be said as to the *Amendment* by the *States*

4. As to the Introduction of the Government

VI[14]

We the People of (*and*) the States of New Hampshire, Massachusetts, Rhode Island and Providence Plantations, Connecticut, New. York, New. Jersey, Pennsylvania, Delaware, Maryland, Virginia, North. Carolina, South. Carolina and Georgia do ordain declare and establish the following Constitution for the Government of ourselves and of our Posterity.

1.

The Stile of this Government shall be the "United People and States of America."

2.

The Government shall consist of supreme legislative, executive and judicial Powers.

3.

The (Supreme) legislative Power shall be vested in a Congress to consist of two separate and distinct Bodies of Men, (one to be called the) *a* House of Representatives, (the other to be called the) *and a* Senate (of) each of which shall in all Cases have a Negative on the other (in all cases not otherwise provided for in this Constitution)

---

[14] Found among the Wilson Papers and in Wilson's handwriting. Portions in parentheses represent parts crossed out. Italics represent later insertions.

COMMITTEE OF DETAIL, VI

4.

The Members of the House of Representatives shall be chosen every second Year (in the Manner following) by the People of the several States comprehended within this Union (the Time and Place and the Manner and the of holding the Elections and the Rules) *The Qualifications of the Electors* shall be (appointed) *prescribed* by the Legislatures of the several States; but the*ir* provisions (which they shall make concerning them shall be subject to the Control of) *concerning them may at any Time be altered and superseded by* the Legislature of the United States.

(No person shall be capable of being chosen) Every Member of the House of Representatives shall be (twenty-five Years of Age) *of the Age of twenty five Years* at least; shall have been a Citizen in the United States for at least three Years before his Election, and shall be, at the Time of his Election, a Resident of the State, (from) *in* which he shall be chosen.

The House of Representatives shall, at its first Formation *and until the Number of Citizens and Inhabitants shall be taken in the Manner hereinafter described* consist of 65 Members, of whom three shall be chosen in New-Hampshire, eight in Massachusetts, &c.

As the (present) Proportions of Numbers in the different States will alter from Time to Time; as some of the States may be hereafter divided; as others may be enlarged by Addition of Territory, or two or more States may be united; and as new States will be erected within the Limits of the United States; the Legislature shall, in each of these cases, possess Authority to regulate the Number of Representatives by the Number of Inhabitants according to the provisions herein after made.

(Representation) *Direct Taxation* shall always be in Proportion to (direct Taxation.) Representation in the House of Representatives.

(In order to ascertain and regulate the Proportions of direct Taxation from Time to Time, the Legislature of the United States shall, within six Years after its first Meeting and within the Term of every ten Years afterwards, cause)

COMMITTEE OF DETAIL, VI

The Proportions of direct Taxation shall be regulated by the whole Number of white and other Free Citizens and Inhabitants of every &c. which Number (shall) shall, (be taken) within six Years after the first Meeting of the Legislature (of the United States,) and within the Term of every ten Years afterwards, be taken in such Manner as the said Legislature shall direct (and appoint).

From the first Meeting of the Legislature until the Number of Citizens and Inhabitants shall be taken (in the Manner beforementioned) *as aforesaid*, direct Taxation shall be in Proportion to the Number of (Inhabitants) *Representatives chosen* in each State.

All Bills for raising or appropriating Money and for fixing the Salaries of the Officers of Government shall originate in the House of Representatives, and shall not be altered or amended by the Senate. No money shall be drawn from the public Treasury, but in Pursuance of Appropriations that shall originate in the House of Representatives.

The House of Representatives shall be the grand Inquest of this Nation; and all Impeachments shall be made by them. Vacancies in the House of Representatives shall be supplied by Writs of Election from the (Supr) Executive (Pow) Authority of the State in *the Representation* (*of*) *from* which they shall happen.

The House of Representatives shall chuse its own Speaker and other Officers

The (Members of the) Senate of the United States shall be chosen (*every sixth year*) by the Legislatures of the several States; Each (of which) *Legislature* shall chuse two Members. (The votes shall not be given by States, but by the Members separately *from each State*.) Each Member shall have one Vote.

The Members of the Senate shall be chosen for six Years; provided that immediately after the first Election they (Members of the Senate) shall (by) be divided by Lot into three Classes as nearly as may be, and numbered one, two and three. The Seats of the Members of the first Class shall be vacated at the Expiration of the second Year, (th) of the second Class

at the Expiration of the fourth Year, of the third Class at the (End) *Expiration* of the sixth Year, (that a) and so on continually, that a third Part of the Members of the Senate may be (biennially) chosen every second Year.

Every Member of the Senate shall be *of the Age of thirty Years* at least (thirty Years of Age), shall have been a citizen in the United States for at least four Years before his Election, and shall be, at the Time of his Election a Resident of the State for which he shall be chosen

The Senate (shall be empowered) *of the United States shall have Power* to make Treaties of (Peace, of Alliance, and of Commerce,) to send Ambassadors, and to appoint the Judges of the Supreme national Court

Each House of the Legislature shall possess the right of originating (Acts) Bills, except in Cases beforementioned

The Senate shall chuse its own President and other Officers.

The Members of each House shall be ineligible to and incapable of holding any Office under the Authority of the United States during the Time for which they shall be respectively elected: And the Members of the Senate shall be ineligible to and incapable of holding any such Office for one Year afterwards.

The *enacting* Stile of the Laws of the United States

In each House (*of the Legislature*) a Majority *of the Members* shall constitute a Quorum to do Business; but a smaller Number may adjourn from Day to Day

Each House of the Legislature shall be the Judge of the Elections Returns, and Qualifications of its own Members

The Times and Places and the Manner of holding the Elections (for) *of* the Members of each House shall be prescribed by the Legislatures of each State; but their Provisions concerning them may, at any Time, be altered and superseded by the Legislature of the United States.

The Legislature of the United States shall have Au-

COMMITTEE OF DETAIL, VI

shall be "be it enacted and it is hereby enacted by the House of Representatives, and by the Senate of the United States in Congress assembled

The Members of each House shall receive a Compensation for their Services, to be (paid) ascertained and paid by the State in which they shall be chosen

The House of Representatives and the Senate when it shall be acting in a legislative Capacity (Each House) shall keep a Journal of its Proceedings, and shall from Time to Time publish them, (except such Parts as in their Judgment require Secrecy;) and the Yeas and Nays of the Members of each House on any Question shall at the Desire of any Member be entered on the Journal at the desire of any Member

Freedom of Speech

thority to establish such Qualifications of the Members of each House (of the Legislature) *with Regard to Property* as to the said Legislature shall seem proper and expedient.

(A Majority *of the Members* of each House shall constitute a Quorum to do Business but a smaller Number than a Majority of them may, in each House, adjourn from Day to Day.)

Each House shall have Authority to (settle) *determine* the Rules and Order of its Proceedings, and (have Power) to punish its own Members *for disorderly* (*and indecent*) *Behaviour*

Each House may expel a Member, but not a second Time for the same Offence.

Neither House shall adjourn for more than three Days without the Consent of the other; nor with such Consent, to any other Place than that at which the two Houses are sitting. But this Regulation shall be applied to the Senate only in its Legislative Capacity.

The Members of each House shall, in all cases, except Treason, Felony &

Breach of the Peace, be privileged from Arrest during their Attendance at Congress, and in going to and returning from it.

VII [15]

An Appeal for the Correction of all Errors both in Law and Fact

That the United States in Congress be authorised — to pass Acts for raising a Revenue, — by levying Duties on all Goods and Merchandise of foreign Growth or Manufacture imported into any Part of the United States — by Stamps on Paper Vellum or Parchment — and by a Postage on all Letters and Packages passing through the general Post-Office, to be applied to such foederal Purposes as they shall deem proper and expedient — to make Rules and Regulations for the Collection thereof — to pass Acts for the Regulation of Trade and Commerce as well with foreign Nations as with each other *to lay and collect Taxes*

That the Executive direct all military Operations

That the Judiciary have authority to hear and determine all Impeachments of foederal Officers; and, by Way of Appeal, in all Cases touching the Rights of Ambassadors — in all Cases of Capture from an Enemy — in all Cases of Piracies and Felonies on the high Seas — *in all Cases of Revenue* — in all Cases in which Foreigners may be interested in the Construction of any Treaty, or which may arise on any Act for regulating Trade or collecting Revenue *or on the Law of Nations, or general commercial or marine Laws*

If any State, or any Body of Men in any State, shall oppose

---

[15] Documents VI and VIII are on two sheets of four pages each. Between them is placed Document VII, consisting of a smaller single sheet of two pages. It is in Wilson's hand, but written with a finer pen. The first portion is evidently an extract from the New Jersey plan and the latter portion (after the break and beginning "The Legislature shall consist") was identified by Professor Jameson as extracts from the original Pinckney Plan (see his *Studies in the History of the Federal Convention of 1787*, 128–132.)

or prevent the carrying into Execution the Acts or Treaties of the United States; the Executive shall be authorised to enforce and compel Obedience by calling forth the Powers of the United States.

That the Rule for Naturalization ought to be the same in every State

The Legislature shall consist of two distinct Branches — a Senate and a House of Delegates, each of which shall have a Negative on the other, and shall be stiled the U. S. in Congress assembled.

Each House shall appoint its own Speaker and other Officers, and settle its own Rules of Proceeding; but neither the Senate nor H. D. shall have the power to adjourn for more than Days, without the (other) Consent of both.

There shall be a President, in which the Ex. Authority of the U. S. shall be vested. It shall be his Duty to inform the Legislature of the Condition of U. S. so far as may respect his Department — to recommend Matters to their Consideration — to correspond with the Executives of the several States — to attend to the Execution of the Laws of the U. S. — to transact Affairs with the Officers of Government, civil and military — to expedite all such Measures as may be resolved on by the Legislature — to inspect the Departments of foreign Affairs — War — Treasury — Admiralty — to reside where the Legislature shall sit — to commission all Officers, and keep the Great Seal of U. S. — He shall, by Virtue of his Office, be Commander in chief of the Land Forces of U. S. and Admiral of their Navy — He shall have Power to convene the Legislature on extraordinary Occasions — to prorogue them, provided such Prorogation shall not exceed Days in the space of any — He may suspend Officers, civil and military

The Legislature of U. S. shall have the exclusive Power — of raising a military Land Force — of equiping a Navy — of rating and causing public Taxes to be levied — of regulating the Trade of the several States as well with foreign Nations as with each other — of levying Duties upon Imports and

Exports — of establishing Post-Offices, and raising a Revenue from them — of regulating Indian Affairs — of coining Money — fixing the Standard of Weights and Measures — of determining in what Species of Money the public Treasury shall be supplied.

The foederal judicial Court shall try Officers of the U. S. for all Crimes &C in their Offices — (and to this Court an Appeal shall be allowed from the Courts of)

The Legislature of U. S. shall have the exclusive Right of instituting in each State a Court of Admiralty for hearing and determining maritime Causes.

The power of impeaching shall be vested in the H. D. — The Senators and Judges of the foederal Court, be a Court for trying Impeachments.

The Legislature of U. S. shall possess the exclusive Right of establishing the Government and Discipline of the Militia of — and of ordering the Militia of any State to any Place within U. S.

VIII[16]

mitted on the same Terms with the original States: But the Legislature may make Conditions with the new States (with Respect to) *concerning* the (then subsisting) *public* Debt (of the United States) which shall be then subsisting

The United States shall guaranty to each State a (A) Republican Form of Government (shall be guarantied to each State by the United States); and (the) shall protect each State (from) against (domestic Violence) *foreign Invasion* and, on the Application of its Legislature (from foreign Invasions) against domestic Violence.

This Constitution ought to be amended whenever such Amendment shall become necessary; and on the Application of the Legislatures of two thirds of the States in the Union, the Legislature of the United States shall call a Convention for that Purpose.

The Members of the Legislature, and the executive and

[16] Found among Wilson papers, a continuation of VI, see above notes 14 and 15.

judicial Officers of the United States and of the several States shall be bound by Oath to support this Constitution.

Resolved, That the Constitution proposed by this Convention, to the People (and States) of the Uni(on)*ted States* for their approbation (should, as soon as may be laid) *be* (to) *laid* before the United States in Congress assembled for their Agreement and Recommendation and (should) *be* afterwards (be) submitted to a Convention chosen in each State under the Recommendation of its Legislature, in order to receive the Ratification of such Convention.

Resolved, That the Ratification of the Conventions of States shall be sufficient for organizing this Constitution: That each assenting (State) *Convention* shall notify its Assent *and Ratification* to the United States in Congress assembled: That the United States in Congress assembled, after receiving the Assent and Ratification of the Conventions of States shall appoint and publish a Day, as early as may be, and appoint a Place for (organizing and) commencing (Oper) Proceedings under this Constitution: That after such Publication or, — in case it shall not be made, — (after on) *after* the Expiration of Days (after) from the Time when the Ratification of the Convention of the State shall have been notified to Congress the Legislatures of the several States shall (chuse) *elect* Members of the Senate, and direct the Election of Members of the House of Representatives, and shall provide for their support: That the Members of the Legislature shall meet at the Time and Place assigned by Congress or, — if Congress shall have assigned not Time and Place, — at such Time and Place as shall have been agreed on by the Majority of the Members elected for each House, and shall as soon as may be after their Meeting chuse the (Governour) *President* of the United States and proceed to (carry) execute this Constitution.

(The Legislature (Senate) of the United States shall have Authority) In all Disputes and Controversies now sub-

(All) *Every* Bill(s), which shall have passed the House of Representatives and the Senate, shall, before (they) *it* be-

sisting, or that may hereafter subsist between two or more States, the Senate shall possess the following Powers. Whenever the Legislature, or the Executive Authority, or the lawful Agent of any State in Controversy with another shall (present a petition) by Memorial to the Senate, state the Matter in Question, and apply for a Hearing, Notice of such Memorial and application shall be given by Order of the Senate to the Legislature or the Executive Authority of the other State in Controversy. (A Day) The Senate shall also assign a Day for the Appearance of the Parties by their Agents before that House. The Agents shall be directed to appoint by joint Consent Commissioners or Judges to constitute a Court for hearing and determining the Matter in Question. But if the Agents cannot agree, the Senate shall name *three Persons* out of each of the several States, and from the List of such Persons each Party shall alternately strike out one (the Party who shall have applied for a Hearing beginning) until the Number shall be reduced to thirteen; and from that Number not

come *a* Law(s) be presented to the Governour of the United States for his (Revisal) Revision; (and) If, upon such Revision, he approve (thereof) of it, he shall signify his Approbation by signing it; But, if, upon such Revision, it shall appear to him improper for (becoming) *being passed into* a Law, he shall return it, together with his Objection against it in Writing, to that House (of Representatives or Senate) in which it shall have originated, who shall enter the Objection at large on their Journal, and proceed to reconsider the Bill. But if after such Reconsideration, two thirds of that House shall, notwithstanding the Objections of the Governour, agree to pass it; it shall, together with his objections, be sent to the other House, (where) *by which* it shall (also) *likewise* be reconsidered; and, if approved by two thirds of the other House also, it shall be a Law. But in all such Cases the Votes of both Houses shall be determined by Yeas and Nays; and the Names of the Persons voting for or against the Bill shall be entered in the Journal(s) of each House respectively — If any

less than seven, nor more than nine Names, as the Senate shall direct, shall, in their Presence, be drawn out by Lot; and the Persons, whose names shall be so drawn, or any five of them, shall be Commissioners or Judges to hear and finally determine the Controversy; provided a major Part of the Judges, who shall hear the cause

Bill shall not be returned by the Governour within Days after it shall have been presented to him, it shall be a Law, unless the Legislature, by their Adjournment, prevent its Return; in which Case it shall be returned on the first Day of the next Meeting of the Legislature.

agree in the Determination. If either Party shall neglect to attend at the Day assigned, without showing (to the Sen) sufficient Reasons for not attending, or, being present, shall refuse to strike, the Senate shall proceed to nominate three Persons out of each State, and the (President) *Secretary or Clerk* of the Senate shall strike in Behalf of the Party absent or refusing. If any of the Parties shall refuse to submit to the Authority of such Court, or shall not appear to prosecute or defend their Claim or Cause; the Court shall nevertheless proceed to pronounce (Sentence or) Judgment. The (Sentence or) Judgment (of the court appointed in the Manner before presented) shall be final and conclusive. The Proceedings shall be transmitted to the (Governour) *President* of the (United States) *Senate* and shall be lodged among the public Records for the security of the Parties concerned. Every (Judge) *Commissioner* shall before he sit in Judgment, take an Oath, to be administered by one of the Judges of the Supreme or Superior Court of the State, where the Cause shall be tried, "well and truly to hear and determine the Matter in Question, according to the best of his Judgment, without Favour, Affection or Hope of Reward."

All Controversies concerning Lands claimed under different Grants of two or more States, whose Jurisdictions, as they respect such Lands, shall have been decided or adjusted subsequent to such Grants, shall, on Application to the Senate, be finally determined, as near as may be in the same Manner

as is before (des) prescribed for deciding Controversies between different States.

IX[17]

We the People of the States of New Hampshire, Massachusetts, Rhode-Island and Providence Plantations, Connecticut, New-York, New-Jersey, Pennsylvania, Delaware, Maryland, Virginia, North-Carolina, South-Carolina and Georgia, do ordain, declare and establish the following Constitution for the Government of ourselves and our Posterity.

1.

The Stile of this Government shall be. "the United States of America".

2.

The Government shall consist of supreme legislative, executive, and judicial Powers.

3.

The legislative Power shall be vested in a Congress, to consist of two separate and distinct Bodies of Men, a House of Representatives, and a Senate; each of which shall in all Cases, have a Negative on the other ⟨To meet on the 1st Monday every December —⟩

4.

The Members of the House of Representatives shall be chosen every second Year, by the People of the several States comprehended within this Union. The Qualifications of the Electors shall be (prescribed by the Legislatures of the several States; but these Provisions concerning them may, at any

[17] Found among the Wilson Papers, and in Wilson's handwriting, but with emendations in Rutledge's hand. Parts in parentheses were crossed out in the original; italics represent additions by Wilson; emendations by Rutledge are in angle brackets ⟨ ⟩.

Time be altered and superseded by the Legislature of the United States) *the same from Time to Time as those of the Electors, in the several States, of the most numerous Branch of their own Legislatures.*

Every Member of the House of Representatives shall be of the Age of twenty five Years at least; shall have been a Citizen in the United States for at least three Years before his Election; and shall be, at the Time of his Election, a Resident of the State in which he shall be chosen.

The House of Representatives shall, at its first Formation, and until the Number of Citizens and Inhabitants shall be taken in the Manner herein after described, consist of sixty five Members, of whom three shall be chosen in New-Hampshire, eight in Massachusetts, one in Rhode-Island and Providence Plantations, five in Connecticut, six in New-York, four in New-Jersey, eight in Pennsylvania, one in Delaware, six in Maryland, ten in Virginia, five in North-Carolina, five in South-Carolina, and three in Georgia.

As the Proportions of Numbers in different States will alter from Time to Time; as some of the States may be hereafter divided; as others may be enlarged by Addition of Territory; as two or more States may be united; and as new States will be erected within the Limits of the United States, the Legislature shall, in each of these Cases (possess authority to) regulate the Number of Representatives by the Number of Inhabitants, according to the Provisions herein after made.

All Bills for raising or appropriating Money, and for fixing the Salaries of the Officers of Government, shall originate in the House of Representatives, and shall not be altered or amended by the Senate. No money shall be drawn from the public Treasury, but in Pursuance of Appropriations that shall originate in the House of Representatives.

The House of Representatives shall (be the grand Inquest of the Nation; and all) ⟨have the sole Power of⟩ Impeachment(s shall be made by them).

Vacancies in the House of Representatives shall be supplied by Writs of Election from the Executive Authority of the State, in the representation from which they shall happen.

The House of Representatives shall chuse its (own) Speaker and other Officers.

5.

The Senate of the United States shall be chosen by the Legislatures of the several States. Each Legislature shall chuse two Members. Each Member shall have one Vote.

The Senators shall be chosen for six Years; but immediately after the first Election they shall be divided, by Lot, into three Classes, as nearly as may be, numbered one, two and three. The Seats of the Members of the first Class shall be vacated at the Expiration of the second Year, of the second Class at the Expiration of the fourth Year, of the third Class at the Expiration of the sixth Year, (and so continually) ⟨so⟩ that a third Part of the Members (of the Senate) may be chosen every second Year.

Every Member of the Senate shall be of the Age of thirty Years at least; shall have been a Citizen in the United States for at least four Years before his Election; and shall be, at the time of his Election, a Resident of the State for which he shall be chosen.

The Senate shall (be comp) chuse its own President and other Officers

6.

(Each House of the Legislature shall possess the Right of originating Bills, except in the Cases beforementioned.)

The Times and Places and the Manner of holding the Elections of the Members of each House shall be prescribed by the Legislature of each State; but their Provisions concerning them may, at any Time, be altered (or superseded) by the Legislature of the United States.

The Legislature of the United States shall have Authority to establish such ⟨uniform⟩ Qualifications of the Members of each House, with Regard to Property, as to the said Legislature shall seem (proper and ⟨fit⟩) expedient.

In each House a Majority of the Members shall constitute a Quorum to do Business; but a smaller Number may adjourn from Day to Day.

COMMITTEE OF DETAIL, IX

Each House shall be the Judge of the Elections, Returns and Qualifications of its own Members.

Freedom of Speech and Debate in the Legislature shall not be impeached or questioned in any Court or Place out of the Legislature; and the Members of each House shall, in all Cases, except Treason, Felony and Breach of the Peace, be privileged from Arrest during their Attendance at Congress, and in going to and returning from it.

Each House (shall have Authority to) *may* determine the Rules of its Proceedings, (and to) *may* punish its (own) Members for disorderly Behaviour. (Each House) *and* may expel a Member, (but not a second Time for the same Offence).

The House of Representatives, and the Senate, when it shall be acting in a legislative Capacity, (Each House) shall keep a Journal of their Proceedings, and shall, from Time to Time, publish them: and the Yeas and Nays of the Members of each House, on any Question, shall at the Desire of (any) ⟨$\frac{1}{5}$th. of the⟩ Member⟨s⟩ be entered on the Journal.

Neither House (shall adjourn for more than three Days;) without the Consent of the other ⟨shall adjourn for more than three Days⟩; nor (without such Consent,) to any other Place than that, at which the two Houses are sitting. But this Regulation shall (be applied) ⟨not extend⟩ to the Senate (only in its legislative Capacity.) ⟨when it shall exercise the Powers mentd. in the Article.⟩

The Members of each House shall be ineligible to, and incapable of holding any Office under the Authority of the United States during the Time, for which they shall be respectively elected: And the Members of the Senate shall be ineligible to, and incapable of holding any such Office for one Year afterwards.

The Members of each House shall receive a Compensation for their Services, to be ascertained and paid by the State, in which they shall be chosen.

The enacting Stile of the Laws of the United States shall be "be it enacted and it is hereby enacted by the House of Representatives and by the Senate of the United States in Congress assembled".

Each House shall possess the Right of Originating Bills, except in the Cases beforementioned.

7.

Every Bill, which shall have passed the House of Representatives and the Senate, shall, before it become a Law, be presented to the (Governour) ⟨President⟩ of the United States for his Revision: If, upon such Revision, he approve of it; he shall signify his Approbation by signing it: But if, upon such Revision, it shall appear to him improper for being passed into a Law; he shall return it, together with his Objections against it, to that House, in which it shall have originated, who shall enter the Objections at large on their Journal, and proceed to reconsider the Bill. But if after such Reconsideration, two thirds of that House shall, notwithstanding the Objections of the (Governour) ⟨President⟩, agree to pass it, it shall, together with his Objections, be sent to the other House, by which it shall likewise be reconsidered, and, if approved by two thirds of the other House also; it shall be a Law. But in all such Cases, the Votes of both Houses shall be determined by Yeas and Nays; and the Names of the Persons voting for or against the Bill shall be entered in the Journal of each House respectively.

If any bill shall not be returned by the (Governour) ⟨President⟩ within ⟨seven⟩ days after it shall have been presented to him, it shall be a Law, unless the Legislature by their Adjournment prevent its Return; in which Case it shall (be returned on the first Day of the next Meeting of the Legislature) ⟨not⟩.

8

The Legislature of the United States shall have the (Right and) Power to lay and collect Taxes, Duties, Imposts and Excises; to regulate (Naturalization and) Commerce ⟨with foreign Nations & amongst the several States⟩; *to establish an uniform Rule for Naturalization throughout the United States*; to coin Money; to regulate the (Alloy and) Value of ⟨foreign⟩ Coin; to fix the Standard of Weights and Measures; to estab-

lish Post-offices; to borrow Money, and emit Bills on the Credit of the United States; to appoint a Treasurer by Ballott; to constitute Tribunals inferior to the Supreme (national) Court; to make Rules concerning Captures on Land or Water; to declare the Law and Punishment of Piracies and Felonies committed on the high Seas, and the Punishment of counterfeiting the ⟨Coin⟩ (and) ⟨of the U. S. &⟩ of Offences against the Law of Nations; (to declare what shall be Treason against the United States;) ⟨& of Treason agst the U: S: or any of them; not to work Corruption of Blood or Forfeit except during the Life of the Party;⟩ to regulate the Discipline of the Militia of the several States; to subdue a Rebellion in any State, on the Application of its Legislature; to make War; to raise Armies; to build and equip Fleets, to (make laws for) call(ing) forth the Aid of the Militia, in order to execute the Laws of the Union, (to) enforce Treaties, (to) suppress Insurrections, and repel invasions; and to make all Laws that shall be necessary and proper for carrying into (full and complete) Execution (the foregoing Powers, and) all other powers vested, by this Constitution, in the Government of the United States, or in any Department or Officer thereof;

(Representation shall)

(Direct Taxation shall always be in Proportion to Representation in the House of Representatives.)

The proportions of direct Taxation shall be regulated by the whole Number of white and other free Citizens and Inhabitants, of every Age, Sex and Condition, including those bound to Servitude for a Term of Years, and three fifths of all other Persons not comprehended in the foregoing Description; which Number shall, within six Years after the first Meeting of the Legislature, and within the Term of every ten Years afterwards, be taken in such Manner as the said Legislature shall direct.

From the first Meeting of the Legislature until the Number of Citizens and Inhabitants shall be taken as aforesaid, direct Taxation shall be in Proportion to the Number of Representatives chosen in each State.

No Tax or Duty shall be laid by the Legislature, on Articles

exported from any State; nor on the emigration or Importation of such Persons as the several States shall think proper to admit; nor shall such emigration or Importation be prohibited.

No Capitation Tax shall be laid, unless in Proportion to the Census herein before directed to be taken.

No Navigation Act shall be passed without the Assent of two thirds of the Members present in each House.

The United States shall not grant any Title of Nobility.

9

The Acts of the Legislature of the United States made in Pursuance of this Constitution, and all Treaties made under the Authority of the United States shall be the supreme Law of the several States, and of their Citizens and Inhabitants; and the Judges in the several States shall be bound thereby in their Decisions, any Thing in the Constitutions or Laws of the several States to the Contrary notwithstanding.

10

No State shall enter into any (Al) Treaty, Alliance (or) Confederation ⟨with any foreign Power nor witht. Const. of U. S. into any agreemt. or compact wh (any other) another State or Power⟩; nor lay any Imposts or Duties on Imports; [18] nor keep Troops or Ships of War in Time of Peace;[18] nor grant Letters of Marque and Reprisal; nor coin Money; nor (emit Bills of Credit), without the Consent of the Legislature of the United States, ⟨emit Bills of Credit.⟩ No State shall, without such Consent engage in any War, unless it shall be actually invaded by Enemies, or the Danger of Invasion be so imminent as not to admit of a Delay, until the Legislature of the United States can be consulted. No State shall grant any Title of Nobility.

11.

The Senate of the United States shall have Power to make Treaties; to send Ambassadors; and to appoint the Judges of the Supreme (national) Court.

[18] This clause was underscored in the original.

COMMITTEE OF DETAIL, IX

In all Disputes and Controversies now subsisting, or that may hereafter subsist between two or more States ⟨respecting (Territory) Jurisdn or Territory⟩, the Senate shall possess the following Powers. Whenever the Legislature, or the Executive Authority, or the lawful Agent of any State, in controversy with another, shall, by Memorial to the Senate, state the Matter in Question, and apply for a Hearing, Notice of such Memorial and Application shall be given, by Order of the Senate, to the Legislature, or the Executive Authority of the other State in Controversy. The Senate shall also assign a Day for the Appearance of the Parties, by their Agents before that House. The Agents shall be directed to appoint, by joint Consent, Commissioners or Judges to constitute a Court for hearing and determining the Matter in Question. But if the Agents cannot agree, the Senate shall name three Persons out of each of the several States; and from the List of such Persons each Party shall alternately strike out one, until the Number shall be reduced to thirteen; and from that Number not less than seven, nor more than nine names, as the Senate shall direct, shall in their Presence, be drawn out by Lot; and the Persons whose Names shall be so drawn, or any five of them shall be Commissioners or Judges to hear and finally determine the Controversy, provided a major*ity* (Part) of the Judges, who shall hear the Cause, agree in the Determination. If either Party shall neglect to attend at the Day assigned, without shewing sufficient Reasons for not attending; or being present, shall refuse to strike, the Senate shall proceed to nominate three Persons out of each State, and the (Secretary or) Clerk of the Senate shall strike in Behalf of the Party absent or refusing. If any of the Parties shall refuse to submit to the Authority of such Court, or shall not appear to prosecute or defend their Claim or Cause; the Court shall nevertheless proceed to pronounce Judgment. The Judgment shall be final and conclusive. The Proceedings shall be transmitted to the President of the Senate, and shall be lodged among the public Records for the Security of the Parties concerned. Every Commissioner shall, before he sit in Judgment, take an Oath, to be administered by one of the Judges of the

Supreme or Superior Court of the State where the Cause shall be tried, "well and truly to hear and determine the Matter in Question according to the best of his Judgment, without Favor, Affection or Hope of Reward."

All controversies concerning Lands claimed under different Grants of two or more States, whose Jurisdictions as they respect such Lands, shall have been decided or adjusted subsequent to such Grants ⟨or any of them⟩ shall, on Application to the Senate, be finally determined, as near as may be, in the same manner as is before prescribed for deciding Controversies between different States.

12.

The Executive Power of the United States shall be vested in a single Person. His Stile shall be, "The President of the United States of America;" and his Title shall be, "His Excellency". He shall be elected by Ballot by the Legislature. He shall hold his Office during the term of seven Years; but shall not be elected a second Time.

He shall from Time to Time give information ⟨to the Legislature⟩ of the State of the (Nation to the Legislature) ⟨Union⟩; he may recommend (Matters) ⟨such measures as he shall judge nesy. & expedt.⟩ to their Consideration, and (he) may convene them on extraordinary Occasions ⟨& in Case of a disagreemt between the 2 Houses with regard to the Time of Adj. he may adjourn them to such Time as he shall think proper.⟩[19] (He shall take Care to the best of his Ability, that the Laws) ⟨It shall be his duty to provide for the due & faithful exec — of the Laws⟩ of the United States (be faithfully executed) ⟨to the best of his ability⟩. He shall commission all the Officers of the United States and (shall) appoint (Officers in all Cases) (⟨such of them whose appts.⟩ them in all cases⟩ not otherwise provided for by this Constitution. He shall receive Ambassadors, and shall correspond with the (Governours and other) ⟨Supreme⟩ Executive*s* (Officers) of the several States.

He shall have power to grant Reprieves and Pardons; but

[19] See Appendix A, CCX.

his Pardon shall not be pleadable in Bar of an Impeachment. He shall be Commander in Chief of the Army and Navy of the United States, and of the Militia of the Several States. He shall, at stated Times, receive for his Services, a fixed Compensation, which shall neither be encreased nor diminished during his Continuance in Office. Before he shall enter on the Duties of his Department, he shall take the following Oath or Affirmation, "I ——— solemnly swear, — or affirm, — "that I will faithfully execute the Office of President of the "United States of America." He shall be (dismissed) *removed* from his Office on Impeachment by the House of Representatives, and Conviction in the Supreme (National) Court, of Treason (or) Bribery or Corruption. In Case of his Impeachment, (Dismission) *Removal*, Death, Resignation or Disability to discharge the Powers and Duties of his (Department) *Office*; the President of the Senate shall exercise those Powers and Duties, until another President of the United States be chosen, or until the President impeached or disabled be acquitted, or his Disability be removed.

13.

All Commissions, Patents and Writs shall be in the Name of "the United (People and) States of America."

14.

The Judicial Power of the United States shall be vested in one Supreme (National) Court, and in such (other) ⟨inferior⟩ Courts as shall, from Time to Time, be constituted by the Legislature of the United States.

The Judges of the Supreme (National) Court shall (be chosen by the Senate by Ballott). (They shall) hold their Offices during good Behaviour. They shall, at stated Times, receive for their Services, a Compensation, which shall not be diminished during their Continuance in Office.

The Jurisdiction of the Supreme (National) Court shall extend to all Cases arising under Laws passed by the Legislature of the United States; to all Cases affecting Ambassadors (and other) ⟨other⟩ public Ministers ⟨& Consuls⟩, to the Trial

of Impeachments of Officers of the United States; to all Cases of Admiralty and Maritime Jurisdiction; to Controversies between ⟨States,—except those wh. regard Jurisdn or Territory, —betwn⟩ a State and a Citizen or Citizens of another State, between Citizens of different States and between ⟨a State or the⟩ Citizens (of any of the States) ⟨thereof⟩ and foreign States, Citizens or Subjects. In Cases of Impeachment, (those) ⟨Cases⟩ affecting Ambassadors (and) other public Ministers ⟨& Consuls⟩, and those in which a State shall be (one of the) ⟨a⟩ Part(ies)⟨y⟩, this Jurisdiction shall be original. In all the other Cases beforementioned, it shall be appellate, with such Exceptions and under such Regulations as the Legislature shall make. The Legislature may (distribute) ⟨assign any part of⟩ th(is)*e* Jurisdiction ⟨above mentd.,—except the Trial of the Executive—⟩, in the Manner and under the Limitations which it shall think proper (among) ⟨to⟩ such (other) ⟨inferior⟩ Courts as it shall constitute from Time to Time.

(Crimes shall be tried) ⟨&⟩ in the State, (in which) ⟨where⟩ they shall be committed; (and) The Trial of (them) ⟨all Criml Offences,—except in Cases of Impeachment—⟩ shall be by Jury.

⟨Judgmts. in Cases of Impeachmt. shall not extend further than to removal from Office & disqualifn. to hold & enjoy any place of Honr. Trust or Profit under the U. S. But the party convicted shall nevertheless be liable & subject to Judl. Trial Judt & Punishment according to (the) Law of (the Land)⟩

New States lawfully constituted or established within the Limits of the United States may be admitted, by the Legislature, into this Government; but to such Admission the Consent of two thirds of the Members present in each House shall be necessary. If a new State shall arise within the Limits of any of the present States; the consent of the Legislatures of such States shall be also necessary to its Admission. If (such) *the* Admission be consented to, the new States shall be admitted on the same Terms with the original States. But the Legislature may make Conditions with the new States concerning the public Debt, which shall be then subsisting.

⟨The free (inhabs) Citizens of each State shall be intitled

to all Privileges & Immunities of free Citizens in the sevl States [20]

Any person charged with Treason Felony or high Misdemeanor who shall flee from Justice & be found in any of the U States shall on demd of the executive power of the State from wh. he fled be delivd. up & removed to the State havg Jurisdn of (the tr) the Offence. —

Full Faith & Credit &c⟩

The United States shall guaranty to each State a Republican form of Government; and shall protect each State against foreign Invasions, and, on the Application of its Legislature, against domestic Violence.

This Constitution ought to be amended whenever such amendment shall become necessary; and on the Application of (two thirds) the Legislatures of two thirds of the States of the Union, the Legislature of the United States shall call a Convention for that Purpose.

The Members of the Legislatures, and the executive and judicial Officers of the United States, and of the several States, shall be bound by Oath to support this Constitution.

(⟨In order to introduce this Governnt⟩)

(Resolved)

(That) this Constitution proposed (by this Convention to the People of the United States for their Approbation should) ⟨shall⟩ be laid before the United States in Congress assembled for their (Agreement and Recommendation) ⟨Approbation⟩ and ⟨that in the opinn. of this Conventn. it shd⟩ be afterwards submitted to a Convention chosen in each State, under the Recommendations of its Legislature in Order to receive the Ratification of such Convention.

Resolved

⟨In order to introde. this Govt it is the opinn of this Convn that⟩ That the Ratification of the Conventions of States shall be sufficient for organizing this Constitution. (That each) each assenting Convention (in each) (shall) ⟨shd.⟩ notify its Assent and Ratification to the United States in

[20] Pinckney claimed to have introduced this clause into the Constitution, see Appendix A, CCCXXXVIII.

Congress assembled: (That the United States in) *that* Congress (assembled), after receiving the Assent and Ratification of the Conventions of States, (shall) ⟨shd.⟩ appoint and publish a Day, as early as may be, and appoint a Place for commencing Proceedings under this Constitution: That after such Publication (or, — in Case it shall not be made — after the expiration of Days from the Time when the Ratification of the Convention of the State shall have been notified to Congress,) the Legislatures of the several States (shall) *shd.* elect Members of the Senate, and direct the Election of Members of the House of Representatives (and shall provide for their support). That the Members of the Legislature (shall) *shd.* meet at the Time and Place assigned by Congress, (or, — if Congress shall have assigned no Time and Place — at such Time and Place as shall have been agreed on by the Majority of the Members elected for each House;) and (shall) ⟨shd.⟩ as soon as may be, after their Meeting, choose the President of the United States, and proceed to execute this Constitution.

McHENRY

Left Baltimore 2 August.

August 4th.

Returned to Philada. The committee of Convention ready to report. Their report in the hands of Dunlop the printer to strike off copies for the members.

MONDAY, AUGUST 6, 1787.

JOURNAL

Monday August 6. 1787.

The House met agreeably to adjournment.

The honorable John Francis Mercer Esq, One of the Deputies from the State of Maryland, attended and took his seat.

The honorable Mr Rutledge, from the Committee to whom were referred the Proceedings of the Convention for the purpose of reporting a Constitution for the establishment of a national Government conformable to these Proceedings, informed the House that the Committee were prepared to report — The report was then delivered in at the Secretary's table, and being read once throughout and copies thereof given to the members — It was moved and seconded to adjourn till wednesday morning

which passed in the negative. [Ayes — 3; noes — 5.]

The house then adjourned till to-morrow morning at 11 o'Clock A. M.

Detail of Ayes and Noes

[Beginning of 8th loose sheet]

	New Hampshire	Massachusetts	Rhode Island	Connecticut	New York	New Jersey	Pennsylvania	Delaware	Maryland	Virginia	North Carolina	South Carolina	Georgia	Questions	Ayes	Noes	Divided
[232]	no	no		no			aye		aye	aye	no	no		To adjourn till wednesday	3	5	

MADISON

Monday August 6th. In Convention

⟨Mr. John Francis Mercer from Maryland took his seat.⟩[1]

Mr. Rutlidge ⟨delivered in⟩ the Report of the Committee of detail as follows;[2] ⟨a printed copy being at the same time furnished to each member.⟩[3]

"We the people of the States of New Hampshire, Massachusetts, Rhode-Island and Providence Plantations, Connecticut, New-York, New-Jersey, Pennsylvania, Delaware, Maryland, Virginia, North-Carolina, South-Carolina, and Georgia, do ordain, declare, and establish the following Constitution for the Government of Ourselves and our Posterity.

Article I

The stile of the [this] Government shall be, "The United States of America"

II

The Government shall consist of supreme legislative, executive, and judicial powers.

III

The legislative power shall be vested in a Congress, to consist of two separate and distinct bodies of men, a House of Representatives and a Senate; each of which shall [,] in all cases [,] have a negative on the other. The Legislature shall meet on the first Monday in December [in] every year.

---

[1] Taken from *Journal.*

[2] Madison originally recorded simply, "The House adjd after receiving from Mr. Rutlidge the report . . . as follows;". The additions were taken from *Journal.*

[3] Madison copied the report into his Debates, and it is his transcript which is given in the text. Differences in the printed report from this copy are noted in the text by square brackets or in foot-notes.

Several copies of the original printed report are in existence, and a number of facsimiles printed by Peter Force. The reprint is readily distinguished: the original report numbered the 6th and 7th articles both VI; the facsimile numbers the 7th and 8th articles both VII.

IV

Sect. 1. The members of the House of Representatives shall be chosen every second year, by the people of the several States comprehended within this Union. The qualifications of the electors shall be the same, from time to time, as those of the electors in the several States, of the most numerous branch of their own legislatures.

Sect. 2. Every member of the House of Representatives shall be of the age of twenty five years at least; shall have been a citizen of [in] the United States for at least three years before his election; and shall be, at the time of his election, a resident of the State in which he shall be chosen.

Sect. 3. The House of Representatives shall, at its first formation, and until the number of citizens and inhabitants shall be taken in the manner herein after described, consist of sixty five Members, of whom three shall be chosen in New Hampshire, eight in Massachusetts, one in Rhode-Island and Providence Plantations, five in Connecticut, six in New-York, four in New-Jersey, eight in Pennsylvania, one in Delaware, six in Maryland, ten in Virginia, five in North-Carolina, five in South-Carolina, and three in Georgia.

Sect. 4. As the proportions of numbers in [the] different States will alter from time to time; as some of the States may hereafter be divided; as others may be enlarged by addition of territory; as two or more States may be united; as new States will be erected within the limits of the United States, the Legislature shall, in each of these cases, regulate the number of representatives by the number of inhabitants, according to the provisions herein after made, at the rate of one for every forty thousand.

Sect. 5. All bills for raising or appropriating money, and for fixing the salaries of the officers of the Government, shall originate in the House of Representatives, and shall not be altered or amended by the Senate. No money shall be drawn from the public Treasury, but in pursuance of appropriations that shall originate in the House of Representatives.

Sect. 6. The House of Representatives shall have the sole

power of impeachment. It shall choose its Speaker and other officers.

Sect. 7. Vacancies in the House of Representatives shall be supplied by writs of election from the executive authority of the State, in the representation from which it shall happen.

V

Sect. 1. The Senate of the United States shall be chosen by the Legislatures of the several States. Each Legislature shall chuse two members. Vacancies may be supplied by the Executive until the next meeting of the Legislature. Each member shall have one vote.

Sect. 2. The Senators shall be chosen for six years; but immediately after the first election they shall be divided, by lot, into three classes, as nearly as may be, numbered one, two and three. The seats of the members of the first class shall be vacated at the expiration of the second year, of the second class at the expiration of the fourth year, of the third class at the expiration of the sixth year, so that a third part of the members may be chosen every second year.

Sect. 3. Every member of the Senate shall be of the age of thirty years at least; shall have been a citizen in the United States for at least four years before his election; and shall be, at the time of his election, a resident of the State for which he shall be chosen.

Sect. 4. The Senate shall chuse its own President and other officers.

VI

Sect. 1. The times and places and [the] manner of holding the elections of the members of each House shall be prescribed by the Legislature of each State; but their provisions concerning them may, at any time, be altered by the Legislature of the United States.

Sect. 2. The Legislature of the United States shall have authority to establish such uniform qualifications of the members of each House, with regard to property, as to the said Legislature shall seem expedient.

Sect. 3. In each House a majority of the members shall constitute a quorum to do business; but a smaller number may adjourn from day to day.

Sect 4. Each House shall be the judge of the elections, returns and qualifications of its own members.

Sect. 5. Freedom of speech and debate in the Legislature shall not be impeached or questioned in any Court or place out of the Legislature; and the members of each House shall, in all cases, except treason [,] felony and breach of the peace, be privileged from arrest during their attendance at Congress, and in going to and returning from it.

Sect 6. Each House may determine the rules of its proceedings; may punish its members for disorderly behaviour; and may expel a member.

Sect. 7. The House of Representatives, and the Senate, when it shall be acting in a legislative capacity, shall keep a Journal of their proceedings, and shall, from time to time, publish them: and the yeas and nays of the members of each House, on any question, shall [,] at the desire of one-fifth part of the members present, be entered on the journal.

Sect. 8. Neither House, without the consent of the other, shall adjourn for more than three days, nor to any other place than that at which the two Houses are sitting. But this regulation shall not extend to the Senate, when it shall exercise the powers mentioned in the article.

Sect. 9. The members of each House shall be ineligible to, and incapable of holding any office under the authority of the United States, during the time for which they shall respectively be elected: and the members of the Senate shall be ineligible to, and incapable of holding any such office for one year afterwards.

Sect. 10. The members of each House shall receive a compensation for their services, to be ascertained and paid by the State, in which they shall be chosen,

Sect. 11. The enacting stile of the laws of the United States shall be, "Be it enacted by the Senate and Representatives in Congress assembled".[4]

[4] Printed copy reads: "Be it enacted, and it is hereby enacted by the House of Representatives, and by the Senate of the United States, in Congress assembled."

The Records for August 15 indicate that section 11 was adopted without amend-

Sect. 12. Each House shall possess the right of originating bills, except in the cases beforementioned.

Sect. 13. Every bill, which shall have passed the House of Representatives and the Senate, shall, before it become a law, be presented to the President of the United States for his revision: if, upon such revision, he approve of it, he shall signify his approbation by signing it: But if, upon such revision, it shall appear to him improper for being passed into a law, he shall return it, together with his objections against it, to that House in which it shall have originated, who shall enter the objections at large on their journal and proceed to reconsider the bill. But if after such reconsideration, two thirds of that House shall, notwithstanding the objections of the President, agree to pass it, it shall together with his objections, be sent to the other House, by which it shall likewise be reconsidered, and [,] if approved by two thirds of the other House also, it shall become a law. But in all such cases, the votes of both Houses shall be determined by yeas and nays; and the names of the persons voting for or against the bill shall be entered on the journal of each House respectively. If any bill shall not be returned by the President within seven days after it shall have been presented to him, it shall be a law, unless the legislature by their adjournment, prevent its return; in which case it shall not be a law.

VII [VI] [5]

Sect. 1. The Legislature of the United States shall have the power to lay and collect taxes, duties, imposts and excises;

To regulate commerce with foreign nations, and among the several States;

---

ment, but the Washington and Brearley copies of the report of the Committee of Detail show a change in wording in accordance with Madison's text. A probable explanation of this is that the Committtee of Detail made this modification after the Report was in print.

[5] In the printed copy, the number VI was repeated, consequently Article VII and all subsequent articles were misnumbered. It is important to remember this in noting subsequent references to articles by number.

To establish an uniform rule of naturalization throughout the United States;

To coin money;

To regulate the value of foreign coin;

To fix the standard of weights and measures;

To establish Post-offices;

To borrow money, and emit bills on the credit of the United States;

To appoint a Treasurer by ballot;

To constitute tribunals inferior to the Supreme Court;

To make rules concerning captures on land and water;

To declare the law and punishment of piracies and felonies committed on the high seas, and the punishment of counterfeiting the coin of the United States, and of offences against the law of nations;

To subdue a rebellion in any State, on the application of its legislature;

To make war;

To raise armies;

To build and equip fleets;

To call forth the aid of the militia, in order to execute the laws of the Union, enforce treaties, suppress insurrections, and repel invasions;

And to make all laws that shall be necessary and proper for carrying into execution the foregoing powers, and all other powers vested, by this Constitution, in the government of the United States, or in any department or officer thereof;

Sect. 2. Treason against the United States shall consist only in levying war against the United States, or any of them; and in adhering to the enemies of the United States, or any of them. The Legislature of the United States shall have power to declare the punishment of treason. No person shall be convicted of treason, unless on the testimony of two witnesses. No attainder of treason shall work corruption of blood, nor forfeiture, except during the life of the person attainted.

Sect. 3. The proportions of direct taxation shall be regulated by the whole number of white and other free citizens

and inhabitants, of every age, sex and condition, including those bound to servitude for a term of years, and three fifths of all other persons not comprehended in the foregoing description, (except Indians not paying taxes) which number shall, within six years after the first meeting of the Legislature, and within the term of every ten years afterwards, be taken in such manner as the said Legislature shall direct.

Sect. 4. No tax or duty shall be laid by the Legislature on articles exported from any State; nor on the migration or importation of such persons as the several States shall think proper to admit; nor shall such migration or importation be prohibited.

Sect- 5. No capitation tax shall be laid, unless in proportion to the Census hereinbefore directed to be taken.

Sect- 6. No navigation act shall be passed without the assent of two thirds of the members present in each House.

Sect. 7. The United States shall not grant any title of Nobility.

VIII [VII]

The Acts of the Legislature of the United States made in pursuance of this Constitution, and all treaties made under the authority of the United States shall be the supreme law of the several States, and of their citizens and inhabitants; and the judges in the several States shall be bound thereby in their decisions; anything in the Constitutions or laws of the several States to the contrary notwithstanding.

IX [VIII]

Sect 1. The Senate of the United States shall have power to make treaties, and to appoint Ambassadors, and Judges of the supreme Court.

Sect. 2. In all disputes and controversies now subsisting, or that may hereafter subsist between two or more States, respecting jurisdiction or territory, the Senate shall possess the following powers. Whenever the Legislature, or the Executive authority, or lawful Agent of any State, in con-

troversy with another, shall by memorial to the Senate, state the matter in question, and apply for a hearing; notice of such memorial and application shall be given by order of the Senate, to the Legislature or the Executive authority of the other State in Controversy. The Senate shall also assign a day for the appearance of the parties, by their agents, before the House. The Agents shall be directed to appoint, by joint consent, commissioners or judges to constitute a Court for hearing and determining the matter in question. But if the Agents cannot agree, the Senate shall name three persons out of each of the several States; and from the list of such persons each party shall alternately strike out one, until the number shall be reduced to thirteen; and from that number not less than seven nor more than nine names, as the Senate shall direct, shall in their presence, be drawn out by lot; and the persons whose names shall be so drawn, or any five of them shall be commissioners or Judges to hear and finally determine the controversy; provided a majority of the Judges, who shall hear the cause, agree in the determination. If either party shall neglect to attend at the day assigned, without shewing sufficient reasons for not attending, or being present shall refuse to strike, the Senate shall proceed to nominate three persons out of each State, and the Clerk of the Senate shall strike in behalf of the party absent or refusing. If any of the parties shall refuse to submit to the authority of such Court; or shall not appear to prosecute or defend their claim or cause, the Court shall nevertheless proceed to pronounce judgment. The judgment shall be final and conclusive. The proceedings shall be transmitted to the President of the Senate, and shall be lodged among the public records, for the security of the parties concerned. Every Commissioner shall, before he sit in judgment, take an oath, to be administred by one of the Judges of the Supreme or Superior Court of the State where the cause shall be tried, "well and truly to hear and determine the matter in ques-"tion according to the best of his judgment, without favor, "affection, or hope of reward."

Sect. 3. All controversies concerning lands claimed under

different grants of two or more States, whose jurisdictions, as they respect such lands shall have been decided or adjusted subsequent to such grants, or any of them, shall, on application to the Senate, be finally determined, as near as may be, in the same manner as is before prescribed for deciding controversies between different States.

X [IX]

Sect. 1. The Executive Power of the United States shall be vested in a single person. His stile shall be "The President of the United States of America;" and his title shall be, "His Excellency". He shall be elected by ballot by the Legislature. He shall hold his office during the term of seven years; but shall not be elected a second time.

Sect. 2. He shall, from time to time, give information to the Legislature, of the state of the Union: he may recommend to their consideration such measures as he shall judge necessary, and expedient: he may convene them on extraordinary occasions. In case of disagreement between the two Houses, with regard to the time of adjournment, he may adjourn them to such time as he thinks proper: he shall take care that the laws of the United States be duly and faithfully executed: he shall commission all the officers of the United States; and shall appoint officers in all cases not otherwise provided for by this Constitution. He shall receive Ambassadors, and may correspond with the supreme Executives of the several States. He shall have power to grant reprieves and pardons; but his pardon shall not be pleadable in bar of an impeachment. He shall be commander in chief of the Army and Navy of the United States, and of the Militia of the Several States. He shall, at stated times, receive for his services, a compensation, which shall neither be increased nor diminished during his continuance in office. Before he shall enter on the duties of his department, he shall take the following oath or affirmation, "I ——— solemnly swear, "(or affirm) that that I will faithfully execute the office of "President of the United States of America." He shall be

removed from his office on impeachment by the House of Representatives, and conviction in the supreme Court, of treason, bribery, or corruption. In case of his removal as aforesaid, death, resignation, or disability to discharge the powers and duties of his office, the President of the Senate shall exercise those powers and duties, until another President of the United States be chosen, or until the disability of the President be removed.

XI [X]

Sect. 1. The Judicial Power of the United States shall be vested in one Supreme Court, and in such inferior Courts as shall, when necessary, from time to time, be constituted by the Legislature of the United States.

Sect. 2. The Judges of the Supreme Court, and of the Inferior Courts, shall hold their offices during good behaviour. They shall, at stated times, receive for their services, a compensation, which shall not be diminished during their continuance in office.

Sect. 3. The Jurisdiction of the Supreme Court shall extend to all cases arising under laws passed by the Legislature of the United States; to all cases affecting Ambassadors, other Public Ministers and Consuls; to the trial of impeachments of Officers of the United States; to all cases of Admiralty and maritime jurisdiction; to controversies between two or more States, (except such as shall regard Territory or Jurisdiction) between a State and Citizens of another State, between Citizens of different States, and between a State or the Citizens thereof and foreign States, citizens or subjects. In cases of impeachment, cases affecting Ambassadors, other Public Ministers and Consuls, and those in which a State shall be party, this jurisdiction shall be original. In all the other cases before mentioned, it shall be appellate, with such exceptions and under such regulations as the Legislature shall make. The Legislature may assign any part of the jurisdiction above mentioned (except the trial of the President of the United States) in the manner, and

under the limitations which it shall think proper, to such Inferior Courts, as it shall constitute from time to time.

Sect. 4. The trial of all criminal offences (except in cases of impeachments) shall be in the State where they shall be committed; and shall be by Jury.

Sect. 5. Judgment, in cases of Impeachment, shall not extend further than to removal from Office, and disqualification to hold and enjoy any office of honour, trust or profit, under the United States. But the party convicted shall, nevertheless be liable and subject to indictment, trial, judgment and punishment according to law.

XII [XI]

No State shall coin money; nor grant letters of marque and reprisals; nor enter into any treaty, alliance, or confederation; nor grant any title of Nobility.

XIII [XII]

No State, without the consent of the Legislature of the United States, shall emit bills of credit, or make any thing but specie a tender in payment of debts; nor lay imposts or duties on imports; nor keep troops or ships of war in time of peace; nor enter into any agreement or compact with another State, or with any foreign power; nor engage in any war, unless it shall be actually invaded by enemies, or the danger of invasion be so imminent, as not to admit of delay, until the Legislature of the United States can be consulted.

XIV [XIII]

The Citizens of each State shall be entitled to all privileges and immunities of citizens in the several States.

XV [XIV]

Any person charged with treason, felony or high misdemeanor in any State, who shall flee from justice, and shall be found in any other State, shall, on demand of the Execu-

tive power of the State from which he fled, be delivered up and removed to the State having jurisdiction of the offence.

XVI [XV]

Full faith shall be given in each State to the acts of the Legislatures, and to the records and judicial proceedings of the Courts and Magistrates of every other State.

XVII [XVI]

New States lawfully constituted or established within the limits of the United States may be admitted, by the Legislature, into this Government; but to such admission the consent of two thirds of the members present in each House shall be necessary. If a new State shall arise within the limits of any of the present States, the consent of the Legislatures of such States shall be also necessary to its admission. If the admission be consented to, the new States shall be admitted on the same terms with the original States. But the Legislature may make conditions with the new States, concerning the public debt which shall be then subsisting.

XVIII [XVII]

The United States shall guaranty to each State a Republican form of Government; and shall protect each State against foreign invasions, and, on the application of its Legislature, against domestic violence.

XIX [XVIII]

On the application of the Legislatures of two thirds of the States in the Union, for an amendment of this Constitution, the Legislature of the United States shall call a Convention for that purpose.

XX [XIX]

The members of the Legislatures, and the Executive and Judicial officers of the United States, and of the several States, shall be bound by oath to support this Constitution.

XXI [XX]

The ratifications of the Conventions of States shall be sufficient for organizing this Constitution.

XXII [XXI]

This Constitution shall be laid before the United States in Congress assembled, for their approbation; and it is the opinion of this Convention, that it should be afterwards submitted to a Convention chosen, under the recommendation of its legislature, in order to receive the ratification of such Convention.

XXIII [XXII]

To introduce this government, it is the opinion of this Convention, that each assenting Convention should notify its assent and ratification to the United States in Congress assembled; that Congress, after receiving the assent and ratification of the Conventions of States, should appoint and publish a day, as early as may be, and appoint a place for commencing proceedings under this Constitution; that after such publication, the Legislatures of the several States should elect members of the Senate, and direct the election of members of the House of Representatives; and that the members of the Legislature should meet at the time and place assigned by Congress, and should, as soon as may be, after their meeting, choose the President of the United States, and proceed to execute this Constitution."

⟨A motion was made to adjourn till Wednesday, in order to give leisure to examine the Report; which passed in the Negative — N. H. no. Mas — no. Ct. no. Pa. ay Md. ay. Virg. ay. N. C. no. S — C. no [6]

The [6] House then adjourned till tomorrow 11 OC.⟩[7]

---

[6] Taken from *Journal*.

[7] See further Appendix A, LXXVIII, LXXIX. Martin stated that "many of the members being absent, we adjourned to the next day." (Appendix A, CXC).

McHENRY

Augt. 6. Convention met. present 8 States. Report delivered in by Mr. Rutledge. read. Convention adjourned till to-morrow to give the members an opportunity to consider the report.

Proposed to Mr. D. Carrol, Mr. Jenifer — Mr. Mercer and Mr. Martin, to meet to confer on the report, and to p[r]epare ourselves to act in unison.[8]

Met at Mr. Carrolls lodgings in the afternoon. I repeated the object of our meeting, and proposed that we should take the report up by paragraphs and give our opinions thereon. Mr. Mercer wished to know of me whether I thought Maryland would embrace such a system. I told him I did not know, but I presumed the people would not object to a wise system. He extended this idea to the other gentlemen. Mr. Martin said they would not; That he was against the system, that a compromise only had enabled its abettors to bring it into its present stage — that had Mr. Jenifer voted with him, things would have taken a different turn. Mr. Jenifer said he voted with him till he saw it was in vain to oppose its progress. I begged the gentlemen to observe some order to enable us to do the business we had convened upon. I wished that we could be unanimous — and would make a proposition to effect it. — I would join the deputation in bringing on a motion to postpone the report, to try the affections of the house to an amendment of the confederation without altering the sovereignty of suffrage; which failing we should then agree to render the system reported as perfect as we could, in the mean while to consider our motion to fail and proceed to confer upon the report agreeably to the intention of our meeting. I. E. That we should now and at our future meetings alter the report to our own judgement to be able to appear unanimous in case our motion failed. —

Mr. Carrol could not agree to this proposition, because he did not think the confederation could be amended to answer

[8] See Appendix A, CLXXXIX and CXCI.

its intentions. I thought that it was susceptable of a revision which would sufficiently invigorate it for the exigencies of the times. Mr. Mercer thought otherwise as did Mr. Jenifer. This proposition to conciliate the deputation was rejected.

Mr. Martin in the course of the conversation observed that he was against two branches — that we was against the people electing the representatives of the national government. That he wished to see the States governments rendered capable of the most vigorous exertions, and so knit together by a confederation as to act together on national emergencies.

Finding that we could come to no conclusions I recommended meeting again to-morrow, for unless we could appear in the convention with some degree of unanimity it would be unnecessary to remain in it, sacrificing time and money without being able to render any service. They agreed to meet to-morrow, except Mr. Martin who said he was going to New York and would not be back till monday following.

It being of importance to know and to fix the opinions of my colleagues on the most consequential articles of the new system; I prepared the following propositions, for that purpose viz.

Art. IV. Sec. 5. Will you use your best endeavours to obtain for the senate an equal authority over money bills with the house of representatives.?

Art. VII. Sect. 6. Will you use your best endeavours to have it made a part of the system that "no navigation act shall be passed without the assent of two thirds of the representation from each State?

In case these alterations cannot be obtained will you give your assent to the 5 sect. of the IV article and 6 sect. of the VII. article as they stand in the report?

Will you also, (in case these alterations are not obtained) agree that the ratification of the conventions of nine States shall be sufficient for organizing the new constitutions?

N. B.[9] Saw Mr. Mercer make out a list of the members names who had attended or were attending in convention

[9] Inserted from a previous page, according to marks which show place for insertion.

with for and against marked opposite most of them — asked carelessly what question occasioned his being so particular upon which he told me laughing that it was no question but that those marked with a for were for a king. I then asked him how he knew that to which he said no matter the thing is so. I took a copy with his permission, and Mr. Martin seeing me about it asked What it was. I told him, in the words Mr. Mercer had told me, when he begged me to let him copy the list which I did.[10]

[11] See Appendix A, CCIII and CCXI.

TUESDAY, AUGUST 7, 1787.

JOURNAL

Tuesday August 7. 1787.

[To refer the report to a Committee of the whole Ayes — 5; noes — 4.

Delaware being represented during the Debate a question was again taken on ye Committee of ye whole Ayes — 3; noes — 6.][1]

On the question to agree to the Preamble to the constitution as reported from the committee to whom were referred the Proceedings of the Convention — it passed unan: in the affirmative [Ayes — 10; noes — 0.][2]

On the question to agree to the first article, as reported, it passed in the affirmative

On the question to agree to the second article, as reported, it passed in the affirmative

It was moved and seconded to alter the second clause of the third article so as to read

"each of which shall in all cases have a negative on the legislative acts of the other"

which passed in the negative [Ayes — 5; noes — 5.]

On the question to strike the following clause out of the third article namely

"each of which shall, in all cases, have a negative on the other"

it passed in the affirmative. [Ayes — 7; noes — 3.]

It was moved and seconded to add the following words to the last clause of the third article

---

[1] Votes 233, 234, Detail of Ayes and Noes.

[2] Vote 235, Detail of Ayes and Noes, but this might be assigned to either of the two questions following.

"unless a different day shall be appointed by law"

which passed in the affirmative [Ayes — 8; noes — 2.][3]

It was moved and seconded to strike out the word "December" and to insert the word "May" in the third article

which passed in the negative. [Ayes — 2; noes — 8.]

It was moved and seconded to insert after the word "Senate" in the third article, the following words, namely

"subject to the negative hereafter mentioned"

which passed in the negative. [Ayes — 1; noes — 9.]

It was moved and seconded to amend the last clause of the third article so as to read as follows namely

"The Legislature shall meet at least once in every year;
" and such meeting shall be on the first monday in December
"unless a different day shall be appointed by law"

which passed in the affirmative

It was moved and seconded to strike out the last clause in the first section of the fourth article

which passed in the negative. [Ayes — 1; noes — 7; divided — 1.]

[To adjourn Ayes — 4; noes — 5.][4]

It was moved and seconded to adjourn till to-morrow morning at 10 o'clock

which passed in the negative [Ayes — 3; noes — 5; divided — 1.]

The House then adjourned till to-morrow morning at 11 o'clock [Ayes — 7; noes — 2.][5]

---

[3] Vote 238, Detail of Ayes and Noes, which states that the amendment was "offered by Mr Randolph".

[4] Vote 242, Detail of Aye and Noes.

[5] Vote 244, Detail of Ayes and Noes. It is not certain that this vote belongs here.

Detail of Ayes and Noes

	New Hampshire	Massachusetts	Rhode Island	Connecticut	New York	New Jersey	Pennsylvania	Delaware	Maryland	Virginia	North Carolina	South Carolina	Georgia	Questions	Ayes	Noes	Divided
[233]	no	no		no			aye	aye	aye	aye	no	aye		To refer the report to a Committee of the whole	5	4	
[234]	no	no		no			no	aye	aye	aye	no	no		Delaware being represented during the Debate a question was again taken on ye Committee of ye whole	3	6	
[235]	aye	aye		aye			aye	aye	aye	aye	aye	aye	aye				
[236]	aye	aye		aye			aye	no	no	no	aye	no	no	To insert the words "legislative acts of the other in the third article	5	5	
[237]	aye	aye		no			aye	aye	no	aye	no	aye	aye	To strike out the words each of wh shall in all cases have a negative on the other 3rd article	7	3	
[238]	no	aye		no			aye	aye	aye	aye	aye	aye	aye	To add an amendnt to the last clause of ye 3. article offered by Mr Randolph	8	2	
[239]	no	no		no			no	no	no	no	no	aye	aye	To strike out the word Decr and insert "May"	2	8	
[240]	no	no		no			no	aye	no	no	no	no	no	To add the words subject to the negative hereafter mentioned	1	9	
[241]	no	no		no			no	aye	dd	no	no	no		To strike out the last clause of the first section of the fourth article	1	7	1
[242]	no	no		no			aye	aye	aye	aye	no	no		To adjourn	4	5	
[243]	aye	aye		aye			no	no	no	no	no	dd		To adjourn till 10 o'Clock	3	5	
[244]	no	no		aye			aye	aye	aye	aye	aye	aye			7	2	

MADISON

Teusday August 7th. In Convention

The Report of the Committee ⟨of detail being⟩ taken up,

Mr. Pinkney moved that it be referred to a Committee of the whole. This was strongly opposed by Mr Ghorum and several others, as likely to produce unnecessary delay; and was negatived. ⟨Delaware Maryd. & Virga. only being in the affirmative.⟩[6]

The ⟨preamble⟩[7] of the Report was agreed to nem. con. So were Art: I & II.[8]

Art: III.[9] considered. Col. Mason doubted the propriety of giving each branch a negative on the other "in all cases". There were some cases in which it was he supposed not intended to be given as in the case of balloting for appointments.

Mr. Govr. Morris moved to ⟨insert⟩ "legislative acts" instead of "all cases"

Mr Williamson 2ds. him.

Mr. Sherman. This will restrain the operation of the clause too much. It will particularly exclude a mutual negative in the case of ballots, which he hoped would take place.

Mr. Ghorum contended that elections ought to be made by *joint ballot.* If separate ballots should be made for the President, and the two branches should be each attached to a favorite, great delay, contention & confusion may ensue. These inconveniences have been felt in Masts. in the election of officers of little importance compared with the Executive of the U. States. The only objection agst. a joint ballot is

---

[6] Taken from *Journal.*

[7] Crossed out: "Caption".

[8] Article 1. "The stile of the Government shall be. 'The United States of America'."

Article II. "The Government shall consist of supreme legislative, executive, and judicial powers."

[9] Article III. "The legislative power shall be vested in a Congress, to consist of two separate and distinct bodies of men, a House of Representatives and a Senate; each of which shall in all cases have a negative on the other. The Legislature shall meet on the first Monday in December every year."

that it may deprive the Senate of their due weight; but this ought not to prevail over the respect due to the public tranquility & welfare.

Mr. Wilson was for a joint ballot in several cases at least; particularly in the choice of the President, and was therefore for the amendment. Disputes between the two Houses, during & concerng the vacancy of the Executive, might have dangerous consequences.

Col. Mason thought the amendment of Govr. Morris extended too far. Treaties are in a subsequent part declared to be laws, they will be therefore subjected to a negative; altho' they are to be made as proposed by the Senate alone. He proposed that the mutual negative should be restrained to "cases requiring the distinct assent" of the two Houses.

Mr. Govr. Morris thought this but a repetition of the same thing; the mutual negative and distinct assent, being equavalent expressions. Treaties he thought were not laws.

Mr ⟨Madison⟩[10] moved to strike out the words "each of which shall in all cases, have a negative on the other; the idea being sufficiently expressed in the preceding member of the Article; vesting the "legislative power" in "distinct bodies". especially as the respective powers and mode of exercising them were fully delineated in a subsequent article.

Genl. Pinkney 2ded. the motion

On a question for inserting legislative Acts as moved by Mr Govr. Morris

N. H. ay. Mas. ay. Ct. ay. Pa. ay. Del. no. Md no. Va. no. N. C. ay. S. C. no. Geo. no. [Ayes — 5; noes — 5.]

On question for agreeing to' Mr M's motion to strike out &c—

N. H. ay. Mas. ay. Ct. no. Pa. ay. Del. ay. Md. no. Va. ay. N- C- no. S. C. ay. Geo. ay. [Ayes — 7; noes — 3.]

Mr ⟨Madison⟩ wished to know the reasons of the Come for fixing by ye. Constitution the time of Meeting for the Legislature; and suggested, that it be required only that one meeting at least should be held every year leaving the time to be fixed or varied by law.

---

[10] Crossed out: "Mr. Pinkney".

Mr. Govr. Mor moved to strike out the sentence. It was improper to tie down the Legislature to a particular time, or even to require a meeting every year. The public business might not require it.

Mr. Pinckney concurred with Mr ⟨Madison⟩

Mr. Ghorum. If the time be not fixed by the Constitution, disputes will arise in the Legislature; and the States will be at a loss to adjust thereto, the times of their elections. In the N. England States, the annual time of meeting had been long fixed by their Charters and Constitutions, and no inconveniency had resulted. He thought it necessary that there should be one meeting at least every year as a check on the Executive department.

Mr. Elseworth was agst. striking out the words. The Legislature will not know till they are met whether the public interest required their meeting or not. He could see no impropriety in fixing the day, as the Convention could judge of it as well as the Legislature.

Mr. Wilson thought on the whole it would be best to fix the day.

Mr. King could not think there would be a necessity for a meeting every year. A great vice in our system was that of legislating too much. The most numerous objects of legislation belong to the States. Those of the Natl. Legislature were but few. The chief of them were commerce & revenue. When these should be once settled, alterations would be rarely necessary & easily made.

Mr ⟨Madison⟩ thought if the time of meeting should be fixed by a law it wd. be sufficiently fixed & there would be no difficulty ⟨then⟩ as had been suggested, on the part of the States in adjusting their elections to it. One consideration appeared to him to militate strongly agst. fixing a time by the Constitution. It might happen that the Legislature might be called together by the public exigencies & finish their Session but a short time before the annual period. In this case it would be extremely inconvenient to reassemble so quickly & without the least necessity. He thought one annual meeting ought to be required; but did not wish to make two unavoidable.

Col. Mason thought the objections against fixing the time insuperable; but that an annual meeting ought to be required as essential to the preservation of the Constitution. The extent of the Country will supply business. And if it should not, the Legislature, besides *legislative*, is to have *inquisitorial* powers, which can not safely be long kept in a State of suspension.

Mr. Sherman was decided for fixing the time, as well as for frequent meetings of the Legislative body. Disputes and difficulties will arise between the two Houses, & between both & the States, if the time be changeable — frequent meetings of Parliament were required at the Revolution in England as an essential safeguard of liberty. So also are annual meetings in most of the American charters and constitutions. There will be business eno' to require it. The Western Country, and the great extent and varying state of our affairs in general will supply objects.

Mr. Randolph[11] was agst. fixing any day irrevocably; but as there was no provision made any where in the Constitution for regulating the periods of meeting, and some precise time must be fixed, untill the Legislature shall make provision, he could not agree to strike out the words altogether. Instead of which he moved ⟨to add the words following — "unless a different day shall be appointed by law."⟩[12]

Mr. ⟨Madison⟩ 2ded. the motion, & on the question

N. H. no. Mas. ay. Ct. no. Pa. ay. Del. ay. Md. ay. Va. ay. N. C. ay. S. C. ay. Geo. ay. [Ayes — 8; noes — 2.]

Mr. Govr. Morris moved to strike out Decr. & insert May. It might frequently happen that our measures ought to be influenced by those in Europe, which were generally planned during the Winter and of which intelligence would arrive in the Spring.

Mr. ⟨Madison⟩ 2ded. the motion. he preferred May to Decr. because the latter would require the travelling to & from the Seat of Govt. in the most inconvenient seasons of the year.

---

[11] Crossed out: "Mr. Pinckney was opposed to".

[12] Revised from *Journal.*

Mr. Wilson. The Winter is the most convenient season for business.

Mr. Elseworth. The summer will interfere too much with private business, that of almost all the probable members of the Legislature being more or less connected with agriculture.

Mr Randolph. The time is of no great moment now, as the Legislature can vary it. On looking into the Constitutions of the States, he found that the times of their elections with which the elections of the Natl. Representatives would no doubt be made to co-incide, would suit better with Decr than May. And it was advisable to render our innovations as little incommodious as possible.

On question for "May" instead of "Decr."

N- H. no. Mas. no. Ct. no. Pa. no. Del. no. Md. no. Va. no. N. C. no. S. C. ay. Geo. ay. [Ayes — 2; noes — 8.]

Mr. Read moved to insert ⟨after the word "Senate" the words "subject⟩[13] to the Negative to be hereafter provided". His object was to give an absolute negative to the Executive — He considered this as so essential to the Constitution, to the preservation of liberty, & to the public welfare, that his duty compelled him to make the motion.

Mr. Govr. Morris 2ded. him. And on the question

N. H. no. Mas. no. Ct. no. Pa. no. Del. ay. Md. no. Va. no. N. C. no. S. C. no. Geo. no. [Ayes — 1; noes — 9.]

Mr. Rutlidge. Altho' it is agreed on all hands that an annual meeting of the Legislature should be made necessary, yet that point seems not to be freed from doubt as the clause stands. On this suggestion. "Once at least in every year." were inserted, nem. con.

Art. III with the foregoing alterations was agd. to nem. con. ⟨and is as follows "The Legislative power shall be vested in a Congress to consist of 2 separate & distinct bodies of men; a House of Reps. & a Senate. The Legislature shall meet at least once in every year, and such meeting shall be on the 1st. monday in Decr. unless a different day shall be appointed by law".⟩[13]

[13] Revised from *Journal*.

"Art IV. Sect. 1.[14] taken up."

Mr. Govr. Morris moved to strike out the last member of the section ⟨beginning with the words⟩ "qualifications" of Electors." in order that some other provision might be substituted which wd. restrain the right of suffrage to freeholders.

Mr. Fitzsimmons 2ded. the motion

Mr. Williamson was opposed to it.

Mr. Wilson. This part of the Report was well considered by the Committee, and he did not think it could be changed for the better. It was difficult to form any uniform rule of qualifications for all the States. Unnecessary innovations he thought too should be avoided. It would be very hard & disagreeable for the same persons, at the same time, to vote for representatives in the State Legislature and to be excluded from a vote for those in the Natl. Legislature.

Mr. Govr. Morris. Such a hardship would be neither great nor novel. The people are accustomed to it and not dissatisfied with it, in several of the States. In some the qualifications are different for the choice of the Govr. & Representatives; In others for different Houses of the Legislature. Another objection agst. the clause as it stands is that it makes the qualifications of the Natl. Legislature depend on the will of the States, which he thought not proper.

Mr. Elseworth. thought the qualifications of the electors stood on the most proper footing. The right of suffrage was a tender point, and strongly guarded by most of the ⟨State⟩ Constitutions. The people will not readily subscribe to the Natl. Constitution, if it should subject them to be disfranchised. The States are the best Judges of the circumstances and temper of their own people.

Col. Mason. The force of habit is certainly not attended to by those gentlemen who wish for innovations on this point. Eight or nine States have extended the right of suffrage beyond

[14] Article IV, Sect. 1. "The members of the House of Representatives shall be chosen every second year, by the people of the several States comprehended within this Union. The qualifications of the electors shall be the same, from time to time, as those of the electors in the several States, of the most numerous branch of their own legislatures."

the freeholders. What will the people there say, if they should be disfranchised. A power to alter the qualifications would be a dangerous power in the hands of the Legislature.

Mr. Butler. There is no right of which the people are more jealous than that of suffrage Abridgments of it tend to the same revolution as in Holland, where they have at length thrown all power into the hands of the Senates, who fill up vacancies themselves, and form a rank aristocracy.

Mr. Dickenson. had a very different idea of the tendency of vesting the right of suffrage in the freeholders of the Country. He considered them as the best guardians of liberty; And the restriction of the right to them as a necessary defence agst. the dangerous influence of those multitudes without property & without principle, with which our Country like all others, will in time abound. As to the unpopularity of the innovation it was in his opinion chemirical. The great mass of our Citizens is composed at this time of freeholders, and will be pleased with it.

Mr Elseworth. How shall the freehold be defined? Ought not every man who pays a tax to vote for the representative who is to levy & dispose of his money? Shall the wealthy merchants and manufacturers, who will bear a full share of the public burdens be not allowed a voice in the imposition of them — ⟨taxation and representation ought to go together.⟩

Mr. Govr. Morris. He had long learned not to be the dupe of words. The sound of Aristocracy therefore, had no effect on him. It was the thing, not the name, to which he was opposed, and one of his principal objections to the Constitution as it is now before us, is that it threatens this Country with an Aristocracy. The aristocracy will grow out of the House of Representatives. Give the votes to people who have no property, and they will sell them to the rich who will be able to buy them. We should not confine our attention to the present moment. The time is not distant when this Country will abound with mechanics & manufacturers who will receive their bread from their employers. Will such men be the secure & faithful Guardians of liberty? Will they be the impregnable barrier agst. aristocracy? — He was as

little duped by the association of the words, "taxation & Representation" — The man who does not give his vote freely is not represented. It is the man who dictates the vote. Children do not vote. Why? because they want prudence. because they have no will of their own. The ignorant & the dependent can be as little trusted with the public interest. He did not conceive the difficulty of defining "freeholders" to be insuperable. Still less that the restriction could be unpopular. $\frac{9}{10}$ of the people are at present freeholders and these will certainly be pleased with it. As to Merchts. &c. if they have wealth & value the right they can acquire it. If not they don't deserve it.

Col. Mason. We all feel too strongly the remains of antient prejudices, and view things too much through a British Medium. A Freehold is the qualification in England, & hence it is imagined to be the only proper one. The true idea in his opinion was that every man having evidence of attachment to & permanent common interest with the Society ought to share in all its rights & privileges. Was this qualification restrained to freeholders? Does no other kind of property but land evidence a common interest in the proprietor? does nothing besides property mark a permanent attachment. Ought the merchant, the monied man, the parent of a number of children whose fortunes are to be pursued in their own ⟨Country⟩, to be viewed as suspicious characters, and unworthy to be trusted with the common rights of their fellow Citizens

Mr. ⟨Madison.⟩ the right of suffrage is certainly one of the fundamental articles of republican Government, and ought not to be left to be regulated by the Legislature. A gradual abridgment of this right has been the mode in which Aristocracies have been built on the ruins of popular forms. Whether the Constitutional qualification ought to be a freehold, would with him depend much on the probable reception such a change would meet with in States where the right was now exercised by every description of people. In several of the States a freehold was now the qualification. Viewing the subject in its merits alone, the freeholders of the Country would be the safest depositories of Republican liberty. In future times a

great majority of the people will not only be without landed, but any other sort of, property. These will either combine under the influence of their common situation; in which case,[15] the rights of property & the public liberty,[16] ⟨will not be secure in their hands:⟩ or which is more probable, they will become the tools of opulence & ambition, in which case there will be equal danger on another side. The example of England has been misconceived (by Col Mason). A very small proportion of the Representatives are there chosen by freeholders. The greatest part are chosen by the Cities & boroughs, in many of which the qualification of suffrage is as low as it is in any one of the U. S. and it was in ⟨the boroughs & Cities⟩ rather than the Counties, that bribery most prevailed, & the influence of the Crown on elections was most dangerously exerted.[17]

Docr. Franklin. It is of great consequence that we shd. not depress the virtue & public spirit of our common people; of which they displayed a great deal during the war, and which contributed principally to the favorable issue of it.

[15] Crossed out: "if the authority be in their hands by the rule of suffrage".

[16] Crossed out: "good, will not he thought bid fair to be very secure".

[17] "Note to Speech of J. Madison of August 7th, 1787.

As appointments for the General Government here contemplated will, in part, be made by the State Governments: all the Citizens in States where the right of suffrage is not limited to the holders of property, will have an indirect share of representation in the General Government. But this does not satisfy the fundamental principle that men cannot be justly bound by laws in making of which they have no part. Persons and property being both essential objects of Government, the most that either can claim, is such a structure of it as will leave a reasonable security for the other. And the most obvious provision of this double character, seems to be that of confining to the holders of property, the object deemed least secure in popular Governments, the right of suffrage for one of the two Legislative branches. This is not without example among us, as well as other Constitutional modifications, favoring the influence of property in the Government. But the United States have not reached the stage of Society in which conflicting feelings of the Class with, and the Class without property, have the operation natural to them in Countries fully peopled. The most difficult of all political arrangements is that of so adjusting the claims of the two Classes as to give security to each, and to promote the welfare of all. The federal principle, which enlarges the sphere of power without departing from the elective basis of it, and controls in various ways the propensity in small republics to rash measures and the facility of forming and executing them, will be found the best expedient yet tried for solving the problem." Madison Papers, Library of Congress, Vol. IV, p. 7. See further Appendix A, CCCXLII and CCCXLIII.

He related the honorable refusal of the American seamen who were carried in great numbers into the British Prisons during the war, to redeem themselves from misery or to seek their fortunes, by entering on board the Ships of the Enemies to their Country; contrasting their patriotism with a contemporary instance in which the British seamen made prisoners by the Americans, readily entered on the ships of the latter on being promised a share of the prizes that might be made out of their own Country. This proceeded he said, from the different manner in which the common people were treated in America & G. Britain. He did not think that the elected had any right in any case to narrow the privileges of the electors. He quoted as arbitrary the British Statute setting forth the danger of tumultuous meetings, and under that pretext, narrowing the right of suffrage to persons having freeholds of a certain value; observing that this Statute was soon followed by another under the succeeding Parliamt. subjecting the people who had no votes to peculiar labors & hardships. He was persuaded also that such a restriction as was proposed would give great uneasiness in the populous States. The sons of a substantial farmer, not being themselves freeholders, would not be pleased at being disfranchised, and there are a great many persons of that description.

Mr. Mercer. The Constitution is objectionable in many points, but in none more than the present. He objected to the footing on which the qualification was put, but particularly to the *mode of election* by the people. The people can not know & judge of the characters of Candidates. The worse possible choice will be made. He quoted the case of the Senate in Virga. as an example in point- The people in Towns can unite their votes in favor of one favorite; & by that means always prevail over the people of the Country, who being dispersed will scatter their votes among a variety of candidates.

Mr. Rutlidge thought the idea of restraining the right of suffrage to the freeholders a very unadvised one. It would create division among the people & make enemies of all those who should be excluded.

On the question for striking out as moved by Mr. Govr. Morris, from the word "qualifications" to the end of the III article

N. H. no. Mas. no. Ct. no. Pa. no. Del. ay. Md. divd. Va. no. N. C. no. S. C. no. Geo. not prest. [Ayes — 1; noes — 7; divided — 1; absent — 1.]

Adjourned[18]

KING

Tuesday 7. Augt 87

3A — a. in all cases have a negative &c — proposed to be altered so that the negative extend only to those legislative acts in the passage whereof each Br. has concurrent authority — It was remarked by Madison yt. the whole clause "each of which shall in all cases have a negative on the other." might be struck out, and the Legislature wd. be well organised — This motion was agreed to, & the words stricken out.

— B. Madison proposed omitting in the Constitution the Time when the Legislature shd. meet — G. Morris in favor of leaving the Time of meeting to the Legislature — He remarked yt. if the Time was fixed in the Constitution, when the Legisl. shd. meet, it wd. be broken for yy wd. not meet at the Time fixed —

Gorham — in favor of meeting once a year and fixing the period — he was for meeting to superintend the conduct of the executive —

Mason — In favor of an annual meeting — They are not only Legislators but they possess inquisitorial powers. They must meet frequently to inspect the Conduct of the public offices —

4. Art. — S. 1 — c. The clause of Qualifications of Electors — G. Morris proposed to strike out the Clause — and to leave

[18] See further Appendix A, LXXX.

it to the Legislature to establish the Qualifications of Electors & Elected — or to add a Clause that the Legislat. may hereafter alter the Qualifications —

Elsworth — If the Legislature can alter the Qualifications, they may disqualify $\frac{3}{4}$ or any greater proportion from being Electors — This wd. go far in favor of Aristocracy — we are safe as it is — because the States have staked yr. Liberties on the Qualifications as yy now stand —

Dickenson — It is said yr. restraining by ye Constitution the rights of Election to Freeholders, is a step towards aristocracy — is this true, No. — we are safe by trusting the owners of the soil — the Owners of the Country — it will not be unpopular — because the Freeholders are the most numerous at this Time — The Danger to Free Governments has not been from Freeholders, but those who are not Freeholders — there is no Danger — because our Laws favor the Division of property — The Freehold will be parcelled among all the worthy men in the State — The Merchants & Mechanicks are safe — They may become Freeholders besides they are represented in ye State Legislatures, which elect the Senate of the US —

Elsworth — Why confine Elections to Freeholders — The rule is this — he who pays and is governed ought to have a right to vote — there is no justice in supposing that Virtue & Talents, are confined to Freeholders —

G. Morris — I disregard sounds — I am not alarmed with the word Aristocracy — but I dread the thing — I will oppose it — and for that reason I think I shall oppose this Constitution, because I think this constitution establishes an Aristocracy — there can be no Aristocracy if the Freeholders are Electors — but there will be, when a great & rich man shall bring his indigent Dependents to vote in Elections — if you don't establish a qualification of property, you will have an Aristocracy — Confing. ye. Electn. to Freeholders will not be unpopular because $\frac{9}{10}$th of the Inhabs. are Freeholders —

Mason — I think every person of full age and who can give evidence of a common Interest with the community shd. be an Elector — under this definition has a Freeholder alone ys.

common Interest —? I think the Father of a Family has this interest — his Children will remain — this is a natural Interest — a Farm & other property is an artificial interest — we are governed by our prejudices in favr. of Engd — there a Twig, a Turf is the Elector —

Madison — I am in favr. of the rigt. of Election being confind. to Freeholders — we are not governed by British Attachments — because the Knights of Shires are elected by Freeholders, but the Members from the Cities & Boroughs are elected by persons qualified by as small property as in any country and wholly without Freeholds — where is the Corruption in England: where is the Crown Influence seen — in the Cities & Boroughs & not in the Counties —

4 A. S. 1

Franklin — I am afraid by depositing the rights of Elections in the Freeholders it will be injurious to the lower class of Freemen — this class have hardy Virtues and gt. Integrity — the late war is a glorious Testimony in favor of plebian Virtue — Military men are sensible of this Truth — I know yt our Seamen prisoners in England refused all Allurements to draw them from yr. Allegiance — they were threatened with Halters but refused — this was not the case with the Brith. Seamen — they entered the American service & pointed out where they might make more marine prisoners — This is the reason — the Americans were all free and equal to any of yr. fellow Citizens — the British once were so — in antient Times every freeman was an Elector — but finally they made a law requiring an Elector to be a Freeholder — this was only in the Shires — The consequence was that the residue of Inhabitants were disgraced — in the next parliament they made a law authorising the Justices to fix the price of Labor — to compel any person not an Elector or Freeholder to labor for a Freeholder at the stated price or to be imprisoned — the English common people from that period lost a large portion of patriotism — [19]

[19] [Endorsed:] 7 & 8 Augt | Qualifications of electors | Ellsworth Mason Gorham Franklin — agt. confing. of the Qual. to Freeholders | Madison Gov. Mor Dickinson — in favour of it

McHENRY

Augt. 7.

Mr. Martin set out for New York on this day so we were without his concurrence in the propositions.[20]

Shewed these propositions to Mr. Carroll Mr. Jenifer and Mr. Mercer in convention. They said in general terms that they believed they should accord with them. I observed to Mr. Carrol that we would meet again in the evening and talk over the subject.[21]

The business of the Convention proceeded.

The preamble or caption and the 1. and 2. article passed without debate, the 3 article was amended so as to leave it with the legislature to appoint after the first meeting, the day for the succeeding meetings.

The IV article gave rise to a long debate, respecting the *qualifications of the electors.*

Mr. Dickinson contended for confining the rights of election in the first branch to *free holders.* No one could be considered as having an interest in the government unless he possessed some of the soil.

The fear of an aristocracy was a theoretical fiction. The owners of the soil could have no interest distinct from the country. There was no reason to dread a few men becoming lords of such an extent of territory as to enable them to govern at their pleasure.

Governeur Morris — thought that wise men should not suffer themselves to be misguided by sound. If the suffrage was to be open to all *freemen* — the government would indubitably be an aristocracy. The system was a system of Aristocracy. It put it in the power of opulent men whose business created numerous dependents to rule at all elections. Hence so soon as we erected large manufactories and our towns

---

[20] See McHenry's notes of August 6.

[21] Crossed out: "that I had my doubt whether the gentlemen had given themselves time to consider the effect of the propositions or the part we ought to take respecting them."

became more populous — wealthy merchants and manufacturers would elect the house of representatives. This was an aristocracy. This could only be avoided by confining the suffrage to *free holders.* Mr. Maddison supported similar sentiments.

The old ideas of taxation and representation were opposed to such reasoning.[22]

Doctor Franklin spoke on this occasion. He observed that in time of war a country owed much to the lower class of citizens. Our late war was an instance of what they could suffer and perform. If denied the right of suffrage it would debase their spirit and detatch them from the interest of the country. One thousand of our seamen were confined in English prisons — had bribes offered them to go on board English vessels which they rejected. An English ship was taken by one of our men of war. It was proposed to the English sailors to join ours in a cruise and share alike with thm in the captures. They immediately agreed to the proposal. This difference of behavior arises from[23] the operation of freedom in America, and the laws in England. One British Statute excluded a number of subjects from a suffrage — These immediately became slaves —

At thee o'clock the house adjourned without coming to any issue.

At five o'clock in the evening I went to Mr. Carrolls lodging to confer with my colleagues on the points I had submitted to their consideration. I found Mr. Carroll alone when We entered upon their merits. He agreed with me that the deputation should oppose a resolute face to the 5 sect of the IV article,[24] and that they ought to reject it. He appeared fully sensible of its tendency — That lodging in the house of representatives the sole right of raising and appropriating money,

---

[22] This is apparently McHenry's comment. What follows, from "Doctor Franklin" to "became slaves" is written on the opposite page of the manuscript, and marked to be inserted.

[23] Crossed out: "this description of men having a right of suffrage."

[24] That money-bills should originate in the House of Representatives alone, and that the Senate should have no right to alter or amend them.

upon which the Senate had only a negative, gave to that branch an inordinate power in the constitution, which must end in its destruction. That without equal powers they were not an equal check upon each other — and that this was the chance that appeared for obtained an equal suffrage, or a suffrage equal to wht we had in the present confedn.

We accorded also that the deputation should in no event consent to the 6 sect. of VII article.[25] He saw plainly that as a quorum consisted of a majority of the members of each house — that the dearest interest of trade were under the controul of four States or of 17 membes in one branch and 8 in the other branch.[26]

We adverted also to the 1st sect of the VII article which enabled the legislature to lay and collect taxes, duties, imposts and excises, and to regulate commerce among the several States. We almost shuddered at the fate of the commerce of Maryland should we be unable to make any change in this extraordinary power.

We agreed that our deputation ought never to assent to this article in its present form or without obtaining such a provision as I proposed.

I now begged his particular attention to my last proposition.[27] By the XXII article we were called upon to agree that the system should be submitted to a convention chosen in each State under the recommendation of its legislature. And that a less number of conventions than the whole agreeing to the system should be sufficient to organise the constitution.

We had taken an oath to support our constitution and frame of government. We had been empowered by a legislature legally constituted to revise the confederation and fit it for the *exigencies of government*, and *preservation of the union.* Could we do this business in a manner contrary to our constitution? I feared (This [28] was said first I *thought*—then I *feared*[29])

[25] "No navigation act shall be passed without the assent of two-thirds of the members present in each house."

[26] Marginal note: "33, 17 and 14, 8."

[27] As to ratification by nine states.

[28] Note by McHenry.

[29] The word "feared" is substituted for a word erased.

we could not. If we relinquished any of the rights or powers of our government to the U. S. of America, we could no otherwise agree to that relinquishment than in the mode our constitution prescribed for making changes or alterations in it.

Mr. Carrol said he had felt his doubts respecting the propriety of this article as it respected Maryland; but he hoped we should be able to get over this difficulty.

Mr. Jenifer now came in to whom Mr. Carroll repeated what we had said upon my propositions and our determinations. Mr. Jenifer agreed to act in unison with us but seemed to have vague ideas of the mischiefs of the system as it stood in the report.

I wished to impress him with the necessity to support us, and touched upon some popular points.

I suggested to him the unfavorable impression it would make upon the people on account of its expence — An army and navy was to be raised and supported, expensive courts of judicature to be maintained, and a princely president to be provided for etc — That it was plain that the revenue for these purposes was to be chiefly drawn from commerce. That Maryland in this case would have this resource taken from her, without the expences of her own government being lessened. — That what would be raised from her commerce and by indirect taxation would far exceed the proportion she would be called upon to pay under the present confederation.

An increase of taxes, and a decrease in the objects of taxation as they respected a revenue for the State would not prove very palatable to our people, who might think that the whole objects of taxation were hardly sufficient to discharge the States obligations.

Mr. Mercer came in, and said he would go with the deputation on the points in question. He would wish it to be understood however, that he did not like the system, that it was weak — That he would produce a better one since the convention had undertaken to go radically to work, that perhaps he would not be supported by any one, but if he was not, he would go with the stream —

WEDNESDAY, AUGUST 8, 1787.

JOURNAL

Wednesday August 8. 1787.

On the question to agree to the first section of the fourth article as reported

it passed unanimously in the affirmative

It was moved and seconded to strike out the word "three" and to insert the word "seven" in the second section of the fourth article

which passed in the affirmative [Ayes — 10; noes — 1.]

It was moved and seconded to amend the second section of the fourth article by inserting the word "of" instead of "in" after the word "citizen" and the words "an inhabitant" instead of the words "a resident"

which passed in the affirmative

[To strike out the word "of" and to substitute "in" after resident in the 2 sect. 4 article Ayes — 4; noes — 7.

To postpone Mr motion in order to take up Mr Dickinsons Ayes — 3; noes — 8.

To insert the word "three" Ayes — 2; noes — 9.

To add One year residence before the election Ayes — 4; noes 6; divided — 1.][1]

On the question to agree to the second section of the fourth article as amended

it passed in the affirmative [Ayes — 11; noes — 0.]

It was moved and seconded to strike out the word "five" and to insert the word "six" before the words "in South Carolina" in the third section of the fourth article

which passed in the negative [Ayes—4; noes—7.]

---

[1] Votes 246–249, Detail of Ayes and Noes.

On the question to agree to the third section of the fourth article as reported

it passed in the affirmative

It was moved and seconded to alter the latter clause of the fourth section of the fourth article so as to read as follows namely

"according to the rule herein after made for direct taxation not exceeding the rate of One for every forty thousand"

which passed in the affirmative [Ayes—9; noes—2.]

It was moved and seconded to add the following clause to the fourth section of the fourth article namely

"Provided that every State shall have at least one representative"

which passed in the affirmative

It was moved and seconded to insert the word "free" before the word "inhabitants" in the fourth section of the fourth article

which passed in the negative. [Ayes—1; noes—10.]

On the question to agree to the fourth section of the fourth article as amended

it passed in the affirmative

It was moved and seconded to strike out the fifth section of the fourth article

which passed in the affirmative [Ayes—7; noes—4.]

And then the House adjourned till to-morrow at 11 o'clock A. M.

Detail of Ayes and Noes

	New Hampshire	Massachusetts	Rhode Island	Connecticut	New York	New Jersey	Pennsylvania	Delaware	Maryland	Virginia	North Carolina	South Carolina	Georgia	Questions	Ayes	Noes	Divided
[245]	aye	aye		no		aye	aye	aye	aye	aye	aye	aye	aye	To strike out "three" and insert seven in ye 2 Sect 4 art.	10	1	
[246]	no	no		no		aye	no	no	aye	aye	no	aye	no	To strike out the word "of" and to substitute "in" after resident in the 2 sect. 4 article	4	7	
[247]	no	no		no		no	no	no	aye	no	no	aye	aye	To postpone Mr motion in order to take up Mr Dickinsons	3	8	
[248]	no	no		no		no	no	no	no	no	no	aye	aye	To insert the word "three"	2	9	
[249]	no	no		no		aye	no	no	dd	no	aye	aye	aye	To add One year residence before the election	4	6	1
[250]	aye	aye		aye		aye	aye	aye	aye	aye	aye	aye	aye	To agree to ye 2 clause of ye 2 sect.			
[251]	no	no		no		no	no	aye	no	no	aye	aye	aye	To give six representatives to So Carolina	4	7	
[252]	aye	aye		aye		no	aye	no	aye	aye	aye	aye	aye	To alter the latter clause of the 4 sect. of the 4. Art. "according to the rule herein after provided for Direct taxation"	9	2	
[253]	no	no		no		aye	no	no	no	no	no	no	no	To insert the word "free" before inhabitants 4 sect. 4 article	1	10	
[254]	no	no		no		aye	aye	aye	aye	aye	no	aye	aye	To strike out the 5 section 4 article	7	4	

MADISON

Wednesday Augst. 8. In Convention

Art: IV. Sect. 1.—Mr. Mercer expressed his dislike of the whole plan, and his opinion that it never could succeed.[2]

Mr. Ghorum. He had never seen any inconveniency from allowing such as were not freeholders to vote, though it had long

[2] See Appendix A, CCXXIII.

been tried. The elections in Phila. N. York & Boston where the Merchants, & Mechanics vote are at least as good as those made by freeholders only. The case in England was not accurately stated yesterday (by Mr. Madison) The Cities & large towns are not the seat of Crown influence & corruption. These prevail in the Boroughs, and not on account of the right which those who are not freeholders have to vote, but of the smallness of the number who vote. The people have been long accustomed to this right in various parts of America, and will never allow it to be abridged. We must consult their rooted prejudices if we expect their concurrence in our propositions.

Mr. Mercer did not object so much to an election by the people at large including such as were not freeholders, as to their being left to make their choice without any guidance. He hinted that Candidates ought to be nominated by the State Legislatures.

On question for agreeing to Art: IV– Sect. 1 it passd. nem. con.

Art. IV. Sect. 2. taken up.[3]

Col. Mason was for opening a wide door for emigrants; but did not chuse to let foreigners and adventurers make laws for us & govern us. Citizenship for three years was not enough for ensuring that local knowledge which ought to be possessed by the Representative. This was the principal ground of his objection to so short a term. It might also happen that a rich foreign Nation, for example Great Britain, might send over her tools who might bribe their way into the Legislature for insidious purposes. He moved that "seven" years instead of "three," be inserted.[4]

Mr. Govr. Morris 2ded. the motion, & on the question, All the States agreed to it except Connecticut.

Mr. Sherman moved to strike out the word "resident" and insert "inhabitant," as less liable to misconstruction.

---

[3] Article IV, Sect. 2. "Every member of the House of Representatives shall be of the age of twenty five years at least; shall have been a citizen of the United States for at least three years before his election; and shall be, at the time of his election, a resident of the State in which he shall be chosen."

[4] See Appendix A, LXVIII.

Mr M⟨adison⟩ 2ded. the motion. both were vague, but the latter least so in common acceptation, and would not exclude persons absent occasionally for a considerable time on public or private business. Great disputes had been raised in Virga. concerning the meaning of residence as a qualification of Representatives which were determined more according to the affection or dislike to the man ⟨in question⟩, than ⟨to⟩ any fixt interpretation of the word.

Mr. Wilson preferred "inhabitant."

Mr. Govr. Morris was opposed to both and for requiring nothing more than a freehold. He quoted great disputes in N. York occasioned by these terms, which were decided by the arbitrary will of the majority. Such a regulation is not necessary. People rarely chuse a nonresident — It is improper as in the 1st. branch, *the people at large,*[5] not the *States*[5] are represented.

Mr. Rutlidge urged & moved that a residence of 7 years shd. be required in the State Wherein the Member shd. be elected. An emigrant from N. England to S. C. or Georgia would know little of its affairs and could not be supposed to acquire a thorough knowledge in less time.

Mr. Read reminded him that we were now forming a *Natil* Govt and such a regulation would correspond little with the idea that we were one people.

Mr. Wilson — enforced the same consideration.

Mr. ⟨Madison⟩ suggested the case of new States in the West, which could have perhaps no representation on that plan.

Mr. Mercer. Such a regulation would present a greater alienship among the States than existed under the old federal system. It would interweave local prejudices & State distinctions in the very Constitution which is meant to cure them. He mentioned instances of violent disputes raised in Maryland concerning the term "residence"

Mr Elseworth thought seven years of residence was by far too long a term: but that some fixt term of previous resi-

[5] Underscored by Madison when he revised his notes.

dence would be proper. He thought one year would be sufficient, but seemed to have no objection to three years.

Mr. Dickenson proposed ⟨that it should read⟩ "inhabitant actually resident for ——— year." This would render the meaning less indeterminate.

Mr. Wilson. If a short term should be inserted in the blank, so strict an expression might be construed to exclude the members of the Legislature, who could not be said to be actual residents in their States whilst at the Seat of the Genl. Government.

Mr. Mercer. It would certainly exclude men, who had once been inhabitants, and returning from residence elswhere to resettle in their original State; although a want of the necessary knowledge could not in such case be presumed.

Mr. Mason thought 7 years too long, but would never agree to part with the principle. It is a valuable principle. He thought it a defect in the plan that the Representatives would be too few to bring with them all the local knowledge necessary. If residence be not required, Rich men of neighbouring States, may employ with success the means of corruption in some particular district and thereby get into the public Councils after having failed in their own State. This is the practice in the boroughs of England.

On the question for postponing in order to consider Mr Dickinsons motion

N. H. no. Mas. no. Ct. no. N. J. no. Pa. no. Del. no. Md. ay. Va. no. N. C. no. S. C. ay. Geo. ay. [Ayes — 3; noes — 8.]

On the question for inserting "inhabitant" in place of "resident" — Agd. to nem. con.

Mr. Elseworth & Col. Mason move to insert "one year" for previous inhabitancy

Mr. Williamson liked the Report as it stood. He thought "resident" a good eno' term. He was agst requiring any period of previous residence. New residents if elected will be most zealous to Conform to the will of their constituents, as their conduct will be watched with a more jealous eye.

Mr. Butler & Mr. Rutlidge moved "three years" instead of "one year" ⟨for previous inhabitancy⟩

On the question for 3 years.

N. H. no. Mas. no. Ct. no. N. J. no. Pa. no. Del. no. Md. no. Va. no. N. C. no. S. C. ay. Geo. ay [Ayes — 2; noes — 9.]

On the question for "1 year"

N. H. no — Mas — no. Ct. no. N. J. ay. Pa. no. Del. no. Md. divd. Va. no- N- C. ay- S. C. ay. Geo — ay [Ayes — 4; noes — 6; divided — 1.]

Art. IV- Sect. 2. As amended in manner preceding, was agreed to nem. con.

Art: IV. Sect. 3. "taken up.[6]

Genl. Pinkney & Mr. Pinkney moved that the number of representatives allotted to S. Carola. be "six"

On the question.

N. H. no. Mas. no. Ct. no. N. J. no. Pa. no. ⟨Delaware ay⟩ [7] Md. no. Va. no. N. C. ay. S. C. ay. Geo. ay. [Ayes — 4; noes — 7.]

⟨The 3. Sect of Art: IV was then agreed to.⟩[7]

Art: IV. Sect. 4. taken up.[8]

Mr. Williamson moved to strike out "according to the provisions hereinafter made" and to insert ⟨the⟩ words ⟨"according⟩ "to the rule hereafter to be provided for direct taxation" — See Art VII. sect. 3.

On the question for agreeing to Mr. Williamson's amendment

N. H- ay. Mas. ay. Ct. ay. N. J. no. Pa. ay. Del. no. Md. ay. Va ay. N. C. ay. S. C. ay. Geo. ay. [Ayes — 9; noes — 2.]

---

[6] Article IV, Sect. 3. "The House of Representatives shall, at its first formation, and until the number of citizens and inhabitants shall be taken in the manner herein after described, consist of sixty-five Members, of whom three shall be chosen in New Hampshire, eight in Massachusetts, one in Rhode-Island and Providence Plantations, five in Connecticut, six in New-York, four in New-Jersey, eight in Pennsylvania, one in Delaware, six in Maryland, ten in Virginia, five in North-Carolina, five in South-Carolina, and three in Georgia."

[7] Taken from *Journal*.

[8] Article IV, Sect. 4. "As the proportions of numbers in different States will alter from time to time; as some of the States may hereafter be divided; as others may be enlarged by addition of territory; as two or more States may be united; as new States will be erected within the limits of the United States, the Legislature shall, in each of these cases, regulate the number of representatives by the number of inhabitants, according to the provisions herein after made, at the rate of one for every forty thousand."

Mr. King wished to know what influence the vote just passed was meant have on the succeeding part of the Report, concerning the admission of slaves into the rule of Representation. He could not reconcile his mind to the article if it was to prevent objections to the latter part. The admission of slaves was a most grating circumstance to his mind, & he believed would be so to a great part of the people of America. He had not made a strenuous opposition to it heretofore because he had hoped that this concession would have produced a readiness which had not been manifested, to strengthen the Genl. Govt. and to mark a full confidence in it. The Report under consideration had by the tenor of it, put an end to all these hopes. In two great points the hands of the Legislature were absolutely tied. The importation of slaves could not be prohibited — exports could not be taxed. Is this reasonable? What are the great objects of the Genl. System? 1. difence agst. foreign invasion. 2. agst. internal sedition. Shall all the States then be bound to defend each; & shall each be at liberty to introduce a weakness which will render defence more difficult? Shall one part of the U. S. be bound to defend another part, and that other part be at liberty not only to increase its own danger, but to withhold the compensation for the burden? If slaves are to be imported shall not the exports produced by their labor, supply a revenue the better to enable the Genl. Govt. to defend their Masters? — There was so much inequality & unreasonableness in all this, that the people of the N⟨orthern⟩ States could never be reconciled ⟨to it⟩. No candid man could undertake to justify it to them. He had hoped that some accommodation wd. have taken place on this subject; that at least a time wd. have been limited for the importation of slaves. He never could agree to let them be imported without limitation & then be represented in the Natl. Legislature. Indeed he could so little persuade himself of the rectitude of such a practice, that he was not sure he could assent to it under any circumstances. At all events, either slaves should not be represented, or exports should be taxable.

Mr. Sherman regarded the slave-trade as iniquitous; but

the point of representation having been Settled after much difficulty & deliberation, he did not think himself bound to make opposition; especially as the present article as amended did not preclude any arrangement whatever on that point in another place of the Report.[9]

Mr. ⟨Madison⟩ objected to 1 for every 40,000 inhabitants ⟨as a perpetual rule⟩.[10] The future increase of population if the Union shd. be permanent, will render the number of Representatives excessive.[11]

Mr. Ghorum. It is not to be supposed that the Govt will last so long as to produce this effect. Can it be supposed that this vast Country including the Western territory will 150 years hence remain one nation?

Mr. Elseworth. If the Govt. should continue so long, alterations may be made in the Constitution in the manner proposed in a subsequent article.

Mr Sherman & Mr. ⟨Madison⟩ moved to insert the words "not exceeding" before the words "1 for every 40,000, which was agreed to nem. con.

Mr Govr. Morris moved to insert "free" before the word "inhabitants." Much he said would depend on this point. He never would concur in upholding domestic slavery. It was a nefarious institution — It was the curse of heaven on the States where it prevailed. Compare the free regions of the Middle States, where a rich & noble cultivation marks the prosperity & happiness of the people, with the misery & poverty which overspread the barren wastes of Va. Maryd. & the other States having slaves. ⟨Travel thro' ye whole Continent & you behold the prospect continually varying with the appearance & disappearance of slavery. The moment you leave ye E. Sts. & enter N. York, the effects of the institution become visible; Passing thro' the Jerseys and entering Pa- every criterion of superior improvement witnesses the change. Proceed Southwdly, & every step you take thro' ye great

[9] See further upon this subject references under August 22 note 2, and August 25 note 7.

[10] Probably but not certainly a later revision.

[11] See Appendix A, CXLIV.

regions of slaves, presents a desert increasing with ye increasing proportion of these wretched beings.⟩[12]

Upon what principle is it that the slaves shall be computed in the representation? Are they men? Then make them Citizens & let them vote? Are they property? Why then is no other property included? The Houses in this City (Philada.) are worth more than all the wretched slaves which cover the rice swamps of South Carolina. The admission of slaves into the Representation when fairly explained comes to this: that the inhabitant of Georgia and S. C. who goes to the Coast of Africa, and in defiance of the most sacred laws of humanity tears away his fellow creatures from their dearest connections & dam⟨n⟩s them to the most cruel bondages, shall have more votes in a Govt. instituted for protection of the rights of mankind, than the Citizen of Pa or N. Jersey who views with a laudable horror, so nefarious a practice. He would add that Domestic slavery is the most prominent feature in the aristocratic countenance of the proposed Constitution. The vassalage of the poor has ever been the favorite offspring of Aristocracy. And What is the proposed compensation to the Northern States for a sacrifice of every principle ot right, of every impulse of humanity. They are to bind themselves to march their militia for the defence of the S. States; for their defence agst those very slaves of whom they complain. They must supply vessels & seamen, in case of foreign Attack. The Legislature will have indefinite power to tax them by excises, and duties on imports: both of which will fall heavier on them than on the Southern inhabitants; for the bohea tea used by a Northern freeman, will pay more tax than the whole consumption of the miserable slave, which consists of nothing more than his physical subsistence and the rag that covers his nakedness. On the other side the Southern States are not to be restrained from importing fresh supplies of wretched Africans, at once to increase the danger of attack, and the difficulty of defence; nay they are to be encouraged to it by an assurance of having their votes in the Natl Govt increased

[12] It is difficult to account for this passage. The MS. seems to show fairly ceratinly that it was a later insertion.

in proportion. and are at the same time to have their exports & their slaves exempt from all contributions for the public service. Let it not be said that direct taxation is to be proportioned to representation. It is idle to suppose that the Genl Govt. can stretch its hand directly into the pockets of the people scattered over so vast a Country. They can only do it through the medium of exports imports & excises. For what then are all these sacrifices to be made? He would sooner submit himself to a tax for paying for all the Negroes in the U. States. than saddle posterity with such a Constitution.

Mr. Dayton 2ded. the motion. He did it he said that his sentiments on the subject might appear whatever might be the fate of the amendment.

Mr. Sherman. did not regard the admission of the Negroes into the ratio of representation, as liable to such insuperable objections. It was the freemen of the Southn. States who were in fact to be represented according to the taxes paid by them, and the Negroes are only included in the Estimate of the taxes. This was his idea of the matter.

Mr Pinkney, considered the fisheries & the Western frontier as more burdensome to the U. S. than the slaves — He thought this could be demonstrated if the occasion were a proper one.

Mr Wilson. thought the motion premature — An agreement to the clause would be no bar to the object of it.

Question On Motion to insert "free" before "inhabitants."

N. H– no. Mas. no. Ct. no. N. J. ay. Pa. no. Del. no. Md. no. Va. no. N. C. no. S. C. no. Geo. no. [Ayes — 1; noes — 10.]

On the suggestion of Mr. Dickenson ⟨the words⟩, "provided that each State shall have one representative at least." — were added nem. con.

Art. IV. sect. 4. as amended was Agreed to nem. con.

Art. IV. sect. 5. taken up [13]

[13] Article IV, Sect. 5. "All bills for raising or appropriating money, and for fixing the salaries of the officers of the Government, shall originate in the House of Representatives, and shall not be altered or amended by the Senate. No money shall be drawn from the public Treasury, but in pursuance of appropriations that shall originate in the House of Representatives."

Mr. Pinkney moved to strike out Sect. 5, As giving no peculiar advantage to the House of Representatives, and as clogging the Govt. If the Senate can be trusted with the many great powers proposed, it surely may be trusted with that of originating money bills.

Mr. Ghorum. was agst. allowing the Senate to *originate;* but ⟨only⟩ to *amend.*

Mr. Govr. Morris. It is particularly proper that the Senate shd. have the right of originating money bills. They will sit constantly. will consist of a smaller number. and will be able to prepare such bills with due correctness; and so as to prevent delay of business in the other House.

Col. Mason was unwilling to travel over this ground again. To strike out the section, was to unhinge the compromise of which it made a part. The duration of the Senate made it improper. He does not object to that duration. On the Contrary he approved of it. But joined with the smallness of the number, it was an argument ⟨against⟩ adding this to the other great powers vested in that body. His idea of an Aristocracy was that it was the govern t. of the few over the many. An aristocratic body, like the screw in mechanics, workig. its way by slow degrees, and holding fast whatever it gains, should ever be suspected of an encroaching tendency —The purse strings should never be put into its hands.

Mr Mercer, considered the exclusive power of originating Money bills as so great an advantage, that it rendered the equality of votes in the Senate ideal & of no consequence.

Mr. Butler was for adhering to the principle which had been settled.

Mr. Wilson was opposed to it on its merits, with out regard to the compromisc

Mr. Elseworth did not think the clause of any consequence, but as it was thought of consequence by some members from the larger States, he was willing it should stand.

Mr. ⟨Madison⟩ was for striking it out: considering it as of no advantage to the large States as fettering the Govt. and as a source of injurious altercations between the two Houses.

On the question for striking out "Sect. 5. art. IV"

N. H. no. Mas. no. Ct. no. N. J. ay. Pa. ay. Del. ay. Md. ay. Va. ay. N. C. no. S. C. ay. Geo. ay. [Ayes — 7; noes — 4.]

Adjd.

KING

Wednesday 8 August —

4. A. 1 — c. The Qualifications of Electors — Gorham, The Qualifications stand well — Gentlemen who say that the Elections in the Cities are unsafe are in an Error — The Members of London, Bristol & Liverpool are as independent as any of the Members of the Shires — The King has no Influence in ye. City Elections — He buys the boroughs and he buys them of the Freeholders — there will be no Danger in allowing the Merchants & Mechanicks to be Electors — they have been Electors Time immemorial in this country as well as in England — We must regard the Habits & prejudices of the people — if you propose a window Tax in N. Eng. you wd. offend the people — If the minister in England shd. propose a poll-Tax he wd. also offend the People — so if you deprive the Mercht. & Mechank. of the Rights of Election you will offend them —

— 2d. Resident — proposed to change the word to Inhabitant — Morris G. proposed Freeholder — Rutledge — Resident for seven years in the State where he is elected — Mason — I am in favor of Residency — if you do not require it — a rich man may send down to the Districts of a state in wh. he does not reside and purchase an Election for his Dependt. We shall have the Eng. Borough corruption — a question was put & negatived by 8 of 11 states to insert Inhabitant for 3 yrs [14] — afterwards the question for One yr. before Election was negatived by 6 of 11 — finally the wd. was established as it stands unanimously — [15]

[14] According to the Journal and Madison the vote on this question was Ayes, 2; noes, 9; and the vote which King gives belongs to the preceding question "to postpone."

[15] [Endorsed:] | August 8th | Qualifications of | electors.

McHENRY

August 8.

The 2 sect. of the IV. article was amended to read 7 insted of three years. It was proposed to add to the section "at least one year preceding his election". negatived. Maryland divided. Mrs. Mercer and Carrol neg. Mr. Jenifer and myself aff.

The fifth section giving the sole power of raising and appropriating money to the house of representatives expunged.

THURSDAY, AUGUST 9, 1787.

JOURNAL

Thursday August 9. 1787.

On the question to agree to the 6 section of the 4. article as reported.

it passed in the affirmative

On the question to agree to the 7. section of the 4 article as reported

it passed in the affirmative

It was moved and seconded to insert the following words in the third clause of the 5 article after the word "executive"

"of the State, in the representation of which the vacancies shall happen"

which passed in the affirmative

It was moved and seconded to strike out the 3rd clause of the 1st section of the 5. article

which passed in the affirmative [Ayes — 1; noes — 8; divided — 1.][1]

It was moved and seconded to add the following words to the 3rd clause of the 1st section of the 5 article, namely

"unless other provision shall be made by the Legislature"

which passed in the negative [Ayes — 4; noes — 6.]

It was moved and seconded to alter the 3rd. clause in the 1st section of the 5. article so as to read as follows, namely

"vacancies happening by refusals to accept resignations or
"otherwise may be supplied by the Legislature of the State
"in the representation of which such vacancies shall happen
"or by the executive thereof until the next meeting of the
"Legislature"

Which passed in the affirmative

[1] Vote 255, Detail of Ayes and Noes. Madison confirms this negative vote.

On the motion to agree to the three first clauses of the 1st section of the 5th article

it passed in the affirmative [Ayes — 8; noes — 2; divided — 1.]

It was moved and seconded to postpone the consideration of the last clause in the first section of the 5. article

which was passed in the negative [Ayes — 2; noes — 8; divided — 1.]

On the question to agree to the last clause in the 1st section of the 5. article

it passed in the affirmative

It was moved and seconded to insert the following words after the word "after" in the 2nd section of the 5 article namely

"they shall be assembled in consequence of"

which passed in the affirmative

On the question to agree to the 2nd section of the 5. article as amended.

it passed in the affirmative

It was moved and seconded to strike out the word "four" and to insert the word "fourteen" in the 3 section of the 5 article

which passed in the negative [Ayes — 4; noes — 7.]

It was moved and seconded to strike out the word "four" and to insert the word "fourteen"[2] in the 3 section of the 5 article

which passed in the negative [Ayes — 4; noes — 7.]

It was moved and seconded to strike out the word "four" and to insert the word "Ten" in the 3 section of the 5 article

which passed in the negative [Ayes — 4; noes — 7.]

It was moved and seconded to strike out the word "four" and to insert the word "nine" in the 3rd section of the 5 article

which passed in the affirmative [Ayes—6; noes—4; divided — 1.]

It was moved and seconded to amend the 3rd section of the 5

[2] "fourteen" is evidently a mistake for "thirteen", so in Vote 260, Detail of Ayes and Noes, and in Madison.

article by inserting the word "of" after the word "citizen" and the words "an inhabitant" instead of the words "a resident"

which passed in the affirmative

On the question to agree to the 3rd section of the 5 article as amended

it passed in the affirmative

On the question to agree to the 4th section of the 5. article as reported

it passed in the affirmative

It was moved and seconded to strike out the words "each House" and to insert the words "the House of representatives" in the 1st section of the 6th article

which passed in the negative [Ayes — 1; noes — 10.]

It was moved and seconded to insert the word "respectively" after the word "State" in the 1st section of the 6. article

which passed in the affirmative

It was moved and seconded to alter the second clause in the first section of the 6th article so as to read as follows namely

"but regulations in each of the foregoing cases may, at "any time, be made or altered by the Legislature of the United "States"

which passed in the affirmative

On the question to agree to the 1st section of the 6th article as amended

it passed in the affirmative.

And then the House adjourned till to-morrow at 11 o'Clock A. M.

DETAIL OF AYES AND NOES

	New Hampshire	Massachusetts	Rhode Island	Connecticut	New York	New Jersey	Pennsylvania	Delaware	Maryland	Virginia	North Carolina	South Carolina	Georgia	Questions	Ayes	Noes	Divided
[255]	no	no		no		no	aye		dd	no	no	no	no	To strike out the 3rd clause of the 1st sect. of the 5 article	1	8	1
[256]	no	no		no		no	no		aye	no	aye	aye	aye	To add the words to ye 1st sect 5 art. unless other provision shall be made by the Legislature	4	6	
[257]	aye	no		aye		aye	aye	ayc	aye	aye	no	dd	aye	To agree to the three first clauses of the 1st sect. of the 5 article	8	2	1
[258]	dd	no		no		no	no	no	no	aye	aye	no	no	To postpone the last clause in the 1st section of the 5 article	2	8	1
[259]	aye	no		no		aye	no	no	no	no	no	aye	aye	fourteen years citizenship to qualify to a seat in the Senate.	4	7	
[260]	aye	no		no		aye	no	no	no	no	no	aye	aye	Thirteen years	4	7	
[261]	aye	no		no		aye	no	no	no	no	no	aye	aye	Ten years	4	7	
[262]	aye	no		no		aye	no	aye	no	aye	dd	aye	aye	Nine years.	6	4	1
[263]	no	no		no		aye	no	no	no	no	no	no	no	To strike out the words "each House" & to insert the words the Ho of represntves in the 1st sect of the 6 article	1	10	

MADISON

Thursday. Augst. 9. in Convention

Art: IV. sect. 6. Mr. Randolph expressed his dissatisfaction at the disagreement yesterday to sect 5. concerning money bills, as endangering the success of the plan, and extremely objectionable in itself; and gave notice that he should move for a reconsideration of the vote.

Mr. Williamson said he had formed a like intention.

Mr. Wilson, gave notice that he shd. move to reconsider the vote, requiring seven instead of three years of Citizenship

as a qualification of candidates for the House of Representatives.

Art. IV. sect. 6 & 7.[3] Agreed to nem. con.

Art. V. sect. 1. taken up.[4]

Mr. Wilson objected to vacancies in the Senate being supplied by the Executives of the States. It was unnecessary as the Legislatures will meet so frequently. It removes the appointment too far from the people; the Executives in most of the States being elected by the Legislatures. As he had always thought the appointment of the Executives by the Legislative department wrong: so it was still more so that the Executive should elect into the Legislative department.

Mr. Randolph though it necessary ⟨in order⟩ to prevent inconvenient chasms in the Senate. In some States the Legislatures meet but once a year. As the Senate will have more power & consist of a smaller number than the other House, vacancies there will be of more consequence. The Executives might be safely trusted ⟨he thought with the appointment for so short a time.⟩

Mr. Elseworth. It is only said that the Executive *may* supply vacancies. When the Legislative meeting happens to be near, the power will not be exerted. As there will be but two members from a State vacancies may be of great moment.

Mr. Williamson. Senators may resign or not accept. This provision is therefore absolutely necessary.

On the question for striking out "vacancies shall be supplied by Executives

N. H. no. Mas. no. Ct. no. N. J. no. Pa. ay. Md. divd. Va. no. N. C. no. S. C. no. Geo. no. [Ayes — 1; noes — 8; divided — 1.]

---

[3] Article IV, Sect. 6. "The House of Representatives shall have the sole power of impeachment. It shall choose its Speaker and other officers."

Sect. 7. "Vacancies in the House of Representatives shall be supplied by writs of election from the executive authority of the State, in the representation from which it shall happen."

[4] Article V, Sect. 1. "The Senate of the United States shall be chosen by the Legislatures of the several States. Each Legislature shall chuse two members. Vacancies may be supplied by the Executive until the next meeting of the Legislature. Each member shall have one vote."

Mr. Williamson moved to insert after "vacancies shall be supplied by the Executives", the following words "unless other provision shall be made by the Legislature" (of the State).

Mr Elseworth. He was willing to trust the Legislature, or the Executive of a State, but ⟨not⟩ to give the former a discretion to refer appointments for the Senate to whom they pleased.

Question on Mr Williamson's motion

N. H. no. Mas. no. Ct. no. N. J. no. Pa. no. Md. ay. Va. no. N- C. ay. S. C. ay- Geo. ay. [Ayes — 4; noes — 6.]

Mr. ⟨Madison⟩ in order to prevent doubts whether resignations could be made by Senators, or whether they could refuse to accept, moved to ⟨strike out the words⟩ after "vacancies". ⟨& insert⟩ the words "happening by refusals to accept, resignations ⟨or otherwise may be supplied by the Legislature of the State in the representation of which such vacancies shall happen, or by the Executive thereof until the next meeting of the Legislature"⟩[5]

Mr. Govr. Morris this is absolutely necessary. otherwise, as members chosen into the Senate are disqualified from being appointed to any office by sect. 9. of this art: it will be in the power of a Legislature by appointing a man a Senator agst. his consent, to deprive the U. S. of his services.

The motion of Mr. ⟨Madison⟩ was agreed to nem. con.

Mr. Randolph called for a division of the Section, so as to leave a distinct question on the last words, "each ⟨member⟩[6] shall have one vote". He wished this last sentence to be postponed until the reconsideration should have taken place on sect. 5. Art. IV. concerning money bills. If that section should not be reinstated his plan would be to vary the representation in the Senate.

Mr. Strong concurred in Mr. Randolphs ideas on this point

Mr. Read did not consider the section as to money bills of any advantage to the larger States and had voted for strik-

[5] Revised from *Journal*.

[6] Crossed out "State".

ing it out as ⟨being⟩ viewed in the same light by the larger States. If it was considered by them as of any value, and as a condition of the equality of votes in the Senate, he had no objection to its being re-instated.

Mr. Wilson — Mr. Elseworth & Mr. — ⟨Madison⟩ urged that it was of ⟨no⟩ advantage to the larger States. and that it might be a dangerous source of contention between the two Houses. All the principal powers of the Natl. Legislature had some relation to money.

Docr. Franklin, considered the two clauses, the originating of money bills, and the equality of votes in the Senate, as essentially connected by the compromise which had been agreed to.

Col. Mason said this was not the time for discussing this point. When the originating of money bills shall be reconsidered, he thought it could be demonstrated that it was of essential importance to restrain the right to the House of Representatives the immediate choice of the people.

Mr. Williamson. The State of N. C. had agreed to an equality in the Senate, merely in consideration that money bills should be confined to the other House: and he was surprised to see the smaller States forsaking the condition on which they had received their equality.

Question on the Section 1. down to the last sentence

N. H ay. Mas. no. Ct. ay. N. J. ay. Pa. no-* Del. ay. Md. ay. ⟨Virga ay⟩ N. C. no. S. C. divd. Geo. ay. [Ayes — 7; noes — 3; divided — 1.]

Mr. Randolph moved that the last sentence "each ⟨member⟩[7] shall have one vote." be postponed

It was observed that this could not be necessary; as in case the section as to originating bills should not be reinstated, and a revision of the Constitution should ensue, it wd. still be proper that the members should ⟨vote⟩ per capita. A postponement of the preceding sentence allowing to each State 2 members wd. have been more proper.

* ⟨In the printed Journal Pennsylvania, ay.⟩

[7] Crossed out "State".

Mr. Mason, did not mean to propose a change of this mode of voting per capita in any event. But as there might be other modes proposed, he saw no impropriety in postponing the sentence. Each State may have two members, ⟨and⟩ yet may have ⟨unequal⟩[8] votes. He said that unless the exclusive originating of money bills should be restored to the House of Representatives, he should, not from obstinacy, but duty and conscience, oppose throughout the equality of Representation in the Senate.

Mr. Govr. Morris. Such declarations were he supposed, addressed to the smaller States in order to alarm them for their equality in the Senate, and induce them agst. their judgments, to concur in restoring the section concerning money bills. He would declare in his turn that as he saw no prospect of amending the Constitution of the Senate & considered the Section ⟨relating to money bills⟩ as intrinsically bad, he would adhere to the section establishing the equality at all events.

Mr. Wilson. It seems to have been supposed by some that the section concerning money bills is desirable to the large States. The fact was that two of those States (Pa. & Va) had uniformly voted agst. it without reference to any other part of the system.

Mr. Randolph, urged as Col. Mason had done that the sentence under consideration was connected with that relating to money ⟨bills⟩, and might possibly be affected by the result of the motion for reconsidering the latter. That the postponement was therefore ⟨not⟩ improper.

Question for postponing "each member shall have one vote."

N. H. divd. Mas. no. Ct. no. N. J. no. Pa. no. Del. no. Md. no. Va. ay. N. C. ay. S. C. no. Geo. no. [Ayes — 2; noes — 8; divided — 1.]

⟨The words were then agreed to as part of the section.⟩[9]

Mr. Randolph then gave notice that he should move to reconsider this whole Sect: 1. Art. V. as connected with the 5. Sect. art. IV. as to which he had already given such notice.

---

[8] Crossed out "different". [9] Taken from *Journal.*

Art. V. sect. 2d. taken up.[10]

Mr. Govr. Morris moved to insert after the words "immediately after", the following "they shall be assembled in consequence of" which was agreed to nem. con. as was then the whole sect 2.

Art: V. sect. 3. taken up.[11]

Mr. Govr. Morris moved to insert 14 instead of 4 years citizenship as a qualification for Senators; urging the danger of admitting strangers into our public Councils. Mr. Pinkney 2ds. him

Mr. Elseworth. was opposed to the motion as discouraging meritorious aliens from emigrating to this Country.

Mr. Pinkney. As the Senate is to have the power of making treaties & managing our foreign affairs, there is peculiar danger and impropriety in opening its door to those who have foreign attachments. He quoted the jealousy of the Athenians on this subject who made it death for any stranger to intrude his voice into their legislative proceedings.

Col. Mason highly approved of the policy of the motion. Were it not that many not natives of this Country had acquired great merit during the revolution, he should be for restraining the eligibility into the Senate, to natives.

Mr. ⟨Madison⟩ was not averse to some restrictions on this subject; but could never agree to the proposed amendment. He thought any restriction ⟨however⟩ in the *Constitution*[12] unnecessary, and improper. unnecessary; because the Natl. Legislre. is to have the right of regulating naturalization, and can by virtue thereof fix different periods of residence as conditions of enjoying different privileges of Citizenship: Im-

[10] Article V, Sect. 2. "The Senators shall be chosen for six years; but immediately after the first election they shall be divided, by lot, into three classes, as nearly as may be, numbered one, two and three. The seats of the members of the first class shall be vacated at the expiration of the second year, of the second class at the expiration of the fourth year, of the third class at the expiration of the sixth year, so that a third part of the members may be chosen every second year."

[11] Article V, Sect. 3. "Exery member of the Senate shall be of the age of thirty years at least; shall have been a citizen of the United States for at least four years before his election; and shall be, at the time of his election, a resident of the State for which he shall be chosen."

[12] Underscoring was a later revision.

proper: because it will give a tincture of illiberality to the Constitution: because it will put it out of the power of the Natl Legislature even by special acts of naturalization to confer the full rank of Citizens on meritorious strangers & because it will discourage the most desirable class of people from emigrating to the U. S. Should the proposed Constitution have the intended effect of giving stability & reputation to our Govts. great numbers of respectable Europeans; men who love liberty and wish to partake its blessings, will be ready to transfer their fortunes hither. All such would feel the mortification of being marked with suspicious incapacitations though they sd. not covet the public honors He was not apprehensive that any dangerous number of strangers would be appointed by the State Legislatures, if they were left at liberty to do so: nor that foreign powers would make use of strangers as instruments for their purposes. Their bribes would be expended on men whose circumstances would rather stifle than excite jealousy & watchfulness in the public.

Mr. Butler was decidely opposed to the admission of foreigners without a long residence in the Country. They bring with them, not only attachments to other Countries; but ideas of Govt. so distinct from ours that in every point of view they are dangerous. He acknowledged that if he himself had been called into public life within a short time after his coming to America, his foreign habits opinions & attachments would have rendered him an improper agent in public affairs. He mentioned the great strictness observed in Great Britain on this subject.

Docr. Franklin was not agst. a reasonable time, but should be very sorry to see any thing like illiberality inserted in the Constitution. The people in Europe are friendly to this Country. Even in the Country with which we have been lately at war, We have now & had during the war, a great many friends not only among the people at large but in both Houses of Parliament. In every other Country in Europe all the people are our friends. We found in the Course of the Revolution, that many strangers served us faithfully — and that many natives took part agst. their Country. When

foreigners after looking about for some other Country in which they can obtain more happiness, give a preference to ours, it is a proof of attachment which ought to excite our confidence & affection.

Mr. Randolph did not know but it might be problematical whether emigrations to this Country were on the whole useful or not: but he could never agree to the motion for disabling them for 14 years to participate in the public honours. He reminded the Convention of the language held by our patriots during the Revolution, and the principles laid down in all our American Constitutions. Many foreigners may have fixed their fortunes among us under the faith of these invitations. All persons under this description with all others who would be affected by such a regulation, would enlist themselves under the banners of hostility to the proposed System. He would go as far as seven years, but no further.

Mr. Wilson said he rose with feelings which were perhaps peculiar; mentioning the circumstance of his not being a native, and the possibility, if the ideas of some gentlemen should be pursued, of his being incapacitated from holding a place under the very Constitution which he had shared in the trust of making. He remarked the illiberal complexion which the motion would give to the System, & the effect which a good system would have in inviting meritorious foreigners among us, and the discouragement & mortification they must feel from the degrading discrimination, now proposed. He had himself experienced this mortification. On his removal into Maryland, he found himself, from defect of residence, under certain legal incapacities, which never ceased to produce chagrin, though he assuredly did not desire & would not have accepted the offices to which they related. To be appointed to a place may be matter of indifference. To be incapable of being appointed, is a circumstance grating, and mortifying.

Mr. Govr. Morris. The lesson we are taught is that we should be governed as much by our reason, and as little by our feelings as possible. What is the language of Reason on this subject? That we should not be polite at the expense

of prudence. There was a moderation in all things. It is said that some tribes of Indians, carried their hospitality so far as to offer to strangers their wives and daughters. Was this a proper model for us? He would admit them to his house, he would invite them to his table, would provide for them comfortable lodgings; but would not carry the complaisance so far as, to bed them with his wife. He would let them worship at the same altar, but did not choose to make Priests of them. He ran over the privileges which emigrants would enjoy among us, though they should be deprived of that of being eligible to the great offices of Government; observing that they exceeded the privileges allowed to foreigners in any part of the world; and that as every Society from a great nation down to a club had the right of declaring the conditions on which new members should be admitted, there could be no room for complaint. As to those philosophical gentlemen, those Citizens of the World, as they called themselves, He owned he did not wish to see any of them in our public Councils. He would not trust them. The men who can shake off their attachments to their own Country can never love any other. These attachments are the wholesome prejudices which uphold all Governments, Admit a Frenchman into your Senate, and he will study to increase the commerce of France: An Englishman, he will feel an equal bias in favor of that of England. It has been said that The Legislatures will not chuse foreigners, at least improper ones. There was no knowing what Legislatures would do. Some appointments made by them, proved that every thing ought to be apprehended from the cabals practised on such occasions. He mentioned the case of a foreigner who left this State in disgrace, and worked himself into an appointment from ⟨another⟩[13] to Congress.

Question on the motion of Mr. Govr. Morris to insert 14 in place of 4 years

N. H. ay. Mas. no. Ct. no. N. J. ay. Pa. no. Del. no. Md. no. Va. no. N. C. no. S. C. ay. Geo. ay. [Ayes—4; noes—7.]

[13] Crossed out "Georgia".

On 13 years, moved Mr. Govr. Morris

N. H. ay. Mas. no. Ct. no. N. J. ay. Pa. no Del. no. Md. no. Va. no. N. C. no. S. C. ay. Geo. ay. [Ayes — 4; noes — 7.]

On 10 years moved by Genl Pinkney

N. H. ay. Mas. no. Ct. no. N. J. ay. Pa. no. Del. no. Md. no. Va. no. N. C. no. S. C. ay. Geo. ay. [Ayes — 4; noes — 7.]

Dr. Franklin reminded the Convention that it did not follow from an omission to insert the restriction in the Constitution that the persons in question wd. be actually chosen into the Legislature.

Mr. Rutlidge. 7 years of Citizenship have been required for the House of Representatives. Surely a longer time is requisite for the Senate, which will have more power.

Mr. Williamson. It is more necessary to guard the Senate in this case than the other House. Bribery & Cabal can be more easily practised in the choice of the Senate which is to be made by the Legislatures composed of a few men, than of the House of Represents. who will be chosen by the people.

Mr. Randolph will agree to 9 years with the expectation that it will be reduced to seven if Mr. Wilson's motion to reconsider the vote fixing 7 years for the House of Representatives should produce a reduction of that period.

On a question for 9 years

N. H. ay. Mas. no. Ct. no. N. J. ay. Pa. no. Del. ay. Md. no. Va. ay. N. C. divd. S. C. ay. Geo. ay. [Ayes — 6; noes — 4; divided — 1.]

The term "Resident" was struck out, & "inhabitant" inserted nem. con.

Art. V Sect. 3. as amended agreed to nem. con.

Sect. 4. agreed to nem. con.[14]

Art. VI. sect. 1. taken up.[15]

Mr. ⟨Madison⟩ — & Mr. Govr. Morris moved to strike

---

[14] Article V, Sect. 4. "The Senate shall chuse its own President and other officers."

[15] Article VI, Sect. 1. "The times and places and manner of holding the elections of the members of each House shall be prescribed by the Legislature of each State; but their provisions concerning them may, at any time, be altered by the Legislature of the United States."

out "each House" & ⟨to insert "the House of Representatives";⟩[16] the right of the Legislatures to regulate the times & places &c. in ⟨the election of Senators⟩ being involved in the right of appointing ⟨them⟩, which was ⟨disagreed to.⟩[17]

Division of the question being called, it was taken on the first part down to "but their provisions concerning &c"

The first part was agreed to nem. con.

Mr. Pinkney & Mr. Rutlidge moved to strike out the remaining part viz but their provisions concerning them may at any time be altered by the Legislature of the United States."[18] The States they contended could & must be relied on in such cases.

Mr Ghorum. It would be as improper take this power from the Natl. Legislature, as to Restrain the British Parliament from regulating the circumstances of elections, leaving this business to the Counties themselves —

Mr ⟨Madison⟩. The necessity of a Genl. Govt. supposes that the State Legislatures will sometimes fail or refuse to consult the common interest at the expense of their local conveniency or prejudices. The policy of referring the appointment of the House of Representatives to the people and not to the Legislatures of the States, supposes that the result will be somewhat influenced by the mode, This view of the question seems to decide that the Legislatures of the States ought not to have the uncontrouled right of regulating the times places & manner of holding elections. These were words of great latitude. It was impossible to foresee all the abuses that might be made of the discretionary power. Whether the electors should vote by ballot or vivâ voce, should assemble at this place or that place; should be divided into districts or all meet at one place, shd all vote for all the representatives; or all in a district vote for a number allotted to the district;

---

[16] Revised from *Journal*. Crossed out "to alter so as to restrain not to extend to the Senate;".

[17] Madison originally recorded "agd. to", but changed this in accordance with *Journal*.

[18] Upon this question and debate, see Appendix A, CXLVI*a*, CLVIII(35), CLXXXII, CCX, CCXXVI, and CCXLVIII.

these & many other points would depend on the Legislatures. and might materially affect the appointments. Whenever the State Legislatures had a favorite measure to carry, they would take care so to mould their regulations as to favor the candidates they wished to succeed. Besides, the inequality of the Representation in the Legislatures of particular States, would produce a like inequality in their representation in the Natl. Legislature, as it was presumable that the Counties having the power in the former case would secure it to themselves in the latter. What danger could there be in giving a controuling power to the Natl. Legislature? Of whom was it to consist? 1. of a Senate to be chosen by the State Legislatures. If the latter therefore could be trusted, their representatives could not be dangerous. 2. of Representatives elected by the same people who elect the State Legislatures; surely then if confidence is due to the latter, it must be due to the former. It seemed as improper in principle — though it might be less inconvenient in practice, to give to the State Legislatures this great authority over the election of the Representatives of the people in the Genl. Legislature, as it would be to give to the latter a like power over the election of their Representatives in the State Legislatures.

Mr. King. If this power be not given to the Natl. Legislature, their right of judging of the returns of their members may be frustrated. No probability has been suggested of its being abused by them. Altho this scheme of erecting the Genl. Govt. on the authority of the State Legislatures has been fatal to the federal establishment, it would seem as if many gentlemen, still foster the dangerous idea.

Mr. Govr. Morris — observed that the States might make false returns and then make no provisions for new elections

Mr. Sherman did not know but it might be best to retain the clause, though he had himself sufficient confidence in the State Legislatures. ⟨The motion of Mr. P. & Mr. R. did not prevail⟩

⟨The word "respectively" was inserted after the word "State"⟩[19]

---

[19] Taken from *Journal*.

On the motion of Mr Read the word "their" was struck out, & "regulations in such cases" inserted in place of "provisions concerning them". ⟨the clause then reading — "but regulations, in each of the foregoing cases may at any time, be made or altered by the Legislature of the U. S.⟩[20] This was meant to give the Natl. Legislature a power not only to alter the provisions of the States, but to make regulations in case the States should fail or refuse altogether.

Art. VI. Sect. 1 — as thus amended was agreed to nem. con.

Adjourned.

KING

5. Art. S. 1 — Wilson moves to strike out the clause authorising the State Executives to supply Vacancies in the Senate observing that the case may be safely lodged with the Senate — Randolph agt. the motion — because the Senate is the Br. where the Interest of the States will be deposited — They ought then to be constantly represented — in case of Treaty, or the election of Ambassadors, each state ought to be present — the State Legislatures may be in recess at the Time of a vacancy in the senate — If the place is not supplied the state may suffer a very great Inconvenience — Wilson — I think Legislators are improper Electors of the Executive — and so the Executive is an unqualified Elector of the Legislators —

G Morris

Liberal & illiberal — The terms are indefinite — The Indians are the most liberal, because when a Stranger comes among them they offer him yr. wife & Daughters for his carnal amusement —

It is said yt. we threw open our Doors — invited the oppressed of all Countries to come & find an Asylum in America — This is true we invited them to come and worship in our Temple but we never invited them to become Priests at our Altar — We shd. cherish the love of our country — This is a whole-

[20] Revised from *Journal*.

some prejudice and is in favor of our Country — Foreigners will not learn our laws & Constitution under 14 yrs. — 7 yrs must be applied to learn to be a Shoe Maker — 14 at least are necessary to learn to be an Amer. Legislator —
Again — that period will be requisite to eradicate the Affections of Education and native Attachments —

Franklin — I am agt. the Term of 14 yrs — it looks illiberal — we have many good Friends in Engld. & other parts of Europe — they ought not to be excluded —
Wilson — agt. the motion for 14 yrs —[21]

McHENRY

August 9.

6 and 7 sects. agreed to without amendment.

The 1 section of the V article underwent an emendatory alteration. The last clause — "each member shall have one vote" — opposed by Mr. Mason, Randolph and a few others on account of the Senate by the loss of the 5 sect of the IV article having the same powers over money bills as the house of representatives. — The whole however was agreed to.

Sect. 2. agreed to after an emendatory addition.

Sect. 3 agreed to after inserting inhabitant for resident, as being less equivocal, and 9 years for 4 years.

Governeur Morris proposed insted of 4 years 14. He would have confined the members he said to natives — but for its appearance and the effects it might have against the system.

Mr. *Mason* had the same wishes, but he could not think of excluding those foreigners who had taken a part and borne with the country the dangers and burdenths of the war.

Mr. Maddison was against such an invidious distinction. The matter might be safely intrusted to the respective legislatures. Doctor Franklin was of the same opinion. Mr. Willson expressed himself feelingly on the same side. It might happen, he said, that he who had been thought worthy of

[21] [Endorsed:] Term of Citizenship | to be a senator | Gov. Morris for 14 yrs | Franklin agt.

being trusted with the framing of the Constitution, might be excluded from it. He had not been born in this country. He considered such exclusing as one of the most galling chains which the human mind could experience, It was wrong to deprive the government of the talents virtue and abilities of such foreigners as might chuse to remove to this country. The corrup of other countries would not come here. Those who were tired in opposing such corruptions would be drawn hither, etc. etc.

Sect. 4 agreed to.

Article VI.

Sect. 1. Agreed to with this amendment insted of "*but their provisions concerning them.*"

adjourned

FRIDAY, AUGUST 10, 1787.

JOURNAL

Friday August 10. 1787.

It was moved and seconded to strike out 2nd sect. of the 6. article in order to introduce the following namely

"That the qualifications of the members of the Legislature "be as follows.

"The members of the House of representatives shall possess "a clear and unincumbered property of

"The Members of the Senate"

which passed in the negative

It was moved and seconded to strike the following words out of the 2nd sect. of the 6. article, namely

"with regard to property"

which passed in the negative. [Ayes — 4; noes — 6.]

On the question to agree to the 2nd sect. of the 6. article as reported.

it passed in the negative. [Ayes — 3; noes — 7.]

It was moved and seconded to reconsider the 2nd sect. of the 4th article

which passed in the affirmative [Ayes — 6; noes — 5.]

and monday next was assigned for the reconsideration [Ayes — 9; noes — 2.]

It was moved and seconded to amend the 3rd sect. of the 6. article to read as follows, namely.

"not less than 33 members of the House of representa-"tives, nor less that 14 members of the Senate, shall consti-"tute a quorum to do business; a smaller number in either "House may adjourn from day to day, but the number neces-"sary to form such quorum may be encreased by an act of "the Legislature on the addition of members in either branch"

which passed in the negative [Ayes — 2; noes — 9.][1]

---

[1] Vote 268, Detail of Ayes and Noes, which notes that the amendment was "offd by Mr. King".

It was moved and seconded to add the following amendment to the 3rd sect. of the 6. article

"and may be authorised to compel the attendance of ab-"sent members in such manner and under such penalties as "each House may provide"

which passed in the affirmative [Ayes — 10; noes — 0; divided — 1.][2]

On the question to agree to the 3rd sect. of the 6. article as amended

it passed in the affirmative

On the question to agree to the 4 sect of the 6 article as reported

it passed in the affirmative

On the question to agree to the 5. sect. of the 6 article as reported

it passed in the affirmative

It was moved and seconded to amend the last clause in the 6 sect. of the 6. article by adding the following words

"with the concurrence of two thirds"

which passed in the affirmative [Ayes — 10; noes — 0; divided — 1.]

On the question to agree to the 6 sect. of the 6 article as amended

it passed in the affirmative

It was moved and seconded to strike out the words

"one fifth part" and to insert the words "of every one Member present" in the latter clause of the 7. sect. of the 6 article

which passed in the negative.[3]

It was moved and seconded to strike out the words "each House" and to insert the words "the House of representatives" in the second clause of the 7 sect of the 6 article — and to add the following words to the section, namely

"and any member of the Senate shall be at liberty to enter his dissent"

---

[2] Vote 269, Detail of Ayes and Noes, which notes that the amendment was Randolph's.

[3] *Journal* (p. 243) ascribes Vote 271 to this question, but there is nothing in the Detail of Ayes and Noes to indicate this, and according to Madison it belongs to the following question.

which passed in the negative [Ayes — 3; noes — 8.][4]
It was moved and seconded to strike the following words out of the 7 sect of the 6 article, namely

"when it shall be acting in a legislative capacity"

and to add the following words to the section

"except such parts thereof as in their judgment require secrecy"

which passed in the affirmative. [Ayes — 7; noes — 3; divided — 1.][5]

And then the House adjourned till to-morrow at 11 o'clock A. M.

DETAIL OF AYES AND NOES

	New Hampshire	Massachusetts	Rhode Island	Connecticut	New York	New Jersey	Pennsylvania	Delaware	Maryland	Virginia	North Carolina	South Carolina	Georgia	Questions	Ayes	Noes	Divided
[264]	no	no		aye		aye	aye		no	no	no	no	aye	To strike out the words "with regard to property"	4	6	
[265]	aye	aye		no		no	no		no	no	no	no	aye	To agree to the 2 sect. of ye 6. article as reported	3	7	
[266]	no	no		aye		no	aye	aye	aye	aye	aye	no	no	To reconsider the 2 sect of 4 art.	6	5	
[267]	aye	no		aye		aye	aye	aye	aye	aye	aye	aye	no	Monday assigned	9	2	
[268]	no	aye		no		no	no	aye	no	no	no	no	no	To agree to the amendmt of ye 3 sect. 6 art. offd by Mr King	2	9	
[269]	aye	aye		aye		aye	dd	aye	aye	aye	aye	aye	aye	To agree to Mr Randolphs amendmt to ye 3 sect 6 art.	10		1
[270]	aye	aye		aye		aye	dd	aye	aye	aye	aye	aye	aye	Two-thirds required to expel a member	10		1
[Beginning of ninth loose sheet]																	
[271]	no	no		no		no	no	no	aye	aye	no	aye	no	To agree to the amendmt proposed to the 7 Sect of the 6 article by Mr Carrol	3	8	
[272]	dd	aye		no		no	no	aye	aye	aye	aye	aye	aye	To agree to Mr Gerry's amendment to the 7 section of the 6 article	7	3	1

[4] Vote 271, Detail of Ayes and Noes, which notes "amendt proposed . . . by Mr. Carrol".

[5] Vote 272, Detail of Ayes and Noes, which notes that it was "Mr. Gerry's amendment".

MADISON

Friday Augst. 10. in Convention

Art. VI. sect. 2. taken up.[6]

Mr. Pinkney — The Committee as he had conceived were instructed to report the proper qualifications of property for the members of the Natl. Legislature; instead of which they have referred the task to the Natl. Legislature itself. Should it be left on this footing, the first Legislature will meet without any particular qualifications of property; and if it should happen to consist of rich men they might fix such such qualifications as may be too favorable to the rich; if of poor men, an opposite extreme might be run into. He was opposed to the establishment of an undue aristocratic influence in the Constitution but he thought it essential that the members of the Legislature, the Executive, and the Judges — should be possessed of competent property to make them independent & respectable. It was prudent when such great powers were to be trusted to connect the tie of property with that of reputation in securing a faithful administration. The Legislature would have the fate of the Nation put into their hands. The President would also have a very great influence on it. The Judges would have not only important causes between Citizen & Citizen but also where foreigners are concerned. They will even be the Umpires between the U. States and individual States as well as between one State & another. Were he to fix the quantum of property which should be required, he should not think of less than one hundred thousand dollars for the President, half of that sum for each of the Judges, and in like proportion for the members of the Natl. Legislature. He would however leave the sums blank. His motion was that the President of the U. S. the Judges, and members of the Legislature should be required to swear that they were respectively possessed of a clear unincumbered

[6] Article VI, Sect. 2. "The Legislature of the United States shall have authority to establish such uniform qualifications of the members of each House, with regard to property, as to the said Legislature shall seem expedient."

Estate to the amount of ——— in the case of the President, &c &c —

Mr. Rutlidge seconded the motion; observing, that the Committee had reported no qualifications because they could not agree on any among themselves, being embarrassed by the danger on ⟨one⟩ side of displeasing the people by making them ⟨high⟩, and on the other of rendering them nugatory by making them low.

Mr. Elseworth. The different circumstances of different parts of the U. S. and the probable difference between the present and future circumstances of the whole, render it improper to have either *uniform* or *fixed* qualifications. Make them so high as to be useful in the S. States, and they will be inapplicable to the E. States. Suit them to the latter, and they will serve no purpose in the former. In like manner what may be accommodated to the existing State of things among us, may be very inconvenient in some future state of them. He thought for these reasons that it was better to leave this matter to the Legislative discretion than to attempt a provision for it in the Constitution.

Doctr Franklin expressed his dislike of every thing that tended to debase the spirit of the common people. If honesty was often the companion of wealth, and if poverty was exposed to peculiar temptation, it was not less true that the possession of property increased the desire of more property- Some of the greatest rogues he was ever acquainted with, were the richest rogues. We should remember the character which the Scripture requires in Rulers, that they should be men hating covetousness- This Constitution will be much read and attended to in Europe, and if it should betray a great partiality to the rich- will not only hurt us in the esteem of the most liberal and enlightened men there, but discourage the common people from removing to this Country.

The Motion of Mr. Pinkney was rejected by so general a *no*, that the States were not called.

Mr ⟨Madison⟩ was opposed to the Section as vesting an improper & dangerous power in the Legislature. The qualifications of electors and elected were fundamental articles in a

Republican Govt. and ought to be fixed by the Constitution. If the Legislature could regulate those of either, it can by degrees subvert the Constitution. A Republic may be converted into an aristocracy or oligarchy as well by limiting the number capable of being elected, as the number authorised to elect. In all cases where the representatives of the people will have a personal interest distinct from that of their Constituents, there was the same reason for being jealous of them, as there was for relying on them with full confidence, when they had a common interest. This was one of the former cases. It was as improper as to allow them to fix their own wages, or their own privileges. It was a power also, which might be made subservient to the views of one faction agst. another. Qualifications founded on artificial distinctions may be devised,[7] by the stronger in order to keep out partizans of ⟨a weaker⟩[8] faction.

Mr. Elseworth, admitted that the power was not unexceptionable; but he could not view it as dangerous. Such a power with regard to the electors would be dangerous because it would be much more liable to abuse.

Mr. Govr. Morris moved to strike out "with regard to property" in order to leave the Legislature entirely at large.

Mr. Williamson. This could surely never be admitted. Should a majority of the Legislature be composed of any particular description of men, of lawyers for example, which is no improbable supposition, the future elections might be secured to their own body.

Mr. ⟨Madison⟩ observed that the British Parliamt. possessed the power of regulating the qualifications both of the electors, and the elected; and the abuse they had made of it was a lesson worthy of our attention. They had made the changes in both cases subservient to their own views, or to the views of political or Religious parties.

Question on the motion to strike out with regard to property

N. H. no. Mas. no. Ct. ay. N. J. ay. Pa. ay. Del. no.* Md. no. Va. no. N. C. no. S. C. no. Geo- ay. [Ayes—4; noes—7.]

* ⟨In the printed Journal Delaware did not vote.⟩

[7] Crossed out "which may exclude obnoxious".

[8] Crossed out "the opposite".

Mr Rutlidge was opposed to leaving the power to the Legislature– He proposed that the qualifications should be the same as for members of the State Legislatures.

Mr. Wilson thought it would be best on the whole to let the Section go out. A uniform rule would probably be never fixed by the Legislature. and this particular power would constructively exclude every other power of regulating qualifications–

On the question for agreeing to Art– VI– sect– 2d

N. H. ay. Mas. ay. Ct. no. N. J. no. Pa. no. Md. no. Va. no. ⟨N. C. no⟩ S. C. no. Geo. ay– [Ayes — 3; noes — 7.]

On Motion of Mr Wilson to reconsider Art: IV. sect. 2. so as to restore 3 in place of seven years of citizenship as a qualification for being elected into the House of Represents.

N. H– no. Mas– no. Ct. ay. N. J. no. Pa. ay. Del. ay. Md. ay. Va. ay. N. C. ay. S. C. no. Geo. no. [Ayes — 6; noes — 5.]

⟨Monday next was then assigned for the reconsideration: all the States being ay– except Massts. & Georgia⟩ [9]

Art: VI. sect. 3. taken up.[10]

Mr. Ghorum contended that less than a Majority ⟨in each House⟩ should be made of Quorum, otherwise great delay might happen in business, and great inconvenience from the future increase of numbers.

Mr. Mercer was also for less than a majority. So great a number will put it in the power of a few by seceding at a critical moment to introduce convulsions, and endanger the Governmt. Examples of secession have already happened in some of the States. He was for leaving it to the Legislature to fix the Quorum, as in Great Britain, where the requisite number is small & no inconveniency has been experienced.

Col. Mason. This is a valuable & necessary part of the plan. In this extended Country, embracing so great a diversity of interests, it would be dangerous to the distant parts to

[9] Taken from *Journal.* Madison originally included this question as a part of the one preceding.

[10] Article VI, sect. 3. "In each House a majority of the members shall constitute a quorum to do business; but a smaller number may adjourn from day to day."

allow a small number of members of the two Houses to make laws. The Central States could always take care to be on the Spot and by meeting earlier than the distant ones, or wearying their patience, and outstaying them, could carry such measures as they pleased. He admitted that inconveniences might spring from the secession of a small number: But he had also known good produced by an apprehension of it. He had known a paper emission prevented by that cause in Virginia. He thought the Constitution as now moulded was founded on sound principles, and was disposed to put into it extensive powers. At the same time he wished to guard agst abuses as much as possible. If the Legislature should be able to reduce the number at all, it might reduce it as low as it pleased & the U. States might be governed by a Juncto– A majority of the number which had been agreed on, was so few that he feared it would be made an objection agst. the plan.

Mr. King admitted there might be some danger of giving an advantage to the Central States; but was of opinion that the public inconveniency on the other side was more to be dreaded.

Mr. Govr. Morris moved to fix the quorum at 33 members in the H. of Reps. & 14 in the Senate. This is a majority of the present number, and will be a bar to the Legislature: fix the number low and they will generally attend knowing that advantage may be taken of their absence. the Secession of a small number ought not to be suffered to break a quorum. Such events in the States may have been of little consequence. In the national Councils, they may be fatal. Besides other mischiefs, if a few can break up a quorum, they may sieze a moment when a particular ⟨part⟩ of the Continent may be in need of immediate aid, to extort, by threatening a secession, some unjust & selfish measure.

Mr. Mercer 2ded. the motion

Mr. King said he had just prepared a motion[11] which instead of fixing the numbers proposed by Mr. Govr Morris as Quorums, made those the lowest numbers, leaving the

[11] In the MS. the word "motion" has a cross (×) above it, evidently referring to the motion as given on the following page and similarly marked.

Legislature at liberty to increase them or not. He thought the future increase of members would render a majority of the whole extremely cumbersome.

Mr. Mercer agreed to substitute Mr. Kings motion in place of Mr. Morris's.

Mr. Elseworth was opposed to it. It would be a pleasing ground of confidence to the people that no law or burden could be imposed on them, by a few men. He reminded the movers that the Constitution proposed to give such a discretion with regard to the number of Representatives that a very inconvenient number was not to be apprehended. The inconveniency of secessions may be guarded agst by giving to each House an authority to require the attendance of absent members.

Mr. Wilson concurred in the sentiments of Mr. Elseworth.

Mr. Gerry seemed to think that some further precautions than merely fixing the quorum might be necessary. He observed that as 17 wd. be a majority of a quorum of 33, and 8 of 14, questions might by possibility be carried in the H. of Reps. by 2 large States, and in the Senate by the same States with the aid of two small ones. — He proposed that the number for a quorum in the H. of Reps. should not exceed 50 ⟨nor be less than 33⟩. leaving the intermediate discretion to the Legislature.

Mr. King. as the quorum could not be altered witht. the concurrence of the President by less than ⅔ of each House, he thought there could be no danger in trusting the Legislature.

Mr Carrol this will be no security agst. a continuance of the quorums at 33 & 14. when they ought to be increased.

On question on Mr. Kings motion ⟨"that not less than 33 in the H. of Reps. nor less than 14 in the Senate shd. constitute a Quorum, which may be increased by a law, on additions of members in either House.⟩ [12]

N. H. no. Mas. ay. Ct. no. N. J. no. Pa. no. Del. ay. Md. no. Va. no. N. C. no. S. C. no. Geo. no. [Ayes — 2; noes — 9.]

Mr. Randolph & Mr. — ⟨Madison⟩ moved to add to the

[12] Taken from *Journal*. In the MS. marked by a cross (×), see above, note 11.

end of Art. VI Sect 3, "and ⟨may⟩ be authorized to compel the attendance of absent members in such manner & under such penalties as each House may provide." Agreed to ⟨by all except Pena — which was divided⟩ [13]

Art: VI. Sect. 3. Agreed to as amended Nem. con.

Sect. 4. } Agreed to nem. con.[14]
Sect. 5. }

Mr. ⟨Madison⟩ observed that the right of expulsion (Art. VI. Sect. 6.)[15] was too important to be exercised by a bare majority of a quorum: and in emergencies of faction might be dangerously abused. He moved that "with the concurrence of ⅔" might be inserted between may & expel.

Mr. Randolph & Mr. Mason approved the idea.

Mr Govr Morris. This power may be safely trusted to a majority. To require more may produce abuses on the side of the minority. A few men from factious motives may keep in a member who ought to be expelled.

Mr. Carrol thought that the concurrence of ⅔ at least ought to be required.

On the question for requiring ⅔ in cases of expelling a member.

N. H. ay– Mas. ay. Ct. ay– N. J– ay. Pa. divd. Del. ay. Md. ay. Va. ay. N– C. ay– S. C. ay. Geo. ay. [Ayes— 10; noes — 0; divided — 1.]

Art. VI– Sect– 6– as thus amended agreed to nem. con.

Art: VI. Sect. 7. taken up.[16]

---

[13] Taken from *Journal*. Crossed out: "nem. con."

[14] Article VI, Sect. 4. "Each House shall be the judge of the elections, returns and qualifications of its own members."

Sect. 5. "Freedom of speech and debate in the Legislature shall not be impeached or questioned in any Court or place out of the Legislature; and the members of each House shall, in all cases, except treason felony and breach of the peace, be privileged from arrest during their attendance at Congress, and in going to and returning from it."

[15] Article VI, Sect. 6. "Each House may determine the rules of its proceedings; may punish its members for disorderly behaviour; and may expel a member."

[16] Article VI, Sect. 7. "The House of Representatives, and the Senate, when it shall be acting in a legislative capacity, shall keep a Journal of their proceedings, and shall, from time to time, publish them: and the yeas and nays of the members of each House, on any question, shall at the desire of one-fifth part of the members present, be entered on the journal."

Mr. Govr Morris urged that if the yeas & nays were proper at all any individual ought to be authorized to call for them: and moved an amendment to that effect. — The small States may otherwise be under a disadvantage, and find it difficult. to get a concurrence of $\frac{1}{5}$

Mr. Randolph 2ded. ye motion.

Mr. Sherman had rather strike out the yeas & nays altogether. they never have done any good, and have done much mischief. They are not proper as the reasons governing the voter never appear along with them.

Mr Elseworth was of the same opinion

Col. Mason liked the Section as it stood. it was a middle way between two extremes.

Mr Ghorum was opposed to the motion for allowing a single member to call the yeas & nays, and recited the abuses of it, in Massts. 1 in stuffing the journals with them on frivolous occasions. 2 in misleading the people who never know the reasons determining the votes.

The motion for allowing a single member to call the yeas & nays was disagd. to nem- con-

Mr. Carrol & Mr. Randolph moved ⟨to strike out the words "each House" and to insert the words "the House of Representatives" in sect- 7. art- 6. and to add to the Section the words "and any member of the Senate shall be at liberty to enter his dissent"⟩[17]

Mr. Govr Morris & Mr Wilson observed that if the minority were to have a right to enter their votes & reasons, the other side would have a right to complain, if it were not extended to them: & to allow it to both, would fill the Journals, like the records of a Court, with replications, rejoinders &c-

Question on Mr Carrols motion to allow a member to ⟨enter his⟩ dissent

N. H- no. Mas. no. Cont. no. N. J. no. Pa. no. Del. no. Md. ay. Va. ay. N. C. no. S. C. ay. Geo. no. [Ayes — 3; noes — 8.]

Mr Gerry moved to strike out the words "when it shall

[17] Taken from *Journal*, but Madison had recorded the substance of the motion.

be acting in its legislative capacity" in order to extend the provision to the Senate when exercising its peculiar authorities ⟨and to insert "except such parts thereof as in their judgment require secrecy" after the words "publish them"⟩. —(It was thought by others that provision should be made with respect to these when that part came under consideration which proposed to vest those ⟨additional⟩ authorities in the Senate.)

On this question for striking out the words "when acting in its Legislative capacity"

N. H. divd. Mas ay. Ct. no. N. J. no. Pa. no. Del. ay. Md. ay. Va. ay– N. C. ay. S. C– ay. Geo. ay– [Ayes—7; noes—3; divided — 1.]

Adjourned

McHENRY

August 10.

Sect. 2. dissented to. Sects. 3. 4 5 and 6 agreed to.[18]

[18] See Appendix A, CXLVI*a*.

SATURDAY, AUGUST 11, 1787.

JOURNAL

Saturday August 11. 1787.

It was moved and seconded to amend the first clause of the 7 sect. of the 6 article to read as follows namely

"Each House shall keep a Journal of it's proceedings, and "shall from time to time publish the same; except such part "of the proceedings of the Senate when acting not in it's "Legislative capacity as may be judged by that House to "require secrecy"

which passed in the negative. [Ayes — 1; noes — 10.][1]

It was moved and seconded to insert in the first clause of the 7 sect of the 6 article after the word "thereof" the following words

"relative to Treaties and military operations"

which passed in the negative. [Ayes — 2; noes — 9.][2]

[On the 1st clause of the 7 sect. of the 6 article as reported

Ayes — 11; noes 0.

except such parts thereof as in their judgment require secrecy.

Ayes — 6; noes — 4; divided — 1.

To agree to the last clause of the 7 sect of the 6 art.

Ayes — 11; noes — 0.][3]

On the question to agree to the 7. sect. of the 6 article as amended

it passed in the affirmative

[To commit the 2nd clause of the 7 sect. 6 art.

Ayes —4; noes — 7.

---

[1] Vote 273, Detail of Ayes and Noes, which notes that it was "Mr. Madison's amendmt".

[2] Vote 274, Detail of Ayes and Noes, which states the question more correctly.

[3] Votes 275–277, Detail of Ayes and Noes.

"nor to any other place than that at which the two Houses are sitting" 8 sect. 6 article Ayes — 10; noes — 1.][4]
It was moved and seconded to alter the 8th sect. of the 6. article to read as follows, namely,

"The Legislature shall at their first assembling determine "on a place at which their future Sessions shall be held: "neither House shall afterwards, during the Session of the "House of Representatives, without the consent of the other, "adjourn for more than three days, nor shall they adjourn to "any other place than such as shall have been fixed by law"

which passed in the negative

It was moved and seconded to prefix the following words to the 8 sect. of the 6 article, namely

"During the session of the Legislature"[5]

and to strike out the last clause of the section

which passed in the affirmative

On the question to agree to the 8 sect. of the 6 article as amended.

it passed in the affirmative

It was moved and seconded to reconsider the 5. sect. of the 4. article

which passed in the affirmative [Ayes—8; noes—2; divided — 1.]

and monday next was assigned for the reconsideration
And then the House adjourned till Monday next at 11 o'Clock A. M.

---

[4] Votes 278–279. Detail of Ayes and Noes. The former probably refers to Section 8 rather than Section 7, see Madison's record.

[5] McHenry reports this on August 14.

DETAIL OF AYES AND NOES

	New Hampshire	Massachusetts	Rhode Island	Connecticut	New York	New Jersey	Pennsylvania	Delaware	Maryland	Virginia	North Carolina	South Carolina	Georgia	Questions	Ayes	Noes	Divided
[273]	no	no		no		no	no	no	no	aye	no	no	no	To agree to Mr Madison's amendmt	1	10	
[274]	no	aye		aye		no	no	no	no	no	no	no	no	except such parts thereof relative to Treaties & military operations.	2	9	
[275]	aye	aye		aye		aye	aye	aye	aye	aye	aye	aye	aye	On the 1st clause of the 7 sect. of the 6 article as reported	11		
[276]	dd	aye		aye		aye	no	no	no	aye	aye	no	aye	except such parts thereof as in their judgment require secrecy.	6	4	1
[277]	aye	aye		aye		aye	aye	aye	aye	aye	aye	aye	aye	To agree to the last clause of the 7 sect of the 6 art.			
[278]	no	aye		no		aye	aye	no	no	aye	no	no	no	To commit the 2nd clause of the 7 sect. 6 art.	4	7	
[279]	aye	aye		aye		aye	aye	aye	aye	no	aye	aye	aye	“ nor to any other place than that at which the two Houses are sitting” 8 sect. 6 article	10	1	
[280]	aye	aye		aye		no	aye	aye	no	aye	aye	dd	aye	To reconsider 5 sect 4 article Monday assigned	8	2	1

MADISON

Saturday Augst. 11. in Convention

Mr ⟨Madison⟩ & Mr. Rutlidge moved "that each House shall keep a journal of its proceeding, & ⟨shall⟩ publish the same from time to time; except such ⟨part⟩ of the proceedings of the Senate, when acting not in its Legislative capacity as may ⟨be judged by⟩ that House ⟨to⟩ require secrecy."

Mr. Mercer. This implies that other powers than legislative will be given to the Senate which he hoped would not be given.

Mr. M⟨adison⟩ & Mr. R's motion. was disagd. to by all the States except Virga.

Mr. Gerry & Mr. Sharman moved to insert after the words "publish them" the following "except such as relate to treaties & military operations." Their object was to give each House a discretion in such cases. — On this question

N. H– no. Mas– ay. Ct. ay. N– J. no. Pa. no. Del– no. Va. no. N. C. no. S. C. no. Geo. no. [Ayes — 2; noes — 8.][6]

Mr. Elseworth. As the clause is objectionable in so many shapes, it may as well be struck out altogether.[7] The Legislature will not fail to publish their proceedings from time to time — The ⟨people⟩ will call for it if it should be improperly omitted.

Mr. Wilson thought the expunging of the clause would be very improper. The people have a right to know what their Agents are doing or have done, and it should not be in the option of the Legislature to conceal their proceedings. Besides as this is a clause in the existing confederation, the not retaining it would furnish the adversaries of the reform with a pre-text by which weak & suspicious minds may be easily misled.

Mr. Mason thought it would give a just alarm to the people, to make a conclave of their Legislature.

Mr. Sherman thought the Legislature might be trusted in this case if in any.

Question on 1st. part of the Section, down to "*publish them*" inclusive: Agreed to nem. con.

Question on the words to follow, to wit except such parts thereof as may in their Judgment require secrecy."[8] N. H. divd. Mas. ay. Ct. ay. N. J– ay. Pa. no. Del– no. Md. no. Va. ay– N. C. ay. S. C. no. Geo. ay—[Ayes — 6; noes — 4; divided — 1.]

The remaining part as to yeas and nays. — agreed to nem. con.

Art VI. sect. 8. taken up.[9]

[6] Vote 274, Detail of Ayes and Noes, includes Maryland in the negative.

[7] On the debate which follows, see Appendix A, CCXII, CCXXVII.

[8] See Appendix A, CCIX.

[9] Article VI, Sect. 8. "Neither House, without the consent of the other, shall

Mr. King remarked[10] that the section authorized the 2 Houses to adjourn to a new place. He thought this inconvenient. The mutability of place had dishonored the federal Govt. and would require as strong a cure as we could devise. He thought a law at least should be ⟨made⟩ necessary to a removal of the Seat of Govt.

Mr ⟨Madison⟩ viewed the subject in the same light, and joined with Mr. King in a motion requiring a law.

Mr. Governr. Morris proposed the additional alteration by inserting the words "during the Session" &c".

Mr. Spaight. this will fix the seat of Govt at N. Y. ⟨The present⟩ Congress will convene them there in the first instance, and they will never be able to remove; especially if the Presidt. should be Northern Man.

Mr Govr Morris. such a distrust is inconsistent with all Govt.

Mr. ⟨Madison⟩ supposed that a central place for the Seat of Govt. was so just and wd. be so much insisted on by the H. of Representatives, that though a law should ⟨be made requisite for⟩[11] the purpose, it could & would be ⟨ob⟩tained. The necessity of a central residence of the Govt wd be much greater under the new than old Govt The members of the ⟨new⟩ Govt wd. be more numerous. They would be taken more from the interior parts of the States: they wd. not, like members of ⟨ye present⟩ Congs. come so often from the distant States by water. As the powers & objects of the new Govt. would be far greater ⟨yn. heretofore⟩, more private individuals wd. have business calling them to the seat of it, and it was more necessary that the Govt should be in that position from which it could contemplate with the most equal eye, and sympathize most equally with, every part of the nation. These considerations he supposed would extort a removal even if a law were made necessary. But in order to quiet suspicions both within & without doors, it might not be

adjourn for more than three days, nor to any other place than that at which the two Houses are sitting. But this regulation shall not extend to the Senate, when it shall exercise the powers mentioned in the article."

[10] Upon this debate, see Appendix A, CCX.

[11] Crossed out "be required of".

amiss to authorize the 2 Houses by a concurrent vote to adjourn at their first meeting to the most proper place, and to require thereafter, the sanction of a law to their removal. ⟨The motion was accordingly moulded into the following form:[12] "the Legislature shall at their first assembling determine on a place at which their future sessions shall be held; neither House shall afterwards, during the session of the House of Reps. without the consent of the other, adjourn for more than three days, nor shall they adjourn to any other place than such as shall have been fixt by law"⟩

Mr. Gerry thought it would be wrong to let the Presidt check the will of the ⟨2⟩ Houses on this subject ⟨at all.⟩

Mr Williamson supported the ideas of Mr. Spaight

Mr Carrol was actuated by the same apprehensions

Mr. Mercer. it will serve no purpose to require the two Houses at their first Meeting to fix on a place. They will never agree.

After some further expressions from others denoting an apprehension that the seat of Govt. might be continued at an improper place if a law should be made necessary to a removal, and ⟨the⟩ motion ⟨above stated with another⟩ for recommitting the section ⟨had been⟩ negatived, the Section was left in the shape it ⟨which it was reported, as to this point. The words "during the session of the legislature were prefixed to the 8th section — and the last sentence "But this regulation shall not extend to the Senate when it shall exercise the powers mentioned in the article" struck out. The 8th. section as amended was then agreed to.⟩[13]

Mr. Randolph moved according to notice to reconsider Art: IV: Sect. 5. concerning money-bills which had been struck out. He argued[14] 1. that he had not wished for this privilege whilst a proportional Representation in the Senate was in contemplation. but since an equality had been fixed in that

[12] Taken from *Journal*.

[13] Taken from *Journal* after crossing out "now bears".

[14] Crossed out "1. that this exclusive privilege in behalf of the House of Representatives would render the plan acceptable". This necessitated the renumbering of the four other points.

house, the large States would require this compensation at least. 2. that it would make the plan more acceptable to the people, because they will consider the Senate as the more aristocratic body, and will expect that the usual guards agst its influence be provided according to the example in G. Britain. 3. the privilege will give some advantage to the House of Reps. if it extends to the originating only — but still more, if it restrains the Senate ⟨from⟩ amend⟨g⟩[15] 4. he called on the smaller States to concur in the measure, as the condition by which alone the compromise had entitled them to an equality in the Senate. He signified that he should propose instead of the original Section, a clause specifying that the bills in question should be for the purpose of Revenue, in order to repel ye. objection agst. the extent of the words "*raising money*," which might happen incidentally, and that the Senate should not so amend or alter as to increase or diminish the sum; in order to obviate the inconveniences urged agst. a restriction of the Senate to a simple affirmative or negative.

Mr. Williamson 2ded. the motion

Mr. Pinkney was sorry to oppose the opportunity gentlemen asked to have the question again opened for discussion, but as he considered it a mere waste of time he could not bring himself to consent to it. He said that notwithstanding what had been said as to the compromise, he always considered this section as making no part of it. The rule of Representation in the 1st. branch was the true condition of that in the 2d. branch. — Several others spoke for & agst the reconsideration, but without going into the merits — on the Question to reconsider

N. H. ay. Mas. ay. Ct. ay. N. J. ay.* Pa. ay. Del. ay. Md. no. Va. ay. N. C. ay. S. C. divd. Geo. ay. [Ayes — 9; noes — 1; divided — 1.] — Monday was then assigned —

Adj'd.[16]

* ⟨In the printed Journal N. Jersey — no.⟩

[15] Originally "may amend."

[16] See further, Appendix A, LXXXI, LXXXII.

McHENRY

Augt. 11.

Sect. 7 agreed to after expunging the words "when it shall be acting in a legislative capacity" and inserting after the words "publish them" except such parts as in their judgement require secrecy —

After much debate agreed to reconsider on monday the 5 sect. of the 4 article.

MONDAY, AUGUST 13, 1787.

JOURNAL

Monday August 13. 1787.

It was moved and seconded to strike out the word "seven" and to insert the word "four" in the 2nd sect. of the 4 article

It was moved and seconded to strike out the word "seven" and to insert the word "nine" in the 2nd sect. of the 4 article

It was moved and seconded to strike out the words "shall have been a citizen of the United States for at least seven years before his election" and to insert between the words "an" and "inhabitant" the words "Citizen and" in the 2nd sect. of the 4 article

which passed in the negative. [Ayes — 4; noes — 7.][1]

On the question to agree to the amendment of "nine"

it passed in the negative. [Ayes — 3; noes — 8.]

On the question to agree to the amendment of "four"

it passed in the negative. [Ayes — 3; noes — 8.]

It was moved and seconded to add the following clause to the 2nd sect. of the 4 article, namely,

"Provided always that the above limitation of seven years "shall not be construed to affect the rights of those who are "now Citizens of the United States"

which passed in the negative. [Ayes — 5; noes — 6.][2]

It was moved and seconded to strike out the word "seven" and to insert the word "five" in the 2nd sect. of the 4. article

which passed in the negative [Ayes — 3; noes — 7; divided — 1.]

---

[1] Vote 281, Detail of Ayes and Noes, which notes that it was "Mr. Hamilton's amendment".

[2] Vote 284, Detail of Ayes and Noes, which notes it was "the Proviso offered . . . by Mr. G. Morris."

On the question to agree to the 2nd sect. of the 4. article as formerly amended

it passed in the affirmative.

On the question shall the word "nine" in the 3rd sect. of the 5. article stand part of the said section

it passed in the affirmative [Ayes — 8; noes — 3.]

[To adjourn. — Ayes — 5; noes — 5; divided — 1.][3]

It was moved and seconded to amend the 5. sect of the 4. article to read as follows, namely,

"all bills for raising money for the purposes of revenue, "or for appropriating the same, shall originate in the House "of representatives; and shall not be so altered or amended "by the Senate, as to encrease or diminish the sum to be "raised, or change the mode of raising or the objects of it's "appropriation"

which passed in the negative. [Ayes — 4; noes — 7.][4]

On the question to agree to the 5 sect. of the 4. article as reported

it passed in the negative. [Ayes — 3; noes — 8.]

[last clause 5 section 4. article Ayes — 1; noes — 10.][5]

And then the House adjourned till to-morrow at 11 o'Clock A. M.

---

[3] Vote 287, Detail of Ayes and Noes.

[4] Vote 288, Detail of Ayes and Noes, which notes that it was "Mr. Randolph's proposition" and that the question was only one on "the first clause".

[5] Vote 290, Detail of Ayes and Noes. There is nothing to indicate that this belongs here, except its relative position.

DETAIL OF AYES AND NOES

	New Hampshire	Massachusetts	Rhode Island	Connecticut	New York	New Jersey	Pennsylvania	Delaware	Maryland	Virginia	North Carolina	South Carolina	Georgia	Questions	Ayes	Noes	Divided
[281]	no	no		aye		no	aye	no	aye	aye	no	no	no	On Mr Hamilton's amendment of the 2nd sect. of the 4 article	4	7	
[282]	aye	no		no		no	no	no	no	no	no	aye	aye	To strike out the word "seven" and to insert the word "nine" 2 sect. 4 art.	3	8	
[283]	no	no		aye		no	no	no	aye	aye	no	no	no	To agree to the amendmt of "four" 2 sect. 4 article.	3	8	
[284]	no	no		aye		aye	aye	no	aye	aye	no	no	no	To agree to the Proviso offered to ye 2 sect of the 4 art. by Mr. G. Morris.	5	6	
[285]	no	no		aye		no	dd	no	aye	aye	no	no	no	instead of the word "seven" to insert "five	3	7	1
[286]	aye	aye		no		aye	no	aye	no	aye	aye	aye	aye	shall the word nine in the 3rd sect of the 5 art: remain.	8	3	
[287]	dd	aye		aye		no	aye	aye	aye	no	no	no	no	To adjourn.—	5	5	1
[288]	aye	aye		no		no	no	no	no	aye	aye	no	no	To agree to the first clause of Mr Randolph's proposition for reinstating the 5 Section 4 article	4	7	
[289]	aye	aye		no		no	no	no	no	no	aye	no	no	To agree to the 5 sect. 4 art. as reported	3	8	
[290]	no	aye		no		no	no	no	no	no	no	no	no	last clause 5 section 4. article	1	10	

MADISON

Monday. Augst. 13. In Convention

Art. IV. Sect. 2. reconsidered —[6]

[6] Article IV, Sect. 2 (as amended). "Every member of the House of Representatives shall be of the age of twenty-five years at least; shall have been a citizen of the United States for at least seven years before his election; and shall be, at the time of his election an inhabitant of the State in which he shall be chosen."

Mr. Wilson & Mr. Randolph moved to strike out "7 years" and insert "4 years," as the requisite term of Citizenship to qualify for the House of Reps. Mr. Wilson said it was very proper the electors should govern themselves by this consideration; but unnecessary & improper that the Constitution should chain them down to it.

Mr. Gerry wished that in future the eligibility might be confined to Natives. Foreign powers will intermeddle in our affairs, and spare no expence to influence them. Persons having foreign attachments will be sent among us & insinuated into our councils, in order to be made instruments for their purposes. Every one knows the vast sums laid out in Europe for secret services — He was not singular in these ideas. A great many of the most influential men in Massts. reasoned in the same manner.

Mr. Williamson moved to insert 9 years instead of seven. He wished this Country to acquire as fast as possible national habits. Wealthy emigrants do more harm by their luxurious examples, than good, by the money, they bring with them.

Col. Hamilton was in general agst. embarrassing the Govt. with minute restrictions. There was on one side the possible danger that had been suggested — on the other side, the advantage of encouraging foreigners was obvious & admitted. Persons in Europe of moderate fortunes will be fond of coming here where they will be on a level with the first Citizens. He moved that the section be so altered as to require merely Citizenship & inhabitancy. The right of determining the rule of naturalization will then leave a discretion to the Legislature on this subject which will answer every purpose.

Mr ⟨Madison⟩ seconded the motion. He wished to maintain the character of liberality which had been professed in all the Constitutions & publications of America. He wished to invite foreigners of merit & republican principles among us. America was indebted to emigration for her settlement & Prosperity. That part of America which had encouraged them most had advanced most rapidly in population, agriculture & the arts. There was a possible danger he admitted that men with foreign predilections might obtain appoint-

ments but it was by no means probable that it would happen in any dangerous degree. For the same reason that they would be attached to their native Country, our own people wd. prefer natives of this Country to them. Experience proved this to be the case. Instances were rare of a foreigner being elected by the people within any short space after his coming among us — If bribery was to be practised by foreign powers, it would not be attempted among the electors, but among the elected; and among natives having full Confidence of the people not among strangers who would be regarded with a jealous eye.

Mr. Wilson. Cited Pennsylva. as a proof of the advantage of encouraging emigrations. It was perhaps the youngest (except Georgia) settlemt. on the Atlantic; yet it was at least among the foremost in population & prosperity. He remarked that almost all the Genl. officers of ⟨the⟩ Pena. line ⟨of the late army⟩ were foreigners. And no complaint had ever been made against their fidelity or merit. Three of her deputies to the Convention (Mr. R. Morris, Mr. Fitzsimmons & himself) were also not natives. He had no objection to Col. Hamiltons motion & would withdraw the one made by himself.[7]

Mr. Butler was strenuous agst. admitting foreigners into our public Councils.

Question on Col. Hamilton's Motion

N. H. no. Mas. no. Ct. ay. N. J. no. Pa. ay. Del. no Md. ay. Va. ay. N. C. no. S. C. no. Geo. no. [Ayes — 4; noes — 7.]

Question on Mr. Williamson's moution, to insert 9 years instead of seven.

N. H. ay. Masts. no. Ct. no. N. J. no. Pa. no. Del. no. Md. no. Va no. N- C. no. S. C. ay. Geo. ay. [Ayes — 3; noes — 8.]

Mr. Wilson's renewed the motion for 4 years instead of 7. & on question

N. H. no Mas. no. Ct. ay. N. J. no. Pa. no. Del. no. Md. ay. Va. ay. N. C. no. S. C. no Geo. no. [Ayes — 3; noes — 8.]

---

[7] See Appendix A, CCCXXXVI.

Mr. Govr. Morris moved to add to the end of the section (art IV. s. 2) a proviso that the limitation ⟨of seven years⟩ should not affect ⟨the rights of⟩ any person now a Citizen.[8]

Mr. Mercer 2ded. the motion. It was necessary he said to prevent a disfranchisement of persons who had become Citizens under the faith ⟨& according to⟩ — the laws & Constitution ⟨from⟩ being on a level in all respects with natives.

Mr. Rutlidge. It might as well be said that all qualifications are disfranchisemts. and that to require the age of 25 years was a disfranchisement. The policy of the precaution was as great with regard to foreigners now Citizens; as to those who are to be naturalized in future.

Mr Sherman. The U. States have not invited foreigners nor pledged their faith that they should enjoy equal privileges with native Citizens. The Individual States alone have done this. The former therefore are at liberty to make any discriminations they may judge requisite.

Mr. Ghorum. When foreigners are naturalized it wd. seem as if they stand on an equal footing with natives. He doubted then the propriety of giving a retrospective force to the restriction.

Mr. ⟨Madison⟩ animadverted on the peculiarity of the doctrine of Mr. Sharman. It was ⟨a subtilty⟩ by which every national engagement might be evaded. By parity of reason, Whenever our public debts, or foreign treaties become inconvenient nothing ⟨more⟩ would be necessary to relieve us from them, than to[9] new model the Constitution. It was said that the *U. S.* as such have not pledged their faith to the naturalized foreigners, & therefore are not bound. Be it so, & that the States alone are bound. Who are to form the New Constitution by which the condition of that class of citizens is to be made worse than the other class? Are not the States ye agents? will they not be the members of it? Did they not appoint this Convention? Are not they to ratify its proceedings? Will not the new Constitution be their Act? If the new Constitution then violates the faith pledged to any

---

[8] Revised from *Journal*.

[9] Crossed out: "abolish them by".

description of people will not the makers of it, will not the States, be the violators. To justify the doctrine it must be said that the States can get rid of their obligation by revising the Constitution, though they could not do it by repealing the law under which foreigners held their privileges. He considered this a matter of real importance. It woud expose us to the reproaches of all those who should be affected by it, reproaches which wd. soon be echoed from the other side of the Atlantic; and would unnecessarily enlist among the Adversaries of the reform a very considerable body of Citizens: We should moreover reduce every State to the dilemma of rejecting it or of violating the faith pledged to a part of its citizens.

Mr. Govr. Morris[10] considered the case of persons under 25 years, as very different from that of foreigners. No faith could be pleaded by the former in bar of the regulation. No assurance had ever been given that persons under that age should be in all cases on a level with those above it. But with regard to foreigners among us, the faith had been pledged that they should enjoy the privileges of Citizens. If the restriction as to age had been confined to natives, & had left foreigners under 25 years, eligible in this case, the discrimination wd. have been an equal injustice on the other side.

Mr. Pinkney remarked that the laws of the States had varied much the terms of naturalization in different parts of America; and contended that the U. S. could not be bound to respect them on such an occasion as the present. It was a sort of recurrence to first principles.

Col– Mason was struck not like (Mr. ⟨Madison⟩), with the *peculiarity*,[11] but the *propriety*[11] of the doctrine of Mr. Sharman. The States have formed different qualifications themselves, for enjoying different rights of citizenship. Greater caution wd. be necessary in the outset of the Govt. than afterwards. All the great objects wd. be then provided for. Every thing would be then set in Motion. If persons among us attached to G– B. should work themselves into our Councils, a turn might be given to our affairs & particularly to our Commer-

[10] Crossed out: "Mr. Randolph remarked".

[11] Underscored by Madison when he revised his notes.

cial regulations which might have pernicious consequences. The great Houses of British Merchants would spare no pains to insinuate the instruments of their views ⟨into the Govt —⟩

Mr. Wilson read the clause in the Constitution of Pena. giving to foreigners after two years residence all the rights whatsoever of Citizens, combined it with the Article of Confederation making the Citizens of one State Citizens of all, inferred the obligation Pena. was under to maintain the faith thus pledged to her citizens of foreign birth, and the just complaints which her failure would authorize: He observed likewise that the Princes & States of Europe would avail themselves of such breach ⟨of faith⟩ to deter their subjects from emigrating to the U. S.[12]

Mr. Mercer enforced the same idea of a breach of faith.

Mr. Baldwin could ⟨not⟩ enter into the force of the arguments agst. extending the disqualification to foreigners now Citizens. The discrimination of the place of birth, was not more objectionable than that of age which all had concurred in the propriety of.

Question on the proviso of Mr Govr. Morris in favor of foreigners now Citizens

N. H. no. Mas. no. Ct. ay. N. J. ay. Pa. ay. Del. no. Maryd. ay. Va. ay. N- C. no. S. C. no. Geo. no. [Ayes — 5; noes — 6.]

Mr. Carrol moved to ⟨insert⟩ "5 years" instead "of seven," ⟨in section 2d. Art: IV⟩[13]

N- H. no. Mas. no. Ct. ay. N. J. no. Pa. divd. Del. no. Md. ay. Va. ay. N. C. no. S. C. no. Geo. no. [Ayes — 3; noes — 7; divided — 1.]

The Section (Art IV. Sec. 2.) ⟨as formerly amended was⟩[13] then agreed to nem. con.

Mr. Wilson moved that (in Art: V. sect. 3)[14] 9 years be reduced to seven. ⟨which was disagd. to and the 3d. Section (art. V.) confirmed by the following vote.⟩[15]

---

[12] See Appendix A, CCCXXXVI.

[13] Revised from *Journal.*

[14] Relating to qualifications of Senators.

[15] Taken from *Journal.* Madison originally gave the vote which follows to the question preceding.

N. H. ay. Mas. ay. Ct. no. N. J. ay. Pa. no. Del. ay. Md. no. Va. ay. N. C. ay. S. C. ay. Geo. ay. [Ayes — 8 ; noes — 3.]

Art. IV. ⟨Sec.⟩ 5. ⟨being⟩ reconsidered.

Mr. Randolph moved that the clause be altered so as to read — "Bills for raising money for the *purpose of revenue* ⟨or for appropriating the same shall originate in the House of Representatives⟩ and shall not be ⟨so⟩ amended or altered by the Senate as to increase or diminish the sum to be raised, or change the mode of levying it, or the object of its appropriation."[15a] — He would not repeat his reasons, but barely remind the members from the smaller States of the compromise by which the larger States were entitled to this privilege.

Col. Mason. This amendment removes all the objections urged agst. the section as it stood at first. By specifying *purposes of revenue*, it obviated the objection that the Section extended to all bills under which money might incidentally arise. By authorizing amendments in the Senate it got rid of the objections that the Senate could not correct errors of any sort, & that it would introduce into the House of Reps. the practice of tacking foreign matter to money bills: These objections being removed, the arguments in favor of the proposed restraint on the Senate ought to have their full force. 1. the Senate did not represent the *people*, but the *States* in their political character. It was improper therefore that it should tax the people. The reason was the same agst. their doing it; as it had been agst. Congs. doing it. Nor was it in any respect necessary in order to cure the evils of our Republican system. He admitted that notwithstanding the superiority of the Republican form over every other, it had its evils. The chief ones, were the danger of the majority oppressing the minority, and the mischievous influence of demagogues. The Genl. Government of itself will cure these. As the States will not concur at the same time in their unjust & oppressive plans, the general Govt. will be able to check &

[15a] Revised from *Journal.*

defeat them, whether they result from the wickedness of the majority, or from the misguidance of demagogues. Again, the Senate is not like the H. of Reps. chosen frequently and obliged to return frequently among the people. They are to be chosen by the Sts for 6 years, will probably settle themselves at the seat of Govt. will pursue schemes for their own aggrandizement — will be able by wearyg out the H. of Reps and taking advantage of their impatience at the close of a long Session, to extort measures for that purpose. If they should be paid as he expected would be yet determined & wished to be so, out of the Natl. Treasury, they will particularly extort an increase of their wages. A bare negative was a very different thing from that of originating bills. The practice in Engld was in point. The House of Lords does not represent nor tax the people, because not elected by the people. If the Senate can originate, they will in the recess of the Legislative Sessions, hatch their mischievous projects, for their own purposes, and have their money bills ready cut & dried, (to use a common phrase) for the meeting of the H. of Reps. He compared the case to Poyning's law — and signified that the House of Reps. might be rendered by degrees like the Parliament of Paris, the mere depository of the decrees of the Senate. As to the compromise so much had passed on that subject that he would say nothing about it. He did not mean by what he had said to oppose the permanency of the Senate. On the contrary he had no repugnance to an increase of it — nor to allowing it a negative, though the Senate was not by its present constitution entitled to it. But in all events he would contend that the pursestrings should be in the hands of the Representatives of the people.

Mr. Wilson was himself directly opposed to the equality of votes granted to the Senate by its present Constitution. At the same time he wished not to multiply the vices of the system. He did not mean to enlarge on a subject which had been so much canvassed, but would remark as an insuperable objection agst. the proposed restriction of money bills to the H. of Reps. that it would be a source of perpetual contentions where there was no mediator to decide them. The Presidt.

here could not like the Executive Magistrate in England interpose by a prorogation, or dissolution. This restriction had been found pregnant with altercation in every State where the Constitution had established it. The House of Reps. will insert the other things in money bills, and by making them conditions of each other, destroy the deliberate liberty of the Senate. He stated the case of a Preamble to a money bill sent up by the House of Commons in the reign of Queen Anne, to the H. of Lords, in which the conduct of the displaced Ministry, who were to be impeached before the Lords, was condemned; the Commons thus extorting a premature judgmt. without any hearing of the Parties to be tried, and the H. of Lords being thus reduced to the poor & disgraceful expedient of opposing to the authority of a law a protest on their Journals agst. its being drawn into precedent. If there was any thing like Poynings law in the present case, it was in the attempt to vest the exclusive right of originating in the H. of Reps. and so far he was agst it. He should be equally so if the right were to be exclusively vested in the Senate. With regard to the pursestrings, it was to be observed that the purse was to have two strings, one of which was in the hands of the H. of Reps. the other in those of the Senate. Both houses must concur in untying, and of what importance could it be which untied first, which last. He could not conceive it to be any objection to the senate's preparing the bills, that they would have leisure for that purpose and would be in the habits of business. War, Commerce, & Revenue were the great objects of the Genl. Government. All of them are connected with money. The restriction in favor of the H. of Represts. would exclude the Senate from originating any important bills whatever —

Mr Gerry. considered this as a part of the plan that would be much scrutinized. Taxation & representation are strongly associated in the minds of the people, and they will not agree that any but their immediate representatives shall meddle with their purses. In short the acceptance of the plan will inevitably fail, if the Senate be not restrained from originating Money bills.

Mr. Govermr. Morris All the arguments suppose the right to originate ⟨money⟩ & to tax, to be exclusively vested in the Senate. — The effects commented on may be produced by a Negative only in the Senate. They can tire out the other House, and extort their concurrence in favorite measures, as well by withholding their negative, as by adhering to a bill introduced by themselves.

Mr ⟨Madison thought⟩ If the substitute offered by Mr. Randolph for the original section is to be adopted it would be proper to allow the Senate at least so to amend as to *diminish* the sums to be raised. Why should they be restrained from checking the extravagance of the other House? — One of the greatest evils incident to Republican Govt. was the spirit of contention & faction. The proposed substitute, which in some respects lessened the objections agst. the section, had a contrary effect with respect to this particular. It laid a foundation for new difficulties and disputes between the two houses. The word *revenue* was ambiguous. In many acts, particularly in the regulations of trade, the object would be twofold. The raising of revenue would be one of them. How could it be determined which was the primary or predominant one; or whether it was necessary that revenue shd: be the sole object, in exclusion even of other incidental effects. When the Contest was first opened with G. B. their power to regulate trade was admitted. Their power to raise revenue rejected. An accurate investigation of the subject afterward proved that no line could be drawn between the two cases. The words *amend or alter*, form an equal source of doubt & altercation. When an obnoxious paragraph shall be sent down from the Senate to the House of Reps it will be called an origination under the name of an amendment. The Senate may actually couch extraneous matter under that name. In these cases, the question will turn on the *degree* of connection between the matter & object of the bill and the ⟨alteration or⟩ amendment offered to it. Can there be a more fruitful source of dispute, or a kind of dispute more difficult to be settled? His apprehensions on this point were not conjectural. Disputes had actually flowed from this source in Virga. where

the Senate can originate no bill. The words "so as to *increase or diminish* the sum to be raised," were liable to the same objections. In levying indirect taxes, which it seemed to be understood were to form the principal revenue of the new Govt. the sum to be raised, would be increased or diminished by a variety of collateral circumstances influencing the consumption, in general, the consumption of foreign or of domestic articles — of this or that particular species of articles, and even by the mode of collection which may be closely connected with the productiveness of a tax. — The friends of the section had argued its necessity from the permanency of the Senate. He could not see how this argumt. applied. The Senate was not more permanent now than in the form it bore in the original propositions of Mr. Randolph and at the time when no objection whatever was hinted agst. its originating money bills. Or if in consequence of a loss of the present question, a proportional vote in the Senate should be reinstated as has been urged as the indemnification the permanency of the Senate will remain the same. — If the right to originate be vested exclusively in the House of Reps. either the Senate must yield agst. its judgment to that House, in which ⟨case⟩ the Utility of the check will be lost — or the Senate will be inflexible & the H. of Reps must adapt its Money bill to the views of the Senate, in which case, the exclusive right will be of no avail. — As to the Compromise of which so much had been said, he would make a single observation. There were 5 States which had opposed the equality of votes in the Senate. viz. Masts. Penna. Virga. N. Carolina & S. Carola. As a compensation for the sacrifice extorted ⟨from them⟩ on this head, the exclusive origination of money bills in the other House had been tendered. Of the five States a majority viz. Penna. Virga. & S. Carola. have uniformly voted agst. the proposed compensation, on its own merits, as rendering the plan of Govt. still more objectionable– Massts has been divided. N. Carolina alone has set a value on the compensation, and voted on that principle. What obligation then can the small States be under to concur agst. their judgments in reinstating the section?

Mr. Dickenson. Experience must be our only guide. Reason may mislead us. It was not Reason that discovered the singular & admirable mechanism of the English Constitution. It was not Reason that discovered or ever could have discovered the odd & in the eye of those who are governed by reason, the absurd mode of trial by Jury. Accidents probably produced these discoveries, and experience has give a sanction to them. This is then our guide. And has not experience verified the utility of restraining money bills to the immediate representatives of the people. Whence the effect may have proceeded he could not say; whether from the respect with which this privilege inspired the other branches of Govt. to the H. of Commons, or from the turn of thinking it gave to the people at large with regard to their rights, but the effect was visible & could not be doubted Shall we oppose to this long experience, the short experience of 11 years which we had ourselves, on this subject — As to disputes, they could not be avoided any way. If both Houses should originate, each would have a different bill to which it would be attached, and for which it would contend. — He observed that all the prejudices of the people would be offended by refusing this exclusive privilege to the H. of Repress. and these prejudices shd. never be disregarded by us when no essential purpose was to be served. When this plan goes forth, it will be attacked by the popular leaders. Aristocracy will be the watchword; the Shibboleth among its adversaries. Eight States have inserted in their Constitutions the exclusive right of originating money bills in favor of the popular branch of the Legislature. Most of them however allowed the other branch to amend. This he thought would be proper for us to do.

Mr Randolph regarded this point as of such consequence, that as he valued the peace of this Country, he would press the adoption of it. We had numerous & monstrous difficulties to combat. Surely we ought not to increase them. When the people behold in the Senate, the countenance of an aristocracy; and in the president, the form at least of a little monarch, will not their alarms be sufficiently raised without

taking from their immediate representatives, a right which has been so long appropriated to them. — The Executive will have more influence over the Senate, than over the H. of Reps — Allow the Senate to originate in this case, & that influence will be sure to mix itself in their deliberations & plans. The Declaration of War he conceived ought not to be in the Senate composed of 26 men only, but rather in the other House. In the other House ought to be placed the origination of the means of war. As to Commercial regulations which may involve revenue, the difficulty may be avoided by restraining the definition to bills for the *mere* or *sole*, purpose of raising revenue. The Senate will be more likely to be corrupt than the H. of Reps and should therefore have less to do with money matters. His principal object however was to prevent popular objections against the plan, and to secure its adoption.

Mr. Rutlidge. The friends of this motion are not consistent in their reasoning. They tell us, that ⟨we ought to be guided by⟩ the long experience of G. B. & not our own experience of 11 years: and yet they themselves propose to depart from it. The *H. of Commons* not only have the exclusive right of originating, but the *Lords* are not allowed to alter or amend a money bill. Will not the people say that this restriction is but a mere tub to the whale. They cannot but see that it is of no real consequence; and will be more likely to be displeased with it as an attempt to bubble them, than to impute it to a watchfulness over their rights. For his part, he would prefer giving the exclusive right to the Senate, if it was to be given ⟨exclusively⟩ at all. The Senate being more conversant in business, and having more leisure, will digest the bills much better, and as they are to have no effect, till examined & approved by the H. of Reps there can be no possible danger. These clauses in the Constitutions of the States had been put in through a blind adherence to the British model. If the work was to be done over now, they would be omitted. The experiment in S. Carolina– where the Senate cannot originate or amend money bills, has shown that it answers no good purpose; and produces the very bad one of

continually dividing & heating the two houses. Sometimes indeed if the matter of the amendment of the Senate is pleasing to the other House they wink at the encroachment; if it be displeasing, then the Constitution is appealed to. Every Session is distracted by altercations on this subject. The practice now becoming frequent is for the Senate not to make formal amendments; but to send down a schedule of the alterations which will procure the bill their assent.

Mr. Carrol. The most ingenious men in Maryd. are puzzled to define the case of money bills, or explain the Constitution on that point; tho' it seemed to be worded with all possible plainness & precision. It is a source of continual difficulty & squabble between the two houses.

Mr. McHenry mentioned an instance of extraordinary subterfuge, to get rid of the apparent force of the Constitution

On Question on the first part of the motion as to the exclusive originating of Money bills in the H. of Reps.

N. H. ay. Mas. ay. Ct. no. N. J. no. Pa. no. Del. no. Md. no. Virga. ay. Mr. Blair & Mr. M. no– Mr. R. Col. Mason and *Genl. Washington ay. N. C. ay. S. C. no. Geo. no [Ayes — 4; noes — 7.]

Question on Originating by H. of Reps & *amending* by Senate. ⟨as reported, Art IV. Sect. 5.⟩[16]

N. H. ay. Mas. ay. Ct. no. N J. no. Pa. no. Del. no. Md. no Va.† ay. ⟨N. C. ay⟩ S. C. no. Geo. no [Ayes — 4; noes — 7.]

⟨Question on the last clause of sect: 5 — Art: IV — viz "No money shall be drawn from the Public Treasury, but in pursuance of *appropriations* that shall originate in the House of Reps. It passed in the negative

N. H. no. Mas. ay Con. no N. J no. Pa. no Del no. Md no Va no. N. C. no. S. C. no. Geo. no.⟩[17] [Ayes — 1; noes —10.]

Adjd.[18]

* he disapproved & till now voted agst., the exclusive privilege, he gave up his judgment he said, because it was not of very material weight with him & was made an essential point with others, who if disappointed, might be less cordial in other points of real weight.

† ⟨In the printed Journ Virga — no⟩

[16] Taken from *Journal*.

[17] Taken from *Journal*, see above, note 5.

[18] See further Appendix A, LXXXIII, LXXXIII*a*.

McHENRY

August 13.

The 2 sect. of the 4 article and the 3 sect. of the 5 article was reconsidered and lengthily debated. The 7 years however in the first and the 9 years in the latter remained and the articles stood as before reconsideration.

TUESDAY, AUGUST 14, 1787.

JOURNAL

Tuesday August 14. 1787.

It was moved and seconded to postpone the consideration of the 9. section of the 6 article in order to take up the following

"The members of each House shall be incapable of hold-"ing any Office under the United States for which they, or "any other for their benefit, receive any salary, fees, or emol-"uments of any kind — and the acceptance of such office shall "vacate their seats respectively"

which passed in the negative. [Ayes — 5; noes — 5; divided — 1.]

It was moved and seconded to amend the 9 section of the 6 article by adding the following clause after the words "be elected"

"except in the army or navy thereof, but in that case "their seats shall be vacated"

Before the question was taken on the last amendment

It was moved and seconded to postpone the consideration of the 9th section of the 6 article until the powers to be vested in the Senate are ascertained

which passed unanimously in the affirmative

It was moved and seconded to strike out the latter clause of the 10 sect. of the 6 article and to insert the following

"to be paid out of the Treasury of the United States"

which passed in the affirmative [Ayes — 9; noes — 2.]

It was moved and seconded to agree to the following amendment to the 10 sect. of the 6 article

"five dollars or the present value thereof per diem during "their attendance & for every thirty miles travel in going to "and returning from Congress"

which passed in the negative [Ayes — 2; noes — 9.]

It was moved and seconded to agree to the following amendment to the 10th sect. of the 6 article

"to be ascertained by law"

which passed in the affirmative

On the question to agree to the 10 section of the 6 article as amended it passed in the affirmative —

and then the House adjourned till to-morrow at 11 o'Clock A M

DETAIL OF AYES AND NOES

	New Hampshire	Massachusetts	Rhode Island	Connecticut	New York	New Jersey	Pennsylvania	Delaware	Maryland	Virginia	North Carolina	South Carolina	Georgia	Questions	Ayes	Noes	Divided
[291]	aye	no		no		no	aye	aye	aye	aye	no	no	dd	To postpone the considn of the 9 sect. of the 6 article	5	5	1
[292]	aye	no		aye		aye	aye	aye	aye	aye	aye	no	aye	To be paid out of the Treasury of the United States.	9	2	
[293]	no	no		aye		no	no	no	no	aye	no	no	no	To agree to five dollars ℔ diem	2	9	

MADISON

Tuesday Aug. 14. In Convention

Article VI. sect. 9. taken up.[1]

Mr. Pinkney argued that the making the members ineligible to offices was *degrading* to them, and the more improper as their election into the Legislature implied that they had the confidence of the people; that it was *inconvenient*, because the Senate might be supposed to contain the fittest men. He hoped to see that body become a School of Public Ministers, a nursery of Statesmen: that it was *impolitic*, because the Legislature would cease to be a magnet to the first talents

[1] Article VI, Sect. 9. "The members of each House shall be ineligible to, and incapable of holding any office under the authority of the United States; during the time for which they shall respectively be elected: and the members of the Senate shall be ineligible to, and incapable of holding any such office for one year afterwards."

and abilities. He moved ⟨to postpone the section in order to take up the following proposition viz — "the members of each House shall be incapable of holding any office under the U. S. for which they or any of others for their benefit receive any salary, fees, or emoluments of any kind — and the acceptance of such office shall vacate their seats respectively"⟩ [2]

Genl. Mifflin 2ded. the motion

Col. Mason ironically proposed to strike out the whole section, as a more effectual expedient for encouraging that exotic corruption which might not otherwise thrive so well in the American Soil — for compleating that Aristocracy which was probably in the contemplation of some among us. and for inviting into the Legislative service, those generous & benevolent characters who will do justice to each other's merit, by carving out offices & rewards for it. In the present state of American morals & manners, few friends it may be thought will be lost to the plan, by ⟨the opportunity⟩ of giving premiums to a mercenary & depraved ambition.

Mr Mercer. It is a first principle in political science, that whenever the rights of property are secured, an aristocracy will grow out of it. Elective Governments also necessarily become aristocratic, because the rulers being few can & will draw emoluments for themselves from the many. The Governments of America will become aristocracies. They are so already. The public measures are calculated for the benefit of the Governors, not of the people. The people are dissatisfied & complain. They change their rulers, and the public measures are changed, but it is only a change of one scheme of emolument to the rulers, for another. The people gain nothing by it, but an addition of instability & uncertainty to their other evils. — Governmts. can only be maintained by *force* or *influence*. The Executive has not *force*, deprive him of influence by rendering the members of the ⟨Legislature⟩ ineligible to Executive offices, and he becomes a mere phantom of authority. The Aristocratic part will not even let him in for a share of the plunder. The Legislature must & will

[2] Revised from *Journal*.

be composed of wealth & abilities, and the people will be governed by a Junto. The Executive ought to have a Council, being members of both Houses. Without such an influence, the war will be between the aristocracy & the people. He wished it to be between the Aristocracy & the Executive. Nothing else can protect the people agst. those speculating Legislatures which are now plundering them throughout the U. States.

Mr. Gerry read a Resolution of the Legislature of Massts. passed before the Act of Congs. recommending the Convention, in which her deputies were instructed not to depart from the rotation established in the 5th. art: of Confederation, nor to agree in any case to give to the members of Congs. a capacity to hold offices under the Government. This he said was repealed in consequence of the Act of Congs. with which the State thought it proper to comply in an unqualified manner. The Sense of the State however was still the same. He could not think with Mr. Pinkney that the disqualification was degrading. Confidence is the road to tyranny. As to Ministers & Ambassadors few of them were necessary. It is the opinion of a great many that they ought to be discontinued, on our part; that none may be sent among us, & that source of influence be shut up. If the Senate were to appoint Ambassadors as seemed to be intended, they will multiply embassies for their own sakes. He was not so fond of those productions as to wish to establish nurseries for them. If they are once appointed, the House of Reps. will be obliged to provide salaries for them, whether they approve of the measures or not. If men will not serve in the Legislature without a prospect of such offices, our situation is deplorable indeed. If our best Citizens are actuated by such mercenary views, we had better chuse a single despot at once. It will be more easy to satisfy the rapacity of one than of many. According to the idea of one Gentleman (Mr. Mercer) our Government it seems is to be a Govt. of plunder. In that case it certainly would be prudent to have but one rather than many to be employed in it. We cannot be too circumspect in the formation of this System. It will be examined on all sides

and with a very suspicious eye. The People who have been so lately in arms agst. G. B. for their liberties, will not easily give them up. He lamented the evils existing at present under our Governments, but imputed them to the faults of those in office, not to the people. The misdeeds of the former will produce a critical attention to the opportunities afforded by the new system to like or greater abuses. As it now stands it is as compleat an aristocracy as ever was framed If great powers should be given to the Senate we shall be governed in reality by a Junto as has been apprehended. He remarked that it would be very differently constituted from Congs 1. there will be but 2 deputies from each State, in Congs. there may be 7. and are generally 5. — 2. they are chosen for six years. those of Congs. annually. 3. they are not subject to recall; those of Congs. are. 4. In Congs. 9 *states* are necessary for all great purposes — here 8 *persons* will suffice. Is it to be presumed that the people will ever agree to such a system? He moved to render the members of the H. of Reps. as well as of the Senate ineligible not only during, but for one year after the expiration of their terms. — If it should be thought that this will injure the Legislature by keeping out of it men of abilities who are willing to serve in other offices it may be required as a qualification for other offices, that the Candidate shall have served a certain time in the Legislature.

Mr Govr. Morris. Exclude the officers of the army & navy, and you form a band having a different interest from & opposed to the civil power: you stimulate them to despise & reproach those "talking Lords who dare not face the foe". Let this spirit be roused at the end of a war, before your troops shall have laid down their arms, and though the Civil authority be "entrenched in parchment to the teeth" they will cut their way to it. He was agst. rendering the members of the Legislature ineligible to offices. He was for rendering them eligible agn. after having vacated their Seats by accepting office. Why should we not avail ourselves of their services if the people chuse to give them their confidence. There can be little danger of corruption either among the people or the Legislatures who are to be the Electors. If they say, we see

their merits, we honor the men, we chuse to renew our confidence in them, have they not a right to give them a preference; and can they be properly abridged of it.

Mr. Williamson; introduced his opposition to the motion by referring to the question concerning "money bills". That clause he said was dead. Its ghost he was afraid would notwithstanding haunt us. It ⟨had been⟩ a matter of conscience with him, to insist upon it as long as there was hope of retaining it. He had swallowed the vote of rejection, with reluctance. He could not digest it. All that was said on the other side was that the restriction was not *convenient.* We have now got a House of Lords which is to originate money-bills. To avoid another *inconveniency*, we are to have a whole Legislature at liberty to cut out offices for one another. He thought a self-denying ordinance for ourselves would be more proper. Bad as the Constitution has been made by expunging the restriction on the Senate concerning money bills he did not wish to make it worse by expunging the present Section. He had scarcely seen a single corrupt measure in the Legislature of N– Carolina, which could not be traced up to office hunting.

Mr Sherman. The Constitution shd. lay as few temptations as possible in the way of those in power. Men of abilities will increase as the Country grows more populous and, and the means of education are more diffused.

Mr. Pinkney– No State has rendered the members of the Legislature ineligible to offices. In S– Carolina the Judges are eligible into the Legislature. It cannot be supposed then that the motion will be offensive to the people. If the State Constitutions should be revised he believed restrictions of this sort wd be rather diminished than multiplied.

Mr. Wilson could not approve of the Section as it stood, and could not give up his judgment to any supposed objections that might arise among the people. He considered himself as acting & responsible for the welfare of millions not immediately represented in this House. He had also asked himself the serious question what he should say to his constituents in case they should call upon him to tell them why he sacrificed his own Judgment in a case where they author-

ized him to exercise it? Were he to own to them that he sacrificed it in order to flatter their prejudices, he should dread the retort: did you suppose the people of Penna. had not good sense enough to receive a good Government? Under this impression he should certainly follow his own Judgment which disapproved of the section. He would remark in addition to the objections urged agst. it. that as one branch of the Legislature was to be appointed by the Legislatures of the States, the other by the people of the States, as both are to be paid by the States, and to be appointable to State offices; nothing seemed to be wanting to prostrate the Natl. Legislature, but to render its members ineligible to Natl offices, & by that means take away its power of attracting those talents which were necessary to give weight to the Governt. and to render it useful to the people. He was far from thinking the ambition which aspired to Offices of dignity and trust, an ignoble or culpable one. He was sure it was not politic to regard it in that light, or to withhold from it the prospect of those rewards, which might engage it in the career of public service. He observed that the State of Penna. which had gone as far as any State into the policy of fettering power, had not rendered the members of the Legislature ineligible to offices of Govt.

Mr Elsworth did not think the mere postponement of the reward would be any material discouragement of merit. Ambitious minds will serve 2 years or 7 years in the Legislature for the sake of qualifying themselves for other offices. This he thought a sufficient security for obtaining the services of the ablest men in the Legislature, although whilst members they should be ineligible to Public offices. Besides, merit will be most encouraged, when most impartially rewarded. If rewards are to circulate only within the Legislature, merit out of it will be discouraged.

Mr. Mercer was extremely anxious on this point. What led to the appointment of this Convention? The corruption & mutability of the Legislative Councils of the States. If the plan does not remedy these, it will not recommend itself: and we shall not be able in our private capacities to support

& enforce it: nor will the best part of our Citizens exert themselves for the purpose. — It is a great mistake to suppose that the paper we are to propose will govern the U. States? It is The men whom it will bring into the Governt. and interest in maintaining it that is to govern them. The paper will only mark out the mode & the form– Men are the substance and must do the business. All Govt. must be by force or influence. It is not the King of France — but 200,000 janisaries of power that govern that Kingdom. There will be no such force here; influence then must be substituted; and he would ask whether this could be done, if the members of the Legislature should be ineligible to offices of State; whether such a disqualification would not determine all the most influential men to stay at home, and & prefer appointments within their respective States.

Mr. Wilson was by no means satisfied with the answer given by Mr. Elseworth to the argument as to the discouragement of merit. The members must either go a second time into the Legislature, and disqualify themselves — or say to their Constituents, we served you before only from the mercenary view of qualifying ourselves for offices, and haveg answered this purpose we do not chuse to be again elected.

Mr. Govr. Morris put the case of a war, and the Citizen the most capable of conducting it, happening to be a member of the Legislature. What might have been the consequence of such a regulation at the commencement, or even in the Course of the late contest for our liberties?

On question for postponing in order to take up Mr. Pinkneys motion, ⟨it was lost.⟩

N– H– ay– Mas. no. Ct no. N. J– no. Pa ay. Del. ay. Md. ay. Va. ay. N. C. no. S– C. no. Geo. ⟨divd.⟩ [Ayes — 5; noes — 5; divided — 1.] [3]

Mr Govr Morris moved to insert, after "office", except offices in the army or navy: ⟨but in that case their offices shall be vacated⟩ [4]

---

[3] Revised from *Journal*. Madison originally recorded "Geo. ay", which would have determined the question in the affirmative.

[4] Taken from *Journal*.

Mr. Broome 2ds. him

M. Randolph had been & should continue uniformly opposed to the striking out of the clause; as opening a door for influence & corruption. No arguments had made any impression on him, but those which related to the case of war, and a co-existing incapacity of the fittest commanders to be employed. He admitted great weight in these, and would agree to the exception proposed by Mr. Govr. Morris.

Mr. Butler & Mr Pinkney urged a general postponemt. ⟨of 9 Sect. art. VI⟩[5] till it should be seen what powers would be vested in the Senate, when it would be more easy to judge of the expediency of allowing the Officers of State to be chosen out of that body. — A general postponement was agreed to nem. con.[6]

Art: VI. sect. 10. taken up — "that members be paid by their respective States." [7]

Mr. Elseworth said that in reflecting on this subject he had been satisfied that too much dependence on the States would be produced by this mode of payment. He moved ⟨to strike out and insert⟩ "that they should" be paid out of the Treasury ⟨of the U. S.⟩ an allowance not exceeding ⟨(blank)⟩[8] dollars per day or the present value thereof,

Mr. Govr Morris. remarked that if the members were to be paid by the States it would throw an unequal burden on the distant States, which would be unjust as the Legislature was to be a national Assembly. He moved that the payment be out of the Natl. Treasury; leaving the quantum to the discretion of the Natl. Legislature. There could be no reason to fear that they would overpay themselves.

Mr. Butler contended for payment by the States; particularly in the case of the Senate, who will be so long out of their respective States, that they will lose sight of their Constituents unless dependent on them for their support.

Mr Langdon was agst. payment by the States. There would

[5] Taken from *Journal*.

[6] See further references under September 3, note 7.

[7] Upon this debate, see above June 12, June 22, and Appendix A, CCX.

[8] Crossed out "four".

be some difficulty in fixing the sum; but it would be unjust to oblige the distant States to bear the expence of their members in travelling to and from the Seat of Govt.

Mr ⟨Madison.⟩ If the H. of Reps. is to be chosen *biennially* — and the Senate to be *constantly* dependent on the Legislatures which are chosen *annually*, he could not see any chance for that stability in the Genl Govt. the want of which was a principal evil in the State Govts. His fear was that the organization of the Govt supposing the Senate to be really independt. for six years, would not effect our purpose. It was nothing more than a combination of the peculiarities of two of the State Govts. which separately had been found insufficient. The Senate was formed on the model of that of Maryld. The Revisionary check, on that of N. York. What the effect of A union of these provisions might be, could not be foreseen. The enlargement of the sphere of the Government was indeed a circumstance which he thought would be favorable as he had on several occasions undertaken to show. He was however for fixing at least two extremes not to be exceeded by the Natl. Legislre. in the payment of themselves.

Mr. Gerry. There are difficulties on both sides. The observation of Mr. Butler has weight in it. On the other side, the State Legislatures may turn out the Senators by reducing their salaries. Such things have been practised.

Col. Mason. It has not yet been noticed that the clause as it now stands makes the House of Represents. also dependent on the State Legislatures; so that both Houses will be made the instruments of the politics of the States whatever they may be.

Mr. Broom could see no danger in trusting the Genl. Legislature with the payment of themselves. The State Legislatures had this power, and no complaint had been made of it–

Mr. Sherman was not afraid that the Legislature would make their own wages too high; but too low, so that men ever so fit could not serve unless they were at the same time rich. He thought the best plan would be to fix a moderate allowance to be paid out of the Natl. Treasy. and let the States make such additions as they might judge fit. He moved that

5 dollars per day be the sum, any further emoluments to be added by the States.

Mr. Carrol had been much surprised at seeing this clause in the Report. The dependence of both houses on the State Legislatures is compleat; especially as the members of the former are eligible to State offices. The States can now say: if you do not comply with our wishes, we will starve you: if you do we will reward you. The new Govt. in this form was nothing more than a second edition of Congress in two volumes, instead of one, and perhaps with very few amendments —

Mr Dickenson took it for granted that all were convinced of the necessity of making the Genl. Govt. independent of the prejudices, passions, and improper views of the State Legislatures. The contrary of This was effected by the section as it stands. On the other hand, there were objections agst taking a permanent standard as Wheat which had been suggested on a former occasion, as well as against leaving the matter to the pleasure of the Natl. Legislature. He proposed that an Act should be passed every 12 years by the Natl. Legislre settling the quantum of their wages. If the Genl. Govt. should be left dependent on the State Legislatures, it would be happy for us if we had never met in this Room.

Mr. Elseworth was not unwilling himself to trust the Legislature with authority to regulate their own wages, but well knew that an unlimited discretion for that purpose would produce strong, tho' perhaps not insuperable objections. He thought changes in the value of money, provided for by his motion in the words, "or the present value thereof."

Mr. L. Martin. As the Senate is to represent the States, the members of it ought to be paid by the States —

Mr. Carrol. The Senate was to represent & manage the affairs of the whole, and not to be the advocates of State interests. They ought then not to be dependent on nor paid by the States.

On the question for paying the Members of the Legislature out of the Natl Treasury, ÷

N. H. ay. Mas. no. Ct. ay. N. J. ay. Pa. ay. Del. ay. Md. ay. Va. ay. N. C. ay. S. C. no. Geo. ay. [Ayes — 9; noes — 2.]

Mr. Elsworth moved that the pay be fixed at 5 dollrs. ⟨or the present value thereof per day during their attendance & for every thirty miles in travelling to & from Congress.⟩[9]

Mr. Strong preferred 4 dollars, leaving the Sts at liberty to make additions

On question for fixing the pay at 5 dollars.

N. H. no. Mas. no. Ct. ay. N. J. no. Pa. no. Del. no. Md. no. Va. ay. N. C. no. S. C. no. Geo. no. [Ayes — 2; noes — 9.]

Mr. Dickenson proposed that the wages of the members of both houses sd. be required to be the same.

Mr. Broome seconded him.

Mr Ghorum. this would be unreasonable. The Senate will be detained longer from home, will be obliged to remove their families, and in time of war perhaps to sit constantly. Their allowance should certainly be higher. The members of the Senates in the States are allowed more, than those of the other house.

Mr Dickenson withdrew his motion

⟨It was moved & agreed to amend the Section by adding– "to be ascertained by law"⟩[9]

The Section (Art VI. sec. 10) as amended– agreed to nem. con.

Adjd.

McHENRY

Augt. 14.

Sect. 8 agreed to, premising the words "during the session of the legislature".[10]

Sect. 9. postponed.

Sect. 10. altered, that the members of both branches be paid out of the treasury of the United States, their pay to be ascertained by law.

[9] Taken from *Journal.*

[10] According to the Journal this action was taken on August 11.

WEDNESDAY, AUGUST 15, 1787.

JOURNAL

Wednesday August 15. 1787.

On the question to agree to the 11 Sect. of the 6 article as reported [1]

it passed in the affirmative

It was moved and seconded to strike out the latter part of the 12 Sect. of the 6 article,

which passed in the affirmative [2]

It was moved and seconded to amend– the 12. sect. of the 6 article as follows

"Each House shall possess the right of originating all Bills "except Bills for raising money for the purposes of revenue "or for appropriating the same and for fixing the salaries of "the Officers of Government which shall originate in the "House of representatives; but the Senate may propose or "concur with amendments as in other cases"

It was moved and seconded to postpone the consideration of the last amendment

which passed in the affirmative. [Ayes — 6; noes — 5.]

It was moved and seconded to agree to the following amendmt of the 13th sect. of the 6 article.

"Every bill which shall have passed the two Houses, "shall, before it become a law, be severally presented to the "President of the United States and to the Judges of the "supreme court, for the revision of each — If, upon such "revision, they shall approve of it, they shall respectively "signify their approbation by signing it — But, if upon such "revision, it shall appear improper to either or both to be

---

[1] See August 6, note 4.

[2] Not reported by Madison, but confirmed by the clause being struck out in Washington's copy of the Report of the Committee of Detail.

"passed into a law; it shall be returned, with the objections "against it, to that House in which it shall have originated, "who shall enter the objections at large on their Journal, and "proceed to reconsider the bill: But, if, after such reconsid-"eration, two thirds of that House, when either the President "or a Majority of the Judges shall object, or three fourths, "where both shall object, shall agree to pass it, it shall, "together with the objections, be sent to the other House, by "which it shall likewise be reconsidered and, if approved by "two thirds, or three fourths of the other House, as the case "may be, it shall become a law"

which passed in the negative [Ayes — 3; noes — 8.][3]

It was moved and seconded to postpone the consideration of the 13th sect. of the 6th article

which passed in the negative [Ayes — 2; noes — 9.]

It was moved and seconded to strike out the words "two thirds" and to insert the words "three fourths" in the 13th sect. of the 6 article

which passed in the affirmative [Ayes — 6; noes — 4; divided — 1.]

It was moved and seconded to amend the first clause of the 13 sect. of the 6 article as follows

"No Bill or resolve of the Senate and House of repre-"sentatives shall become a Law, or have force until it shall "have been presented to the President of the United States "for his revision"

which passed in the negative. [Ayes — 3; noes — 8.]

[No money shall be drawn from the Treasy of the U. S. but in conseq. of approns by law. withdrawn.

To adjourn Ayes — 3; noes — 7.][4]

It was moved and seconded to strike out the word "seven" and to insert the words "ten ("sundays excepted") in the 13th sect. of the 6 article

which passed in the affirmative [Ayes — 9; noes — 2.]

---

[3] Vote 295, Detail of Ayes and Noes, which notes that it was "Mr. Madison's amendment to the negative by addg the Judiciary".

[4] Votes 299–300, Detail of Ayes and Noes, but there is no reason beyond that of relative position (*i. e.* between Votes 298 and 301) for inserting these questions here.

On the question to agree to the 13 sect. of the 6 article as amended

it passed in the affirmative

And then the House adjourned till to-morrow at 11 o'Clock A. M.

DETAIL OF AYES AND NOES

	New Hampshire	Massachusetts	Rhode Island	Connecticut	New York	New Jersey	Pennsylvania	Delaware	Maryland	Virginia	North Carolina	South Carolina	Georgia	Questions	Ayes	Noes	Divided
[294]	aye	aye		no		no	no	no	no	aye	aye	aye	aye	To postpone the amendmt offered to the 12th section	6	5	
[295]	no	no		no		no	no	aye	aye	aye	no	no	no	To agree to Mr Madison's amendment to the negative by addg the Judiciary	3	8	
[296]	no	no		no		no	no	aye	aye	no	no	no	no	To postpone the considn of the 13. sect. 6 article	2	9	
[297]	no	no		aye		no	dd	aye	aye	aye	aye	aye	no	"three fourths," instead of "two thirds" 13 sect 6 art.	6	4	1
[298]	no	aye		no		no	no	aye	no	no	aye	no	no	To agree to the amendmt "no bill or resolve"	3	8	
[299]						withdrawn								No money shall be drawn from the Treasy of the U. S. but in conseq. of approns by law.			
[300]	no	no	no			no		aye	aye	aye	no	no	no	To adjourn			
[301]	no	no	aye			aye	aye	aye	aye	aye	aye	aye	aye	To insert ten days sundays excepted	9	2	

[End of ninth loose sheet]

MADISON

Wednesday August 15. in Convention

⟨Art: VI.⟩ sect. 11.[5] Agreed to nem. con.

⟨Art: VI⟩ Sect– 12. taken up.[6]

[5] Article VI, Sect. 11. "The enacting stile of the laws of the United States shall be. 'Be it enacted by the Senate and Representatives in Congress assembled'." See August 6, note 4.

[6] Article VI, Sect. 12. "Each House shall possess the right of originating bills, except in the cases beforementioned."

Mr. Strong move⟨d⟩[7] to amend ⟨the article so as to read — "Each House shall possess the right of originating all bills, except bills for raising money for the purposes of revenue, or for appropriating the same and for fixing the salaries of the officers of the Govt. which shall originate in the House of Representatives; but the Senate may propose or concur with amendments as in other cases"⟩[8]

Col. Mason. 2ds. the motion. He was extremely earnest to take this power from the Senate, who he said could already sell the whole Country by means of Treaties.

Mr Ghorum urged the amendment as of great importance. The Senate will first acquire the habit of preparing money bills, and then the practice will grow into an exclusive right of preparing them.

Mr. Gouvernr. Morris opposed it as unnecessary and inconvenient.

Mr. Williamson– some think this restriction on the Senate essential to liberty — others think it of no importance. Why should not the former be indulged. he was for an efficient and stable Govt: but many would not strengthen the Senate if not restricted in the case of money bills. The friends of the Senate would therefore lose more than they would gain by refusing to gratify the other side. He moved to postpone the subject till the powers of the Senate should be gone over.

Mr. Rutlidge 2ds. the motion.

Mr. Mercer should hereafter be agst. returning to a reconsideration of this section. He contended, (alluding to Mr. Mason's observations) that the Senate ought not to have the power of treaties. This power belonged to the Executive department; adding that Treaties would not be final so as to alter the laws of the land, till ratified by legislative authority. This was the case of Treaties in Great Britain; particularly the late Treaty of Commerce with France.

Col. Mason. did not say that a Treaty would repeal a law; but that the Senate by means of treaty might alienate territory &c. without legislative sanction. The cessions of the Brit-

[7] The Journal reports a previous motion, see above note 2.

[8] Revised from *Journal*.

ish Islands in W– Indies by Treaty alone were an example – If Spain should possess herself of Georgia therefore the Senate might by treaty dismember the Union. He wished the motion to be decided now, that the friends of it might know how to conduct themselves.

On question for postponing Sect: 12. ⟨it passed in the affirmative.⟩

N. H. ay. Mas. ay Ct. no. ⟨N. J. no⟩ Pena no. ⟨Del. no⟩ Maryd. no. Va. ay. N. C. ay. S. C. ay– Geo. ay. — [Ayes — 6; noes — 5.][9]

Mr. Ma⟨dison⟩ moved that all acts before they become laws should be submitted both to the Executive and Supreme Judiciary Departments, that if either of these should object $\frac{2}{3}$ of each House, if both should object, $\frac{3}{4}$ of each House, should be necessary to overrule the objections and give to the acts the force of law. — ⟨See the motion at large in the Journal of this date, page 258 [253]. & insert it here.⟩

Mr. Wilson seconds the motion

Mr. Pinkney opposed the interference of the Judges in the Legislative business: it will involve them in parties, and give a previous tincture to their opinions.

Mr. Mercer heartily approved the motion. It as an axiom that the Judiciary ought to be separate from the Legislative: but equally so that it ought to be independent of that department. The true policy of the axiom is that legislative usurpation and oppression may be obviated. He disapproved of the Doctrine that the Judges as expositors of the Constitution should have authority to declare a law void. He thought laws ought to be well and cautiously made, and then to be uncontroulable.

Mr. Gerry. This motion comes to the same thing with what has been already negatived.

Question on the motion of Mr M⟨adison⟩

N– H. no. Mass. no. Ct. no. N. J. no. Pa. no. Del. ay. Maryd. ay. Virga. ay. N. C. no. S. C. no. Geo. no. [Ayes — 3; noes — 8.]

---

[9] Revised from *Journal.*

Mr. Govr. Morris regretted that something like the proposed check could not be agreed to. He dwelt on the importance of public Credit, and the difficulty of supporting it without some strong barrier against the instability of legislative Assemblies. He suggested the idea of requiring three fourths of each house to *repeal* laws where the President should not concur. He had no great reliance on the revisionary power as the Executive was now to be constituted (elected by the Congress). The legislature will contrive to soften down the President. He recited the history of paper emissions, and the perseverance of the legislative assemblies in repeating them, with all the distressing effects ⟨of such measures⟩ before their eyes. Were the National legislature formed, and a war was now to break out, this ruinous expedient would be again resorted to, if not guarded against. The requiring $\frac{3}{4}$ to repeal would, though not a compleat remedy, prevent the hasty passage of laws, and the frequency of those repeals which destroy faith in the public, and which are among our greatest calamities. —

Mr Dickenson was strongly impressed with the remark of Mr. Mercer as to the power of the Judges to set aside the law. He thought no such power ought to exist. He was at the same time at a loss what expedient to substitute. The Justiciary of Aragon he observed became by degrees the lawgiver.

Mr. Govr. Morris, suggested the expedient of an absolute negative in the Executive. He could not agree that the Judiciary which was part of the Executive, should be bound to say that a direct violation of the Constitution was law. A controul over the legislature might have its inconveniences. But view the danger on the other side. The most virtuous citizens will often as members of a legislative body concur in measures which afterwards in their private capacity they will be ashamed of. Encroachments of the popular branch of the Government ought to be guarded agst. The Ephori at Sparta became in the end absolute. The Report of the Council of Censors in Pennsylva points out the many invasions of the legislative department on the Executive numerous as the

latter* is, within the short term of seven years, and in a State where a strong party is opposed to the Constitution, and watching every occasion of turning the public resentments agst. it. If the Executive be overturned by the popular branch, as happened in England, the tyranny of one man will ensue – In Rome where the Aristocracy overturned the throne, the consequence was different. He enlarged on the tendency of the legislative Authority to usurp on the Executive and wished the section to be postponed, in order to consider of some more effectual check than requiring $\frac{2}{3}$ only to overrule the negative of the Executive.

Mr Sherman. Can one man be trusted better than all the others if they all agree? This was neither wise nor safe. He disapproved of Judges meddling in politics and parties. We have gone far enough in forming the negative as it now stands.

Mr. Carrol– when the negative to be overruled by $\frac{2}{3}$ only was agreed to, the *quorum* was not fixed. He remarked that as a majority was now to be the quorum, 17, in the larger, and 8 in the smaller house might carry points. The Advantage that might be taken of this seemed to call for greater impediments to improper laws. He thought the controuling power however of the Executive could not be well decided, till it was seen how the formation of that department would be finally regulated. He wished the consideration of the matter to be postponed.

Mr. Ghorum saw no end to these difficulties and postponements. Some could not agree to the form of Government before the powers were defined. Others could not agree to the powers till it was seen how the Government was to be formed. He thought a majority as large a quorum as was necessary. It was the quorum almost every where fixt in the U. States.

Mr. Wilson; after viewing the subject with all the coolness and attention possible was most apprehensive of a dissolution of the Govt from the legislature swallowing up all the other powers. He remarked that the prejudices agst the Executive

* The Executive consists at this time of abt. 20 members.

resulted from a misapplication of the adage that the parliament was the palladium of liberty. Where the Executive was really formidable, *King* and *Tyrant*, were naturally associated in the minds of people; not *legislature* and *tyranny*. But where the Executive was not formidable, the two last were most properly associated. After the destruction of the King in Great Britain, a more pure and unmixed tyranny sprang up in the parliament than had been exercised by the monarch. He insisted that we had not guarded agst. the danger on this side by a sufficient self-defensive power either to the Executive or Judiciary department–

Mr Rutlidge was strenuous agst postponing; and complained much of the tediousness of the proceedings.

Mr Elseworth held the same language. We grow more & more skeptical as we proceed. If we do not decide soon, we shall be unable to come to any decision.

The question for postponement passed in the negative: ⟨Del: & Maryd only being in the affirmative.⟩[10]

Mr. Williamson moved to change " $\frac{2}{3}$ of each house" into "$\frac{3}{4}$" as requisite to overrule the dissent of the President. He saw no danger in this, and preferred giving the power to the Presidt. alone, to admitting the Judges into the business of legislation.

Mr. Wilson 2ds. the motion; referring to and repeating the ideas of Mr. Carroll.

On this motion for $\frac{3}{4}$. ⟨instead of two thirds; it passed in the affirmative⟩ [11]

N– H– no– Mas. no. Ct. ⟨ay⟩ N– J. no. Pena. divd. Del– ay. Md. ay. Va. ay. N. C. ay. S. C. ay. Geo. no. [Ayes — 6; noes — 4; divided — 1.] [12]

Mr. ⟨Madison,⟩ observing that if the negative of the President was confined to *bills;* it would be evaded by acts under the form and name of Resolutions, votes &c — proposed that "or resolve" should be added after "*bill*" in the beginning of sect 13. with an exception as to votes of adjournment &c.

[10] Taken from *Journal.*

[11] Revised from *Journal.*

[12] Madison originally recorded Connecticut's vote as "no", which made the total vote a negative. The vote was changed to conform to *Journal.*

— after a short and rather confused conversation on the subject, the question was put & rejected, the States being as follows,

N. H. no– Mas. ay– Ct. no. N– J. no– Pena. no. Del ay. Md. no. Va. no. N. C. ay. S. C. no. Geo. no. [Ayes — 3; noes — 8.]

"*Ten* days (Sundays excepted)" instead of "*seven*" were allowed to the President for returning bills with his objections ⟨N. H. & Mas: only voting agst. it. The 13 sect: of art. VI as amended was then agreed to.⟩ [13]

Adjourned.[14]

McHENRY

August 15.

Sect. 11. agreed to.

Sect. 12 postponed.

Sect. 13. Agreed to with the alteration of $\frac{3}{4}$ of each house instead of *two thirds*.

[13] Taken from *Journal*.

[14] See further, Appendix A, LXXXIV.

THURSDAY, AUGUST 16, 1787.

JOURNAL

Thursday August 16. 1787.

It was moved and seconded to agree to the following as the 14 section of the 6. article.

"every order, resolution or vote, to which the concurrence "of the Senate and House of representatives may be necessary "(except on a question of adjournment, and in the cases here-"inafter mentioned) shall be presented to the President for his "revision; and before the same shall have force, shall be ap-"proved by him, or, being disapproved by him, shall be repassed "by the Senate and House of representatives, according to the "rules and limitations prescribed in the case "of a bill"

which passed in the affirmative. [Ayes — 9; noes — 1][1]

It was moved and seconded to insert the following proviso after the first clause of the 1st section of the 7-article.

"Provided that no Tax, Duty or Imposition shall be laid "by the Legislature of the United States on articles exported "from any State"

It was moved and seconded to postpone the consideration of the Proviso

which passed in the affirmative. [Ayes — 10; noes — 1.]

It was moved and seconded to add the words "and post roads" after the words "post offices" in the 7 clause of the 1st sect of the 7. article

which passed in the affirmative. [Ayes — 6; noes — 5.]

It was moved and seconded to strike the words "and emit bills" out of the 8. clause of the 1 section of the 7 article

which passed in the affirmative. [Ayes — 9; noes — 2.]

---

[1] Vote 195, Detail of Ayes and Noes, see *Records* of July 20, note 3; see also note 3 below.

[To adjourn Ayes — 4; noes — 7.][2]
separate questions being taken on the 1, 2, 3, 4, 5, 6, 7 and 8 clauses of the 1. sect. of the 7 article as amended

They passed in the affirmative.

And then the House adjourned till to-morrow at 11 o'Clock A. M.

Detail of Ayes and Noes

[Beginning of p. 12 of blank book][3]

	New Hampshire	Massachusetts	Rhode Island	Connecticut	New York	New Jersey	Pennsylvania	Delaware	Maryland	Virginia	No Carolina	So Carolina	Georgia	Questions	ayes	noes	divided
[302]	aye	aye		aye		aye	aye	aye	no	aye	aye	aye	aye	To postpone the Proviso to the 1st clause 1st sect. 7 article	10	1	
[303]	no	aye		no		no	no	aye	aye	aye	no	aye	aye	To add the words "and Post roads" after "Post offices"	6	5	
[304]	aye	aye		aye		no	aye	aye	no	aye	aye	aye	aye	To strike out the words "and emit bills" 8 clause, 1 section, 7 article	9	2	
[305]	no	no		no		aye	no	no	aye	aye	aye	no	no	To adjourn			

MADISON

Thursday. August 16. in Convention.

Mr. Randolph, having thrown into a new form the motion, putting votes, Resolutions &c. on a footing with Bills, renewed it ⟨as follows. "Every order resolution or vote, to which the concurrence of the Senate & House of Reps. may be necessary (except on a question of adjournment and in the cases here-

[2] Vote 305, Detail of Ayes and Noes, but there is no reason for placing it here, except that it follows Vote 304.

[3] At this point the secretary began keeping the Detail of Ayes and Noes in a bound blank book. On page 1 he apparently started to copy some of the more important votes from the loose sheets. He had thus copied Votes 17, 29, 30, 32, 34–37, 39–41, when he stopped and, leaving ten blank pages, commenced recording the votes of August 16 on page 12. After filling up pages 12–16, he turned back to page 2 and recorded the last votes on that and the page following.

inafter mentioned) shall be presented to the President for his revision; and before the same shall have force shall be approved by him, or being disapproved by him shall be repassed by the Senate & House of Reps according to the rules & limitations prescribed in the case of a Bill")[4]

Mr. Sherman thought it unnecessary, except as to votes taking money out of the Treasury which might be provided for in another place.

On Question as moved by Mr Randolph

N- H. ay. Mas: not present, Ct. ay. N. J. no. Pa. ay. Del. ay. Md. ay. Va. ay. N - C. ay. S. C. ay. Geo. ay. [Ayes — 9; noes — 1; absent — 1.]

⟨The Amendment was made a Section 14. of Art VI.⟩[4]

Art: VII. Sect. 1. taken up.[5]

Mr. L. Martin asked what was meant by the Committee of detail ⟨in the expression⟩ "*duties*" and "*imposts*".[6] If the meaning were the same, the former was unnecessary; if different, the matter ought to be made clear.

Mr Wilson, *duties* are applicable to many objects to which the word *imposts* does not relate. The latter are appropriated to commerce; the former extend to a variety of objects, as stamp duties &c.

Mr. Carroll reminded the Convention of the great difference of interests among the States, and doubts the propriety in that point of view of letting a majority be a quorum.

Mr. Mason urged the necessity of connecting with the power of levying taxes duties &c, ⟨the prohibition in Sect 4 of art VI[7]⟩ that no tax should be laid on exports. He was unwilling to trust to its being done in a future article. He hoped the Northn. States did not mean to deny the Southern this security. It would hereafter be as desirable to the former when the latter should become the most populous. He pro-

---

[4] Taken from *Journal*.

[5] Article VII, Sect. 1. "The Legislature of the United States shall have the power to lay and collect taxes, duties, imposts and excises;"

[6] See Appendix A, CLVIII(48).

[7] Misprint of original Report of the Committe of Detail for Art. VII, see *Records* of August 6, note 5.

fessed his jealousy for the productions of the Southern or as he called them, the staple States. ⟨He moved to insert the following amendment: "provided that no tax duty or imposition, shall be laid by the Legislature of the U. States on articles exported from any State"⟩[8]

Mr Sherman had no objection to the proviso here, other than it would derange the parts of the report as made by the Committee, to take them in such an order.

Mr. Rutlidge. It being of no consequence in what order points are decided, he should vote for the clause as it stood, but on condition that the subsequent part relating to negroes should also be agreed to.

Mr. Governeur Morris considered such a proviso as inadmissible any where. It was so radically objectionable, that it might cost the whole system the support of some members. He contended that it would not in some cases be equitable to tax imports without taxing exports; and that taxes on exports would be often the most easy and proper of the two.

Mr. ⟨Madison⟩ 1. the power of taxing exports is proper in itself, and as the States cannot with propriety exercise it separately, it ought to be vested in them collectively. 2. it might with particular advantage be exercised with regard to articles in which America was not rivalled in foreign markets, as Tobo. &c. The contract between the French Farmers Genl. and Mr. Morris stipulating that if taxes sd. be laid in America on the export of Tobo. they sd. be paid by the Farmers, shewed that it was understood by them, that the price would be thereby raised in America, and consequently the taxes be paid by the European Consumer. 3. it would be unjust to the States whose produce was exported by their neighbours, to leave it subject to be taxed by the latter. This was a grievance which had already filled N. H. Cont. N. Jery. Del: and N. Carolina with loud complaints, as it related to imports, and they would be equally authorized by taxes ⟨by the States⟩ on exports. 4. The Southn. States being most in danger and most needing naval protection, could the less complain if the

[8] Taken from *Journal.*

burden should be somewhat heaviest on them. 5. we are ⟨not⟩ providing for the present moment only, and time will equalize the situation of the States in this matter. ⟨He was for these reasons, agst the motion⟩

Mr. Williamson considered the clause proposed agst taxes on exports as reasonable and necessary.

Mr. Elseworth was agst. Taxing exports; but thought the prohibition stood in the most proper place, and was agst. deranging the order reported by the Committee

Mr. Wilson was decidedly agst prohibiting general taxes on exports. He dwelt on the injustice and impolicy of leaving N. Jersey Connecticut &c any longer subject to the exactions of their commercial neighbours.

Mr Gerry thought the legislature could not be trusted with such a power. It might ruin the Country. It might be exercised partially, raising one and depressing another part of it.

Mr Govr Morris. However the legislative power may be formed, it will if disposed be able to ruin the Country — He considered the taxing of exports to be in many cases highly politic. Virginia has found her account in taxing Tobacco. All Countries having peculiar articles tax the exportation of them; as France her wines and brandies. A tax here on lumber, would fall on the W. Indies & punish their restrictions on our trade. The same is true of live-stock and in some degree of flour. In case of a dearth in the West Indies, we may extort what we please. Taxes on exports are a necessary source of revenue. For a long time the people of America will not have money to pay direct taxes. Seize and sell their effects and you push them into Revolts —

Mr. Mercer was strenuous against giving Congress power to tax exports. Such taxes were impolitic, as encouraging the raising of articles not meant for exportation. The States had now a right where their situation permitted, to tax both the imports and exports of their uncommercial neighbours. It was enough for them to sacrifice one half of it. It had been said the Southern States had most need of naval protection. The reverse was the case. Were it not for promoting the carrying trade of the Northn States, the Southn States could let

their trade go into foreign bottoms, where it would not need our protection. Virginia by taxing her tobacco had given an advantage to that of Maryland.

Mr. Sherman. To examine and compare the States in relation to imports and exports will be opening a boundless field. He thought the matter had been adjusted, and that imports were to be subject, and exports not, to be taxed. He thought it wrong to tax exports except it might be such articles as ought not to be exported. The complexity of the business in America would render an equal tax on exports impracticable. The oppression of the uncommercial States was guarded agst. by the power to regulate trade between the States. As to compelling foreigners, that might be done by regulating trade in general. The Government would not be trusted with such a power. Objections are most likely to be excited by considerations relating to taxes & money. A power to tax exports would shipwreck the whole.

Mr. Carrol was surprised that any objection should be made to an exception of exports from the power of taxation.

It was finally agreed that the question concerning exports shd. lie over for the place in which the exception stood in the report.[9] ⟨Maryd. alone voting agst it⟩ [10]

Sect: 1. (art. VII) agreed to: Mr. Gerry alone answering no.

Clause for regulating commerce with foreign nations &c. agreed to nem. con.

for[11] coining money. agd. to nem. con.

for regulating foreign coin. do. do.

for fixing the standard of weights & measures. do. do.

"To establish post-offices". Mr Gerry moved to add, and post-roads. Mr. Mercer 2ded. & on question

N– H– no– Mas– ay– Ct. no. N. J– no. Pena, no. Del. ay. Md. ay. Va. ay. N. C. no. S. C. ay. Geo. ay. [Ayes 6; noes — 5.]

Mr. Govr Morris moved to strike out "and emit bills on

---

[9] See further August 21, note 15.

[10] Taken from *Journal*.

[11] Madison omits clause 3, "to establish an uniform rule of naturalization", included in the Journal.

the credit of the U. States"[12] — If the United States had credit such bills would be unnecessary: if they had not unjust & useless.

Mr Butler, 2ds. the motion.

Mr. Madison, will it not be sufficient to prohibit the making them a *tender?* This will remove the temptation to emit them with unjust views. And promissory notes in that shape may in some emergencies be best.

Mr. Govr. Morris. striking out the words will leave room still for notes of a *responsible* minister which will do all the good without the mischief. The Monied interest will oppose the plan of Government, if paper emissions be not prohibited.

Mr. Ghorum was for striking out, without inserting any prohibition. if the words stand they may suggest and lead to the measure.

Col Mason had doubts on the subject. Congs. he thought would not have the power unless it were expressed. Though he had a mortal hatred to paper money, yet as he could not foresee all emergences, he was unwilling to tie the hands of the Legislature. He observed that the late war could not have been carried on, had such a prohibition existed.

Mr Ghorum- The power as far as it will be necessary or safe, is involved in that of borrowing.

Mr Mercer was a friend to paper money, though in the present state & temper of America, he should neither propose nor approve of such a measure. He was consequently opposed to a prohibition of it altogether. It will stamp suspicion on the Government to deny it a discretion on this point. It was impolitic also to excite the opposition of all those who were friends to paper money. The people of property would be sure to be on the side of the plan, and it was impolitic to purchase their further attachment with the loss of the opposite class of Citizens

Mr. Elseworth thought this a favorable moment to shut and bar the door against paper money. The mischiefs of the various experiments which had been made, were now

[12] Upon this question, see Appendix A, CLVIII (50), CCCXIV.

fresh in the public mind and had excited the disgust of all the respectable part of America. By withholding the power from the new Governt. more friends of influence would be gained to it than by almost any thing else– Paper money can in no case be necessary– Give the Government credit, and other resources will offer– The power may do harm, never good.

Mr. Randolph, nothwithstanding his antipathy to paper money, could not agree to strike out the words, as he could not foresee all the occasions that might arise.

Mr Wilson. It will have a most salutary influence on the credit of the U. States to remove the possibility of paper money. This expedient can never succeed whilst its mischiefs are remembered. And as long as it can be resorted to, it will be a bar to other resources.

Mr. Butler. remarked that paper was a legal tender in no Country in Europe. He was urgent for disarming the Government of such a power.

Mr Mason was still averse to tying the hands of the Legislature *altogether*. If there was no example in Europe as just remarked it might be observed on the other side, that there was none in which the Government was restrained on this head.

Mr. Read, thought the words, if not struck out, would be as alarming as the mark of the Beast in Revelations.

Mr. Langdon had rather reject the whole plan than retain the three words "(and emit bills").[13]

On the motion for striking out

N. H. ay– Mas. ay. Ct. ay. N–J. no. Pa. ay. Del. ay. Md. no. Va. ay.* N. C– ay. S. C. ay. Geo. ay. [Ayes — 9; noes — 2.]

The clause for borrowing money, agreed to nem. con.

Adjd

* This vote in the affirmative by Virga. was occasioned by the acquiescence of Mr. Madison who became satisfied that striking out the words would not disable the Govt from the use of public notes as far as they could be safe & proper; & would only cut off the pretext for a paper currency and particularly for making the bills a tender either for public or private debts.

[13] See Appendix A, CCIII.

McHENRY

16 Augt.

Agreed to Article VII from Sec: 1. to the paragraph "borrow money and emit bills on the credit of the united States inclusive, with the addition of the words "and post roads" and the omission of "*and emit bills*".

Mr. Martin appeared in convention.

FRIDAY, AUGUST 17, 1787.

JOURNAL

Friday August 17. 1787.

It was moved and seconded to insert the word "joint" before the word "ballot" in the 9 clause of the 1 sect. 7 article

which passed in the affirmative [Ayes — 7; noes — 3.]

It was moved and seconded to strike out the 9 clause of the 1. sect. of the 7 article

which passed in the negative [Ayes — 4; noes — 6.]

[To strike out the words "and punishmt 11 [12] clause 1 sect 7 art Ayes — 7; noes — 3.][1]

It was moved and seconded to alter the first part of the 12th clause 1 sect. 7 article to read as follows

"To punish piracies and felonies committed on the high seas"

which passed in the affirmative [Ayes — 7; noes — 3.]

It was moved and seconded to insert the words "define and" between the word "To" and the word "punish" in the 12 clause

which passed in the affirmative

It was moved and seconded to amend the second part of the 12 clause as follows

"To punish the counterfeiting of the securities and current coin of the United States, and offences against the law of nations"

which passed in the affirmative

["or without, when the Legislature cannot. Ayes — 5; noes — 3; divided — 2.][2]

---

[1] Vote 308, Detail of Ayes and Noes.

[2] Vote 310, Detail of Ayes and Noes.

On the question to agree to the 13 clause of the 1st sect. 7 article amended as follows

"To subdue a rebellion in any State against the govern-"ment thereof on the application of it's Legislature, or with-"out when the Legislature cannot meet"

it passed in the negative [Ayes — 4; noes — 5.]

["To subdue rebellion" Ayes — 2; noes — 4; divided — 1.][3]

It was moved and seconded to strike out the word "make" and to insert the word "declare" in the 14th clause

which passed in the negative [Ayes — 4; noes — 5.]

It was moved and seconded to strike out the 14 clause

which passed in the negative.

The question being again taken to strike out the word "make" and to insert the word "declare" in the 14. clause

it passed in the affirmative [Ayes — 8; noes — 1.]

It was moved and seconded to add the words

"and to make peace" to the 14 clause

which passed in the negative [Ayes — 0; noes — 10.]

Separate questions having been taken on the 9, 10, 11, 12, and 14 clauses of the 1st section, 7 article as amended.

They passed in the affirmative

And the House adjourned till to-morrow at 11 o'Clock A. M.

[3] Vote 312, Detail of Ayes and Noes, see below, note 7.

DETAIL OF AYES AND NOES

	New Hampshire	Massachusetts	Rhode Island	Connecticut	New York	New Jersey	Pennsylvania	Delaware	Maryland	Virginia	No Carolina	So Carolina	Georgia	Questions	ayes	noes	divided
[306]	aye	aye		no		no	aye		no	aye	aye	aye	aye	To appoint a Treasurer by joint ballot	7	3	
[307]	no	no		no			aye	aye	aye	no	no	aye	no	To strike out the 9 clause of ye 1 sect 7 article	4	6	
[308]	no	aye		no			aye	aye	no	aye	aye	aye	aye	To strike out the words "and punishmt 11 clause 1 sect 7 art	7	3	
[309]	aye	aye		no			aye	aye	aye	no	no	aye	aye	To punish piracies & felonies committed on the high seas.	7	3	
[310]	aye	no		aye			dd	no	no	aye	dd	aye	aye	"or without, when the Legislature cannot.	5	3	2
[311]	aye	no		aye				no	no	aye	no	no	aye	To agree to the 13 clause as amended			
[312]	aye			no					no	no	dd	aye	no	"To subdue rebellion"			
[313]	no			no			aye	aye	no	aye	aye	no	no	To strike out "make" to insert "declare"	4	5	
[314]	no			aye			aye	aye	aye	aye	aye	aye	aye	The last question repeated	8	1	
[315]	no	no		no			no	no	no	no	no	no	no	To add "to make peace" to ye 12 clause			

MADISON

Friday August 17th. in Convention

Art VII. sect. 1. resumed. On the clause "to appoint Treasurer by ballot".

Mr Ghorum moved to insert "joint" before ballot, as more convenient as well as reasonable, than to require the separate concurrence of the Senate.

Mr. Pinkney 2ds. the motion. Mr Sherman opposed it as favoring the larger States.

Mr. Read moved to strike out the clause, leaving the appointment of the Treasurer as of other officers to the Executive. The Legislature was an improper body for

appointments. Those of the State legislatures were a proof of it— The Executive being responsible would make a good choice.

Mr Mercer 2ds. the motion of Mr Read.

On the motion for inserting the word "joint" before ballot

N. H– ay. Mas. ay. Ct. no. N. J. no. Pa. ay. Md. no. Va. ay– N– C. ay. S. C. ay. Geo– ay– [Ayes — 7; noes — 3.]

Col. Mason in opposition to Mr. Reads motion desired it might be considered to whom the money would belong; if to the people, the legislature representing the people ought to appoint the keepers of it.

On striking out the clause as amended by inserting "Joint"

N. H. no– Mas. no. Ct. no. Pa. ay– Del– ay. Md. ay. Va. no. N. C. no. S– C– ay. Geo. no– [Ayes — 4; noes — 6.]

"To constitute inferior tribunals" agreed to nem. con.

"To make rules as to captures on land & water"– do do

"To declare the law and punishment of piracies and felonies &c" &c considered.

Mr. ⟨Madison⟩ moved to strike out "and punishment" &c–

Mr. Mason doubts the safety of it, considering the strict rule of construction in criminal cases. He doubted also the propriety of taking the power in all these cases wholly from the States.

Mr Governr Morris thought it would be necessary to extend the authority farther, so as to provide for the punishment of counterfeiting in general. Bills of exchange for example might be forged in one State and carried into another:

It was suggested by some other member that *foreign* paper might be counterfeited by Citizens; and that it might be politic to provide by national authority for the punishment of it.

Mr Randolph did not conceive that expunging "the punishment" would be a constructive exclusion of the power. He doubted only the efficacy of the word "declare".

Mr Wilson was in favor of the motion– Strictness was not necessary in giving authority to enact penal laws; though necessary in enacting & expounding them.

On motion for striking out "and punishment" as moved by Mr ⟨Madison⟩
N. H. no. Mas. ay. Ct no. Pa ay. Del. ay– Md no. Va. ay. N– C– ay. S– C. ay– Geo. ay. [Ayes — 7; noes — 3.]

Mr Govr Morris moved to strike out "declare the law" and insert "punish" before "piracies". and on the question

N– H– ay. Mas– ay. Ct. no. Pa. ay. Del. ay. Md ay. Va. no. N. C– no. S. C– ay. Geo– ay. [Ayes — 7; noes — 3.]

Mr. M⟨adison,⟩ and Mr. Randolph moved to insert, "define &." before "punish".

Mr. Wilson thought "felonies" sufficiently defined by Common law.

Mr. Dickenson concurred with Mr Wilson

Mr Mercer was in favor of the amendment.

Mr M⟨adison.⟩ felony at common law is vague.[4] It is also defective. One defect is supplied by Stat: of Anne as to running away with vessels which at common law was a breach of trust only. Besides no foreign law should be a standard farther than is expressly adopted — If the laws of the States were to prevail on this subject, the citizens of different States would be subject to different punishments for the same offence at sea — There would be neither uniformity nor stability in the law — The proper remedy for all these difficulties was to vest the power proposed by the term "define" in the Natl. legislature.

Mr Govr. Morris would prefer *designate* to *define*, the latter being as he conceived, limited to the preexisting meaning. ——— It was said by others to be applicable to the creating of offences also, and therefore suited the case both of felonies & of piracies. ⟨The motion of Mr. M. & Mr. R was agreed to.⟩[5]

Mr. Elseworth enlarged the motion so as to read "to define and punish piracies and felonies committed on the high seas, counterfeiting the securities and current coin of the U. States, and offences agst. the law of Nations" which was agreed to, nem con.

"To subdue a rebellion in any State, on the application of its legislature"

---

[4] See Appendix A, CCXV.

[5] Taken from *Journal*.

Mr Pinkney moved to strike out "on the application of its legislature"

Mr Govr. Morris 2ds.

Mr L– Martin opposed it as giving a dangerous & unnecessary power. The consent of the State ought to precede the introduction of any extraneous force whatever.

Mr. Mercer supported the opposition of Mr. Martin.

Mr Elseworth proposed to add after "legislature" "or Executive".

Mr Govr Morris. The Executive may possibly be at the head of the Rebellion. The Genl Govt. should enforce obedience in all cases where it may be necessary.

Mr. Ellsworth. In many cases The Genl. Govt. ought not to be able to interpose unless called upon. He was willing to vary his motion so as to read, "⟨or without it⟩[6] when the legislature cannot meet."

Mr. Gerry was agst. letting loose the myrmidons of the U. States on a State without its own consent. The States will be the best Judges in such cases. More blood would have been spilt in Massts in the late insurrection, if the Genl. authority had intermeddled.

Mr. Langdon was for striking out as moved by Mr. Pinkney. The apprehension of the national force, will have a salutary effect in preventing insurrections.

Mr Randolph– If the Natl. Legislature is to judge whether the State legislature can or cannot meet, that amendment would make the clause as objectionable as the motion of Mr Pinkney.

Mr. Govr. Morris. We are acting a very strange part. We first form a strong man to protect us, and at the same time wish to tie his hands behind him, The legislature may surely be trusted with such a power to preserve the public tranquillity.

On the motion to add "or without it (application) when the legislature cannot meet"

N. H. ay. Mas. no. Ct ay. Pa. divd. Del. no. Md. no. Va.

[6] Crossed out "& of the Executive"; revised from *Journal*.

ay. N– C. divd. S. C. ay. Geo. ay. [Ayes — 5; noes — 3; divided — 2.] so agreed to —

Mr. ⟨Madison⟩ and Mr. Dickenson moved ⟨to insert as explanatory,⟩ after "State" — "against the Government thereof" There might be a rebellion agst the U– States. — ⟨which was⟩ Agreed to nem– con.

On the clause as amended

N. H. ay. Mas–* abst. Ct ay. Pen. abst. Del. no. Md. no. Va. ay. N– C. no. S. C. no– Georg. ay — ⟨so it was⟩ lost [Ayes — 4; noes — 4; absent — 2.]

"To[7] make war"

Mr Pinkney opposed the vesting this power in the Legislature.[8] Its proceedings were too slow. It wd. meet but once a year. The Hs. of Reps. would be too numerous for such deliberations. The Senate would be the best depositary, being more acquainted with foreign affairs, and most capable of proper resolutions. If the States are equally represented in Senate, so as to give no advantage to large States, the power will notwithstanding be safe, as the small have their all at stake in such cases as well as the large States. It would be singular for one– authority to make war, and another peace.

Mr Butler. The Objections agst the Legislature lie in a great degree agst the Senate. He was for vesting the power in the President, who will have all the requisite qualities, and will not make war but when the Nation will support it.

Mr. M⟨adison⟩ and Mr Gerry moved to insert "*declare*," striking out "*make*" war; leaving to the Executive the power to repel sudden attacks.

Mr Sharman thought it stood very well. The Executive shd. be able to repel and not to commence war. "Make" better than "declare" the latter narrowing the power too much.

Mr Gerry never expected to hear in a republic a motion to empower the Executive alone to declare war.

* ⟨In the printed Journal Mas. no⟩

[7] Crossed out "Mr. Dickenson moved". A considerable blank space was left apparently for the insertion of the motion and the action upon it. This may have been Vote 312, Detail of Ayes and Noes, see the Journal above.

[8] See Appendix A, CCCXXVI.

Mr. Elseworth. there is a material difference between the cases of making *war*, and making *peace*. It shd. be more easy to get out of war, than into it. War also is a simple and overt declaration. peace attended with intricate & secret negociations.

Mr. Mason was agst giving the power of war to the Executive, because not ⟨safely⟩ to be trusted with it; or to the Senate, because not so constructed as to be entitled to it. He was for clogging rather than facilitating war; but for facilitating peace. He preferred "*declare*" to "*make*".

On the Motion to insert *declare* — in place of *Make*, ⟨it was agreed to.⟩

N. H. no. Mas. abst. Cont. no.* Pa ay. Del. ay. Md. ay. Va. ay. N. C. ay. S. C. ay. Geo- ay. [Ayes — 7; noes — 2; absent — 1.]

Mr. Pinkney's motion to strike out whole clause, disagd. to without call of States.

Mr Butler moved to give the Legislature power of peace, as they were to have that of war.

Mr Gerry 2ds. him. 8 Senators may possibly exercise the power if vested in that body, and 14 if all should be present; and may consequently give up part of the U. States. The Senate are more liable to be corrupted by an Enemy than the whole Legislature.

On the motion for adding "and peace" after "war"

N. H. no. Mas. no. Ct. no. Pa. no. Del. no. Md. no. Va. no. N. C. ⟨no⟩ [9] S. C no. Geo. no. [Ayes — 0; noes — 10.]

Adjourned

* On the remark by Mr. King that "*make*" war might be understood to "conduct" it which was an Executive function, Mr. Elseworth gave up his objection ⟨and the vote of Cont was changed to — ay.⟩[10]

[9] Madison originally left a blank after "N. C."

[10] The Journal shows that the question was repeated.

McHENRY

August 17.

Agreed "to appoint a treasurer by joint Ballot; To constitute tribunals inferior to the supreme court; To make rules concerning captures on land and water;

expunged the next section and inserted

To define and punish piracies and felonies committed on the high seas;

To punish counterfeiting the securities and the current coin of the United States.

Struck out the clause To subdue a rebellion etc.

Debated the difference between a power to declare war, and to make war — amended by substituting declare — adjourned without a question on the clause.

SATURDAY, AUGUST 18, 1787.

JOURNAL

Saturday August 18. 1787.

The following additional powers proposed to be vested in the Legislature of the United States having been submitted to the consideration of the Convention — It was moved and seconded to refer them to the Committee to whom the proceedings of the Convention were referred

which passed in the affirmative

The propositions are as follows

To dispose of the unappropriated lands of the United States

To institute temporary governments for new States arising thereon

To regulate affairs with the Indians as well within as without the limits of the United States

To exercise exclusively Legislative authority at the seat of the general Government, and over a district around the same, not exceeding   square miles: the consent of the Legislature of the State or States comprising such district being first obtained

To grant charters of incorporation in cases where the public good may require them, and the authority of a single State may be incompetent

To secure to literary authors their copy rights for a limited time

To establish an University

To encourage, by proper premiums and provisions, the advancement of useful knowledge and discoveries

To authorise the Executive to procure and hold for the use of the United States landed property for the erection of forts, magazines, and other necessary buildings

To fix and permanently establish the seat of Government of

the United-States in which they shall possess the exclusive right of soil and jurisdiction

To establish seminaries for the promotion of literature and the arts and sciences

To grant charters of incorporation

To grant patents for useful inventions

To secure to authors exclusive rights for a certain time

To establish public institutions, rewards and immunities for the promotion of agriculture, commerce, trades, and manufactures.

That Funds which shall be appropriated for payment of public Creditors shall not during the time of such appropriation be diverted or applied to any other purpose — and to prepare a clause or clauses for restraining the Legislature of the United States from establishing a perpetual revenue

To secure the payment of the public debt.

To secure all Creditors, under the new Constitution, from a violation of the public faith. when pledged by the authority of the Legislature

To grant letters of marque and reprisal

To regulate Stages on the post-roads.

It was moved and seconded That a Committee to consist of a Member from each State be appointed to consider the necessity and expediency of the debts of the several States being assumed by the United States

which passed in the affirmative [Ayes — 6; noes — 4; divided — 1.][1]

and a Committee was appointed by ballot of the honorable Mr Langdon, Mr King, Mr Sherman, Mr Livingston, Mr Clymer, Mr Dickinson, Mr Mc Henry, Mr Mason, Mr Williamson, Mr C. C. Pinckney, and Mr Baldwin.

It was moved and seconded to agree to the following resolution, namely

Resolved That this Convention will meet punctually at 10 o'clock every morning (Sundays excepted) and sit till four o'clock in the afternoon, at which time the President shall

[1] Vote 316, Detail of Ayes and Noes, which notes that it was "Mr. Rutledge's proposition".

adjourn the Convention and that no motion for adjournment be allowed.

which passed in the affirmative [Ayes — 9; noes — 2.]

It was moved and seconded to insert the words "and support" between the word "raise" and the word "armies" in the 14. clause, 1 sect, 7 article

which passed in the affirmative

It was moved and seconded to strike out the words "build and equip" and to insert the words "provide and maintain" in the 15 clause, 1 sect. 7 article

which passed in the affirmative

It was moved and seconded to insert the following as a 16th clause, in the 1 sect. of the 7. article

"To make rules for the government and regulation of the land and naval forces"

which passed in the affirmative

It was moved and seconded to annex the following proviso to the last clause

"provided that in time of peace the army shall not consist "of more than thousand men"

which passed[2] in the negative.

It was moved and seconded to insert the following as a clause in the 1 sect. of the 7 article

"to make laws for regulating and disciplining the militia "of the several States, reserving to the several States the "appointment of their militia Officers"

It was moved and seconded to postpone the last clause in order to take up the following

"To establish an uniformity of exercise and arms for the "militia — and rules for their government when called into "service under the authority of the United States: and to "establish and regulate a militia in any State where it's Legis-"lature shall neglect to do it"

It was moved and seconded to refer the last two motions to a Committee

which passed in the affirmative

---

[2] Crossed out "nem con".

and they were referred to the Committee of eleven. [Ayes — 8; noes — 2; divided — 1.]

And then the House adjourned till monday next at 10 o'clock A. M.

DETAIL OF AYES AND NOES.

	New Hampshire	Massachusetts	Rhode Island	Connecticut	New York	New Jersey	Pennsylvania	Delaware	Maryland	Virginia	No Carolina	So Carolina	Georgia	Questions	ayes	noes	divided
[316]	no	aye		aye		no	dd	no	no	aye	aye	aye	aye	To refer Mr Rutledge's proposition respecting the public debt to a Committee of a Member from each State	6	4	1
[317]	aye	aye		aye		aye	no	aye	no	aye	aye	aye	aye	To meet at 10 o'clock to adjourn at 4.	9	2	
[318]	aye	aye		no		no	aye	aye	dd	aye	aye	aye	aye	To commit the two motions respectg militia to the Committee of 11.	8	2	1

MADISON

Saturday August 18. in Convention

⟨Mr– Madison[3] submitted in order to be referred to the Committee of detail the following powers as proper to be added to those of the General Legislature

"To dispose of the unappropriated lands of the U. States"

"To institute temporary Governments for New States arising therein"

"To regulate affairs with the Indians as well within as without the limits of the U. States

[3] Madison's original record stood: — "Mr. Pinkney proposed for consideration several additional powers which had occurred to him. Mr. M. proposed the following, to be referred to a committee." Then follow ten numbered powers. This was all stricken out and the record as here given taken from the printed Journal. Madison's original list corresponds with this, except: in the 2d he had "thereon" instead of "therein" (the Journal also has "thereon"); in the 4th he had "comprehending" instead of "comprising"; and there was one in addition, — "7 To secure to the inventors of useful machines and implements the benefits thereof for a limited time."

"To exercise exclusively Legislative authority at the seat of the General Government, and over a district around the same not, exceeding square miles; the Consent of the Legislature of the State or States comprising the same, being first obtained"

"To grant charters of incorporation in cases where the Public good may require them, and the authority of a single State may be incompetent"

"To secure to literary authors their copyrights for a limited time"

"To establish an University"

"To encourage by premiums & provisions, the advancement of useful knowledge and discoveries"

"To authorize the Executive to procure and hold for the use of the U — S. landed property for the erection of Forts, Magazines, and other necessary buildings"

These propositions were referred to the Committee of detail which had prepared the Report and at the same time the following which were moved by Mr. Pinkney:[4] — in both cases unanimously.

"To fix and permanently establish the seat of Government of the U. S. in which they shall possess the exclusive right of soil & jurisdiction"

"To establish seminaries for the promotion of literature and the arts & sciences"

"To grant charters of incorporation"

"To grant patents for useful inventions"

"To secure to Authors exclusive rights for a certain time"

"To establish public institutions, rewards and immunities for the promotion of agriculture, commerce, trades and manufactures"

"That funds which shall be appropriated for the payment of public Creditors, shall not during the time of such appropriation, be diverted or applied to any other purpose– and that

[4] It is hardly possible that all of these could have been suggested by Pinckney alone. The last five would seem to have been suggested by Gerry, Rutledge and Mason, see below.

the Committee prepare a clause or clauses for restraining the Legislature of the U. S. from establishing a perpetual revenue"

"To secure the payment of the public debt"

"To secure all creditors under the New Constitution from a violation of the public faith when pledged by the authority of the Legislature"

"To grant letters of mark and reprisal"

"To regulate Stages on the post roads")

Mr Mason introduced the subject of regulating the militia.[5] He thought such a power necessary to be given to the Genl. Government. He hoped there would be no standing army in time of peace, unless it might be for a few garrisons. The Militia ought therefore to be the more effectually prepared for the public defence. Thirteen States will never concur in any one system, if the displining of the Militia be left in their hands. If they will not give up the power over the whole, they probably will over a part as a select militia. He moved as an addition to the propositions just referred to the Committee of detail, & to be referred in like manner, "a power to regulate the militia".

Mr. Gerry remarked that some provision ought to be made in favor of public Securities,[6] and something inserted concerning letters of marque, which he thought not included in the power of war. He proposed that these subjects should also go to a Committee.

Mr. Rutlidge moved to refer a clause "that funds appropriated to public creditors should not be diverted to other purposes."

Mr. Mason was much attached to the principle, but was afraid such a fetter might be dangerous in time of war. He suggested the necessity of preventing the danger of perpetual revenue which must of necessity subvert the liberty of any Country. If it be objected to on the principal of Mr. Rut-

[5] Upon this subject see August 21, August 22, and August 23 (with references under note 4.)

[6] Charges as to Gerry's motives in making this proposal, and Gerry's defense, will be found in Appendix A, CLVII, CLXII, CLXXV, CLXXXIX, CXCIX, see also August 25. On the subject of the indebtedness of the Confederation, see below August 21–24, and August 25 (with references under note 5.)

lidge's motion that Public Credit may require perpetual provisions, that case might be excepted; it being declared that in other cases, no taxes should be laid for a longer term than years. He considered the caution observed in Great Britain on this point as the paladium of the public liberty.

Mr. Rutlidge's motion was referred — He then moved that a Grand Committee ⟨be appointed to⟩ consider the necessity and expediency of the U– States assuming all the State debts — A regular settlement between the Union & the several States would never take place. The assumption would be just as the State debts were contracted in the common defence. It was necessary, as the taxes on imports the only sure source of revenue were to be given up to the Union. It was politic, as by disburdening the people of the State debts it would conciliate them to the plan.

Mr. King and Mr Pinkney seconded the motion

(Col. Mason interposed a motion that the Committee prepare a clause for restraining perpetual revenue, which was agreed to nem– con.)

Mr. Sherman thought it would be better to authorize the Legislature to assume the State debts, than to say positively it should be done. He considered the measure as just and that it would have a good effect to say something about the Matter.

Mr. Elseworth differed from Mr. Sherman — As far as the State debts ought in equity to be assumed, he conceived that they might and would be so.

Mr. Pinkney observed that a great part of the State debts were of such a nature that although in point of policy and true equity ⟨they ought⟩, yet would they not be viewed in the light of fœderal expenditures.

Mr. King thought the matter of more consequence than Mr Elseworth seemed to do; and that it was well worthy of commitment. Besides the considerations of justice and policy which had been mentioned. it might be remarked that the State Creditors an active and formidable party would otherwise be opposed to a plan which transferred to the Union the best resources of the States without transferring the State

debts at the same time. The State Creditors had generally been the strongest foes to the impost-plan. The State debts probably were of greater amount than the fœderal. He would not say that it was practicable to consolidate the debts, but he thought it would be prudent to have the subject considered by a Committee.

On Mr. Rutlidge's motion, that Come be appointed to consider of the assumption &c

N. H. no. Mas. ay– Ct ay. N– J. no. Pa divd. Del. no. Md no. Va. ay. N. C. ay. S. C ay. Geo– ay. [Ayes — 6; noes — 4; divided — 1.]

Mr. Gerry's motion to provide for[7] ⟨public securities⟩ for stages on post-roads, and for letters of marque and reprisal, were committed nem. con.

Mr. King suggested that all unlocated lands of particular States ought to be given up if State debts were to be assumed. — Mr Williamson concurred in the idea.

A Grand Committee was appointed consisting of ⟨(The Come. appointed by ballot were — Mr. Langdon, Mr. King, Mr. Sharman. Mr. Livingston. Mr. Clymer, Mr. Dickenson, Mr. McHenry, Mr. Mason, Mr– Williamson, Mr. C. C. Pinkney, Mr. Baldwin.)⟩[8]

Mr. Rutlidge remarked on the length of the Session, the probable impatience of the public and the extreme anxiety of many members of the Convention to bring the business to an end; concluding with a motion that the Convention meet henceforward, precisely at 10 oC. A. M. and that precisely at 4 oC. P. M., the President adjourn the House without motion for the purpose. and that no motion to adjourn sooner be allowed [9]

On this question

N– H. ay. Mas– ay. Ct ay. N. J– ay. Pa. no– Del. ay. Md no. Va. ay. N– C– ay. S. C. ay– Geo. ay.

[Ayes — 9; noes — 2.]

Mr. Elseworth observed that a Council had not yet been provided for the President. He conceived there ought to be

[7] Crossed out "securing public debts". [8] Taken from *Journal.*

[9] See May 25 note 1, and Appendix A, LXXXVIII, XC, CXLI.

one. His proposition was that it should be composed of the President of the Senate– the Chief-Justice, and the Ministers as they might be estabd. for the departments of foreign & domestic affairs, war finance, and marine, who should advise but not conclude the President.

Mr Pinkney wished the proposition to lie over, as notice had been given for a like purpose by Mr. Govr. Morris who was not then on the floor. His own idea was that the President shd. be authorized to call for advice or not as he might chuse. Give him an able Council and it will thwart him; a weak one and he will shelter himself under their sanction.

Mr Gerry was agst. letting the heads of the departments, particularly of finance have any thing to do in business connected with legislation. He mentioned the Chief Justice also as particularly exceptionable. These men will also be so taken up with other matters as to neglect their own proper duties.

Mr. Dickenson urged that the great appointments should be made by the Legislature, in which case they might properly be consulted by the Executive — but not if made by the Executive himself — This subject by general Consent lay over; & the House proceeded to the clause "To raise armies".

Mr. Ghorum moved to add "and support" after "raise". Agreed to nem. con. and then the clause agreed to nem – con– as amended

Mr Gerry took notice that there was ⟨no⟩ check here agst. standing armies in time of peace. The existing Congs. is so constructed that it cannot of itself maintain an army. This wd. not be the case under the new system. The people were jealous on this head, and great opposition to the plan would spring from such an omission. He suspected that preparations of force were now making agst. it. (he seemed to allude to the activity of the Govr. of N. York at this crisis in disciplining the militia of that State.) He thought an army dangerous in time of peace & could never consent to a power to keep up an indefinite number. He proposed that there shall not be kept up in time of peace more than thousand troops. His idea was that the blank should be filled with two or three thousand.

Instead of "to build and equip fleets" — "to provide & maintain a navy" agreed to nem. con as a more convenient definition of the power.

"To make rules for the Government and regulation of the land & naval forces," — added from the existing Articles of Confederation.

Mr. L. Martin and Mr. Gerry now regularly moved "provided that in time of peace the army shall not consist of more than   thousand men." [10]

Genl. Pinkney asked whether no troops were ever to be raised untill an attack should be made on us?

Mr. Gerry. if there be no restriction, a few States may establish a military Govt.

Mr. Williamson, reminded him of Mr. Mason's motion for limiting the appropriation of revenue as the best guard in this case.

Mr. Langdon saw no room for Mr. Gerry's distrust of the Representatives of the people.

Mr. Dayton. preparations for war are generally made in peace; and a standing force of some sort may, for ought we know, become unavoidable. He should object to no restrictions consistent with these ideas.

The motion of Mr. Martin & Mr. Gerry was disagreed to nem. con.

Mr. Mason moved as an additional power "to make laws for the regulation and discipline of the Militia of the several States reserving to the States the appointment of the Officers". He considered uniformity as necessary in the regulation of the Militia throughout the Union.

Genl Pinkney mentioned a case during the war in which a dissimilarity in the militia of different States had produced the most serious mischiefs. Uniformity was essential. The States would never keep up a proper discipline of their militia.

Mr. Elseworth was for going as far in submitting the militia to the Genl Government as might be necessary, but thought the motion of Mr. Mason went too far. He ⟨moved⟩

[10] On this motion see Appendix A, CLVIII (51), CXCII.

that the militia should have the same arms ⟨& exercise and be under rules established by the Genl Govt. when in actual service of the U. States and when States neglect to provide regulations for militia, it shd. be regulated & established by the Legislature of U. S.⟩[11] The whole authority over the Militia ought by no means to be taken away from the States whose consequence would pine away to nothing after such a sacrifice of power. He thought the Genl Authority could not sufficiently pervade the Union for such a purpose, nor could it accommodate itself to the local genius of the people. It must be vain to ask the States to give the Militia out of their hands.

Mr Sherman 2ds. the motion.

Mr Dickenson. We are come now to a most important matter, that of the sword. His opinion was that the States never would nor ought to give up all authority over the Militia. He proposed to restrain the general power to one fourth part at a time, which by rotation would discipline the whole Militia.

Mr. Butler urged the necessity of submitting the whole Militia to the general Authority, which had the care of the general defence.

Mr. Mason– had suggested the idea of a select militia. He was led to think that would be in fact as much as the Genl. Govt could advantageously be charged with. He was afraid of creating insuperable objections to the plan. He withdrew his original motion, and moved a power "to make laws for regulating and disciplining the militia, not exceeding one tenth part in any one year, and reserving the appointment of officers to the States."

Genl Pinkney, renewed Mr. Mason's original motion. For a part to be under the genl. and a part under the State Govts. wd be an incurable evil. he saw no room for such distrust of the Genl Govt.

Mr. Langdon 2ds. Genl. Pinkney's renewal. He saw no more reason to be afraid of the Genl. Govt than of the State Govts. He was more apprehensive of the confusion of the different authorities on this subject, than of either.

---

[11] Revised from *Journal.*

Mr Madison thought the regulation of the Militia naturally appertaining to the authority charged with the public defence. It did not seem in its nature to be divisible between two distinct authorities. If the States would trust the Genl. Govt. with a power over the public treasure, they would from the same consideration of necessity grant it the direction of the public force. Those who had a full view of the public situation wd. from a sense of the danger, guard agst. it: the States would not be separately impressed with the general situation, nor have the due confidence in the concurrent exertions of each other.

Mr. Elseworth– considered the idea of a select militia as impracticable; & if it were not it would be followed by a ruinous declension of the great body of the Militia. The States will never submit to the same militia laws. Three or four shilling's as a penalty will enforce obedience better in New England, than forty lashes in some other places.

Mr. Pinkney thought the power such an one as could not be abused, and that the States would see the necessity of surrendering it. He had however but a scanty faith in Militia. There must be ⟨also⟩ a real military force — This alone can ⟨effectually answer the purpose.⟩ The United States had been making an experiment without it, and we see the consequence in their rapid approaches toward anarchy.*

Mr Sherman, took notice that the States might want their Militia for defence agst invasions and insurrections, and for enforcing obedience to their laws. They will not give up this point– In giving up that of taxation, they retain a concurrent power of raising money for their own use.

Mr. Gerry thought this the last point remaining to be surrendered. If it be agreed to by the Convention, the plan will have as black a mark as was set on Cain. He had no such confidence in the Genl. Govt. as some Gentlemen possessed, and believed it would be found that the States have not.

Col. Mason. thought there was great weight in the remarks of Mr. Sherman– and moved an exception to his motion

* ⟨This had reference to the disorders particularly which had occurred in Massachts. which had called for the interposition of the federal troops.⟩

"of such part of the Militia as might be required by the States for their own use."

Mr. Read doubted the propriety of leaving the appointment of the Militia officers in the States. In some States they are elected by the legislatures; in others by the people themselves. He thought at least an appointment by the State Executives ought to be insisted on.

On committing to the grand Committee last appointed, the latter motion of Col. Mason, & the original one revived by Gel Pinkney

N. H- ay. Mas. ay. Ct no. N- J. no. Pa ay. Del. ay. Md. divd. Va ay. N. C. ay- S. C. ay. Geo. ay. [Ayes — 8; noes — 2; divided — 1.]

Adjourned [12]

McHENRY

Augt. 18.

To make war, to raise armies "to build and equip fleets amended to "declare war, to raise and support armies, to provide and maintain fleets" to which was added "to make rules for the government and regulation of the land and naval forces.

The next clause postponed.

---

[12] In the New York *Daily Advertiser* of this date a report was mentioned that a project was in embryo for the establishment of a monarchy, at the head of which it was contemplated to place the Bishop of Osnaburgh (J. C. Hamilton, *History of the Republic of the United States*, III, 330). See further Appendix A, XLI, LXXXIX, XCII, CVII, CXVI.

MONDAY, AUGUST 20, 1787.

JOURNAL

Monday August 20th. 1787.

It was moved and seconded to refer the following propositions to the Committee of five.

which passed in the affirmative.

Each House shall be the Judge of it's own privileges, and shall have authority to punish by imprisonment every person violating the same: or who, in the place where the Legislature may be sitting and during the time of it's session, shall threaten any of it's members for any thing said or done in the House: or who shall assault any of them therefor — or who shall assault, or arrest any witness or other person ordered to attend either of the Houses in his way going or returning; or who shall rescue any person arrested by their order.

Each Branch of the Legislature, as well as the supreme Executive shall have authority to require the opinions of the supreme Judicial Court upon important questions of law, and upon solemn occasions

The privileges and benefit of the writ of habeas corpus shall be enjoyed in this government in the most expeditious and ample manner: and shall not be suspended by the Legislature except upon the most urgent and pressing occasions, and for a limited time not exceeding   months.

The liberty of the Press shall be inviolably preserved.

No Troops shall be kept up in time of peace, but by consent of the Legislature

The military shall always be subordinate to the civil power, and no grants of money shall be made by the Legislature for supporting military land forces for more than one year at a time

No Soldier shall be quartered in any house in time of peace without consent of the Owner.

No person holding the Office of President of the United States — a Judge of their supreme Court — Secretary for the Department of foreign affairs — of Finance — of Marine — of War — or of

shall be capable of holding at the same time any other office of trust or emolument under the United States, or an individual State.

No religious test or qualification shall ever be annexed to any oath of office under the authority of the United States:

The United States shall be for ever considered as one Body-corporate and politic in law, and entitled to all the rights, privileges and immunities which to Bodies Corporate do, or ought to appertain.

The Legislature of the United States shall have the power of making the great seal, which shall be kept by the President of the United States or in his absence by the President of the Senate, to be used by them as the occasion may require ——— It shall be called the great Seal of the United-States and shall be affixed to all laws.

all commissions and writs shall run in the name of the United States.

The jurisdiction of the supreme court shall be extended to all controversies between the United States and an individual State — or the United States and the Citizen of an individual State.

To assist the President in conducting the Public affairs there shall be a Council of State composed of the following Officers.

1. The Chief Justice of the supreme Court, who shall from time to time recommend such alterations of, and additions to, the Laws of the United-States as may in his opinion be necessary to the due administration of Justice, and such as may promote useful learning and inculcate sound morality throughout the Union: He shall be President of the Council in the absence of the President.

2. The Secretary of domestic-affairs who shall be appointed by the President and hold his office during pleasure It shall

be his duty to attend to matters of general police, the state of agriculture and manufactures, the opening of roads and navigations, and the facilitating communications through the United States, and he shall from time to time recommend such measures and establishments as may tend to promote those objects.
3 The Secretary of Commerce and Finance who shall also be appointed by the President during pleasure. It shall be his duty to superintend all matters relating to the public finances, to prepare and report Plans of revenue and for the regulation of expenditures, and also to recommend such things as may in his judgment promote the commercial interests of the United-States.
4. The Secretary of foreign affairs who shall also be appointed by the President during pleasure — It shall be his duty to correspond with all foreign Ministers, prepare plans of Treaties, and consider such as may be transmitted from abroad — and generally to attend to the Interests of the United States, in their connections with foreign Powers.
5. The Secretary of war who shall also be appointed by the President during pleasure. — It shall be his duty to superintend every thing relating to the war Department such as the raising and equipping of Troops, the care of military Stores, public Fortifications, arsenals, and the like — also in time of war to prepare and recommend Plans of offence and defence.
6 The Secretary of the Marine who shall also be appointed by the President during pleasure — It shall be his duty to superintend every thing relating to the marine Department, the public ships, Dock-yards, naval stores, and Arsenals — also in time of war to prepare and recommend Plans of offence and defence.
The President shall also appoint a Secretary of State to hold his office during pleasure; who shall be Secretary of the Council of State, and also public Secretary to the President. — It shall be his duty to prepare all public dispatches from the President, which he shall countersign.

The President may from time to time submit any matter to the discussion of the Council of State, and he may require

the written opinions of any one or more of the Members; But he shall in all cases exercise his own judgment, and either conform to such opinions or not as he may think proper: and every officer above mentioned shall be responsible for his opinion on the affairs relating to his particular Department.

Each of the Officers abovementioned shall be liable to impeachment and removal from office for neglect of duty, malversation, or corruption

That the Committee be directed to report qualifications for the President of the United-States — and a mode for trying the supreme Judges in cases of impeachment.

It was moved and seconded to postpone the consideration of the 17 clause, 1 sect. 7 article

which passed in the affirmative

It was moved and seconded to insert the following clause in the 1. sect. 7 article

"To make sumptuary laws"

which passed in the negative [Ayes — 3; noes — 8.]

It was moved and seconded to insert the following clause in the 1st sect. of the 7 article

"To establish all offices"

which passed in the negative [Ayes — 2; noes — 9.]

On the question to agree to the last clause of the 1st sect. 7 article, as reported,

it passed in the affirmative.

[To commit the 2nd section 7 article Ayes — 5; noes — 5; divided — 1.] [1]

It was moved and seconded to insert the words "some overt-act of" after the word "in" in the 2 sect. 7 article and to strike out the word "and" before the words "in adhering" and to insert the word "or"

which passed in the affirmative [2]

[1] Vote 321, Detail of Ayes and Noes, but it is not certain that it belongs here rather than just preceding the motion to commit.

[2] Brearley's notes on his copy of the Report of the Committee of Detail confirm these changes.

It was moved and seconded to strike out the words "or any of them" 2 section 7 article

which passed in the affirmative

It was moved and seconded to postpone the consideration of the 2nd sect. 7 article in order to take up the following.

"Whereas it is essential to the preservation of Liberty to "define precisely and exclusively what shall constitute the "crime of Treason it is therefore ordained declared and es-"tablished that if a man do levy war against the United States "within their Territories or be adherent to the enemies of "the United States within the said territories giving to them "aid and comfort within their Territories or elsewhere, and "thereof be provably attainted of open deed by the People "of his condition he shall be adjudged guilty of treason"

On the question to postpone

it passed in the negative. [Ayes — 2; noes — 8.]

It was moved and seconded to strike out the words "against the United States" 1st line, 2 sect. 7 article

which passed in the affirmative [Ayes — 8; noes — 2.]

It was moved and seconded to insert the words "to the same overt-act." after the word "witnesses" 2 sect. 7 article

which passed in the affirmative [Ayes — 8; noes — 3.]

It was moved and seconded to strike the words "some overt-act" out of the 1st line, 2 sect. 7 article [3]

which passed in the affirmative

It was moved and seconded to insert the words

"Sole and exclusive" before the word "power" in the 2 clause, 2 sect, 7 article.

which passed in the negative [Ayes — 5; noes — 6.]

It was moved and seconded to re-instate the words

"against the United States" in the first line, 2 sect. 7 article

which passed in the affirmative [Ayes — 6; noes — 5.]

It was moved and seconded to strike out the words "of the United States" in the 3rd line 2 sect. 7 article

which passed in the affirmative

[3] Refers to insertion made by an earlier vote of this same day.

It was moved and seconded to amend the 1st clause of the 2 sect. 7 article to read

"Treason against the United States shall consist only "in levying war against them, or in adhering to their enemies"

which passed in the affirmative

It was moved and seconded to add the words

"giving them aid and comfort" after the word "enemies" in the 2 section, 7 article.

which passed in the affirmative [Ayes — 8; noes — 3.]

It was moved and seconded to add after the words "overt act" the words "or on confession in open court" 2 section, 7 article.

which passed in the affirmative [Ayes — 7; noes — 3; divided — 1.]

On the question to agree to the 2nd section of the 7 article as amended

it passed in the affirmative.

It was moved and seconded to strike the words

"white and other" out of the 3rd sect. 7 article

which passed in the affirmative.

It was moved and seconded to strike out the word

"six" and to insert the word "three" in the 3rd section of the 7 article.

which passed in the affirmative. [Ayes — 9; noes — 2.]

It was moved and seconded to add the following clause to the 3rd section of the 7 article

"That from the first meeting of the Legislature of the "United States until a Census shall be taken, all monies for "supplying the public Treasury, by direct taxation shall be "raised from the several States according to the number of "their representatives respectively in the first Branch"

Before a question was taken on the last motion

The House adjourned.

DETAIL OF AYES AND NOES

	New Hampshire	Massachusetts	Rhode Island	Connecticut	New York	New Jersey	Pennsylvania	Delaware	Maryland	Virginia	No Carolina	So Carolina	Georgia	Questions	ayes	noes	divided
[319]	no	no		no		no	no	aye	aye	no	no	no	aye	"To make sumptuary laws"	3	8	
[320]	no	aye		no		no	no	no	aye	no	no	no	no	To establish all Offices"	2	9	
[321]	no	no		no		aye	aye	no	aye	aye	dd	no	aye	To commit the 2nd section 7 article.	5	5	1
[322]		no		no		aye	no	no	no	aye	no	no	no	To postpone ye 2nd sect. 7 art. to take up a substitute	2	8	
[323]		aye		aye		aye	aye	aye	aye	no	no	aye	aye	To strike out "agt the United States" 1st line 2 sect. 7 article	8	2	
[324]	aye	aye		aye		no	aye	aye	aye	no	no	aye	aye	"To the same overt act"	8	3	
[325]	aye	aye		no		no	aye	aye	no	no	no	aye	no	To insert the words "sole & exclusive" before the word power" 2 sect. 7 article	5	6	
[326]	no	no		aye		aye	no	no	aye	aye	aye	no	aye	To reinstate the words "against the United States"	6	5	
[327]	aye	aye		no		aye	aye	no	aye	aye	aye	aye	no	"and comfort"	8	3	
[328]	aye	no		aye		aye	aye	aye	aye	aye	dd	no	no	"or on confession in open Court"	7	3	1
[329]	aye	aye		aye		aye	aye	aye	aye	aye	aye	no	no	To strike out "six" and insert "three" 3 sect, 7 article	9	2	

MADISON

Monday August 20 — in Convention.

⟨Mr. Pinkney [4] submitted to the House, in order to be

[4] This whole section was taken from *Journal*; Madison's original record was as follows: — "Mr. Pinkney submitted sundry propositions — 1. authorising the Legislature to imprison for insult. 2. to require opinion of the Judges. 3. securing the benefit of the habeas corpus. 4. preserving the liberty of the press. 5 guarding agst billeting of soldiers. 6. agst. raising troops without the consent of the Legislature. 7. rendering the great officers of the Union incapable of other offices either under the Genl Govt. or the State Govts. 8. forbidding religious tests. 9 declaring

referred to the Committee of detail, the following propositions — "Each House shall be the Judge of its own privileges, and shall have authority to punish by imprisonment every person violating the same; or who, in the place where the Legislature may be sitting and during the time of its Session, shall threaten any of its members for any thing said or done in the House, or who shall assault any of them therefor — or who shall assault or arrest any witness or other person ordered to attend either of the Houses in his way going or returning; or who shall rescue any person arrested by their order."

"Each branch of the Legislature, as well as the Supreme Executive shall have authority to require the opinions of the supreme Judicial Court upon important questions of law, and upon solemn occasions"

"The privileges and benefit of the Writ of Habeas corpus shall be enjoyed in this Government in the most expeditious and ample manner; and shall not be suspended by the Legislature except upon the most urgent and pressing occasions, and for a limited time not exceeding months."

"The liberty of the Press shall be inviolably preserved"

"No troops shall be kept up in time of peace, but by consent of the Legislature"

"The military shall always be subordinate to the Civil power, and no grants of money shall be made by the Legislature for supporting military Land forces, for more than one year at a time"

"No soldier shall be quartered in any House in time of peace without consent of the owner."

"No person holding the office of President of the U. S., a Judge of their Supreme Court, Secretary for the department of Foreign Affairs, of Finance, of Marine, of War, or of ,

---

the U. States to be a body politic and corporate. 10 providing a great seal to be affixed to laws &c. 11. extending the jurisdiction of the Judiciary to controversies between the United States & States or individuals. — these were referred to the Committee of detail for consideration & report.

"Mr. Govr. Morris and Mr Pinkney proposed a sett of resolutions organizing the Executive department — referred to the Committee of detail."

Cf. Appendix A, CXXIX, note 2.

shall be capable of holding at the same time any other office of Trust or Emolument under the U. S. or an individual State"

"No religious test or qualification shall ever be annexed to any oath of office under the authority of the U. S."

"The U. S. shall be for ever considered as one Body corporate and politic in law, and entitled to all the rights privileges, and immunities, which to Bodies corporate do or ought to appertain"

"The Legislature of the U. S. shall have the power of making the great Seal which shall be kept by the President of the U. S. or in his absence by the President of the Senate, to be used by them as the occasion may require. — It shall be called the great Seal of the U. S. and shall be affixed to all laws."

"All Commissions and writs shall run in the name of the U. S."

"The Jurisdiction of the supreme Court shall be extended to all controversies between the U. S. and an individual State, or the U. S. and the Citizens of an individual State"

These propositions were referred to the Committee of detail without debate or consideration of them, by the House.

Mr. Govr. Morris 2ded. by Mr. Pinkney submitted the following propositions which were in like manner referred to the Committee of Detail.

"To assist the President in conducting the Public affairs there shall be a Council of State composed of the following officers — 1. The Chief Justice of the Supreme Court, who shall from time to time recommend such alterations of and additions to the laws of the U. S. as may in his opinion be necessary to the due administration of Justice, and such as may promote useful learning and inculcate sound morality throughout the Union: He shall be President of the Council in the absence of the President

2. The Secretary of Domestic Affairs who shall be appointed by the President and hold his office during pleasure. It shall be his duty to attend to matters of general police, the State

of Agriculture and manufactures, the opening of roads and navigations, and the facilitating communications thro' the U. States; and he shall from time to time recommend such measures and establishments as may tend to promote those objects.

3. The Secretary of Commerce and Finance who shall also be appointed by the President during pleasure. It shall be his duty to superintend all matters relating to the public finances, to prepare & report plans of revenue and for the regulation of expenditures, and also to recommend such things as may in his Judgment promote the commercial interests of the U. S.

4. The Secretary of foreign affairs who shall also be appointed by the President during pleasure. It shall be his duty to correspond with all foreign Ministers, prepare plans of Treaties, & consider such as may be transmitted from abroad; and generally to attend to the interests of the U– S– in their connections with foreign powers.

5. The Secretary of War who shall also be appointed by the President during pleasure. It shall be his duty to superintend every thing relating to the war-Department, such as the raising and equipping of troops, the care of military Stores — public fortifications, arsenals & the like — also in time of war to prepare & recommend plans of offence and Defence.

6. The Secretary of the Marine who shall also be appointed during pleasure — It shall be his duty to superintend every thing relating to the Marine-Department, the public Ships, Dock-Yards, Naval-Stores & arsenals — also in the time of war to prepare and recommend plans of offence and defence.

The President shall also appoint a Secretary of State to hold his office during pleasure; who shall be Secretary to the Council of State, and also public Secretary to the President. It shall be his duty to prepare all public despatches from the President which he shall countersign

The President may from time to time submit any matter to the discussion of the Council of State, and he may require the written opinions of any one or more of the members: But he shall in all cases exercise his own judgment, and either

Conform to such opinions or not as he may think proper; and every officer abovementioned shall be responsible for his opinion on the affairs relating to his particular Department.

Each of the officers abovementioned shall be liable to impeachment & removal from office for neglect of duty malversation, or corruption")[4a]

Mr Gerry moved "that the Committee be instructed to report proper qualifications for the President, and a mode of trying ⟨the Supreme⟩ Judges ⟨in cases of⟩ impeachment.[5]

The clause "to call forth the aid of the Militia &c– was postponed till report should be made as to the power over the Militia referred yesterday to the Grand Committee ⟨of eleven⟩.

Mr. Mason moved to enable Congress "to enact sumptuary laws." No Government can be maintained unless the manners be made consonant to it. Such a discretionary power may do good and can do no harm. A proper regulation of excises & of trade may do a great deal but it is best to have an express provision. It was objected to sumptuary laws that they were contrary to nature. This was a vulgar error. The love of distinction it is true is natural; but the object of sumptuary laws is not to extinguish this principle but to give it a proper direction.

Mr. Elseworth, The best remedy is to enforce taxes & debts. As far as the regulation of eating & drinking can be reasonable, it is provided for in the power of taxation.

Mr Govr. Morris argued that sumptuary laws tended to create a landed Nobility, by fixing in the great-landholders and their posterity their present possessions.

Mr Gerry. the law of necessity is the best sumptuary law.

On Motion of Mr. Mason "as to sumptuary laws"

N. H. no. Mas– no. Ct no. N. J. no. Pa. no. Del. ay. Md. ay. Va. no. N– C. no– S. C. no. Geo. ay. [Ayes — 3; noes — 8.]

"And to make all laws necessary and proper for carrying into execution the foregoing powers, and all other powers

---

[4a] See above, note 4.

[5] Revised from *Journal.*

vested, by this Constitution, in the Government of the U. S. or any department or officer thereof."[6]

Mr. M⟨adison⟩ and Mr. Pinkney moved to insert between "laws" and "necessary" "and establish all offices". it appearing to them liable to cavil that the latter was not included in the former.

Mr. Govr. Morris. Mr. Wilson, Mr Rutlidge and Mr. Elseworth urged that the amendment could not be necessary.

On the motion for inserting "and establish all offices"

N. H. no. Mas. ay. Ct. no. N. J. no. Pa. no. Del. no. Md. ay. Va. no. N– C– no. S. C. no. Geo. no. [Ayes — 2; noes — 9.]

The clause as reported was then agreed to nem con.

Art: VII sect. 2. concerning Treason which see[7]

Mr. M⟨adison,⟩ thought the definition too narrow. It did not appear to go as far as the Stat. of Edwd. III. He did not see why more latitude might not be left to the Legislature. It wd. be as safe as in the hands of State legislatures; and it was inconvenient to bar a discretion which experience might enlighten, and which might be applied to good purposes as well as be abused.

Mr Mason was for pursuing the Stat: of Edwd. III.

Mr. Govr Morris was for giving to the Union an exclusive right to declare what shd. be treason. In case of a contest between the U– S– and a particular State, the people of the latter must, under the disjunctive terms of the clause, be traitors to ⟨one⟩ or other authority.

Mr Randolph thought the clause defective in adopting the words "in adhering" only. The British Stat: adds. "giving them aid ⟨and⟩[8] comfort" which had a more extensive meaning.

---

[6] See Appendix A, CLXI.

[7] Article VII, Sect. 2. "Treason against the United States shall consist only in levying war against the United States, or any of them; and in adhering to the enemies of the United States, or any of them. The Legislature of the United States shall have power to declare the punishment of treason. No person shall be convicted of treason, unless on the testimony of two witnesses. No attainder of treason shall work corruption of bloods nor forfeiture, except during the life of the person attainted."

[8] Crossed out "or".

Mr. Elseworth considered the definition as the same in fact with that of the Statute.

Mr. Govr Morris "adhering" does not go so far as giving aid ⟨and⟩[8a] Comfort" or the latter words may be restrictive of "adhering". in either case the Statute is not pursued.

Mr Wilson held "giving aid and comfort" to be explanatory, not operative words; and that it was better to omit them —

Mr Dickenson, thought the addition of "giving aid & comfort" unnecessary & improper; being too vague and extending too far– He wished to know what was meant by the "testimony of two witnesses", whether they were to be witnesses to the same overt act or to different overt acts. He thought also that proof of an overt-act ought to be expressed as essential in the case.

Docr Johnson considered "giving aid & comfort" as explanatory of "adhering" & that something should be inserted in the definition concerning overt-acts. He contended that Treason could not be both agst. the U. States — and individual States; being an offence agst the Sovereignty which can be but one in the same community–

Mr. M⟨adison⟩ remarked that "and" before "in adhering" should be changed into "or" otherwise both offences ⟨viz of levying war, & of adhering to the Enemy⟩ might be necessary to constitute Treason. He added that as the definition here was of treason against *the U. S.* it would seem that the individual States wd. be left in possession of a concurrent power so far as to define & punish treason particularly agst. themselves; which might involve double punishmt.

It was moved that the whole clause be recommitted ⟨which was lost, the votes being equally divided.⟩

N– H– no. Mas– no– Ct no– N– J ay– Pa ay– Del– no– Md. ay. Va. ay– N C– divd S– C–no. Geo– ay. — [Ayes — 5; noes — 5; divided — 1.]

Mr. Wilson & Docr. Johnson moved, that "or any of them" after "United States" be struck out in order to remove the embarrassment: which was agreed to nem. con —

[8a] Crossed out " or ".

Mr M⟨adison⟩ This has not removed the embarrassment. The same Act might be treason agst. the United States as here defined — and agst a particular State according to its laws.

Mr Elseworth — There can be no danger to the Genl authority from this; as the laws of the U. States are to be paramount.

Docr Johnson was still of opinion there could be no Treason agst a particular State. It could not even at present, as the Confederation now stands; the Sovereignty being in the Union; much less can it be under the proposed System.

Col. Mason. The United States will have a qualified sovereignty only. The individual States will retain a part of the Sovereignty. An Act may be treason agst. a particular State which is not so against the U. States. He cited the Rebellion of Bacon in Virginia as an illustration of the doctrine.

Docr. Johnson: That case would amount to Treason agst the Sovereign, the supreme Sovereign, the United States —

Mr. King observed that the controversy relating to Treason might be of less magnitude than was supposed; as the legislature might punish capitally under other names than Treason.

Mr. Govr Morris and Mr Randolph wished to substitute the words of the British Statute
⟨and moved to postpone Sect. 2. art VII in order to consider the following substitute — "Whereas it is essential to the preservation of liberty to define precisely and exclusively what shall constitute the crime of Treason, it is therefore ordained, declared & established, that if a man do levy war agst. the U. S. within their territories, or be adherent to the enemies of the U. S. within the said territories, giving them aid and comfort within their territories or elsewhere, and thereof be provably attainted of open deed by the People of his condition, he shall be adjudged guilty of Treason"⟩[9]

On this question

N. H Mas– no. Ct. no. N. J– ay Pa. no. Del. no. Md.

---

[9] Taken from *Journal*.

no. Va.– ay. N. C. no– S. C. no. Geo– no. [Ayes — 2; noes — 8.]

It was moved to strike out "agst United States" after "treason" so as to define treason generally — and on this question

Mas. ay — Ct. ay. N — J. ay. Pa ay. Del. ay. Md. ay. Va. no. N. C. no. S. C ay. Geo. ay. [Ayes — 8; noes — 2.]

It was then moved to insert after "two witnesses" the words "to the same overt act".

Docr Franklin wished this amendment to take place — prosecutions for treason were generally virulent; and perjury too easily made use of against innocence

Mr. Wilson. much may be said on both sides. Treason may sometimes be practised in such a manner, as to render proof extremely difficult — as in a traitorous correspondence with an Enemy.

On the question — as to same overt act

N— H— ay— Mas— ay— Ct. ay. N. J. no— Pa. ay— Del— ay— Md ay. Va no— N. C. no— S. C. ay— Geo— ay– [Ayes — 8; noes — 3.]

Mr King moved to insert before the word "power" the word "sole", giving the U. States the exclusive right to declare the punishment of Treason.

Mr Broom 2ds. the motion–

Mr Wilson in cases of a general nature, treason can only be agst the U– States. and in such they shd have the sole right to declare the punishment — yet in many cases it may be otherwise. The subject was however intricate and he distrusted his present judgment on it.

Mr King this amendment results from the vote defining treason generally by striking out agst. the U. States; which excludes any treason agst particular States. These may however punish offences as high misdemesnors.

On inserting the word "sole". ⟨It passed in the negative⟩

N– H. ay– Mas– ay. Ct no– N. J– no– Pa ay. Del. ay. Md no– Va– no– N– C– no– S. C. ay– Geo– no.— [Ayes — 5; noes — 6.]

Mr. Wilson. the clause is ambiguous now. "Sole"

ought either to have been inserted—or "against the U- S." to be reinstated.

Mr King no line can be drawn between levying war and adhering to enemy—agst the U. States and agst an individual States—Treason agst the latter must be so agst the former.

Mr Sherman, resistance agst. the laws of the U- States as distinguished from resistance agst the laws of a particular State, forms the line–

Mr. Elseworth– the U. S. are sovereign on one side of the line dividing the jurisdictions — the States on the other — each ought to have power to defend their respective Sovereignties.

Mr. Dickenson, war or insurrection agst a member of the Union must be so agst the whole body; but the Constitution should be made clear on this point.

The clause was reconsidered nem. con—& then, Mr. Wilson & Mr. Elseworth moved to reinstate "agst the U. S.". after "Treason"—on which question

N- H- no- Mas. no. Ct. ay- N- J- ay- Pa no- Del. no- Md ay. Va. ay- N- C. ay- S- C- no- Geo. ay— [Ayes—6; noes — 5.]

Mr M—⟨adison⟩ was not satisfied with the footing on which the clause now stood. As treason agst the U- States involves Treason agst. particular States, and vice versa, the same act may be twice tried & punished by the different authorities— Mr Govr Morris viewed the matter in the same lights—

⟨It was moved & 2ded to amend the Sentence to read— "Treason agst. the U. S. shall consist only in levying war against them, or in adhering to their enemies" which was agreed to.⟩[10]

Col- Mason moved to insert the words "giving ⟨them⟩ aid comfort". as restrictive of "adhering to their Enemies &c"– the latter he thought would be otherwise too indefinite— This motion was agreed to ⟨Cont: Del: & Georgia only being in the Negative.⟩[10]

Mr L. Martin — moved to insert after conviction &c— "or

---

[10] Taken from *Journal.*

on confession in open court" — and on the question, (the negative States thinking the words superfluous) ⟨it was agreed to⟩ N. H: ay– Mas– no– Ct. ay. N– J. ay– Pa. ay. Del. ay– Md ay– Va ay. N– C– divd S– C– no. Geo– no.

[Ayes — 7; noes — 3; divided — 1.]

Art: VII. Sect— 2. as amended was then agreed to nem—con.[11]

Sect— 3— taken up.[12] "white & other" struck out nem con. as superfluous.

Mr Elseworth moved to required the first census to be taken within "three" instead of "six" years from the first meeting of the Legislature — and on question

N— H— ay. Mas— ay Ct ay— N J— ay— Pa ay— Del. ay. Md ay Va ay— N— C— ay— S— C. no— Geo— no. [Ayes — 9; noes — 2.]

Mr King asked what was the precise meaning of *direct* taxation? No one answd.

Mr. Gerry moved ⟨to add to the 3d. Sect. art. VII, the following clause. "That from the first meeting of the Legislature of the U. S. until a Census shall be taken all monies for supplying the public Treasury by direct taxation shall be raised from the several States according to the number of their Representatives respectively in the first branch"⟩ [13]

Mr. Langdon. This would bear unreasonably hard on N. H. and he must be agst it.

Mr. Carrol. opposed it. The number of Reps. did not admit of a proportion exact enough for a rule of taxation —

⟨Before any question the House⟩ [14]

Adjourned.[15]

---

[11] See further Appendix A, CL, CLVIII (88–91).

[12] Article VII, Sect. 3. "The proportions of direct taxation shall be regulated by the whole number of white and other free citizens and inhabitants, of every age, sex and condition, including those bound to servitude for a term of years, and three fifths of all other persons not comprehended in the foregoing description, (except Indians not paying taxes) which number shall, within six years after the first meeting of the Legislature, and within the term of every ten years afterwards, be taken in such manner as the said Legislature shall direct."

[13] Taken from *Journal*, but Madison had recorded the substance of this motion.

[14] Taken from *Journal*.

[15] See further, Appendix A, LXXXV–LXXXIX.

McHENRY

August 20.

The following one agreed to.

Sect. 2. Amended to read. Treason against the U. S. shall consist only in levying war against them, or in adhering to their enemies giving them aid and comfort. The legislature shall have power to declare the punishment of treason. No person shall be convicted of treason unless on confession in open court, or the testimony of two witnesses to the same overt act.

Mr. Mason moved to add to the 1 sect of the VII article.

To make sumptuary laws.

Governeur Morris. sump. laws were calculated to continue great landed estates for ever in the same families — If men had no temptation to dispose of their money they would not sell their estates.

Negatived.

Amended section 3 by striking out the words in the second line *white and other*, and the word six in the 5 line and substituting the word three — but adjourned without a question on the section.

TUESDAY, AUGUST 21, 1787.

JOURNAL

Tuesday August 21. 1787.

The honorable Mr Livingston, from the Committee of eleven to whom were referred

a proposition respecting the debts of the several States, entered on the Journal of the 18 instant

and a proposition respecting the militia

entered on the Journal of the 18 instant

informed the House that the Committee were prepared to report — and had directed him to submit the same to the consideration of the House.

The report was then delivered in at the Secretary's-table, and, being read throughout, is as follows.

"The Legislature of the United-States shall have power "to fulfil the engagements which have been entered into by "Congress, and to discharge as well the debts of the United "States, as the debts incurred by the several States during "the late war, for the common defence and general welfare."

"To make laws for organizing, arming, and disciplining "the militia, and for governing such part of them as may be "employed in the service of the United States, reserving to "the States respectively, the appointment of the Officers, "and the authority of training the militia according to the "discipline prescribed by the United States"

It was moved and seconded to postpone the consideration of the above report

which passed in the affirmative

On the question to agree to the 3rd sect. of the 7 article as amended

it passed in the affirmative [Ayes — 10; noes — 1.]

It was moved and seconded to add the following clause to the 3rd sect. of the 7 article

"And all accounts of supplies furnished, services per-"formed, and monies advanced by the several States, to the "United States; or by the United States to the several States "shall be adjusted by the same rule."

The last motion being withdrawn,

It was moved and seconded to add the following clause to the 3rd section of the 7th article.

"By this rule the several quotas of the States shall be "determined in settling the expences of the late war"

It was moved and seconded to postpone the consideration of the last motion

which passed in the affirmative.

It was moved and seconded to add the following clause to the 3rd sect. of the 7 article

That from the first meeting of the Legislature of the United States until a Census shall be taken, all monies for supplying the public Treasury, by direct taxation, shall be raised from the several States according to the number of their representatives respectively in the first Branch.

It was moved and seconded to annex the following amendment to the last motion.

"subject to a final liquidation by the foregoing rule when "a Census shall have been taken"

On the question to agree to the amendment

it passed in the affirmative

On the question to agree to the Proposition and amendment it passed in the negative. [Ayes — 2; noes — 8; divided — 1.][1]

On the question to take up the amendment offered to the 12 sect of the 6 article, entered on the Journal of the 15th instant, and then postponed

it passed in the negative [Ayes — 5; noes — 6.]

It was moved and seconded to add the following clause to the 3rd sect. 7 article

"and whenever the Legislature of the United States shall

[1] Vote 331, Detail of Ayes and Noes, which notes that the original "Proposition" was "made by Mr. Gerry". *Journal* (p. 273) misprinted it "Ellsworth".

"find it necessary that revenue should be raised by direct "taxation, having apportioned the same, according to the "above rule, on the several States, requisitions shall be made "of the respective States to pay into the Continental Treasury "their respective quotas within a time in the said requisition "specified, and in case of any of the States failing to comply "with such requisitions, then and then only to devise and "pass acts directing the mode and authorising the collection "of the same."

which passed in the negative [Ayes — 1; noes — 7; divided — 1.][2]

It was moved and seconded to insert the following clause after the word "duty" in the first line 4 sect. 7 article

"for the purpose of revenue"

which passed in the negative. [Ayes — 3; noes — 8.]

It was moved and seconded to amend the first clause of the 4 sect. 7 article by inserting the following words

"unless by consent of two thirds of the legislature"

which passed in the negative [Ayes — 5; noes — 6.]

On the question to agree to the first clause of the 4 section of the 7 article, as reported,

it passed in the affirmative. [Ayes — 7; noes — 4.]

It was moved and seconded to insert the word "free" before the word "persons" in the 4 sect. of the 7 article.

Before the question was taken on the last motion

The House adjourned

[2] Vote 333, Detail of Ayes and Noes, which notes that it was "Mr. Martin's proposition".

DETAIL OF AYES AND NOES

	New Hampshire	Massachusetts	Rhode Island	Connecticut	New York	New Jersey	Pennsylvania	Delaware	Maryland	Virginia	No Carolina	So Carolina	Georgia	Questions	ayes	noes	divided
[330]	aye	aye		aye		aye	aye	no	aye	aye	aye	aye	aye	To agree to the 3 sect. 7 article as amended	10	1	
[331]	no	aye		no		no	no	no	no	no	dd	aye	no	To agree to the Proposition made by Mr Gerry until a Census be taken &ca	2	8	1
[332]	aye	no		aye		no	no	no	aye	aye	aye	no	no	To take up the amendmt offered to ye 12 sect. 4 art. entered on the Journal of the 15. august	5	6	
[333]				no		aye	no	no	dd	no	no	no	no	To agree to Mr. Martin's proposition respecting direct taxation	1	7	1
[334]	no	no		no		aye	aye	aye	no	no	no	no	no	To agree "to the words" for the purpose of revenue" 1st line 4 sect. 7 article	3	8	
[335]	aye	aye		no		aye	aye	aye	no	no	no	no	no	"unless by two-thirds of the Legislature" 1 line–4 sect. 7 article	5	6	
[336]	no	aye		aye		no	no	no	aye	aye	aye	aye	aye	To agree to ye 1st clause —4 sect. 7 article	7	4	

MADISON

Tuesday August 21. in Convention

Governour Livingston, from the Committee of Eleven to whom was referred the propositions respecting the debts of the several States, and also the Militia, entered on the 18th. inst: delivered the following report: [3]

"The Legislature of the U. S. shall have power to fulfil the engagements which have been entered into by Congress, and to discharge as well the debts of the U– S: as the debts

[3] Taken from *Journal.* Madison originally recorded substance in brief.

incurred by the several States during the late war, for the common defence and general welfare"[4]

"To make laws for organizing arming and disciplining the Militia, and for governing such part of them as may be employed in the service of the U— S reserving to the States respectively, the appointment of the officers, and the authority of training the Militia according to the discipline prescribed by the U. States")

Mr. Gerry considered giving the power only, without adopting the obligation, as destroying the security now enjoyed by the public creditors of the U— States. He enlarged on the merit of this class of citizens, and the solemn faith which had been pledged under the existing Confederation. If their situation should be changed as here proposed great opposition would be excited agst. the plan — He urged also that as the States had made different degrees of exertion to sink their respective debts, those who had done most would be alarmed, if they were now to be saddled with a share of the debts of States which had done least.

Mr. Sherman. It means neither more nor less than the confederation as it relates to this subject.

Mr Elseworth moved that the Report delivered in by Govr. Livingston should lie on the table. Agreed to nem. con.[5]

Art: VII. sect. 3. resumed.[6] — Mr. Dickenson moved to postpone this in order to reconsider Art: IV. sect. 4. and to *limit* the number of representatives to be allowed to the large States. Unless this were done the small States would be reduced to entire insignificancy, and encouragement given to the importation of slaves.

Mr. Sherman would agree to such a reconsideration, but did not see the necessity of postponing the section before the House. — Mr. Dickenson withdrew his motion.

---

[4] On the phrase "common defence and general welfare", see Appendix A, CXXIII, CCCLXXII.

[5] See further, August 18 (with references under note 6), August 22–24, August 25 (with references under note 5).

[6] Relating to direct taxation and census.

Art: VII. sect. 3. then agreed to ⟨10 ays. Delaware alone being no.⟩[7]

Mr. Sherman moved ⟨to add to sect 3, the following clause "and all accounts of supplies furnished, services performed, and monies advanced by the several States to the U— States, or by the U. S. to the several States shall be adjusted by the same rule."⟩[8]

Mr. Governr. Morris 2ds. the motion.

Mr. Ghorum, thought it wrong to insert this in the Constitution. The Legislature will no doubt do what is right. The present Congress have such a power and are now exercising it.

Mr Sherman unless some rule be expressly given none will exist under the new system.

Mr. Elseworth. ⟨Though⟩ The contracts of Congress will be binding, there will be no rule for executing them on the States; — and one ought to be provided.

Mr Sherman withdrew his motion to make way for one of Mr Williamson to add to sect- 3. "By this rule the ⟨several⟩ quotas of the States ⟨shall be determined in⟩ Settling the expences of the late war"–[9]

Mr. Carrol brought into view the difficulty that might arise on this subject from the establishment of the Constitution as intended without the *Unanimous* consent of the States

Mr Williamson's motion was postponed nem. con.

Art: VI sect. 12.[10] which had been postponed Aug: 15. was now called for by Col. Mason. who wished to know how the proposed amendment as to money bills would be decided, before he agreed to any further points.

Mr. Gerry's motion of yesterday that previous to a census, direct taxation be proportioned on the States according to the number of Representatives, was taken up– He observed that the principal acts of Government would probably take place within that period, and it was but reasonable that the States should pay in proportion to their share in them.

---

[7] Taken from *Journal.*

[8] Taken from *Journal.* Madison originally recorded the substance of the motion.

[9] Revised from *Journal.*

[10] Article VI, Sect. 12. "Each House shall possess the right of originating bills."

Mr. Elseworth thought such a rule unjust– there was a great difference between the number of Represents. and the number of inhabitants as a rule in this case. Even if the former were proportioned as nearly as possible to the latter, it would be a very inaccurate rule– A State might have one Representative only, that had inhabitants enough for 1½ or more, if fractions could be applied — &c —. He proposed to amend the motion by adding ⟨the words "subject to a final liquidation by the foregoing rule when a census shall have been taken."⟩[11]

Mr. M⟨adison.⟩ The last appointment of Congs., on which the number of Representatives was founded, was conjectural and meant only as a temporary rule till a Census should be established.

Mr. Read. The requisitions of Congs. had been accommodated to the impoverishments produced by the war; and to other local and temporary circumstances —

Mr. Williamson opposed Mr Gerry's motion

Mr Langdon was not here when N. H. was allowed three members. If it was more than her share; he did not wish for them.

Mr. Butler contended warmly for Mr Gerry's motion as founded in reason and equity.

Mr. Elseworth's proviso to Mr. Gerry's motion was agreed to nem con.

Mr. King thought the power of taxation given to the Legislature rendered the motion of Mr Gerry altogether unnecessary.

On Mr Gerry's motion as amended

N– H– no Mas– ay. Ct no N– J– no. Pa. no– Del. no– Md no– Va no– N– Ci– divd. S– C. ay. Geo. no– [Ayes — 2; noes — 8; divided — 1.]

On a question Shall art: VI sect. 12 with the amendment to it proposed & entered on the 15 instant,[12] as called for by Col Mason be now taken up? ⟨it passed in the Negative.⟩

N. H. ay– Mas– no– Ct ay– N– J– no– Pa no– Del– no–

[11] Taken from *Journal*. Madison originally recorded the substance of the motion.

[12] This wording may have been revised from *Journal*.

Md ay. Va ay. N– C– ay– S– C– no– Geo. no– [Ayes — 5; noes — 6.]

Mr L. Martin. The power of taxation is most likely to be criticised by the public. Direct taxation should not be used but in cases of absolute necessity; and then the States will be best Judges of the mode. He therefore moved ⟨the following addition to sect: 3. Art: VII "And whenever the Legislature of the U: S: shall find it necessary that revenue should be raised by direct taxation, having apportioned the same, according to the above rule on the several States, — requisitions shall be made of the respective States to pay into the Continental Treasury their respective quotas within a time in the said requisitions specified; and in case of any of the States failing to comply with such requisitions, then and then only to devise and pass acts directing the mode, and authorizing the collection of the same"⟩[13]

Mr McHenry 2ded. the motion — there was no debate, and on the question

N— H— no— Ct. no. N. J. ay. Pena. no. Del. no. Md. divd. (Jenifer & Carrol no). Va. no. N. C. no. S. C. no. Geo. no. [Ayes — 1; noes — 8; divided — 1.][14]

Art. VII. sect. 4.[15] — Mr. Langdon. by this section the States are left at liberty to tax exports. N. H. therefore with other non-exporting States, will be subject to be taxed by the States exporting its produce. This could not be admitted. It seems to be feared that the Northern States will oppress the trade of the Southn. This may be guarded agst by requiring the concurrence of $\frac{2}{3}$ or $\frac{3}{4}$ of the legislature in such cases.

Mr Elseworth— It is best as it stands— The power of

[13] Taken from *Journal*. Madison originally recorded the substance. See Appendix A, CLVIII (49), CLXXXIX, CXCI.

[14] Detail of Ayes and Noes (Vote 333) omits New Hampshire.

[15] Article VII, Sect. 4. "No tax or duty shall be laid by the Legislature on articles exported from any State; nor on the migration or importation of such persons as the several States shall think proper to admit; nor shall such migration or importation be prohibited."

Upon this question, see above, July 23, and August 16, and Appendix A, II, CXLVI*a*, CCLXV, CCCXXXVI.

regulating trade between the States will protect them agst each other — Should this not be the case, the attempts of one to tax the produce of another passing through its hands, will force a direct exportation and defeat themselves — There are solid reasons agst. Congs taxing exports. 1. it will discourage industry, as taxes on imports discourage luxury. 2. The produce of different States is such as to prevent uniformity in such taxes. there are indeed but a few articles that could be taxed at all; as Tobo. rice & indigo, and a tax on these alone would be partial & unjust. 3. The taxing of exports would engender incurable jealousies.

Mr Williamson. Tho' N— C. has been taxed by Virga by a duty on 12,000 Hhs of her Tobo. exported thro' Virga yet he would never agree to this power. Should it take take place, it would destroy the last hope of an adoption of the plan.

Mr. Govr Morris. These local considerations ought not to impede the general interest. There is great weight in the argument, that the exporting States will tax the produce of their uncommercial neighbours. The power of regulating the trade between Pa & N. Jersey will never prevent the former from taxing the latter. Nor will such a tax force a direct exportation from N— Jersey— The advantages possessed by a large trading City, outweigh the disadvantage of a moderate duty; and will retain the trade in that channel— If no tax can be laid on exports, an embargo cannot be laid, though in time of war such a measure may be of critical importance —Tobacco, lumber, and live-stock are three objects belonging to different States, of which great advantage might be maed by a power to tax exports — To these may be added Ginseng and Masts for Ships by which a tax might be thrown on other nations. The idea of supplying the West Indies with lumber from Nova Scotia, is one of the many follies of lord Sheffield's pamphlets. The State of the Country also, will change, and render duties on exports, as skins, beaver & other peculiar raw materials, politic in the view of encouraging American Manufactures.

Mr. Butler was strenuously opposed to a power over exports; as unjust and alarming to the staple States.

Mr. Langdon suggested a prohibition on the States from taxing the produce of other States exported from their harbours.

Mr. Dickenson. The power of taxing exports may be inconvenient at present; but it must be of dangerous consequence to prohibit it with respect to all articles and for ever. He thought it would be better to except particular articles from the power.

Mr. Sherman— It is best to prohibit the National legislature in all cases. The States will never give up all power over trade. An enumeration of particular articles would be difficult invidious and improper.

Mr M⟨adison⟩ As we ought to be governed by national and permanent views, it is a sufficient argument for giving ye power over exports that a tax, tho' it may not be expedient at present, may be so hereafter.[16] A proper regulation of exports may & probably will be necessary hereafter, and for the same purposes as the regulation of — imports; viz, for revenue — domestic manufactures[17] — and procuring equitable regulations from other nations. An Embargo may be of absolute necessity, and can alone be effectuated by the Genl. authority. The regulation of trade between State and State can not effect more than indirectly to hinder a State from taxing its own exports; by authorizing its Citizens to carry their commodities freely into a neighbouring State which might decline taxing exports in order to draw into its channel the trade of its neighbours — As to the fear of disproportionate burdens on the more exporting States, it might be remarked that it was agreed on all hands that the revenue wd. principally be drawn from trade, and as only a given revenue would be needed, it was not material whether all should be drawn wholly from imports — or half from those, and half from exports — The imports and exports must be pretty nearly equal in every State — and relatively the same among the different States.

Mr Elseworth did not conceive an embargo by the Congress interdicted by this section.

[16] Crossed out: "for the general good of the Union".

[17] See Appendix A, CCCLXIV, CCCXC.

Mr. McHenry conceived that power to be included in the power of war.

Mr. Wilson. Pennsylvania exports the produce of Maryd. N. Jersey, Delaware & will by & by when the River Delaware is opened, export for N— York. In favoring the general power over exports therefore, he opposed the particular interest of his State. He remarked that the power had been attacked by reasoning which could only have held good in case the Genl Govt. had been *compelled*, instead of *authorized*, to lay duties on exports. To deny this power is to take from the Common Govt. half the regulation of trade — It was his opinion that a power over exports might be more effectual than that over imports in obtaining beneficial treaties of commerce.

Mr. Gerry was strenuously opposed to the power over exports. It might be made use of to compel the States to comply with the will of the Genl Government, and to grant it any new powers which might be demanded — We have given it more power already than we know how will be exercised — It will enable the Genl Govt to oppress the States, as much as Ireland is oppressed by Great Britain.

Mr. Fitzimmons would be agst. a tax on exports to be laid immediately; but was for giving a power of laying the tax when a proper time may call for it — This would certainly be the case when America should become a manufacturing country — He illustrated his argument by the duties in G— Britain on wool &c.

Col. Mason — If he were for reducing the States to mere corporations as seemed to be the tendency of some arguments, he should be for subjecting their exports as well as imports to a power of general taxation — He went on a principle often advanced & in which he concurred, that "a majority when interested will oppress the minority". This maxim had been verified by our own Legislature (of Virginia). If we compare the States in this point of view the 8 Northern States have an interest different from the five Southn. States, — and have in one branch of the legislature 36 votes agst 29. and in the other, in the proportion of 8 agst 5. The Southern

States had therefore good ground for their suspicions. The case of Exports was not the same with that of imports. The latter were the same throughout the States: the former very different. As to Tobacco other nations do raise it, and are capable of raising it as well as Virga. &c. The impolicy of taxing that article had been demonstrated by the experiment of Virginia —

Mr Clymer remarked that every State might reason with regard to its particular productions, in the same manner as the Southern States. The middle States may apprehend an oppression of their wheat flour, provisions, &c. and with more reason, as these articles were exposed to a competition in foreign markets not incident to Tobo. rice &c — They may apprehend also combinations agst. them between the Eastern & Southern States as much as the latter can apprehend them between the Eastern & middle — He moved as a qualification of the power of taxing Exports that it should be restrained to regulations of trade, ⟨by inserting after the word "duty" Sect 4 art VII the words⟩ [18] "for the purpose of revenue."

On Question on Mr. Clymer's motion

N. H— no— Mas. no. Ct. no. N. J— ay. Pa ay. Del. ay. Md. no. Va. no. N— C. no. Geo. no. [Ayes — 3; noes — 7.] [19]

Mr. M⟨adison,⟩ In order to require ⅔ of each House to tax exports — as a lesser evil than a total prohibition ⟨moved to insert the words "unless by consent of two thirds of the Legislature"⟩,[20] Mr Wilson 2ds. and on this question, ⟨it passed in the Negative.⟩

N. H. ay. Mas— ay. Ct. no. N. J. ay. Pa. ay. Del. ay. Md. no. Va. no. (⟨Col. Mason, Mr. Randolph Mr. Blair no.⟩ Genl Washington & J. M. ay.) N. C. no. S— C. no. Geo. no. [Ayes — 5; noes — 6.]

Question on sect: 4. art VII. as far as to [21] "no tax shl. be laid on exports — ⟨It passed in the affirmative⟩ —

N. H. no. Mas. ay. Ct. ay. N— J. no. Pa. no— Del. no.

---

[18] Revised from *Journal.*

[19] Detail of Ayes and Noes (Vote 334) includes South Carolina in the negative.

[20] Revised from *Journal.*

[21] "as far as to" renders the clause meaningless; it may be a later insertion.

Md ay. Va. ay (Genl W. & J. M. no.)[22] N. C. ay. S. C. ay. Geo— ay. [Ayes — 7; noes — 4.]

Mr L— Martin, proposed to vary the sect: 4. art VII so as to allow a prohibition or tax on the importation of slaves.[23] 1. As five slaves are to be counted as 3 free men in the apportionment of Representatives; such a clause wd. leave an encouragement to this trafic. 2 slaves weakened one part of the Union which the other parts were bound to protect: the privilege of importing them was therefore unreasonable — 3. it was inconsistent with the principles of the revolution and dishonorable to the American character to have such a feature in the Constitution.

Mr Rutlidge did not see how the importation of slaves could be encouraged by this section. He was not apprehensive of insurrections and would readily exempt the other States from[24] ⟨the obligation to protect the Southern against them.⟩. — Religion & humanity had nothing to do with this question — Interest alone is the governing principle with Nations — The true question at present is whether the Southn. States shall or shall not be parties to the Union. If the Northern States consult their interest, they will not oppose the increase of Slaves which will increase the commodities of which they will become the carriers.

Mr. Elseworth was for leaving the clause as it stands. let every State import what it pleases. The morality or wisdom of slavery are considerations belonging to the States themselves — What enriches a part enriches the whole, and the States are the best judges of their particular interest. The old confederation had not meddled with this point, and he did not see any greater necessity for bringing it within the policy of the new one:

Mr Pinkney. South Carolina can never receive the plan if it prohibits the slave trade. In every proposed extension of the powers of Congress, that State has expressly & watchfully excepted that of meddling with the importation of negroes.

[22] See Appendix A, CXXXIV.

[23] Upon this question see further, references under August 22, note 2, and August 25, note 7.

[24] Crossed out "being protected agst. them".

If the States be all left at liberty on this subject, S. Carolina may perhaps by degrees do of herself what is wished, as Virginia & Maryland have already done.

Adjourned[25]

McHENRY

Augt. 21.

passed the 3 sect.

Took up 4 sect. adjourned, after passing the first clause to the word State 2 line inclusive.

[25] See further, Appendix A, XC.

WEDNESDAY, AUGUST 22, 1787.

JOURNAL

Wednesday August 22nd 1787.

The motion, made yesterday, to insert the word "free" before the word "persons" in the 4 section of the 7 article, being withdrawn,

It was moved and seconded to commit the two remaining clauses of the 4 section, and the 5 section of the 7 article

which passed in the affirmative. [Ayes — 7; noes — 3.]

It was moved and seconded to com't the 6th section of the 7 article

which passed in the affirmative [Ayes — 9; noes — 2.]

and a Committee (of a Member from each State) was appointed by ballot of the honorable Mr Langdon, Mr King, Mr Johnson, Mr Livingston, Mr Clymer, Mr Dickinson, Mr L. Martin, Mr Madison, Mr Williamson, Mr C. C. Pinckney, & Mr Baldwin. — to whom the 2 remaining clauses of the 4th & ye 5 & 6 sections were referred.

The honorable Mr Rutledge, from the Committee to whom sundry propositions were referred on the 18 and 20th instant, informed the House that the Committee were prepared to report — he then read the report in his place — and the same, being delivered in at the Secretary's table, was again read throughout, and is as follows

The Committee report that in their opinion the following additions should be made to the report now before the Convention vizt

at the end of the 1st clause of the 1st section of the 7 article add

"for payment of the debts and necessary expences of the "United States — provided that no law for raising any branch

"of revenue, except what may be specially appropriated for "the payment of interest on debts or loans shall continue in "force for more than years"

at the end of the 2nd clause, 2 sect. 7 article add

"and with Indians, within the Limits of any State, not "subject to the laws thereof"

at the end of the 16 clause of the 2 sect. 7 article add

"and to provide, as may become necessary, from time to "time, for the well managing and securing the common prop-"erty and general interests and welfare of the United States "in such manner as shall not interfere with the Governments "of individual States in matters which respect only their "internal Police, or for which their individual authorities "may be competent"

at the end of the 1st section 10 article add

"he shall be of the age of thirty five years, and a Citizen "of the United States, and shall have been an Inhabitant "thereof for Twenty one years"

after the 2nd section of the 10th article insert the following as a 3rd section.

"The President of the United States shall have a Privy-"Council which shall consist of the President of the Senate, "the Speaker of the House of representatives, the Chief-"Justice of the Supreme-Court, and the principal Officer in "the respective departments of foreign affairs, domestic-"affairs, War, Marine, and Finance, as such departments of "office shall from time to time be established — whose duty "it shall be to advise him in matters respecting the execution "of his Office, which he shall think proper to lay before them: "But their advice shall not conclude him, nor affect his respon-"sibility for the measures which he shall adopt"

at the end of the 2nd section of the 11 article add

"The Judges of the Supreme Court shall be triable by the "Senate, on impeachment by the House of representatives"

Between the 4 & 5 lines of the 3rd section of the 11 article, after the word "controversies" — insert

"between the United States and an individual State, or "the United States and an individual person"

It was moved and seconded to rescind the order of the House respecting the hours of meeting and adjournment

which passed in the negative [Ayes — 4; noes — 7.]

It was moved and seconded to insert the following clause after the 2nd section of the 7 article

"The Legislature shall pass no bill of attainder, nor any ex post facto laws."

which passed in the affirmative [Ayes—7; noes—3; divided — 1.]

It was moved and seconded to take up the report of the Committee of five,

It was moved and seconded to postpone the consideration of the report, in order that the Members may furnish themselves with copies of the report,

which passed in the affirmative. [Ayes — 6; noes — 5.]

It was moved and seconded to take up the report of the Committee of eleven, entered on the Journal of the 21st instant

which passed in the affirmative.

It was moved and seconded to amend the first clause of the report to read as follows.

"The Legislature shall fulfil the engagements and dis-"charge the debts of the United States"

It was moved and seconded to alter the amendment by striking out the words "discharge the debts" and insert the words "liquidate the claims"

which passed in the negative

On the question to agree to the clause as amended, namely,

"The Legislature shall fulfil the engagements and dis-"charge the debts of the United States"

it passed in the affirmative [Ayes — 11; noes — 0.][1]

It was moved and seconded to strike the following words out of the second clause of the report

"and the authority of training the militia according to the "discipline prescribed by the United States"

Before the question was taken on the last motion

The House adjourned

---

[1] Vote 342, Detail of Ayes and Noes, which notes that it was "Mr Morris's amendment".

Detail of Ayes and Noes

	New Hampshire	Massachusetts	Rhode Island	Connecticut	New York	New Jersey	Pennsylvania	Delaware	Maryland	Virginia	No Carolina	So Carolina	Georgia	Questions	ayes	noes	divided
[337]	no			aye		aye	no	no	aye	aye	aye	aye	aye	To commit ye remaing clauses of the 4th & the 5 sect 7 article	7	3	
[338]	aye	aye		no		no	aye	aye	aye	aye	aye	aye	aye	To commit the 6th section 7 article	9	2	
[339]	no	aye		no		no	aye	aye	aye	no	no	no	no	To rescind the order of the House respecting the hours of meeting and adjournment	4	7	
[340]	aye	aye		no		no	no	aye	aye	aye	dd	aye	aye	To agree to the clause after the 2nd sect. 7 article	7	3	1
[341]	no	aye		no		aye	no	no	aye	aye	aye	no	aye	To postpone the considn of the report of the Committee of five	6	5	
[342]	aye	aye		aye		aye	aye	aye	aye	aye	aye	aye	aye	To agree to Mr Morris's amendment of the 1st clause of the report of the Committee of eleven	11		

MADISON

Wednesday August 22. in Convention

Art. VII sect 4. resumed.[2] Mr. Sherman was for leaving the clause as it stands. He disapproved of the slave trade: yet as the States were now possessed of the right to import slaves, as the public good did not require it to be taken from them, & as it was expedient to have as few objections as possible to the proposed scheme of Government, he thought it best to leave the matter as we find it. He observed that the abolition of slavery seemed to be going on in the U. S.

[2] Upon this question, see above, July 23, August 8, and August 21, and Appendix A, CXLVIII, CLI, CLVIII (56–60), CLXXI, CCXII, CCLI, CCLIII, CCCXXXIV, CCCXXXV, also below August 25 (with references under note 7), August 28 and August 29.

& that the good sense of the several States would probably by degrees compleat it. He urged on the Convention the necessity of despatch⟨ing its business.⟩

Col. Mason. This infernal trafic originated in the avarice of British Merchants. The British Govt. constantly checked the attempts of Virginia to put a stop to it. The present question concerns not the importing States alone but the whole Union. The evil of having slaves was experienced during the late war. Had slaves been treated as they might have been by the Enemy, they would have proved dangerous instruments in their hands. But their folly dealt by the slaves, as it did by the Tories. He mentioned the dangerous insurrections of the slaves in Greece and Sicily; and the instructions given by Cromwell to the Commissioners sent to Virginia, to arm the servants & slaves, in case other means of obtaining its submission should fail. Maryland & Virginia he said had already prohibited the importation of slaves expressly. N. Carolina had done the same in substance. All this would be in vain if S. Carolina & Georgia be at liberty to import. The Western people are already calling out for slaves for their new lands; and will fill that Country with slaves if they can be got thro' S. Carolina & Georgia. Slavery discourages arts & manufactures. The poor despise labor when performed by slaves. They prevent the immigration of Whites, who really enrich & strengthen a Country. They produce the most pernicious effect on manners. Every master of slaves is born a petty tyrant. They bring the judgment of heaven on a Country. As nations can not be rewarded or punished in the next world they must be in this. By an inevitable chain of causes & effects providence punishes national sins, by national calamities. He lamented that some of our Eastern brethren had from a lust of gain embarked in this nefarious traffic. As to the States being in possession of the Right to import, this was the case with many other rights, now to be properly given up. He held it essential in every point of view, that the Genl. Govt. should have power to prevent the increase of slavery.

Mr. Elsworth. As he had never owned a slave could not

judge of the effects of slavery on character. He said however that if it was to be considered in a moral light we ought to go farther and free those already in the Country. — As slaves also multiply so fast in Virginia & Maryland that it is cheaper to raise than import them, whilst in the sickly rice swamps foreign supplies are necessary, if we go no farther than is urged, we shall be unjust towards S. Carolina & Georgia — Let us not intermeddle. As population increases; poor laborers will be so plenty as to render slaves useless. Slavery in time will not be a speck in our Country. Provision is already made in Connecticut for abolishing it. And the abolition has already taken place in Massachusetts. As to the danger of insurrections from foreign influence, that will become a motive to kind treatment of the slaves.

Mr. Pinkney — If slavery be wrong, it is justified by the example of all the world. He cited the case of Greece Rome & other antient States; the sanction given by France England, Holland & other modern States. In all ages one half of mankind have been slaves. If the S. States were let alone they will probably of themselves stop importations. He wd. himself as a Citizen of S. Carolina vote for it. An attempt to take away the right as proposed will produce serious objections to the Constitution which he wished to see adopted.

General Pinkney declared it to be his firm opinion that if himself & all his colleagues were to sign the Constitution & use their personal influence, it would be of no avail towards obtaining the assent of their Constituents. S. Carolina & Georgia cannot do without slaves. As to Virginia she will gain by stopping the importations. Her slaves will rise in value, & she has more than she wants. It would be unequal to require S. C. & Georgia to confederate on such unequal terms. He said the Royal assent before the Revolution had never been refused to S. Carolina as to Virginia. He contended that the importation of slaves would be for the interest of the whole Union. The more slaves, the more produce to employ the carrying trade; The more consumption also, and the more of this, the more of revenue for the common treasury. He admitted it to be reasonable that slaves should be dutied

like other imports, but should consider a rejection of the clause as an exclusion of S. Carola from the Union.

Mr. Baldwin had conceived national objects alone to be before the Convention, not such as like the present were of a local nature. Georgia was decided on this point. That State has always hitherto supposed a Genl Governmt to be the pursuit of the central States who wished to have a vortex for every thing — that her distance would preclude her from equal advantage — & that she could not prudently purchase it by yielding national powers. From this it might be understood in what light she would view an attempt to abridge one of her favorite prerogatives. If left to herself, she may probably put a stop to the evil. As one ground for this conjecture, he took notice of the sect of which he said was a respectable class of people, who carryed their ethics beyond the mere *equality of men*, extending their humanity to the claims of the whole animal creation.

Mr. Wilson observed that if S. C. & Georgia were themselves disposed to get rid of the importation of slaves in a short time as had been suggested, they would never refuse to Unite because the importation might be prohibited. As the Section now stands all articles imported are to be taxed. Slaves alone are exempt. This is in fact a bounty on that article.

Mr. Gerry thought we had nothing to do with the conduct of the States as to Slaves, but ought to be careful not to give any sanction to it.

Mr. Dickenson considered it as inadmissible on every principle of honor & safety that the importation of slaves should be authorized to the States by the Constitution. The true question was whether the national happiness would be promoted or impeded by the importation, and this question ought to be left to the National Govt. not to the States particularly interested. If Engd. & France permit slavery, slaves are at the same time excluded from both those Kingdoms. Greece and Rome were made unhappy by their slaves. He could not believe that the Southn. States would refuse to confederate on the account apprehended; especially as the power was

not likely to be immediately exercised by the Genl. Government.

Mr Williamson stated the law of N. Carolina on the subject, to wit that it did not directly prohibit the importation of slaves. It imposed a duty of £5. on each slave imported from Africa. £10. on each from elsewhere, & £50 on each from a State licensing manumission. He thought the S. States could not be members of the Union if the clause should be rejected, and that it was wrong to force any thing down, not absolutely necessary, and which any State must disagree to.

Mr. King thought the subject should be considered in a political light only. If two States will not agree to the Constitution as stated on one side, he could affirm with equal belief on the other, that great & equal opposition would be experienced from the other States. He remarked on the exemption of slaves from duty whilst every other import was subjected to it, as an inequality that could not fail to strike the commercial sagacity of the Northn. & middle States.

Mr. Langdon was strenuous for giving the power to the Genl. Govt. He cd. not with a good conscience leave it with the States who could then go on with the traffic, without being restrained by the opinions here given that they will themselves cease to import slaves.

Genl. Pinkney thought himself bound to declare candidly that he did not think S. Carolina would stop her importations of slaves in any short time, but only stop them occasionally as she now does. He moved to commit the clause that slaves might be made liable to an equal tax with other imports which he he thought right & wch. wd. remove one difficulty that had been started.

Mr. Rutlidge. If the Convention thinks that N. C; S. C. & Georgia will ever agree to the plan, unless their right to import slaves be untouched, the expectation is vain. The people of those States will never be such fools as to give up so important an interest. He was strenuous agst. striking out the Section, and seconded the motion of Genl. Pinkney for a commitment.

Mr Govr. Morris wished the whole subject to be committed including the clauses relating to taxes on exports & to a navigation act. These things may form a bargain among the Northern & Southern States.

Mr. Butler declared that he never would agree to the power of taxing exports.

Mr. Sherman said it was better to let the S. States import slaves than to part with them, if they made that a sine qua non. He was opposed to a tax on slaves imported as making the matter worse, because it implied they were *property*. He acknowledged that if the power of prohibiting the importation should be given to the Genl. Government that it would be exercised. He thought it would be its duty to exercise the power.

Mr. Read was for the commitment provided the clause concerning taxes on exports should also be committed.

Mr. Sherman observed that that clause had been agreed to & therefore could not committed.

Mr. Randolph was for committing in order that some middle ground might, if possible, be found. He could never agree to the clause as it stands. He wd. sooner risk the constitution — He dwelt on the dilemma to which the Convention was exposed. By agreeing to the clause, it would revolt the Quakers, the Methodists, and many others in the States having no slaves. On the other hand, two States might be lost to the Union. Let us then, he said, try the chance of a commitment.

On the question for committing the remaining part of Sect 4 & 5. of art: 7. N. H. no. Mas. abst. Cont. ay N. J. ay Pa. no. Del. no Maryd ay. Va ay. N. C. ay S. C. ay. Geo. ay. [Ayes — 7; noes — 3; absent — 1.]

Mr. Pinkney & Mr. Langdon moved to commit sect. 6. as to navigation act ⟨by two thirds of each House.⟩

Mr. Gorham did not see the propriety of it. Is it meant to require a greater proportion of votes? He desired it to be remembered that the Eastern States had no motive to Union but a commercial one. They were able to protect themselves. They were not afraid of external danger, and did not need the aid of the Southn. States.

Mr. Wilson wished for a commitment in order to reduce the proportion of votes required.

Mr. Elsworth was for taking the plan as it is. This widening of opinions has a threatening aspect. If we do not agree on this middle & moderate ground he was afraid we should lose two States, with such others as may be disposed to stand aloof, should fly into a variety of shapes & directions, and most probably into several confederations and not without bloodshed.

On Question for committing 6 sect. as to navigation Act to a member from each State — N. H. ay— Mas. ay. Ct no. N. J. no. Pa. ay. Del. ay. Md. ay. Va. ay. N. C. ay. S. C. ay. Geo. ay. [Ayes — 9; noes — 2.]

The Committee appointed were Mr. Langdon, King, Johnson, Livingston, Clymer, Dickenson, L. Martin,[3] Madison, Williamson, C. C. Pinkney, & Baldwin.

To this committee were referred also the two clauses above mentioned, of the 4 & 5. sect: of art. 7.

Mr. Rutlidge, from the Committee to whom were referred on the 18 & 20th. instant the propositions of Mr. Madison & Mr. Pinkney, made the Report following. —

☞ (⟨Here insert⟩ ——— the Report ⟨from⟩ the Journal of the Convention of this date.) —

A motion to rescind the order of the House respecting the hours of meeting & adjourning, was negatived:

⟨Mass: Pa. Del. Mard. . . . . ay
N. H. Con: N. J. Va. N. C. S. C. Geo. no⟩[4]

Mr. Gerry[5] & Mr. McHenry moved to insert after the 2d. sect. art: 7. the clause following, to wit, "The Legislature shall pass no bill of attainder nor ⟨any⟩[4] ex post facto law" *

Mr. Gerry urged the necessity of this prohibition, which he said was greater in the National than the State Legislature, because the number of members in the former being fewer, they were on that account the more to be feared.

* ⟨the proceedings on this motion involving the two questions on "attainders & ex post facto laws." are not so fully stated in the printed Journal.⟩

[3] See Appendix A, CLXXXIX.

[4] Taken from *Journal*.

[5] See Appendix A, CLI.

Mr. Govr. Morris thought the precaution as to ex post facto laws unnecessary; but essential as to bills of attainder

Mr Elseworth contended that there was no lawyer, no civilian who would not say that ex post facto laws were void of themselves. It cannot then be necessary to prohibit them.

Mr. Wilson was against inserting anything in the Constitution as to ex post facto laws. It will bring reflexions on the Constitution — and proclaim that we are ignorant of the first principles of Legislation, or are constituting a Government which will be so.

The question being divided, The first part of the motion relating to bills of attainder was agreed to nem. contradicente.

On the second part relating to ex post facto laws —

Mr Carrol remarked that experience overruled all other calculations. It had proved that in whatever light they might be viewed by civilians or others, the State Legislatures had passed them, and they had taken effect.

Mr. Wilson. If these prohibitions in the State Constitutions have no effect, it will be useless to insert them in this Constitution. Besides, both sides will agree to the principle & will differ as to its application.

Mr. Williamson. Such a prohibitory clause is in the Constitution of N. Carolina, and tho it has been violated, it has done good there & may do good here, because the Judges can take hold of it

Docr. Johnson thought the clause unnecessary, and implying an improper suspicion of the National Legislature.

Mr. Rutlidge was in favor of the clause.

On the question for inserting the prohibition of ex post facto laws.

N— H— ay— Mas. ay. Cont. no. N. J— no. Pa. no. Del— ay. Md. ay. Virga. ay N— C. divd. S. C. ay— Geo. ay. [Ayes — 7; noes — 3; divided — 1.]

The report of the committee of 5. made by Mr. Rutlidge, was taken up & then postponed that each member Might furnish himself with a copy.

The Report of the Committee of Eleven delivered in & entered on the Journal of the 21st. inst. was then taken up.

and the first clause containing the words "The Legislature of the U. S. *shall have power* to fulfil the engagements which have been entered into by Congress" being under consideration,[6]

Mr. Elsworth argued that they were unnecessary. The U— S— heretofore entered into Engagements by Congs who were their Agents. They will hereafter be bound to fulfil them by their new agents.

Mr Randolph thought such a provision necessary; for though the U. States will be bound, the new Govt will have no authority in the case unless it be given to them.

Mr. Madison thought it necessary to give the authority in order to prevent misconstruction. He mentioned the attempts made by the Debtors to British subjects to shew that contracts under the old Government, were dissolved by the Revolution which destroyed the political identity of the Society.

Mr Gerry thought it essential that some explicit provision should be made on this subject, so that no pretext might remain for getting rid of the public engagements.

Mr. Govr. Morris moved by way of amendment to substitute — "The Legislature *shall* discharge the debts & fulfil the engagements ⟨of the U. States⟩".

It was moved to vary the amendment by striking out "discharge the debts" & to insert "liquidate the claims", which being negatived,

The amendment moved by Mr. Govr. Morris was agreed to all the States being in the affirmative.

It was moved & 2ded. to strike the following words — out of the 2d. clause of the report "and the authority of training the Militia according to the discipline prescribed by the U— S." ⟨Before a question was taken⟩[7]

The House adjourned[8]

---

[6] See further, August 18 (with references under note 6), August 21, August 23–24, and August 25 (with references under note 5).

[7] Taken from *Journal*.

[8] See further, Appendix A, XCI–XCIII.

McHENRY

August 22.

Committed the remainder of the 4 sect. with the 5 and 6.

The 4 sect promitting the importation of Slaves gave rise to much desultory debate.

Every 5 slaves counted in representation as one elector without being equal in point of strength to one *white* inhabitant.

This gave the slave States an advantage in representation over the others.

The slaves were moreover exempt from duty on importation.

They served to render the representation from such States aristocratical.

It was replied — That the population or increase of slaves in Virginia exceeded their calls for their services — That a prohibition of Slaves into S. Carolina Georgia etc — would be a monopoly in their favor. These States could not do without Slaves — Virginia etc would make their own terms for such as they might sell.

Such was the situation of the country that it could not exist without slaves — That they could confederate on no other condition.

They had enjoyed the right of importing slaves when colonies.

They enjoyed as States under the confederation — And if they could not enjoy it under the proposed government, they could not associate or make a part of it.

Several additions were reported by the Committee.

Mr. Martin shewed us some restrictory clauses drawn up for the VII article respecting commerce — which we agreed to bring forward. —

Moved that the legislature should pass no ex post facto laws or bills of attainder.

G. Morris Willson Dr. Johnson etc thought the first an unnecessary guard as the principles of justice law et[c] were

a perpetual bar to such — To say that the legis. shall not pass an ex post facto law is the same as to declare they shall not do a thing contrary to common sense — that they shall not cause that to be a crime which is no crime —

Carried in the affirmative.

THURSDAY, AUGUST 23, 1787.

JOURNAL

Thursday August 23rd 1787.

It was moved and seconded to postpone the consideration of the second clause of the report of the Committee of eleven in order to take up the following

"To establish an uniform and general system of discipline "for the militia of these States, and to make laws for organ-"izing, arming, disciplining and governing such part of them "as may be employed in the service of the United States, re-"serving to the States respectively the appointment of the "Officers and all authority over the militia not herein given "to the general Government"

On the question to postpone

it passed in the negative [Ayes — 3; noes — 8.]

It was moved and seconded to postpone the consideration of the second clause of the report of the Committee of eleven in order to take up the following

"To establish an uniformity of arms, exercise, and organ-"ization for the militia — and to provide for the government "of them when called into the service of the United States"

On the question to postpone

it passed in the affirmative [Ayes — 1; noes — 10.] [1]

It was moved and seconded to recommit the 2nd clause of the report of the Committee of eleven

which passed in the negative.

[1] Vote 344, Detail of Ayes and Noes, which notes that the motion to postpone was in order "to take up Mr Elsworths amendt". The Journal states that the question "passed in the affirmative", but the Detail of Ayes and Noes records a negative vote, which is confirmed by Madison, and the subsequent action of the Convention makes an affirmative vote impossible.

On the question to agree to the first part of the 2nd clause of the report, namely

"To make laws for organizing, arming, and disciplining "the militia, and for governing such part of them as may be "employed in the service of the United States"

it passed in the affirmative [Ayes — 9; noes — 2.]

It was moved and seconded to amend the next part of the 2nd clause of the report to read

"reserving to the States, respectively, the appointment "of the Officers under the rank of general Officers

it passed in the negative. [Ayes — 2; noes — 9.]

On the question to agree to the following part of the 2nd clause of the report, namely,

"reserving to the States, respectively, the appointment of "the Officers"

it passed in the affirmative

On the question to agree to the following part of the 2nd clause of the report, namely,

"and the authority of training the militia according to the "discipline prescribed by the United States"

it passed in the affirmative [Ayes — 7; noes — 4.] [2]

It was moved and seconded to agree to the 7 section of the 7 article, as reported,

which passed in the affirmative [Ayes — 11; noes — 0.]

It was moved and seconded to insert the following clause after the 7 section of the 7 article.

"No person holding any office of profit or trust under the "United States, shall without the consent of the Legislature "accept of any present, emolument, office, or title of any kind "whatever, from any king, prince, or foreign State"

which passed in the affirmative

It was moved and seconded to amend the 8th article to read as follows

"This Constitution and the Laws of the United States "made in pursuance thereof, and all treaties made under the "authority of the United-States, shall be the supreme law of

[2] Vote 347, Detail of Ayes and Noes, which makes an evident mistake in giving the total.

"the several States, and of their Citizens and inhabitants; "and the Judges in the several States shall be bound thereby "in their decisions; any thing in the constitutions or laws of "the several States to the contrary notwithstanding"

which passed in the affirmative

On the question to agree to the 8 article as amended

it passed in the affirmative

It was moved and seconded to strike the following words out of the 18 clause of the 1st section 7 article

"enforce treaties"

which passed in the affirmative

It was moved and seconded to alter the first part of the 18 clause of the 1st section, 7 article to read

"To provide for calling forth the militia to execute the laws "of the Union, suppress insurrections, and repel invasions"

which passed in the affirmative

On the question to agree to the 18th clause of the 1st section, 7 article, as amended

it passed in the affirmative.

It was moved and seconded to agree to the following proposition, as an additional power to be vested in the Legislature of the United States.

"To negative all laws passed by the several States inter-"fering, in the opinion of the Legislature, with the general "interests and harmony of the Union — provided that two "thirds of the Members of each House assent to the same."

It was moved and seconded to commit the proposition

which passed in the negative. [Ayes — 5; noes — 6.]

The Proposition was then withdrawn.

It was moved and seconded to amend the 1st section of the 7. article to read

"The Legislature shall fulfil the engagements and dis-"charge the debts of the United-States, and shall have the "power to lay and collect taxes, duties, imposts, and excises."

which passed in the affirmative

It was moved and seconded to amend the first clause of the first section 9. article to read

"The Senate shall have power to treat with foreign na-

"tions, but no Treaty shall be binding on the United States "which is not ratified by a Law."

It was moved and seconded to postpone the consideration of the amendment.

which passed in the negative. [Ayes — 5; noes — 5.] [3]

On the question to agree to the amendment.

it passed in the negative [Ayes — 1; noes — 8; divided — 1].

It was moved and seconded to postpone the considn of the first clause of the 1st sect. 9 article

which passed in the affirmative

It was moved and seconded to insert the words

"and other public ministers" after the word "ambassadors" in the first section 9 article

which passed in the affirmative

Separate questions being taken on postponing the several clauses of the first sect. 9 article

they passed in the affirmative.

It was moved and seconded to take up the 1st section of the 9 article, in order to it's being committed

which passed in the affirmative.

and it was referred to the Committee of five.

and then the House adjourned

---

[3] Vote 350, Detail of Ayes and Noes, which notes that it was "Mr Morris's amendment".

DETAIL OF AYES AND NOES

	New Hampshire	Massachusetts	Rhode Island	Connecticut	New York	New Jersey	Pennsylvania	Delaware	Maryland	Virginia	No Carolina	So Carolina	Georgia	Questions	ayes	noes	divided
[343]	no	no		no		aye	no	no	aye	no	no	no	aye	To postpone ye 2nd clause of the report of the Comme	3	8	
[p. 13]																	
[344]	no	no		aye		no	no	no	no	no	no	no	no	To postpone ye 2 clause of the report to take up Mr Elsworths amendt	1	10	
[345]	aye	aye		no		aye	aye	aye	no	aye	aye	aye	aye	To agree to the 1st part of ye 2d clause of the report of the Committee of eleven	9	2	
[346]	aye	no		no		no	no	no	no	no	no	aye	no	To agree to the appointment of the Genl Officers of the militia by the genl Govt	2	9	
[347]	aye	aye		aye		aye	aye	no	aye	no	aye	no	no	To agree to the last clause of the report	8	3	
[348]	aye	aye		aye		aye	aye	aye	aye	aye	aye	aye	aye	"The United States shall not grant titles of nobility"			
[349]	aye	no		no		no	aye	aye	aye	aye	no	no	no	To commit the motion for giving a negative to the Legislature of the U. S. over the State laws.	5	6	
[350]		no		no		aye	aye	aye	aye	aye	no	no	no	To postpone Mr Morris's amendment to the 1st clause 1st sect. 9 article	5	5	
[351]		no		no		no	aye	no	no	no	dd	no	no	To agree to the amendment	1	8	1

MADISON

In Convention Thursday Aug: 23. 1787

The Report of the Committee of Eleven made Aug: 21. being taken up, and the following clause being under consideration to wit "To make laws for organizing, arming & disciplining the Militia, and for governing such parts of them

as may be employed in the service of the U. S. reserving to the States respectively, the appointment of the officers, and authority of training the militia according to the discipline prescribed" — [4]

Mr Sherman moved to strike out the last member — "and authority of training &c. He thought it unnecessary. The States will have this authority of course if not given up.

Mr. Elsworth doubted the propriety of striking out the sentence. The reason assigned applies as well to the other reservation of the appointment to offices. He remarked at the same time that the term discipline was of vast extent and might be so expounded as to include all power on the subject.

Mr. King, by way of explanation, said that by *organizing* the Committee meant, proportioning the officers & men — by *arming*, specifying the kind size and caliber of arms — & by *disciplining* prescribing the manual exercise evolutions &c.

Mr. Sherman withdrew his motion

Mr Gerry, This power in the U— S. as explained is making the States drill-sergeants. He had as lief let the Citizens of Massachusetts be disarmed, as to take the command from the States, and subject them to the Genl Legislature. It would be regarded as a system of Despotism.

Mr Madison observed that "*arming*" as explained did not did not extend to furnishing arms; nor the term "disciplining" to penalties & Courts martial for enforcing them.

Mr. King added, to his former explanation that *arming* meant not only to provide for uniformity of arms, but included authority to regulate the modes of furnishing, either by the militia themselves, the State Governments, or the National Treasury: that *laws* for disciplining, must involve penalties and every thing necessary for enforcing penalties.

Mr. Dayton moved to postpone the paragraph, in order to take up the following proposition

"To establish an uniform & general system of discipline for the Militia of these States, and to make laws for organiz-

[4] Upon this question, see above August 18, 21, and 22, and below September 14, also Appendix A, CLVIII (52–55), CLXXV, CLXXXIX, CXCI, CCX, CCLXXII, CCCXV.

ing, arming, disciplining & governing *such part of them as may be employed in the service of the U. S.*, reserving to the States respectively the appointment of the officers, and all authority over the Militia not herein given to the General Government"

On the question to postpone in favor of this proposition: ⟨it passed in the Negative⟩

N. H. no. Mas— no. Ct no. N. J. ay. P. no. Del. no. Maryd ay. Va. no. N. C. no. S. C. no. Geo. ay. [Ayes — 3; noes — 8.]

Mr. Elsworth & Mr. Sherman moved to postpone the 2d. clause in favor of the following

"To establish an uniformity of arms, exercise & organization for the Militia, and to provide for the Government of them when called into the service of the U. States"

The object of this proposition was to refer the plan for the Militia to the General Govt. but leave the execution of it to the State Govts.

Mr Langdon said He could not understand the jealousy expressed by some Gentleman. The General & State Govts. were not enemies to each other, but different institutions for the good of the people of America. As one of the people he could say, the National Govt. is mine, the State Govt is mine — In transferring power from one to the other—I only take out of my left hand what it cannot so well use, and put it into my right hand where it can be better used.

Mr. Gerry thought it was rather taking out of the right hand & putting it into the left. Will any man say that liberty will be as safe in the hands of eighty or a hundred men taken from the whole continent, as in the hands of two or three hundred taken from a single State?

Mr. Dayton was against so absolute a uniformity. In some States there ought to be a greater proportion of cavalry than in others. In some places rifles would be most proper, in others muskets &c—

Genl Pinkney preferred the clause reported by the Committee, extending the meaning of it to the case of fines &c—

Mr. Madison. The primary object is to secure an effectual discipline of the Militia. This will no more be done if left

to the States separately than the requisitions have been hitherto paid by them. The States neglect their Militia now, and the more they are consolidated into one nation, the less each will rely on its own interior provisions for its safety & the less prepare its Militia for that purpose; in like manner as the Militia of a State would have been still more neglected than it has been if each County had been independently charged with the care of its Militia. The Discipline of the Militia is evidently a *National* concern, and ought to be provided for in the *National* Constitution.

Mr L— Martin was confident that the States would never give up the power over the Militia; and that, if they were ⟨to do so,⟩ the militia would be less attended to by the Genl. than by the State Governments.

Mr Randolph asked what danger there could be that the Militia could be brought into the field and made to commit suicide on themselves. This is a power that cannot from its nature be abused, unless indeed the whole mass should be corrupted. He was for trammelling the Genl Govt. whenever there was danger. but here there could be none— He urged this as an essential point; observing that the Militia were every where neglected by the State Legislatures, the members of which courted popularity too much to enforce a proper discipline. Leaving the appointment of officers to the States protects the people agst. every apprehension that could produce murmur.

On Question on Mr. Elsworth's Motion

N. H. no. Mas— no— Ct. ay. N. J. no. Pa. no. Del. no. Md. no. Va no— N— C. no. S. C no. Geo. no. [Ayes — 1; noes — 10.]

A motion was then made to recommit the 2d clause which was negatived.

On the question to agree to the 1st. part of the clause, namely

"To make laws for organizing arming & disciplining the Militia, and for governing such part of them as may be employed in the service of the U. S".

N. H ay. Mas. ay. Ct. no. N. J. ay. Pa. ay. Del. ay. Md

no. Va ay. N—C—ay. S. C. ay. Geo. ay. [Ayes—9 noes—2.]

Mr. Madison moved to amend the next part of the clause so as to read "reserving to the States respectively, the appointment of the officers, *under the rank of General officers.*"

Mr. Sherman considered this as absolutely inadmissible. He said that if the people should be so far asleep as to allow the Most influential officers of the Militia to be appointed by the Genl. Government, every man of discernment would rouse them by sounding the alarm to them—

Mr. Gerry. Let us at once destroy the State Govts have an Executive for life or hereditary, and a proper Senate, and then there would be some consistency in giving full powers to the Genl Govt. but as the States are not to be abolished, he wondered at the attempts that were made to give powers inconsistent with their existence. He warned the Convention agst pushing the experiment too far. Some people will support a plan of vigorous Government at every risk. Others of a more democratic cast will oppose it with equal determination. And a Civil war may be produced by the conflict.

Mr. Madison. As the greatest danger is that of disunion of the States, it is necessary to guard agst. it by sufficient powers to the Common Govt. and as the greatest danger to liberty is from large standing armies, it is best to prevent them by an effectual provision for a good Militia—

On the Question to agree to Mr. Madison's motion

N—H—ay—Mas—no—Ct no—N—J—no—Pa no—Del—no—Md no—Va no—N—C—no—S—C—ay—Geo—*ay. [Ayes—3; noes—8.]

On the question to agree to the "reserving to the States the appointment of the officers". It was agreed to nem: contrad:

On the question on the clause "and the authority of training the Militia according to the discipline prescribed by the U. S"—

N. H. ay. Mas. ay. Ct. ay—N—J—ay. Pa. ay—Del. no. Md. ay. Va. no—N—C. ay. S. C. no. Geo. no—[Ayes—7; noes—4.]

* ⟨In the printed Journal-Geo: no⟩

On the question to agree ⟨to⟩ Art. VII— sect. 7. ⟨as reported⟩[5] It passed nem: contrad:

Mr Pinkney urged the necessity of preserving foreign Ministers & other officers of the U. S. independent of external influence and moved to insert — after Art VII sect 7. the clause following — "No person holding any office of profit or trust under the U. S. shall without the consent of the Legislature, accept of any present, emolument, office or title of any kind whatever, from any King, Prince or foreign State which passed nem: contrad.[6]

Mr. Rutlidge moved to amend Art: VIII to read as follows,

"This Constitution & the laws of the U. S. made in pursuance thereof, and all Treaties made under the authority of the U. S. shall be the supreme law of the several States and of their citizens and inhabitants; and the Judges in the several States shall be bound thereby in their decisions, any thing in the Constitutions or laws of the several States, to the contrary notwithstanding" —[7]

which was agreed to, nem: contrad:

Art: IX being next for consideration,[8]

Mr Govr Morris argued agst. the appointment of officers by the Senate. He considered the body as too numerous for the purpose; as subject to cabal; and as devoid of responsibility. — If Judges were to be tried by the Senate according to a late report of a Committee it was particularly wrong to let the Senate have the filling of vacancies which its own decrees were to create.

Mr. Wilson was of the same opinion & for like reasons.

The art IX— being waved— and art VII. sect 1. resumed,[9]

Mr Govr Morris moved to strike the following words out

[5] Article VII, Sect. 7. "The United States shall not grant any title of Nobility."

[6] See Appendix A, CCXII.

[7] See Appendix A, CXCII, CCCXCVIII.

[8] Article IX, Sect. 1. "The Senate of the United States shall have power to make treaties, and to appoint Ambassadors, and Judges of the supreme Court."

[9] Article VII, Sect. 1 (clause 18). "To call forth the aid of the militia, in order to execute the laws of the Union, enforce treaties, suppress insurrections, and repel invasions;".

of the 18 clause "enforce treaties" as being superfluous since treaties were to be "laws" . . . . . . which was agreed to nem: contrad:

Mr Govr Morris moved to alter 1st. part. of 18. clause — sect. 1. art. VII so as to read "to provide for calling forth the militia to execute the laws of the Union,[10] suppress insurrections and repel invasions". which was agreed to nem: contrad

On the question then to agree to the 18 clause of sect. 1. art: 7. as amended it passed in the affirmative nem: contradicente.

Mr C— Pinkney moved to add as an additional power to be vested in the Legislature of the U. S. "To negative all laws passed by the several States interfering in the opinion of the Legislature with the General interests and harmony of the Union;" provided that two thirds of the members of each House assent to the same" This principle he observed had formerly been agreed to.[11] He considered the precaution as essentially necessary: The objection drawn from the predominance of the large ⟨States⟩ had been removed by the equality established in the Senate— Mr. Broome 2ded. the proposition.

Mr. Sherman thought it unnecessary; the laws of the General Government being Supreme & paramount to the State laws according to the plan, as it now stands.

Mr. Madison proposed that it should be committed— He had been from the beginning a friend to the principle; but thought the modification might be made better.

Mr. Mason wished to know how the power was to be exercised. Are all laws whatever to be brought up? Is no road nor bridge to be established without the Sanction of the General Legislature? Is this to sit constantly in order to receive & revise the State Laws? He did not mean by these remarks to condemn the expedient, but he was apprehensive that great objections would lie agst. it.

[10] See Appendix A, CCX.

[11] See above June 8 (with references under note 3), July 17, and Appendix A, XCI, CCCXXVI, CCCLXXXIII.

Mr. Williamson thought it unnecessary, & having been already decided, a revival of the question was a waste of time.

Mr. Wilson considered this as the key-stone wanted to compleat the wide arch of Government we are raising. The power of self-defence had been urged as necessary for the State Governments— It was equally necessary for the General Government. The firmness of Judges is not of itself sufficient Something further is requisite— It will be better to prevent the passage of an improper law, than to declare it void when passed.

Mr. Rutlidge. If nothing else, this alone would damn and ought to damn the Constitution. Will any State ever agree to be bound hand & foot in this manner. It is worse than making mere corporations of them whose bye laws would not be subject to this shackle.

Mr Elseworth observed that the power contended for wd. require either that all laws of the State Legislatures should previously to their taking effect be transmitted to the Genl Legislature, or be repealable by the Latter; or that the State Executives should be appointed by the Genl Government, and have a controul over the State laws. If the last was meditated let it be declared.[12]

Mr. Pinkney declared that he thought the State Executives ought to be so appointed with such a controul. & that it would be so provided if another Convention should take place.

Mr Governr. Morris did not see the utility or practicability of the proposition of Mr. Pinkney, but wished it to be referred to the consideration of a Committee.

Mr Langdon was in favor of the proposition. He considered it as resolvable into the question whether the extent of the National Constitution was to be judged of by the Genl or the State Governments.

On the question for commitment, ⟨it passed in the negative.⟩

N— H. ay. Masts: no. Cont. no N. J. no. Pa. ay. Del: ay. Md. ay. Va. ay. N. C. no. S. C. no. Geo. no. [Ayes — 5; noes — 6.] [13]

---

[12] See Appendix A, CLXIII.

[13] See Appendix A, CXXXVII.

Mr Pinkney then withdrew his proposition.

The 1st sect. of art: VII being so amended as to read "The Legislature *shall* fulfil the engagements and discharge the debts of the U. S, & shall have the power to lay & collect taxes duties imposts & excises", ⟨was agreed to⟩ [14]

Mr. Butler expressed his dissatisfaction lest it should compel payment as well to the Blood-suckers who had speculated on the distresses of others, as to those who had fought & bled for their country. He would be ready he said tomorrow to vote for a discrimination between those classes of people, and gave notice that he should move for a reconsideration.

Art IX. sect. 1. being resumed, to wit "The Senate of the U. S. shall have power to make treaties, and to appoint Ambassadors, and Judges of the Supreme Court."

Mr. ⟨Madison⟩ observed that the Senate represented the States alone, and that for this as well as other obvious reasons it was proper that the President should be an agent in Treaties.[15]

Mr. Govr. Morris did not know that he should agree to refer the making of Treaties to the Senate at all, but for the present wd. move to add as an amendment to the section, after "Treaties" — "but no Treaty shall be binding on the U. S. which is not ratified by a law."

Mr Madison suggested the inconvenience of requiring a legal *ratification* of treaties of alliance for the purposes of war &c &c

Mr. Ghorum. Many other disadvantages must be experienced if treaties of peace and all negociations are to be previously ratified — and if not prevously, the Ministers would be at a loss how to proceed— What would be the case in G. Britain if the King were to proceed in this maner? American Ministers must go abroad not instructed by the same Authority (as will be the case with other Ministers) which is to ratify their proceedings.

Mr. Govr. Morris. As to treaties of alliance, they will oblige foreign powers to send their Ministers here, the very

---

[14] See further August 18 (with references under note 6), August 21–22, August 24, August 25 (with references under note 5).

[15] Upon this question and its determination, see Appendix A, CCLXXIV—CCLXXVI.

thing we should wish for. Such treaties could not be otherwise made, if his amendment shd. succeed. In general he was not solicitous to multiply & facilitate Treaties. He wished none to be made with G. Britain, till she should be at war. Then a good bargain might be made with her. So with other foreign powers. The more difficulty in making treaties, the more value will be set on them.

Mr. Wilson. In the most important Treaties, the King of G. Britain being obliged to resort to Parliament for the execution of them, is under the same fetters as the amendment of Mr. Morris will impose on the Senate. It was refused yesterday to permit even the Legislature to lay duties on exports. Under the clause, without the amendment, the Senate alone can make a Treaty, requiring all the Rice of S. Carolina to be sent to some one particular port.

Mr. Dickinson concurred in the amendment, as most safe and proper, tho' he was sensible it was unfavorable to the little States; wch would otherwise have an *equal* share in making Treaties.

Docr. Johnson thought there was something of solecism in saying that the acts of a Minister with plenipotentiary powers from one Body, should depend for ratification on another Body. The Example of the King of G. B. was not parallel. Full & compleat power was vested in him— If the Parliament should fail to provide the necessary means of execution, the Treaty would be violated.

Mr. Ghorum in answer to Mr. Govr Morris, said that negociations on the spot were not to be desired by us, especially if the whole Legislature is to have any thing to do with Treaties. It will be generally influenced by two or three men, who will be corrupted by the Ambassadors here. In such a Government as ours, it is necessary to guard against the Government itself being seduced.

Mr. Randolph observing that almost every Speaker had made objections to the clause as it stood, moved in order to a further consideration of the subject, that the Motion of Mr. Govr. Morris should be postponed, and on this question ⟨It was lost the States being equally divided.⟩

Massts. no. Cont. no. N. J— ay— Pena. ay. Del. ay. Md. ay. Va. ay—N. C. no. S. C. no—Geo. no. [Ayes — 5; noes — 5.]

On Mr. Govr. Morris Motion

Masts. no. Cont no. N. J. no. Pa. ay— Del. no— Md. no. Va. no. N. C divd S. C. no. Geo— no. [Ayes — 1; noes — 8; divided — 1.]

The several clauses of Sect: 1. art IX, were then separately postponed after inserting "and other public Ministers" next after "Ambassadors."

Mr. Madison hinted for consideration, whether a distinction might not be made between different sorts of Treaties — Allowing the President & Senate to make Treaties eventual and of Alliance for limited terms — and requiring the concurrence of the whole Legislature in other Treaties.

The 1st Sect. art IX. was finally referred nem: con: to the committee of Five, and the House then

Adjourned.[16]

McHENRY

August 23.

7 sect. agreed to.

On motion, on a proposition reported and amended agreed that "*The legislature* shall fulfil the engagements and discharge the debts of the U. S." To make the first clause in the VII article — Amended the first clause in the report of the said article by striking out the words, *the legislature of the U. S.* Added in the said article after the clause "to provide and maintain fleets."

To organize and discipline the militia and govern such part of them as may be employed in the service of the U. S. reserving to the States respectively the appointment of the officers and the authority of training the militia according to the discipline prescribed by the U. S."

Expunged in the VIII article the words *the acts of the legis-*

[16] See further, Appendix A, XCIV.

lature of the U. S. and *of this constitution*, so as that the constitution and laws made in pursuance thereof etc should be the supreme laws of the several States —

The IX article being taken up, It was motioned that no treaty should be binding till it received the sanction of the legislature.

It was said[17] that a minister could not then be instructed by the Senate who were to appoint him, or if instructed there could be no certainty that the house of representatives would agree to confirm what he might agree to under these instructions.

To this it was answered[18] that all treaties which contravene a law of England or require a law to give them operation or effect are inconclusive till agreed to by the legislature of Great Britain.

Except in such cases the power of the King without the concurrence of the parliament conclusive.

Mr. Maddison. the Kings power over treaties final and original except in granting subsidies or dismembering the empire. These required parliamentary acts.

Commiteed.

Adjourned.

---

[17] By Gorham.

[18] By Wilson.

FRIDAY, AUGUST 24, 1787.

JOURNAL

Friday August 24. 1787.

The honorable Mr Livingston, from the Committee of eleven to whom were referred the two remaining clauses of the 4th section, and the 5th and 6th sections of the 7 article, informed the House that the Committee were prepared to report. The report was then delivered in at the Secretary's table, was once read, and is as follows.

"Strike out so much of the 4th section of the 7th article as "was referred to the Committee and insert "The migration "or importation of such persons as the several States now "existing shall think proper to admit, shall not be prohibited "by the Legislature prior to the year 1800 — but a Tax or "Duty may be imposed on such migration or importation at a "rate not exceeding the average of the Duties laid on Imports."

"The 5th section to remain as in the report"

"The 6th section to be stricken out"

It was moved and seconded to reconsider the 1st clause 1st sect. 7 article

which passed in the affirmative

and to-morrow was assigned for the reconsideration [Ayes — 7; noes — 2.]

It was moved and seconded to postpone the consideration of the 2nd and 3rd sections 9 article.

which passed in the negative. [Ayes — 3; noes — 7.]

It was moved and seconded to strike out the 2nd and 3rd sections of the 9th article

which passed in the affirmative [Ayes — 8; noes — 2.]

Separate questions being taken on the 1st 2nd and 3rd clauses of the 1st section — 10th article, as reported,

they passed in the affirmative.

It was moved and seconded to strike out the word "Legislature" and to insert the word "People" in the 1st section 10th article.

which passed in the negative [Ayes — 2; noes — 9.]

It was moved and seconded to insert the word "joint" before the word "ballot" in the 1st section of the 10th article

which passed in the affirmative [Ayes — 7; noes — 4.]

It was moved and seconded to add after the word "Legislature" in the 1st section 10th article the words "each State having one vote"

which passed in the negative. [Ayes — 5; noes — 6.]

It was moved and seconded to insert after the word "Legislature" in the 1st sect. of the 10 article the words "to which election a majority of the votes of the Members present shall be required"

which passed in the affirmative [Ayes — 10; noes — 1.]

On the question to agree to the following clause

"and in case the numbers for the two highest in votes "should be equal, then the President of the Senate shall have "an additional casting voice"

it passed in the negative.

It was moved and seconded to agree to the following amendment to the first sect. of the 10th article

"shall be chosen by electors to be chosen by the People of the several States"

which passed in the negative. [Ayes — 5; noes — 6.]

It was moved and seconded to postpone the consideration of the two last clauses of the 1st sect. 10 article

which passed in the negative

It was moved and seconded to refer the two last clauses of the 1st sect. 10 article. to a committee of a Member from each State.

which passed in the negative. [Ayes — 5; noes — 5; divided — 1.]

On the question to agree to the following clause

"shall be chosen by electors"

it passed in the negative [Ayes — 4; noes — 4; divided — 2.]

The consideration of the remaining clauses of the 1st section

10 article was postponed till to-morrow on the request of the Deputies of the State of New Jersey.

On the question to transpose the word "information" and to insert it after the word "Legislature" in the first clause of the 2 sect. 10 article

it passed in the affirmative

It was moved and seconded to strike out the words "he may" and to insert the word "and" before the word "recommend" in the second clause of the 2 sect. 10 article

which passed in the affirmative

It was moved and seconded to insert the word "and" after the word "occasions" in the 2 sect. 10 article;

which passed in the affirmative

It was moved and seconded to insert the word "shall" before the words "think proper" 2 sect. 10 article.

which passed in the affirmative

It was moved and seconded to strike out the words "officers" and to insert the words "to offices" after the word "appoint" in the 2 sect. of the 10 article

which passed in the affirmative

It was moved and seconded to insert the words "or by law" after the word "constitution" in the 2nd section of the 10th article

which passed in the negative. [Ayes — 1; noes — 9.]

It was moved and seconded to strike out the words "and shall "appoint to offices in all cases not otherwise provided for by "this Constitution" and to insert the following

"and shall appoint to all offices established by this Con-"stitution, except in cases herein otherwise provided for, and "to all offices which may here after be created by law."

which passed in the affirmative [Ayes — 6; noes — 4.][1]

It was moved and seconded to add the following clause to the last amendment

"except where by Law the appointment shall be vested in "the[2] Executives of the several States"

[1] Vote 363, Detail of Ayes and Noes, which notes that it was "Mr. Dickinson's amendment".

[2] Crossed out "legislatures or", this striking out was an amendment. See Madison's record below.

which passed in the negative [3]

It was moved and seconded to agree to the following order

"That the order respecting the adjournment at four be repealed, and that in future the House assemble at ten and adjourn at three

which passed in the affirmative [Ayes — 10; noes — 0.]

The House adjourned

Detail of Ayes and Noes

	New Hampshire	Massachusetts	Rhode Island	Connecticut	New York	New Jersey	Pennsylvania	Delaware	Maryland	Virginia	No Carolina	So Carolina	Georgia	Questions	ayes	noes	divided
[352]	no	aye		aye		aye		aye	no	aye		aye	aye	To reconsider the 1st sec. 7 article to-morrow	7	2	
[353]	aye	no		no		no		no	no	no	aye	no	aye	To postpone ye 2 sect. 9 article	3	7	
[354]	aye	aye		aye		aye		aye	aye	aye	no	aye	no	To strike out the 2 & 3 sections 9th article	8	2	
[355]	no	no		no		no	aye	aye	no	no	no	no	no	To strike out the word Legislature, and insert the word "People" 1st sect. 10 article	2	9	
[356]	aye	aye		no		no	aye	aye	no	aye	aye	aye	no	To insert the word joint before the word ballot.	7	4	
[357]	no	no		aye		aye	no	aye	aye	no	no	no	aye	"each State having One vote"	5	6	
[358]	aye	aye		aye		no	aye	aye	aye	aye	aye	aye	aye	a majority of the votes of Members present required	10	1	
[359]	no	no		aye		aye	aye	aye	no	aye	no	no	no	To be elected by the Electors.	5	6	
[360]	no	no		dd		aye	aye	aye	aye	aye	no	no	no	To commit ye 2 last clauses 1 sect. 10 art.	5	5	1
[361]	no			dd		aye	aye	aye	dd	aye	no	no	no	To be elected by Electors.	4	4	2
[362]	no	no		aye		no	no	no	no	no		no	no	To add the words "or by law" 2 sect. 10 art.	1	9	
[363]	no	no		aye		aye	aye	no	aye	aye		no	aye	To agree to Mr. Dickinson's amendment	6	4	
[364]	aye	aye		aye		aye	aye	aye	aye	aye		aye	aye	To adjourn at 3 o'Clock			

[3] See below note 12.

MADISON

Friday August 24. 1787. In Convention

Governour Livingston, from the Committee of Eleven, to whom were referred the two remaining clauses of the 4th. Sect & the 5 & 6 Sect: of the 7th. art: delivered in the following Report:

"Strike out so much of the 4th. sect: as was referred to the Committee and insert — "The migration or importation of "such persons as the several States now existing shall think "proper to admit, shall not be prohibited by the Legislature "prior to the year 1800, but a tax or duty may be imposed on "such migration or importation at a rate not exceeding the "average of the duties laid on imports."

"The 5 Sect: to remain as in the Report" [4]

"The 6 Sect. to be stricken out" [4]

Mr. Butler, according to notice, moved that clause 1st. sect. 1. of art VII, as to the discharge of debts, be reconsidered tomorrow— He dwelt on the division of opinion concerning the domestic debts, and the different pretensions of the different classes of holders. Genl. Pinkney 2ded. him.

Mr. Randolph wished for a reconsideration in order to better the expression, and to provide for the case of the State debts as is done by Congress.

On the question for reconsidering

N— H. no. Mas: ay. Cont. ay N. J. ⟨ay.⟩[5] Pena. absent. Del. ay— Md. no. Va. ay— N. C. absent, S. C. ay. Geo. ay. [Ayes — 7; noes — 2; absent — 2.] — and tomorrow assigned for the reconsideration.

Sect: 2 & 3 of art: IX being taken up,[6]

Mr Rutlidge said this provision ⟨for deciding controversies

[4] Article VII, Sect. 5. "No capitation tax shall be laid, unless in proportion to the Census hereinbefore directed to be taken."

Sect. 6. "No navigation act shall be passed without the assent of two thirds of the members present in each House."

[5] New Jersey's vote changed from "no" to "ay" to conform to *Journal.*

[6] Relating to disputes between states and over land questions — modeled on procedure in Articles of Confederation.

between the States⟩ was necessary under the Confederation, but will be rendered unnecessary by the National Judiciary now to be established, and moved to strike it out.

Docr. Johnson 2ded. the Motion

Mr. Sherman concurred: so did Mr Dayton.

Mr. Williamson was for postponing instead of striking out, in order to consider whether this might not be a good provision, in cases where the Judiciary were interested or too closely connected with the parties—

Mr. Ghorum had doubts as to striking out, The Judges might be connected with the States being parties — He was inclined to think the mode proposed in the clause would be more satisfactory than to refer such cases to the Judiciary —

On the Question for postponing ⟨the 2d and 3d Section, it passed in the negative⟩

N. H. ay. Masts. no. ⟨Cont. no⟩ N. J. no. Pena abst. Del. no. Md. no. Va no. N. C. ⟨ay⟩ S— C no. Geo. ay. [Ayes — 3; noes — 7; absent — 1.][7]

Mr. Wilson urged the striking out, the Judiciary being a better provision.

On Question for striking out 2 & 3 Sections Art: IX

N. H. ay. Mas: ay. Ct. ay. N. J— ay. Pa. abst. Del— ay. Md. ay. Va ay. N. C. no. S. C. ay— Geo. no. [Ayes — 8; noes — 2; absent — 1.]

Art X. sect. 1. "The executive power of the U— S— shall be vested in a single person. His stile shall be "The President of the U— S. of America" and his title shall be "His Excellency". He shall be elected by ballot by the Legislature. He shall hold his office during the term of seven years; but shall not be elected a second time.

On the question for vesting the power in a *single person* — It was agreed to nem: con: So also on the *Stile* and *title* —

Mr. Rutlidge moved to insert "joint" before the word "ballot", as the most convenient mode of electing.

Mr. Sherman objected to it as depriving the *States* represented in the *Senate* of the negative intended them in that house,

[7] Vote of Connecticut inserted, and that of North Carolina changed to conform to *Journal*.

Mr. Ghorum said it was wrong to be considering, at every turn whom the Senate would represent. The public good was the true object to be kept in view— Great delay and confusion would ensue if the two Houses shd vote separately, each having a negative on the choice of the other.

Mr. Dayton. It might be well for those not to consider how the Senate was constituted, whose interest it Was to keep it out of sight. — If the amendment should be agreed to, a *joint* ballot would in fact give the appointment to one House. He could never agree to the clause with such an amendment. There could be no ⟨doubt⟩[8] of the two Houses separately concurring in the same person for President. The importance & necessity of the case would ensure ⟨a concurrence⟩.

Mr. Carrol moved to strike out, "by the Legislature" and insert "by the people" — Mr Wilson 2ded. him & on the question

N. H. no. Massts. no. Cont. no. N. J. no. Pa. ay. Del. ay. Md no. Va. no N. C. no. S. C. no. Geo. no. [Ayes — 2; noes — 9.]

Mr Brearly was opposed to the motion for inserting the word "joint". The argument that the small States should not put their hands into the pockets of the large ones did not apply in this case.

Mr. Wilson urged the reasonableness of giving the larger States a larger share of the appointment, and the danger of delay from a disagreement of the two Houses. He remarked also that the Senate had peculiar powers balancing the advantage given by a joint balot in this case to the other branch of the Legislature.

Mr. Langdon. This general officer ought to be elected by the joint & general voice. In N. Hampshire the mode of separate votes by the two Houses was productive of great difficulties. The Negative of the Senate would hurt the feelings of the man elected by the votes of the other branch. He was for inserting "joint" tho' unfavorable to N. Hampshire as a small State.

Mr. Wilson remarked that as the President of the Senate

[8] Crossed out "danger".

was to be the President of the U— S. that Body in cases of vacancy might have an interest in throwing dilatory obstacles in the way, if its separate concurrence should be required.

Mr. Madison. If the amendment be agreed to the rule of voting will give to the largest State, compared with the smallest, an influence as 4 to 1 only, altho the population is as 10 to 1. This surely cannot be unreasonable as the President is to act for the *people* not for the *States*. The President of the *Senate* also is to be occasionally President of the U. S. and by his negative alone can make $\frac{3}{4}$ of the other branch necessary to the passage of a law — This is another advantage enjoyed by the Senate.

On the question for inserting "joint", ⟨it passed in the affirmative⟩

N. H. ay. Masts ay— Ct. no. N. J. no. Pa. ay— Del. ay. Md. no. Va. ay. N. C. ay. S. C. ay. Geo. no. [Ayes — 7; noes — 4.]

Mr. Dayton then moved to insert, after the word "Legislatures" the words "each State having one vote" Mr Brearly 2ded. him, and on the question ⟨it passed in the negative⟩

N. H. no. Mas. no. Ct. ay. N. J. ay. Pa. no. Del. ay. Md ay. Va. no. N. C. no. S. C. no. Geo. ay [Ayes — 5; noes — 6.]

Mr. Pinkney moved to insert after the word "Legislature" the words "to which election a majority of the votes of the members present shall be required" &

On this question, ⟨it passed in the affirmative⟩

N. H. ay. Mas. ay. Ct. ay. N. J. no. Pa. ay. Del. ay— Md. ay— Va. ay— N. C. ay— S. C. ay— Geo. ay. [Ayes — 10; noes — 1.]

Mr Read moved "that in case the numbers for the two highest in votes should be equal, then the President of the Senate shall have an additional casting vote", which was disagreed to by a general negative.

Mr. Govr Morris opposed the election of the President by the Legislature. He dwelt on the danger of rendering the Executive uninterested in maintaining the rights of his Station, as leading to Legislative tyranny. If the Legislature have the Executive dependent on them, they can perpetuate

& support their usurpations by the influence of tax-gatherers & other officers, by fleets armies &c. Cabal & corruption are attached to that mode of election: so also is ineligibility a second time. Hence the Executive is interested in Courting popularity in the Legislature by sacrificing his Executive rights; & then he can go into that Body, after the expiration of his Executive Office, and enjoy there the fruits of his policy. To these considerations he added that rivals would be continually intriguing to oust the President from his place. To guard against all these evils he moved that the President "shall be chosen by Electors to be chosen by the people of the several States" Mr Carrol 2ded. him & on the question ⟨it passed in the negative⟩

N. H. no. Mas. no. Ct. ay. N— J— ay. Pa. ay. Del. ay. Md. no— Va. ay. N— C— no— S— C— no— Geo— no. [Ayes — 5; noes — 6.]

Mr. Dayton moved to postpone the consideration of the two last clauses of sect. 1. art. X. which was disagreed to without a count of the States.

Mr Broome moved to refer the two clauses to a Committee of a Member from each State. & on the question, ⟨it failed the States being equally divided.⟩

N— H— no— Mas— no. Ct. divd. N— J— ay. Pa. ay. Del. ay. Md. ay— Va. ay. N— C— no. S. C. no— Geo. no. [Ayes — 5; noes — 5; divided — 1.]

On the question taken on the first part of Mr. Govr Morris's Motion to wit "shall be chosen by electors" as an abstract question, ⟨it failed the States being equally divided —⟩

N—H— no. Mas. abst. Ct. divd. ⟨N. Jersey ay⟩[9] Pa ay. Del. ay. Md. divd. Va ay— N— C— no. S. C. no. Geo. no. [Ayes — 4; noes — 4; divided — 2; absent — 1.]

The consideration of the remaining clauses of sect 1. art X. was then posponed till tomorrow at the instance of the Deputies of New Jersey —

Sect. 2. Art: X[10] being taken up. the word information was transposed & inserted after "Legislature"

[9] Taken from *Journal*.

[10] Relating to the powers and duties of the President.

On motion of Mr Govr Morris, "he may" was struck out, & "and" inserted before "recommend" in the clause 2d. sect— 2d art: X. in order to make it the *duty* of the President to recommend, & thence prevent umbrage or cavil at his doing it —

Mr. Sherman objected to the sentence "and shall appoint officers in all cases not otherwise provided for by this Constitution". He admitted it to be proper that many officers in the Executive Department should be so appointed — but contended that many ought not, as general officers in the Army in time of peace &c. Herein lay the corruption in G. Britain. If the Executive can model the army, he may set up an absolute Government; taking advantage of the close of a war and an army commanded by his creatures. James 2d. was not obeyed by his officers because they had been appointed by his predecessors not by himself. He moved to insert "or by law" after the word "Constitution".

On Motion of Mr Madison "officers" was struck out and "to offices" inserted, in order to obviate doubts that he might appoint officers without a previous creation of the offices by the Legislature.

On the question for inserting "or by law as moved by Mr. Sherman

N. H. no. Mas. no. Ct. ay. N. J. no. Pena. no. Del. no. Md. no. Va. no. N. C. absent. S. C. no. Geo. no. [Ayes — 1; noes — 9; absent — 1.]

Mr. Dickinson moved to strike out the words "and shall appoint to offices in all cases not otherwise provided for by this Constitution" and insert — "and shall appoint to all offices established by this Constitution, except in cases herein otherwise provided for, and to all offices which may hereafter be created by law."

Mr Randolph observed that the power of appointments was a formidable one both in the Executive & Legislative hands — and suggested whether the Legislature should not be left at liberty to refer appointments in some cases, to some State Authority.

Mr. Dickenson's motion, ⟨it passed in the affirmative⟩

N. H. no. Mas— no— Ct ay— N— J— ay. Pa. ay— Del. no. Md ay. Va. ay— N— C. abst. S. C no. Geo— ⟨ay⟩ [Ayes — 6; noes — 4; absent — 1.] [11]

Mr. Dickinson then moved to annex to his last amendment "except where by law the appointment shall be vested in the Legislatures or Executives of the several States". Mr. Randolph 2ded. the motion

Mr. Wilson— If this be agreed to it will soon be a standing instruction from the State Legislatures to pass no law creating offices, unless the appts be referred to them.

Mr. Sherman objected to "Legislatures" in the motion, which was struck out by consent of the movers.

Mr. Govr. Morris — This would be putting it in the power of the States to say, "You shall be viceroys but we will be viceroys over you" —

The motion was negatived without a Count of the States —[12]

Ordered ⟨unaminously⟩[13] that the order respecting the adjournment at 4 oClock be repealed, & that in future the House assemble at 10 OC. & adjourn at 3 oC.[14]

Adjourned

McHENRY

Augt. 24.

2 and 3 sect. struck out. The 10 article give rise to various debate. Amended to read that the election of the president of the U. S. be by *joint ballot.* It was moved to add each State having one vote — Conn: Jer. Mar. Georg.[15] ay. N. H. Mass. Penns. Vir. N. C. and S. C. no. It was moved

[11] Madison originally had Georgia recorded as voting "no", which made the total vote a tie, and the determination of the question in the negative. This was changed to conform to *Journal* and the subsequent proceedings.

[12] McHenry is probably correct in stating that the house adjourned when the question was going to be put", see August 25, note 15.

[13] Taken from *Journal.*

[14] See May 25, note 1.

[15] Detail of Ayes and Noes (Vote 357) and Madison both include Delaware in the affirmative.

that the president be elected by the people[16] 3 states affirm — 7 neg.

On what respects his ineligibility Gov. Morris observed.

That in the strength of the Executive would be found the strength of America. Ineligibility operates to weaken or destroy the constitution.

The president will have no interest beyond his period of service.

He will for peace and emolument to himself and friends agree to acts that will encrease the power and agrandize the bodies which elect him.

The legislature will swallow up the whole powers of the constitution; but to do this effectually they must possess the Executive. This will lead them to tempt him, and the shortness of his reign will subject him to be tempted and overcome.

The legislature has great and various appointments in their power. This will create them an extensive influence which may be so used as to put it out of the power of the Executive to prevent them from arriving at supremacy.

On the other hand give the Executive a chance of being re-chosen and he will hold his prerogatives with all possible tenaciousness.

postponed the question.

Proceeded, and made some amendments to the 2 sect. Adjourned when the question was going to be put whether the legislature might enable the State Executives or legislatures to appoint officers to certain offices.[17]

---

[16] According to the Journal, Detail of Ayes and Noes and Madison, this question was the first one upon Article X for which a vote was taken, and the vote is given as Ayes, 2; noes, 9.

[17] Both the Journal and Madison report this motion as negatived, but McHenry is probably correct. See August 25, note 15.

SATURDAY, AUGUST 25, 1787.

JOURNAL

Saturday August 25. 1787.

It was moved and seconded to postpone the first clause of the first section 7 article, in order to take up the following amendment

"all debts contracted and engagements entered into, by or "under the authority of Congress shall be as valid against the "United States under this constitution as under the confed- "eration."

which passed in the affirmative

On the question to agree to the amendment

it passed in the affirmative [Ayes — 10; noes — 1.] [1]

It was moved and seconded to add the following clause to the first clause of the 1st sect. 7 article

"for the payment of said debts and for the defraying the "expences that shall be incurred for the common defence and "general welfare"

which passed in the negative. [Ayes — 1; noes — 10.]

It was moved and seconded to amend the report of the Committee of eleven, entered on the Journal of the 24th instant as follows

to strike out the words "the year eighteen hundred" and to insert the words "the year eighteen hundred and eight"

which passed in the affirmative [Ayes — 7; noes — 4.]

It was moved and seconded to amend the first clause of the report to read

The importation of Slaves into such of the States as shall

---

[1] Vote 365, Detail of Ayes and Noes, which notes that it was "Mr. Randolph's amendment".

permit the same shall not be prohibited by the Legislature of the U. S. until the year 1808.

which passed in the negative [2]

On the question to agree to the first part of the report as amended, namely.

"The migration or importation of such persons as the "several States now existing shall think proper to admit "shall not be prohibited by the Legislature prior to the year "1808."

it passed in the affirmative. [Ayes — 7; noes — 4.]

It was moved and seconded to strike out the words "average of the duties laid on Imports" and to insert the words

"common impost on articles not enumerated"

which passed in the affirmative

It was moved and seconded to amend the second clause of the report to read

"but a tax or duty may be imposed on such importation "not exceeding ten dollars for each person"

which passed in the affirmative.

On the question to agree to the second clause of the report as amended

it passed in the affirmative

On the question to postpone the farther consideration of the report

it passed in the affirmative

It was moved and seconded to amend the 8th article to read

"This Constitution and the Laws of the United States, "which shall be made in pursuance thereof and all treaties "made or which shall be made under the authority of the "United-States shall be the supreme law of the several States, "and of their citizens and inhabitants; and the Judges in the "several States shall be bound thereby in their decisions; "any thing in the constitutions or laws of the several States "to the contrary notwithstanding"

which passed in the affirmative

[2] *Journal* (p. 292) ascribes Vote 369, Detail of Ayes and Noes, to this question, but there is no apparent reason for this, and probably it is the same as reported by Madison (see below note 15) and McHenry.

It was moved and seconded to agree to the following propositions

"The Legislature of the United States shall not oblige "Vessels belonging to Citizens thereof, or to foreigners, to "enter or pay duties, or imposts in any other State than in "that to which they may be bound, or to clear out in any "other than the State in which their cargoes may be laden "on board — Nor shall any privilege, or immunity, be granted "to any vessels on entering, clearing out, or paying duties "or imposts in one State in preference to another"

"Should it be judged expedient by the Legislature of the "United States that one or more ports for collecting duties "or imposts other than those ports of entrance and clearance "already established by the respective States should be established, the Legislature of the U. S. shall signify the same "to the Executive of the respective States ascertaining the "number of such ports judged necessary; to be laid by the "said Executives before the Legislatures of the States at their "next session; and the legislature of the U. S. shall not have "the power of fixing or establishing the particular ports for "collecting duties or imposts in any State except the Legislature of such State shall neglect to fix and establish the same "during their first session to be held after such notification "by the legislature of the U. S. to the executive of such State.

"all duties, imposts, and excises, prohibitions or restraints "laid or made by the Legislature of the U. S. shall be uniform "and equal throughout the United States"

It was moved and seconded to refer the above propositions to a Committee of a Member from each State

which passed in the affirmative

and a Committee was appointed by ballot of the honorable Mr Langdon, Mr Gorham, Mr Sherman, Mr Dayton, Mr Fitz Simmons, Mr Read, Mr Carrol Mr Mason, Mr Williamson, Mr Butler and Mr Few.

[To agree to Mr Sherman's amendment Ayes — 3; noes — 6; divided — 1.] [3]

[3] Vote 369, Detail of Ayes and Noes.

It was moved and seconded to add the words
"and other public Ministers" after the word "Ambassadors" 2 sect. 10 article
which passed in the affirmative. [Ayes — 10; noes — 0.]
It was moved and seconded to strike the words "and may correspond with the supreme executives of the several States" out of ye 2 sect. 10 article
which passed in the affirmative [Ayes — 9; noes — 1.]
[————Ayes — 1; noes — 9.][4]
It was moved and seconded to insert the words "except in cases of impeachment" after the word "pardons" 2 sect. 10 article
which passed in the affirmative
On the question to agree to the following clause
"but his pardon shall not be pleadable in bar"
it passed in the negative [Ayes — 4; noes — 6.]
The House adjourned.

[4] Vote 372, Detail of Ayes and Noes. See below, note 18.

DETAIL OF AYES AND NOES

	New Hampshire	Massachusetts	Rhode Island	Connecticut	New York	New Jersey	Pennsylvania	Delaware	Maryland	Virginia	No. Carolina	So. Carolina	Georgia	Questions	ayes	noes	divided
[365]	aye	aye		aye		aye	no	aye	aye	aye	aye	aye	aye	To agree to Mr Randolph's amendment to the 1st clause, 1st section, 7 article.			
[366]	no	no		aye		no	no	no	no	no	no	no	no	To agree to the amendmt of ye 1st clause 1 sect. 7 article	1	10	
[367]	aye	aye		aye		no	no	no	aye	no	aye	aye	aye	To agree to the amendment of 20 years.	7	4	
[368]	aye	aye		aye		no	no	no	aye	no	aye	aye	aye	To agree to the first clause of ye report of eleven entd on the journal 24 instt	7	4	
[369]	no	no		aye			no	no	dd	aye	no	no	aye	to agree to Mr Sherman's amendment			
[370]	aye	aye		aye			aye	aye	aye	aye	aye	aye	aye	To add the words & other pub: Ministers			
[371]	aye	aye		aye			aye	aye	no	aye	aye	aye	aye	To strike out the words "correspond with the Executives"	9	1	
[372]	no	no		aye			no	no	no	no	no	no	no		1	9	
[373]	aye	no		no			no	no	aye	no	aye	aye	no	but his pardon shall not be pleadable in bar	4	6	

MADISON

Saturday August. 25. 1787— In Convention

The 1st. clause of 1 sect. of art: VII being reconsidered[5]

Col. Mason objected to the term, "*shall*" — fullfil the engagements & discharge the debts &c as too strong. It may be impossible to comply with it. The Creditors should be kept in the same plight. They will in one respect be necessarily and properly in a better. The Government will be more able

[5] Upon this subject, see above August 18 (with references under note 6), August 21–24, and Appendix A, CCV, CCXII, CCLII, CCLIV, CCLVI, CCLXVIII, CCCLXXII.

to pay them. The use of the term *shall* will beget speculations and increase the pestilent practice of stock-jobbing. There was a great distinction between original creditors & those who purchased fraudulently of the ignorant and distressed. He did not mean to include those who have bought Stock in open market. He was sensible of the difficulty of drawing the line in this case, but He did not wish to preclude the attempt. Even fair purchasers, at 4, 5, 6, 8 for 1 did not stand on the same footing with the first Holders, supposing them not to be blameable. The interest they receive even in paper is equal to their purchase money. What he particularly wished was to leave the door open for buying up the securities, which he thought would be precluded by the term "shall" as requiring *nominal payment*, & which was not inconsistent with his ideas of public faith. He was afraid also the word "*shall*," might extend to all the old continental paper.

Mr Langdon wished to do no more than leave the Creditors in statu quo.

Mr. Gerry said that for himself he had no interest in the question being not possessed of more of the securities than would, by the interest, pay his taxes. He would observe however that as the public had received the value of the literal amount, they ought to pay that value to some body. The frauds on *the soldiers* ought to have been foreseen. These poor & ignorant people could not but part with their securities. There are other creditors who will part with any thing rather than be cheated of the capital of their advances. The interest of the States he observed was different on this point, some having more, others less than their proportion of the paper. Hence the idea of a scale for reducing its value had arisen. If the public faith would admit, of which he was not clear, he would not object to a revision of the debt so far as to compel restitution to the ignorant & distressed, who have been defrauded. As to Stock-jobbers he saw no reason for the censures thrown on them — They keep up the value of the paper. Without them there would be no market.

Mr. Butler said he meant neither to increase nor diminish the security of the Creditors.

Mr. Randolph moved to postpone the clause in favor of the following "All debts contracted & engagements entered "into, by or under the authority of Congs. shall be as valid "agst the U. States under this constitution as under the Con-"federation"

Docr Johnson. The debts are debts of the U— S— of the great Body of America. Changing the Government cannot change the obligation of the U— S— which devolves of course on the New Government. Nothing was in his opinion necessary to be said. If any thing, it should be a mere declaration as moved by Mr. Randolph.

Mr. Govr. Morris, said he never had become a public Creditor that he might urge with more propriety the compliance with public faith. He had always done so and always would, and preferr'd the term "*shall*" as the most explicit. As to *buying up* the debt, the term "*shall*" was not inconsistent with it, if provision be first made for paying the interest: if not, such an expedient was a mere evasion. He was content to say nothing as the New Government would be bound of course — but would prefer the clause with the term "*shall*", because it would create many friends to the plan.

On Mr. Randolph's Motion

N— H— ay— Mas. ay. Ct ay— N. J. ay— Pa. no Del. ay— ⟨Maryd. ay⟩[6] Va. ay— N. C— ay— S. C. ay Geo. ay— [Ayes — 10; noes — 1.]

Mr. Sherman thought it necessary to connect with the clause for laying taxes duties &c an express provision for the object of the old debts &c — and moved to add to the 1st. clause of 1st. sect— of art VII "for the payment of said debts and for the defraying the expences that shall be incurred for the common defence and general welfare".

The proposition, as being unnecessary was disagreed to, Connecticut alone, being in the affirmative.

The Report of the Committee of eleven (see friday the 24th. instant) being taken up,[7]

[6] Taken from *Journal*.

[7] Compromise upon importation of slaves and navigation acts. Upon this subject and upon the compromise in general see above July 23, August 8, August 21,

Genl Pinkney moved to strike out the words "the year eighteen hundred" ⟨as the year limiting the importation of slaves,⟩ and to insert the words "the year eighteen hundred and eight"

Mr. Ghorum 2ded. the motion

Mr. Madison. Twenty years will produce all the mischief that can be apprehended from the liberty to import slaves. So long a term will be more dishonorable to the National character than to say nothing about it in the Constitution.

On the motion; ⟨which passed in the affirmative.⟩

N— H— ay. Mas. ay— Ct. ay. N. J. no. Pa. no. Del— no. Md. ay. Va. no. N— C. ay. S— C. ay. Geo. ay. [Ayes — 7; noes — 4.]

Mr. Govr. Morris was for making the clause read at once, "importation of slaves into N. Carolina, S— Carolina & Georgia". ⟨shall not be prohibited &c.⟩ This he said would be most fair and would avoid the ambiguity by which, under the power with regard to naturalization, the liberty reserved to the States might be defeated. He wished it to be known also that this part of the Constitution was a compliance with those States. If the change of language however should be objected to by the members from those States, he should not urge it.[8]

Col: Mason was not against using the term "slaves" but agst naming N— C— S— C. & Georgia, lest it should give offence to the people of those States.

Mr Sherman liked a description better than the terms proposed, which had been declined by the old Congs & were not pleasing to some people. Mr. Clymer concurred with Mr. Sherman

Mr. Williamson said that both in opinion & practice he was, against slavery; but thought it more in favor of

August 22 (with references under note 2), August 24, and below August 28 and 29; also Appendix A, CXXXIV, CXXXVII, CLVIII (60–64), CLXXI, CC*a*, CCII, CCXII, CCXVII, CCXXVII, CCXXXIX, CCLXIX, CCLXXX, CCCXXXII, CCCXXXIII, CCCXXXVI.

[8] On the avoidance of the term "slaves", see Appendix A, CXLVIII, CLVIII (57), CCLXXX, CCCXXXII.

humanity, from a view of all circumstances, to let in S— C & Georgia on those terms, than to exclude them from the Union —

Mr. Govr. Morris withdrew his motion.

Mr. Dickenson wished the clause to be confined to the States which had not themselves prohibited the importation of slaves, and for that purpose moved to amend the clause so as to read "The importation of slaves into such of the States as shall permit the same shall not be prohibited by the Legislature of the U— S— until the year 1808". — which was disagreed to nem: cont:*

The first part of the report was then agreed to, amended as follows. "The migration or importation of such persons as the several States now existing shall think proper to admit, shall not be prohibited by the Legislature prior to the year 1808." ⟨N. H. Mas. Con. Md. N. C. S. C: Geo: . . . . . ay
N. J. Pa. Del. Virga . . . . no⟩
[Ayes — 7; noes — 4.] [10]

Mr. Baldwin in order to restrain & more explicitly define "the average duty" moved to strike out of the 2d. part the words "average of the duties laid on imports" and insert "common impost on articles not enumerated" which was agreed to nem: cont:

Mr. Sherman was agst. this 2d part, as acknowledging men to be property, by taxing them as such under the character of slaves,

Mr. King & Mr. Langdon considered this as the price of the 1st part.

Genl. Pinkney admitted that it was so.

Col: Mason. Not to tax, will be equivalent to a bounty on the importation of slaves.

Mr. Ghorum thought that Mr Sherman should consider the duty, not as implying that slaves are property, but as a discouragement to the importation of them.

*⟨ In the printed Journal. Cont. Virga. & Georgia voted in the affirmative.⟩[9]

[9] An error of *Journal*, see above note 2.

[10] Taken from *Journal*.

Mr Govr, Morris remarked that as the clause now stands it implies that the Legislature may tax freemen imported.[11]

Mr. Sherman in answer to Mr. Ghorum observed that the smallness of the duty shewed revenue to be the object, not the discouragement of the importation.

Mr. Madison thought it wrong to admit in the Constitution the idea that there could be property in men. The reason of duties did not hold, as slaves are not like merchandise, consumed. &c

Col. Mason (in answr. to Govr. Morris) the provision as it stands was necessary for the case of Convicts in order to prevent the introduction of them.

It was finally agreed nem: contrad: to make the clause read "but a tax or duty may be imposed on such importation not exceeding ten dollars for each person", and then the 2d. part as amended was agreed to.

Sect 5— art— VII was agreed to nem: con: as reported.[12]

Sect. 6. art. VII. in the Report was, postponed.

On motion of Mr. Madison 2ded. by Mr Govr Morris art VIII was reconsidered and after the words "all treaties made," were inserted nem: con: the words "or which shall be made" This insertion was meant to obviate all doubt concerning the force of treaties prëexisting, by making the words "all treaties made" to refer to them, as the words inserted would refer to future treaties.

Mr. Carrol & Mr. L. Martin expressed their apprehensions, and the probable apprehensions of their constituents, that under the power of regulating trade the General Legislature, might favor the ports of particular States, by requiring vessels destined to or from other States to enter & clear thereat, as vessels belonging or bound to Baltimore, to enter & clear at Norfolk &c They moved the following proposition

"The Legislature of the U— S. shall not oblige vessels belonging to citizens thereof, or to foreigners, to enter or pay duties or imposts in any other State than in that to which they may be bound, or to clear out in any other than the

[11] See Appendix A, CXLVIII, CLVIII(57), CCLXXX, CCCXXXII CCCXXXIV.

[12] "No capitation tax" etc.

State in which their cargoes may be laden on board; nor shall any privilege or immunity be granted to any vessels on entering or clearing out or paying duties or imposts in one state in preference to another" [13]

Mr Ghorum thought such a precaution unnecessary; & that the revenue might be defeated, if vessels could run up long rivers, through the jurisdiction of different States without being required to enter, with the opportunity of landing & selling their cargoes by the way.

Mr McHenry & Genl Pinkney made the following propositions

"Should it be judged expedient by the Legislature of the U— S— that one or more ports for collecting duties or imposts other than those ports of entrance & clearance already established by the respective States, should be established, the Legislature of the U— S— shall signify the same to the Executives of the respective States, ascertaining the number of such ports judged necessary; to be laid by the said Executives before the Legislatures of the States at their next Session; and the Legislature of the U— S— shall not have the power of fixing or establishing the particular ports for collecting duties or imposts in any State, except the Legislature of such State shall neglect to fix and establish the same during their first Session to be held after such notification by the Legislature of the U— S— to the Executive of such State"

"All duties imposts & excises, prohibitions or restraints laid or made by the Legislature of the U— S— shall be uniform and equal throughout the U— S—" [14]

These several propositions were referred, nem: con: to a committee composed of a member from each State, The committee appointed by ballot were Mr. Langdon, Mr. Ghorum, Mr. Sherman, Mr Dayton, Mr. Fitzimmons, Mr. Read, Mr. Carrol, Mr. Mason, Mr. Williamson, Mr. Butler, Mr. Few.

On The question now taken on Mr. Dickinson motion of yesterday, allowing appointments to offices, to be referred by

[13] Upon this subject see McHenry, below, and Appendix A, CXXXVIII, CLVIII (67–68), CCLXV, also below August 31 and September 12–15.

[14] See Appendix A, CLVIII (67–68.)

the Genl. Legislature to the Executives of the several States" as a farther amendment to sect. 2. art. X.,[15] the votes were

N. H. no Mas. no. Ct ay. Pa. no— Del. no. Md divided[16]— Va. ay— N— C— no— S. C. no. Geo. ay— [Ayes— 3; noes — 6; divided — 1.]

In amendment of the same section, "other public Ministers" were inserted after "ambassadors".[17]

Mr. Govr Morris moved to strike out of the section — "and may correspond with the supreme Executives of the several States" as unnecessary and implying that he could not correspond with others. Mr. Broome 2ded. him.

On the question

N. H. ay. Mas. ay. Ct. ay. Pa. ay. Del. ay. Md. no. Va. ay. N. C. ay— S. C. ay. Geo— ay. [Ayes — 9; noes — 1.]

"Shall receive ambassadors & other public Ministers". agreed, to nem. con.

Mr. Sherman moved to amend the "power to grant reprieves & pardon" so as to read "to grant reprieves until the ensuing session of the Senate, and pardons with consent of the Senate."

On the question

N— H— no. Mas. no. Ct. ay— Pa no Md. no. Va. no. N. C. no. S. C. no. Geo. no. [Ayes — 1; noes — 8.][18]

"except in cases of impeachment" inserted nem: con: after "pardon"

On the question to agree to — "but his pardon shall not be pleadable in bar"

---

[15] On August 24 Sherman had objected to the clause in Article X, Section 2 which empowered the President to "appoint officers in all cases not otherwise provided for by this Constitution." Sherman's proposed modification was defeated, one amendment by Dickinson was adopted and a second one offered by Dickinson. According to both the Journal and Madison Dickinson's second motion was negatived, but McHenry states that the House adjourned "when the question was going to be put." McHenry was probably correct as this question is now brought up without any recorded motion to reconsider. This is doubtless the amendment attributed to Sherman in Vote 369, Detail of Ayes and Noes (see above, notes 2 and 3).

[16] See McHenry's statement below.

[17] Vote 370, Detail of Ayes and Noes, records the vote as Ayes, 10; noes, 0.

[18] Probably the same as Vote 372, Detail of Ayes and Noes, which includes Delaware in the negative.

N. H. ay— Mas— no. Ct. no— Pa. no— Del. no. Md. ay. Va. no. N— C— ay— S. C. ay— Geo. no. [Ayes — 4; noes — 6.]

Adjourned

McHENRY

Augt. 25.

The clause in the 2 sect. X article, "he shall commission all the officers of the U. S. and shall appoint officers in all cases not otherwise provided for by this constitution, was moved to be amended by adding, except where by law the Executive of the several States shall have the power — Amendment negatives. Maryland divided — D. C. and J. against Martin and myself affirm.[19]

Moved several propositions to restrict the legislature from giving any preference in duties, or from obliging duties to be collected in a manner injurious to any State, and from establishing new ports of entrance and clerance, unless neglected to be established by the States after application — Opposed by Massachusetts — Mr. Gorahm said it might be very proper to oblige vessels, for example, to stop at Norfolk on account of the better collection of the revenue.

Mr. King thought it improper to deliberate long on such propositions but to take the sense of the house immediately upon them.

I moved to have them committed to a committee consisting of a member from each State. Committed.

Proceeded a little further in the 2 sect.

Mr. C. Pinkney gave notice that he would move that the consent of $\frac{3}{4}$ of the whole legislature be necessary to the enacting a law respecting the regulation of trade or the formation of a navigation act.

Adjourned to monday.

[19] See above note 15.

The Legislature [20] of the United States shall not oblige Vessels belonging to Citizens thereof, or to foreigners to enter or pay duties or imposts in any other State than in that to which they may be bound, or to clear out in any other than the State in which their Cargoes may be laden on board; Nor shall any priviledge, or immunity be granted to any Vessels on entering clearing out or paying duties or imposts in one State in preference to another — Nor shall vessels owned by Citizens of one State have any preference of vessels owned by Citizens of another State.

[20] Found among the McHenry MSS., but not in his handwriting.

MONDAY, AUGUST 27, 1787.

JOURNAL

Monday August 27. 1787.

It was moved and seconded to insert the words "after conviction" after the words "reprieves and pardons" 2 sect. 10 article. — (Motion withdrawn).

It was moved and seconded to amend the clause giving the command of the militia to the executive to read

"and of the militia of the several States when called into the actual service of the United States"

which passed in the affirmative. [Ayes — 6; noes — 2.]

It was moved and seconded to postpone the consideration of the following clause. 2 section. 10 article

"He shall be removed from his office on impeachment by "the House of representatives, and conviction in the supreme "Court, of treason, bribery, or corruption"

which passed in the affirmative

It was moved and seconded to postpone the last clause of the 2 section, 10 article.

which passed in the affirmative

It was moved and seconded to add the following clause to the oath of office to be taken by the supreme Executive

"and will to the best of my judgment and power, pre-"serve, protect and defend the Constitution of the United "States"

which passed in the affirmative [Ayes — 7; noes — 1.]

It was moved and seconded to insert the words

"both in Law and Equity" after the words "United States" 1 line, 1 sect, 11th article

which passed in the affirmative [Ayes — 6; noes — 2.][1]

[1] Detail of Ayes and Noes ascribes the same question to Votes 376 and 377, and

On the question to agree to the 1st sect. 11 article as amended.
it passed in the affirmative. [Ayes — 6; noes — 2.][1]

It was moved and seconded to add the following clause after the word "behaviour" 2 section. 11 article

"Provided that they may be removed by the Executive on "the application by the Senate and House of representatives"

which passed in the negative [Ayes — 1; noes — 7.]

On the question to agree to the 2nd section of the 11 article as reported

it passed in the affirmative[2]

It was moved and seconded to insert the words

"encreased or" before the word "diminished" in the 2nd section 11th article.

which passed in the negative. [Ayes — 1; noes — 5; divided — 1.]

It was moved and seconded to add the following words to the 2nd section 11 article

"nor encreased by any act of the Legislature, which shall "operate before the expiration of three years after the pass-"ing thereof."

which passed in the negative [Ayes — 2; noes — 5.]

It was moved and seconded to postpone the following clause 3 section 11 article

"to the trial of impeachments of officers of the United "States"

which passed in the affirmative.

It was moved and seconded to add the following words after the word "controversies" 3 sect. 11 article

"to which the United States shall be a Party"

which passed in the affirmative

It was moved and seconded to insert the words "this constitution the" before the word "laws" 2 line 3 sect, 11 article.

which passed in the affirmative

It was moved and seconded to strike out the words "passed

---

is evidently in error in reading "2 Sect.", instead of "1 Sect." Madison gives these same votes at this point in the day's proceedings, and they are assigned to the two questions in the Journal on Section 1 of Article XI.

[2] *Journal* (p. 297) ascribes Vote 376, Detail of Ayes and Noes, to this question.

by the Legislature" and to insert after the words "United States" the words "and treaties made or which shall be made under their authority"

which passed in the affirmative

It was moved and seconded to insert the word "controversies" before the words "between two" or

which passed in the affirmative

It was moved and seconded to postpone the following clause "in cases of impeachment"

which passed in the affirmative

It was moved and seconded to insert the words

"the United States or" before the words "a State shall be a party"

which passed in the affirmative

It was moved and seconded to agree to the following amendment.

In all the other cases beforementioned original jurisdiction shall be in the Courts of the several States but with appeal both as to Law and fact to the courts of the United States, with such exceptions and under such regulations, as the Legislatures shall make.

The last motion being withdrawn,

It was moved and seconded to amend the clause to read

"In cases of impeachment, cases affecting Ambassadors, "other public Ministers and Consuls, and those in which a "State shall be Party, this jurisdiction shall be original In "all the other cases before mentioned it shall be appellate "both as to law and fact with such exceptions and under such "regulations as the Legislature shall make"

which passed in the affirmative

It was moved and seconded to add the following clause to the last amendment.

"But in cases in which the United States shall be a Party "the jurisdiction shall be original or appellate as the Legisla-"ture may direct"

[To strike out the words "original or" Ayes — 6; noes — 2.] [3]

[3] Vote 381, Detail of Ayes and Noes, but this is inserted here merely because it is the only place that it seems to fit in with the proceedings.

which passed in the negative [Ayes — 3; noes — 5.][4]

On the question to reconsider the 3rd section 11 article

it passed in the affirmative

It was moved and seconded to strike out the words

"The jurisdiction of the Supreme Court" and to insert the words "The Judicial Power"

which passed in the affirmative

It was moved and seconded to strike out the words "this "jurisdiction shall be original" and to insert the words "The "supreme Court shall have original jurisdiction"

which passed in the affirmative

It was moved and seconded to agree to the following amendment

"In all the other cases before mentioned the judicial power "shall be exercised in such manner as the Legislature shall "direct"

which passed in the negative [Ayes — 2; noes — 6.][5]

It was moved and seconded to strike out the last clause of the 3rd sect. 11 article

which passed in the affirmative [Ayes — 8; noes — 0.]

It was moved and seconded to insert the words "both in law and equity" before the word "arising" in the first line, 3rd section, 11 article.

which passed in the affirmative.

It was moved and seconded to insert after the words "between citizens of different States" the words "between Citizens of the same State claiming lands under grants of different States

which passed in the affirmative

The House adjourned

---

[4] Vote 382, Detail of Ayes and Noes, but inserted here merely because of its relative position and that it is a negative vote.

[5] Vote 383, Detail of Ayes and Noes, but inserted here merely because it is a negative vote preceding Vote 384.

DETAIL OF AYES AND NOES

	New Hampshire	Massachusetts	Rhode Island	Connecticut	New York	New Jersey	Pennsylvania	Delaware	Maryland	Virginia	No Carolina	So Carolina	Georgia	Questions	ayes	noes	divided
[374]	aye			aye			aye	no	aye	aye		no	aye	To amend the clause giving the command of the militia to the Executive.	6	2	
[375]	aye			aye			aye	no	aye	aye		aye	aye	To amend the oath of office by the President	7	1	
[376]	aye			aye			aye	no	no	aye		aye	aye	To agree to the 2 Sect. 11 art.	6	2	
[377]	aye			aye			aye	no	no	aye		aye	aye				
[378]	no			aye			no	no	no	no		no	no	To agree to the amendt to ye 2 sect. 11 article	1	7	
[379]	no			no			no	no	dd	aye		no		amendt to ye 2 sect. 11 article	1	5	1
[380]	no			no			no	no	aye	aye		no		amendt to ye 2 sect. 11 article	2	5	
[381]	aye			aye			no	no	aye	aye		aye	aye	To strike out the words "original or"	6	2	
[382]	aye			no			aye	aye	no	no		no	no	amendment to 3 sect 11 article	3	5	
[383]	no			no			no	aye	no	aye		no	no	amendmt 3 sect. 11 art.	2	6	
[384]	aye			aye			aye	aye	aye	aye		aye	aye	To strike out the last clause 3 sect			

MADISON

Monday Augst. 27th. 1787. In Convention

Art X. sect. 2. being resumed,[6]

Mr. L. Martin moved to insert the words "after conviction" after the words "reprieves and pardons"

Mr. Wilson objected that pardon before conviction might be necessary in order to obtain the testimony of accomplices. He stated the case of forgeries in which this might particularly happen. — Mr L. Martin withdrew his motion.

Mr. Sherman moved to amend the clause giving the Executive the command of the Militia, so as to read "and of the Militia of the several States, *when called into the actual service of the U— S—*" and on the Question

N— H. ay. Mas. abst. Ct. ay. N— J. abst Pa ay. Del. no.

[6] Relating to the powers and duties of the President.

Md ay. Va. ay. N— C. abst. S. C— no. Geo— ay, [Ayes — 6; noes — 2; absent — 3.][7]

The clause for removing the President on impeachment by the House of Reps and conviction in the supreme Court, of Treason, Bribery or corruption, was postponed nem: con: at the instance of Mr. Govr. Morris, who thought the Tribunal an improper one, particularly, if the first judge was to be of the privy Council.

Mr. Govr. Morris objected also to the President of the Senate being provisional successor to the President, and suggested a designation of the Chief Justice.

Mr. Madison added as a ground of objection that the Senate might retard the appointment of a President in order to carry points whilst the revisionary power was in the President of their own body, but suggested that the Executive powers during a vacancy, be administered by the persons composing the Council to the President.

Mr Williamson suggested that the Legislature ought to have power to provide for occasional successors. & moved that the last clause (of 2 sect. X art:) ⟨relating to a provisional successor to the President⟩ be postponed.

Mr Dickinson 2ded. the postponement. remarking that it was too vague. What is the extent of the term "disability" & who is to be the judge of it?

The postponement was agreed to nem: con:

Col: Mason & Mr. Madison, moved to add to the oath to be taken by the supreme Executive "and will to the best of my judgment and power preserve protect and defend the Constitution of the U. S."

Mr. Wilson thought the general provision for oaths of office, in a subsequent place, rendered the amendment unnecessary —

On the question

N. H. ay— Mas— abst Ct ay— Pa ay. Del. no. Md. ay. Va. ay— N. C. abst S. C. ay. Geo. ay. [Ayes — 7; noes — 1; absent — 2.]

---

[7] See also statement by Martin in Appendix A, CLVIII (79).

Art: XI being taken up.[8]

Docr. Johnson suggested that the judicial power ought to extend to equity as well as law — and moved to insert the words "both in law and equity" after the words "U. S." in the 1st line of sect 1.

Mr. Read objected to vesting these powers in the same Court—

On the question

N. H. ay. ⟨Mas. absent⟩ Ct ay. ⟨N. J. abst⟩ P. ay— Del. no. Md no. Virga. ay. ⟨N— C— abst.⟩ S. C. ay. Geo. ay. [Ayes — 6; noes — 2; absent — 3.]

On the question to agree to Sect. 1. art. XI. as amended

N— H— ay— ⟨Mas. abst.⟩ Ct. ay— Pa ay— ⟨N— J— abst⟩ Del. no. Md. no. Va. ay. ⟨N— C— abst⟩ S. C. ay Geo. ay. [Ayes — 6; noes — 2; absent — 3.]

Mr. Dickinson moved as an amendment to sect. 2— art XI[9] after the words "good behavior" the words "provided that they may be removed by the Executive on the application ⟨by⟩ the Senate and House of Representatives."

Mr. Gerry 2ded. the motion

Mr Govr. Morris thought it a contradiction in terms to say that the Judges should hold their offices during good behavior, and yet be removeable without a trial. Besides it was fundamentally wrong to subject Judges to so arbitrary an authority.

Mr. Sherman saw no contradiction or impropriety if this were made part of the Constitutional regulation of the Judiciary establishment. He observed that a like provision was contained in the British Statutes.

Mr. Rutlidge: If the supreme Court is to judge between the U. S. and particular States, this alone is an insuperable objection to the motion.

[8] Article XI, Sect. 1. "The Judicial Power of the United States shall be vested in one Supreme Court, and in such inferior Courts as shall, when necessary, from time to time, be constituted by the Legislature of the United States."

[9] Article XI, Sect. 2. "The Judges of the Supreme Court, and of the Inferior Courts, shall hold their offices during good behaviour. They shall, at stated times, receive for their services, a compensation, which shall not be diminished during their continuance in office."

Mr. Wilson considered such a provision in the British Government as less dangerous than here, the House of Lords & House of Commons being less likely to concur on the same occasions. Chief Justice Holt, he remarked, had *successively* offended by his independent conduct, both houses of Parliament. Had this happened at the same time, he would have been ousted. The Judges would be in a bad situation if made to depend on every gust of faction which might prevail in the two branches of our Govt

Mr. Randolph opposed the motion as weakening too much the independence of the Judges.

Mr Dickinson was not apprehensive that the Legislature composed of different branches constructed on such different principles, would improperly unite for the purpose of displacing a Judge—

On the question for agreeing to Mr. Dickinson's Motion

N. H. no. ⟨Mas. abst⟩ Ct. ay. ⟨N. J. abst⟩ Pa. no. Del. no. Md no. Va. no ⟨N. C. abst⟩. S— C— no— Geo— no. [Ayes — 1; noes — 7; absent — 3.]

⟨On the question on Sect. 2 art: XI as reported. Del. & Maryd. only no—⟩[10]

Mr. Madison & Mr. McHenry moved to reinstate the words "increased or" before the word "diminished" in the 2d. Sect: art XI.

Mr. Govr. Morris opposed it for reasons urged by him on a former occasion—

Col: Mason contended strenuously for the motion. There was no weight he said in the argument drawn from changes in the value of the metals, because this might be provided for by an increase of salaries so made as not to affect persons in office, and this was the only argument on which much stress seemed to have been laid.

Genl. Pinkney. The importance of the Judiciary will require men of the first talents: large salaries will therefore be necessary, larger than the U. S. can allow in the first instance. He was not satisfied with the expedient mentioned by Col:

[10] Taken from *Journal* which is probably in error as to the vote, see above notes 1 and 2.

Mason. He did not think it would have a good effect or a good appearance, for new Judges to come in with higher salaries than the old ones.

Mr Govr Morris said the expedient might be evaded & therefore amounted to nothing. Judges might resign, & then be re-appointed to increased salaries.

On the question

N. H. no— Ct no. Pa no. Del. no— Md. divd Va ay— S. C. no— Geo. abst. ⟨also Masts— N. J. & N— C—⟩ [Ayes — 1; noes — 5; divided — 1; absent — 4.]

Mr. Randolph & Mr. Madison then moved to add the following words to sect 2. art XI. "nor increased by any Act of the Legislature which shall operate before the expiration of three years after the passing thereof"

On this question

N. H. no. Ct. no— Pa. no. Del. no. Md ay— Va ay— S. C. no. Geo— abst ⟨also Mas. N. J. & N. C.⟩ [Ayes — 2; noes — 5; absent — 4.]

Sect. 3— art. XI.[11] being taken up— the following clause was postponed — viz. "to the trial of impeachments of officers of the U. S." by which the jurisdiction of the supreme Court was extended to such cases.

Mr Madison & Mr. Govr. Morris moved to insert after the word "controversies" the words "to which the U— S— shall be a party" — which was agreed to nem: con:

Docr. Johnson moved to insert the words "this Constitution and the" before the word "laws"

Mr Madison doubted whether it was not going too far to extend the jurisdiction of the Court generally to cases arising Under the Constitution, & whether it ought not to be limited to cases of a Judiciary Nature. The right of expounding the Constitution in cases not of this nature ought not to be given to that Department.

The motion of Docr. Johnson was agreed to nem: con: it being generally supposed that the jurisdiction given was constructively limited to cases of a Judiciary nature—

[11] Relating to the jurisdiction of the Supreme Court.

On motion of Mr Rutlidge, the words "passed by the Legislature" were struck out, and after the words "U. S" were inserted nem. con: the words "and treaties made or which shall be made under their authority"—conformably to a preceding amendment in another place.

The clause "in cases of impeachment", was postponed.

Mr. Govr. Morris wished to know what was meant by the words "In all the cases before mentioned it (jurisdiction) shall be appellate with such exceptions &c," whether it extended to matters of fact as well as law — and to cases of Common law as well as Civil law.

Mr. Wilson. The Committee he believed meant facts as well as law & Common as well as Civil law. The jurisdiction of the federal Court of Appeals had he said been so construed.[12]

Mr. Dickinson moved to add after the word "appellate" the words "both as to law & fact which was agreed to nem: con:

Mr. Madison[13] & Mr. Govr. Morris moved to strike out the beginning of the 3d sect. "The jurisdiction of the supreme Court" & to insert the words "the Judicial power" which was agreed to nem: con:

The following motion was disagreed to, to wit to insert "In all the other cases before mentioned the Judicial power shall be exercised in such manner as the Legislature shall direct" ⟨Del. Virga ay

N. H Con. P. M. S. C. G no⟩ [Ayes — 2; noes — 6.] [14]

On a question for striking out the last sentence of sect. 3. "The Legislature may assign &c—"

N. H. ay— Ct ay. Pa ay. Del— ay— Md ay— Va ay— S— C. ay— Geo. ay. [Ayes — 8; noes — 0.]

Mr. Sherman moved to insert after the words "between Citizens of different States" the words, "between Citizens of the same State claiming lands under grants of different

[12] See Appendix A, CXXXIV.

[13] The preceding line was crossed out: "It was moved but disagreed to." This would seem to correspond to Votes 381 and 382, Detail of Ayes and Noes. See above notes 3 and 4.

[14] Taken from *Journal*. See above note 5.

States" — according to the provision in the 9th. art: of the Confederation — which was agreed to nem: con:[15]

Adjourned[16]

McHENRY

Monday 27 Augt.

Amended the Presidential oath of office — made some other amendments — postponed what follows from the oath to the end.

Agreed to the 1. 2 and 3 sect. of the XI article with amendments.

MASON[17]

The judicial power of the United States shall be vested in one Supreme Court and in such Courts of Admiralty as Congress shall establish in any of the States. And also in Courts of Admiralty to be established in such of the States as Congress shall direct.

The jurisdiction of the supreme courts shall extend to all cases in law and equity arising under this Constitution, the laws of the United States and treaties made or which shall be made under their authority; to all cases affecting ambassadors, other public ministers and consuls; to all cases of admiralty and maritime jurisdiction; to controversies to which the United States shall be a party, to controversies between two or more States; between *citizens of the same State* claiming lands of different States, and between *a State and the citizens thereof* and foreign States, citizens or subjects.

In all cases affecting ambassadors, other public ministers

[15] See further Appendix A, CLVIII (83–87), CCVIII, CCXIV, CCXV, CCXXVIII, CCCVI, CCCXIV.

[16] See further Appendix A, XCIV.

[17] This document, not in Mason's handwriting, was found among the Mason Papers. It seems to represent a plan for the organization and jurisdiction of the judiciary, which must have been prepared about this time by some one familiar with the work of the Convention. There is no evidence that it was presented to the Convention. It is reprinted here from K. M. Rowland, *Life of George Mason*, II, 385–386.

and consuls, and those in which a State shall be a party, and suits between persons claiming lands under grants of different States the Supreme Court shall have original jurisdiction, and in all the other cases before mentioned the Supreme Courts shall have appellate jurisdiction as to law only, except in cases of equity and admiralty and maritime jurisdiction in which last mentioned cases the Supreme Court shall have appellate jurisdiction, both as to law and fact.

In all cases of admiralty and maritime jurisdiction, the Admiralty Courts appointed by Congress shall have original jurisdiction, and an appeal may be made to the Supreme Court of Congress for any sum and in such manner as Congress may by law direct.

In all other cases not otherwise provided for the *Superior* State Courts shall have original jurisdiction, and an appeal may be made to the Supreme federal Court in all cases where the subject in controversy or the decree or judgment of the State court shall be of the value of one thousand dollars and in cases of less value the appeal shall be to the High Court of Appeals, Court of Errors or other Supreme Court of the State where the suit shall be tried.

The trial of all crimes, except in case of impeachment shall be in the Superior Court of that State where the offence shall have been committed in such manner as the Congress shall by law direct except that the trial shall be by a jury. But when the crime shall not have been committed within any one of the United States the trial shall be at such place and in such manner as Congress shall by law direct, except that such trial shall also be by a jury.[18]

[18] For a transcription of this document from the original manuscript see Volume IV.

TUESDAY, AUGUST 28, 1787.

JOURNAL

Tuesday August 28. 1787

The honorable Mr Sherman from the Committee to whom were referred several propositions entered on the Journal of the 25 instant informed the House that the Committee were prepared to report — The report was then delivered in at the Secretary's table, was read, and is as follows.

The Committee report that the following be inserted after the 4 clause of the 7 section

"Nor shall any regulation of commerce or revenue give "preference to the ports of one State over those of another "or oblige Vessels bound to or from any State to enter, clear, "or pay duties in another.

And all tonnage, duties, imposts, and excises, laid by the "Legislature shall be uniform throughout the United States"

It was moved and seconded to strike out the words

"it shall be appellate" and to insert the words "the Supreme Court shall have appellate jurisdiction" 3 sect. 11 article

which passed in the affirmative [Ayes — 9; noes — 1.][1]

It was moved and seconded to amend the 4th section of the 11th article to read as follows.

"The trial of all crimes (except in cases of impeachment) "shall be by Jury — and such trial shall be held in the State "where the said crimes shall have been committed; but when "not committed within any State then the trial shall be at "such place or places as the Legislature may direct."

which passed in the affirmative

---

[1] Vote 385, Detail of Ayes and Noes. In this and the four votes following the vote of Massachusetts is recorded in the Rhode Island column.

It was moved and seconded to add the following amendment to the 4 sect. 11 article

"The privilege of the writ of Habeas Corpus shall not be "suspended; unless where in cases of rebellion or invasion "the public safety may require it."

which passed in the affirmative [Ayes — 7; noes — 3.][2]

On the question to agree to the 5. section 11 article as reported

it passed in the affirmative.

It was moved and seconded to insert the words "nor emit bills of credit" after the word "money" in the 12 article

which passed in the affirmative. [Ayes — 8; noes — 1; divided — 1.][3]

It was moved and seconded to insert the following clause after the last amendment.

"nor make any thing but gold and silver coin a tender in payment of debts"

which passed in the affirmative [Ayes — 11; noes — 0.][4]

It was moved and seconded to add the following clause to the last amendment.

"nor pass any bill of attainder or ex post facto laws"

which passed in the affirmative [Ayes — 7; noes — 3.][5]

It was moved and seconded to insert after the word "reprisal" the words "nor lay embargoes"

which passed in the negative. [Ayes — 3; noes — 8.]

It was moved and seconded to transfer the following words from the 13 to the 12 article

"nor lay imposts or duties on imports"

which passed in the negative. [Ayes — 4; noes — 7.]

Separate questions being taken on the several clauses of the 12 article, as amended,

they passed in the affirmative.

It was moved and seconded to insert after the word "imports" in the 13th article the words "or exports"

which passed in the affirmative [Ayes — 6; noes — 5.]

[2] Vote 386, Detail of Ayes and Noes. *Journal* (p. 302) mistakenly ascribes this vote to the next question.

[3] Vote 387, Detail of Ayes and Noes.

[4] Vote 390, Detail of Ayes and Noes.

[5] Vote 391, Detail of Ayes and Noes. See below note 19.

DETAIL OF AYES AND NOES

	New Hampshire	Massachusetts	Rhode Island	Connecticut	New York	New Jersey	Pennsylvania	Delaware	Maryland	Virginia	No Carolina	So Carolina	Georgia	Questions	ayes	noes	divided
[385]	aye		aye	aye			aye	aye	no	aye	aye	aye	aye	The supreme Court shall have appellate jurisd	9	1	
[386]	aye		aye	aye			aye	aye	aye	aye	no	no	no	unless where in cases of rebellion &ca Ha Cor:	7	3	
[387]	aye		aye	aye			aye	aye	dd	no	aye	aye	aye	nor emit bills of credit	8	1	1
[388][6]	aye		aye	no		no	aye	aye	aye	aye	aye	aye	aye		9	2	
[389][7]	aye		no	aye		aye	aye	aye	aye	no	aye	aye	aye				
[page 14]																	
[390]	aye	aye		aye		aye	aye	aye	aye	aye	aye	aye	aye	nor make any thing but gold or silver coin a tender in payment of debts	11		
[391]	aye			no		aye	aye	aye	no	no	aye	aye	aye	nor pass any bill of attainder or ex post facto laws.			
[392]	no	aye		no		no	no	aye	no	no	no	aye	no	"nor lay embargoes."	3	8	
[393]	aye	no		no		aye	no	aye	no	no	aye	no	no	lay imposts or dues on imports	4	7	
[394]	aye	aye		no		aye	aye	aye	no	no	aye	no	no	"or exports" 13 article.	6	5	
[395]	aye	no		aye		aye	aye	aye	no	aye	aye	aye	aye	"nor wh such consent but for the use of the Treasy of the U S.			
[396]	aye	no		aye		aye	aye	aye	no	aye	aye	aye	aye	on the first clause 13 article	9	2	
[397]	aye	aye		aye		aye	aye	aye	aye	aye	aye	no	dd	To agree to ye 14 article	9	1	1

[6] This vote is not accounted for.

[7] This vote probably belongs to the Records of September 5 (see note 1a of that date).

It was moved and seconded to add after the word "exports" in the 13th article the words "nor with such consent but for the use of the treasury of the United States"

which passed in the affirmative [Ayes — 9; noes — 2.]

[on the first clause 13 article Ayes — 9; noes — 2.][8]

Separate questions being taken on the several clauses of the 13th article, as amended,

they passed in the affirmative

On the question to agree to the 14 article as reported it passed in the affirmative [Ayes — 9; noes — 1; divided — 1.]

It was moved and seconded to strike out the words "high misdemeanor," and to insert the words "other crime"

which passed in the affirmative

On the question to agree to the 15th article as amended

it passed in the affirmative

The House adjourned.

MADISON

Tuesday August 28. 1787— In Convention

Mr. Sherman from the Committee to whom were referred several propositions on the 25th. instant, made the following report —

That there be inserted after the 4 clause of 7th. section

"Nor shall any regulation of commerce or revenue give "preference to the ports of one State ⟨over⟩[9] those of another, "or oblige vessels bound to or from any State to enter clear "or pay duties in another and all tonnage, duties, imposts "& excises laid by the Legislature shall be uniform through-"out the U. S–" Ordered to lie on the table.

Art XI sect. 3. "It was moved to strike out the words "it shall be appellate" & to insert the words "the supreme Court shall have appellate jurisdiction", — in order to prevent uncertainty whether "it" referred to the *supreme Court*, or to the *Judicial power*.

On the question

[8] Vote 396, Detail of Ayes and Noes.

[9] Crossed out: "to".

N. H. ay. Mas. ay. Ct. ay. N. J. abst. Pa. ay. Del. ay. Md. no. Va. ay. N C ay. S. C. ay. Geo. ay. [Ayes — 9; noes — 1; absent — 1.][10]

Sect. 4— was so amended nem: con: as to read "The trial of all crimes (except in cases of impeachment) shall be by jury, and such trial shall be held in the State where the said crimes shall have been committed; but when not committed within any State, then the trial shall be at such place or places as the Legislature may direct". The object of this amendment was to provide for trial by jury of offences committed out of any State.

Mr. Pinkney, urging the propriety of securing the benefit of the Habeas corpus in the most ample manner, moved "that it should not be suspended but on the most urgent occasions, & then only for a limited time not exceeding twelve months"[11]

Mr. Rutlidge was for declaring the Habeas Corpus inviolable— He did ⟨not⟩ conceive that a suspension could ever be necessary at the same time through all the States—

Mr. Govr Morris moved that "The privilege of the writ of Habeas Corpus shall not be suspended, unless where in cases of Rebellion or invasion the public safety may require it".

Mr. Wilson doubted whether in any case ⟨a suspension⟩ could be necessary, as the discretion now exists with Judges, in most important cases to keep in Gaol or admit to Bail.

The first part of Mr. Govr. Morris' ⟨motion,⟩ to the word "unless" was agreed to nem: con: — on the remaining part;

N. H. ay. Mas. ay. Ct. ay. Pa. ay. Del. ay. Md. ay. Va. ay. N. C. no. S. C. no. Geo. no. [Ayes — 7; noes — 3.]

Sect. 5. of art: XI.[12] was agreed to *nem: con:* *

* ⟨The vote on this section as stated in the printed journal is not unanimous: The statement here probably the right one.⟩[13]

---

[10] See Appendix A, CLXXXIX, CXCII, CXCIX.

[11] Upon this question, see Appendix A, CLVIII (65–66), CXCII.

[12] Article XI, Sect. 5 "Judgment, in cases of Impeachment, shall not extend further than to removal from Office, and disqualification to hold and enjoy any office of honour, trust or profit, under the United States. But the party convicted shall, nevertheless be liable and subject to indictment, trial, judgment and punishment according to law."

[13] See above note 2.

Art: XII being taken up.[14]

Mr. Wilson & Mr. Sherman moved to insert after the words "coin money" the words "nor emit bills of credit, nor make any thing but gold & silver coin a tender in payment of debts" making these prohibitions absolute, instead of ⟨making the measures allowable⟩ (as in the XIII art:) *with the consent of the Legislature of the U. S.*[15]

Mr. Ghorum thought the purpose would be as well secured by the provision of art: XIII which makes the consent of the Genl. Legislature necessary, and that in that mode, no opposition would be excited; whereas an absolute prohibition of paper money would rouse the most desperate opposition from its partizans—[16]

Mr. Sherman thought this a favorable crisis for crushing paper money. If the consent of the Legislature could authorize emissions of it, the friends of paper money would make every exertion to get into the Legislature in order to license it.

The question being divided: on the 1st. part — "nor emit bills of credit"

N. H. ay. Mas. ay. Ct. ay. Pa. ay— Del. ay. Md divd.[17] Va. no. N— C— ay— S— C. ay. Geo. ay. [Ayes — 8; noes — 1; divided — 1.]

The remaining part of Mr. Wilson's & Sherman's motion, was agreed to nem: con:

Mr King moved to add, in the words used in the Ordinance of Congs establishing new States, a prohibition on the States to interfere in private contracts.

Mr. Govr. Morris. This would be going too far. There are a thousand laws relating to bringing actions — limitations of actions & which affect contracts— The Judicial power of the U— S— will be a protection in cases within their jurisdiction; and within the State itself a majority must rule, whatever may be the mischief done among themselves.

[14] Article XII. "No state shall coin money; nor grant letters of marque and reprisals; nor enter into any treaty, alliance, or confederation; nor grant any title of Nobility."

[15] Upon this question, see Appendix A, CXXIII, CLVIII (70–72), CCXXIX, CCCLXXV.

[16] Crossed out "of that expedient sort of medicines".

[17] Martin voted in the negative, see Appendix A, CLVIII (69).

Mr. Sherman. Why then prohibit bills of credit?

Mr. Wilson was in favor of Mr. King's motion.

Mr. Madison admitted that inconveniences might arise from such a prohibition but thought on the whole it would be overbalanced by the utility of it. He conceived however that a negative on the State laws could alone secure the effect. Evasions might and would be devised by the ingenuity of the Legislatures—

Col: Mason. This is carrying the restraint too far. Cases will happen that can not be foreseen, where some kind of interference will be proper, & essential— He mentioned the case of limiting the period for bringing actions on open account — that of bonds after a certain ⟨lapse of time,⟩ — asking whether it was proper to tie the hands of the States from making provision in such cases?

Mr. Wilson. The answer to these objections is that *retrospective* interferences only are to be prohibited.

Mr. Madison. Is not that already done by the prohibition of ex post facto laws, which will oblige the Judges to declare such interferences null & void.

Mr. Rutlidge moved instead of Mr. King's Motion to insert — "nor pass bills of attainder nor retrospective* laws" on which motion

N. H. ay— Ct. no. N. J. ay. Pa. ay. Del. ay. Md. no. Virga. no. N— C. ay. S. C. ay. Geo. ay. [Ayes — 7; noes — 3.][18]

Mr. Madison moved to insert after the word "reprisal" (art. XII) the words "nor lay embargoes". He urged that such acts ⟨by the States⟩ would be unnecessary — impolitic — & unjust—

Mr. Sherman thought the States ought to retain this power in order to prevent suffering & injury to their poor.

Col: Mason thought the amendment would be not only improper but dangerous, as the Genl. Legislature would not

* ⟨In the printed Journal "ex post facto"⟩ [19]

[18] See Appendix A, CLVIII (70–72).

[19] The Journal is correct, according to marginal notes in the Washington and Brearley copies of the Report of the Committee of Detail.

sit constantly and therefore could not interpose at the necessary moments— He enforced his objection by appealing to the necessity of sudden embargoes during the war, to prevent exports, particularly in the case of a blockade—

Mr Govr. Morris considered the provision as unnecessary; the power of regulating trade between State & State, already vested in the Genl— Legislature, being sufficient.

On the question

N. H. no. Mas. ay. Ct. no. N. J. no. Pa. no. Del. ay. Md. no. Va. no. N. C. no. S. C. ay. Geo. no. [Ayes — 3; noes — 8.]

Mr Madison moved that the words "nor lay imposts or duties on imports" be transferred from art: XIII where the consent of[20] the Genl. Legislature may license the act — into art: XII which will make the prohibition on the States absolute. He observed that as the States interested in this power by which they could tax the imports of their neighbours passing thro' their markets, were a majority,[21] they could give the consent of the Legislature, to the injury of N. Jersey, N. Carolina &c — [22]

Mr. Williamson 2ded. the motion

Mr. Sherman thought the power might safely be left to the Legislature[23] of the U. States.

Col: Mason, observed that particular States might wish to encourage by impost duties certain manufactures for which they enjoyed natural advantages, as Virginia, the manufacture[24] of Hemp &c.

Mr. Madison— The encouragment of Manufacture in that mode requires duties not only on imports directly from foreign Countries, but from the other States in the Union, which would revive all the mischiefs experienced from the want of a Genl. Government over commerce.

On the question

N. H. ay. Mas. no. Ct. no. N. J— ay. Pa. no. Del: ay. Md. no. Va. no N. C. ay. S. C. no. Geo. no. [Ayes — 4; noes — 7.]

[20] Crossed out "Congress may authorize them".

[21] Crossed out: "of the consent of Congress might be given".

[22] See Appendix A, CCXII.

[23] Crossed out "Govt."

[24] Crossed out "culture and".

Art: XII as amended agreed to nem: con: [25]

Art: XIII being taken up.[26] Mr. King moved to insert after the word "imports" the words "or exports" so as to prohibit the States from taxing either. — & on this question ⟨it passed in the affirmative.⟩

N. H— ay. Mas. ay. Ct no. N. J. ay. P. ay. Del. ay. Md no. Va. no. N. C. ay. S. C. no. Geo. no. [Ayes — 6; noes noes — 5.]

Mr. Sherman moved to add, after the word "exports" — the words "nor with such consent but for the use of the U. S." — so as to carry the proceeds of all State duties on imports & exports, into the common Treasury.[27]

Mr. Madison liked the motion as preventing all State imposts — but lamented the complexity we were giving to the commercial system.

Mr. Govr. Morris thought the regulation necessary to prevent the Atlantic States from endeavouring to tax the Western States — & promote their interest by opposing the navigation of the Mississippi which would drive the Western people into the arms of G. Britain.

Mr. Clymer thought the encouragement of the Western Country was suicide on the old States— If the States have such different interests that they can not be left to regulate their own manufactures without encountering the interests of other States, it is a proof that they are not fit to compose one nation.

Mr. King was afraid that the regulation moved by Mr Sherman would too much interfere with a policy of States respecting their manufactures, which may be necessary. Revenue he reminded the House was the object of the general Legislature.

[25] See Appendix A, CCXII.

[26] Article XIII. "No State, without the consent of the Legislature of the United States, shall emit bills of credit, or make any thing but specie a tender in payment of debts; nor lay imposts or duties on imports; nor keep troops or ships of war in time of peace; nor enter into any agreement or compact with another State, or with any foreign power; nor engage in any war, unless it shall be actually invaded by enemies, or the danger of invasion be so imminent, as not to admit of delay, until the Legislature of the United States can be consulted."

[27] Upon this question see Appendix A, CCCXC.

On Mr. Sherman's motion

N. H. ay. Mas. no. Ct. ay. N. J. ay. Pa. ay. Del. ay. Md. no. Va. ay. N. C. ay. S. C. ay. Geo. ay. [Ayes — 9; noes — 2.]

Art XIII was then agreed to as amended.

Art. XIV was taken up.[28]

Genl. Pinkney was not satisfied with it. He seemed to wish some provision should be included in favor of property in slaves.

On the question ⟨on art: XIV.⟩

N. H. ay. Mas. ay. Ct. ay. N. J. ay— Pa. ay. Del. ay. Md. ay— Va. ay. N— C— ay. S— C. no. Geo. divided [Ayes — 9; noes — 1; divided — 1.]

Art: XV. being taken up.[29] the words "high misdemesnor," were struck out, and "other crime" inserted, in order to comprehend all proper cases: it being doubtful whether "high misdemeanor" had not a technical meaning too limited.

Mr. Butler and Mr Pinkney moved "to require fugitive slaves and servants to be delivered up like criminals."

Mr. Wilson. This would oblige the Executive of the State to do it, at the public expence.

Mr Sherman saw no more propriety in the public seizing and surrendering a slave or servant, than a horse.

Mr. Butler withdrew his proposition in order that some particular provision might be made apart from this article.

Art XV as amended was then agreed to nem: con:

Adjourned[30]

---

[28] Article XIV. "The Citizens of each State shall be entitled to all privileges and immunities of citizens in the several States."

[29] Article XV. "Any person charged with treason, felony or high misdemeanor in any State, who shall flee from justice, and shall be found in any other State, shall, on demand of the Executive power of the State from which he fled, be delivered up and removed to the State having jurisdiction of the offence."

[30] See further, Appendix A, XCVI.

McHENRY

Augt. 28.

4 Sect. Amended. 5 sect. agreed to.

XII article amended by adding that no State shall emit bills of credit, nor make any thing but specie a tender in debts.

XIII amended so [th]at all duties laid by a State shall accrue to the use of the U. S.

WEDNESDAY, AUGUST 29, 1787.

JOURNAL

Wednesday August 29 1787.

It was moved and seconded to commit the 16th article together with the following proposition

To establish uniform laws upon the subject of bankruptcies and respecting the damages arising on the protest of foreign bills of exchange.

which passed in the affirmative [Ayes — 9; noes — 2.]

It was moved and seconded to commit the following proposition

Whensoever the act of any State, whether legislative executive or judiciary shall be attested and exemplified under the seal thereof, such attestation and exemplification shall be deemed in other State as full proof of the existence of that act — and it's operation shall be binding in every other State, in all cases to which it may relate, and which are within the cognizance and jurisdiction of the State, wherein the said act was done

which passed in the affirmative

It was moved and seconded to commit the following proposition

Full faith ought to be given in each State to the public acts, records, and judicial proceedings of every other State; and the Legislature shall by general laws determine the Proof and effect of such acts, records, and proceedings

which passed in the affirmative

and the foregoing Propositions together with the 16 article were referred to the honorable Mr Rutledge, Mr Randolph, Mr Gorham, Mr Wilson and Mr Johnson

It was moved and seconded to postpone the report of the

Comme entd on ye Journal of the 24 instant take up the following proposition

That no act of the Legislature for the purpose of regulating the commerce of the United States with foreign powers or among the several States shall be passed without the assent of ⅔rds of the Members of each House.

which passed in the negative [Ayes — 4; noes — 7.]

On the question to agree to the report of the Committee of eleven entered on the Journal of the 24 instant

it passed in the affirmative

It was moved and seconded to agree to the following proposition to be inserted after the 15 article

"If any Person bound to service or labor in any of the "United States shall escape into another State, He or She "shall not be discharged from such service or labor in conse-"quence of any regulations subsisting in the State to which "they escape; but shall be delivered up to the person justly "claiming their service or labor"

which passed in the affirmative [Ayes — 11; noes — 0.]

It was moved and seconded to strike out the two last clauses of the 17 article

which passed in the affirmative [Ayes — 9; noes — 2.] [1]

It was moved and seconded to strike the following words out of the 17th article.

"but to such admission the consent of two thirds of the "Members present in each House shall be necessary"

It was moved and seconded to agree to the following proposition, as a substitute for the 17 article.

"New States may be admitted by the Legislature into this "union: but no new State shall be erected within the limits "of any of the present States without the consent of the Legis-"lature of such State as well as of the general Legislature."

Separate questions being taken on the different clauses of the proposition

they passed in the affirmative [Ayes — 6; noes — 5.]

The House adjourned

[1] Vote 401, Detail of Ayes and Noes. *Journal* (p. 307) mistakenly ascribes this vote to the question following.

DETAIL OF AYES AND NOES

	New Hampshire	Massachusetts	Rhode Island	Connecticut	New York	New Jersey	Pennsylvania	Delaware	Maryland	Virginia	No Carolina	So Carolina	Georgia	Questions	ayes	noes	divided
[398]	no	no		aye		aye	aye	aye	aye	aye	aye	aye	aye	To commit the 16 article &ca			
[399]	no	no		no		no	no	no	aye	aye	aye	no	aye	To postpone the report of the Committee entd on the Journal 24 Augt			
[400]	aye	aye		aye		aye	aye	aye	aye	aye	aye	aye	aye	To agree to the amendmt to the 15 article.			
[401]	aye	aye		aye		aye	aye	aye	no	no	aye	aye	aye	To strike out the two last clauses of the 17 article	9	2	
[402]	no	aye		no		no	aye	no	no	aye	aye	aye	aye	To agree to the substitute for the 17 article	6	5	

MADISON

Wednesday August 29th. 1787. In Convention

Art: XVI. taken up.[2]

Mr. Williamson moved to substitute in place of it, the words of the Articles of Confederation on the same subject. He did ⟨not⟩ understand precisely the meaning of the article.

Mr. Wilson & Docr. Johnson supposed the meaning to be that Judgments in one State should be the ground of actions in other States, & that acts of the Legislatures should be included,[3] for the sake of Acts of insolvency &c —

Mr. Pinkney moved to commit art XVI, with the following proposition, "To establish uniform laws upon the subject of bankruptcies, and respecting the damages arising on the protest of foreign bills of exchange"

Mr Ghorum was for agreeing to the article, and committing the ⟨proposition.⟩

[2] Article XVI. "Full faith shall be given in each State to the acts of the Legislatures, and to the records and judicial proceedings of the Courts and Magistrates of every other State."

[3] Crossed out "as they may sometimes serve the like purpose as act".

Mr. Madison was for committing both. He wished the Legislature might be authorized to provide for the *execution* of Judgments in other States, under such regulations as might be expedient— He thought that this might be safely done and was justified by the nature of the Union.

Mr. Randolph said there was no instance of one nation executing judgments of the Courts of another nation. He moved the following proposition.

"Whenever the Act of any State, whether Legislative Executive or Judiciary shall be attested & exemplified under the seal thereof, such attestation and exemplification, shall be deemed in other States as full proof of the existence of that act — and its operation shall be binding in every other State, in all cases to which it may relate, and which are within the cognizance and jurisdiction of the State, wherein the said act was done."

On the question for committing art: XVI with Mr. Pinkney's motion

N. H. no. Mas. no. Ct. ay. N. J. ay. Pa ay. Del. ay. Md. ay. Va. ay. N. C. ay. S. C. ay. Geo. ay. [Ayes — 9; noes — 2.]

The motion of Mr. Randolph was also committed nem: con:

Mr. Govr. Morris moved to commit also the following proposition on the same subject.

"Full faith ought to be given in each State to the public acts, records, and judicial proceedings of every other State; and the Legislature shall by general laws, determine the proof and effect of such acts, records, and proceedings". and it was committed nem: contrad:

The committee appointed for these references, were Mr. Rutlidge, Mr. Randolph, Mr. Gorham, Mr Wilson, & Mr Johnson.

Mr. Dickenson mentioned to the House that on examining Blackstone's Commentaries, he found that the terms "ex post facto" related to criminal cases only;[4] that they would

[4] See below, September 14 and Appendix A, CCXII.

not consequently restrain the States from retrospective laws in civil cases, and that some further provision for this purpose would be requisite.

Art. VII Sect. 6 by ye. Committee ⟨of eleven⟩ reported to be struck out[5] (see the 24 instant) being now taken up,

Mr. Pinkney moved to postpone the Report in favor of the following proposition — "That no act of the Legislature for the purpose of regulating the commerce of the U— S. with foreign powers, or among the several States, shall be passed without the assent of two thirds of the members of each House—" — He remarked that there were five distinct commercial interests— 1. the fisheries & W. India trade, which belonged to the N. England States. 2. the interest of N. York lay in a free trade. 3. Wheat & flour the Staples of the two Middle States, (N. J. & Penna.)— 4 Tobo. the staple of Maryd. & Virginia ⟨& partly of N. Carolina.⟩[6] 5. Rice & Indigo, the staples of S. Carolina & Georgia. These different interests would be a source of oppressive regulations if no check to a bare majority should be provided. States pursue their interests with less scruple than individuals. The power of regulating commerce was a pure concession on the part of the S. States. They did not need. the protection of the N. States at present.

Mr. Martin 2ded. the motion

Genl. Pinkney said it was the true interest of the S. States to have no regulation of commerce; but considering the loss brought on the commerce of the Eastern States by the revolution, their liberal conduct towards the views* of South Carolina, and the interest the weak Southn. States had in being united with the strong Eastern States, he thought it proper that no

* He meant the permission to import slaves. An understanding on the two subjects of *navigation* and *slavery*, had taken place between those parts of the Union, which explains the vote on the Motion depending, as well as the language of Genl. Pinkney & others.

[5] Requiring two-thirds of both houses to pass navigation acts. On this question see August 22 and Appendix A, CXV, CXXXII, CLV, CXCIII, CCXVI, CCXVII, CCCXXXVI. As this subject was a matter of compromise in connection with the slave-trade, see references under August 25, note 7.

[6] Probably but not certainly a later insertion.

fetters should be imposed on the power of making commercial regulations; and that his constituents though prejudiced against the Eastern States, would be reconciled to this liberality— He had himself, he said, prejudices agst the Eastern States before he came here, but would acknowledge that he had found them as liberal and candid as any men whatever.

Mr. Clymer. The diversity of commercial interests, of necessity creates difficulties, which ought not to be increased by unnecessary restrictions. The Northern & middle States will be ruined, if not enabled to defend themselves against foreign regulations.

Mr. Sherman, alluding to Mr. Pinkney's enumeration of particular interests, as requiring a security agst. abuse of the power; observed that, the diversity was of itself a security. adding that to require more than a majority to decide a question was always embarrassing as had been experienced in cases requiring the votes of nine States in Congress.

Mr. Pinkney replied that his enumeration meant the five minute interests— It still left the two great divisions of Northern & Southern Interests.

Mr. Govr. Morris. opposed the object of the motion as highly injurious— Preferences to american ships will multiply them, till they can carry the Southern produce cheaper than it is now carried- — A navy was essential to security, particularly of the S. States, and can only be had by a navigation act encouraging american bottoms & seamen— In those points of view then alone, it is the interest of the S. States that navigation acts should be facilitated. Shipping he said was the worst & most precarious kind of property. and stood in need of public patronage.

Mr Williamson was in favor of making two thirds instead of a majority requisite, as more satisfactory to the Southern people. No useful measure he believed had been lost in Congress for want of nine votes As to the weakness of the Southern States, he was not alarmed on that account. The sickliness of their climate for invaders would prevent their being made an object. He acknowledged that he did not think the motion requiring $\frac{2}{3}$ necessary in itself, because if

a majority of Northern States should push their regulations too far, the S. States would build ships for themselves: but he knew the Southern people were apprehensive on this subject and would be pleased with the precaution.

Mr. Spaight was against the motion. The Southern States could at any time save themselves from oppression, by building ships for their own use.

Mr. Butler differed from those who considered the rejection of the motion as no concession on the part of the S. States. He considered the interests of these and of the Eastern States, to be as different as the interests of Russia and Turkey. Being notwitstanding desirous of conciliating the affections of the East: States, he should vote agst. requiring $\frac{2}{3}$ instead of a majority.

Col: Mason. If the Govt. is to be lasting, it must be founded in the confidence & affections of the people, and must be so constructed as to obtain these. The *Majority* will be governed by their interests. The Southern States are the *minority* in both Houses. Is it to be expected that they will deliver themselves bound hand & foot to the Eastern States, and enable them to exclaim, in the words of Cromwell on a certain occasion — "the lord hath delivered them into our hands.

Mr. Wilson took notice of the several objections and remarked that if every peculiar interest was to be secured, *unanimity* ought to be required. The majority he said would be no more governed by interest than the minority— It was surely better to let the latter be bound hand and foot than the former. Great inconveniences had, he contended, been experienced in Congress from the article of confederation requiring nine votes in certain cases.

Mr. Madison. went into a pretty full view of the subject. He observed that the disadvantage to the S. States from a navigation act, lay chiefly in a temporary rise of freight, attended however with an increase of Southn. as well as Northern Shipping — with the emigration of Northern seamen & merchants to the Southern States — & with a removal of the existing[7] & injurious retaliations among the States ⟨on each

[7] Crossed out "& fetters".

other⟩. The power of foreign nations to obstruct our retaliating measures[8] on them by a corrupt influence would also be less if a majority shd be made competent than if $\frac{2}{3}$ of each House shd. be required to legislative acts in this case. An abuse of the power would be qualified with all these good effects. But he thought an abuse was rendered improbable by the provision of 2 branches — by the independence of the Senate, by the negative[9] of the Executive, by the interest of Connecticut & N. Jersey which were agricultural, not commercial States; by the interior interest which was also agricultural in the most commercial States— by the accession of Western States which wd. be altogether agricultural. He added that the Southern States would derive an essential advantage in the general security afforded by the increase of our maritime strength. He stated the vulnerable situation of them all, and of Virginia in particular. The increase of the Coasting trade, and of seamen, would also be favorable to the S. States, by increasing, the consumption of their produce. If the Wealth of the Eastern should in a still greater proportion be augmented, that wealth wd. contribute the more to the public wants, and be otherwise a national benefit.[10]

Mr. Rutlidge was agst. the motion of his colleague. It did not follow from a grant of the power to regulate trade, that it would be abused. At the worst a navigation act could bear hard a little while only on the S. States. As we are laying the foundation for a great empire, we ought to take a permanent view of the subject and not look at the present moment only. He reminded the House of the necessity of securing the West India trade to this country. That was the great object, and a navigation Act was necessary for obtaining it.

Mr. Randolph said that there were features so odious in the Constitution as it now stands, that he doubted whether he should be able to agree to it. A rejection of the motion would compleat the deformity of the system. He took notice of the argument in favor of giving the power over trade to a

[8] Crossed out "and with successful retaliation on the injurious restrictions of foreign powers".

[9] Crossed out "controul".

[10] See Appendix A, CCCXC.

majority, drawn from the opportunity foreign powers would have of obstructing retaliating measures, if two thirds were made requisite. He did not think there was weight in that consideration— The difference between a majority & two thirds did not afford room for such an opportunity. Foreign influence would also be more likely to be exerted on the President who could require three fourths by his negative— He did not mean however to enter into the merits. What he had in view was merely to pave the way for a declaration which he might be hereafter obliged to make if an accumulation of obnoxious ingredients should take place, that he could not give his assent to the plan.

Mr Gorham. If the Government is to be so fettered as to be unable to relieve the Eastern States what motive can they have to join in it, and thereby tie their own hands from measures which they could otherwise take for themselves. The Eastern States were not led to strengthen the Union by fear for their own safety. He deprecated the consequences of disunion, but if it should take place it was the Southern part of the Continent that had the most reason to dread them. He urged the improbability of a combination against the interest of the Southern States, the different situations of the Northern & Middle States being a security against it. It was moreover certain that foreign ships would never be altogether excluded especially those of Nations in treaty with us.

On the question to postpone in order to take up Mr. Pinkney's Motion

N— H. no. Mas. no. Ct. no N. J. no. Pa. no. Del. no. Md. ay. Va ay. N. C. ay— S— C. no— Geo. ay, [Ayes — 4 noes — 7.]

The Report of the Committee for striking out sect: 6. requiring two thirds of each House to pass a navigation act was then agreed to, nem: con:

Mr Butler moved to insert after art: XV. "If any person bound to service or labor in any of the U— States shall escape into another State, he or she shall not be discharged from such service or labor, in consequence of any regulations subsisting in the State to which they escape, but shall be delivered up

to the person justly claiming their service or labor," which was agreed to nem: con:[11]

Art: XVII being taken up,[12] Mr. Govr. Morris moved to strike out the two last sentences, to wit "If the admission be consented to, the new States shall be admitted on the same terms with the original States— But the Legislature may make conditions with the new States, concerning the public debt, which shall be then subsisting". — He did not wish to bind down the Legislature to admit Western States on the terms here stated.

Mr Madison opposed the motion, insisting that the Western States neither would nor ought to submit to a Union which degraded them from an equal rank with the other States.

Col. Mason— If it were possible by just means to prevent emigrations to the Western Country, it might be good policy. But go the people will as they find it for their interest, and the best policy is to treat them with that equality which will make them friends[13] not enemies.

Mr Govr Morris. did not mean to discourage the growth of the Western Country. He knew that to be impossible. He did not wish however to throw the power into their hands.

Mr Sherman, was agst. the motion, & for fixing an equality of privileges by the Constitution.

Mr Langdon was in favor of the Motion. he did not know but circumstances might arise which would render it inconvenient to admit new States on terms of equality.

Mr. Williamson was for leaving the Legislature free. The existing *small* States enjoy an equality now, and for *that* reason are admitted to it in the Senate. This reason is not applicable to ⟨new⟩ Western States.

On Mr Govr Morris's motion for striking out.

N. H. ay— Mas. ay—Ct ay. N—J. ay. Pa. ay. Del. ay. Md. no Va. no. N— C— ay. S—C— ay. Geo. ay, [Ayes —9; noes —2.]

Mr. L— Martin & Mr Govr. Morris moved to strike out

---

[11] See above August 28, and Appendix A, CXV and CCXII, also references under August 25, note 7.

[12] Relating to the admission of new states.

[13] Crossed out "firm"

of art XVII "but to such admission the consent of two thirds "of the members present shall be necessary." Before any question was taken on this motion,

Mr Govr. Morris moved the following proposition as a substitute for the XVII art: "New States may be admitted by the Legislature into this Union: but no new State shall be erected within the limits of any of the present States, without the consent of the Legislature of such State, as well as of the Genl. Legislature"[14]

The first part to Union inclusive was agreed to nem: con:

Mr. L— Martin opposed the latter part— Nothing he said would so alarm the limited States as to make the consent of the large States claiming the Western lands, necessary to the establishment of new States within their limits. It is proposed to guarantee the States. Shall Vermont be reduced by force in favor of the States claiming it? Frankland & the Western country of Virginia were in a like situation.

On Mr Govr. Morris's Motion to substitute &c ⟨it was agreed to⟩ —

N. H. no. Mas. ay. Ct. no. N. J. no. Pa. ay. Del. no. Md no. Va. ay. N. C. ay. S. C. ay. Geo. ay. [Ayes — 6; noes — 5.]

Art: XVII — before the House, as amended.

Mr. Sherman was against it. He thought it unnecessary. The Union cannot dismember a State without its consent.

Mr Langdon thought there was great weight in the argument of Mr. Luther Martin, and that the proposition substituted ⟨by Mr. Govr. Morris⟩ would excite a dangerous opposition to the plan.

Mr. Govr Morris thought on the contrary that the small States would be pleased with the regulation, as it holds up the idea of dismembering the large States.

Mr. Butler. If new States were to be erected without the consent of the dismembered States, nothing but confusion would ensue. Whenever taxes should press on the people, demagogues would set up their schemes of new States.

[14] Upon the significance of the wording of this article, see Appendix A, CCCIV.

Docr. Johnson agreed in general with the ideas of Mr Sherman, but was afraid that as the clause stood, Vermont would be subjected to N— York, contrary to the faith pledged by Congress. He was of opinion that Vermont ought to be compelled to come into the Union.

Mr Langdon said his objections were connected with the case of Vermont. If they are not taken in, & remain exempt from taxes, it would prove of great injury to N. Hampshire and the other neighbouring States

Mr Dickinson hoped the article would not be agreed to. He dwelt on the impropriety of requiring the small States to secure the large ones in their extensive claims of territory.

Mr. Wilson— When the *majority* of a State wish to divide they can do so. The aim of those in opposition to the article, he perceived, was that the Genl. Government should abet the *minority*, & by that means divide a State against its own consent.

Mr Govr. Morris. If the forced division of the States is the object of the new System, and is to be pointed agst one or two States, he expected, the gentleman from these[15] would pretty quickly leave us.

Adjourned[16]

McHENRY

Agt. 29.

XIIII and XV agreed to.[17] XVI. article committed.

[15] Madison originally wrote "the gentleman in the Chair (George Washington)". Martin's remarks the next day would indicate that the reference was more general.

[16] See further, Appendix A, XCVII.

[17] According to the Journal and Madison, on August 28.

THURSDAY, AUGUST 30, 1787.

JOURNAL

Thursday August 30. 1787.

[To commit the substitute offered to the 17 article Ayes — — 3; noes — 8.][1]

It was moved and seconded to postpone the substitute for the 17 article, agreed to yesterday, in order to take up the following amendment.

The Legislature shall have power to admit other States into the Union, and new States to be formed by the division or junction of States now in the Union, with the consent of the Legislature of such states.

which passed in the negative. [Ayes — 5; noes — 6.][2]

It was moved and seconded to strike out the words "the limits" and to insert the words "the jurisdiction" in the substitute offered to the 17 article.

which passed in the affirmative [Ayes — 7; noes — 4.]

It was moved and seconded to insert the words "hereafter formed or" after the words "shall be" in the substitute for the 17 article

which passed in the affirmative. [Ayes — 9; noes — 2.]

It was moved and seconded to postpone the consideration of the substitute to the 17 article as amended in order to take up the following

"The Legislature of the United States shall have power "to erect new States within as well as without the territory "claimed by the several States or either of them and admit "the same into the Union: Provided that nothing in this

[1] Vote 403, Detail of Ayes and Noes.

[2] Vote 404, Detail of Ayes and Noes, which notes that the proposal was in order "to take up Mr Sherman's motion".

"Constitution shall be construed to affect the claim of the "United States to vacant lands ceded to them by the late "treaty of Peace"

which passed in the negative [Ayes — 3; noes — 8.][3]

On the question to agree to the substitute offered to the 17 article, amended as follows.

"New States may be admitted by the Legislature into "this Union: but no new State shall be hereafter formed or "erected within the jurisdiction of any of the present States "without the consent of the Legislature of such State as well "as of the general Legislature

which passed in the affirmative [Ayes — 8; noes — 3.]

It was moved and seconded to add the following clause to the last amendment.

"Nor shall any State be formed by the junction of two or "more States or parts thereof without the consent of the "Legislatures of such States as well as of the Legislature of "the United States"

which passed in the affirmative

It was moved and seconded to add the following clause to the last amendment

"Provided nevertheless that nothing in this Constitution "shall be construed to affect the claim of the United States "to vacant lands ceded to them by the late Treaty of peace."

The last motion being withdrawn —

It was moved and seconded to agree to the following proposition.

Nothing in this Constitution shall be construed to alter the claims of the United States or of the individual States to the western territory but all such claims may be examined into and decided upon by the supreme Court of the United States

It was moved and seconded to postpone the last proposition in order to take up the following.

The Legislature shall have power to dispose of and make all needful rules and regulations respecting the territory or other property belonging to the United States: and nothing

[3] Vote 407, Detail of Ayes and Noes, which notes that this was a "proposition from Maryland". See below, note 15.

in this Constitution contained shall be so construed as to prejudice any claims either of the United States or of any particular State

It was moved and seconded to add the following clause to the last proposition

"But all such claims may be examined into and decided "upon by the Supreme Court of the United States"

which passed in the negative [Ayes — 2; noes — 8.]

On the question to agree to the following proposition

"The Legislature shall have power to dispose of and make "all needful rules and regulations respecting the territory or "other property belonging to the United States: and nothing "in this Constitution contained shall be so construed as to "prejudice any claims either of the United States or of any "particular State"

it passed in the affirmative [4]

On the question to agree to the first clause of the 18 article — it passed in the affirmative

It was moved and seconded to strike out the word "foreign" in the 18 article

which passed in the affirmative [Ayes — 10; noes — 1.][5]

It was moved and seconded to strike out the words "on the "application of it's Legislature against"

which passed in the negative [Ayes — 3; noes — 8.]

It was moved and seconded to strike out the words "domestic violence" and insert the word "insurrections" in the 18 article

which passed in the negative [Ayes — 5; noes — 6.]

It was moved and seconded to insert the words "or Executive" after the word "Legislature"

which passed in the affirmative [Ayes — 8; noes — 2.][6]

---

[4] *Journal* (p. 311) assigns to this question Vote 410, Detail of Ayes and Noes. This is probably a mistake, for there is no reason in favor of it except that it follows Vote 409. It, however, also precedes Vote 411, and the latter position accords with Madison's original record. See below, notes 18 and 20.

[5] Vote 410, Detail of Ayes and Noes. See above note 4.

[6] Vote 413, Detail of Ayes and Noes. In the Maryland column in the MS. "aye" is crossed out, and the summary gives an eleventh vote as divided. Madison records Maryland's vote as divided.

Detail of Ayes and Noes

	New Hampshire	Massachusetts	Rhode Island	Connecticut	New York	New Jersey	Pennsylvania	Delaware	Maryland	Virginia	No Carolina	So Carolina	Georgia	Questions	ayes	noes	divided
[403]	no	no		no		aye	no	aye	aye	no	no	no	no	To commit the substitute offered to the 17 article	3	8	
[404]	aye	aye		aye		no	aye	no	no	no	no	aye	no	To postpone the substitute to take up Mr Sherman's motion	5	6	
[405]	aye	aye		aye		aye	aye	no	no	aye	aye	aye	aye	To add the words "hereafter formed or"	9	2	
[406]	aye	aye		aye		no	aye	aye	aye	aye	no	no	no	To strike the words "limits" out & to insert "jurisdict."	7	4	
[407]	no	no		no		aye	no	aye	aye	no	no	no	no	To postpone the substitute to ye 17 article in order to take up the proposition from Maryland	3	8	
[408]	aye	aye		aye		no	aye	no	no	aye	aye	aye	aye	To agree to the substitute to ye 17 article as amended	8	3	
[409]	no	no		no		aye	no	no	aye	no		no	no	To agree to the amendmt offered by Maryland	2	8	
[410]	aye	aye		aye		aye	aye	aye	no	aye	aye	aye	aye		10	1	
[411]	no	no		no		aye	aye	aye	no	no	no	no	no	To strike out "on application of it's Legislature"	3	8	
[412]	no	no		no		aye	no	no	no	aye	aye	ay	aye	To insert "insurrections"	5	6	
[413][6]	aye	no		aye		aye	aye	aye		no	aye	aye	aye	To insert "or Executive"	8	2	1
[414]	no	no		no		no	no	no	aye	no	no	no	no	in the recess of the Legislature			
[415]	aye	aye		aye		aye	aye	no	no	aye	aye	aye	aye	To agree to ye 18 article as amended			
[416]	aye	aye		dd		aye	aye	aye	dd	aye	no	aye	aye	To agree to the 20 article	8	1	2
[417]	no	no		no		aye	no	aye	aye	no	no	no	no	To take up the report of the Committee of eleven	3	8	

[6] See footnote on p. 459.

It was moved and seconded to add the following clause to the last amendment

"in the recess of the Legislature"

which passed in the negative. [Ayes — 1; noes — 10.]

Separate questions being taken on the several clauses of the 18 article as amended

they passed in the affirmative [Ayes — 9; noes — 2][7]

On the question to agree to the 19 article as reported

it passed in the affirmative

It was moved or seconded to add the words "or affirmation" after the word "oath" 20 article

which passed in the affirmative.

On the question to agree to the 20 article as amended

it passed in the affirmative [Ayes — 8; noes — 1; divided — 2.]

It was moved and seconded to add the following clause to the 20 Article.

"But no religious test shall ever be required as a qualifica-"tion to any office or public trust under the authority of the "United States"

which passed unan: in the affirmative

It was moved and seconded to take up the report of the Committee of eleven.

which passed in the negative [Ayes — 3; noes — 8.]

The House adjourned

MADISON

Thursday August 30th. 1787. In Convention

Art XVII resumed for a question on it as amended by Mr. Govr. Morris's substitutes

Mr. Carrol moved to strike out so much of the article as requires the consent of the State to its being divided.[8] He was aware that the object of this prerequisite might be to prevent domestic disturbances, but such was our situation with regard to the Crown lands, and the sentiments of Maryland on that subject, that he perceived we should again be at sea, if no

[7] Vote 415, Detail of Ayes and Noes. Madison records this vote as on the last clause.

[8] Upon this debate, see Appendix A, CLVIII (92–99).

guard was provided for the right of the U. States to the back lands. He suggested that it might be proper to provide that nothing in the Constitution should affect the Right of the U. S. to lands ceded by G. Britain in the Treaty of peace, and proposed a committment to a member from each State. He assurred the House that this was a point of a most serious nature. It was desirable above all things that the act of the Convention might be agreed to unanimously. But should this point be disregarded, he believed that all risks would be run by a considerable minority, sooner than give their concurrence.

Mr. L. Martin 2ded. the motion for a committment.

Mr. Rutlidge is it to be supposed that the States are to be cut up without their own consent. The case of Vermont will probably be particularly provided for. There could be no room to fear, that Virginia or N— Carolina would call on the U. States to maintain their Government over the Mountains.

Mr. Williamson said that N. Carolina was well disposed to give up her Western lands, but attempts at compulsion was not the policy of the U. S. He was for doing nothing in the constitution in the present case, and for leaving the whole matter in Statu quo.

Mr Wilson was against the committment. Unanimity was of great importance, but not to be purchased by the majority's yielding to the minority. He should have no objection to leaving the case of New States as heretofore. He knew of nothing that would give greater or juster alarm than the doctrine, that a political society is to be torne asunder without its own consent—

On Mr. Carrol's motion for commitment

N. H. no[9] Mas. no. Ct. no. N. J. ay. Pa. no. Del— ay— Md. ay— Va. no— N— C. no. S. C. no. Geo. no. [Ayes — 3; noes — 8.]

Mr Sherman moved to postpone the substitute for art: XVII agreed to yesterday in order to take up the following amendment "The Legislature shall have power to admit

[9] New Hampshire's vote was changed from "ay" to "no". This may have been a later correction

other States into the Union, and new States to be formed by the division or junction of States now in the Union, with the consent of the Legislature of such State" (The first part was meant for the case of Vermont to secure its admission)

On the question, ⟨it passed in the Negative⟩

N. H. ay. Mas. ay. Ct. ay. N. J. no. Pa. ay. Del. no. Md. no. Va. no. N. C. no. S. C ay. Geo. no. [Ayes — 5; noes — 6.]

Docr. Johnson [10] moved to insert the words "hereafter formed or" after the words "shall be" in the substitute for art: XVII, (the more clearly to save Vermont as being already formed into a State, from a dependence on the consent of N. York to her admission.)

⟨The motion was agreed to Del. & Md. only dissenting.⟩ [11]

Mr Governr. Morris moved to strike out the word "limits" in the substitute, and insert the word "jurisdiction" (This also was meant to guard the case of Vermont, the jurisdiction of N. York not extending over Vermont which was in the exercise of sovereignty, tho' Vermont was within the asserted limits of New York)

On this question

N— H— ay— Mas— ay. Ct ay— N. J. no. Pa. ay. ⟨Del. ay⟩ [12] Md. ay. Va ay— N. C. no. S. C. no. Geo. no. [Ayes — 7; noes — 4.]

Mr. L. Martin, urged the unreasonableness of forcing & guaranteeing the people of Virginia beyond the Mountains, the Western people, of N. Carolina. & of Georgia, & the people of Maine, to continue under the States now governing them, without the consent of those States to their separation. Even if they should become the *majority*, the majority of *Counties*, as in Virginia may still hold fast the dominion over them. Again the majority may place [13] the seat of Government entirely among themselves & for their own conveniency, and still keep the injured parts of the States in subjection, under the guarantee of the Genl. Government

[10] A line preceding was crossed out: "The word 'limits' was struck out of". Notice the order of questions in the Journal.

[11] Taken from *Journal*.

[12] Probably taken from *Journal*.

[13] Crossed out "hold".

agst. domestic violence. He wished Mr Wilson had thought a little sooner of the value of *political* bodies.[14] In the beginning, when the rights of the small States were in question, they were phantoms, ideal beings. Now when the Great States were to be affected, political Societies were of a sacred nature. He repeated and enlarged on the unreasonableness of requiring the small States to guarantee the Western claims of the large ones. — It was said yesterday by Mr Govr Morris, that if the large States were to be split to pieces without their consent, their representatives here would take their leave. If the Small States are to be required to guarantee them in this manner, it will be found that the Representatives of other States will with equal firmness take their leave of the Constitution on the table.

It was moved by Mr. L. Martin to postpone the substituted article, in order to take up the following.[15]

"The Legislature of the U— S— shall have power to erect New States within as well as without the territory claimed by the several States or either of them, and admit the same into the Union: provided that nothing in this constitution shall be construed to affect the claim of the U— S. to vacant lands ceded to them by the late treaty of peace— which passed in the negative: ⟨N. J. Del. & Md. only ay.⟩[16]

On the question to agree to Mr. Govr. Morris's substituted article as amended in the words following,

"New States may be admitted by the Legislature into the Union: but no new State shall be hereafter formed or erected within the jurisdiction of any of the present States without the consent of the Legislature of such State as well as of the General Legislature"

N. H. ay. Mas. ay. Ct. ay. N. J— no— Pa. ay. Del. no. Md. no. Va. ay. N— C. ay— S. C— ay. Geo. ay. [Ayes — 8; noes — 3.]

---

[14] Crossed out "Counties".

[15] Crossed out after Martin's name "(*as understood*)". See above note 3. Martin records this motion in quite different words and gives New Hampshire's vote and Connecticut's vote in the affirmative, see Appendix A, CLVIII (96).

[16] Taken from *Journal;* see also note 15.

Mr. Dickinson moved to add the following clause to the last —

"Nor shall any State be formed by the junction of two or more States or parts thereof, without the consent of the Legislatures of such States, as well as of the Legislature of the U. States". which was agreed to without a count of the Votes.

Mr Carrol moved to add — "Provided nevertheless that nothing in this Constitution shall be construed to affect the claim of the U. S. to vacant lands ceded to them by the Treaty of peace". This he said might be understood as relating to lands not claimed by any particular States. but he had in view also some of the claims of particular States.

Mr. Wilson was agst. the motion. There was nothing in the Constitution affecting one way or the other the claims of the U. S. & it was best to insert nothing, leaving every thing on that litigated subject in statu quo.

Mr. Madison considered the claim of the U. S. as in fact favored by the jurisdiction of the Judicial power of the U— S— over controversies to which they should be parties. He thought it best on the whole to be silent on the subject. He did not view the proviso of Mr. Carrol as dangerous; but to make it neutral and fair, it ought to go farther & declare that the claims of particular States also should not be affected.

Mr. Sherman thought the proviso harmless, especially with the addition suggested by Mr. Madison in favor of the claims of particular States.

Mr. Baldwin did not wish any undue advantage to be given to Georgia. He thought the proviso proper with the addition proposed. It should be remembered that if Georgia has gained much by the Cession in the Treaty of peace, she was in danger during the war, of a Uti possidetis.

Mr. Rutlidge thought it wrong to insert a proviso where there was nothing which it could restrain, or on which it could operate.

Mr. Carrol withdrew his motion and moved the following,

"Nothing in this Constitution shall be construed to alter the claims of the U. S. or of the individual States to the West-

ern territory, but all such claims shall be examined into & decided upon, by the Supreme Court of the U. States."

Mr Govr Morris moved to postpone this in order to take up the following. "The Legislature shall have power to dispose of and make all needful rules and regulations respecting the territory or other property belonging to the U. States; and nothing in this constitution contained, shall be so construed as to prejudice any claims either of the U— S— or of any particular State," — The postponemt. agd. to nem. con.

Mr. L. Martin moved to amend the proposition of Mr Govr Morris by adding — "But all such claims may be examined into & decided upon by the supreme Court of the U— States".

Mr. Govr. Morris. this is unnecessary, as all suits to which the U. S— are parties— are already to be decided by the Supreme Court.

Mr. L. Martin, it is proper in order to remove all doubts on this point.

Question on Mr. L— Martin's amendatory motion

N— H— no. Mas— no. Ct. no. N. J. ay. Pa. no. Del. no. Md. ay. Va. no — States not farther called the negatives being sufficient & the point given up.[17]

The Motion of Mr. Govr. Morris was then agreed to, ⟨Md. alone dissenting.⟩[18]

Art: XVIII being taken up,[19] — the word "foreign" was struck out. ⟨nem: con: as superfluous, being implied in the term "invasion"⟩[20]

Mr. Dickinson moved to strike out "on the application of its Legislature against" He thought it of essential impor-

---

[17] See Vote 409, Detail of Ayes and Noes.

[18] "nem. con:" crossed out and this substituted from *Journal*. Probably a mistake, see below note 20, and above note 4.

[19] Article XVIII. "The United States shall guaranty to each State a Republican form of Government; and shall protect each State against foreign invasions, and, on the application of its Legislature, against domestic violence.

[20] Madison originally recorded: "nem: con: Maryland being in the negative. It was thought to be superfluous as implied in the term invasion". Apparently when he saw *Journal* ascribing Maryland's negative vote to another question, Madison modified his records accordingly. See above note 18.

tance to the tranquillity of the U— S. that they should in all cases suppress domestic violence, which may proceed from the State Legislature itself, or from disputes between the two branches where such exist

Mr. Dayton mentioned the Conduct of Rho. Island as shewing the necessity of giving latitude to the power of the U— S. on this subject.

On the question

N. H. no. Mas. no. Ct. no. N. J. ay. Pa. ay. Del. ay— Md. no. Va. no. N. C. no. S. C. no. Geo— no [Ayes — 3; noes — 8.]

On a question for striking out "domestic violence" ⟨and insertg. "insurrections" — it passed in the negative.⟩ N. H. no. Mas. no. Ct. no. N. J. ay. Pa. ⟨no⟩ Del no. Md. no. Va. ay. N. C. ay. S. C. ay. Geo. ay [Ayes — 5; noes — 6.][21]

Mr. Dickinson moved to insert the words, "or Executive" after the words "application of its Legislature" — The occasion itself he remarked might hinder the Legislature from meeting.

On this question

N. H. ay. Mas. no. Ct. ay. N. J. ay. Pa. ay. Del. ay. Md divd. Va. no. N. C. ay. S. C. ay. Geo. ay. [Ayes — 8; noes — 2; divided — 1.]

Mr. L— Martin moved to subjoin to the last amendment the words "in the recess of the Legislature" On which question

N. H. no. Mas. no. Ct. no. Pa. no. Del. no. Md. ay. Va. no. N. C. no. S. C. no. Geo— no. [Ayes — 1; noes —9.][22]

On Question on the last clause as amended

N. H. ay. Mas— ay. Ct. ay— N. J. ay— Pa. ay. Del. no. Md. no. Va. ay. N— C— ay— S— C. ay. Geo— ay, [Ayes — 9; noes — 2.]

Art: XIX taken up.[23]

---

[21] Madison originally recorded "Pa. ay." which would have determined the question in the affirmative. Later he made his record conform to *Journal.*

[22] The Journal includes New Jersey in the negative.

[23] Article XIX. "On the application of the Legislatures of two thirds of the States in the Union, for an amendment of this Constitution, the Legislature of the United States shall call a Convention for that purpose.

Mr. Govr. Morris suggested that the Legislature should be left at liberty to call a Convention, whenever they please.

The art: was agreed to nem: con:

Art: XX. taken up.[24] — "or affirmation" was added after "oath."

Mr. Pinkney. moved to add to the art: — "but no religious test shall ever be required as a qualification to any office or public trust under the authority of the U. States"[25]

Mr. Sherman thought it unnecessary, the prevailing liberality being a sufficient security agst. such tests.

Mr. Govr. Morris & Genl. Pinkney approved the motion,

The motion was agreed to nem: con: ⟨and then the whole Article, N— C. only no — & Md. divided.⟩[26]

Art: XXI. taken up. viz: "The ratifications of the Conventions of States shall be sufficient for organizing this Constitution."

Mr. Wilson proposed to fill the blank with "seven" that being a majority of the whole number & sufficient for the commencement of the plan.

Mr. Carrol moved to postpone the article in order to take up the Report of the Committee of Eleven (see Tuesday Augst: 28) — and on the question

N. H— no. Mas— no. Ct. no. N. J. ay. Pa. no. Del. ay. Md. ay. Va. no. N. C. no. S. C. no. Geo. no. [Ayes — 3; noes — 8.]

Mr. Govr. Morris thought the blank ought to be filled in a twofold way, so as to provide for the event of the ratifying States being contiguous which would render a smaller number sufficient, and the event of their being dispersed, which wd require a greater number for the introduction of the Government.

Mr. Sherman. observed that the States being now confederated by articles which require unanimity in changes, he

[24] Article XX. "The members of the Legislatures, and the Executive and Judicial officers of the United States, and of the several States, shall be bound by oath to support this Constitution."

[25] See Pinckney's proposal August 20, and Appendix A, CLVIII (100), CXCII CXCVI, CCVIII.

[26] Taken from *Journal*, which gives Connecticut's vote also as divided.

thought the ratification in this case of ten States at least ought to be made necessary.

Mr Randolph was for filling the blank with "Nine" that being a respectable majority of the whole, and being a number made familiar by the constitution of the existing Congress.

Mr Wilson mentioned "eight" as preferable.

Mr. Dickinson asked whether the concurrence of Congress is to be essential to the establishment of the system, whether the refusing States in the Confederacy could be deserted — and whether Congress could concur in contravening the system under which they acted?

Mr. Madison. remarked that if the blank should be filled with "seven" eight, or "nine" — the Constitution as it stands might be put in force over the whole body of the people. tho' less than a majority of them should ratify it.

Mr. Wilson. As the Constitution stands, the States only which ratify can be bound. We must he said in this case go to the original powers of Society, The House on fire must be extinguished, without a scrupulous regard to ordinary rights.

Mr. Butler was in favor of "nine". He revolted at the idea, that one or two States should restrain the rest from consulting their safety.

Mr. Carrol moved to fill the blank with "the thirteen". unanimity being necessary to dissolve the existing confederacy which had been unanimously established.

Mr King thought this amendt. necessary, otherwise as the Constitution now stands it will operate on the whole though ratified by a part only.

Adjourned

McHENRY

Augt. 30.

XVII article debated by Maryland obtained an alteration so that the claim of the U. S. to the Crown lands or Western territory may be decided upon by the supreme judiciary —

XVIIII agreed to.

Endeavoured to recall the house to the reported propositions from maryland, to prevent the U. S. from giving prefe[re]nces to one State above another or to the shipping of one State above another, in collecting or laying duties. — The house averse to taking any thing up till this system is got through. XXI. adjourned on this article.

Proposed to have a private conference with each other to-morrow before meeting of the convention to take measures for carrying out propositions. etc —

FRIDAY, AUGUST 31, 1787.

JOURNAL

Friday August 31. 1787.

It was moved and seconded to insert the words "between the said States" after the word "constitution" in the 20 [21][1] article

which passed in the affirmative [Ayes — 9; noes — 1.]

It was moved and seconded to postpone the consideration of the 20 [21][1] article to take up the reports of Committees which have not been acted on

which passed in the negative. [Ayes — 5; noes — 5; divided — 1.]

[To postpone the 21 to take up the 22 articles Ayes — 5; noes — 6.][2]

It was moved and seconded to strike the words "conventions of" out of the 21st article

which passed in the negative [Ayes — 4; noes — 6.]

It was moved and seconded to fill up the blank in the 21st article with the word "Thirteen"

which passed in the negative [Ayes — 1; noes — 9.]

It was moved and seconded to fill up the blank in the 21st article with the word "Ten"

which passed in the negative [Ayes — 4; noes — 7.]

It was moved and seconded to fill up the blank in the 21st article as follows.

"any seven or more States entitled to 33 Members at least "in the House of representatives according to the allotment "made in the 3rd sect. 4th article.

---

[1] Error due to misnumbering of printed Report of Committee of Detail. See August 6, note 5.

[2] Vote 420, Detail of Ayes and Noes, in which the summary of the vote is obviously incorrect.

It was moved and seconded to fill up the blank in the 21st article with the word "nine"

which passed in the affirmative [Ayes — 8; noes — 3.]

On the question to agree to the 21st article as amended.

it passed in the affirmative [Ayes — 10; noes — 1.]

It was moved and seconded to strike the words "for their approbation" out of the 22nd article

which passed in the affirmative [Ayes — 7; noes — 4.]

It was moved and seconded to agree to the following amendment to the 22nd article

"This Constitution shall be laid before the United States "in Congress assembled — and it is the opinion of this Con-"vention that it should afterwards be submitted to a Conven-"tion chosen in each State in order to receive the ratification "of such Convention: to which end the several Legislatures "ought to provide for the calling Conventions within their "respective States as speedily as circumstances will permit."

which passed in the negative [Ayes — 4; noes — 7.]

It was moved and seconded to postpone the consideration of the 22nd article

which passed in the negative. [Ayes — 3; noes — 8.]

On the question to agree to the 22nd article as amended.

it passed in the affirmative [Ayes — 10; noes — 1.]

It was moved and seconded to fill up the blank in the 23rd article with the word "Nine"

which passed in the affirmative

It was moved and seconded to agree to the 23rd article as far as the words

"assigned by Congress" inclusive

which passed in the affirmative

It was moved and seconded to postpone the remainder of the 23rd article

which passed in the negative [Ayes — 4; noes — 7.]

It was moved and seconded to strike the words

"choose the President of the United States and" out of the 23rd article

which passed in the affirmative [Ayes — 8; noes — 2; divided — 1.]

On the question to agree to the 23rd article as amended.

it passed in the affirmative

It was moved and seconded to take up the report of the Committee of eleven entered on the journal of the 28th instant

On the question to agree to the following clause of the report, to be inserted after the 4th section of the 7th article,

"nor shall any regulation of commerce or revenue give "preference to the ports of One State over those of another"

it passed in the affirmative

On the question to agree to the following clause of the report

"or oblige Vessels bound to or from any State to enter "clear or pay duties in another"

it passed in the affirmative [Ayes — 8; noes — 2.][3]

It was moved and seconded to strike out the word "tonnage"

which passed in the affirmative.

On the question to agree to the following clause of the report

"and all duties, imposts, and excises, laid by the Legisla-"ture, shall be uniform throughout the United States"

it passed in the affirmative

It was moved and seconded to refer such parts of the Constitution as have been postponed, and such parts of reports as have not been acted on to a Committee of a Member from each State

which passed in the affirmative

and a Committee was appointed by ballot of The honorable Mr Gilman, Mr King, Mr Sherman, Mr Brearley, Mr G. Morris, Mr Dickinson, Mr Carrol, Mr Madison, Mr Williamson, Mr Butler and Mr Baldwin.

The House adjourned.[4]

---

[3] Vote 432, Detail of Ayes and Noes. *Journal* (p. 318) mistakenly ascribes this vote to the second question following.

[4] *Journal* (p. 319) inserts here Vote 433, Detail of Ayes and Noes; but this probably belongs in *Records* of September 1.

DETAIL OF AYES AND NOES

	New Hampshire	Massachusetts	Rhode Island	Connecticut	New York	New Jersey	Pennsylvania	Delaware	Maryland	Virginia	No Carolina	So Carolina	Georgia	Questions	ayes	noes	divided
[418]	aye	aye		aye		aye	aye		no	aye	aye	aye	aye	To add the words "between the said States" to ye 21 article	9	1	
[419]	aye	no		dd		no	aye	aye	aye	no	no	no	aye	To postpone the 20 article to take up reports of Committees	5	5	1
[420]	no	no		aye		no	aye	aye	aye	aye	no	no	no	To postpone the 21 to take up the 22 articles	5	5	
[421]	no	no		aye		no	aye	no	aye	no		no	aye	To strike out the words "the Conventions of"	4	6	
[422]	no	no		no		no	no	no	aye	no		no	no	To fill up the blank with "thirteen 21 article 13.			
[423]	no	no		aye		aye	no	no	aye	no	no	no	aye	to fill up "Ten	4	7	
[424]	aye	aye		aye		aye	aye	aye	aye	no	no	no	aye	To fill up the blank in the 21 article wh "nine"	8	3	
[425]	aye	aye		aye		aye	aye	aye	no	aye	aye	aye	aye	To agree to the 21 article as amended	10	1	
[426]	aye	no		aye		no	aye	aye	no	aye	aye	aye	no	To strike out "for their approbation" 22 article	7	4	
[427]	aye	aye		no		no	aye	aye	no	no	no	no	no	To agree to the amendmt offered to ye 22 article	4	7	
[428]	no	no		no		aye	no	no	aye	no	aye	no	no	To postpone the 22 article.	3	8	
[429]	aye	aye		aye		aye	aye	aye	no	aye	aye	aye	aye	To agree to ye 22 article as amended	10	1	
[430]	no	aye		no		no	no	aye	no	aye	aye	no	no	To postpone the latter clause of ye 23 article	4	7	
[431]	no	aye		aye		aye	aye	aye	dd	aye	aye	no	aye	To strike out the words choose the Presidt of the U. S. and"			
[432]	no			aye		aye	aye	aye	aye	aye	aye	no	aye	To agree to the 2nd clause of the report Committee of eleven.	8	2	

MADISON

Friday August 31st. 1787. In Convention.

Mr. King moved to add to the end of art: XXI the words "between the said States" so as to confine the operation of the Govt. to the States ratifying it.

On the question

N. H. ay. Mas. ay. Ct. ay. N— J— ay. Pa. ay. Md. no. Virga. ay. N. C. ay. ⟨S. C. ay.⟩[5] Geo. ay. [Ayes — 9; noes — 1.]

Mr. Madison proposed to fill the blank in the article with "Any seven or more States entitled to thirty three members at least in the House of Representatives according to the allotment made in the 3 Sect: of art: 4." This he said would require the concurrence of a majority of both the States and people.

Mr. Sherman doubted the propriety of authorizing less than all the States to execute the Constitution, considering the nature of the existing Confederation. Perhaps all the States may concur, and on that supposition it is needless to hold out a breach of faith.

Mr. Clymer and Mr. Carrol moved to postpone the consideration of Art: XXI in order to take up the Reports of Committees not yet acted on— On this question, ⟨the States were equally divided.⟩ N. H. ay. Mas. no. Ct. divd. N. J— no. Pa. ay— Del— ay. Md. ay. Va. no. N. C no. S. C. no. G. ay. [Ayes — 5; noes — 5; divided — 1.]

Mr Govr. Morris[6] moved to strike out "Conventions of the" after "ratifications". leaving the States to pursue their own modes of ratification.

Mr. Carrol mentioned the mode of altering the Constitution of Maryland pointed out therein, and that no other mode could be pursued in that State.

---

[5] Taken from *Journal*.

[6] A line preceding was crossed out: "A motion was then made & rejected, for postponing art. XXI, in order to take up art. XXII." Copied from *Journal*, but Madison afterwards found that he had the same record a little farther on.

Mr. King thought that striking out "Conventions". as the requisite mode was equivalent to giving up the business altogether. Conventions alone, which will avoid all the obstacles from the complicated formation of the Legislatures, will succeed, and if not positively required by the plan, its enemies will oppose that mode.

Mr. Govr. Morris said he meant to facilitate the adoption of the plan, by leaving the modes approved by the several State Constitutions to be followed.

Mr. Madison considered it best to require Conventions; Among other reasons, for this, that the powers given to the Genl. Govt. being taken from the State Govts the Legislatures would be more disinclined than conventions composed in part at least of other men; and if disinclined, they could devise modes apparently promoting, but really. thwarting the ratification. The difficulty in Maryland was no greater than in other States, where no mode of change was pointed out by the Constitution, and all officers were under oath to support it. The people were in fact, the fountain of all power, and by resorting to them, all difficulties were got over. They could alter constitutions as they pleased. It was a principle in the Bills of rights, that first principles might be resorted to.

Mr. McHenry said that the officers of Govt. in Maryland were under oath to support the mode of alteration prescribed by the Constitution.

Mr Ghorum urged the expediency of "Conventions" also Mr. Pinkney, for reasons, formerly urged on a discussion of this question.

Mr. L. Martin insisted on a reference to the State Legislatures. He urged the danger of commotions from a resort to the people & to first principles in which the Governments might be on one side & the people on the other. He was apprehensive of no such consequences however in Maryland, whether the Legislature or the people should be appealed to. Both of them would be generally against the Constitution. He repeated also the peculiarity in the Maryland Constitution.

Mr. King observed that the Constitution of Massachusetts

was made unalterable till the year 1790, yet this was no difficulty with him. The State must have contemplated a recurrence to first principles before they sent deputies to this Convention.

Mr. Sherman moved to postpone art. XXI. & to take up art: XXII on which question,

N. H. no. Mas. no. Ct. ay— N. J. no— P. ay— Del— ay— Md ay. Va. ay. ⟨N. C. no⟩[7] S. C. no— Geo— no— [Ayes — 5; noes — 6.]

On Mr Govr. Morris's motion to strike out "Conventions of the," ⟨it was negatived.⟩

N. H. no. Mas. no. Ct. ay. N. J. no. Pa ay. Del. no. Md. ay— Va no— S— C no— Geo. ay. [Ayes — 4; noes — 6.]

On filling the blank ⟨in Art: XXI⟩ with "thirteen" moved by Mr. Carrol, & L. Martin

N. H. no. Mas. no. Ct. no. — All no— except Maryland.

Mr. Sherman & Mr. Dayton moved to fill the blank with "ten"

Mr. Wilson supported the motion of Mr. Madison, requiring a majority both of the people and of States.[8]

Mr Clymer was also in favor of it.

Col: Mason was for preserving ideas familiar to the people. Nine States had been required in all great cases under the Confederation & that number was on that account preferable

On the question for "ten"

N. H. no. Mas. no. Ct ay. N. J— ay. Pa. no. Del— no. Md. ay. Va. no. N. C. no. S. C. no. Geo. ay. [Ayes — 4; noes — 7.]

On question for "nine"

N— H. ay. Mas. ay. Ct. ay— N— J. ay. Pa. ay— Del. ay. Md. ay— Va. no. N. C. no. S. C. no. Geo— ay, [Ayes—8; noes—3.]

Art: XXI. ⟨ as amended⟩ was then agreed to by all the States, Maryland excepted, & Mr. Jenifer being, ay—[9]

---

[7] Taken from *Journal*.

[8] Crossed out "to fill the blank with any seven or more States containing a majority".

[9] See further Appendix A, XLI, LXIX, LXXVI, LXXXI, CXXXIX, CLVIII (101–106), CLXXXIX, CXCII, CXCIX, CCV, CCXXX.

Art. XXII taken up, to wit, "This Constitution shall be laid before the U— S. in Congs. assembled for their approbation; and it is the opinion of this Convention that it should be afterwards submitted to a Convention chosen, ⟨in each State⟩ under the recommendation of its Legislature, in order to receive the ratification of such Convention"

Mr. Govr. Morris & Mr. Pinkney moved to strike out the words "for their approbation"[10] On this question

N. H. ay. Mas. no. Ct. ay. N—J. ay.* Pa. ay. Del. ay. Md. no Va. ay. N. C— ay. S. C— ay. Geo. no. [Ayes — 8; noes — 3.]

Mr Govr. Morris & Mr. Pinkney then moved to amend the art: so as to read

"This Constitution shall be laid before the U. S. in Congress assembled; and it is the opinion of this Convention that it should afterwards be submitted to a Convention chosen in each State, in order to receive the ratification of such Convention: to which end the several Legislatures ought to provide for the calling Conventions within their respective States as speedily as circumstances will permit". — Mr. Govr. Morris said his object was to impress in stronger terms the necessity of calling Conventions in order to prevent enemies to the plan, from giving it the go by. When it first appears, with the sanction of this Convention, the people will be favorable to it. By degrees the State officers, & those interested in the State Govts will intrigue & turn the popular current against it.[11]

Mr. L— Martin believed Mr. Morris to be right, that after a while the people would be agst. it. but for a different reason from that alledged. He believed they would not ratify it unless hurried into it by surprize.

Mr. Gerry enlarged on the idea of Mr. L. Martin in which he concurred, represented the system as full of vices, and dwelt on the impropriety of destroying the existing Confederation, without the unanimous Consent of the parties to it:

* ⟨In the printed Journal N— Jersey— no.⟩

[10] See Appendix A, CLVIII (103).

[11] See Appendix A, CXCII.

Question on Mr Govr. Morris's and Mr. Pinckney's motion

N. H— ay. Mas. ay. Ct no. N— J. no. Pa. ay. Del— ay. Md. no. Va no. N— C— no— S— C. no. Geo. no— [Ayes — 4; noes — 7.]

Mr. Gerry moved to postpone art: XXII.

Col: Mason 2ded. the motion, declaring that he would sooner chop off his right hand than put it to the Constitution as it now stands. He wished to see some points not yet decided brought to a decision, before being compelled to give a final opinion on this article. Should these points be improperly settled, his wish would then be to bring the whole subject before another general Convention.

Mr. Govr Morris was ready for a postponement. He had long wished for another Convention, that will have the firmness to provide a vigorous Government, which we are afraid to do.

Mr. Randolph stated his idea to be, in case the final form of the Constitution should not permit him to accede to it, that the State Conventions should be at liberty to propose amendments to be submitted to another General Convention which may reject or incorporate them, as shall be judged proper.

On the question for postponing

N. H. no. Mas. no. Ct no. N. J— ay— Pa. no. Del. no. Md ay— Va. no. N. C. ay. S— C. no. Geo. no. [Ayes — 3; noes — 8.]

On the question on Art: XXII

N. H. ⟨ay.⟩[12] Mas. ay. Ct. ay. N. J. ay. Pa. ay— Del. ay. Md. no. Va ay. N— C. ay. S— C. ay. Geo. ay. [Ayes — 10; noes — 1.]

Art: XXIII being taken up.[13] as far the words "assigned

[12] Apparently Madison left a blank after "N. H." and later inserted an affirmative vote according to *Journal*.

[13] Article XXIII. "To introduce this government, it is the opinion of this Convention, that each assenting Convention should notify its assent and ratification to the United States in Congress assembled; that Congress, after receiving the assent and ratification of the Conventions of States, should appoint and publish a day, as early as may be, and appoint a place for commencing proceedings under this Constitution; that after such publication, the Legislatures of the several States should

by Congress" inclusive, was agreed to nem: con: the blank having been first filled with the word "nine" as of course.

On a motion for postponing the residue of the clause, concerning the choice of the President &c,

N. H. no. Mas. ay. Ct. no. N— J. no. Pa. no. Del. ay. Md. no. Va. ay. N. C. ay. S— C. no. Geo. no. [Ayes — 4; noes — 7.]

Mr. Govr. Morris then moved to strike out the words "choose the President of the U. S. and" — this point, of choosing the President not being yet finally determined, & on this question

N— H— no. Mas. ay. Ct. ay. N. J. ay. Pa. ay. Del. ay. Md. divd. Va. ay. N— C. ay— S. C. ay—* Geo. ay [Ayes—9; noes — 1; divided — 1.]

Art: XXIII as amended was then agreed to nem: con:

The report of the grand Committee of eleven made by Mr. Sherman was then taken up (see Aug: 28).

On the question to agree to the following clause, to be inserted after sect— 4. art: VII. "nor shall any regulation of commerce or revenue give preference to the ports of one State over those of another".[14] Agreed to nem: con:

On the clause "or oblige vessels bound to or from any State to enter clear or pay duties in another"

Mr. Madison thought the restriction wd. be inconvenient, as in the River Delaware, if a vessel cannot be required to make entry below the jurisdiction of Pennsylvania.

Mr. Fitzimmons admitted that it might be inconvenient, but thought it would be a greater inconveniency to require vessels bound to Philada. to enter below the jurisdiction of the State.

Mr. Gorham & Mr. Langdon, contended that the Govt would be so fettered by this clause, as to defeat the good pur-

* ⟨In the printed Journal- S. C. — no.⟩

elect members of the Senate, and direct the election of members of the House of Representatives; and that the members of the Legislature should meet at the time and place assigned by Congress, and should, as soon as may be, after their meeting, choose the President of the United States, and proceed to execute this Constitution."

[14] See August 25, note 13.

pose of the plan. They mentioned the situation of the trade of Mas. & N. Hampshire, the case of Sandy Hook which is in the State of N. Jersey, but where precautions agst smuggling into N. York, ought to be established by the Genl. Government.

Mr. McHenry said the clause would not shreen a vessel from being obliged to take an officer on board as a security for due entry &c—.

Mr Carrol was anxious that the clause should be agreed to. He assured the House, that this was a tender point in Maryland.

Mr Jenifer urged the necessity of the clause in the same point of view

On the question for agreeing to it

N. H. no. Ct ay. N. J. ay. Pa. ay. Del. ay. Md ay. Va. ay. N— C— ay. S— C. no. Geo. ay, [Ayes — 8; noes — 2.][15]

The word "tonnage" was struck out, nem: con: as comprehended in "duties"

On question On the clause of the Report "and all duties, imposts & excises, laid by the Legislature shall be uniform throughout the U. S." It was agreed to nem: con: *

On motion of Mr. Sherman it was agreed to refer such parts of the Constitution as have been postponed, and such parts of Reports as have not been acted on, to a Committee of a member from each State; the Committee appointed by ballot, being— Mr Gilman, Mr. King. Mr Sherman. Mr. Brearley, Mr. Govr. Morris, Mr. Dickinson, Mr. Carrol, Mr. Madison, Mr. Williamson, Mr. Butler & Mr. Baldwin.

(The House adjourned)

* ⟨In printed Journal N H. and S. C. entered as in the negative.⟩[16]

[15] McHenry includes Massachusetts in the negative.

[16] An error of *Journal*. See above note 3.

McHENRY

Augt. 31.

Filled up the blank in the XXI article with 9: 8 States afirm: 3 Neg. Maryland moved to fill it up with 13 but stood alone on the question. G. W. was for 7.

Struck out *for their approbation* in the 22 Article. filled up the blank in the 23 article with 9, and amended the last clause by striking out *choose the president of the U. S. and.*

The system being thus far agreed to the restrictory propositions from Maryland were taken up — and carried — against them N. Hamp. Massachus.[17] and S. Carolina.

Refered to a grand committee all the sections of the system under postponement and a report of a committee of 5 with several motions.

Adjourned.

[17] Massachusetts's vote was not recorded by the Journal or Madison.

SATURDAY, SEPTEMBER 1, 1787.

JOURNAL

Saturday September 1. 1787.

The honorable Mr Brearley from the Committee of eleven to whom such parts of the Constitution, as have been postponed, and such parts of reports, as have not been acted on, were referred — informed the House that the Committee were prepared to report partially —

The following report was then read "That in lieu of the 9th section of the 6th article the following be inserted

The Members of each House shall be ineligible to any civil Office under the authority of the United States during the time for which they shall respectively be elected —And no Person holding any office under the United States shall be a Member of either House during his continuance in office.

The honorable Mr Rutledge from the Committee to whom sundry propositions, entered on the Journal of the 28th ultimo were referred, informed the House that the Committee were prepared to report. — The following report was then read.

That the following additions be made to the report vizt

after the word "States" in the last line on the margin of the 3rd page,[1] add

"To establish uniform laws on the subject of bankrupt-"cies" — and insert the following as the 16th article vizt.

"Full faith and credit ought to be given in each State to "the public Acts, Records, and Judicial proceedings of every "other State, and the Legislature shall by general laws pre-

---

[1] Article VII, Section 1 (relating to the powers of Congress) had been amended (August 21–23) by adopting a modified report of a committee upon "state debts" and "militia", and this amendment had apparently been written in the margin of the printed Report of the Committee of Detail.

"scribe the manner in which such acts, records, and proceed-"ings shall be proved, and the effect which judgments obtained "in one State shall have in another.

It was moved and seconded to adjourn [Ayes — 7; noes — 1; divided — 1.][2]

The House adjourned till Monday next at 10 o'clock A. M.

Detail of Ayes and Noes

	New Hampshire	Massachusetts	Rhode Island	Connecticut	New York	New Jersey	Pennsylvania	Delaware	Maryland	Virginia	No Carolina	So Carolina	Georgia	Questions	ayes	noes	divided
[433]	dd	aye		no				aye	aye	aye	aye	aye	aye	To adjourn			

MADISON

Saturday Sepr. 1. 1787. In Convention.

Mr. Brearley from the Comme. of eleven to which were referred yesterday, the postponed part of the Constitution, & parts of Reports not acted upon, made the following partial report.

That in lieu of the 9th. sect: of art: 6. the words following be inserted viz "The members of each House shall be ineligible to any civil office under the authority of the U. S. during the time for which they shall respectively be elected, and no person holding an office under the U. S. shall be a member of either House during his continuance in office."

Mr Rutlidge from the Committee to whom were referred sundry propositions (see Aug: 29), together with art: XVI, reported that the following additions be made to the Report — viz.

After the word "States" in the last line on the Margin of the 3d. page (see the printed Report)[3] — add "to establish uniform laws on the subject of Bankruptcies"

and insert the following as Art: XVI — viz

[2] Vote 433, Detail of Ayes and Noes. *Journal* (p. 319) assigns this to the records of August 31.

[3] See above, note 1.

"Full faith and credit ought to be given in each State to the public acts, records, and Judicial proceedings of every other State, and the Legislature shall by general laws prescribe the manner in which such acts, Records, & proceedings shall be proved, and the effect which Judgments obtained in one State, shall have in another".

After receiving these reports

The House adjourned to 10 oC. on Monday next [4]

McHENRY

Septmbr. 1.

Adjourned to let the committee *sit.*

[4] See further, Appendix A, XCIX, C.

MONDAY, SEPTEMBER 3, 1787.

JOURNAL

Monday Septr 3rd 1787.

It was moved and seconded to strike out the words

"judgments obtained in one State shall have in another" and to insert the word "thereof" after the word "effect" in the report from the Committee of five entered on the Journal of the 1st instant

which passed in the affirmative [Ayes — 6; noes — 3.]

It was moved and seconded to strike out the words "ought to" and to insert the word "shall" and to strike out the word "shall" and to insert the word "may" in the report entered on the Journal of the 1st instant.

which passed in the affirmative.

On the question to agree to the report amended as follows.

Full faith and credit shall be given in each State to the public Acts, records, and judicial proceedings of every other State, and the Legislature may by general laws prescribe the manner in which such acts, records, and proceedings shall be proved and the effect thereof"

which passed in the affirmative

On the question to agree to the following clause of the report

"To establish uniform laws on the subject of bankruptcies"

it passed in the affirmative [Ayes — 9; noes — 1.]

[To adjourn Ayes — 2; noes — 8.][2]

It was moved and seconded to postpone the consideration of the report from Committee of eleven entered on the Journal of the 1st instant, in order to take up the following

---

[1] Vote 434, Detail of Ayes and Noes, which notes that this was "Mr. Morris's amendmt".

[2] Vote 436, Detail of Ayes and Noes.

The Members of each House shall be incapable of holding any office under the United States for which they or any other for their benefit receive any salary, fees, or emoluments of any kind and the acceptance of such office shall vacate their seats respectively

On the question to postpone

it passed in the negative. [Ayes — 2; noes — 8.]

[To adjourn Ayes — 4; noes — 6.][3]

It was moved and seconded to insert the word "created" before the word "during" in the report of the Committee of eleven

which passed in the negative [Ayes — 5; noes — 5.]

It was moved and seconded to insert the words "created or the emoluments whereof shall have been encreased" before the word "during" in the report of the Committee.

which passed in the affirmative [Ayes—5; noes—4; divided — 1.]

[on the last question Ayes — 5; noes — 3; divided — 1.][4]

Separate questions having been taken on the report as amended they passed in the affirmative

and the report, as amended, is as follows

"The Members of each House shall be ineligible to any "civil office under the authority of the United States created, "or the emoluments whereof shall have been encreased dur-"ing the time for which they shall respectively be elected — "and no person holding any office under the United States "shall be a Member of either House during his continuance "in Office."

The House then adjourned.

---

[3] Vote 438, Detail of Ayes and Noes.

[4] Vote 441, Detail of Ayes and Noes.

DETAIL OF AYES AND NOES

	New Hampshire	Massachusetts	Rhode Island	Connecticut	New York	New Jersey	Pennsylvania	Delaware	Maryland	Virginia	No Carolina	So Carolina	Georgia	Questions	ayes	noes	divided
[434]		aye		aye		aye	aye		no	no	aye	aye	no	To agree to Mr Morris's amendmt to the report of the Come of five.	6	3	
[435]	aye	aye		no		aye	aye		aye	aye	aye	aye	aye	To establish uniform laws on the subject of bankruptcies	9	1	
[436]	no	no		no		no	no		aye	aye	no	no	no	To adjourn	2	8	
[437]	no	no		no		no	aye		no	no	aye	no	no		2	8	
[438]	no	no		no		no	aye		aye	aye	aye	no	no	To adjourn	4	6	
[439]	aye	aye		no		no	aye		no	aye	aye	no	no	To agree to the amendment "created"	5	5	
[440]	aye	aye		no		no	aye		no	aye	aye	no	dd	"created, or the emoluments whereof shall have been encreased"	5	4	1
[441]	aye	aye		no			aye		no	aye	aye	no	dd	on the last question	5	3	1

MADISON

Monday Sepr. 3. 1787. In Convention

Mr. Govr. Morris moved to amend the Report concerning the respect to be paid to Acts Records &c of one State, in other States (see Sepr. 1.) by striking out "judgments obtained in one State shall have in another" and to insert the word "thereof" after the word "effect"

Col: Mason favored the motion, particularly if the "effect" was to be restrained to judgments & Judicial proceedings

Mr. Wilson remarked, that if the Legislature were not allowed to *declare the effect* the provision would amount to nothing more than what now takes place among all Independent Nations.

Docr. Johnson thought the amendment as worded would authorize the Genl. Legislature to declare the effect of Legislative acts of one State, in another State.

Mr. Randolph considered it as strengthening the general

objection agst. the plan, that its definition of the powers of the Government was so loose as to give it opportunities of usurping all the State powers. He was for not going farther than the Report, which enables the Legislature to provide for the effect of *Judgments.*

On the amendment as moved by Mr Govr. Morris Mas. ay. Ct ay. N. J. ay. Pa. ay. Md. no. Va no. N. C. ay. S. C. ay. Geo. no. [Ayes — 6; noes — 3.][5]

On motion of Mr. Madison, "ought to" was struck out, and "shall" inserted; and "shall" between "Legislature" & "by general laws" struck out, and "may" inserted, nem: con:

On the question to agree to the report as amended viz "Full faith & credit shall be given in each State to the public acts, records & judicial proceedings of every other State, and the Legislature may by general laws prescribe the manner in which such acts records & proceedings[6] shall be proved, and the effect thereof" Agreed to witht. a count of Sts.

The clause in the Report "To establish uniform laws on the subject of Bankruptcies" being taken up.

Mr. Sherman observed that Bankruptcies were in some cases punishable with death by the laws of England— & He did not chuse to grant a power by which that might be done here.

Mr Govr Morris said this was an extensive & delicate subject. He would agree to it because he saw no danger of abuse of the power by the Legislature of the U— S.

On the question to agree to the clause

N. H. ay. Mas. ay. Ct. no. N. J— ay— Pa. ay. Md ay. Va. ay. N. C. ay. S. C. ay— Geo. ay. [Ayes — 9; noes — 1.]

Mr. Pinkney moved to postpone the Report of the Committee of Eleven (see Sepr. 1) in order to take up the following,

"The members of each House shall be incapable of holding any office under the U— S— for which they or any other for their benefit, receive any salary, fees or emoluments of

[5] Crossed out "N. H. ay— " and "Del. —".

[6] Crossed out: "judicial".

any kind, and the acceptance of such office shall vacate their seats respectively."[7] He was strenuously opposed to an ineligibility of members to office, and therefore wished to restrain the proposition to a mere incompatibility. He considered the eligibility of members of the Legislature to the honorable offices of Government, as resembling the policy of the Romans, in making the temple of virtue the road to the temple of fame.

On this question

N. H. no. Mas. no. Ct no— N— J. no. Pa ay. Md. no Va. no. N. C. ay. S. C— no. Geo. no. [Ayes — 2; noes — 8.]

Mr King moved to insert the word "created" before the word "during" in the Report of the Committee. This he said would exclude[8] the members of the first Legislature under the Constitution, as most of the Offices wd. then be created.

Mr. Williamson 2ded. the motion,[9] He did not see why members of the Legislature should be ineligible to *vacancies* happening during the term of their election,[10]

Mr Sherman was for entirely incapacitating members of the Legislature. He thought their eligibility to offices would give too much influence to the Executive. He said the incapacity ought at least to be extended to cases where salaries should be *increased*, as well as *created*, during the term of the member. He mentioned also the expedient by which the restriction could be evaded to wit: an existing officer might be translated to an office created, and a member of the Legislature be then put into the office vacated.

Mr Govr. Morris contended that the eligibility of members to office wd. lessen the influence of the Executive. If they cannot be appointed themselves, the Executive will appoint their relations & friends, retaining the service & votes of

[7] Upon this subject see above, Virginia Plan, May 29, June 12, June 22–23, June 26, Report of Committee of Detail, August 14, September 1, and Appendix A, CXLVI*a*, CLVIII (40–42), CXCI, CCX, CCXXXVI, CCLXXVII.

[8] Crossed out "most who".

[9] Crossed out "tho'".

[10] Crossed out "since they could not be influenced by an event wht. was in this contingency."

the members for his purposes in the Legislature. Whereas the appointment of the members deprives him of such an advantage.

Mr. Gerry. thought the eligibility of members would have the effect of opening batteries agst. good officers, in order to drive them out & make way for members of the Legislature.

Mr Gorham was in favor of the amendment. Without it we go further than has been done in any of the States, or indeed any other Country, The experience of the State Governments where there was no such ineligibility, proved that it was not necessary; on the contrary that the eligibility was among the inducements for fit men to enter into the Legislative service

Mr. Randolph was inflexibly fixed against inviting men into the Legislature by the prospect of being appointed to offices.

Mr. Baldwin remarked that the example of the States was not applicable. The Legislatures there are so numerous that an exclusion of their members would not leave proper men for offices. The case would be otherwise in the General Government.

Col: Mason. Instead of excluding merit, the ineligibility will keep out corruption, by excluding office-hunters.

Mr. Wilson considered the exclusion of members of the Legislature as increasing the influence of the Executive as observed by Mr Govr Morris at the same time that it would diminish, the general energy of the Government. He said that the legal disqualification for office would be odious to those who did not wish for office, but did not wish either to be marked by so degrading a distinction —

Mr Pinkney. The first Legislature will be composed of the ablest men to be found. The States will select such to put the Government into operation. Should the Report of the Committee or even the amendment be agreed to, The great offices, even those of the Judiciary Deparment which are to continue for life, must be filled whilst those most capable of filling them will be under a disqualification

On the question on Mr. King's motion

N— H. ay. Mas. ay— Ct. no. N. J. no. Pa. ay. Md. no. Va. ay N— C. ay. S— C. no. Geo— no. [Ayes — 5; noes — 5.]

The amendment being thus lost by the equal division of the States, Mr Williamson moved to insert the words "created or the emoluments whereof shall have been increased" before the word "during" in the Report of the Committee

Mr. King 2ded. the motion. &

On the question

N— H— ay— Mas— ay— Ct. no. N— J. no. Pa. ay. Md. no. Va. ay. N— C. ay. S. C. no. Geo— divided. [Ayes — 5; noes — 4; divided — 1.]

The last clause rendering a Seat in the Legislature & an office incompatible was agreed to nem: con:

The Report as amended & agreed to is as follows.

"The members of each House shall be ineligible to any Civil office under the authority of the U. States, created, or the emoluments whereof shall have been increased during the time for which they shall respectively be elected — And no person holding any office under the U. S. shall be a member of either House during his continuance in office."

Adjourned

TUESDAY, SEPTEMBER 4, 1787.

JOURNAL

Tuesday September 4th

The honorable Mr Brearley from the Committee of eleven informed the House that the Committee were prepared to report partially — He then read the report in his place; it was afterwards delivered in at the Secretary's table — and was again read: and is as follows.[1]

The Committee of eleven to whom sundry resolutions &ca were referred on the 31st ultimo, report that in their opinion the following additions and alterations should be made to the report before the Convention — viz

The first clause of the first Sect. of the 7th article to read as follows. "The Legislature shall have power to lay and collect taxes, duties, imposts, and excises, to pay the debts and provide for the common defence and general welfare of the United States.

At the end of 2nd clause of the 1st sect. 7 art. add "and with the Indian tribes.

In the place of the 9 article 1st sect. to be inserted

"The Senate of the United States shall have power to try all impeachments; but no person shall be convicted without the concurrence of two thirds of the Members present.

after the word Excellency in the 1st sect 10 article to be inserted "He shall hold his office during the term of four years, and together with the Vice President, chosen for the same term, be elected in the following manner.

Each State shall appoint in such manner as it's Legisla-

---

[1] In this report in the Journal there are four penciled interlineations in another handwriting than that of the Secretary. Those are indicated in the present text by enclosing in angle brackets. See Madison's note, below.

ture may direct, a number of Electors equal to the whole number of Senators, and Members of the House of representatives to which the State may be entitled in the legislature.

The Electors shall meet in their respective States, and vote by ballot for two Persons, of whom one at least shall not be an inhabitant of the same State with themselves. — and they shall make a list of all the Persons voted for, and of the number of votes for each, which list they shall sign and certify, and transmit sealed to the seat of the general Government, directed to the President of the Senate.

The President of the Senate shall in that House open all the certificates, and the votes shall be then and there counted — The Person having the greatest number of votes shall be the President, if such number be a majority of ⟨the whole number⟩[2] of the Electors ⟨appointed⟩[3] and if there be more than One, who have such Majority, and have an equal number of votes, then the Senate shall ⟨immediately⟩[4] choose by ballot one of them for President: but if no Person have a majority, then from the five highest on the list, the Senate shall choose by ballot the President — and in every case after the choice of the President, the Person having the greatest number of votes shall be Vice President: but if there should remain two or more, who have equal votes, the Senate shall choose from them the Vice President.

The Legislature may determine the time of chusing and assembling the Electors, and the manner of certifying and transmitting their votes.

Sect. 2. No Person except a natural born Citizen, or a Citizen of the U. S. at the time of the adoption of this Constitution shall be eligible to the office of President: nor shall any Person be elected to that office, who shall be under the age of 35 years, and who has not been in the whole, at least 14 years a resident within the U. S.

---

[2] In place of "that" crossed out. None of the other copies of this report includes the words "the whole number", but there seems to be no record of a later amendment inserting them.

[3] "appointed", an amendment of September 5.

[4] "immediately", an amendment of September 6.

Sect. 3. The Vice President shall be ex officio, President of the Senate, except when they sit to try the impeachment of the President, in which case the Chief Justice shall preside, and excepting also when he shall exercise the powers and duties of President, in which case, and in case of his absence, the Senate shall chuse a President pro tempore — The Vice President when acting as President of the Senate shall not have a vote unless the House be equally divided

Sect. 4. The President by and with the advice and consent of the Senate, shall have power to make treaties: and he shall nominate and by and with the advice and consent of the Senate shall appoint Ambassadors and other public Ministers, Judges of the supreme Court, and all other officers of the U. S. whose appointments are not otherwise herein provided for. But no Treaty ⟨except Treaties of Peace⟩[5] shall be made without the consent of two thirds of the Members present

after the words "into the service of the U. S. in the 2 sect. 10 art. add "and may require the opinion in writing of the principal officer in each of the executive departments, upon any subject relating to the duties of their respective offices.

The latter part of the 2 sect 10 art to read as follows.

He shall be removed from his office on impeachment by the House of representatives, and conviction by the Senate, for treason or bribery, and in case of his removal as aforesaid, death, absence, resignation or inability to discharge the powers or duties of his office the Vice President shall exercise those powers and duties until another President be chosen, or until the inability of the President be removed.

On the question to agree to the first clause of the report.

it passed in the affirmative

On the question to agree to the second clause of the report

it passed in the affirmative

It was moved and seconded to postpone the consideration of the 3rd clause of the report

which passed in the affirmative

---

[5] Amendment of September 7.

It was moved and seconded to postpone the consideration of the remainder of the report

which passed in the negative [Ayes — 1; noes — 10.][6]

After some time passed in debate.

It was moved and seconded to postpone the consideration of the remainder of the report, and that the Members take copies thereof —

which passed in the affirmative [Ayes — 7; noes — 3.]

It was moved and seconded to refer the following motion to the committee of eleven.

To prepare and report a plan for defraying the expences of this Convention

which passed in the affirmative

[To adjourn Ayes — 11; noes — 0.][7]

The House adjourned

DETAIL OF AYES AND NOES

	New Hampshire	Massachusetts	Rhode Island	Connecticut	New York	New Jersey	Pennsylvania	Delaware	Maryland	Virginia	No Carolina	So Carolina	Georgia	Questions	ayes	noes	divided
[442]	no	no		no		no	no	no	no	no	aye	no	no	To postpone the report	2	9	
[443]	aye	aye		no		no	no	aye	aye	aye		aye	aye	To postpone	7	3	
[444]	aye	aye		aye		aye	aye	aye	aye	aye	aye	aye	aye	To adjourn			

[End of page 14]

MADISON

Tuesday Sepr. 4. 1787. In Convention

Mr. Brearley from the Committee of eleven made a further partial Report as follows[8]

---

[6] Vote 442, Detail of Ayes and Noes, which is obviously mistaken in the summary of the vote.

[7] Vote 444, Detail of Ayes and Noes.

[8] Among the unbound Madison Papers is a copy of this report endorsed "Reptt. of Come. of 11". Subsequently it was endorsed

"(Appointd Aug. 31) Sepr. 4.— the first clause (including "Common defence &

"The Committee of Eleven to whom sundry resolutions &c were referred on the 31st. of August, report that in their opinion the following additions and alterations should be made to the Report before the Convention, viz

* (1.) The first clause of sect: 1. art. 7. to read as follow — 'The Legislature shall have power to lay and collect taxes duties imposts & excises, to pay the debts and provide for the common defence & general welfare[9]. ⟨of the U. S.⟩'

(2). At the end of the 2d. clause of sect. 1. art. 7. add 'and with the Indian tribes'.

(3) In the place of the 9th. art: Sect. 1. to be inserted 'The Senate of the U— S— shall have power to try all impeachments; but no person shall be convicted without the concurrence of two thirds of the members present.'[10]

(4) After the word 'Excellency' in sect. 1. art. 10. to be inserted. 'He shall hold his office during the term of four years, and together with the vice-President, chosen for the same term, be elected in the following manner, viz. Each State shall appoint in such manner as its Legislature may direct, a number of electors equal to the whole number of Senators and members of the House of Representatives, to which the State may be entitled in the Legislature. The Electors shall meet in their respective States, and vote by ballot for two persons, of whom one at least shall not be an inhabitant of the same State with themselves; and they shall make a list of all the persons voted for, and of the number of votes for each, which list they shall sign and certify and transmit sealed to the Seat of the. Genl. Government, directed to the President of the Senate — The President of the Senate

* ⟨This is an exact copy. The variations in that in the printed Journal are occasioned by its incorporation of subsequent amendments. This remark is applicable to other cases.⟩[11]

Genl. welfare passed nem: con: and, as appears, without debate. Quer. if this report be not in the handwriting of Mr. Sherman? | more probably in that of Mr. Brearley".

In this copy some abbreviations are used, the punctuation differs slightly, and the paragraphs are not numbered, otherwise it is identical with Madison's copy, except in three instances noted below.

[9] See Appendix A, CCCLXXII.

[10] See Appendix A, CLXX.

[11] See above, note 1.

shall in that House open all the certificates; and the votes shall be then & there counted. The Person having the greatest number of votes shall be the President, if such number be a majority of that of the electors; and if there be more than one who have such a majority, and have an equal number of votes, then the Senate shall immediately[12] choose by ballot one of them for President: but if no person have a majority. then from the five highest on the list, the Senate shall choose by ballot the President. And in every case after the choice of the President, the person having the greatest number of votes shall be vice-president: but if there should remain two or more who have equal votes, the Senate shall choose from them the vice-President. The Legislature may determine the time of choosing and assembling the Electors, and the manner of certifying and transmitting their votes.'[12a]

(5) 'Sect. 2. No person except a natural born citizen or a Citizen of the U— S— at the time of the adoption of this Constitution shall be eligible to the office of President; nor shall any person be elected to that office, who shall be under the age of thirty five years, and who has not been in the whole, at least fourteen years a resident within the U— S.'

(6) 'Sect— 3— The vice-president shall be ex officio President of the Senate, except when they sit to try the impeachment of the President, in which case the Chief Justice shall preside, and excepting also when he shall exercise the powers and duties of President, in which case & in case of his absence, the Senate shall chuse a President pro tempore.— The vice President when acting as President of the Senate shall not have a vote unless the House be equally divided.'

(7) 'Sect— 4 The President by and with the advice and Consent of the Senate, shall have power to make Treaties; and he shall nominate and by and with the advice and consent of the Senate shall appoint ambassadors, and other public Ministers,[13] Judges of the Supreme Court, and all other Officers

---

[12] Madison himself seems to have been misled here: "immediately" was inserted by an amendment on Sept. 6. It is omitted in the Brearley draft among the Madison Papers, and in McHenry's copy. [12a] See Appendix A, CC*a*.

[13] Brearley copy has interlined "& consuls" above "Ministers".

of the U— S—, whose appointments are not otherwise herein provided for. But no Treaty[14] shall be made without the consent of two thirds of the members present.'

(8) After the words "into the service of the U S." in sect. 2. art: 10. add 'and may require the opinion in writing of the principal Officer in each of the Executive Departments, upon any subject relating to the duties of their respective offices.'

The latter part of Sect. 2. Art: 10. to read as follows.

(9) "He shall be removed from his office on impeachment by the House of Representatives, and conviction by the Senate, for Treason, or bribery, and in case of his removal as aforesaid, death, absence, resignation or inability to discharge the powers or duties of his office, the vice-president shall exercise those powers and duties until another President be chosen, or until the inability of the President be removed.'

The (1st.) clause of the Report was agreed to nem. con.

The (2) clause was also agreed to nem: con:

The (3) clause was postponed in order to decide previously on the mode of electing the President —

The (4) clause was accordingly taken up.

Mr. Gorham disapproved of making the next highest after the President, the vice-President, without referring the decision to the Senate in case the next highest should have less than a majority of votes. as the regulation stands a very obscure man with very few votes may arrive at that appointment

Mr Sherman said the object of this clause of the report of the Committee was to get rid of the ineligibility, which was attached to the mode of election by the Legislature, & to render the Executive independent of the Legislature. As the choice of the President was to be made out of the five highest, obscure characters were sufficiently guarded against in that case: And he had no objection to requiring the vice-President to be chosen in like manner, where the choice was not decided by a majority in the first instance

[14] Brearley copy has interlined "except treaties of peace" to be inserted after "Treaty".

Mr. Madison was apprehensive that by requiring both the President & vice President to be chosen out of the five highest candidates, the attention of the electors would be turned too much to making candidates instead of giving their votes in order to a definitive choice, Should this turn be given to the business, the election would in fact be consigned to the Senate altogether. It would have the effect at the same time, he observed, of giving the nomination of the candidates to the largest States.

Mr Govr Morris concurred in, & enforced the remarks of Mr. Madison.

Mr Randolph & Mr Pinkney wished for a particular explanation & discussion of the reasons for changing the mode of electing the Executive.

Mr. Govr. Morris said he would give the reasons of the Committee and his own. The 1st. was the danger of intrigue & faction if the appointmt. should be made by the Legislature. 2 the inconveniency of an ineligibility required by that mode in order to lessen its evils. 3 The difficulty of establishing a Court of Impeachments, other than the Senate which would not be so proper for the trial nor the other branch for the impeachment of the President, if appointed by the Legislature, 4. No body had appeared to be satisfied with an appointment by the Legislature. 5. Many were anxious even for an immediate choice by the people— 6— the indispensable necessity of making the Executive independent of the Legislature. — As the Electors would vote at the same time throughout the U. S. and at so great a distance from each other, the great evil of cabal was avoided. It would be impossible also to corrupt them. A conclusive reason for making the Senate instead of the Supreme Court the Judge of impeachments, was that the latter was to try the President after the trial of the impeachment.

Col: Mason confessed that the plan of the Committee had removed some capital objections, particularly the danger of cabal and corruption. It was liable however to this strong objection, that nineteen times in twenty the President would be chosen by the Senate, an improper body for the purpose.

Mr. Butler thought the mode not free from objections, but much more so than an election by the Legislature, where as in elective monarchies, cabal faction & violence would be sure to prevail.

Mr. Pinkney stated as objections to the mode 1. that it threw the whole appointment in fact into the hands of the Senate. 2—The Electors will be strangers to the several candidates and of course unable to decide on their comparative merits. 3. It makes the Executive reeligible which will endanger the public liberty. 4. It makes the same body of men which will in fact elect the President his Judges in case of an impeachment.

Mr. Williamson had great doubts whether the advantage of reeligibility would balance the objection to such a dependence of the President on the Senate for his reappointment. He thought at least the Senate ought to be restrained to the *two* highest on the list

Mr. Govr. Morris said the principal advantage aimed at was that of taking away the opportunity for cabal. The President may be made if thought necessary ineligible on this as well as on any other mode of election. Other inconveniences may be no less redressed on this plan than any other.

Mr. Baldwin thought the plan not so objectionable when well considered, as at first view. The increasing intercourse among the people of the States, would render important characters less & less unknown; and the Senate would consequently be less & less likely to have the eventual appointment thrown into their hands.

Mr. Wilson. This subject has greatly divided the House, and will also divide people out of doors. It is in truth the most difficult of all on which we have had to decide. He had never made up an opinion on it entirely to his own satisfaction. He thought the plan on the whole a valuable improvement on the former. It gets rid of one great evil, that of cabal & corruption; & Continental Characters will multiply as we more & more coalesce, so as to enable the electors in every part of the Union to know & judge of them. It clears the way also for a discussion of the question of re-eligibility on its own

merits, which the former mode of election seemed to forbid. He thought it might be better however to refer the eventual appointment to the Legislature than to the Senate, and to confine it to a smaller number than five of the Candidates. The eventual election by the Legislature wd. not open cabal anew, as it would be restrained to certain designated objects of choice, and as these must have had the previous sanction of a number of the States: and if the election be made as it ought as soon as the votes of the electors are opened & it is known that no one has a majority of the whole, there can be little danger of corruption— Another reason for preferring the Legislature to the Senate in this business, was that the House of Reps. will be so often changed as to[15] be free from the influence & faction to which the permanence of the Senate may subject that branch —

Mr. Randolph preferred the former mode of constituting the Executive, but if the change was to be made, he wished to know why the eventual election was referred to the *Senate* and not to the *Legislature?* He saw no necessity for this and many objections to it. He was apprehensive also that the advantage of the eventual appointment would fall into the hands of the States near the Seat of Government.

Mr Govr. Morris said the *Senate* was preferred because fewer could then, say to the President, you owe your appointment to us. He thought the President would not depend so much on the Senate for his re-appointment as on his general good conduct.

The further consideration of the Report was postponed that each member might take a copy of the remainder of it.

The following motion was referred to the Committee of Eleven — to wit, — "To prepare & report a plan for defraying the expences of the Convention"

* Mr. Pinkney moved a clause declaring "that each House should be judge of the privilege of its own members.[16] Mr Govr. Morris 2ded. the motion

*⟨This motion not inserted in the printed Journal⟩

[15] Crossed out "break from its accustomed spirit of faction & intrigue in which the Senate retains".

[16] See Appendix A, CCLXXXVII.

Mr. Randolph & Mr. Madison expressed doubts as to the propriety of giving such a power, & wished for a postponement.

Mr Govr. Morris thought it so plain a case that no postponement could be necessary.

Mr. Wilson thought the power involved, and the express insertion of it needless. It might beget doubts as to the power of other public bodies, as Courts &c. Every Court is the judge of its own privileges.

Mr Madison distinguished between the power of Judging of privileges previously & duly established, and the effect of the motion which would give a discretion to each House as to the extent of its own privileges. He suggested that it would be better to make provision for ascertaining by *law*, the privileges of each House, than to allow each House to decide for itself. He suggested also the necessity of considering what privileges ought to be allowed to the Executive.

Adjourned [17]

McHENRY

Sepr. 3. and 4 Employed chiefly by the committee.

Agreed on report of the com. that the 1 clause of the 1 sect. of the 7 art. read vz.

> "The legislature shall have power to lay and collect taxes duties imposts and excises, to pay the debts and provide for the common defence and general welfare of the U. S."

Also to add at the end of the 2 clause of the 1 sect of the 7 art. "and with the Indian tribes."

+ Took up in the report "in the place of the 9 art. 1 sec. —"The senate of the U. S. shall have power to try all impeachments but no person shall be convicted without the concurrence of ⅔ of the members present. postponed.

The committee report in part as follows[18] . . .

---

[17] See Appendix A, CI, CII.

[18] The rest of the report is like that in Madison, (except in the one instance noted above, see note 12), and is accordingly omitted here.

No provision in the above for a new election in case of the death or removal of the President.

Upon looking over the constitution it does not appear that the national legislature can *erect light houses* or *clean out or preserve the navigation of harbours* — This expence ought to be borne by commerce — of course by the general treasury into which all the revenue of commerce must come —

Is it proper to declare all the navigable waters or rivers and within the U. S. common high ways? Perhaps a power to restrain any State from demanding tribute from citizens of another State in such cases is comprehended in the power to regulate trade between State and State.

This to be further considered. A motion to be made on the light house etc, to-morrow.

WEDNESDAY, SEPTEMBER 5, 1787.

JOURNAL

Wednesday September 5. 1787.

The honorable Mr Brearley from the Committee of eleven informed the House that the Committee were prepared to report farther — He then read the report in his place — and, the same being delivered in at the Secretary's table, was again read, and is as follows.

To add to the clause "To declare war" the words "and grant letters of marque and reprisal" agreed[1]

To add to the clause "To raise and support armies" the words "But no appropriation of money to that use shall be for a longer term than two years" agreed[1]

Instead of the twelfth section of the 6th article say

all Bills for raising revenue shall originate in the House of representatives and shall be subject to alterations and amendments by the Senate: No money shall be drawn from the Treasury but in consequence of appropriations made by law. postponed[1]

Immediately before the last clause of the first section of the seventh article

To exercise exclusive legislation in all cases whatsoever over such district (not exceeding ten miles square) as may by cession of particular States and the acceptance of the Legislature become the seat of the Government of the United States, and to exercise like authority over all Places purchased for the erection of Forts, Magazines, Arsenals, Dock Yards and other needful buildings. agd[1]

"To promote the progress of science and useful arts by securing for limited times to Authors and Inventors the exclusive right to their respective writings and discoveries. agreed[1]

[1] In margin opposite paragraph preceding.

On the question to agree to the first clause of the report
it passed in the affirmative
On the question to agree to the second clause of the report
it passed in the affirmative
It was moved and seconded to postpone the consideration of the third clause of the report
which passed in the affirmative. [Ayes—9; noes — 2.] [1a]
It was moved and seconded to insert the following words after the word "purchased" in the fourth clause of the report "by the consent of the Legislature of the State"
which passed in the affirmative
On the question to agree to the fourth clause of the report as amended
it passed in the affirmative
On the question to agree to the fifth clause of the report
it passed in the affirmative.
The following resolution and order - - - - reported from the Committee of eleven were read.
Resolved
"That the United States in Congress be requested to allow "and cause to be paid to the Secretary and other officers of "this Convention such sums in proportion to their respective "times of service as are allowed to the Secretary and similar "Officers of Congress"

Ordered That the Secretary make out and transmit to the Treasury Office of the United States an account for the said services, and for the incidental expences of this Convention.

Separate questions being taken on the foregoing resolve and Order
They passed in the affirmative
It was moved and seconded to take up the remainder of the report from the Committee of eleven entered on the Journal of the 4. instant

---

[1a] According to Madison the vote on this question is the same as Vote 389, Detail of Ayes and Noes (see August 28). Probably the secretary did not have a new page ready on which to record the first vote taken (the two questions preceding being agreed to unanimously) and made use of a convenient blank space.

It was moved and seconded to postpone the consideration of the report in order to take up the following.

"He shall be elected by joint ballot by the Legislature, to "which election a majority of the votes of the Members present "shall be required: He shall hold his office during the term of "seven years: but shall not be elected a second "time" —

On the question to postpone

it passed in the negative. [Ayes — 2; noes — 8; divided — 1.]

It was moved and seconded to strike out the words

"if such number be a majority of that of the Electors"

which passed in the negative. [Ayes — 1; noes — 10.]

It was moved and seconded to strike out the word "Senate" and to insert the word "Legislature"

which passed in the Negative [Ayes — 3; noes — 7; divided — 1.]

It was moved and seconded to strike out the words "such majority" and to insert the words "one third."

which passed in the negative [Ayes — 2; noes — 9.]

[To strike out the word "five" to insert "three" Ayes — 2; noes — 9.][2]

It was moved and seconded to strike out the word "five" and to insert the word "thirteen"

which passed in the negative. [Ayes — 2; noes — 9.]

It was moved and seconded to add after the word "electors" the words "who shall have balloted"

which passed in the negative. [Ayes — 4; noes — 7.]

It was moved and seconded to add after the words "if such number be a majority of the whole number of the Electors" the word "appointed"

which passed in the affirmative [Ayes — 9; noes — 2.]

It was moved and seconded to insert after the words "The Legislature may determine the time of chusing and assembling the Electors" the words "and of their giving their votes"

which passed in the affirmative

The House adjourned

---

[2] Vote 449, Detail of Ayes and Noes.

DETAIL OF AYES AND NOES

[page 15]

	New Hampshire	Massachusetts	Rhode Island	Connecticut	New York	New Jersey	Pennsylvania	Delaware	Maryland	Virginia	No Carolina	So Carolina	Georgia	Questions	ayes	noes	divided
[445]	dd	no		no		no	no	no	no	no	aye	aye	no	To postpone the report for electg the Presidt by electors, to take up the report for electg him by the Legislature	2	8	1
[446]	no	no		no		no	no	no	no	no	aye	no	no	To strike out the words if such number &ca	1	10	
[447]	dd	no		no		no	aye	no	no	aye	no	aye	no	To strike out the word "Senate" to insert "Legislature"	3	7	1
[448]	no	no		no		no	no	no	no	aye	aye	no	no	To strike out the words "such majority" to insert "One third"	2	9	
[449]	no	no		no		no	no	no	no	aye	aye	no	no	To strike out the word "five" to insert "three"	2	9	
[450]	no	no		no		no	no	no	no	no	aye	aye	no	To strike out "five" to insert "thirteen"	2	9	
[451]	no	no		no		no	aye	no	aye	aye	aye	no	no	To add the words "who shall have ballotted"	4	7	
[452]	aye	aye		aye		aye	aye	aye	aye	no	no	aye	aye	To add the word "appointed" after the words "whole number of Electors"	9	2	

MADISON

Wednesday Sepr. 5. 1787 In Convention.

Mr. Brearley from the Committee of Eleven made a farther report as follows,

(1) To add to the clause "to declare war" the words "and grant letters of marque and reprisal"

(2) To add to the clause "to raise and support armies" the words "but no appropriation of money to that use shall be for a longer term than two years"

(3) Instead of sect: 12. art. 6. say — "All bills for raising

revenue shall originate in the House of Representatives, and shall be subject to alterations and amendments by the Senate: No money shall be drawn from the Treasury, but in consequence of appropriations made by law."

(4) Immediately before the last clause of Sect. 1. art. 7 — insert "To exercise exclusive legislation in all cases whatsoever over such district (not exceeding ten miles square) as may by Cession of particular States and the acceptance of the Legislature become the seat of the Government of the U— S— [3] and to exercise like authority over all places purchased for the erection of Forts, Magazines, Arsenals, Dock-Yards, and other needful buildings"

(5) "To promote the progress of Science and useful arts by securing for limited times to authors & inventors, the exclusive right to their respective writings and discoveries"

This report being taken up. — The (1) clause was agreed to nem. con:

To the (2) clause Mr. Gerry objected that it admitted of appropriations to an army. for two years instead of one, for which he could not conceive a reason— that it implied there was to be a standing army which he inveighed against as dangerous to liberty, as unnecessary even for so great an extent of Country as this. and if necessary, some restriction on the number & duration ought to be provided: Nor was this a proper time for such an innovation. The people would not bear it.

Mr Sherman remarked that the appropriations were permitted only, not required to be for two years. As the Legislature is to be biennally elected, it would be inconvenient to require appropriations to be for one year, as there might be no Session within the time necessary to renew them. He should himself he said like a reasonable restriction on the number and continuance of an army in time of peace.

The clause (2). was agreed to nem: con:

The (3)clause, Mr. Govr. Morris moved to postpone — It had been agreed to in the Committee on the ground of com-

[3] See Appendix A, CCCVII.

promise, and he should feel himself at liberty to dissent to it; if on the whole he should not be satisfied with certain other parts to be settled. — Mr. Pinkney 2ded. the motion

Mr. Sherman was for giving immediate ease to those who looked on this clause as of great moment, and for trusting to their concurrence in other proper measures.

On the question for postponing

N— H— ay— Mas— no. Ct. ay. N— J— ay— Pa. ay— Del. ay. Md ay— Va. no. N— C— ay— S. C ay— Geo ay. [Ayes — 9; noes — 2.]

So much of the (4) clause as related to the seat of Government was agreed to nem: con:

On the residue, to wit, "to exercise like authority over all places purchased for forts &c.

Mr Gerry contended that this power might be made use of to enslave any particular State by buying up its territory, and that the strongholds proposed would be a means of awing the State into an undue obedience to the Genl. Government —

Mr. King thought himself the provision unnecessary, the power being already involved: but would move to insert after the word "purchased" the words "by the consent of the Legislature of the State" This would certainly make the power safe.

Mr. Govr Morris 2ded. the motion, which was agreed to nem: con: as was then the residue of the clause as amended.

The (5) clause was agreed to nem: con:

The following resolution & order being reported from the Committee of eleven, to wit,

"Resolved that the U— S— in Congress be requested to allow and cause to be paid to the Secretary and other officers of this Convention such sums in proportion to their respective times of service, as are allowed to the Secretary & similar officers of Congress."

"Ordered that the Secretary make out & transmit to the Treasury office of the U. S. an account for the said Services, & for the incidental expenses of this convention"[4]

[4] See also Appendix A, V, and upon payment of individual delegates, IV. XXXVIII, XLIII, XLIV, LII, LXI, XCIII, and Appendix B, and notes.

The resolution & order were separately agreed to nem: con:

Mr. Gerry gave notice that he should move to reconsider articles XIX. XX. XXI. XXII.

Mr. Williamson gave like notice as to the Article fixing the number of Representatives, which he thought too small. He wished also to allow Rho: Island more than one, as due to her probable number of people, and as proper to stifle any pretext arising from her absence on the occasion.

The Report made yesterday as to the appointment of the Executive being then taken up. Mr. Pinkney renewed his opposition to the mode, arguing 1. that the electors will not have sufficient knowledge of the fittest men, & will be swayed by an attachment to the eminent men of their respective States — Hence 2dly the dispersion of the votes would leave the appointment with the Senate, and as the President's reappointment will thus depend on the Senate he will be the mere creature of that body. 3. He will combine with the Senate agst the House of Representatives. 4. This change in the mode of election was meant to get rid of the ineligibility of the President a second time, whereby he will become fixed for life under the auspices of the Senate

Mr. Gerry did not object to this plan of constituting the Executive in itself, but should be governed in his final vote by the powers that may be given to the President.

Mr. Rutlidge was much opposed to the plan reported by the Committee. It would throw the whole power into the Senate. He was also against a re-eligibility. He moved to postpone the Report under consideration & take up the original plan of appointment by the Legislature. to wit. "He shall be elected by joint ballot by the Legislature to which election a majority of the votes of the members present shall be required: He shall hold his office during the term of Seven years; but shall not be elected a second time"

On this motion to postpone

N— H— divd. Mas. no— Ct no— N— J. no. Pa. no— Del— no. Md. no— Va. no. N. C. ay— S. C. ay— Geo. no. [Ayes — 2; noes — 8; divided — 1.]

Col. Mason admitted that there were objections to an appointment by the Legislature as originally planned. He had not yet made up his mind; but would state his objections to the mode proposed by the Committee. 1. It puts the appointment in fact into the hands of the Senate, as it will rarely happen that a majority of the whole votes will fall on any one candidate: and as the Existing President will always be one of the 5 highest, his re-appointment will of course depend on the Senate. 2. Considering the powers of the President & those of the Senate, if a coalition should be established between these two branches, they will be able to subvert the Constitution. — The great objection with him would be removed by depriving the Senate of the eventual election. He accordingly moved to strike out the words "if such number be a majority of that of the electors"

Mr. Williamson 2ded. the motion. He could not agree to the clause without some such modification. He preferred making the highest tho' not having a majority of the votes, President, to a reference of the matter to the Senate. Referring the appointment to the Senate lays a certain foundation for corruption & aristocracy.

Mr. Govr Morris thought the point of less consequence than it was supposed on both sides. It is probable that a majority of the votes will fall on the same man, As each elector is to give two votes, more than $\frac{1}{4}$ will give a majority. Besides as one vote is to be given to a man out of the State, and as this vote will not be thrown away, $\frac{1}{2}$ the votes will fall on characters eminent & generally known. Again if the President shall have given satisfaction, the votes will turn on him of course, and a majority of them will reappoint him, without resort to the Senate: If he should be disliked, all disliking him, would take care to unite their votes so as to ensure his being supplanted.

Col: Mason those who think there is no danger of there not being a majority for the same person in the first instance, ought to give up the point to those who think otherwise.

Mr Sherman reminded the opponents of the new mode proposed that if the Small States had the advantage in the

Senate's deciding among the five highest candidates, the Large States would have in fact the nomination of these candidates

On[5] the motion of Col: Mason

N. H. no— Mas. no. Ct. no. N. J. no. Pa. no. Del. no. Md. ay.* Va. no— N. C. ay. S— C. no. Geo. no [Ayes — 2; noes — 9.]

Mr. Wilson moved to strike out "Senate" and insert the word "Legislature"

Mr Madison considered it as a primary object to render an eventual resort to any part of the Legislature improbable. He was apprehensive that the proposed alteration would turn the attention of the large States too much to the appointment of candidates, instead of aiming at an effectual appointment of the officer, as the large States would predominate in the Legislature which would have the final choice out of the Candidates. Whereas if the Senate in which the small States predominate should have the final choice, the concerted effort of the large States would be to make the appointment in the first instance conclusive.

Mr Randolph. We have in some revolutions of this plan made a bold stroke for Monarchy. We are now doing the same for an aristocracy. He dwelt on the tendency of such an influence in the Senate over the election of the President in addition to its other powers, to convert that body into a real & dangerous Aristocracy —

Mr Dickinson was in favor of giving the eventual election to the Legislature, instead of the Senate — It was too much influence to be superadded to that body —

On the question moved by Mr Wilson

N. H— divd. Mas. no— Ct no— N— J— no. Pa. ay. Del— no. Md. no. Va. ay— N— C. no— S. C. ay. Geo. no. [Ayes — 3; noes — 7; divided — 1.]

* ⟨In printed Journal Maryland — no⟩

[5] The lines preceding were crossed out: "Mr. Wilson remarked that striking the words out would have the effect of inducing the large States to throw away the vote to be given to a person out of the State in order to increase the chances of its own Citizen."

Mr Madison & Mr. Williamson moved to strike out the word "majority" and insert "one third" so that the eventual power might not be exercised if less than a majority, but not less than $\frac{1}{3}$ of the Electors should vote for the same person—

Mr. Gerry objected that this would put it in the power of three or four States to put in whom they pleased.

Mr. Williamson. There are seven States which do not contain one third of the people — If the Senate are to appoint, less than one sixth of the people will have the power —

On the question

N. H— no. Mas. no— Ct no— N. J— no. Pa. no. Del. no. Md. no— Va. ay. N— C. ay. S. C no. Geo. no. [Ayes — 2; noes — 9.]

Mr Gerry suggested that the eventual election should be made by six Senators and seven Representatives chosen by joint ballot of both Houses.

Mr King observed that the influence of the Small States in the Senate was somewhat balanced by the influence of the large States in bringing forward the candidates,* and also by the Concurrence of the small States in the Committee in the clause vesting the exclusive origination of Money bills in the House of Representatives.

Col: Mason moved to strike out the word "five" and insert the word "three" as the highest candidates for the Senate to choose out of —

Mr. Gerry 2ded. the motion

Mr. Sherman would sooner give up the plan. He would prefer seven or thirteen.

On the question moved by Col Mason and Mr Gerry

N. H. no— Mas. no— Ct. no. N— J. no. Pa no. ⟨Delaware⟩ Md. ⟨no⟩[6] Va ay— N— C— ay— S. C. no— Geo— no. [Ayes — 2; noes — 8.]

* This explains the compromise mentioned above by Mr. Govr Morris- Col: Mason Mr. Gerry & other members from large States set great value on this privilege of originating money bills. Of this the members from the small States, with some from the large States who wished a high mounted Govt, endeavored to avail themselves, by making that privilege, the price of arrangements in the constitution favorable to the small States, and to the elevation of the Government.

Mr Spaight and Mr. Rutlidge moved to strike out "five" and insert "thirteen" — to which all the States disagreed — except N— C. & S— C—

Mr Madison & Mr. Williamson moved to insert after "Electors" the words "who shall have balloted" so that the non voting electors not being counted might not increase the number necessary as a majority of the whole — to decide the choice without the agency of the Senate —

On this question

N. H— no. Mas— no. Ct. ⟨no⟩.[6] N. J— no. Pa ay. Del. no. Md. ay. Va ay— N— C. ay. S— C— no. Geo. no [Ayes — 4; noes — 7.]

Mr. Dickinson moved, in order to remove ambiguity from the intention of the clause as explained by the vote, to add, after the words "if such number be a majority of the whole "number of the Electors" the word "appointed"

On this motion

N. H. ay. Mas— ay— ⟨Con: ay⟩[7] N— J— ay— Pa ay. ⟨Delaware⟩ Md. ay— Va. no. N. C. no. S— C. ay— Geo. ay. [Ayes — 8; noes — 2.]

Col: Mason. As the mode of appointment is now regulated, he could not forbear expressing his opinion that it is utterly inadmissible. He would prefer the Government of Prussia to one which will put all power into the hands of seven or eight men, and fix an Aristocracy worse than absolute monarchy.

The words "and of their giving their votes" being inserted on motion for that purpose, after the words "The Legislature may determine the time of chusing and assembling the Electors"

The House adjourned.

---

[6] Vote changed from "ay" to "no" to conform to *Journal.*

[7] Taken from *Journal.*

McHENRY

Septr. 5 —

The greatest part of the day spent in desultory conversation on that part of the report respecting the mode of chusing the President — adjourned without coming to a conclusion —

THURSDAY, SEPTEMBER 6, 1787.

JOURNAL

Thursday September 6 —— 1787.

It was moved and seconded to insert the following words after the words "may be entitled in the Legislature" in the 5. clause of the report entered on the Journal of the 4th instant.

"But no Person shall be appointed an Elector who is a "Member of the Legislature of the United States or who "holds any office of profit or trust under the United States"

which passed in the affirmative

It was moved and seconded to insert the word "seven" instead of "four" in the fourth clause of the report.

which passed in the negative [Ayes — 3; noes — 8.][1]

It was moved and seconded to insert the word "six" instead of "four"

which passed in the negative [Ayes — 2; noes — 9.][2]

[To agree to the word "four" Ayes — 10; noes — 1.

To agree to the clause respectg Presidt & V. Presidt Ayes — 10; noes — 1.

To agree to the appointment of Electors. Ayes — 9; noes — 2.][3]

It was moved and seconded to insert the words "under the seal of the State" after the word "transmit" in the sixth clause of the report

which passed in the negative.

[To agree to Ayes — 10; noes — 1.

---

[1] Vote 453, Detail of Ayes and Noes. [2] Vote 454, Detail of Ayes and Noes.

[3] Votes 455–457, Detail of Ayes and Noes. From this point on in this day's records it seems hopeless to determine the order of questions and votes. The editor has tried simply to remove some of the confusion by assigning votes from Detail of Ayes and Noes to their respective questions, and distributing the balance as seems probable.

The person having the greatest number of votes shall be the Presidt Ayes — 8; noes — 2; divided — 1

Provided that number be a majority of the

Ayes — 8; noes — 3.][4]

It was moved and seconded to insert the words "and who shall have given their votes" after the word "appointed" in the 7 clause of the report.

which passed in the negative. [Ayes — 5; noes — 6.][5]

[Ayes — 10; noes — 1.][6]

It was moved and seconded to insert the words "in presence of the Senate and House of representatives" after the word "counted"

which passed in the affirmative

It was moved and seconded to insert the word "immediately" before the word "choose"

which passed in the affirmative [Ayes — 9; noes — 2.][7]

[and that not less than $\frac{2}{3}$ of the whole number of Senators be present — (In presence of the S & Ho of representatives)

Ayes — 6; noes — 4.][8]

It was moved and seconded to insert the words "of the Electors" after the word "votes"

which passed in the affirmative [Ayes — 11; noes — 0.][9]

It was moved and seconded to agree to the following clause

"That the Electors meet at the seat of the general Government"

which passed in the negative. [Ayes — 1; noes — 10.][10]

It was moved and seconded to agree to the following clause "But The election shall be on the same day throughout the United States" after the words "transmitting their votes"

which passed in the affirmative [Ayes — 8; noes — 3.][11]

It was moved and seconded to strike out the words "The

[4] Vote 459–461, Detail of Ayes and Noes.

[5] Vote 462, Detail of Ayes and Noes.

[6] Vote 463, Detail of Ayes and Noes. Probably is the same as Madison reports on eventual choice of President by Senate.

[7] Vote 470, Detail of Ayes and Noes, probably belongs here although the wording is slightly different.

[8] Vote 464, Detail of Ayes and Noes.

[9] Vote 467, Detail of Ayes and Noes, probably belongs here.

[10] Vote 458, Detail of Ayes and Noes.

[11] Vote 468, Detail of Ayes and Noes.

Senate shall immediately choose by ballot" &ca and to insert the words "The House of representatives shall immediately choose by ballot one of them for President, the Members from each State having one vote"

which passed in the affirmative [Ayes — 10; noes — 1.][12]

[Ho of representatives to elect Ayes — 8; noes — 3.][13]

It was moved and seconded to agree to the following amendment

"But a quorum for this purpose shall consist of a Member "or Members from two thirds of the States"

which passed in the affirmative ["Unanimous"][14]

On the question to agree to the following amendment

"and also of a Majority of the whole number of the House of representatives"

it passed in the negative [Ayes — 5; noes — 6.][15]

[and in every case after the choice of the Presidt the Person having the greatest number of votes Ayes — 10; noes — 1.][16]

The several amendments being agreed to, on separate questions,

The first sect. of the report is as follows.

"He shall hold his office during the term of four years, and together with the Vice President, chosen for the same term, be elected in the following manner.

Each State shall appoint, in such manner as it's legislature may direct, a number of Electors equal to the whole number of Senators and Members of the House of representatives to which the State may be entitled in the Legislature.

"But no Person shall be appointed an Elector who is a mem-"ber of the Legislature of the United States, or who holds "any office of profit or trust under the United States.

The Electors shall meet in their respective States and "vote by ballot for two Persons of whom one at least shall "not be an inhabitant of the same State with themselves. — "and they shall make a list of all the Persons voted for, and "of the number of votes for each, which list they shall sign

---

[12] Vote 465, Detail of Ayes and Noes.

[13] Vote 469, Detail of Ayes and Noes.

[14] Vote 471, Detail of Ayes and Noes.

[15] Vote 472, Detail of Ayes and Noes.

[16] Vote 466, Detail of Ayes and Noes.

DETAIL OF AYES AND NOES

	New Hampshire	Massachusetts	Rhode Island	Connecticut	New York	New Jersey	Pennsylvania	Delaware	Maryland	Virginia	No Carolina	So Carolina	Georgia	Questions	ayes	noes	divided
[453]	aye	no		no		no	no	no	no	aye	aye	no	no	To insert the word "seven" instead of "four"	3	8	
[454]	no	no		no		no	no	no	no	no	aye	aye	no	To insert the word "six" instead of four.	2	9	
[455]	aye	aye		aye		aye	aye	aye	aye	aye	no	aye	aye	To agree to the word "four"	10	1	
[456]	aye	aye		aye		aye	aye	aye	aye	aye	no	aye	aye	To agree to the clause respectg Presidt & V. Presidt	10	1	
[457]	aye	aye		aye		aye	aye	aye	aye	aye	no	no	aye	To agree to the appointment of Electors."	9	2	
[458]	no	no		no		no	no	no	no	no	aye	no	no	That the Electors meet at ye seat of the genl Govt	1	10	
[459]	aye	aye		aye		aye	aye	aye	aye	aye	no	aye	aye	To agree to	10	1	
[460]	dd	no		no		aye	aye	aye	aye	aye	aye	aye	aye	The person having the greatest number of votes shall be Presidt	8	2	1
[461]	aye	aye		aye		aye	no	aye	aye	no	no	aye	aye	Provided that number be a Majority of the	8	3	
[462]	no	aye		no		no	aye	no	no	aye	aye	aye	no	and who shall have given their votes ☞			
[463]	aye	aye		aye		aye	aye	aye	aye	aye	no	aye	aye		10	1	
[464]	aye			no		no	no	no	aye	aye	aye	aye	aye	and that not less than ⅔ of the whole number of Senators be present. — (In ☞ presence of the S & Ho of representatives.)			
[465]	aye	aye		aye		aye	aye	no	aye	aye	aye	aye	aye	House of representatives shall chuse by ballot the President, the Members ☞ from each State having one vote	10	1	
[466]	aye	aye		aye		aye	aye	aye	aye	aye	no	aye	aye	and in every case after the choice of the Presidt the Person having the greatest number of votes	10	1	
[467]	aye	aye		aye		aye	aye	aye	aye	aye	aye	aye	aye	☞ to insert the words "of the Electors" after the last clause	11		
[468]	aye	no		aye		no	aye	no	aye	aye	aye	aye	aye	☞ The election shall be on the same day throughout the United States.	8	3	
[469]	aye	aye		aye		no	aye	no	no	aye	aye	aye	aye	Ho of representatives. to elect	8	3	
[470]	aye	aye		aye		no	aye	aye	aye	aye	no	aye	aye	To insert the word "immediately" after the word "shall elect	9	2	
[471]						Unanimous								But a quorum for this purpose shall consist of a Member or Members from ⅔rds of ye States.			
[472]	no	aye		aye		no	aye	no	no	aye	aye	no	no	and also a majority of the whole number of the House of representatives.	5	6	

"and certify, and transmit sealed to the seat of the general "Government, directed to the President of the Senate.

"The President of the Senate shall in the presence of the "Senate and House of representatives open all the certificates "and the votes shall then be counted.

The Person having the greatest number of votes shall be "the President (if such number be a majority of the whole "number of the Electors appointed) and if there be more "than one who have such majority, and have an equal num-"ber of votes, then the House of representatives shall imme-"diately choose by ballot one of them for President, the "representation from each State having one vote — But if "no Person have a majority, then from the five highest on "the list, the House of representatives shall, in like manner, "choose by ballot the President —— In the choice of a "President by the House of representatives a quorum shall "consist of a Member or Members from two thirds of the "States. and the concurrence of a majority of all the States, "shall be necessary to such choice. —— and, in every case after "the choice of the President, the Person having the greatest "number of votes of the Electors shall be the vice-President: "But, if there should remain two or more who have equal "votes, the Senate shall choose from them the Vice President" "The Legislature may determine the time of chusing the "Electors and of their giving their votes: and the manner of "certifying and transmitting their votes — But the election "shall be on the same day throughout the United States"

MADISON

Thursday Sepr. 6. 1787 — In Convention

Mr. King and Mr. Gerry moved to insert in the (5) clause of the Report (see Sepr 4) after the words "may be entitled in the Legislature" the words following — "But no person shall be appointed an elector who is a member of the Legislature of the U. S. or who holds any office of profit or trust under the U. S." which passed nem: con:

Mr. Gerry proposed, as the President was to be elected by the Senate out of the five highest candidates, that if he should not at the end of his term be re-elected by a majority of the Electors, and no other candidate should have a majority, the eventual election should be made by the Legislature — This he said would relieve the President from his particular dependence on the Senate for his continuance in office.

Mr. King liked the idea, as calculated to satisfy particular members & promote unanimity; & as likely to operate but seldom.

Mr Read opposed it, remarking that if individual members were to be indulged, alterations would be necessary to satisfy most of them—

Mr Williamson espoused it as a reasonable precaution against the undue influence of the Senate.

Mr Sherman liked the arrangement as it stood, though he should not be averse to some amendments. He thought he said that if the Legislature were to have the eventual appointment instead of the Senate, it ought to vote in the case by States, in favor of the snall States, as the large States would have so great an advantage in nominating the candidates—

Mr. Govr Morris thought favorably of Mr. Gerry's proposition. It would free the President from being tempted in naming to Offices. to Conform to the will of the Senate, & thereby virtually give the appointments to office, to the Senate.

Mr Wilson said that he had weighed carefully the report of the Committee for remodelling the constitution of the Executive; and on combining it with other parts of the plan, he was obliged to consider the whole as having a dangerous tendency to aristocracy; as throwing a dangerous power into the hands of the Senate, They will have in fact, the appointment of the President, and through his dependence on them, the virtual appointment to offices; among others the offices of the Judiciary Department. They are to make Treaties; and they are to try all impeachments. In allowing them thus to make the Executive & Judiciary appointments, to be the Court of impeachments, and to make Treaties which are to be laws of the land, the Legislative, Executive & Judiciary

powers are all blended in one branch of the Government. The power of making Treaties involves the case of subsidies, and here as an additional evil, foreign influence is to be dreaded— According to the plan as it now stands, the President will not be the man of the people as he ought to be, but the Minion of the Senate. He cannot even appoint a tide-waiter without the Senate— He had always thought the Senate too numerous a body for making appointments to office. The Senate, will moreover in all probability be in constant Session. They will have high salaries. And with all those powers, and the President in their interest, they will depress the other branch of the Legislature, and aggrandize themselves in proportion. Add to all this, that the Senate sitting in Conclave, can by holding up to their respective States various and improbable candidates, contrive so to scatter their votes, as to bring the appointment of the President ultimately before themselves— Upon the whole, he thought the new mode of appointing the President, with some amendments, a valuable improvement; but he could never agree to purchase it at the price of the ensuing parts of the Report, nor befriend a system of Which they make a part—[17]

Mr. Govr. Morris expressed his wonder at the observations of Mr. Wilson so far as they preferred the plan in the printed Report to the new modification of it before the House, and entered into a comparative view of the two, with an eye to the nature of Mr. Wilsons objections to the last. By the first the Senate he observed had a voice in appointing the President out of all the Citizens of the U. S. — by this they were limited to five candidates previously nominated to them, with a probability of being barred altogether by the successful ballot of the Electors. Here surely was no increase of power. They are now to appoint Judges nominated to them by the President. Before they had the appointment without any agency whatever of the President. Here again was surely no additional power. If they are to make Treaties as the plan now stands, the power was the same in the printed plan—

[17] See Appendix A, CXLIX.

If they are to try impeachments, the Judges must have been triable by them before. Wherein then lay the dangerous tendency of the innovations to establish an aristocracy in the Senate? As to the appointment of officers, the weight of sentiment in the House, was opposed to the exercise of it by the President alone; though it was not the case with himself — If the Senate would act as was suspected, in misleading the States into a fallacious disposition of their votes for a President, they would, if the appointment were withdrawn wholly from them, make such representations in their several States where they have influence, as would favor the object of their partiality.

Mr. Williamson. ⟨replying to Mr. Morris: observed that⟩[18] The aristocratic complexion proceeds from the change in the mode of appointing the President which makes him dependent on the Senate.

Mr. Clymer[19] said that the aristocratic part to which he could never accede was that in the printed plan, which gave the Senate the power of appointing to Offices.

Mr. Hamilton said that he had been restrained from entering into the discussions by his dislike of the Scheme of Govt in General; but as he meant to support the plan to be recommended, as better than nothing, he wished in this place to offer a few remarks. He liked the new modification, on the whole, better than that in the printed Report. In this the President was a Monster elected for seven years, and ineligible afterwards; having great powers, in appointments to office, & continually tempted by this constitutional disqualification to abuse them in order to subvert the Government — Although he should be made re-eligible, Still if appointed by the Legislature, he would be tempted to make use of corrupt influence to be continued in office — It seemed peculiarly desirable therefore that Some other mode of election should be devised. Considering the different views of different States, & the different districts Northern Middle & Southern, he con-

[18] Probably but not certainly a later insertion.

[19] Crossed out "observed that the parts of the Report ought to be regarded as distinct".

curred with those who thought that the votes would not be concentered, and that the appointment would consequently in the present mode devolve on the Senate. The nomination to offices will give great weight to the President — Here then is a mutual connection & influence, that will perpetuate the President, and aggrandize both him & the Senate. What is to be the remedy? He saw none better than to let the highest number of ballots, whether a majority or not, appoint the President. What was the objection to this? Merely that too small a number might appoint. But as the plan stands, the Senate may take the candidate having the smallest number of votes, and make him President.

Mr. Spaight & Mr. Williamson moved to insert "seven" instead of "four" years for the term of the President —*

On this motion

N. H. ay. Mas. no. Ct. no— N. J. no— Pa no. Del— no. Md. no. Va. ay. N. C— ay. S. C. no. Geo— no. [Ayes — 3; noes — 8.]

Mr. Spaight & Mr. Williamson then moved to insert "six" instead of "four". On which motion

N. H. no. Mas. no. Ct no. N. J. no. Pa. no. Del. no. Md. no. Va. no, N. C— ay. S. C. ay— Geo. no [Ayes — 2; noes — 9.]

On the term "four" all the States were ay, except N. Carolina, no.

On the question ⟨(Clause 4. in the Report)⟩ for Appointing President by electors — down to the words, — "entitled in the Legislature" inclusive. "See

N. H— ay— Mas: ay. ⟨Cont: ay⟩ [20] N. J. ay— Pa. ay. Del— ay. Md ay, Va ay. N. C. no— S— C— no— Geo— ay. [Ayes — 9; noes — 2.]

⟨It was moved that the Electors meet at the seat of the Genl. Govt. which passed in the Negative. N. C. only being ay.⟩[21]

* An ineligibility wd. have followed (tho'. it wd. seem from the vote not in the opinion of all.) this prolongation of the term.

[20] Taken from *Journal*.

[21] Taken from *Journal*. Madison is in error in copying this here, as he has the same question and vote in his own records a little farther on.

It was moved to insert the words "under the seal of the State" after the word "transmit" ⟨in 4th clause of the Report⟩ which was disagreed to; as was another motion to insert the words "and who shall have given their votes" after the word "appointed" ⟨in the 4th Clause of the Report⟩ as added yesterday on motion of Mr. Dickinson.

On several motions. the words "in presence of the Senate and House of Representatives" were inserted after the word "Counted" and the word "immediately" before the word "choose"; and the words "of the Electors" after the word "votes".

Mr. Spaight said if the election by Electors is to be crammed down, he would prefer their meeting altogether and deciding finally without any reference to the Senate and moved "That the Electors meet at the seat of the General Government—"

Mr Williamson 2ded. the motion, on which all the States were in the negative except N: Carolina.

On motion the words "But the election shall be on the same day throughout the U— S—" were added after the words "transmitting their votes." N. H. ay. Mas. no. Ct. ay. N. J. no. Pa. ay. Del. no. Md. ay. Va. ay. N. C. ay. S. C. ay. Geo. ay [Ayes — 8; noes — 3.] [22]

On a question on the sentence in clause (4). "if such number be a majority of that of the electors" ⟨appointed."⟩

N— H— ay— Mas. ay. Ct ay. N. J. ay— Pa no— Del— ay. Md. ay. Va no— N. C. no. S— C. ay Geo. ay. [Ayes — 8; noes — 3.]

On a question on the clause referring the eventual appointment of the President to the Senate

N— H— ay. Mas. ay. Ct. ay. N. J. ay. Pa ay. Del— ay— Va ay. N. C. no Here the call ceased.

Mr Madison made a motion requiring $\frac{2}{3}$ at least of the Senate to be present at the choice of a President— Mr. Pinkney 2ded, the motion

Mr. Gorham thought it a wrong principle to require more than a majority in any case. In the present case it might

[22] It is possible that this vote was copied from *Journal.*

prevent for a long time any choice of a President On the question moved by Mr M— & Mr. P.

N. H. ay: Mas. abst Ct. no. N. J. no. Pa. no. Del. no. Md. ay. Va. ay. N— C. ay. S— C. ay. Geo. ay [Ayes — 6; noes — 4; absent — 1.]

Mr. Williamson suggested as better than an eventual choice by the Senate, that this choice should be made by the Legislature, voting *by States* and not *per capita.*

Mr. Sherman suggested the House of Reps. as preferable to "the Legislature", and moved, accordingly,

To strike out the words "The Senate shall immediately choose &c." and insert "The House of Representatives shall immediately choose by ballot one of them for President, the members from each State having one vote."

Col: Mason liked the latter mode best as lessening the aristocratic influence of the Senate.

On the motion of Mr. Sherman

N. H. ay. Mas. ay— Ct. ay— N. J. ay. Pa ay. Del. no. Md. ay. Va ay. N— C. ay— S— C. ay. Geo. ay, [Ayes — 10; noes — 1.]

Mr. Govr Morris suggested the idea of providing that in all cases, the President in office, should not be one of the five Candidates; but be only re-eligible in case a majority of the electors should vote for him— (This was another expedient for rendering the President independent of the Legislative body for his continuance in office)

Mr. Madison remarked that as a majority of members wd. make a quorum in the H— of Reps. it would follow from the amendment of Mr Sherman giving the election to a majority of States, that the President might be elected by two States only, Virga. & Pena. which have 18 members, if these States alone should be present

On a motion that the eventual election of Presidt. in case of *an equality* of the votes of the electors be referred to the House of Reps.

N. H. ay. Mas. ay. N. J. no. Pa. ay. Del. no. Md. no. Va. ay. N— C. ay. S. C. ay— Geo— ay, [Ayes — 8; noes — 3.]

Mr. King moved to add to the amendment of Mr. Sherman

"But a quorum for this purpose shall consist of a member or members from two thirds of the States," and also of a majority of the whole number of the House of Representatives."

Col Mason liked it as obviating the remark of Mr Madison — The motion as far as "States" inclusive was agd. to

On the residue to wit. "and also of a majority of the whole number of the House of Reps. ⟨it passed in the Negative⟩

N. H. no. Mas. ay. Ct. ay. N. J. no. Pa. ay. Del. no. Md. **no.** Va. ay— N— C— ay— S— C— no— Geo— no. [Ayes — 5; noes — 6.]

The Report relating to the appointment of the Executive stands as amended, as follows,[23]

"He shall hold his office during the term of four years, and together with the vice-President, chosen for the same term, be elected in the following manner.

Each State shall appoint in such manner as its Legislature may direct, a number of electors equal to the whole number of Senators and members of the House of Representatives, to which the State may be entitled in the Legislature:

But no person shall be appointed an Elector who is a member of the Legislature of the U. S. or who holds any office of profit or trust under the U. S.

The Electors shall meet in their respective States and vote by ballot for two persons, of whom one at least shall not be an inhabitant of the same State with themselves; and they shall make a list of all the persons voted for, and of the number of votes for each; which list they shall sign and certify, and transmit sealed to the Seat of the General Government, directed to the President of the Senate.

The President of the Senate shall in the presence of the Senate and House of Representatives open all the certificates & the votes shall then be counted.

---

[23] Upon the method of electing the president, see above June 1–2, June 9, July 17–26, August 24, September 4–5, also (mainly on the compromise) Appendix A, XLI, CXXXVII, CLII, CLVIII (74–77), CLXXIII, CXCVIII, CCXIII, CCXV, CCXXII, CCXXVII, CCXXXIV, CCLXIII, CCLXXXVI, CCLXXXVIII, CCXCI, CCC, CCCII, CCCIII, CCCV, CCCXVIII, CCCXLV–CCCXLIX, CCCLII.

The person having the greatest number of votes shall be the President (if such number be a majority of the whole number of electors appointed) and if there be more than one who have such a majority, and have an equal number of votes, then the House of Representatives shall immediately choose by ballot one of them for President, the Representation from each State having one vote— But if no person have a majority, then from the five highest on the list, the House of Representatives shall in like manner choose by ballot the President— In the choice of a President by the House of Representatives, a Quorum shall consist of a member or members from two thirds of the States, (* and the concurrence of a majority of all the States shall be necessary to such choice–)—And in every case after the choice of the President, the person having the greatest number of votes of the Electors shall be the vice-president: But, if there should remain two or more who have equal votes, the Senate shall choose from them the vice-President.

The Legislature may determine the time of choosing the Electors, and of their giving their votes; and the manner of certifying and transmitting their votes — But the election shall be on the same day throughout the U— States."

Adjourned [25]

* Note. this clause was not inserted on this day, but on the 7th Sepr. See Friday the 7th[24]

McHENRY

Sepr. 6.

Spoke to Gov Morris Fitzimmons and Mr Goram to insert a power in the confederation enabling the legislature to erect piers for protection of shipping in winter and to preserve the navigation of harbours — Mr Gohram against. The other two gentlemen for it — Mr Gov: thinks it may be done under the words of the 1 clause 1 sect 7 art. amended — "and provide for the common defence and general welfare. — If this

[24] This may be a later insertion. [25] See further, Appendix A, CIII.

comprehends such a power, it goes to authorise the legisl. to grant exclusive privileges to trading companies etc.

Mr. Willson remarked on the report of the committee considered together That it presented to him a most dangerous appearance. He was not affraid of names — but he was of aristocracy.

What was the amount of the report.

1. The Senate in certain events, (which by such management as may be expected would always happen —) is to chuse the President.

2. The Senate may make treaties and alliances.

3 They may appoint almost all officers.

4 May try impeachments.

Montesqu– says, an officer is the officer of those who appoint him. This power may in a little time render the Senate independent of the people.

The different branches should be independent of each other. They are combined and blended in the Senate.

The Senate may exercise, the powers of legislation, and Executive and judicial powers. To make treaties legislative, to appoint officers Executive for the Executive has only the nomination — To try impeachments judicial. If this is not ARISTOCRACY I know not what it is.

Gov. Morris observed that the report had lessened not increased the powers of the Senate. That their powers were greater in the printed paper.

Col Hamilton.

In general the choice will rest in the Senate — take this choice from them and the report is an improvement on the printed paper.

In the printed paper a destroying monster is created. He is not re eligible, he will therefore consider his 7 years as 7 years of lawful plunder. Had he been made re eligible by the legislature, it would not have removed the evil, he would have purchased his re election.

At present the people may make a choice — but hereafter it is probable the choice of a president would centre in the Senate.

As the report stands — the President will use the power of nominating to attach the Senate to his interest. He will act by this means continually on their hopes till at length they will boeth act as one body. Let the election of the president be confined to electors, and take from the Senate the power to try impeachments, and the report will be much preferable to the printed paper.

He does not agree with those persons who say they will vote against the report because they cannot get all parts of it to please them — He will take any system which promises to save America from the dangers with which she is threatened. —

The report amended by placing the choice of the President in the house of representatives, each State having one vote.

Adjourned.

FRIDAY, SEPTEMBER 7, 1787.

JOURNAL

Friday September 7. 1787.

It was moved and seconded to insert the following clause after the words "throughout the United States" in the first sect. of the report.

"The Legislature may declare by law what officer of the "United States shall act as President in case of the death, "resignation, or disability of the President and Vice Presi-"dent; and such Officer shall act accordingly, until such "disability be removed, or a President shall be elected"

which passed in the affirmative [Ayes — 6; noes — 4; divided — 1.][1]

It was moved and seconded to insert the following amendment after the words "a member or members from two thirds of the States" in the 1st sect of the report.

"and the concurrence of a majority of all the States shall be necessary to make such choice."

which passed in the affirmative.

On the question to agree to the 2nd sect. of the report.

it passed in the affirmative.

[The V: Presidt shall ex officio be Presidt of the Senate. Ayes — 8; noes — 2.][2]

Separate questions having been taken on the several clauses of the 3rd sect. of the report

They passed in the affirmative.

[To insert "& the Ho of representatives" 5 sect of ye report Ayes — 1; noes — 10.

foreign Ministers Ayes — 4; noes — 7][3].

[1] Vote 473, Detail of Ayes and Noes. [2] Vote 474, Detail of Ayes and Noes.

[3] Votes 475 and 476, Detail of Ayes and Noes.

It was moved and seconded to amend the 2nd clause of the 4 sect of the report to read

"Ambassadors, other public Ministers, and Consuls"

which passed in the affirmative

[By & with the consent of the Senate appoint Ministers &ca
Ayes — 11; noes — 0.

Judges of the Supreme Court Ayes — 11; noes — 0.

and all other officers Ayes — 9; noes — 2.][4]

It was moved and seconded to postpone the consideration of the 4 sect. of the report in order to take up the following.

That it be an instruction to the Committee of the States to prepare a clause or clauses for establishing an Executive Council, as a Council of State, for the President of the United States, to consist of six Members, two of which from the Eastern, two from the middle, and two from the southern States with a rotation and duration of office similar to that of the Senate; such Council to be appointed by the Legislature or by the Senate.

On the question to postpone

it passed in the negative [Ayes — 3; noes — 8.][5]

[To agree to the last question Ayes — 11; noes — 0.][6]

It was moved and seconded to agree to the following clause

That the President shall have power to fill up all vacancies that may happen during the recess of the Senate by granting commissions which shall expire at the end of the next session of the Senate.

which passed in the affirmative

It was moved and seconded to insert the words (except treaties of Peace) after the word Treaty in the 4 sect of the report

which passed in the affirmative

[To agree to Mr Madison's amendmt Ayes — 3; noes — 8.][7]

— On the question to agree to the 4 sect. of the report as amended

it passed in the affirmative [Ayes — 8; noes — 3][8]

[4] Votes 477–479, Detail of Ayes and Noes.

[5] Vote 482, Detail of Ayes and Noes. *Journal* (pp. 340–341) mistakenly assigns Vote 480 to this question, see Madison's note below.

[6] Vote 483, Detail of Ayes and Noes.

[7] Vote 480, Detail of Ayes and Noes.

[8] Vote 481, Detail of Ayes and Noes.

It was moved and seconded to agree to the follow'g amendment.

"But no Treaty of peace shall be entered into, whereby the United States shall be deprived of any of their present Territory or rights without the concurrence of two thirds of the Members of the Senate present

The House adjourned

DETAIL OF AYES AMD NOES

	New Hampshire	Massachusetts	Rhode Island	Connecticut	New York	New Jersey	Pennsylvania	Delaware	Maryland	Virginia	No Carolina	So Carolina	Georgia	Questions	ayes	noes	divided
[473]	dd	no		no		aye	aye	no	aye	aye	no	aye	aye	To agree to the provision in case of the Presidts disability	6	4	1
[474]	aye	aye		aye		no	aye	aye	no	aye		aye	aye	The V: Presidt shall ex officio be Presidt of the Senate.	8	2	
[475]	no	no		no		no	aye	no	no	no	no	no	no	To insert "& the Ho of representatives" 5 sect of ye report	1	10	
[476]	no	no		no		no	aye	no	aye	no	aye	aye	no	foreign Ministers			
[477]	aye	aye		aye		aye	aye	aye	aye	aye	aye	aye	aye	By & with the consent of the Senate appoint Ministers &ce			
[478]	aye	aye		aye		aye	aye	aye	aye	aye	aye	aye	aye	Judges of the Supreme Court			
[479]	aye	aye		aye		aye	no	aye	aye	aye	aye	no	aye	and all other officers	9	2	
[480]	no	no		no		no	no	no	aye	no	no	aye	aye	To agree to Mr Madison's amendmt	3	8	
[481]	aye	aye		aye		no	no	aye	aye	aye	aye	aye	no	To agree to ye 4 sect of ye report	8	3	
[482]	no	no		no		no	no	no	aye	aye	no	no	aye	To postpone the clause and may require the opinion &ce	3	8	
[483]	aye	aye		aye		aye	aye	aye	aye	aye	aye	aye	aye	To agree to the last question	11		

MADISON

Friday Sepr. 7. 1787. In Convention

The mode of constituting the Executive being resumed, Mr- Randolph moved ⟨to insert in the first Section of the report made yesterday⟩[9]

"The Legislature may declare by law what officer of the U. S— shall act as President in case of the death, resignation, or disability of the President and Vice-President; and such officer shall act accordingly until the time of electing a President shall arrive."

Mr. Madison observed that this, as worded, would prevent a supply of the vacancy by an intermediate election of the President, and moved to substitute — "until such disability be removed, or a President shall be elected —" * Mr. Governr. Morris 2ded. the motion, which was agreed to.

It seemed to be an objection to the provision with some, that according to the process established for chusing the Executive, there would be difficulty in effecting it at other than the fixed periods; with others, that the Legislature was restrained in the temporary appointment to "*officers*" of the *U. S:* ⟨They wished it to be at liberty to appoint others than such.⟩

On the motion of Mr. Randolph as amended, it passed in the affirmative

N. H. divided. Mas. no. Ct. no. N. J. ay. Pa. ay. Del— no. Md. ay. Va. ay. N— C— no— S. C. ay— Geo. ay [Ayes — 6; noes — 4; divided — 1.]

Mr. Gerry moved "that in the election of President by the House of Representatives, no State shall vote by less than three members, and where that number may not be allotted to a State, it shall be made up by its Senators; and a concurrence of a majority of all the States shall be necessary to make such choice". Without some such provision five individuals might possibly be competent to an election, these

* ⟨In the printed Journal this amendment is put into the original Motion.⟩

[9] Taken from *Journal.*

being a majority of two thirds of the existing number of States; and two thirds being a quorum for this business.

Mr. Madison 2ded. the motion[10]

Mr. Read observed that the States having but one member only in the House of Reps. would be in danger of having no vote at all in the election: the sickness or absence either of the Representative or one of the Senators would have that effect

Mr. Madison replied that, if one member of the House of Representatives should be left capable of voting for the State, the states having one Representative only would still be subject to that danger. He thought it an evil that so small a number at any rate should be authorized, to elect. Corruption would be greatly facilitated by it. The mode itself was liable to this further weighty objection that the representatives of a *Minority* of the people, might reverse the choice of a *majority* of the *States* and of the *people*— He wished some cure for this inconveniency might yet be provided—

Mr Gerry withdrew the first part of his motion; and on the, — . . .

Question on the 2d. part viz, "and a concurrence of a majority of all the States shall be necessary to make such choice" to follow the words "a member or members from two thirds of the States" — It was agreed to nem: con:

The ⟨section 2.⟩[11] (see Sepr. 4)

requiring that the President should be a natural-born Citizen, &c & have been resident for fourteen years, & be thirty five years of age, was agreed to nem: con:

⟨Section 3.⟩[12] (see Sepr. 4). "The vice President shall be ex officio President of the Senate"[13]

Mr. Gerry opposed this regulation. We might as well put the President himself at the head of the Legislature. The close intimacy that must subsist between the President

---

[10] Crossed out "adding that otherwise three members might possibly elect them being from their several States and a quorum being made up by the representatives of two large States".

[11] Crossed out: "clause (2)".

[12] Crossed out "Clause (6)".

[13] Upon the Vice-President, see CLVIII (78), CCXXVI, CCXCVII, CCXCIX.

& vice-president makes it absolutely improper. He was agst. having any vice President.

Mr Govr Morris. The vice president then will be the first heir apparent that ever loved his father — If there should be no vice president, the President of the Senate would be temporary successor, which would amount to the same thing.

Mr Sherman saw no danger in the case. If the vice-President were not to be President of the Senate, he would be without employment, and some member by being made President must be deprived of his vote, unless when an equal division of votes might happen in the Senate, which would be but seldom.

Mr. Randolph concurred in the opposition to the clause.

Mr. Williamson, observed that such an officer as vice-President was not wanted. He was introduced only for the sake of a valuable mode of election which required two to be chosen at the same time.

Col: Mason, thought the office of vice-President an encroachment on the rights of the Senate; and that it mixed too much the Legislative & Executive, which as well as the Judiciary departments, ought to be kept as separate as possible. He took occasion to express his dislike of any reference whatever of the power to make appointments to either branch of the Legislature. On the other hand he was averse to vest so dangerous a power in the President alone. As a method for avoiding both, he suggested that a privy Council of six members to the president should be established; to be chosen for six years by the Senate, two out of the Eastern two out of the middle, and two out of the Southern quarters of the Union, & to go out in rotation two every second year; the concurrence of the Senate to be required only in the appointment of Ambassadors, and in making treaties. which are more of a legislative nature. This would prevent the constant sitting of the Senate which he thought dangerous, as well as keep the departments separate & distinct. It would also save the expence of constant sessions of the Senate. He had he said always considered the Senate as too unwieldy & expensive for appointing officers, especially the smallest, such

as tide waiters &c. He had not reduced his idea to writing, but it could be easily done if it should be found acceptable.

On the question shall the vice President be ex officio President of the Senate?

N— H. ay— Mas. ay— Ct. ay. N. J. no. Pa. ay. Del. ay— Mas— no. Va ay— N— C— abst S. C. ay— Geo. ay. [Ayes — 8; noes — 2; absent — 1.]

The other parts of the same ⟨Section⟩ (3) were then agreed to.

The ⟨Section 4.⟩[14] — to wit, "The President by & with the advice and consent of the Senate shall have power to make Treaties &c"

Mr. Wilson moved to add, after the word "Senate" the words, "and House of Representatives". As treaties he said are to have the operation of laws, they ought to have the sanction of laws also. The circumstance of secrecy in the business of treaties formed the only objection; but this he thought, so far as it was inconsistent with obtaining the Legislative sanction, was outweighed by the necessity of the latter.

Mr. Sherman thought the only question that could be made was whether the power could be safely trusted to the Senate. He thought it could; and that the necessity of secrecy in the case of treaties forbade a reference of them to the whole Legislature.

Mr Fitzsimmons 2ded. the motion of Mr Wilson, & on the question[15]

N. H. no. Mas. no. Ct. no. N. J. no. Pa ay. Del. no. Md. no Va. no. N. C. no. S. C. no. Geo. no. [Ayes — 1; noes — 10.]

The first sentence as to making treaties, was then Agreed to: nem: con:

— "He shall nominate &c Appoint ambassadors &c."

Mr. Wilson objected to the mode of appointing, as blending a branch of the Legislature with the Executive. Good laws are of no effect without a good Executive; and there can be

[14] Crossed out "(7) clause".

[15] See further, September 8, Appendix A, CXLIX, CLII, CLXX, CCXXV, CCXXVIII, CCLXXII, CCLXXIV, CCCXXII, CCCXXVI.

no good Executive without a responsible appointment of officers to execute. Responsibility is in a manner destroyed by such an agency of the Senate — He would prefer the Council proposed by Col: Mason, provided its advice should not be made obligatory on the President[16]

Mr. Pinkney was against joining the Senate in these appointments, except in the instances of Ambassadors who he thought ought not to be appointed by the President

Mr. Govr. Morris said that as the President was to nominate, there would be responsibility, and as the Senate was to concur, there would be security. As Congress now make appointments there is no responsibility.

Mr Gerry— The idea of responsibility in the nomination to offices is chimerical— The President can not know all characters, and can therefore always plead ignorance.

Mr King. As the idea of a Council proposed by Col. Mason has been supported by Mr. Wilson, he would remark that most of the inconveniencies charged on the Senate are incident to a Council of Advice. He differed from those who thought the Senate would sit constantly. He did not suppose it was meant that all the minute officers were to be appointed by the Senate, or any other original source, but by the higher officers of the departments to which they belong. He was of opinion also that the people would be alarmed at an unnecessary creation of New Corps which must increase the expence as well as influence of the Government.[17]

On the question on these words in the clause viz — "He shall nominate & by & with the advice and consent of the Senate, shall appoint ambassadors, and other public ministers (and Consuls) Judges of the supreme Court" Agreed to: nem: con: the insertion of "(and consuls" having first taken place.

On the question on the following words "And all other officers of U. S—"[18]

---

[16] See Appendix A, CXLIX.

[17] See Appendix A, CLXXXIV.

[18] See further Appendix A, CXXXVII, CXLIX, CLVIII (80), CCXXVIII, CCXLI, CCXLIII, CCXLV, CCLXXVII, CCLXXXVII, CCCV, CCCXVII, CCCXXVI, CCCLXXXIII, also CXXVIII.

N. H— ay— Mas ay. Ct ay. N— J— ay. Pa. no. Del. ay. Md. ay. Va ay. N— C. ay. S— C. no. Geo. ay. [Ayes 9; noes — 2.]

On[19] motion of Mr. Spaight — "that the President shall have power to fill up all vacancies that may happen during the recess of the Senate by granting Commissions which shall expire at the end of the next Session of the Senate" It was agreed to nem: con:

Section 4.[20] "The President by and with the advice and consent of the Senate shall have power to make Treaties" — "*But no treaty shall be made without the consent of two thirds of the members present*" — this last being before the House.[21]

Mr Wilson thought it objectionable to require the concurrence of ⅔ which puts it in the power of a minority to controul the will of a majority.

Mr. King concurred in the objection; remarking that as the Executive was here joined in the business, there was a check which did not exist in Congress where The concurrence of ⅔ was required.

Mr. Madison moved to insert after the word "treaty" the words "except treaties of peace" allowing these to be made with less difficulty than other treaties — It was agreed to nem: con:

Mr. Madison then moved to authorize a concurrence of two thirds of the Senate to make treaties of peace, without the concurrence of the President". — The President he said would necessarily derive so much power and importance from a state of war that he might be tempted, if authorized, to impede a treaty of peace. Mr. Butler 2ded. the motion

Mr Gorham thought the precaution unnecessary as the means of carrying on the war would not be in the hands of the President, but of the Legislature.

Mr. Govr Morris thought the power of the President in

---

[19] Several lines preceding were crossed out, they contained Mason's motion for a Council of State repeated below. From the Journal and Detail of Ayes and Noes, it seems as if this motion might have been offered at this time, but not voted upon till later.

[20] Crossed out "Clause (7)".

[21] See Appendix A, CCIV, CCXVII.

this case harmless; and that no peace ought to be made without the concurrence of the President, who was the general Guardian of the National interests.

Mr. Butler was strenuous for the motion, as a necessary security against ambitious & corrupt Presidents. He mentioned the late perfidious policy of the Statholder in Holland; and the artifices of the Duke of Marlbro' to prolong the war of which he had the management.

Mr. Gerry was of opinion that in treaties of peace a greater rather than less proportion of votes was necessary, than in other treaties. In Treaties of peace the dearest interests will be at stake, as the fisheries, territory &c. In treaties of peace also there is more danger to the extremities of the Continent, of being sacrificed, than on any other occasions.

Mr. Williamson thought that Treaties of peace should be guarded at least by requiring the same concurrence as in other Treaties.

On the motion of Mr. Madison & Mr. Butler

N. H. no. Mas. no. Ct. no. N. J. no. Pa. no. Del— no. Md. ay— Va no— N. C. no. S. C. ay. Geo. ay. [Ayes — 3; noes — 8.]

On the part of the clause concerning treaties amended by the exception as to Treaties of peace.

N. H. ay. Mas. ay. Ct. ay. N. J. no. Pa. no. Del. ay. Md. ay. Va. ay. N— C. ay. S— C. ay— Geo. no. [Ayes — 8; noes — 3.]

"and may require the opinion in writing of the principal officer in each of the Executive Departments, upon any subject relating to the duties of their respective offices." being before the House

Col: Mason* said that in rejecting a Council to the President we were about to try an experiment on which the most despotic Governments had never ventured— The Grand Signor himself had his Divan. He moved to postpone the

* ⟨In the printed Journal— Mr- Madison is erroneously substituted for Col: Mason—⟩[22]

[22] See above, note 5, and Appendix A, CCCXXXVII.

consideration of the clause in order to take up the following

"That it be an instruction to the Committee of the States to prepare a clause or clauses for establishing an Executive Council, as a Council of State for the President of the U. States, to consist of six members, two of which from the Eastern, two from the middle, and two from the Southern States, with a Rotation and duration of office similar to those of the Senate; such Council to be appointed by the Legislature or by the Senate".

Doctor Franklin 2ded. the motion. We seemed he said too much to fear cabals in appointments by a number, and to have too much confidence in those of single persons. Experience shewed that caprice, the intrigues of favorites & mistresses, &c were nevertheless the means most prevalent in monarchies. among instances of abuse in such modes of appointment, he mentioned the many bad Governors appointed in G. B. for the Colonies. He thought a Council would not only be a check on a bad President but be a relief to a good one.

Mr. Govr. Morris. The question of a Council was considered in the Committee, where it was judged that the Presidt. by persuading his Council— to concur in his wrong measures, would acquire their protection for them—

Mr. Wilson approved of a Council, in preference to making the Senate a party to appointmts.

Mr. Dickinson was for a Council. It wd. be a singular thing if the measures of the Executive were not to undergo some previous discussion before the President

Mr Madison was in favor of the instruction to the Committee proposed by Col. Mason.

⟨The motion of Mr. Mason was negatived. Maryd. ay. S. C. ay. Geo. ay— N. H. no. Mas. no. Ct. no. N. J. no Pa. no. Del. no. Va. no. N C no.⟩[23] [Ayes — 3; noes — 8.]

On the question, "authorizing the President to call for the opinions of the Heads of Departments, in writing": it

[23] Taken from *Journal*, which is in erorr as to the vote. See above note 5.

passed in the affirmative,[24] N. H. only being no.* ⟨The clause was then unanimously agreed to.⟩

Mr Williamson & Mr. Spaight moved "that no Treaty of Peace affecting Territorial rights shd be made without the concurrence of two thirds of the ⟨members of the Senate present.⟩

Mr. King— It will be necessary to look out for securities for some other rights, if this principle be established; he moved to extend the motion to — "all present rights of the U. States".

Adjourned[25]

*⟨not so stated in the Printed Journal; but comformable to the result afterwards appearing.⟩

McHENRY

Sepr. 7.

Made some further progress in the report.

Mr. Mason moved to postpone the section giving the President power to require the advice of the heads of the great departments to take up a motion — to appoint a council of State, to consist of 6 members — two from the Eastern, two from the middle and two from the Southern States — who should in conjunction with the President make all appointments and be an advisory body — to be elected by the legislature, to be in for 6 years with such succession as provided for the Senate.

3 States for postponing 8 against it — so it was lost.

Adjourned.

[24] Crossed out "N. H. ay & all the rest ay". See Vote 482, Detail of Ayes and Noes, and note 5.

[25] See further Appendix A, CIV.

SATURDAY, SEPTEMBER 8, 1787.

JOURNAL

Saturday September 8. 1787.

It was moved and seconded to strike the words ("except Treaties of Peace") out of the 4 sect. of the report.

which passed in the affirmative. [Ayes — 8; noes — 3.]

It was moved and seconded to strike out the last clause of the 4 sect. of the report

which passed in the negative [Ayes — 1; noes — 9; divided — 1.]

It was moved and seconded to agree to the following amendment.

"two thirds of all the Members of the Senate to make a treaty"

which passed in the negative [Ayes — 3; noes — 8.]

It was moved and seconded to agree to the following amendment.

"a majority of all the Members of the Senate to make a treaty"

which passed in the negative [Ayes — 5; noes — 6.]

It was moved and seconded to agree to the following amendment.

"No Treaty shall be made unless two thirds of the whole number of Senators be present

which passed in the negative. [Ayes — 5; noes — 6.]

It was moved and seconded to agree to the following amendment.

"But no Treaty shall be made before all the Members of "the Senate are summoned and shall have time to attend"

which passed in the negative [Ayes — 3; noes — 8.]

It was moved and seconded to agree to the following amendment

"neither shall any appointment be made as aforesaid unless to offices established by the Constitution or by law

which passed in the negative [Ayes — 5; noes — 6.]

It was moved and seconded to insert the words

"or other high crimes and misdemeanors against the State" after the word "bribery"

which passed in the affirmative [Ayes — 7; noes — 4.]

It was moved and seconded to strike out the words

"by the Senate" after the word "conviction"

which passed in the Negative [Ayes — 2; noes — 9.]

It was moved and seconded to strike out the word "State" after the word "against" and to insert the words "United States"

which passed in the affirmative. ["unanimous"]

On the question to agree to the last clause of the report.

it passed in the affirmative [Ayes — 10; noes — 1.]

It was moved and seconded to add the following clause after the words "United States"

"The Vice President and other civil Officers of the United "States shall be removed from Office on impeachment and "conviction as aforesaid"

which passed in the affirmative ["unanimous"]

It was moved and seconded to amend the 3rd clause of the report, entered on the Journal of the 5 instant, to read as follows — instead of the 12 sect. 6 article.

"all Bills for raising revenue shall originate in the House "of representatives: but the Senate may propose or concur "with amendments as on other bills." no money shall be drawn from the Treasury but in consequence of appropriations made by law.

which passed in the affirmative.[1]

[all bills for raising revenue shall originate in the Ho of representatives Ayes — 9; noes — 2.][2]

It was moved and seconded to amend the 3rd clause of the report, entered on the Journal of the 4 instant, to read as follows

[1] Vote 496, Detail of Ayes and Noes. No vote being recorded. the assumption is that it was unanimous as in Votes 493 and 495.

[2] Vote 497, Detail of Ayes and Noes.

DETAIL OF AYES AND NOES

	New Hampshire	Massachusetts	Rhode Island	Connecticut	New York	New Jersey	Pennsylvania	Delaware	Maryland	Virginia	No Carolina	So Carolina	Georgia	Questions	ayes	noes	divided
[484]	aye	aye		aye		no	aye	no	no	aye	aye	aye	aye	To strike out "except Treaties of Peace."	8	3	
[485]	no	no		dd		no	no	aye	no	no	no	no	no	To strike out the clause respectg Treaties.	1	9	1
[486]	no	no		no		no	no	no	no	no	aye	aye	aye	⅔rds of all the Members of the Senate to make a treaty	3	8	
[487]	no	aye		aye		no	no	aye	no	no	no	aye	aye	a majority of all the Members of the Senate to make a treaty	5	6	
[488]	no	no		no		no	no	no	aye	aye	aye	aye	aye	no treaty shall be made unless ⅔rds of the whole number of Senators be present	5	6	
[489]	no	no		no		no	no	no	no	no	aye	aye	aye	But no treaty shall be made before all the members of the Senate are summoned & shall have time to attend	3	8	
[page 16]																	
[490]	no	aye		aye		aye	no	no	no	no	aye	no	aye	neither shall any appointment be made as aforesaid unless to offices established by the Constitution or by law.	5	6	
[491]	aye	aye		aye		no	no	no	aye	aye	aye	no	aye	To insert after the word "bribery" "or other high crimes and misdemeanors, against the State"	7	4	
[492]	no	no		no		no	aye	no	no	aye	no	no	no	To strike out the words "by the Senate"	2	9	
[493]						unanimous.								To insert the "United States" instead of the "State"			
[494]	aye	aye		aye		aye	no	aye	aye	aye	aye	aye	aye	To agree to the clause respectg the impeachmt of the Presidt			
[495]						unanimous								The Vice Presidt and other civil officers of the U. S. shall be removed from office on impeachment & conviction as aforesaid			
[496]														But the Senate may propose or concur with amendments as in other Bills.			
[497]	aye	aye		aye		aye	aye	no	no	aye	aye	aye	aye	all bills for raising revenue shall originate in the Ho of representatives	9	2	
[498]	aye	aye		aye		aye	no	aye	aye	no	aye	aye	aye	To agree to the resolution that the Senate be the court of impeachment	9	2	
[499]	no	aye		aye		no	no	no	no	no	no	no	aye	The Legislature shall have the sole right of establishing offices not herein provided for	3	8	
[500]	aye	no		aye		aye	no	aye	aye	no	aye	no	aye	He may convene both or either of the Houses on extraordinary occasions. 2 sect. 10 art.	7	4	
[501]	no	no		no		no	aye	aye	aye	aye	aye	no	no	To reconsider the number of representatives	5	6	

In the place of the 1st sect. 9 article. insert

"The Senate of the United States shall have power to try "all impeachments: but no person shall be convicted without "the concurrence of two thirds of the Members present: and "every Member shall be on oath"

which passed in the affirmative [Ayes — 9; noes — 2.]

It was moved and seconded to agree to the following clause

"The Legislature shall have the sole right of establishing offices not herein provided for"

which passed in the negative [Ayes — 3; noes — 8.]

It was moved and seconded to amend the 3rd clause of the 2nd sect. 10 article to read

"He may convene both or either of the Houses on extraordinary occasions"

which passed in the affirmative [Ayes — 7; noes — 4.]

It was moved and seconded to appoint a Committee of five to revise the style of and arrange the articles agreed to by the House

which passed in the affirmative

And a Committee was appointed by ballot of the honorable Mr Johnson, Mr Hamilton, Mr G. Morris, Mr Madison and Mr King.

[To reconsider the number of representatives Ayes — 5; noes — 6.][3]

The House adjourned.

MADISON

Saturday September 8th. In convention

The last Report of Committee of Eleven ⟨(see Sepr. 4)⟩ was resumed.

Mr. King moved to strike out the "exception of Treaties of peace" from the general clause requiring two thirds of the Senate for making Treaties

Mr. Wilson wished the requisition of two thirds to be struck

[3] Vote 501, Detail of Ayes and Noes. *Journal* (p. 347) assigns this to September 10.

out altogether If the majority cannot be trusted, it was a proof, as observed by Mr. Ghorum, that we were not fit for one Society.

A reconsideration of the whole clause was agreed to.

Mr. Govr. Morris was agst. striking out the "exception of Treaties of peace" If two thirds of the Senate should be required for peace, the Legislature will be unwilling to make war for that reason, on account of the Fisheries or the Mississippi, the two great objects of the Union.[4] Besides, if a Majority of the Senate be for peace, and are not allowed to make it, they will be apt to effect their purpose in the more disagreeable mode, of negativing the supplies for the war.

Mr. Williamson remarked that Treaties are to be made in the branch of the Govt. where there may be a majority of the States without a majority of the people, Eight men may be a majority of a quorum, & should not have the power to decide the conditions of peace. There would be no danger, that the exposed States, as S. Carolina or Georgia, would urge an improper war for the Western Territory.

Mr. Wilson If two thirds are necessary to make peace, the minority may perpetuate war, against the sense of the majority.

Mr. Gerry enlarged on the danger of putting the essential rights of the Union in the hands of so small a number as a majority of the Senate, representing perhaps, not one fifth of the people. The Senate will be corrupted by foreign influence.

Mr. Sherman was agst leaving the rights, established by the Treaty of Peace, to the Senate, & moved to annex a "proviso that no such rights shd be ceded without the sanction of the Legislature.

Mr Govr. Morris seconded the ideas of Mr Sherman.

Mr. Madison observed that it had been too easy in the present Congress to make Treaties altho' nine States were required for the purpose.

On the question for striking "except Treaties of peace"

[4] See Appendix A, CCIV.

N. H. ay. Mas. ay. Ct. ay. N. J. no. Pa. ay. Del. no. Md. no— Va. ay. N. C.— ay. S. C. ay. Geo— ay [Ayes — 8; noes — 3.]

Mr. Wilson & Mr Dayton move to strike out the clause requiring two thirds of the Senate for making Treaties. — on which,

N. H no— Mas— no— Ct. divd. N— J. no. Pa. no Del. ay. Md. no. Va. no. N. C. no S. C. no. Geo. no. [Ayes — 1; noes — 9; divided — 1.]

Mr Rutlidge & Mr. Gerry moved that "no Treaty be made without the consent of ⅔ of all the members of the Senate" — according to the example in the present Congs

Mr. Ghorum. There is a difference in the case, as the President's consent will also be necessary in the new Govt.

On the question

N— H. no— Mass no— (Mr. Gerry ay) Ct. no. N. J— no. Pa. no. Del. no. Md. no. Va. no. N. C. ay. S. C. ay. Geo. ay. [Ayes — 3; noes — 8.]

Mr. Sherman movd, that "no Treaty be made without a Majority of the whole number ⟨of the Senate⟩ — Mr. Gerry seconded him.

Mr Williamson. This will be less security than ⅔ as now required.

Mr Sherman— It will be less embarrassing.

On the question, ⟨it passed in the negative.⟩

N. H. no. Mas. ay. Ct. ay. N. J. no. Pa. no. Del. ay. Md. no. Va. no. N— C— no. S. C. ay. Geo. ay. [Ayes — 5; noes — 6.]

Mr. Madison movd. that a Quorum of the Senate consist of ⅔ of all the members.

Mr. Govr. Morris — This will put it in the power of one man to break up a Quorum.

Mr. Madison, This may happen to any Quorum.

On the Question ⟨it passed in the negative⟩

N. H. no. Mas. no. Ct. no. N. J. no. Pa. no— Del. no— Md. ay. Va. ay. N. C. ay. S. C. ay. Geo. ay. [Ayes — 5; noes — 6.]

Mr. Williamson & Mr Gerry movd. "that no Treaty shd.

be made witht previous notice to the members, & a reasonable time for their attending."

On the Question

All the States no, except N— C— S. C. & Geo. ay.

On a question on clause of the Report of the Come. of Eleven relating to Treaties by ⅔ of the Senate. All the States were⟩ ay — except Pa N. J. & Geo. no.

Mr. Gerry movd. that no officer shall be appd but to offices created by the Constitution or by law." — This was rejected as unnecessary by six no's and five ays;

⟨The Ayes. Mas. Ct. N. J. N. C. Geo. — Noes— N. H. Pa.: Del. Md Va. S. C.⟩[5] [Ayes — 5; noes — 6.]

The clause referring to the Senate, the trial of impeachments agst. the President, for Treason & bribery, was taken up.[6]

Col. Mason. Why is the provision restrained to Treason & bribery only? Treason as defined in the Constitution will not reach many great and dangerous offences. Hastings is not guilty of Treason. Attempts to subvert the Constitution may not be Treason as above defined— As bills of attainder which have saved the British Constitution are forbidden, it is the more necessary to extend: the power of impeachments. He movd. to add after "bribery" "or maladministration". Mr. Gerry seconded him—

Mr Madison So vague a term will be equivalent to a tenure during pleasure of the Senate.

Mr Govr Morris, it will not be put in force & can do no harm— An election of every four years will prevent maladministration.

Col. Mason withdrew "maladministration" & substitutes "other high crimes & misdemeanors" ⟨agst. the State"⟩[7]

On the question thus altered

N. H— ay. Mas. ay— Ct. ay. ⟨N. J. no⟩ Pa no. Del. no. Md ay. Va. ay. N. C. ay. S. C. ay.* Geo. ay. [Ayes — 8; noes — 3.]

* ⟨In the printed Journal. S. Carolina — no.⟩

[5] Taken from *Journal*.

[6] See Appendix A, CXLIX, CLVIII (81–82), CLXX, CCCVI, CCCXCII.

[7] Revised from *Journal*.

Mr. Madison, objected to a trial of the President by the Senate, especially as he was to be impeached by the other branch of the Legislature, and for any act which might be called a misdemesnor. The President under these circumstances was made improperly dependent. He would prefer the supreme Court for the trial of impeachments, or rather a tribunal of which that should form a part.

Mr Govr Morris thought no other tribunal than the Senate could be trusted. The Supreme Court were too few in number and might be warped or corrupted. He was agst. a dependence of the Executive on the Legislature, considering the Legislative tyranny the great danger to be apprehended; but there could be no danger that the Senate would say untruly on their oaths that the President was guilty of crimes or facts, especially as in four years he can be turned out. —

Mr Pinkney disapproved of making the Senate the Court of Impeachments, as rendering the President too dependent on the Legislature. If he opposes a favorite law, the two Houses will combine agst him, and under the influence of heat and faction throw him out of office.

Mr. Williamson thought there was more danger of too much lenity than of too much rigour towards the President, considering the number of cases in which the Senate was associated with the President —

Mr Sherman regarded the Supreme Court as improper to try the President, because the Judges would be appointed by him.

On motion by Mr. Madison to strike out the words — "by the Senate" after the word "Conviction"

N— H. no. Mas— no. Ct. no. N. J. no— Pa. ay— Del— no. Md. no. Va. ay— N. C. no. S— C— no. Geo. no. [Ayes — 2; noes — 9.]

In the amendment of Col: Mason just agreed to, the word "State" after the words misdemeanors against" was struck out, and the words "United States" inserted, ⟨unanimously⟩[8] in order to remove ambiguity—

On the question to agree to clause as amended,

[8] Taken from *Journal*.

N. H. ay. Mas. ay. ⟨Cont ay⟩[8a] N. J. ay. Pa. no. ⟨Del. ay⟩[8a] Md. ay— Va. ay. N— C. ay. S. C. ay. Geo. ay [Ayes—10; noes—1.]

On motion "The vice-President and other Civil officers of the U. S. shall be removed from office on impeachment and conviction as aforesaid" was added to the clause on the subject of impeachments.

The clause of the report made on the 5th. Sepr. & postponed was taken up, to wit—"All bills for raising revenue shall originate in the House of Representatives; and shall be subject to alterations and amendments by the Senate. No money shall be drawn from the Treasury but in consequence of appropriations made by law."

It was moved to strike out the words "and shall be subject to alterations and amendments by the Senate" and insert the words used in the Constitution of Massachusetts on the same subject—"but the Senate may propose or concur with amendments as in other bills"—which was agreed too nem: con:[9]

On the question On the first part of the clause—"All bills for raising revenue shall originate in the house of Representatives" *

N. H. ay. Mas. ay. Ct. ay. N. J. ay Pa. ay. Del. no. Md. no. Va. ay. N. C. ay. S. C. ay. Geo. ay. [Ayes—9; noes—2.]

Mr. Govr Morris moved to add to clause (3) of the report made on Sept. 4. the words "and every member shall be on oath" which being agreed to, and a question taken on the clause ⟨so amended⟩ viz—"The Senate of the U. S. shall have power to try all impeachments: but no person shall be convicted without the concurrence of two thirds of the members present: and every member shall be on oath"

N. H. ay— Mas. ay. Ct. ay. N. J— ay. Pa. no— Del—

* This was a conciliatory vote, the effect of the compromise formerly alluded to. See Note Wednesday Sepr. 5.

[8a] Taken from *Journal*.

[9] Upon this subject, see June 13 (references under note 13), and Appendix A, CXLVI*a*, CLXXXI, CCX.

ay— Md ay. Va. no. N. C. ay. S. C. ay. Geo. ay. [Ayes —9; noes — 2.]

Mr. Gerry repeated his motion above made on this day, in the form following "The Legislature shall have the sole right of establishing offices not herein provided for". which was again negatived: ⟨Mas. Cont. & Geo. only being ay.⟩[10]

Mr. McHenry observed that the President had not yet been any where authorized to convene the Senate, and moved to amend Art X. sect. 2. by striking out the words "He may convene them (the Legislature) on extraordinary occasions" & insert "He may convene both or either of the Houses on extraordinary occasions" — This he added would also provide for the case of the Senate being in Session at the time of convening the Legislature.

Mr. Wilson said he should vote agst the motion because it implied that the senate might be in Session, when the Legislature was not, which he thought improper.

On the question

N. H. ay— Mas. no. Ct. ay. N. J. ay. Pa. no. Del— ay. Md. ay. Va. no— N. C. ay. S. C. no. Geo. ay. [Ayes — 7; noes — 4.]

A Committee was then appointed by Ballot to revise the stile of and arrange the articles which had been agreed to by the House. The Committee consisted of Mr. Johnson, Mr. Hamilton, Mr Govr. Morris, Mr. Madison and Mr. King.

Mr. Williamson moved that previous to this work of the Committee the clause relating to the number of the House of Representatives shd. be reconsidered for the purpose of increasing the number.[11]

Mr Madison 2ded. the Motion

Mr. Sherman opposed it— he thought the provision on that subject amply sufficient.

Col: Hamilton expressed himself with great earnestness and anxiety in favor of the motion. He avowed himself a friend to a vigorous Government, but would declare at the same time, that he held it essential that the popular branch

---

[10] Taken from *Journal*.

[11] See Appendix A, CCXVIII.

of it should be on a broad foundation. He was seriously of opinion that the House of Representatives was on so narrow a scale as to be really dangerous, and to warrant a jealousy in the people for their liberties. He remarked that the connection between the President & Senate would tend to perpetuate him, by corrupt influence. It was the more necessary on this account that a numerous representation in the other branch of the Legislature should be established.

On the motion of Mr. Williamson to reconsider, ⟨it was negatived,⟩

* N— H— no. Mas. no. Ct. no. N. J. no. Pa. ay. Del. ay. Md. ay. Va ay— N. C. ay. S. C. no. Geo. no. [Ayes — 5; noes — 6.]

Adjd [12]

* ⟨This motion & vote are entered on the Printed journal of the ensuing morning.⟩

McHENRY

Septr. 8 —

Agreed to the whole report with some amendments — and refered the printed paper etc to a committee of 5 to revise and place the several parts under their proper heads — with an instruction to bring in draught of a letter to Congres.

Committee Gov. Morris
Maddison
Hamilton
Dr. Johnson
King—

Maryland gave notice that she had a proposition of much importance to bring forward — but would delay it till Monday it being near the hour to adjourn.

[12] See further Appendix A, CV.

MONDAY, SEPTEMBER 10, 1787.

JOURNAL

Monday September 10. 1787.

It was moved and seconded to reconsider the 19th article
which passed in the affirmative [Ayes — 9; noes — 1; divided — 1.]

It was moved and seconded to amend the 19 article by adding the following clause.

Or the Legislature may propose amendments to the several States, for their approbation, but no amendments shall be binding, until consented to by the several States.

It was moved and seconded to insert the words "two thirds of" before the words "the several States"
which passed in the negative [Ayes — 5; noes — 6.]

It was moved and seconded to insert the words "three fourths"
which passed in the affirmative. ["unanimous"]

It was moved and seconded to postpone the consideration of the amendment in order to take up the following.

"The Legislature of the United States, whenever two "thirds of both Houses shall deem necessary, or on the ap-"plication of two thirds of the Legislatures of the several "States, shall propose amendments to this Constitution which "shall be valid to all intents and purposes as part thereof, "when the same shall have been ratified by three fourths at "least of the Legislatures of the several States, or by Conven-"tions in three fourths thereof, as one or the other mode "of ratification may be proposed by the Legislature of the "United-States: Provided that no amendments which may "be made prior to the year 1808. shall in any manner affect "the 4th and 5th Sections of article the 7th

On the question to postpone
it passed in the affirmative

On the question to agree to the last amendment.

it passed in the affirmative [Ayes — 9; noes — 1; divided— 1.]

It was moved and seconded to reconsider the 21st and 22nd articles

which passed in the affirmative [Ayes — 7; noes — 3; divided — 1.][1]

It was moved and seconded to postpone the 21st article in order to take up the following.

Resolved that the foregoing plan of a Constitution be transmitted to the United States in Congress assembled in order that if the same shall be agreed to by them it may be communicated to the Legislatures of the several States to the end that they may provide for it's final ratification by referring the same to the consideration of a Convention of Deputies in each State to be chosen by the People thereof, and that it be recommended to the said Legislatures in their respective acts for organizing such Convention to declare that, if the said Convention shall approve of the said Constitution, such approbation shall be binding and conclusive upon the State, and further that if the said Convention should be of opinion that the same upon the assent of any nine States thereto ought to take effect between the States so assenting — such opinion shall thereupon be also binding upon such State and the said Constitution shall take effect between the States assenting thereto.

On the question to postpone

it passed in the negative [Ayes — 1; noes — 10.]

On the question to agree to the 21st article

it passed in the affirmative [Ayes — 11; noes — 0.]

It was moved and seconded to restore the words "for their approbation" to the 22nd article

it passed in the negative

It was moved and seconded to refer the following to the Committee of revision.

"That it be an instruction to the Committee to prepare an

---

[1] Votes 506 & 507, Detail of Ayes and Noes.

"address to the People to accompany the present constitu-
"tion, and to be laid with the same before the United States
"in Congress.

which passed in the affirmative.

Detail of Ayes and Noes

	New Hampshire	Massachusetts	Rhode Island	Connecticut	New York	New Jersey	Pennsylvania	Delaware	Maryland	Virginia	No Carolina	So Carolina	Georgia	Questions	ayes	noes	divided
[502]	dd	aye		aye		no	aye	aye	aye	aye	aye	aye	aye	To reconsider the XIX article	9	1	1
[503]	aye	no		no		no	aye	aye	aye	aye	no	no	no	To agree to the amendment of "two-thirds"	5	6	
[504]						unanimous								To agree to the amendment of "three-fourths"			
[505]	dd	aye		aye		aye	aye	no	aye	aye	aye	aye	aye	To agree to the amendment of article XIXth	9	1	1
[506]	dd	no		aye		aye	no	aye	aye	aye	aye	no	aye	To reconsider the XXIInd article	7	3	1
[507]	dd	no		aye		aye	no	aye	aye	aye	aye	no	aye	To reconsider the XXIst article	7	3	1
[508]	no	no		aye		no	no	no	no	no	no	no	no	To postpone the 21st Article.	1	10	
[509]	aye	aye		aye		aye	aye	aye	aye	aye	aye	aye	aye	To agree to the 21st article.	11		

MADISON

Monday Sepr. 10. 1787. In Convention

Mr Gerry moved to reconsider art XIX. viz, "On the application of the Legislatures of two thirds of the States in the Union, for an amendment of this Constitution, the Legislature of the U. S. shall call a Convention for that purpose." ⟨(see Aug." 6.)⟩

This Constitution he said is to be paramount to the State Constitutions. It follows, hence, from this article that two thirds of the States may obtain a Convention, a majority of which can bind the Union to innovations that may subvert

the State-Constitutions altogether. He asked whether this was a situation proper to be run into—

Mr. Hamilton 2ded. the motion, but he said with a different view from Mr. Gerry— He did not object to the consequences stated by Mr. Gerry— There was no greater evil in subjecting the people of the U. S. to the major voice than the people of a particular State— It had been wished by many and was much to have been desired that an easier mode for introducing amendments had been provided by the articles of Confederation. It was equally desirable now that an easy mode should be established for supplying defects which will probably appear in the new System. The mode proposed was not adequate. The State Legislatures will not apply for alterations but with a view to increase their own powers— The National Legislature will be the first to perceive and will be most sensible to the necessity of amendments, and ought also to be empowered, whenever two thirds of each branch should concur to call a Convention— There could be no danger in giving this power, as the people would finally decide in the case.

Mr Madison remarked on the vagueness of the terms, "call a Convention for the purpose." as sufficient reason for reconsidering the article. How was a Convention to be formed? by what rule decide? what the force of its acts?

On the motion of Mr. Gerry to reconsider

N. H. divd. Mas. ay— Ct. ay. N. J— no. Pa ay. Del. ay. Md. ay. Va. ay. N— C. ay. S. C. ay. Geo. ay. [Ayes — 9; noes — 1; divided — 1.]

Mr. Sherman moved to add to the article ""or the Legislature may propose amendments to the several States for their approbation, but no amendments shall be binding until consented to by the several States"

Mr. Gerry 2ded. the motion

Mr. Wilson moved to insert "two thirds of" before the words "several States"— on which amendment to the motion of Mr. Sherman

N. H. ay. Mas. ⟨no⟩ Ct. no. N. J. ⟨no⟩ Pa. ay— Del— ay

Md. ay. Va. ay. N. C. no. S. C. no. Geo. no. [Ayes — 5; noes — 6.][2]

Mr. Wilson then moved to insert "three fourths of" before "the several Sts" which was agreed to nem: con:

Mr. Madison moved to postpone the consideration of the amended proposition in order to take up the following,

"The Legislature of the U— S— whenever two thirds of both Houses shall deem necessary, or on the application of two thirds of the Legislatures of the several States, shall propose amendments to this Constitution, which shall be valid to all intents and purposes as part thereof, when the same shall have been ratified by three fourths at least of the Legislatures of the several States, or by Conventions in three fourths thereof, as one or the other mode of ratification may be proposed by the Legislature of the U. S:"

Mr. Hamilton 2ded. the motion.

Mr. Rutlidge said he never could agree to give a power by which the articles relating to slaves might be altered by the States not interested in that property and prejudiced against it. In order to obviate this objection, these words were added to the proposition: "* provided that no amendments which may be made prior to the year 1808. shall in any manner affect the 4 & 5 sections of the VII article"—[3] The postponement being agreed to,

On the question On the proposition of Mr. Madison & Mr. Hamilton as amended

N. H. divd. Mas. ay. Ct. ay. N. J. ay. Pa. ay. Del. no. Md. ay. Va ay. N. C. ay S. C. ay. Geo. ay. [Ayes — 9; noes — 1; divided — 1.]

Mr. Gerry moved to reconsider art: XXI & XXII from the latter of which "for the approbation of Congs." had been struck out.[4]. He objected to proceeding to change the Govern-

* ⟨The Printed Journal makes the succeeding proviso as to sections 4 & 5 of art: VII, moved by Mr. Rutlidge, part of the proposition of Mr. Madison.⟩

[2] Madison originally recorded both Massachusetts and New Jersey as voting "ay". This made the total vote on the question affirmative. Later he revised his record to conform to *Journal*.

[3] See Appendix A, CCCXXXII.

[4] "from . . . out" possibly a later insertion.

ment without the approbation of Congress as being improper and giving just umbrage to that body. He repeated his objections also to an annulment of the confederation with so little scruple or formality.[5]

Mr. Hamilton concurred with Mr. Gerry as to the indecorum of not requiring the approbation of Congress. He considered this as a necessary ingredient in the transaction. He thought it wrong also to allow nine States as provided by art XXI. to institute a new Government on the ruins of the existing one. He wd propose as a better modification of the two articles (XXI & XXII) that the plan should be sent to Congress in order that the same if approved by them, may be communicated to the State Legislatures, to the end that they may refer it to State Conventions; each Legislature declaring that if the convention of the State should think the plan ought to take effect among nine ratifying States, the same shd take effect accordingly.

Mr. Gorham— Some States will say that nine States shall be sufficient to establish the plan— others will require unanimity for the purpose— And the different and conditional ratifications will defeat the plan altogether.

Mr. Hamilton— No Convention convinced of the necessity of the plan will refuse to give it effect on the adoption by nine States. He thought this mode less exceptionable than the one proposed in the article, and would attain the same end,

Mr Fitzimmons remarked that the words "for their approbation" had been struck out in order to save Congress from the necessity of an Act inconsistent with the Articles of Confederation under which they held their authority.

Mr. Randolph declared if no change should be made in this part of the plan, he should be obliged to dissent from the whole of it. He had from the beginning he said been convinced that radical changes in the system of the Union were necessary. Under this conviction he had brought forward a set of republican propositions as the basis and outline of a

---

[5] See Appendix A, CXCIX.

reform. These Republican propositions had however, much to his regret been widely, and in his opinion, irreconcileably departed from — In this state of things it was his idea and he accordingly meant to propose, that the State Conventions shd. be at liberty to offer amendments to the plan, — and that these should be submitted to a second General Convention, with full power to settle the Constitution finally— He did not expect to succeed in this proposition, but the discharge of his duty in making the attempt, would give quiet to his own mind.

Mr. Wilson was against a reconsideration for any of the purposes which had been mentioned.

Mr King thought it would be more respectful to Congress to submit the plan generally to them; than in such a form as expressly and necessarily to require their approbation or disapprobation. The assent of nine States he considered as sufficient; and that it was more proper to make this a part of the Constitution itself, than to provide for it by a supplemental or distinct recommendation.

Mr. Gerry urged the indecency and pernicious tendency of dissolving in so slight a manner, the solemn obligations of the articles of confederation. If nine out of thirteen can dissolve the compact, Six out of nine will be just as able to dissolve the new one hereafter.

Mr. Sherman was in favor of Mr. King's idea of submitting the plan generally to Congress. He thought nine States ought to be made sufficient: but that it would be best to make it a separate act and in some such form as that intimated by Col: Hamilton, than to make it a particular article of the Constitution.

On the question for reconsidering the two articles. XXI & XXII —

N. H. divd. Mas. no Ct. ay. N. J. ay. Pa. no Del. ay. Md. ay— Va. ay. N. C. ay. S. C. no .Geo. ay. [Ayes — 7; noes — 3; divided — 1.][6]

[6] The votes of Massachusetts, Pennsylvania, and South Carolina were changed from "ay" to "no". In the case of South Carolina this may have been a later revision, in the case of the other two, probably not.

Mr. Hamilton then moved to postpone art XXI in order to take up the following, containing the ideas he had above expressed. viz

Resolved that the foregoing plan of a Constitution be transmitted to the U. S. in Congress assembled, in order that if the same shall be agreed to by them, it may be communicated to the Legislatures of the several States, to the end that they may provide for its final ratification by referring the same to the Consideration of a Convention of Deputies in each State to be chosen by the people thereof, and that it be recommended to the said Legislatures in their respective acts for organizing such convention to declare, that if the said Convention shall approve of the said Constitution, such approbation shall be binding and conclusive upon the State, and further that if the said Convention should be of opinion that the same upon the assent of any nine States thereto, ought to take effect between the States so assenting, such opinion shall thereupon be also binding upon such State, and the said Constitution shall take effect between the States assenting thereto"

Mr. Gerry 2ded. the motion.

Mr. Wilson. This motion being seconded, it is necessary now to speak freely He expressed in strong terms his disapprobation of the expedient proposed, particularly the suspending the plan of the Convention on the approbation of Congress. He declared it to be worse than folly to rely on the concurrence of the Rhode Island members of Congs. in the plan. Maryland had voted on this floor; for requiring the unanimous assent of the 13 States to the proposed change in the federal System. N— York has not been represented for a long time past in the Convention. Many individual deputies from other States have spoken much against the plan. Under these circumstances Can it be safe to make the assent of Congress necessary. After spending four or five months in the laborious & arduous task of forming a Government for our Country, we are ourselves at the close throwing insuperable obstacles in the way of its success.

Mr. Clymer thought that the mode proposed by Mr.

Hamilton would fetter & embarrass Congs. as much as the original one, since it equally involved a breach of the articles of Confederation.

Mr. King concurred with Mr. Clymer. If Congress can accede to one mode, they can to the other. If the approbation of Congress be made necessary, and they should not approve, the State Legislatures will not propose the plan to Conventions; or if the States themselves are to provide that nine States shall suffice to establish the System, that provision will be omitted, every thing will go into confusion, and all our labor be lost.

Mr. Rutlidge viewed the matter in the same light with Mr. King

On the question to postpone in order to take up Col: Hamiltons motion

N. H— no. Mas. no. Ct. ay. N. J. no. Pa no. Del. no. Md. no. Va. no. N— C. no. S. C. no. Geo. no. [Ayes — 1; noes — 10.]

⟨A Question being then taken on the article XXI. It was agreed to, unanimously.⟩[7]

Col: Hamilton withdrew the remainder of the motion to postpone art XXII, observing that his purpose was defeated by the vote just given;

Mr. Williamson & Mr. Gerry moved to re-instate the words "for the approbation of Congress" in art: XXII. which was disagreed to nem: con:

Mr. Randolph took this opportunity to state his objections to the System. They turned on the Senate's being made the Court of Impeachment for trying the Executive — on the necessity of ¾ instead of ⅔ of each house to overrule the negative of the President — on the smallness of the number of the Representative branch, — on the want of limitation to a standing army — on the general clause concerning necessary and proper laws — on the want of some particular restraint on Navigation acts — on the power to lay duties on exports — on the Authority of the general Legislature to interpose

[7] Taken from *Journal.*

on the application of the *Executives* of the States — on the want of a more definite boundary between the General & State Legislatures — and between the General and State Judiciaries — on the the unqualified power of the President to pardon treasons — on the want of some limit to the power of the Legislature in regulating their own compensations. With these difficulties in his mind, what course he asked was he to pursue? Was he to promote the establishment of a plan which he verily believed would end in Tyranny? He was unwilling he said to impede the wishes and Judgment of the Convention— but he must keep himself free, in case he should be honored with a Seat in the Convention of his State, to act according to the dictates of his judgment. The only mode in which his embarrassments could be removed, was that of submitting the plan to Congs. to go from them to the State Legislatures, and from these to State Conventions having power to adopt reject or amend; the process to close with another general Convention with full power to adopt or reject the alterations proposed by the State Conventions, and to establish finally the Government— He accordingly proposed a Resolution to this effect.

Docr Franklin 2ded. the motion

Col: Mason urged & obtained that the motion should lie on the table for a day or two to see what steps might be taken with regard to the parts of the system objected to by Mr Randolph

Mr Pinkney moved "that it be an instruction to the Committee for revising the stile and arrangement of the articles agreed on, to prepare an Address to the people, to accompany the present Constitution, and to be laid with the same before the U— States in Congress"

* The motion itself was referred to the Committee. nem: con:

* Mr. Randolph moved to refer to the Committee also a motion relating to pardons in cases of Treason — which was agreed to nem: con:

Adjourned

* ⟨These motions not entered in the printed Journal.⟩

Proceedings of Convention Referred to the Committee of Style and Arrangement.[1]

We the People of the States of New-Hampshire, Massachusetts, Rhode-Island and Providence Plantations, Connecticut, New-York, New-Jersey, Pennsylvania, Delaware, Maryland, Virginia, North-Carolina, South-Carolina, and Georgia, do ordain, declare and establish the following Constitution for the Government of Ourselves and our Posterity.

ARTICLE I.

The stile of this Government shall be, "The United States of America."

II.

The Government shall consist of supreme legislative, executive and judicial powers.

III.

The legislative power shall be vested in a Congress, to consist of two separate and distinct bodies of men, a House of Representatives, and a Senate. The Legislature shall meet at least once in every year, and such meeting shall be on the first Monday in December unless a different day shall be appointed by law.

IV.

Sect. 1. The Members of the House of Representatives shall be chosen every second year, by the people of the several states comprehended within this Union. The qualifications of the electors shall be the same, from time to time, as those of the electors in the several States, of the most numerous branch of their own legislatures.

Sect. 2. Every Member of the House of Representatives shall be of the age of twenty-five years at least; shall have been a citizen of the United States for at least seven years before his election; and shall be, at the time of his election, an inhabitant of the State in which he shall be chosen.

[1] Compiled by the editor from the proceedings of the Convention.

Sect. 3. The House of Representatives shall, at its first formation, and until the number of citizens and inhabitants shall be taken in the manner herein after described, consist of sixty-five members, of whom three shall be chosen in New-Hampshire, eight in Massachusetts, one in Rhode-Island and Providence Plantations, five in Connecticut, six in New-York, four in New-Jersey, eight in Pennsylvania, one in Delaware, six in Maryland, ten in Virginia, five in North-Carolina, five in South-Carolina, and three in Georgia.

Sect. 4. As the proportions of numbers in the different states will alter from time to time; as some of the States may hereafter be divided; as others may be enlarged by addition of territory; as two or more States may be united; as new States will be erected within the limits of the United States, the Legislature shall, in each of these cases, regulate the number of representatives by the number of inhabitants, according to the rule hereinafter made for direct taxation not exceeding the rate of one for every forty thousand. Provided that every State shall have at least one representative.

Sect. 6.[2] The House of Representatives shall have the sole power of impeachment. It shall choose its Speaker and other officers.

Sect. 7. Vacancies in the House of Representatives shall be supplied by writs of election from the executive authority of the State, in the representation from which they shall happen.

V.

Sect. 1. The Senate of the United States shall be chosen by the Legislatures of the several States. Each Legislature shall chuse two members. Vacancies happening by refusals to accept, resignations or otherwise may be supplied by the Legislature of the State in the representation of which such vacancies shall happen, or by the executive thereof until the next meeting of the Legislature. Each member shall have one vote.

Sect. 2. The Senators shall be chosen for six years; but

[2] Sect. 5 was struck out.

immediately after they shall be assembled in consequence of the first election they shall be divided, by lot, into three classes, as nearly as may be, numbered one, two and three. The seats of the members of the first class shall be vacated at the expiration of the second year, of the second class at the expiration of the fourth year, of the third class at the expiration of the sixth year, so that a third part of the members may be chosen every second year.

Sect. 3. Every member of the Senate shall be of the age of thirty years at least; shall have been a citizen of the United States for at least nine years before his election; and shall be, at the time of his election, an inhabitant of the State for which he shall be chosen.

Sect 4. The Senate shall chuse its own President and other officers.

VI.

Sect. 1. The times and places and the manner of holding the elections of the members of each House shall be prescribed by the Legislature of each State respectively; but regulations in each of the foregoing cases may, at any time, be made or altered by the Legislature of the United States.

Sect. 3.[3] In each House a majority of the members shall constitute a quorum to do business; but a smaller number may adjourn from day to day, and may be authorised to compel the attendance of absent members in such manner and under such penalties as each House may provide.

Sect. 4. Each House shall be the judge of the elections, returns and qualifications of its own members.

Sect. 5. Freedom of speech and debate in the Legislature shall not be impeached or questioned in any court or place out of the Legislature; and the members of each House shall, in all cases, except treason, felony and breach of the peace, be privileged from arrest during their attendance at Congress, and in going to and returning from it.

Sect. 6. Each House may determine the rules of its pro-

[3] Sect. 2 was struck out.

ceedings; may punish its members for disorderly behaviour; and may, with the concurrence of two thirds, expel a member.

Sect. 7. The House of Representatives, and the Senate, shall keep a journal of their proceedings, and shall, from time to time, publish them, except such parts thereof as in their judgment require secrecy; and the yeas and nays of the members of each House, on any question, shall, at the desire of one-fifth part of the members present, be entered on the journal.

Sect. 8. During the session of the Legislature neither House, without the consent of the other, shall adjourn for more than three days, nor to any place than that at which the two Houses are sitting.

Sect. 9. The Members of each House shall be ineligible to any civil office under the authority of the United States created, or the emoluments whereof shall have been encreased during the time for which they shall respectively be elected — and no person holding any office under the United States shall be a Member of either House during his continuance in Office.

Sect. 10. The members of each House shall receive a compensation for their services, to be paid out of the Treasury of the United States, to be ascertained by law.

Sect. 11. The enacting stile of the laws of the United States shall be. "Be it enacted, by the Senate and Representatives in Congress assembled.

Sect. 12. All Bills for raising revenue shall originate in the House of representatives: but the Senate may propose or concur with amendments as on other bills. No money shall be drawn from the Treasury but in consequence of appropriations made by law.

Sect. 13. Every bill, which shall have passed the House of Representatives and the Senate, shall, before it become a law, be presented to the President of the United States, for his revision; if, upon such revision, he approve of it, he shall signify his approbation by signing it: But if, upon such revision, it shall appear to him improper for being passed into a law, he shall return it, together with his objections against it, to

that House in which it shall have originated, who shall enter the objections at large on their Journal, and proceed to reconsider the bill. But if, after such reconsideration, three-fourths of that House shall, notwithstanding the objections of the President, agree to pass it, it shall, together with his objections, be sent to the other House, by which it shall likewise be reconsidered, and, if approved by three-fourths of the other House also, it shall become a law. But, in all such cases, the votes of both Houses shall be determined by Yeas and Nays; and the names of the persons voting for or against the bill shall be entered in the Journal of each House respectively. If any bill shall not be returned by the President within ten days (Sundays excepted) after it shall have been presented to him, it shall be a law, unless the Legislature, by their adjournment, prevent its return; in which case it shall not be a law.

Sect. 14. Every order, resolution or vote, to which the concurrence of the Senate and House of Representatives may be necessary (except on a question of adjournment, and in the cases hereinafter mentioned) shall be presented to the President for his revision; and before the same shall have force, shall be approved by him, or, being disapproved by him, shall be repassed by the Senate and House of representatives, according to the rules and limitations prescribed in the case of a bill.

VII.

Sect. 1. The Legislature shall have power to lay and collect taxes, duties, imposts and excises, to pay the debts and provide for the common defence and general welfare of the United States.

To regulate commerce with foreign nations, and among the several States; and with the Indian tribes.

To establish an uniform rule of naturalization throughout the United States;

To coin money;

To regulate the value of foreign coin;

To fix the standard of weights and measures;

To establish post-offices and post-roads;

To borrow money on the credit of the United States;

To appoint a Treasurer by joint ballot;

To constitute tribunals inferior to the supreme court;

To make rules concerning captures on land and water;

To define and punish piracies and felonies committed on the high seas, to punish the counterfeiting of the securities, and current coin of the United States, and offences against the law of nations;

To declare war; and grant letters of marque and reprisal.

To raise and support armies; but no appropriation of money to that use shall be for a longer term than two years.

To provide & maintain a navy;

To make rules for the government and regulation of the land and naval forces.

To provide for calling forth the militia to execute the laws of the Union, suppress insurrections, and repel invasions;

To make laws for organizing, arming, and disciplining the militia, and for governing such part of them as may be employed in the service of the United States, reserving to the States, respectively, the appointment of the Officers, and the authority of training the militia according to the discipline prescribed by the United States.

To establish uniform laws on the subject of bankruptcies.

To exercise exclusive legislation in all cases whatsoever over such district (not exceeding ten miles square) as may by cession of particular States and the acceptance of the Legislature become the seat of the Government of the United States, and to exercise like authority over all Places purchased, by the consent of the Legislature of the State, for the erection of Forts, Magazines, Arsenals, Dock Yards and other needful buildings.

To promote the progress of science and useful arts by securing for limited times to Authors and Inventors the exclusive right to their respective writings and discoveries.

And to make all laws that shall be necessary and proper for carrying into execution the foregoing powers, and all other powers vested, by this Constitution, in the government of the United States, or in any department or officer thereof.

All[4] debts contracted and engagements entered into, by or under the authority of Congress shall be as valid against the United States under this constitution as under the confederation.

Sect. 2. Treason against the United States shall consist only in levying war against them, or in adhering to their enemies, giving them aid and comfort. The Legislature shall have power to declare the punishment of treason. No person shall be convicted of treason, unless on the testimony of two witnesses to the same overt act, or on confession in open court. No attainder of treason shall work corruption of blood, nor forfeiture, except during the life of the person attainted. The Legislature shall pass no bill of attainder nor any ex post facto laws.

Sect. 3. The proportions of direct taxation shall be regulated by the whole number of free citizens and inhabitants, of every age, sex, and condition, including those bound to servitude for a term of years, and three fifths of all other persons not comprehended in the foregoing description, (except Indians not paying taxes) which number shall, within three years after the first meeting of the Legislature, and within the term of every ten years afterwards, be taken in such manner as the said Legislature shall direct.

Sect. 4. No tax or duty shall be laid by the Legislature on articles exported from any State. The migration or importation of such persons as the several States now existing shall think proper to admit shall not be prohibited by the Legislature prior to the year 1808 — but a tax or duty may be imposed on such importation not exceeding ten dollars for each person. Nor shall any regulation of commerce or revenue give preference to the ports of one State over those of another, or oblige Vessels bound to or from any State to enter, clear, or pay duties in another.

And all duties, imposts, and excises, laid by the Legislature, shall be uniform throughout the United States.

[4] The correct location of this clause is uncertain. It was considered and adopted in connection with the "powers of Congress", and so is inserted here.

COMMITTEE OF STYLE

Sect. 5. No capitation tax shall be laid, unless in proportion to the census herein before directed to be taken.

Sect. 7.[5] The United States shall not grant any title of nobility. No person holding any office of profit or trust under the United States, shall without the consent of the Legislature accept of any present, emolument, office, or title of any kind whatever, from any king, prince or foreign State.

VIII.

This Constitution and the Laws of the United States which shall be made in pursuance thereof, and all treaties made or which shall be made under the authority of the United States shall be the supreme law of the several States, and of their citizens and inhabitants; and the judges in the several States shall be bound thereby in their decisions; any thing in the constitutions or laws of the several States to the contrary notwithstanding.

IX.

Sect. 1. The Senate of the United States shall have power to try all impeachments: but no person shall be convicted without the concurrence of two thirds of the Members present: and every Member shall be on oath.

X.

Sect. 1. The Executive power of the United States shall be vested in a single person. His stile shall be, "The President of the United States of America;" and his title shall be, "His Excellency." He shall hold his office during the term of four years, and together with the Vice President, chosen for the same term, be elected in the following manner.

Each State shall appoint, in such manner as it's legislature may direct, a number of Electors equal to the whole number of Senators and Members of the House of representatives to which the State may be entitled in the Legislature. But no Person shall be appointed an Elector who is a member of the

[5] Sect. 6 was struck out.

Legislature of the United States, or who holds any office of profit or trust under the United States.

The Electors shall meet in their respective States and vote by ballot for two Persons of whom one at least shall not be an inhabitant of the same State with themselves. — and they shall make a list of all the Persons voted for, and of the number of votes for each, which list they shall sign and certify, and transmit sealed to the seat of the general Government, directed to the President of the Senate.

The President of the Senate shall in the presence of the Senate and House of representatives open all the certificates and the votes shall then be counted.

The Person having the greatest number of votes shall be the President (if such number be a majority of the whole number of the Electors appointed) and if there be more than one who have such a majority, and have an equal number of votes, then the House of representatives shall immediately choose by ballot one of them for President, the representation from each State having one vote — But if no Person have a majority, then from the five highest on the list, the House of representatives shall, in like manner, choose by ballot the President — In the choice of a President by the House of representatives a quorum shall consist of a Member or Members from two thirds of the States, and the concurrence of a majority of all the States shall be necessary to such choice. — and, in every case after the choice of the President, the Person having the greatest number of votes of the Electors shall be the vice-President: But, if there should remain two or more who have equal votes, the Senate shall choose from them the Vice President

The Legislature may determine the time of chusing the Electors and of their giving their votes — But the election shall be on the same day throughout the United States

The Legislature may declare by law what officer of the United States shall act as President in case of the death, resignation, or disability of the President and Vice President; and such Officer shall act accordingly, until such disability be removed, or a President shall be elected

COMMITTEE OF STYLE

Sect. 2. No Person except a natural born Citizen, or a Citizen of the U. S. at the time of the adoption of this Constitution shall be eligible to the office of President: nor shall any Person be elected to that office, who shall be under the age of 35 years, and who has not been in the whole, at least 14 years a resident within the U. S.

Sect. 3. The Vice President shall be ex officio, President of the Senate, except when they sit to try the impeachment of the President, in which case the Chief Justice shall preside, and excepting also when he shall exercise the powers and duties of President, in which case, and in case of his absence, the Senate shall chuse a President pro tempore— The Vice President when acting as President of the Senate shall not have a vote unless the House be equally divided

Sect. 4. The President by and with the advice and consent of the Senate, shall have power to make treaties: and he shall nominate and by and with the advice and consent of the Senate shall appoint Ambassadors, other public Ministers and Consuls, Judges of the supreme Court, and all other officers of the U. S. whose appointments are not otherwise herein provided for. But no Treaty shall be made without the consent of two thirds of the Members present.

The President shall have power to fill up all vacancies that may happen during the recess of the Senate by granting commissions which shall expire at the end of the next session of the Senate.

Sect. 2.[6] He shall, from time to time, give to the Legislature information of the State of the Union: and recommend to their consideration such measures as he shall judge necessary, and expedient: he may convene both or either of the Houses on extraordinary occasions, and in case of disagreement between the two Houses, with regard to the time of adjournment, he may adjourn them to such time as he shall think proper: he shall take care that the laws of the United States be duly and faithfully executed: he shall commission all the officers of the United States; and shall appoint to all

[6] Original numbering, the sections above numbered 2–4 were insertions.

offices established by this constitution except in cases herein otherwise provided for, and to all offices which may hereafter be created by law. He shall receive Ambassadors, other public Ministers and Consuls. He shall have power to grant reprieves and pardons except in cases of impeachment. He shall be Commander in Chief of the Army and Navy of the United States, and of the Militia of the several States when called into the actual service of the United States; and may require the opinion in writing of the principal officer in each of the executive departments upon any subject relating to the duties of their respective offices. He shall, at stated times, receive for his services, a compensation, which shall neither be encreased nor diminished during his continuance in office. Before he shall enter on the duties of his department, he shall take the following Oath or Affirmation, "I———— solemnly swear (or affirm) that I will faithfully execute the Office of President of the United States of America, and will to the best of my judgment and power, preserve, protect and defend the Constitution of the United States." He shall be removed from his office on impeachment by the House of representatives, and conviction by the Senate, for treason or bribery or other high crimes and misdemeanors against the United States; the Vice President and other civil Officers of the United States shall be removed from Office on impeachment and conviction as aforesaid; and in case of his removal as aforesaid, death, absence, resignation or inability to discharge the powers or duties of his office the Vice President shall exercise those powers and duties until another President be chosen, or until the inability of the President be removed.

XI.

Sect. 1. The Judicial Power of the United States both in law and equity shall be vested in one Supreme Court, and in such Inferior Courts as shall, when necessary, from time to time, be constituted by the Legislature of the United States.

Sect. 2. The Judges of the Supreme Court, and of the Inferior courts, shall hold their offices during good behaviour. They shall, at stated times, receive for their services, a com-

pensation, which shall not be diminished during their continuance in office.

Sect. 3. The Judicial Power shall extend to all cases both in law and equity arising under this Constitution and the laws of the United States, and treaties made or which shall be made under their authority; to all cases affecting Ambassadors, other Public Ministers and Consuls; to all cases of Admiralty and Maritime Jurisdiction; to Controversies to which the United States shall be a party, to controversies between two or more States (except such as shall regard Territory and Jurisdiction) between a State and citizens of another State, between citizens of different States, between citizens of the same State claiming lands under grants of different States, and between a State or the citizens thereof and foreign States, citizens or subjects. In cases affecting Ambassadors, other Public Ministers and Consuls, and those in which a State shall be party, the Supreme Court shall have original jurisdiction. In all other cases beforementioned the Supreme Court shall have appellate jurisdiction both as to law and fact with such exceptions and under such regulations as the Legislature shall make.

Sect. 4. The trial of all crimes (except in cases of impeachments) shall be by jury and such trial shall be held in the State where the said crimes shall have been committed; but when not committed within any State then the trial shall be at such place or places as the Legislature may direct.

The privilege of the writ of Habeas Corpus shall not be suspended; unless where in cases of rebellion or invasion the public safety may require it.

Sect. 5. Judgment, in cases of Impeachment, shall not extend further than to removal from office, and disqualification to hold and enjoy any office of honour, trust or profit under the United States. But the Party convicted shall nevertheless, be liable and subject to indictment, trial, judgment and punishment, according to law.

XII.

No State shall coin money; nor emit bills of credit, nor make anything but gold or silver coin a tender in payment of debts; nor pass any bill of attainder or ex post facto laws; nor grant letters of marque and reprisal, nor enter into any treaty, alliance, or confederation; nor grant any title of nobility.

XIII.

No State, without the consent of the Legislature of the United States shall lay imposts or duties on imports or exports, nor with such consent but for the use of the treasury of the United States; nor keep troops or ships of war in time of peace; nor enter into any agreement or compact with another State, or with any foreign power; nor engage in any war, unless it shall be actually invaded by enemies, or the danger of invasion be so imminent, as not to admit of a delay, until the Legislature of the United States can be consulted.

XIV.

The citizens of each State shall be entitled to all privileges and immunities of citizens of the several States.

XV.

Any person charged with treason, felony, or other crime in any State, who shall flee from justice, and shall be found in any other State, shall, on demand of the Executive Power of the State from which he fled, be delivered up and removed to the State having jurisdiction of the offence.

If any Person bound to service or labor in any of the United States shall escape into another State, He or She shall not be discharged from such service or labor in consequence of any regulations subsisting in the State to which they escape; but shall be delivered up to the person justly claiming their service or labor.

XVI.

Full faith and credit shall be given in each State to the public Acts, records, and judicial proceedings of every other

State, and the Legislature may by general laws prescribe the manner in which such acts, records, and proceedings shall be proved and the effect thereof.

XVII.

New States may be admitted by the Legislature into this Union: but no new State shall be hereafter formed or erected within the jurisdiction of any of the present States, without the consent of the Legislature of such State as well as of the general Legislature. Nor shall any State be formed by the junction of two or more States or parts thereof without the consent of the Legislatures of such States as well as of the Legislature of the United States.

The Legislature shall have power to dispose of and make all needful rules and regulations respecting the territory or other property belonging to the United States: and nothing in this Constitution contained shall be so construed as to prejudice any claims either of the United States or of any particular State.

XVIII.

The United States shall guaranty to each State a Republican form of government; and shall protect each State against invasions, and, on the application of its Legislature or Executive, against domestic violence.

XIX.

The Legislature of the United States, whenever two thirds of both Houses shall deem necessary, or on the application of two thirds of the Legislatures of the several States, shall propose amendments to this Constitution which shall be valid to all intents and purposes as parts thereof, when the same shall have been ratified by three fourths at least of the Legislatures of the several States, or by Conventions in three fourths thereof, as one or the other mode of ratification may be proposed by the Legislature of the United-States: Provided that no amendments which may be made prior to the year 1808. shall in any manner affect the 4th and 5th Sections of article the 7th

XX.

The Members of the Legislatures, and the executive and judicial officers of the United States, and of the several States, shall be bound by oath or affirmation to support this Constitution.

But no religious test shall ever be required as a qualification to any office or public trust under the authority of the United States.

XXI.

The ratification of the Conventions of nine States shall be sufficient for organising this Constitution between the said States.

XXII.

This Constitution shall be laid before the United States in Congress assembled, and it is the opinion of this Convention that it should be afterwards submitted to a Convention chosen in each State, under the recommendation of its Legislature, in order to receive the ratification of such Convention.

XXIII.

To introduce this government, it is the opinion of this Convention, that each assenting Convention should notify its assent and ratification to the United States in Congress assembled; that Congress, after receiving the assent and ratification of the Conventions of nine States, should appoint and publish a day, as early as may be, and appoint a place for commencing proceedings under this Constitution; that after such publication, the Legislatures of the several States should elect Members of the Senate, and direct the election of Members of the House of Representatives; and that the Members of the Legislature should meet at the time and place assigned by Congress and should, as soon as may be, after their meeting, proceed to execute this Constitution.

That it be an instruction to the Committee to prepare an address to the People to accompany the present constitution,

COMMITTEE OF STYLE

and to be laid with the same before the United States in Congress.[7]

Mr. Randolph moved to refer to the Committee also a motion relating to pardons in cases of Treason — which was agreed to nem: con:[7]

---

[7] Action taken by the Convention at the close of the proceedings on September 10.

TUESDAY, SEPTEMBER 11, 1787.

JOURNAL

Tuesday September 11. 1787.

The House met — but the Committee of revision not having reported, and there being no business before the Convention

The House adjourned.

MADISON

Tuesday Sepr. 11. 1787. In Convention

The report of the Committee of Stile & arrangement[1] not being made & being waited for,

the House Adjourned

---

[1] Upon the work of the Committee of Style and Arrangement, in particular the share of Gouverneur Morris, see Appendix A, CLVI, CCCXIV, CCCLXXIX.

WEDNESDAY, SEPTEMBER 12, 1787.

JOURNAL

Wednesday September 12. 1787.

The honorable Mr Johnson from the Committee of revision informed the House that the Committee were prepared to report the Constitution as revised and arranged.

The report was then delivered in at the Secretary's table[1] — and having been once read throughout.

Ordered that the Members be furnished with printed copies thereof.[1]

The draught of a letter to Congress being at the same time reported — was read once throughout, and afterwards agreed to by paragraphs.

It was moved and seconded to reconsider the 13th sect. of the 6th article

which passed in the affirmative

It was moved and seconded to strike out the words three fourths and to insert the words "two thirds" in the 13 sect of the 6th article

which passed in the affirmative [Ayes — 6; noes — 4; divided — 1.]

It was moved and seconded to appoint a Committee to prepare a Bill of rights

which passed in the negative [Ayes — 0; noes — 10.][2]

---

[1] No copy found among the secretary's papers.

[2] Vote 511, Detail of Ayes and Noes. From this point on the records of the Journal are more unsatisfactory than ever, and it is impossible to reach any satisfactory conclusion with regard to the various questions and votes. At the request of John Quincy Adams, when he was preparing the Journal for publication, Madison first sent him extracts from his notes of the last two days, and later, as far as he was able, filled in the blanks of a list of ayes and noes submitted to him by Adams. See Appendix A, CCCXXIV, CCCXXVIII, CCCXXX, CCCXXXVII.

It was moved and seconded to reconsider the 13th article in order to add the following clause

at the end of the 13 article.

"Provided nothing herein contained shall be construed to "restrain any State from laying duties upon exports, for the "sole purpose of defraying the charges of inspecting, packing, "storing, and indemnifying the losses in keeping the Com- "modities, in the care of public Officers, before exportation"

It was agreed to reconsider[3]

DETAIL OF AYES AND NOES

	New Hampshire	Massachusetts	Rhode Island	Connecticut	New York	New Jersey	Pennsylvania	Delaware	Maryland	Virginia	No Carolina	So Carolina	Georgia	Questions	ayes	noes	divided
[510]	dd	no		aye		aye	no	no	aye	no	aye	aye	aye	⅔rds of the Legislature instead of ¾ths to repass a law.			
[511]	no			no		no	no	no	no	no	no	no	no	To appoint a Committee to prepare a Bill of rights	0	10	
[512]	aye			aye		aye	aye	aye	aye	ye	aye	aye	aye				
[513]	no			aye		no	aye	no	aye	aye	aye	aye	aye	To agree to Commodities	7	3	

LETTER TO CONGRESS[3a]

We have now the Honor to submit to the Consideration of the United States in Congress assembled that Constitution which has appeared to us the most advisable.

The Friends of our Country have long seen and desired that the Power of making war Peace and Treaties, that of levying Money & regulating Commerce and the correspondent executive and judicial Authorities should be fully and effectually vested in the general Government of the Union.

[3] Vote 512, Detail of Ayes and Noes, might be assigned to this question. *Journal* (p. 369) assigns Vote 513. Votes 512 and 513 may belong under September 13.

[3a] This document was among the papers of the Convention turned over to the Secretary of State by President Washington in 1796. It is in the handwriting of Gouverneur Morris.

But the Impropriety of delegating such extensive Trust to one Body of Men is evident. Hence results the Necessity of a different Organization.

It is obviously impracticable - - - - in the fœderal Government of these States to secure all Rights of independent Sovereignty to each and yet provide for the Interest and Safety of all. Individuals entering into Society must give up a Share of Liberty to preserve the Rest. The Magnitude of the Sacrifice must depend as well on Situation and Circumstances as on the Object to be obtained. It is at all Times difficult to draw with Precision the Line between those Rights which must be surrendered and those which may be reserved And on the present Occasion this Difficulty was encreased by a Difference among the several States as to their Situation Extent Habits and particular Interests.

In all our Deliberations on this Subject we kept steadily in our View that which appears to us the greatest Interest of every true American The Consolidation[3b] of our Union in which is involved our Prosperity Felicity Safety perhaps our national Existence. This important Consideration seriously and deeply impressed on our Minds led each State in the Convention to be less rigid on Points of inferior Magnitude than might have been otherwise expected. And thus the Constitution which we now present is the Result of a Spirit of Amity and of that mutual Deference & Concession which the Peculiarity of our political Situation rendered indispensible.[3c]

That it will meet the full and entire approbation of every State is not perhaps to be expected But each will doubtless consider that had her Interests been alone consulted the Consequences might have been particularly disagreeable or injurious to others. That it is liable to as few Exceptions as could reasonably have been expected we hope and believe That it may promote the lasting Welfare of that Country so dear to us all and secure her Freedom and Happiness is our most ardent Wish —[3d]

[3b] See Appendix A, CCCLI. [3c] See Appendix A, CCXXV, CCCXIII.

[3d] [Endorsed:] Draught of the letter from the Convention to Congress, to accompany the Constitution.

MADISON

Wednesday Sepr 12. 1787— In Convention

Docr. Johnson from the Committee of stile &c— reported a digest of the plan, of which printed copies were ordered to be furnished to the members— He also reported a letter to accompany the plan to, Congress. (here insert a transcript ⟨of the former from the annexed sheet as *printed* * and of the latter from the draft as finally agreed to⟩ [4]

Mr. WILLIAMSON moved to reconsider the clause requiring three fourths of each House to overrule the negative of the President, in order to strike out $\frac{3}{4}$ and insert $\frac{2}{3}$. He had he remarked himself proposed $\frac{3}{4}$ instead of $\frac{2}{3}$, but he had since been convinced that the latter proportion was the best. The former puts too much in the power of the President.

Mr. SHERMAN was of the same opinion; adding that the States would not like to see so small a minority and the President, prevailing over the general voice. In making laws regard should be had to the sense of the people. who are to be bound by them, and it was more probable that a single man should mistake or betray this sense than the Legislature

Mr Govr MORRIS. Considering the difference between the two proportions numerically, it amounts in one House to two members only; and in the other to not more than five, according to the numbers of which the Legislature is at first to be composed — It is the interest moreover of the distant States to prefer $\frac{3}{4}$ as they will be oftenest absent and need the interposing check of the President. The excess rather than the deficiency of laws was to be dreaded. The example of N. York shows that $\frac{2}{3}$ is not sufficient to answer the purpose.

Mr. HAMILTON added his testimony to the fact that $\frac{2}{3}$ in N. York had been ineffectual either where a popular object, or a legislative faction operated; of which he mentioned some instances.

* ⟨This is a literal copy of the printed Report.[4] The Copy in the printed Journal contains some of the alterations subsequently made in the House.⟩

[4] There is no such transcript among the Madison Papers. A copy of the printed report is given below.

Mr. Gerry. It is necessary to consider the danger on the other side also. $\frac{2}{3}$ will be a considerable, perhaps a proper security. $\frac{3}{4}$ puts too much in the power of a few men — The primary object of the revisionary check in the President is not to protect the general interest, but to defend his own department. If $\frac{3}{4}$ be required, a few Senators having hopes from the nomination of the President to offices, will combine with him and impede proper laws. Making the vice-President Speaker increases the danger,

Mr. Williamson was less afraid of too few than of too many laws. He was most of all afraid that the repeal of bad laws might be rendered too difficult by requiring $\frac{3}{4}$ to overcome the dissent of the President.

Col: Mason had always considered this as one of the most exceptionable parts of the System. As to the numerical argument of Mr. Govr. Morris, little arithmetic was necessary to understand that $\frac{3}{4}$ was more than $\frac{2}{3}$, whatever the numbers of the Legislature might be. The example of New York depended on the real merits of the laws. The Gentlemen citing it, had no doubt given their own opinions. But perhaps there were others of opposite opinions who could equally paint the abuses on the other side. His leading view was to guard against too great an impediment to the repeal of laws.

Mr. Govr. Morris dwelt on the danger to the public interest from the instability of laws, as the most to be guarded against. On the other side there could be little danger. If one man in office will not consent when he ought, every fourth year another can be substituted. This term was not too long for fair experiments. Many good laws are not tried long enough to prove their merit. This is often the case with new laws opposed to old habits. The Inspection laws of Virginia & Maryland to which all are now so much attached were unpopular at first.

Mr. Pinkney was warmly in opposition to $\frac{3}{4}$ as putting a dangerous power in the hands of a few Senators headed by the President.

Mr. Madison. When $\frac{3}{4}$ was agreed to, the President was

to be elected by the Legislature and for seven years — He is now to be elected by the people and for four years. The object of the revisionary power is twofold. 1. to defend the Executive Rights 2. to prevent popular or factious injustice. It was an important principle in this & in the State Constitutions to check legislative injustice and incroachments. The Experience of the States had demonstrated that their checks are insufficient. We must compare the danger from the weakness of $\frac{2}{3}$ with the danger from the strength of $\frac{3}{4}$. He thought on the whole the former was the greater. As to the difficulty of repeals, it was probable that in doubtful cases the policy would soon take place of limiting the duration of laws so as to require renewal instead of repeal.

The reconsideration being agreed to On the question to insert $\frac{2}{3}$ in place of $\frac{3}{4}$.

N— H— divd. Mas. no. Ct. ay. N— J. ay. Pa. no. Del. no. Md. ay. Mr McHenry no. Va no. Genl. Washington Mr. Blair, Mr. Madison no. Col. Mason, Mr. Randolph ay. N— C.— ay. S— C. ay. Geo. ay. [Ayes — 6; noes — 4; divided — 1.]

Mr. Williamson, observed to the House that no provision was yet made for juries in Civil cases and suggested the necessity of it.[5]

Mr. Gorham. It is not possible to discriminate equity cases from those in which juries are proper. The Representatives of the people may be safely trusted in this matter.

Mr. Gerry urged the necessity of Juries to guard agst. corrupt Judges. He proposed that the Committee last appointed should be directed to provide a clause for securing the trial by Juries.

Col: Mason perceived the difficulty mentioned by Mr. Gorham. The jury cases cannot be specified. A general principle laid down on this and some other points would be sufficient. He wished the plan had been prefaced with a Bill of Rights, & would second a Motion if made for the purpose — It would give great quiet to the people; and with the aid of

[5] See Appendix A, CXXV, CXLVI*a*, CL, CLIII, CLVIII (85–86), CLXX, CLXXXIX, CXCVIII, CXCIX, CCVI, CCXV, CCXXVIII, CCXXX.

the State declarations, a bill might be prepared in a few hours.[6]

Mr Gerry concurred in the idea & moved for a Committee to prepare a Bill of Rights. Col: Mason 2ded the motion.

Mr. Sherman. was for securing the rights of the people where requisite. The State Declarations of Rights are not repealed by this Constitution; and being in force are sufficient — There are many cases where juries are proper which cannot be discriminated. The Legislature may be safely trusted.

Col: Mason. The Laws of the U. S. are to be paramount to State Bills of Rights. On the question for a Come to prepare a Bill of Rights

N. H. no. Mas. abst. Ct no. N— J— no. Pa. no. Del— no. Md no. Va no. N— C. no. S— C— no— Geo— no. [Ayes — 0; noes — 10; absent — 1.]

The Clause relating to exports being reconsidered, at the instance of Col: Mason, Who urged that the restriction on the States would prevent the incidental duties necessary for the inspection & safe-keeping of their produce, and be ruinous to the Staple States, as he called the five Southern States, he moved as follows — 'provided nothing herein contained shall be construed to restrain any State from laying duties upon exports for the sole purpose of defraying the Charges of inspecting, packing, storing and indemnifying the losses, in keeping the commodities in the care of public officers, before exportation," In answer to a remark which he anticipated, to wit, that the States could provide for these expences, by a tax in some other way, he stated the inconveniency of requiring the Planters to pay a tax before the actual delivery for exportation.[7]

Mr Madison 2ded the motion — It would at least be harmless; and might have the good effect of restraining the States to bona fide duties for the purpose, as well as of authorizing explicitly such duties; tho' perhaps the best guard against

[6] Upon a Bill of Rights, see Appendix A, CXLV, CXLIX, CLXXIII, CLXXXIX, CXCII, CXCVIII, CCXLII.

[7] See Appendix A, CLVIII (73), CLXXXIV, also August 25, note 13.

an abuse of the power of the States on this subject, was the right in the Genl. Government to regulate trade between State & State.

Mr Govr Morris saw no objection to the motion. He did not consider the dollar per Hhd laid on Tobo in Virga. as a duty on exportation, as no drawback would be allowed on Tobo. taken out of the Warehouse for internal consumption,

Mr. Dayton was afraid the proviso wd. enable Pennsylva. to tax N. Jersey under the idea of Inspection duties of which Pena. would Judge.

Mr. Gorham & Mr. Langdon, thought there would be no security if the proviso shd. be agreed to, for the States exporting thro' other States, agst. oppressions of the latter. How was redress to be obtained in case duties should be laid beyond the purpose expressed?

Mr. Madison — There will be the same security as in other cases — The jurisdiction of the supreme Court must be the source of redress. So far only had provision been made by the plan agst. injurious acts of the States. His own opinion was, that this was insufficient, —. A negative on the State laws alone. could meet all the shapes which these could assume. But this had been overruled.

Mr Fitzimons. Incidental duties on Tobo. & flour. never have been & never can be considered as duties on exports —

Mr Dickinson. Nothing will save States in the situation of N. Hampshire N Jersey Delaware &c. from being oppressed by their Neighbors, but requiring the assent of Congs to inspection duties, He moved that this assent shd accordingly be required

Mr. Butler 2ded the motion.

Adjourned

McHENRY

Monday Sepr. 10, 11 and 12.

Spent in attempts to amend several parts of the system.

12 — amended the sect art from $\frac{3}{4}$ to $\frac{2}{3}$, — as it stood in the printed report at first.

COMMITTEE OF STYLE

Report of Committee of Style[8]

WE, the People of the United States, in order to form

a more perfect union, to establish justice, insure domestic tranquillity, provide for the common defence, promote the general welfare, and secure the blessings of liberty to ourselves and our posterity, do ordain and establish this Constitution for the United States of America.

ARTICLE I.

Sect. 1. ALL legislative powers herein granted shall be vested in a Congress of the United States, which shall consist of a Senate and House of Representatives.

Sect. 2. The House of Representatives shall be composed of members chosen every second year by the people of the several states, and the electors in each state shall have the qualifications requisite for electors of the most numerous branch of the state legislature.

⟨(*a*)⟩ No person shall be a representative who shall not have attained to the age of twenty-five years, and been seven years a citizen of the United States, and who shall not, when elected, be an inhabitant of that state in which he shall be chosen.

⟨(*b*)⟩ Representatives and direct taxes shall be apportioned among the several states which may be included within this Union, according to their respective numbers, which shall be determined by adding to the whole number of free persons, including those bound to servitude for a term of years, and excluding Indians not taxed, three fifths of all other persons. The actual enumeration shall be made within three years after the first meeting of the Congress of the United States, and

[8] Madison's copy of this report is a printed broadside, preserved, with other printed papers, in Volume XV of "Writings to Madison." It shows additions, alterations and interlineations in Madison's handwriting, and these are indicated here by enclosing in angle brackets. Underscoring was likewise done by pen. At the top of his copy Madison wrote:

"As Reported by Come. of revision, or Stile & arrangement. Sepr. 12. consisting of Mr Johnson Mr Hamilton Mr. Morris, Mr. Madison & Mr King."

within every subsequent term of ten years, in such manner as they shall by law direct. The number of representatives shall not exceed one for every forty thousand, but each state shall have at least one representative: and until such enumeration shall be made, the state of New-Hampshire shall be entitled to chuse three, Massachusetts eight, Rhode-Island and Providence Plantations one, Connecticut five, New-York six, New-Jersey four, Pennsylvania eight, Delaware one, Maryland six, Virginia ten, North-Carolina five, South-Carolina five, and Georgia three.

⟨(*c*)⟩ When vacancies happen in the representation from any state, the Executive authority thereof shall issue writs of election to fill such vacancies.

⟨(*d*)⟩ The House of Representatives shall choose their Speaker and other officers; and they shall have the sole power of impeachment.

Sect. 3. The Senate of the United States shall be composed of two senators from each state, chosen by the legislature thereof, for six years: and each senator shall have one vote.

⟨(*a*)⟩ Immediately after they shall be assembled in consequence of the first election, they shall be divided ⟨*(by lot)⟩ as equally as may be into three classes. The seats of the senators of the first class shall be vacated at the expiration of the second year, of the second class at the expiration of the fourth year, and of the third class at the expiration of the sixth year, so that one-third may be chosen every second year: and if vacancies happen by resignation, or otherwise, during the recess of the Legislature of any state, the Executive thereof may make temporary appointments until the next meeting of the Legislature.

⟨(*b*)⟩ No person shall be a senator who shall not have attained to the age of thirty years, and been nine years a citizen of the United States, and who shall not, when elected, be an inhabitant of that state for which he shall be chosen.

* ⟨The words "by lot"—were not in the Report as printed; but were inserted in manuscript, as a topografical error, departing from the text of the Report referred to the Committee of Style and arrangement.⟩

COMMITTEE OF STYLE

⟨(*c*)⟩ The Vice-President of the United States shall be, ex officio,[9] President of the senate, but shall have no vote, unless they be equally divided.

⟨(*d*)⟩ The Senate shall choose their other officers, and also a President pro tempore, in the absence of the Vice-President, or when he shall exercise the office of President of the United States.

⟨(*e*)⟩ The Senate shall have the sole power to try all impeachments. When sitting for that purpose, they shall be on oath. When the President of the United States is tried, the Chief Justice shall preside: And no person shall be convicted without the concurrence of two-thirds of the members present.

⟨(*f*)⟩ Judgment in cases of impeachment shall not extend further than to removal from office, and disqualification to hold and enjoy any office of honor, trust or profit under the United States: but the party convicted shall nevertheless be liable and subject to indictment, trial, judgment and punishment, according to law.

Sect. 4. The times, places and manner of holding elections for senators and representatives, shall be prescribed in each state by the legislature thereof: but the Congress may at any time by law make or alter such regulations.

⟨(*a*)⟩ The Congress shall assemble at least once in every year, and such meeting shall be on the first Monday in December, unless they shall by law appoint a different day.

Sect. 5. Each House shall be the judge of the elections, returns and qualifications of its own members, and a majority of each shall constitute a quorum to do business: but a smaller number may adjourn from day to day, and may be authorized to compel the attendance of absent members, in such manner, and under such penalties as each house may provide.

⟨(*a*)⟩ Each house may determine the rules of its proceedings; punish its members for disorderly behaviour, and, with the concurrence of two-thirds, expel a member.

⟨(*b*)⟩ Each house shall keep a journal of its proceedings, and

[9] "ex-officio" crossed out by Madison.

from time to time publish the same, excepting such parts as may in their judgment require secrecy; and the yeas and nays of the members of either house on any question shall, at the desire of one-fifth of those present, be entered on the journal.

⟨(*c*)⟩ Neither house, during the session of Congress, shall, without the consent of the other, adjourn for more than three days, nor to any other place than that in which the two houses shall be sitting.

Sect. 6. The senators and representatives shall receive a compensation for their services, to be ascertained by law, and paid out of the treasury of the United States. They shall in all cases, except treason, felony and breach of the peace, be privileged from arrest during their attendance at the session of their respective houses, and in going to and returning from the same; and for any speech or debate in either house, they shall not be questioned in any other place.

⟨(*a*)⟩ No senator or representative shall, during the time for which he was elected, be appointed to any civil office under the authority of the United States, which shall have been created, or the emoluments whereof shall have been encreased during such time; and no person holding any office under the United States, shall be a member of either house during his continuance in office.

Sect. 7. The enacting stile of the laws shall be, "Be it enacted by the senators and representatives in Congress assembled."

⟨(*a*)⟩ All bills for raising revenue shall originate in the house of representatives: but the senate may propose or concur with amendments as on other bills.

⟨(*b*)⟩ Every bill which shall have passed the house of representatives and the senate, shall, before it become a law, be presented to the president of the United States. If he approve he shall sign it, but if not he shall return it, with his objections to that house in which it shall have originated, who shall enter the objections at large on their journal, and proceed to reconsider it. If after such reconsideration two-

thirds of that house shall agree to pass the bill, it shall be sent, together with the objections, to the other house, by which it shall likewise be reconsidered, and if approved by two-thirds of that house, it shall become a law. But in all such cases the votes of both houses shall be determined by yeas and nays, and the names of the persons voting for and against the bill shall be entered on the journal of each house respectively. If any bill shall not be returned by the President within ten days (Sundays excepted) after it shall have been presented to him, the same shall be a law, in like manner as if he had signed it, unless the Congress by their adjournment prevent its return, in which case it shall not be a law.[10]

⟨(*c*)⟩ Every order, resolution, or vote to which the concurrence of the Senate and House of Representatives may be necessary (except on a question of adjournment) shall be presented to the President of the United States; and before the same shall take effect, shall be approved by him, or, being disapproved by him, shall be repassed by * *three-fourths* of the Senate and House of Representatives, according to the rules and limitations prescribed in the case of a bill.

Sect. 8. The Congress may by joint ballot appoint a treasurer. They shall have power.

⟨(*a*)⟩ To lay and collect taxes, duties, imposts and excises; to pay the debts and provide for the common defence and general welfare[12] of the United States. ⟨but all duties imposts & excises shall be uniform throughout the U. States.⟩[13]

⟨(*b*)⟩ To borrow money on the credit of the United States.

* ⟨In the entry of this Report in the printed Journal "two thirds" are substituted for "three fourths".[11] This change was made after the Report was received.⟩

[10] This paragraph has caused a great deal of confusion. The Report of the Committee of Detail on August 6 provided for a two-thirds vote of both houses to overrule the president's veto. On August 15 this was changed to three-fourths. The Committee on Style seem to have changed this back to two-thirds in this paragraph, but left it as three-fourths in the next. On September 12th, this was changed again to two-thirds.

[11] Madison is in error. The *Journal* reading is identical with his own. See above note 10.

[12] See Appendix A, CCLXXXI, CCCXLIV, CCCLXXII.

[13] Interlined by Madison.

⟨(*c*)⟩ To regulate commerce with foreign nations, among the several states, and with the Indian tribes.

⟨(*d*)⟩ To establish an uniform rule of naturalization[14] and uniform laws on the subject of bankruptcies throughout the United States.

⟨(*e*)⟩ To coin money, regulate the value thereof, and of foreign coin, and fix the standard of weights and measures.

⟨(*f*)⟩ To provide for the punishment of counterfeiting the securities and current coin of the United States.

⟨(*g*)⟩ To establish post offices and post roads.

⟨(*i*)⟩ To promote the progress of science and useful arts, by securing for limited times to authors and inventors the exclusive right to their respective writings and discoveries.

⟨(*j*)⟩ To constitute tribunals inferior to the supreme court.

⟨(*k*)⟩ To define and punish piracies and felonies committed on the high seas, and ⟨*(punish)⟩ offences against the law of nations.

⟨(*l*)⟩ To declare war, grant letters of marque and reprisal, and make rules concerning captures on land and water.

⟨(*m*)⟩ To raise and support armies: but no appropriation of money to that use shall be for a longer term than two years.

⟨(*n*)⟩ To provide and maintain a navy.

⟨(*o*)⟩ To make rules for the government and regulation of the land and naval forces.

⟨(*p*)⟩ To provide for calling forth the militia to execute the laws of the union, suppress insurrections and repel invasions.

⟨(*q*)⟩ To provide for organizing, arming and disciplining the militia, and for governing such part of them as may be employed in the service of the United States, reserving to the States respectively, the appointment of the officers, and the authority of training the militia according to the discipline prescribed by Congress.

⟨(*r*)⟩ To exercise exclusive legislation in all cases whatsoever, over such district (not exceeding ten miles square) as may, by cession of particular States, and the acceptance of

* (punish) a typographical omission

[14] "naturalization", see Appendix A, CCL.

Congress, become the seat of government of the United States, and to exercise like authority over all places purchased by the consent of the legislature of the state in which the same shall be, for the erection of forts, magazines, arsenals, dock-yards, and other needful buildings — And

⟨(*s*)⟩ To make all laws which shall be necessary and proper for carrying into execution the foregoing powers, and all other powers vested by this constitution in the government of the United States, or in any department or officer thereof.

Sect. 9. The migration or importation of such persons as the several states now existing shall think proper to admit, shall not be prohibited by the Congress prior to the year one thousand eight hundred and eight, but a tax or duty may be imposed on such importation, not exceeding ten dollars for each person.

⟨(*a*)⟩ The privilege of the writ of habeas corpus shall not be suspended, unless when in cases of rebellion or invasion the public safety may require it.

⟨(*b*)⟩ No bill of attainder shall be passed, nor any ex post facto law.

⟨(*c*)⟩ No capitation tax shall be laid, unless in proportion to the census herein before directed to be taken.

⟨(*d*)⟩ No tax or duty shall be laid on articles exported from any state. ⟨No preference shall be given by any regulation of commerce or revenue to the ports of one State over those of another — nor shall vessels bound to or from one State be obliged to enter, clear or pay duties in another.⟩[15]

⟨(*e*)⟩ No money shall be drawn from the treasury, but in consequence of appropriations made by law.

⟨(*f*)⟩ No title of nobility shall be granted by the United States. And no person holding any office of profit or trust under them, shall, without the consent of the Congress, accept of any present, emolument, office, or title, of any kind whatever, from any king, prince, or foreign state.

Sect. 10. No state shall coin money,[16] nor emit bills of

[15] Interlined by Madison.

[16] The "n" of every "nor" in this section was crossed out by Madison.

credit, nor make any thing but gold or silver coin a tender in payment of debts, nor pass any bill of attainder, nor ex post facto laws, nor laws altering or impairing the obligation of contracts; nor grant letters of marque and reprisal, nor enter into any treaty, alliance, or confederation, nor grant any title of nobility.

⟨(*a*)⟩ No state shall, without the consent of Congress, lay imposts or duties on imports or exports, nor with such consent, but to the use of the treasury of the United States.[17] Nor[18] keep troops nor ships of war in time of peace, nor enter into any agreement or compact with another state, nor with any foreign power; nor engage in any war, unless it shall be actually invaded by enemies, or the danger of invasion be so imminent, as not to admit of delay until the Congress can be consulted.

II.

Sect. 1. The executive power shall be vested in a president of the United States of America. He shall hold his office during the term of four years, and, together with the vice-president, chosen for the same term, be elected in the following manner:

⟨(*a*)⟩ Each state shall appoint, in such manner as the legislature thereof may direct, a number of electors, equal to the whole number of senators and representatives to which the state may be entitled in Congress: but no senator or representative shall be appointed an elector, nor any person holding an office of trust or profit under the United States.

⟨(*b*)⟩ The electors shall meet in their respective states, and vote by ballot for two persons, of whom one at least shall not be an inhabitant of the same state with themselves. And they shall make a list of all the persons voted for, and of the number of votes for each; which list they shall sign and cer-

[17] Marginal note by Madison marked to be inserted at this point: "provided that no State shall be restrained from imposing the usual duties on produce exported from such State for the sole purpose of defraying the charges of inspecting packing storing & indemnifying the losses on such produce while in the custody of public officers. But all such regulations shall in case of abuse be subject to the revision & controul of Congress."

[18] "Nor" crossed out, and "No State shall without the consent of Congress" interlined by Madison.

tify, and transmit sealed to the seat of the general government, directed to the president of the senate. The president of the senate shall in the presence of the senate and house of representatives open all the certificates, and the votes shall then be counted. The person having the greatest number of votes shall be the president, if such number be a majority of the whole number of electors appointed; and if there be more than one who have such majority, and have an equal number of votes, then the house of representatives shall immediately chuse by ballot one of them for president; and if no person have a majority, then from the five highest on the list the said house shall in like manner choose the president. But in choosing the president, the votes shall be taken by states, and not per capita,[19] the representation from each state having one vote. A quorum for this purpose shall consist of a member or members from two-thirds of the states, and a majority of all the states shall be necessary to a choice. In every case, after the choice of the president by the representatives,[20] the person having the greatest number of votes of the electors shall be the vice-president. But if there should remain two or more who have equal votes, the senate shall choose from them by ballot the vice-president.

⟨(*c*)⟩ The Congress may determine the time of choosing the electors, and the time in[21] which they shall give their votes; but the election shall be on the same day[22] throughout the United States.

⟨(*d*)⟩ No person except a natural born citizen, or a citizen of the United States, at the time of the adoption of this constitution, shall be eligible to the office of president; neither shall any person be eligible to that office who shall not have attained to the age of thirty-five years, and been fourteen years a resident within the United States.

⟨(*e*)⟩ In case of the removal of the president from office, or

[19] "and not per capita" crossed out by Madison.

[20] "by the representatives" crossed out by Madison.

[21] "time in" crossed out and "day on" substituted by Madison.

[22] "but the election shall be on the same day" crossed out and "which day shall be the same" interlined by Madison.

of his death, resignation, or inability to discharge the powers and duties of the said office, the same shall devolve on the vice-president, and the Congress may by law provide for the case of removal, death, resignation or inability, both of the president and vice-president, declaring what officer shall then act as president, and such officer shall act accordingly, until the disability be removed, or the period for chusing another president arrive.[23]

⟨(*f*)⟩ The president shall, at stated times, receive a fixed compensation for his services, which shall neither be encreased nor diminished during the period for which he shall have been elected.

⟨(*g*)⟩ Before he enter on the execution of his office, he shall take the following oath or affirmation: "I ———, do solemnly swear (or affirm) that I will faithfully execute the office of president of the United States, and will to the best of my judgment and power, preserve, protect and defend the constitution of the United States."

Sect. 2. The president shall be commander in chief of the army and navy of the United States, and of the militia of the several States[24]: he may require the opinion, in writing, of the principal officer in each of the executive departments, upon any subject relating to the duties of their respective offices, when called into the actual service of the United States,[24] and he shall have power to grant reprieves and pardons for offences against the United States, except in cases of impeachment.

⟨(*a*)⟩ He shall have power, by and with the advice and consent of the senate, to make treaties, provided two-thirds of the senators present concur; and he shall nominate, and by and with the advice and consent of the senate, shall appoint ambassadors, other public ministers and consuls, judges of the supreme court, and all other officers of the United States, whose appointments are not herein otherwise provided for.

[23] "the period for chusing another president arrive" crossed out, and "a president be chosen" inserted by Madison.

[24] Madison indicated by signs that the clause "when called into the actual service of the United States" should follow immediately after "militia of the several States".

⟨(*b*)⟩ The president shall have power to fill up all vacancies that may happen during the recess of the senate, by granting commissions which shall expire at the end of their next session.

Sect. 3. He shall from time to time give to the Congress information of the state of the union, and recommend to their consideration such measures as he shall judge necessary and expedient: he may, on extraordinary occasions, convene both houses, or either of them, and in case of disagreement between them, with respect to the time of adjournment, he may adjourn them to such time as he shall think proper: he shall receive ambassadors and other public ministers: he shall take care that the laws be faithfully executed, and shall commission all the officers of the United States.

Sect. 4. The president, vice-president, and all civil officers of the United States, shall be removed from office on impeachment for, and conviction of treason, bribery, or other high crimes and misdemeanors.

III.

Sect. 1. The judicial power of the United States, both in law and equity, shall be vested in one supreme court, and in such inferior courts as the Congress may from time to time ordain and establish. The judges, both of the supreme and inferior courts, shall hold their offices during good behaviour, and shall, at stated times, receive for their services, a compensation, which shall not be diminished during their continuance in office.

Sect. 2. The judicial power shall extend to all cases, both in law and equity, arising under this constitution, the laws of the United States, and treaties made, or which shall be made, under their authority. To all cases affecting ambassadors, other public ministers and consuls. To all cases of admiralty and maritime jurisdiction. To controversies to which the United States shall be a party. To controversies between two or more States; between a state and citizens of another state; between citizens of different States; between citizens of the same state claiming lands under grants of differ-

ent States, and between a state, or the citizens thereof, and foreign States, citizens or subjects.

In cases affecting ambassadors, other public ministers and consuls, and those in which a state shall be a party, the supreme court shall have original jurisdiction. In all the other cases before mentioned, the supreme court shall have appellate jurisdiction, both as to law and fact, with such exceptions, and under such regulations as the Congress shall make.

The trial of all crimes, except in cases of impeachment, shall be by jury; and such trial shall be held in the state where the said crimes shall have been committed; but when not committed within any state, the trial shall be at such place or places as the Congress may by law have directed.

Sect. 3. Treason against the United States, shall consist only in levying war against them, or in adhering to their enemies, giving them aid and comfort. No person shall be convicted of treason unless on the testimony of two witnesses to the same overt act, or on confession in open court.

The Congress shall have power to declare the punishment of treason, but no attainder of treason shall work corruption of blood nor forfeiture, except during the life of the person attainted.

IV.

Sect. 1. Full faith and credit shall be given in each state to the public acts, records, and judicial proceedings of every other state. And the Congress may by general laws prescribe the manner in which such acts, records and proceedings shall be proved, and the effect thereof.

Sect. 2. The citizens of each state shall be entitled to all privileges and immunities of citizens in the several states.

A person charged in any state with treason, felony, or other crime, who shall flee from justice, and be found in another state, shall on demand of the executive authority of the state from which he fled be delivered up, and removed to the state having jurisdiction of the crime.

No person legally held to service or labour in one state, escaping into another, shall in consequence of regulations

COMMITTEE OF STYLE

subsisting therein be discharged from such service or labor, but shall be delivered up on claim of the party to whom such service or labour may be due.

Sect. 3. New states may be admitted by the Congress into this union; but no new state shall be formed or erected within the jurisdiction of any other state; nor any state be formed by the junction of two or more states, or parts of states, without the consent of the legislatures of the states concerned as well as of the Congress.

The Congress shall have power to dispose of and make all needful rules and regulations respecting the territory or other property belonging to the United States: and nothing in this Constitution shall be so construed as to prejudice any claims of the United States, or of any particular state.

Sect. 4. The United States shall guarantee to every state in this union a Republican form of government, and shall protect each of them against invasion; and on application of the legislature or executive, against domestic violence.

V.

The Congress, whenever two-thirds of both houses shall deem necessary, or on the application of two-thirds[25] of the legislatures of the several states, shall propose amendments to this constitution, which shall be valid to all intents and purposes, as part thereof, when the same shall have been ratified by three-fourths at least of[26] the legislatures[27] of the several states, or by conventions in three-fourths thereof, as the one or the other mode of ratification may be proposed by the Congress: Provided, that no amendment which may be made prior to the year 1808 shall in any manner affect the and[28] sections of[29] article

25 "of two-thirds" crossed out by Madison, and inserted again after "legislatures".

26 "three-fourths at least of" crossed out by Madison.

27 "of three-fourths" inserted by Madison.

28 "and" crossed out, and "1 & 4 clauses in the 9" inserted by Madison.

29 "the first" interlined by Madison.

VI.

All debts contracted and engagements entered into before the adoption of this Constitution shall be as valid against the United States under this Constitution as under the confederation.

This constitution, and the laws of the United States which shall be made in pursuance thereof; and all treaties made, or which shall be made, under the authority of the United States, shall be the supreme law of the land; and the judges in every state shall be bound thereby, any thing in the constitution or laws of any state to the contrary notwithstanding.

The senators and representatives beforementioned, and the members of the several state legislatures, and all executive and judicial officers, both of the United States and of the several States, shall be bound by oath or affirmation, to support this constitution; but no religious test shall ever be required as a qualification to any office or public trust under the United States.

VII.

The ratification of the conventions of nine States, shall be sufficient for the establishment of this constitution between the States so ratifying the same.

THURSDAY, SEPTEMBER 13, 1787.

JOURNAL

Thursday September 13. 1787.

The honorable Mr Johnson from the Committee of revision reported the following as a substitute for the 22nd and 23rd articles[1]
Resolved that the preceeding Constitution be laid before the United States in Congress assembled, and that it is the opinion of this Convention that it should afterwards be submitted to a Convention of Delegates, chosen in each State by the People thereof, under the recommendation of it's Legislature; for their assent and ratification. and that each Convention assenting to, and ratifying, the same should give notice thereof to the United States in Congress assembled.

Resolved that it is the opinion of this Convention that as soon as the Conventions of nine States, shall have ratified this Constitution, the United States in Congress assembled should fix a day, on which Electors should be appointed by the States which shall have ratified the same: and a day on which the Electors should assemble to vote for the President: and the Time and Place for commencing proceedings under this constitution That after such publication the electors should be appointed, and the Senators and Representatives elected: That the Electors should meet on the Day fixed for the Election of the President, and should transmit their votes certified, signed, sealed, and directed, as the Constitution requires, to the Secretary of the United States in Congress assembled, that the Senators and representatives should convene at the Time and place assigned, that the Senators should appoint a President of the Senate for the sole purpose of receiving,

[1] Note in margin "Present from N H".

opening, and counting the votes for President; and that after he shall be chosen, the Congress together with the President should without delay proceed to execute this Constitution

[To postpone the report respecting the 22nd and 23rd Ayes — 9; noes — 1.][2]

The clause offered to the House yesterday to be added to the 13th article being withdrawn — It was moved and seconded to agree to the following amendment to the 13th article

Provided that no State shall be restrained from imposing the usual Duties on produce exported from such State, for the sole purpose of defraying the charges of inspecting, packing, storing, and indemnifying the losses on such produce, while in the custody of public Officers: but all such regulations shall, in case of abuse, be subject to the revision and controul of Congress.

which passed in the affirmative. [Ayes — 7; noes — 3.][3]

It was moved and seconded to proceed to the comparing of the report, from the Committee of revision, with the articles which were agreed to by the House; and to them referred for arrangement.

which passed in the affirmative

and the same was read by paragraphs, compared, and in some places corrected and amended.

[To agree to add "for two years" Ayes — 1; noes — 10.

to insert "service" instead of "servitude" Ayes — 11; noes — 0.

To strike out the words "and direct taxes" Ayes — 3; noes — 8.

______________ Ayes — 3; noes — 8.

To rescind the rule for adjournment Ayes — 6; noes — 5.

______________ Ayes — 3; noes — 7; divided — 1.

To strike out the word "to" before establish justice Ayes — 8; noes — 2.][4]

---

[2] Vote 514, Detail of Ayes and Noes. Votes 512–513, Detail of Ayes and Noes, might be repeated here. They are as likely to belong to this day's records as to those of September 12.

[3] Vote 515, Detail of Ayes and Noes.

[4] Votes 516–522, Detail of Ayes and Noes.

DETAIL OF AYES AND NOES.

	New Hampshire	Massachusetts	Rhode Island	Connecticut	New York	New Jersey	Pennsylvania	Delaware	Maryland	Virginia	No Carolina	So Carolina	Georgia	Questions	ayes	noes	divided
[512]	aye			aye		aye	aye	aye	aye	aye	aye	aye	aye				
[513]	no			aye		no	aye	no	aye	aye	aye	aye	aye	To agree to Commodities	7	3	
[514]	aye			no		aye	aye	aye	aye	aye	aye	aye	aye	To postpone the report respecting the 22nd and 23rd	9	1	
[515]	aye	aye		aye			no	no	aye	aye	aye	no	aye		7	3	
[516]	no	aye		no		no	no	no	no	no	no	no	no	To agree to add "for two years"	1	10	
[517]	aye	aye		aye		aye	aye	aye	aye	aye	aye	aye	aye	to insert "service" instead of "servitude"			
[518]	no	no		no		aye	no	aye	aye	no	no	no	no	To strike out the words "and direct Taxes"	3	8	
[519]	no	no		no		no	aye	no	aye	aye	no	no	no		3	8	
[520]	aye	aye		no		no	no	no	no	aye	aye	aye	aye	To rescind the rule for adjournment	6	5	
[521]	no	no		no		no	aye	no	aye	no	aye	dd	no		3	7	1
[522]	aye	aye		aye		no		aye	aye	no	aye	aye	aye	To strike out the word "to" before establish justice			

MADISON

Thursday Sepr. 13. 1787. In Convention

Col. Mason — He had moved without success for a power to make sumptuary regulations. He had not yet lost sight of his object. After descanting on the extravagance of our manners, the excessive consumption of foreign superfluities, and the necessity of restricting it, as well with œconomical as republican views, he moved that a Committee be appointed to report articles of Association for encouraging by the advice the influence and the example of the members of the Convention, œconomy frugality and american manufactures.

Docr Johnson 2ded the motion which was without debate agreed to — nem: con: and a Committee appointed, consisting

of Col: Mason, Docr. Franklin, Mr. Dickenson, Docr Johnson, and Mr. Livingston.*

Col: Mason renewed his proposition of yesterday on the subject of inspection laws, with an additional clause giving to Congress a controul over them in case of abuse — as follows,

"Provided that no State shall be restrained from imposing the usual duties on produce exported from such State, for the sole purpose of defraying the charges of inspecting, packing, storing, and indemnifying the losses on such produce, while in the custody of public officers: but all such regulations shall in case of abuse, be subject to the revision and controul of Congress —"[5]

There was no debate & on the question

N— H— ay. Mas. ay. Ct. ay. Pa. no. Del. no. Md. ay. Va. ay. N— C— ay. S. C. no— Geo. ay. [Ayes — 7; noes — 3.]

The Report from the Committee of stile and arrangement, was taken up, in order to be compared with the articles of the plan as agreed to by the House & referred to the Committee, and to receive the final corrections and sanction of the Convention.

Art: 1— sect. 2— On motion of Mr. Randolph the word "servitude" was struck out, and "service" ⟨†unanimously⟩ inserted, the former being thought to express the condition of slaves, & the latter the obligations of free persons.

Mr Dickenson & Mr. Wilson moved to strike out "and direct taxes," from sect. 2. art. 1. as improperly placed in a clause relating merely to the Constitution of the House of Representatives.

Mr. Govr. Morris. The insertion here was in consequence of what had passed on this point; in order to exclude the appearance of counting the Negroes in *the Representation* — The including of them may now be referred to the object of direct taxes, and incidentally only to that of Representation —

* ⟨This motion & appointment of the Comittee, not in the printed Journal. No report was made by the Come.⟩ † ⟨See page 372 of the printed Journal.⟩

[5] See also August 25, note 13.

On the motion to strike out "and direct taxes" from this place

N— H— no— Mas— no— Ct. no. N— J— ay. Pa. no. Del. ay. Md ay. Va. no— N. C. no. S. C. no. Geo. no. [Ayes — 3; noes — 8.]

Art. I. sect. ⟨7⟩." — "if any bill shall not be returned by the president within ten days (sundays excepted) after it shall have been presented to him &c"

Mr. Madison, & moved to insert between "after" and "it," ⟨in sect. 7. art. I⟩ the words "the day on which" — in order to prevent a question whether the day on which the bill be presented, ought to be counted or not as one of the ten days —

Mr Randolph 2ded the Motion.

Mr. Governur Morris. The amendment is unnecessary. The law knows no fractions of days —

A number of members being very impatient & calling for the question[6]

N. H. no. Mas. no. Ct. no. N— J. no. Pa. ay. Del. no— Md ay— Va ay. N— C. no. S— C. no. Geo. no— [Ayes — 3; noes — 8.]

Docr. Johnson made a further report from the Committee of stile &c of the following resolutions to be substituted for 22 & 23 articles

Resolved that the preceding Constitution be laid before the U— States in Congress assembled, and that it is the opinion of this Convention, that it should afterwards be submitted to a Convention of Delegates chosen in each State by the people thereof, under the recommendation of its Legislature, for their assent & ratification; & that each Convention assenting & ratifying the same should give notice thereof to the U— S— in Congs. assembled—

"Resolved that it is the opinion of this Convention that as soon as the Conventions of nine States, shall have ratified this Constitution, the U— S— in Congs. assembled should fix a day on which electors should be appointed by the States

[6] See Appendix A, CXCII.

which shall have ratified the same; and a day on which the Electors should assemble to vote for the President; and the time and place for commencing proceedings under this Constitution — That after such publication the Electors should be appointed, and the Senators and Representatives elected: That the Electors should meet on the day fixed for the election of the President, and should transmit their votes certified signed, sealed and directed, as the Constitution requires, to the Secretary of the U— States in Congs assembled: that the Senators and Representatives should convene at the time & place assigned; that the Senators should appoint a President for the sole purpose of receiving, opening, and counting the votes for President, and after that he shall be chosen, the Congress, together with the President should without delay proceed to execute this Constitution."[7]

Adjourned

McHENRY

13 Sepr.

Recd. read and compared the new printed report with the first printed amended report. Made some verbal alterations, and inserted the propositions moved by Maryland which had been overlooked.

[7] The proceedings on these resolutions are not given in the Journal nor by Madison; in the report to Congress September 28, 1787, they are dated September 17.

FRIDAY, SEPTEMBER 14, 1787.

JOURNAL

Friday Septemr 14. 1787.

The[1] report from the Committee of revision, as corrected and amended yesterday, being taken up, was read, debated by paragraphs, amended, and agreed to as far as the first clause of the 10 section of the first article inclusive

The House adjourned.[2]

---

[1] Crossed out: "It was moved and seconded to reconsider the 3 clause of the 2d sect. 1st article which passed in the negative. It was moved and seconded to add the words 'which shall then fill such vacancies' after the words 'meeting of the Legislature' in the 2d clause of the 3d sect. 1st article which passed in the affirmative." See further Detail of Ayes and Noes, Votes 523–540.

[2] *Journal* (pp. 377–378) adds the following amendments, which may have been taken from the interlineations of the Brearley copy or may have been supplied by Madison: — "Add at the end of the first clause of the eighth section, first article, 'but all duties, imposts and excises, shall be uniform throughout the United States.' Add at the end of the fifth clause of the ninth section, first article, 'no preference shall be given by any regulation of commerce or revenue to the ports of one state over those of another. Nor shall vessels bound to or from one state, be obliged to enter, clear or pay duties in another.' Add at the end of the sixth clause of the ninth section, first article, 'and a regular statement and account of the receipts and expenditures of all publick money shall be published from time to time.'"

Journal (pp. 378–379) adds the following changes, evidently compiled from the interlineations of the Brearley copy: — "Article first, second section, clause fifth. Strike out the word 'they.' Article first, section third, clause second. Add at the end of the clause, after the word 'legislature,' the words 'which shall then fill such vacancies.' Article first, section third, clause fourth. Strike out the words 'ex officio.' Article first, section third, clause sixth. After the word 'oath' insert 'or affirmation.' Article first, section eighth, clause third. After the word 'nations,' insert the word 'and.' Article first, section ninth, clause first. Strike out the word 'several,' and between the words 'as' and 'the,' insert the words 'any of.' Alter the third clause so as to read, 'no bill of attainder, or ex post facto law shall be passed.' In the fourth clause, after the word 'capitation,' insert the words 'or other direct.' Article first, section tenth, clause first, was variously amended, to read as follows: 'No State shall enter into any treaty, alliance, or confederation, grant letters of marque and reprisal, coin money, emit bills of credit, make any thing but gold or silver coin a tender in payment of debts, pass any bill of attainder, ex post facto law, or law impairing the obligation of contracts, or grant any title of nobility.'"

DETAIL OF AYES AND NOES

	New Hampshire	Massachusetts	Rhode Island	Connecticut	New York	New Jersey	Pennsylvania	Delaware	Maryland	Virginia	No Carolina	So Carolina	Georgia	Questions	ayes	noes	divided
[523]	no	no		no		no	aye	aye	aye	aye	aye	no	no	To reconsider ye 2d clause of the 3rd sect. 1st article	5	6	
[524]	no	no		no		no	no	no	no	aye	no	no	no		1	10	
[525]	no	no		aye		no	no	no	no	no	no	aye	aye		3	8	
[526]	no	no		no		aye	no	no	aye	no	aye	no	aye	To reconsider the 1st clause of the 5 sect. 1st article	4	7	
[527]	aye	aye		aye		aye	dd	no	aye	aye	aye	aye	aye		1		
[528]	no	no		no		no	no	no	aye	aye	aye	no	aye		4	7	
[529]	no	aye		no		no	aye	no	no	no	no	aye	no				
[530]	no	no		aye		aye	no	aye	aye	no	aye	aye	aye		7	4	
[Page 2][3]																	
[531]	aye	no		aye		aye	no	aye	aye	no	aye	aye	aye	To strike out the Treasurer	8	3	
[532]	aye	aye		aye		no	aye	aye	aye	no	aye	aye	no	To reconsider ye 10 clause 8 sect. 1 Article	8	3	
[533]	aye	no		aye		aye	no	aye	no	no	aye	aye	no	To strike out the word "punish"	6	5	
[534]	no	no		no		no	aye	no	no	aye	no	no	aye	To grant letters of incorporation for Canals &ca			
[535]	no	no		dd		no	aye	no	no	aye	aye	aye	no	To establish an University	4	6	1
[536]	no	no		no		no	no	no	no	aye	no	no	aye		2	9	
[537]	no	no		no		no	no	no	no	no	no	no	no	To reconsider the ex post facto clause			
[538]	aye	aye		no		no	no	no	aye	aye	no	aye	no	To insert The liberty of the Press shall be inviolably preserd	5	6	
[539]	aye			no		aye	aye	aye	aye	aye	aye	no	aye	To insert the words "or enumeration			
[540]		aye		aye		aye	aye	aye	aye	aye	aye	aye	aye				

[3] See above, August 16, note 3.

MADISON

Friday Sepr. 14th. 1787 In Convention

The Report of the Committee of stile & arrangement being resumed,

Mr. Williamson moved to reconsider in order to increase the number of Representatives fixed for the first Legislature. His purpose was to make an addition of one half generally to the number allotted to the respective States; and to allow two to the smallest States.

On this motion

N. H. no— Mas. no. Ct no. N. J— no. Pa ay— Del. ay. Md ay. Va. ay. N C. ay. S— C. no. Geo. no [Ayes — 5; noes — 6.]

Art. 1. sect. 3.—the words *"by lot" were struck out nem: con: on motion of Mr. Madison, that some rule might prevail in the rotation that would prevent both the members from the same State from going out at the same time —

"Ex officio" struck out of the same section as superfluous; nem: con: ⟨and "or affirmation" after "oath" inserted also unanimously — ⟩

Mr Rutlidge and Mr. Govr. Morris moved "that persons impeached be suspended from their office until they be tried and acquitted"

Mr. Madison — The President is made too dependent already on the Legislature, by the power of one branch to try him in consequence of an impeachment by the other. This intermediate suspension, will put him in the power of one branch only — They can at any moment, in order to make way for the functions of another who will be more favorable to their views, vote a temporary removal of the existing magistrate —

Mr. King ⟨concurred⟩ in the opposition to the amendment

On the question to agree to it

N— H. no. Mas. no— Ct. ay— N— J. no. Pa. no. Del—

* ⟨"By lot" had been reinstated from the Report of five made Aug. 6. as a correction of the printed report by the Come of stile & arrangement.⟩

no. Md no. Va. no. N— C. no. S. C. ay, Geo. ay, [Ayes — 3; noes — 8.]

Art. 1. sect. 4. "except as to the places of choosing Senators" added nem: con: to the end of the first clause, in order to exempt the seats of Govt in the States from the power of Congress —[4]

Art. 1. Sect. 5.[5] "Each House shall keep a Journal of its proceedings, and from time to time publish the same, excepting such parts as may in their judgment require secrecy."

Col: Mason & Mr. Gerry moved to insert after the word "parts" the words "of the proceedings of the Senate"[6] so as to require publication of all the proceedings of the House of Representatives.

It was intimated on the other side that cases might arise where secrecy might be necessary in both Houses — Measures preparatory to a declaration of war in which the House of Reps. was to concur, were instanced.

On the question, ⟨it passed in the negative⟩

⟨N. H. no. (Rh. I. ab:.) Mas. no. Con: no. (N. Y. abs) N. J. no. Pen. ay. Del— no. Mary. ay. Virg. no. N. C. ay. S. C. divd. Geor. no⟩ [Ayes — 3; noes — 7; divided — 1.][7]

Mr Baldwin observed that the clause. art. 1. sect 6. declaring that no member of Congs, "during the time for which he was elected; shall be appointed to any Civil office under the authority of the U. S. which shall have been created, or the emoluments whereof shall have been increased during such time", would not extend to offices *created by the Constitution ;* and the salaries of which would be created, *not increased* by Congs. at their first session — The members of the first

---

[4] See Appendix A, CCX.

[5] Detail of Ayes and Noes, Vote 526, records a question to reconsider the 1st clause of this section, which was defeated.

[6] In the margin of his copy of the draft of September 12, Mason has worded this proposed change: "of the journals of the senate," and has written opposite it — "refused".

[7] Crossed out: "Seven States were in the Negative: three in the affirmative: one divided." Madison evidently inserted the vote in the text from the list sent to him by John Quincy Adams (see above September 12, note 2). This is Vote 521, Detail of Ayes and Noes.

Congs consequently might evade the disqualification in this instance. — He was neither seconded nor opposed; nor did any thing further pass on the subject.

Art. 1. Sect. 8." The Congress "may by joint ballot appointed a Treasurer"

Mr Rutlidge moved to strike out this power, and let the Treasurer be appointed in the same manner with other officers.

Mr. Gorham & Mr. King said that the motion, if agreed, to would have a mischievous tendency. The people are accustomed & attached to that mode of appointing Treasurers, and the innovation will multiply objections to the System.

Mr. Govr. Morris remarked that if the Treasurer be not appointed by the Legislature, he will be more narrowly watched, and more readily impeached —

Mr. Sherman — As the two Houses appropriate money, it is best for them to appoint the officer who is to keep it; and to appoint him as they make the appropriation, not by joint, but several votes:

Genl Pinkney. The Treasurer is appointed by joint ballot in South Carolina. The consequence is that bad appointments are made, and the Legislature will not listen to the faults of their own officer.

On the motion to strike out

N. H— ay. Mas. no. Ct. ay. N. J. ay. Pa. no. Del— ay— Md ay. Va. no. N—C. ay. S. C. ay. Geo— ay. [Ayes — 8; noes — 3.]

Art. I. sect. 8: ⟨"but all such duties imposts & excises, shall be uniform throughout the U— S—" was unanimously annexed to the power of taxation.⟩

To define & punish piracies and felonies on the high seas, and "punish" offences against the law of nations.[8]

Mr. Govr. Morris moved to strike out "punish" before the words "offences agst. the law of nations." so as to let these be *definable* as well as punishable, by virtue of the preceding member of the sentence.

[8] Detail of Ayes and Noes, Vote 532, records the adoption of a motion to reconsider this clause.

Mr. Wilson hoped the alteration would by no means be made. To pretend to *define* the law of nations which depended on the authority of all the Civilized Nations of the World, would have a look of arrogance. that would make us ridiculous.

Mr. Govr The word *define* is proper when applied to *offences* in this case; the law of ⟨nations⟩ being often too vague and deficient to be a rule.

On the question to strike out the word "punish" ⟨it passed in the affirmative⟩

N— H. ay. Mas— no. Ct. ay. N— J. ay. Pa. no. Del. ay Md. no. Va. no. N . C— ay— S— C— ay. Geo— no. [Ayes — 6; noes — 5.]

Docr. Franklin moved * to add after the words "post roads" Art ⟨I⟩ Sect. 8. "a power to provide for cutting canals where deemed necessary"[9]

Mr Wilson 2ded. the motion

Mr Sherman objected. The expence in such cases will fall on the U-- States, and the benefit accrue to the places where the canals may be cut.

Mr Wilson. Instead of being an expence to the U. S. they may be made a source of revenue.

Mr. Madison suggested an enlargement of the motion into a power "to grant charters of incorporation where the interest of the U. S. might require & the legislative provisions of individual States may be incompetent". His primary object was however to secure an easy communication between the States which the free intercourse now to be opened, seemed to call for— The political obstacles being removed, a removal of the natural ones as far as possible ought to follow. Mr. Randolph 2ded. the proposition.

Mr King thought the power unnecessary.

Mr Wilson. It is necessary to prevent *a State* from obstructing the *general* welfare.

* ⟨This motion by Dr. Franklin not stated in the printed Journal, as are some other motions.⟩

[9] Upon this discussion, see Appendix A, CCLVII–CCLX, CCLXXVIII, CCCL, CCCLIII, CCCLXXIV.

Mr King— The States will be prejudiced and divided into parties by it— In Philada. & New York, It will be referred to the establishment of a Bank, which has been a subject of contention in those Cities. In other places it will be referred to mercantile monopolies.

Mr. Wilson mentioned the importance of facilitating by canals, the communication with the Western Settlements— As to Banks he did not think with Mr. King that the power in that point of view would excite the prejudices & parties apprehended. As to mercantile monopolies they are already included in the power to regulate trade.

Col: Mason was for limiting the power to the single case of Canals. He was afraid of monopolies of every sort, which he did not think were by any means already implied by the Constitution as supposed by Mr. Wilson.

The motion being so modified as to admit a distinct question specifying & limited to the case of canals.

N— H— no— Mas. no. Ct. no— N— J— no— Pa ay. Del. no— Md. no. Va. ay. N— C— no— S— C. no— Geo. ay. [Ayes — 3; noes — 8.]

The other part fell of course, as including the power rejected.

Mr. Madison & Mr. Pinkney then moved to insert in the list of powers vested in Congress a power — "to establish an University, in which no preferences or distinctions should be allowed on account of religion."[10]

Mr Wilson supported the motion

Mr Govr Morris. It is not necessary. The exclusive power at the Seat of Government, will reach the object.

On the question

N. H. no— Mas. no. Cont. divd. Dr. Johnson ay— Mr. Sherman no. N. J— no. Pa ay. Del. no. Md. no. Va. ay. N— C— ay— S— C— ay. Geo— no. [Ayes—4; noes—6; divided—1.]

Col: Mason, being sensible that an absolute prohibition of standing armies in time of peace might be unsafe, and wishing at the same time to insert something pointing out and

[10] See Appendix A, CCLV, CCCXC.

guarding against the danger of them, moved to preface the clause (Art I sect. 8) "To provide for organizing, arming and disciplining the Militia &c" with the words "And that the liberties of the people may be better secured against the danger of standing armies in time of peace" Mr. Randolph 2ded. the motion

Mr Madison was in favor of it. It did not restrain Congress from establishing a military force in time of peace if found necessary; and as armies in time of peace are allowed on all hands to be an evil, it is well to discountenance them by the Constitution, as far as will consist with the essential power of the Govt. on that head.

Mr Govr. Morris opposed the motion as setting a dishonorable mark of distinction on the military class of Citizens

Mr Pinkney & Mr. Bedford concurred in the opposition.

On the question

N. H— no— Mas— no— Ct no. N— J— no. Pa. no. Del. no. ⟨Maryd no⟩[11] Va ay— N. C. no. S. C. no. Geo. ay. [Ayes — 2; noes — 9.]

Col: Mason moved to strike out from the clause (art I sect 9.) "No bill of attainder nor any expost facto law shall be passed" the words "nor any ex post facto law".[12] He thought it not sufficiently clear that the prohibition meant by this phrase was limited to cases of a criminal nature— and no Legislature ever did or can altogether avoid them in Civil cases.

Mr. Gerry 2ded. the motion but ⟨with a view⟩ to extend the prohibition to "Civil cases", which he thought ought to be done.

On the question; all the States were — no[13]

Mr Pinkney & Mr. Gerry, moved to insert a declaration "that the liberty of the Press should be inviolably observed —"[14]

---

[11] Taken from *Journal*.

[12] Detail of Ayes and Noes, Vote 537, makes this a motion "to reconsider the ex post facto clause", which is more in keeping with Gerry's remarks in seconding it.

[13] Crossed out "N. H. no. Mas. no. . . . Geo. no."

[14] See Pinckney's proposition on August 20, and Appendix A, CLXXIII, CXCII.

Mr. Sherman— It is unnecessary— The power of Congress does not extend to the Press. On the question, ⟨it passed in the negative⟩

N— H— no—* Mas— ay— Ct no. N— J. no. Pa no. Del. no. Md ay. Va. ay. N. C. no. S. C. ay. Geo— no. [Ayes —4; noes — 7.][15]

Art. I. Sect. 9. "no capitation tax shall be laid, unless &c"

Mr Read moved to insert after "capitation" the words. "or other direct tax" He was afraid that some liberty might otherwise be taken to saddle the States with a readjustment by this rule, of past Requisitions of Congs — and that his amendment by giving another cast to the meaning would take away the pretext. Mr Williamson 2ded. the motion, which was agreed to,

On motion of Col: Mason "or enumeration" inserted after, as explanatory of "Census" ⟨Con. & S. C. only. no.⟩[16]

At the end of the clause "no tax or duty shall be laid on articles exported from any State" was added the following amendment conformably to a vote on the day of viz — no preference shall be given by any regulation of commerce or revenue to the ports of one State over those of another; nor shall vessels bound to or from one State, be obliged to enter, clear or pay duties in another.[17]

Col. Mason moved a clause requiring "that an Account of the public expenditures should be annually published" Mr Gerry 2ded. the motion

Mr Govr. Morris urged that this wd. be impossible in many cases.

Mr. King remarked, that the term expenditures went to every minute shilling. This would be impracticable. Congs. might indeed make a monthly publication, but it would be in such general Statements as would afford no satisfactory information.

Mr. Madison proposed to strike out "annually" from the

* ⟨In the printed Journal N. Hampshire ay.⟩

[15] McHenry agrees with Detail of Ayes and Noes, Vote 538, in making the vote Ayes, 5; noes, 6.

[16] Taken from *Journal.*

motion & insert "from time to time". which would enjoin the duty of frequent publications and leave enough to the discretion of the Legislature. Require too much and the difficulty will beget a habit of doing nothing. The articles of Confederation require half-yearly publications on this subject— A punctual compliance being often impossible, the practice has ceased altogether—

Mr Wilson 2ded. & supported the motion— Many operations of finance cannot be properly published at certain times.

Mr, Pinkney was in favor of the motion.

Mr. Fitzimmons— It is absolutely impossible to publish expenditures in the full extent of the term.

Mr. Sherman thought "from time to time" the best rule to be given.

"Annual" was struck out — & those words — inserted nem: con:

The motion of Col. Mason so amended was then agreed to nem: con: and added after — "appropriations by law as follows— "And a regular statement and account of the receipts & expenditures of all public money shall be published from time to time."[17]

The first clause of Art I. sect 10 — was altered so as to read— "No State shall enter into any Treaty alliance or confederation; grant letters of marque and reprisal; coin money; emit bills of credit; make any thing but gold & silver coin a tender in payment of debts; pass any bill of attainder, ex post law, or law impairing the obligation of contracts,[18] or grant any title of nobility."[17]

Mr Gerry entered into observations inculcating the importance of public faith, and the propriety of the restraint put on the States from impairing the obligation of contracts — Alledging that Congress ought to be laid under the like prohibitions. he made a motion to that effect. He was not 2ded

Adjourned.

[17] This paragraph is possibly a later insertion. If so it was taken from *Journal*. See above note 2.

[18] "obligation of contracts", see above August 28 and Appendix A, CCXXIX, CCCXCVIII.

McHENRY

14 Septr.

Moved by Dr. Franklin seconded by Mr. Willson, to empowed Congress to open and establish canals.

This being objected to — moved by Virginia To empower Congress to grant charters of incorporation in cases where the U. S. may require them and where the objects of them cannot be obtained by a State.

Negatived.

Moved To authorize Congress to establish an university to which and the honors and emoluments of which all persons may be admitted without any distinction of religion whatever. Congress enabled to erect such an institution in the place of the general government. Thus Congress to possess exclusive jurisdiction.

Neg. 6 Noes. 3 ay. 1 State divided.

Moved — And the liberty of the press shall be inviolable. 6 noes. 5 ays.

SATURDAY, SEPTEMBER 15, 1787.

JOURNAL

Saturday September 15. 1787.[1]

[1] Crossed out "It was moved and seconded to appoint a Committee to prepare an address to the People of the United States to accompany the Constitution which passed in the negative. It was moved and seconded to reconsider the 3rd clause, 2nd sect, 1st article. which passed in the affirmative It was moved and seconded to —"

See further Votes 541–566, Detail of Ayes and Noes.

Journal (pp. 383–385) adds the following amendments, evidently compiled from the interlineations of the Brearley copy: —

Article second, section first, clause first. Strike out the words "in the following manner," and insert in their stead the words "as follows."

Section first, clause second. Transpose the words "shall be appointed an elector," to the end of the clause; and instead of the word "nor" read "or."

Section first, clause third. Strike out the words "and not per capita," and the words "by the representatives."

Section first, clause fourth. Strike out the words "time in," and insert the words "day on;" strike out "but the election shall be on the same day," and insert "which day shall be the same."

Section first, clause seventh. Instead of "receive a fixed compensation for his services," read "receive for his services a compensation."

In the oath to be taken by the president, strike out the word "judgment," and insert "abilities."

Section second, clause first. After the words "militia of the several states," add the words "when called into the actual service of the United States."

Section second, clause second. After the words "provided for," add "and which shall be established by law."

Article third, section first. Strike out the words "both in law and equity."

Section second, clause first. Strike out the word "both." . . .

Article fourth, section second, clause second. Instead of "and removed," read "to be removed."

Section second, clause third. For "of regulations subsisting," read "of any law or regulation." . . .

Article fourth, section fourth. After the word "executive," insert "when the legislature cannot be convened."

Detail of Ayes and Noes

	New Hampshire	Massachusetts	Rhode Island	Connecticut	New York	New Jersey	Pennsylvania	Delaware	Maryland	Virginia	North Carolina	South Carolina	Georgia	Questions	ayes	noes	divided
[541]	no	no		no		no	aye	aye	aye	aye	no		no	To address the People	4	6	
[542]	aye	no		aye		no	dd	aye	aye	aye	aye	aye	aye	To reconsider the 3rd clause, 2nd sect. 1st Article.	8	2	1
[543]	aye	no		no		no	no	aye	aye	no	aye	no	aye	To add a Member to Rhode Island	5	6	
[544]	no	no		no		no	no	no	aye	aye	aye	aye	aye	To add a Member to North Carolina			
[545]	aye	aye		aye		aye	aye	aye	aye	no	aye	aye	aye		10	1	
[546]	no	no		no		no	dd	no	no	aye	aye	no	aye		3	7	1
[547]	aye	aye		dd		aye	no	aye	aye	no	no	aye	no	Tonnage Tonnage	6	4	1
[548]	aye	aye		no		no	aye	no	aye	aye	no	aye	aye				
[549]	no	no		dd		no	no	no	no	aye	no	no	aye		2	8	1
[550]	aye	no		aye		aye	aye	no	dd	no	aye	no	no				
[551]	dd	no		aye		no	no	dd	aye	aye	aye	no	aye				
[552]	no	no		aye		no	aye	aye	aye	aye	aye	aye	aye				
[553]	no	no		no		no	no	no	no	no	no	aye	no		1	10	
[554]	no	no		no		no	no	no	no	no	no	no	no				
[Page 3]																	
[555]	no	aye		no		no	no	aye	no	no	no	no	no				
[556]	dd	aye		aye		aye	no	no	no	no	no	no	no				
[557]	no	no		aye		no	no	no	no	no	no	no	no		1	10	
[558]	no	no		aye		aye	no	aye	no	no	no	no	no		3	8	
[559]	no	no		aye		aye	no	dd	no	no	no	no	no		2	8	1
[560]	dd	no		no		no	no	aye	aye	no	aye	no	no		3	7	1
[561]	no	no		no		no	no	aye	no	no		no	no				
[562]	dd	no		no		aye	no	aye	aye	no		no	no				
[563]	no	no		no		no	no	no	aye	aye		no	aye		3	7	
[564]	no	no		no		no	no	no	no	no		no	no				
[565]	aye	aye		aye		aye	aye	aye	aye	aye		aye	aye				
[566]	aye	aye		aye		aye	aye	aye	aye	aye		aye	aye	The Constitution unanimously agreed to			

MADISON

Saturday Sepr 15th. 1787. In Convention

Mr. Carrol reminded the House that no address to the people had yet been prepared. He considered it of great importance that such an one should accompany the Consti-

tution. The people had been accustomed to such on great occasions, and would expect it on this— He moved that a Committee be appointed for the special purpose of preparing an Address.

Mr Rutledge objected on account of the delay it would produce and the impropriety of addressing the people before it was known whether Congress would approve and support the plan— Congress, if an address be thought proper can prepare as good a one— The members of the Convention can also explain the reasons of what has been done to their respective Constituents.

Mr Sherman concurred in the opinion that an address was both unnecessary and improper.

On the motion of Mr. Carrol

N— H. no. Mas. no— Ct. no. N— J— no. Pa ay. Del. ay. Md. ay— Va. ay. N— C.* abst. S. C. no.* Geo. no— [Ayes — 4; noes — 6; absent — 1.]

Mr. Langdon. Some gentlemen have been very uneasy that no increase of the number of Representatives has been admitted. It has in particular been thought that one more ought to be allowed to N. Carolina. He was of opinion that an additional one was due both to that State & to Rho: Island. & moved to reconsider for that purpose.

Mr. Sherman. When the Committee of eleven reported the apportionment— five Representatives were thought the proper share of N— Carolina. Subsequent information however seemed to entitle that State to another—

On the motion to reconsider

N— H— ay— Mas— no. Ct ay— N— J. no— Pen. divd. Del. ay. Md. ay. Va. ay— N. C. ay. S— C. ay. Geo. ay. [Ayes — 8; noes — 2; divided — 1.]

Mr Langdon moved to add 1 member to each of the Representations of N— Carolina & Rho: Island.

Mr. King was agst. any change whatever as opening the door for delays. There had been no official proof that the numbers of N— C are greater than before estimated. And he never could sign the Constitution if Rho: Island is to be

*⟨In the printed Journal N. Carolina— no & S. Carol: omitted.⟩

allowed two members that is, one fourth of the number allowed to Massts, which will be known to be unjust.

Mr. Pinkney urged the propriety of increasing the number of Reps allotted to N. Carolina.

Mr. Bedford contended for an increase in favor of Rho: Island, and of Delaware also

On the question for allowing two Reps. to Rho: Island ⟨it passed in the negative⟩

N. H— ay. Mas. no. Ct. no. N. J. no. Pa. no. Del. ay. Md. ay. Va. no. N. C— ay. S. C. no— Geo— ay. [Ayes — 5; noes — 6.]

On the question for allowing six to N. Carolina, ⟨it passed in the negative⟩

N. H. no. Mas. no. Ct. no—N. J. no. Pa. no. Del— no—Md. ay. Va. ay. N—C. ay. S— C. ay. Geo. ay. [Ayes — 5; noes — 6.]

Art 1. sect. 10. (paragraph) 2) "No State shall, without the consent of Congress lay imposts or duties on imports or exports; nor with such consent, but to the use of the Treasury of the U. States"—

In consequence of the proviso moved by Col: Mason: and agreed to on the 13 Sepr, this part of the section was laid aside in favor of the following substitute viz. "No State shall, without the consent of Congress, lay any imposts or duties on imports or exports, except what may be absolutely necessary for executing its Inspection laws; and the nett produce of all duties and imposts, laid by any State on imports or exports, shall be for the use of the Treasury of the U— S—; and all such laws shall be subject to the revision and controul of the Congress"

On a motion to strike out the last part "and all such laws shall be subject to the revision and controul of ⟨the⟩ Congress" ⟨it passed in the Negative.⟩

N. H. no. Mas. no. Ct no— N. J. no. Pa divd. Del. no. Md. no Va ay— N— C— ay. S. C. no Geo. ay. [Ayes — 3; noes — 7; divided — 1.]

The substitute was then agreed to: ⟨Virga. alone being in the Negative.⟩[2]

[2] Taken from *Journal*, which ascribes Vote 545, Detail of Ayes and Noes, to this question. The correctness of this is doubtful.

The remainder of the paragraph being under consideration — viz — "nor keep troops nor ships of war in time of peace, nor enter into any agreement or compact with another State, nor with any foreign power. Nor engage in any war, unless it shall be actually invaded by enemies, or the danger of invasion be so imminent as not to admit of delay, until Congress can be consulted"

Mr. Mc.Henry & Mr. Carrol moved that "no State shall be restrained from laying duties of tonnage for the purpose of clearing harbours and erecting light-houses".

Col. Mason in support of this explained and urged the situation of the Chesapeak which peculiarly required expences of this sort.

Mr. Govr. Morris. The States are not restrained from laying tonnage as the Constitution now Stands. The exception proposed will imply the Contrary, and will put the States in a worse condition than the gentleman (Col Mason) wishes.

Mr. Madison. Whether the States are now restrained from laying tonnage duties depends on the extent of the power "to regulate commerce". These terms are vague but seem to exclude this power of the States— They may certainly be restrained by Treaty. He observed that there were other objects for tonnage Duties as the support of Seamen &c. He was more & more convinced that the regulation of Commerce was in its nature indivisible and ought to be wholly under one authority.[3]

Mr. Sherman. The power of the U. States to regulate trade being supreme can controul interferences of the State regulations ⟨when⟩ such interferences happen; so that there is no danger to be apprehended from a concurrent jurisdiction.

Mr. Langdon insisted that the regulation of tonnage was an essential part of the regulation of trade, and that the States ought to have nothing to do with it. On motion "that no "State shall lay any duty on tonnage without the Consent "of Congress"

N. H— ay— Mas. ay. Ct. divd. N. J. ay. Pa. no. Del.

[3] See Appendix A, CCCLXVI.

ay. Md. ay. Va. no. N— C. no. S— C. ay. Geo. no. [Ayes — 6; noes — 4; divided — 1.]

The remainder of the paragraph was then remoulded and passed as follows viz— "No State shall without the consent of Congress, lay any duty of tonnage, keep troops or ships of war in time of peace, enter into any agreement or compact with another State, or with a foreign power, or engage in war, unless actually invaded, or in such imminent danger as will not admit of delay"

Art II. sect. 1. (paragraph 6) "or the period for chusing another president arrive" was changed into "or a President ⟨shall⟩ be elected" comformably to a vote of the day of

Mr. Rutlidge and Docr Franklin moved to annex to the end paragraph 7. sect. 1. art II— "and he (the President) shall not receive, within that period, any other emolument from the U. S. or any of them." on which question

N— H. ay— Mas. ay. Ct. no. N. J. no. Pa ay. Del. no. Md. ay— Va. ay. N. C. no. S— C. ay. Geo— ay. [Ayes — 7; noes — 4.]

Art: II. sect. 2. "he shall have power to grant reprieves and pardons for offences against the U. S. &c"

Mr Randolph moved to "except cases of treason". The prerogative of pardon in these cases was too great a trust. The President may himself be guilty. The Traytors may be his own instruments.

Col: Mason supported the motion.

Mr Govr Morris had rather there should be no pardon for treason, than let the power devolve on the Legislature.

Mr Wilson. Pardon is necessary for cases of treason, and is best placed in the hands of the Executive. If he be himself a party to the guilt he can be impeached and prosecuted.

Mr. King thought it would be inconsistent with the Constitutional separation of the Executive & Legislative powers to let the prerogative be exercised by the latter — A Legislative body is utterly unfit for the purpose. They are governed too much by the passions of the moment. In Massachusetts, one assembly would have hung all the insurgents in that

State: the next was equally disposed to pardon them all. He suggested the expedient of requiring the concurrence of the Senate in Acts of Pardon.

Mr. Madison admitted the force of objections to the Legislature, but the pardon of treasons was so peculiarly improper for the President that he should acquiesce in the transfer of it to the former, rather than leave it altogether in the hands of the latter. He would prefer to either an association of the Senate as a Council of advice, with the President.

Mr Randolph could not admit the Senate into a share of the Power. the great danger to liberty lay in a combination between the President & that body —

Col: Mason. The Senate has already too much power — There can be no danger of too much lenity in legislative pardons, as the Senate must con concur, & the President moreover can require $\frac{2}{3}$ of both Houses[4]

On the motion of Mr. Randolph

N. H. no— Mas. no— Ct. divd. N— J— no. Pa. no— Del. no. Md no— Va ay— N— C. no— S. C. no. Geo— ay. [Ayes — 2; noes — 8; divided — 1.]

Art II. sect. 2. (paragraph 2) To the end of this, Mr Governr. Morris moved to annex "but the Congress may by law vest the appointment of such inferior Officers as they think proper, in the President alone, in the Courts of law, or in the heads of Departments." Mr Sherman 2ded. the motion

Mr. Madison. It does not go far enough if it be necessary at all — Superior Officers below Heads of Departments ought in some cases to have the appointment of the lesser offices.

Mr Govr Morris There is no necessity. Blank Commissions can be sent —

On the motion

N. H. ay. Mas— no— Ct ay. N. J. ay. Pa. ay. Del. no. Md. divd Va no. N. C. ay— S C no. Geo— no— [Ayes — 5; noes — 5; divided — 1.]

The motion being lost by the equal division ⟨of votes,⟩ It was urged that it be put a second time, some such provision

---

[4] See also Appendix A, CLVIII (79).

being too necessary, to be omitted. and on a second question it was agreed to nem. con.

⟨Art II Sect. 1. The words, "and not per capita" — were struck out as superfluous — and the words "by the Representatives" also — as improper, the choice of President being in another mode as well as eventually by the House of Reps—

Art: II. Sect. 2. After "Officers of the U. S. whose appointments are not otherwise provided for," were added the words "and which shall be established by law".⟩[5]

Art III. sect. 2. parag: 3.. Mr. Pinkney & Mr. Gerry moved to annex to the end. "And a trial by jury shall be preserved as usual in civil cases."

Mr. Gorham. The constitution of Juries is different in different States and the trial itself is *usual* in different cases in different States,

Mr. King urged the same objections

Genl. Pinkney also. He thought such a clause in the Constitution would be pregnant with embarassments

The motion was disagreed to nem: con:

Art. IV. sect 2. parag: 3. the term "legally" was struck out, and "under the laws thereof" inserted ⟨after the word "State,"⟩[6] in compliance with the wish of some who thought the term ⟨legal⟩ equivocal, and favoring the idea that slavery was legal in a moral view—

Art. IV. sect 3. "New States may be admitted by the Congress into this Union: but no new State shall be formed or erected within the jurisdiction of any other State; nor any State be formed by the junction of two or more States, or parts of States, without the consent of the Legislatures of the States concerned as well as of the Congs."

Mr Gerry moved to insert after "or parts of States" the words "or a State and part of a State" which was disagreed to by a large majority; it appearing to be supposed that the case was comprehended in the words of the clause as reported by the Committee.

⟨Art. IV. sect. 4. After the word "Executive" were in-

[5] Based upon *Journal* (p. 383). See above note 1.

[6] Crossed out "in another place". Change accords with *Journal*, p. 384.

serted the words "when the Legislature cannot be Convened")[7]

Art— V. "The Congress, whenever two thirds of both Houses shall deem necessary, or on the application of two thirds of the Legislatures of the several States shall propose amendments to this Constitution, which shall be valid to all intents and purposes as part thereof, when the same shall have been ratified by three fourths at least of the Legislatures of the several States, or by Conventions in three fourths thereof, as the one or the other mode of ratification may be proposed by the Congress: Provided that no amendment which may be made prior to the year 1808 shall in any manner affect the ⟨1 & 4 clauses in the 9.⟩ section of article I "

Mr. Sherman expressed his fears that three fourths of the States might be brought to do things fatal to particular States, as abolishing them altogether or depriving them of their equality in the Senate. He thought it reasonable that the proviso in favor of the States importing slaves should be extended so as to provide that no State should be affected in its internal police, or deprived of its equality in the Senate.

Col: Mason thought the plan of amending the Constitution exceptionable & dangerous. As the proposing of amendments is in both the modes to depend, in the first immediately, and in the second, ultimately, on Congress, no amendments of the proper kind would ever be obtained by the people, if the Government should become oppressive, as he verily believed would be the case.[8]

Mr. Govr. Morris & Mr. Gerry moved to amend the article so as to require a Convention on application of ⅔ of the Sts

Mr Madison did not see why Congress would not be as

[7] Taken from *Journal*, see above note 1.

[8] In the margin of his copy of the draft of September 12, Mason had written:

"Article 5th —By this article Congress only have the power of proposing amendments at any future time to this constitution and should it prove ever so oppressive, the whole people of America can't make, or even propose alterations to it; a doctrine utterly subversive of the fundamental principles of the rights and liberties of the people."

See also Appendix A, CCLXIX.

much bound to propose amendments applied for by two thirds of the States as to call a call a Convention on the like application. He saw no objection however against providing for a Convention for the purpose of amendments, except only that difficulties might arise as to the form, the quorum &c. which in Constitutional regulations ought to be as much as possible avoided.

The motion of Mr. Govr Morris and Mr. Gerry was agreed to nem: con (see: the first part of the article as finally past)

Mr Sherman moved to strike out of art. V. after "legislatures" the words "of three fourths" and so after the word "Conventions" leaving future Conventions to act in this matter, like the present Conventions according to circumstances.

On this motion

N— H— divd. Mas— ay— Ct ay. N— J. ay— Pa no. Del— no. Md no. Va no. N. C. no. S— C. no. Geo— no. [Ayes — 3; noes — 7; divided — 1.]

Mr Gerry moved to strike out the words "or by Conventions in three fourths thereof"

On this motion

N— H— no. Mas. no— Ct. ay. N— J. no. Pa no— Del— no. Md no. Va. no. N— C. no. S. C. no— Geo— no. [Ayes — 1; noes — 10.]

M— Sherman moved according to his idea above expressed to annex to the end of the article a further proviso "that no State shall without its consent be affected in its internal police, or deprived of its equal suffrage in the Senate",

Mr. Madison. Begin with these special provisos, and every State will insist on them, for their boundaries, exports &c.

On the motion of Mr. Sherman

N. H— no. Mas. no. Ct ay. N. J. ay— Pa no. Del— ay. Md. no. Va. no N. C. no. S. C. no. Geo. no. [Ayes — 3; noes — 8.]

Mr. Sherman then moved to strike out art V altogether

Mr Brearley 2ded. the motion, on which

N. H. no. Mas. no. Ct. ay. N. J. ay. Pa. no. Del. divd.

Md. no. Va. no. N. C. no. S. C. no. Geo. no [Ayes — 2; noes — 8; divided — 1.]

Mr. Govr Morris moved to annex a further proviso— "that no State, without its consent shall be deprived of its equal suffrage in the Senate"

This motion being dictated by the circulating murmurs of the small States was agreed to without debate, no one opposing it, or on the question, saying no.[9]

Col: Mason expressing his discontent at the power given to Congress by a bare majority to pass navigation acts, which he said would not only enhance the freight, a consequence he did not so much regard — but would enable a few rich merchants in Philada N. York & Boston, to monopolize the Staples of the Southern States & reduce their value perhaps 50 Per Ct — moved a further proviso "that no law in nature of a navigation act be passed before the year 1808, without the consent of ⅔ of each branch of the Legislature[10]

On this motion

N. H. no. Mas— no. Ct no. N— J. no— Pa no. Del. no. Md ay. Va. ay. N. C abst S. C. no— Geo— ay. [Ayes — 3; noes — 7; absent — 1.]

Mr Randolph animadverting on the indefinite and dangerous power given by the Constitution to Congress, expressing the pain he felt at differing from the body of the Convention, on the close of the great & awful subject of their labours, and anxiously wishing for some accommodating expedient which would relieve him from his embarrassments, made a motion importing "that amendments to the plan might be offered by the State Conventions, which should be submitted to and finally decided on by another general Convention"[11] Should this proposition be disregarded, it would he said be impossible for him to put his name to the instrument. Whether he should oppose it afterwards he would not then decide but he would not deprive himself of the freedom to do so in his own State, if that course should be prescribed by his final judgment—

[9] See Appendix A, CCC.

[10] See Appendix A, CLI.

[11] Upon this proposal, see above August 31 and September 10, and Appendix A, CXXXI, CLXIV, CCXXXV.

Col: Mason 2ded. & followed Mr. Randolph in animadversions on the dangerous power and structure of the Government, concluding that it would end either in monarchy, or a tyrannical aristocracy; which, he was in doubt. but one or other, he was sure. This Constitution had been formed without the knowledge or idea of the people. A second Convention will know more of the sense of the people, and be able to provide a system more consonant to it. It was improper to say to the people, take this or nothing. As the Constitution now stands, he could neither give it his support or vote in Virginia; and he could not sign here what he could not support there. With the expedient of another Convention as proposed, he could sign.[12]

Mr. Pinkney. These declarations from members so respectable at the close of this important scene, give a peculiar solemnity to the present moment. He descanted on the consequences of calling forth the deliberations & amendments of the different States on the subject of Government at large. Nothing but confusion & contrariety could spring from the experiment. The States will never agree in their plans— And the Deputies to a second Convention coming together under the discordant impressions of their Constituents, will never agree. Conventions are serious things, and ought not to be repeated— He was not without objections as well as others to the plan. He objected to the contemptible weakness & dependence of the Executive. He objected to the power of a majority only of Congs over Commerce. But apprehending the danger of a general confusion, and an ultimate decision by the Sword, he should give the plan his support.[13]

Mr. Gerry, stated the objections which determined him to withhold his name from the Constitution.[14] 1. the duration and re-eligibility of the Senate. 2. the power of the House of Representatives to conceal their journals. 3— the power

[12] For Mason's objections, see below (with references under note 21).

[13] See Appendix A, CLXX.

[14] See King's copy of these below, also Appendix A, CXXVIII, CXXXIII, CLVII, CLXXV.

of Congress over the places of election. 4 the unlimited power of Congress over their own compensations. 5 Massachusetts has not a due share of Representatives allotted to her. 6. $\frac{3}{5}$ of the Blacks are to be represented as if they were freemen 7. *Under* the power over commerce, monopolies may be established. 8. The vice president being made head of the Senate. He could however he said get over all these, if the rights of the Citizens were not rendered insecure 1. by the general power of the Legislature to make what laws they may please to call necessary and proper. 2. raise armies and money without limit. 3. to establish a tribunal without juries, which will be a Star-chamber as to Civil cases. Under such a view of the Constitution, the best that could be done he conceived was to provide for a second general Convention.

On the question on the proposition of Mr Randolph. All the States answered– no

On the question to agree to the Constitution. as amended.[15] All the States ay.

The Constitution was then ordered to be engrossed.

And the House adjourned[16]

McHENRY

15 Sepr.

Maryland moved.

No State shall be prohibited from laying such duties of tonnage as may be sufficient for improving their harbors and keeping up lights, but all acts laying such duties shall be subject to the approbation or repeal of Congress.

[15] In addition to the changes noted above in the *Records*, September 13–15, the following have been compiled from the Baldwin, Brearley and Washington copies of the draft of September 12: —

Article 1, Section 7, paragraph 1 — "The enacting stile . . . " struck out.

Article II, Section 1, paragraph 3 — "government of the United States" substituted for "general government".

Article II, Section 1, paragraph 8 — the dash "—" after "I" struck out.

Article III, Section 3, paragraph 2 — "or" substituted for "nor" before "forfeiture" and the comma "," after "forfeiture" struck out.

[16] The session continued until 6 P.M. See Appendix A, CIX.

Moved to amend it viz. No State without the consent of Congress shall lay a duty of tonnage. Carryed in the affirmative

6 ays 4 Noes, 1 divided.

Made several verbal amendment in the progression on the system.

Added to the V article amended "No State without its consent shall be deprived of its equal suffrage in the Senate.

Mr. Mason moved in substance that no navigation act be passed without the concurrence of ⅔ of the members present in each house.

Negatived.

Mr. Randolp moved that it be recommended to appoint a second convention with plenary powers to consider objections to the system and to conclude one binding upon the States.

rejected unanimously—

The question being taken on the system agreed to unanimously—

Ordered to be engrossed and 500 copies struck— Adjourned till monday the *17th.*

provided[17] that any state may lay additional duties on shipping for the support of Lights, piers marks or Buoys or for the deepening or improvement of Harbours.

The legislature shall have power to erect piers buoys or marks and to deepen or clean harbours for facilitating or improving navigation—

No State shall be prohibited from laying such duties of tonnage as may be sufficient for improving their harbours and keeping up lights or buoys, but all acts laying such duties shall be subject to the approbation or repeal of Congress. Amended. 6 ay. 4 noes. 1 divided.

---

[17] On a loose scrap of paper among the McHenry MSS.

KING

Mr. Gerry's objections
The appointment of the Senate for six years — and no rotation
The Power given to the Legislature over their Journals
The Power given to the Legislators to pay themselves
Massachusetts has not her propo. of reptives.
Three fifths of the Blacks, being classed as Taxables
The Power given respectg. Commerce will enable the Legislature to create corporations and monopolies
The V. P destroys the Independce. of the Legislature
Freemen giving up certain rights should be secured in others
The Legislature allowed to make any laws they please
The Constitution has given away every mode of revenue from the States
The Judiciary will be a Star Chamber
Many other objections which he would not enumerate[18]

Gerry's Objections.[19]

1

Duration & no rotation of Senators

2

Secrecy of Journals

3

The Times places & manner of choosing Representatives subjected to ye G. Govt.

4

Senate & Reps. pay ym selves from the general Treasury —

The Army, the Militia, the power in the last clause to make any laws pursut. to ye Conn. to carry the same into Effect — The Sovereignty or Liberty of the States will be destroyed, and the Judicial will be oppressive —
The foregoing are the reasons of my Dissent[20]

---

[18] [On back of sheet:] no no no no | aye aye aye aye aye aye

[19] This document in Gerry's handwriting was found among the King MSS. with the other notes on the Convention.

[20] [Endorsed:] Reasons of Gerry's Dissent from Consn.

5

Mass. has not her proportn.
of Reps. and $\frac{3}{5}$ of the Negroes
are Represented

6

Commercial powers authorise
monopolies & Companys —

7

Vice president dangerous
The foregoing I give up

MASON[20a]

[In addition to the items noted above in the *Records*, Mason had made the following notes on his copy of the draft of September 12:]

In the beginning of the 4th clause of the 3rd section of the 1st Article, strike out the words — *the vice-president of the United States*, and instead of them insert — a vice-president of the United States shall be chosen in the manner hereinafter directed who refused

In the 1st clause of the 10th section of the same Article strike out ex post facto laws — and after the words *obligation of* insert — previous. refused

In the latter end of the 3rd clause of the 2nd Article — enquire of the committee about the senate chusing the vice president

In the 7th clause of the 1st section of the 2nd Article — strike out the words *during the period for which he shall have been elected* — and instead of them insert — so as in any manner to affect the person in office at the time of such increase or diminution.

At the end of the 1st clause of the 2nd section of the 2nd Article add the words — or Treason; but he may grant re-

[20a] Taken from K. M. Rowland, *Life of George Mason*, II, 383–385.

prieves in cases of treason, until the end of the next ensuing session of Congress.

Section 4th of the same Article — Inconsistency between this and the 7th clause of the 3rd section of the 1st Article — amend by inserting after the word *office* the words — and disqualified from holding or enjoying — any office of honor, trust or profit under the United States.

Article 3rd, section 1 — before the word *diminished* — insert — encreased or —

In the 2nd clause of the 2nd section of the 3rd Article — strike out the word *Fact* — and insert — Equity.

In the 3rd section of 3rd Article — *corruption of blood* inaccurately expressed; and no exception or provision for the wife, who may be innocent, and ought not to be involved in ruin from the guilt of the husband.

Section 2nd, Article 4th — The citizens of one State having an estate in another, have not secured to them the right of removing their property as in the 4th Article of the Confederation — amend by adding the following clause: and every citizen having an estate in two or more States shall have a right to remove his property from one State to another.

(not proposed)

Objections to this Constitution of Government.[21]

There is no Declaration of Rights, and the laws of the general government being paramount to the laws and constitution of the several States, the Declaration of Rights in the separate States are no security. Nor are the people secured even in the enjoyment of the benefit of the common law ⟨which stands here upon no other foundation than its having been adopted by the respective acts forming the constitutions of the several States⟩.

---

[21] This was written by Mason on the blank pages of his copy of the draft of September 12. Mason supplied copies of this in one form or another to several people, and it was finally printed in pamphlet form. Angle brackets indicate additions or changes made before printing. (It is reprinted here from Rowland's *Life of George Mason*, II, 387–390).

See above August 31, and Appendix A, CXXVI, CXXXIV, CXXXVII, CLI, CLV, CXCIV, CCII.

In the House of Representatives there is not the substance but the shadow only of representation; which can never produce proper information in the legislature, or inspire confidence in the people; the laws will therefore be generally made by men little concerned in, and unacquainted with their effects and consequences. ⟨This objection has been in some degree lessened by an amendment, often before refused and at last made by an erasure, after the engrossment upon parchment of the word *forty* and inserting *thirty*, in the third clause of the second section of the first article.⟩

The Senate have the power of altering all money bills, and of originating appropriations of money, and the salaries of the officers of their own appointment, in conjunction with the president of the United States, although they are not the representatives of the people or amenable to them.

These with their other great powers, viz.: their power in the appointment of ambassadors and all public officers, in making treaties, and in trying all impeachments, their influence upon and connection with the supreme Executive from these causes, their duration of office and their being a constantly existing body, almost continually sitting, joined with their being one complete branch of the legislature, will destroy any balance in the government, and enable them to accomplish what ursurpations they please upon the rights and liberties of the people.

The Judiciary of the United States is so constructed and extended, as to absorb and destroy the judiciaries of the several States; thereby rendering law as tedious, intricate and expensive, and justice as unattainable, by a great part of the community, as in England, and enabling the rich to oppress and ruin the poor.

The President of the United States has no Constitutional Council, a thing unknown in any safe and regular government. He will therefore be unsupported by proper information and advice, and will generally be directed by minions and favorites; or he will become a tool to the Senate — or a Council of State will grow out of the principal officers of the great departments; the worst and most dangerous of all ingredients for such a Council in a free country; ⟨for they may be induced to join

in any dangerous or oppressive measures, to shelter themselves, and prevent an inquiry into their own misconduct in office. Whereas, had a constitutional council been formed (as was proposed) of six members, viz.: two from the Eastern, two from the Middle, and two from the Southern States, to be appointed by vote of the States in the House of Representatives, with the same duration and rotation of office as the Senate, the executive would always have had safe and proper information and advice; the president of such a council might have acted as Vice-President of the United States *pro tempore*, upon any vacancy or disability of the chief magistrate; and long continued sessions of the Senate, would in a great measure have been prevented.⟩ From this fatal defect has arisen the improper power of the Senate in the appointment of public officers, and the alarming dependence and connection between that branch of the legislature and the supreme Executive.

Hence also sprung that unnecessary ⟨and dangerous⟩ officer the Vice-President, who for want of other employment is made president of the Senate, thereby dangerously blending the executive and legislative powers, besides always giving to some one of the States an unnecessary and unjust pre-eminence over the others.

The President of the United States has the unrestrained power of granting pardons for treason, which may be sometimes exercised to screen from punishment those whom he had secretly instigated to commit the crime, and thereby prevent a discovery of his own guilt.

By declaring all treaties supreme laws of the land, the Executive and the Senate have, in many cases, an exclusive power of legislation; which might have been avoided by proper distinctions with respect to treaties, and requiring the assent of the House of Representatives, where it could be done with safety.

By requiring only a majority to make all commercial and navigation laws, the five Southern States, whose produce and circumstances are totally different from that of the eight Northern and Eastern States, may ⟨will⟩ be ruined, for such rigid and premature regulations may be made as will enable

the merchants of the Northern and Eastern States not only to demand an exhorbitant freight, but to monopolize the purchase of the commodities at their own price, for many years, to the great injury of the landed interest, and ⟨the⟩ impoverishment of the people; and the danger is the greater as the gain on one side will be in proportion to the loss on the other. Whereas requiring two-thirds of the members present in both Houses would have produced mutual moderation, promoted the general interest, and removed an insuperable objection to the adoption of this ⟨the⟩ government.

Under their own construction of the general clause, at the end of the enumerated powers, the Congress may grant monopolies in trade and commerce, constitute new crimes, inflict unusual and severe punishments, and extend their powers ⟨power⟩ as far as they shall think proper; so that the State legislatures have no security for the powers now presumed to remain to them, or the people for their rights.

There is no declaration of any kind, for preserving the liberty of the press, or the trial by jury in civil causes ⟨cases⟩; nor against the danger of standing armies in time of peace.

The State legislatures are restrained from laying export duties on their own produce.

Both the general legislature and the State legislature are expressly prohibited making *ex post facto* laws; though there never was nor can be a legislature but must and will make such laws, when necessity and the public safety require them; which will hereafter be a breach of all the constitutions in the Union, and afford precedents for other innovations.

This government will set out ⟨commence⟩ a moderate aristocracy: it is at present impossible to foresee whether it will, in its operation, produce a monarchy, or a corrupt, tyrannical ⟨oppressive⟩ aristocracy; it will most probably vibrate some years between the two, and then terminate in the one or the other.

The general legislature is restrained from prohibiting the further importation of slaves for twenty odd years; though such importations render the United States weaker, more vulnerable, and less capable of defence.

MONDAY, SEPTEMBER 17, 1787.

JOURNAL

Detail of Ayes and Noes

	New Hampshire	Massachusetts	Rhode Island	Connecticut	New York	New Jersey	Pennsylvania	Delaware	Maryland	Virginia	North Carolina	South Carolina	Georgia	Questions	ayes	noes	divided
[567]	aye	aye		aye		aye	aye	aye	aye	aye	aye	aye	aye	The Constitution unanimously agreed to.			
[568]	aye	aye		aye		aye	aye	aye	aye	aye	aye	dd	aye				
[569]	aye	aye		aye		aye	aye	aye	no	aye	aye	aye	aye	To deliver over the Journals and papers to the President.			

MADISON

Monday Sepr. 17. 1787. In Convention

The engrossed Constitution being read,

Docr. Franklin rose with a speech in his hand, which he had reduced to writing for his own conveniency, and which Mr. Wilson read in the words following.[1]

Mr. President

I confess that there are several parts of this constitution which I do not at present approve, but I am not sure I shall never approve them: For having lived long, I have experi-

[1] Franklin seems to have sent copies of this speech in his own handwriting to several of his friends, and one of these soon found its way into print (see Carey's *American Museum*, II, pp. 558–559). After examining several of these copies, it seems probable that Madison's copy represents the speech as it was read. The others all embody subsequent modifications. See further Appendix A, CXXVIII, CLXXXVII, CC.

enced many instances of being obliged by better information or fuller consideration, to change opinions even on important subjects, which I once thought right, but found to be otherwise. It is therefore that the older I grow, the more apt I am to doubt my own judgment, and to pay more respect to the judgment of others. Most men indeed as well as most sects in Religion, think themselves in possession of all truth, and that whereever others differ from them it is so far error. Steele, a Protestant in a Dedication tells the Pope, that the only difference between our Churches in their opinions of the certainty of their doctrines is, the Church of Rome is infallible and the Church of England is never in the wrong. But though many private persons think almost as highly of their own infallibility as of that of their sect, few express it so naturally as a certain french lady, who in a dispute with her sister, said "I don't know how it happens, Sister but I meet with no body but myself, that's always in the right" — *Il n'y a que moi qui a toujours raison.*"

In these sentiments, Sir, I agree to this Constitution with all its faults, if they are such; because I think a general Government necessary for us, and there is no form of Government but what may be a blessing to the people if well administered, and believe farther that this is likely to be well administered for a course of years, and can only end in Despotism, as other forms have done before it, when the people shall become so corrupted as to need despotic Government, being incapable of any other. I doubt too whether any other Convention we can obtain may be able to make a better Constitution. For when you assemble a number of men to have the advantage of their joint wisdom, you inevitably assemble with those men, all their prejudices, their passions, their errors of opinion, their local interests, and their selfish views. From such an Assembly can a perfect production be expected? It therefore astonishes me, Sir, to find this system approaching so near to perfection as it does; and I think it will astonish our enemies, who are waiting with confidence to hear that our councils are confounded like those of the Builders of Babel; and that our States are on the point of separation, only to meet hereafter for the

purpose of cutting one another's throats. Thus I consent, Sir, to this Constitution because I expect no better, and because I am not sure, that it is not the best. The opinions I have had of its errors, I sacrifice to the public good — I have never whispered a syllable of them abroad — Within these walls they were born, and here they shall die — If every one of us in returning to our Constituents were to report the objections he has had to it, and endeavor to gain partizans in support of them, we might prevent its being generally received, and thereby lose all the salutary effects & great advantages resulting naturally in our favor among foreign Nations as well as among ourselves, from our real or apparent unanimity. Much of the strength & efficiency of any Government in procuring and securing happiness to the people, depends. on opinion, on the general opinion of the goodness of the Government, as well as well as of the wisdom and integrity of its Governors. I hope therefore that for our own sakes as a part of the people, and for the sake of posterity, we shall act heartily and unanimously in recommending this Constitution (if approved by Congress & confirmed by the Conventions) wherever our influence may extend, and turn our future thoughts & endeavors to the means of having it well administered.

On the whole, Sir, I cannot help expressing a wish that every member of the Convention who may still have objections to it, would with me, on this occasion doubt a little of his own infallibility— and to make manifest our unanimity, put his name to this instrument." — He then moved that the Constitution be signed by the members and offered the following as a convenient form viz. "Done in Convention, by the unanimous consent of *the States* present the 17th. of Sepr. &c — In Witness whereof we have hereunto subscribed our names."

This ambiguous form had been drawn up by Mr. G. M. in order to gain the dissenting members, and put into the hands of Docr. Franklin that it might have the better chance of success.

Mr. Gorham said if it was not too late he could wish, for the purpose of lessening objections to the Constitution, that

the clause declaring "the number of Representatives shall not exceed one for every forty thousand —" which had produced so much discussion, might be yet reconsidered, in order to strike out 40,000 & insert "thirty thousand" This would not he remarked establish that as an absolute rule, but only give Congress a greater latitude which could not be thought unreasonable.[2]

Mr. King & Mr Carrol seconded & supported the ideas of Mr Gorham.

When the President rose, for the purpose of putting the question,[3] he said that although his situation had hitherto restrained him from offering his sentiments on questions depending in the House, and it might be thought, ought now to impose silence on him, yet he could not forbear expressing his wish that the alteration proposed might take place. It was much to be desired that the objections to the plan recommended might be made as few as possible — The smallness of the proportion of Representatives had been considered by many members of the Convention, an insufficient security for the rights & interests of the people. He acknowledged that it had always appeared to himself among the exceptionable parts of the plan;[4] and late as the present moment was for admitting amendments, he thought this of so much consequence that it would give much satisfaction to see it adopted.*

No opposition was made to the proposition of Mr. Gorham and it was agreed to unanimously

On the question to agree to the Constitution enrolled in order to be signed. It was agreed to all the States answering ay.

Mr Randolph then rose and with an allusion to the observations of Docr Franklin, apologized for[5] his refusing to sign the Constitution, notwithstanding the vast majority & vener-

* (This was the only occasion on which the President entered at all into the discussions of the Convention).

[2] Upon this change to 30,000 see Appendix A, CXLVII, CLVIII (39), CCXVIII, CCXLVI.

[3] Crossed out "he made a few observations".

[4] Crossed out "of such peculiar importance was its amendments, he could not therefore suppress his approbation of the mo".

[5] Crossed out: "yielding to his own judgment against so".

able names that would give sanction to its wisdom and its worth.[6] He said however that he did not mean by this refusal to decide that he should oppose the Constitution without doors. He meant only to keep himself free to be governed by his duty as it should be prescribed by his future judgment — He refused to sign, because he thought the object of the convention would be frustrated by the alternative which it presented to the people. Nine States will fail to ratify the plan and confusion must ensue. With such a view of the subject he ought not, he could not, by pledging himself to support the plan, restrain himself from taking such steps as might appear to him most consistent with the public good.

Mr. Govr. Morris said that he too had objections, but considering the present plan[7] as the best that was to be attained, he should take it with all its faults. The majority had determined in its favor and by that determination he should abide. The moment this plan goes forth all other considerations will be laid aside— and the great question will be, shall there be a national Government or not? and this must take place or a general anarchy will be the alternative — He remarked that the signing in the form proposed related only to the fact that the *States* present were unanimous.

Mr. Williamson suggested that the signing should be confined to the letter accompanying the Constitution to Congress. which might perhaps do nearly as well, and would he found be satisfactory to some members* who disliked the Constitution. For himself he did not think a better plan was to be expected and had no scruples against putting his name to it.

Mr Hamilton expressed his anxiety that every member should sign. A few characters of consequence, by opposing or even refusing to sign the Constitution, might do infinite mischief by kindling the latent sparks which lurk under an enthusiasm in favor of the Convention which may soon subside. No man's ideas were more remote from the plan than

* He alluded[8] to Mr. Blount for one.

[6] Upon Randolph's refusal to sign, see above September 15, and Appendix A, CXIV, CXXXI, CXXXVII, CCV.

[7] Crossed out "results of all deliberations".

[8] Crossed out "probably".

his own were known to be; but is it possible to deliberate between anarchy and Convulsion on one side, and the chance of good to be expected from the plan on the other.

Mr Blount said he had declared that he would not sign, so as to pledge himself in support of the plan, but he was relieved by the form proposed and would without committing himself attest the fact that the plan was the unanimous act of the States in Convention.

Docr. Franklin expressed his fears from what Mr Randolph had said, that he thought himself alluded to in the remarks offered this morning to the House. He declared that when drawing up that paper he did not know that any particular member would refuse to sign his name to the instrument, and hoped to be so understood. He professed a high sense of obligation to Mr. Randolph for having brought forward the plan in the first instance, and for the assistance he had given in its progress, and hoped that he would yet lay aside his objections, and, by concurring with his brethren, prevent the great mischief which the refusal of his name might produce

Mr. Randolph could not but regard the signing in the proposed form, as the same with signing the Constitution. The change of form therefore could make no difference with him. He repeated that in refusing to sign the Constitution, he took a step which might be the most awful of his life, but it was dictated by his conscience, and it was not possible for him to hesitate, much less, to change. He repeated also his persuasion, that the holding out this plan with a final alternative to the people, of accepting or rejecting it in toto, would really produce the anarchy & civil convulsions which were apprehended from the refusal of individuals to sign it.

Mr Gerry described the painful feelings of his situation, and the embarrassment under which he rose to offer any further observations on the subject wch. had been finally decided. Whilst the plan was depending, he had treated it with all the freedom he thought it deserved— He now felt himself bound as he was disposed to treat it with the respect due to the Act of the Convention— He hoped he should not violate that respect in declaring on this occasion his fears

that a Civil war may result from the present crisis of the U. S— In Massachusetts, particularly he saw the danger of this calamitous event— In that State there are two parties, one devoted to Democracy, the worst he thought of all political evils, the other as violent in the opposite extreme. From the collision of these in opposing and resisting the Constitution, confusion was greatly to be feared. He had thought it necessary for this & other reasons that the plan should have been proposed in a more mediating shape, in order to abate the heat and opposition of parties— As it had been passed by the Convention, he was persuaded it would have a contrary effect— He could not therefore by signing the Constitution pledge himself to abide by it at all events. The proposed form made no difference with him. But if it were not otherwise apparent, the refusals to sign should never be known from him. Alluding to the remarks of Docr. Franklin, he could not he said but view them as levelled at himself and the other gentlemen who meant not to sign;

Genl Pinkney— We are not likely to gain many converts by the ambiguity of the proposed form of signing. He thought it best to be candid and let the form speak the substance— If the meaning of the signers be left in doubt, his purpose would not be answered— He should sign the Constitution with a view to support it with all his influence, and wished to pledge himself accordingly—

Docr. Franklin. It is too soon to pledge ourselves before Congress and our Constituents shall have approved the plan.

Mr Ingersol did not consider the signing, either as a mere attestation of the fact, or as pledging the signers to support the Constitution at all events; but as a recommendation, of what, all things considered, was the most eligible.

On the motion of Docr. Franklin

N. H. ay. Mas. ay— Ct. ay— N. J. ay— Pa. ay— Del— ay. Md. ay. Va. ay— ⟨N. C. ay⟩[9] S. C. divd.* Geo. ay. [Ayes — 10; noes — 0; divided — 1.]

* Genl Pinkney & Mr. Butler disliked the equivocal form of the signing, and on that account voted in the negative

[9] Taken from *Journal*.

Mr. King suggested that the Journals of the Convention should be either destroyed, or deposited in the custody of the President. He thought if suffered to be made public, a bad use would be made of them by those who would wish to prevent the adoption of the Constitution—[10]

Mr Wilson prefered the second expedient. he had at one time liked the first best; but as false suggestions may be propagated it should not be made impossible to contradict them—

A question was then put on depositing the Journals and other papers of the Convention in the hands of the President, On which,

N— H— ay. Mtts ay. Ct. ay— N. J. ay. Pena. ay. Del. ay. Md.* no. Va. ay. N. C. ay— S. C. ay. Geo. ay. [Ayes 10; noes — 1.]

The President having asked what the Convention meant should be done with the Journals &c, whether copies were to be allowed to the members if applied for. It was Resolved nem: con: "that he retain the Journal and other papers, subject to the order of Congress, if ever formed under the Constitution.[11]

The members then proceeded to sign the instrument.

Whilst the last members were signing it Doctr. Franklin looking towards the Presidents Chair, at the back of which a rising sun happened to be painted, observed to a few members near him, that Painters had found it difficult to distinguish in their art a rising from a setting sun. I have, said he, often and often in the course of the Session, and the vicissitudes of my hopes and fears as to its issue, looked at that behind the President without being able to tell whether it was rising or setting: But now at length I have the happiness to know that it is a rising and not a setting Sun.

The Constitution being signed by all the Members except

* This negative of Maryland was occasioned by the language of the instructions to the Deputies of that State, which required them to report to the State, the *proceedings* of the Convention.

[10] See further appendix A, CX, CXI, CCCXX.

[11] For the subsequent history of these papers, see Introduction.

Mr Randolph, Mr Mason, and Mr. Gerry who declined giving it the sanction of their names,[12] the Convention dissolved itself by an Adjournment sine die———

⟨☞ The few alterations and corrections made in these debates which are not in my hand writing, were dictated by me and made in my presence by John C. Payne.

James Madison⟩

McHENRY

Monday 17 Sepr. 1787.

Read the engrossed constitution. Altered the representation in the house of representatives from 40 to thirty thousand.

Dr. Franklin put a paper into Mr Willsons hand to read containing his reasons for assenting to the constitution. It was plain, insinuating persuasive — and in any event of the system guarded the Doctor's fame.

Mr Randolp Mr Mason and Mr Gerry declined signing— The other members signed—

Being opposed to many parts of the system I make a remark why I signed it and mean to support it.

1sly I distrust my own judgement, especially as it is opposite to the opinion of a majority of gentlemen whose abilities and patriotism are of the first cast; and as I have had already frequent occasions to be convinced that I have not always judged right.

2dly Alterations may be obtained, it being provided that the concurrence of $\frac{2}{3}$ of the Congress may at any time introduce them.

3dly Comparing the inconveniences and the evils which we labor under and may experience from the present confederation, and the little good we can expect from it — with the possible evils and probable benefits and advantages promised

[12] See above note 6, and Appendix A, CVIII, CX, CXXIV, CXXXVII, CLVI, CLXXXIX, CCXLII, CCXLIV, CCCLIX, CCCLXII.

us by the new system, I am clear that I ought to give it all the support in my power.

Philada. 17 Sepr. 1787 James McHenry.

Major Jackson Secry. to carry it to Congress — Injunction of secrecy taken off. Members to be provided with printed copies — adjourned sine die — Gentn. of Con. dined together at the City Tavern.[14]

[14] See Appendix A, CX.

THE CONSTITUTION OF THE UNITED STATES[1]

We the People of the United States, in Order to form a more perfect Union, establish Justice, insure domestic Tranquility, provide for the common defence, promote the general Welfare, and secure the Blessings of Liberty to ourselves and our Posterity, do ordain and establish this Constitution for the United States of America.

Article. I.

Section. 1. All legislative Powers herein granted shall be vested in a Congress of the United States, which shall consist of a Senate and House of Representatives.

Section. 2. The House of Representatives shall be composed of Members chosen every second Year by the People of the several States, and the Electors in each State shall have ⟨the⟩ Qualifications requisite for Electors of the most numerous Branch of the State Legislature.

No Person shall be a Representative who shall not have attained to the Age of twenty five Years, and been seven Years a Citizen of the United States, and who shall not, when elected, be an Inhabitant of that State in which he shall be chosen.

Representatives and direct Taxes shall be apportioned among the several States which may be included within this Union, according to their respective Numbers, which shall be determined by adding to the whole Number of free Persons, including those bound to Service for a Term of Years, and excluding Indians not taxed, three fifths of all other Persons. The actual Enumeration shall be made within three Years after the first Meeting of the Congress of the United States,

---

[1] The Constitution is engrossed on four sheets of parchment (23½″ × 27½″). The present copy attempts to reprint the original exactly, except that interlineations are indicated by enclosing them in angle brackets ⟨ ⟩. The indented note at the end is in the original.

and within every subsequent Term of ten Years, in such Manner as they shall by Law direct. The Number of Representatives shall not exceed one for every thirty[9] Thousand, but each State shall have at Least one Representative; and until such enumeration shall be made, the State of New Hampshire shall be entitled to chuse three, Massachusetts eight, Rhode-Island and Providence Plantations one, Connecticut five, New-York six, New Jersey four, Pennsylvania eight, Delaware one, Maryland six, Virginia ten, North Carolina five, South Carolina five, and Georgia three.

When vacancies happen in the Representation from any State, the Executive Authority thereof shall issue Writs of Election to fill such Vacancies.

The House of Representatives shall chuse their Speaker and other Officers; and shall have the sole Power of Impeachment.

Section. 3. The Senate of the United States shall be composed of two Senators from each State, chosen by the Legislature thereof, for six Years; and each Senator shall have one Vote.

Immediately after they shall be assembled in Consequence of the first Election, they shall be divided as equally as may be into three Classes. The Seats of the Senators of the first Class shall be vacated at the Expiration of the second Year, of the second Class at the Expiration of the fourth Year, and of the third Class at the Expiration of the sixth Year, so that one third may be chosen every second Year; and if Vacancies happen by Resignation, or otherwise, during the Recess of the Legislature of any State, the Executive thereof may make temporary Appointments until the next Meeting of the Legislature, which shall then fill such Vacancies.

No Person shall be a Senator who shall not have attained to the Age of thirty Years, and been nine Years a Citizen of the United States, and who shall not, when elected, be an inhabitant of that State for which he shall be chosen.

The Vice President of the United States shall be Presi-

[9] An erasure in the manuscript.

dent of the Senate, but shall have no Vote, unless they be equally divided.

The Senate shall chuse their other Officers, and also a President pro tempore, in the Absence of the Vice President, or when he shall exercise the Office of President of the United States.

The Senate shall have the sole Power to try all Impeachments. When sitting for that Purpose, they shall be on Oath or Affirmation. When the President of the United States ⟨is tried,⟩ the Chief Justice shall preside: And no Person shall be convicted without the Concurrence of two thirds of the Members present.

Judgment in Cases of Impeachment shall not extend further than to removal from Office, and disqualification to hold and enjoy any Office of honor, Trust or Profit under the United States: but the Party convicted shall nevertheless be liable and subject to Indictment, Trial, Judgment and Punishment, according to Law.

Section. 4. The Times, Places and Manner of holding Elections for Senators and Representatives, shall be prescribed in each State by the Legislature thereof; but the Congress may at any time by Law make or alter such Regulations, except as to the Places of chusing Senators.

The Congress shall assemble at least once in every Year, and such Meeting shall be on the first Monday in December, unless they shall by Law appoint a different Day.

Section. 5. Each House shall be the Judge of the Elections, Returns and Qualifications of its own Members, and a Majority of each shall constitute a Quorum to do Business; but a smaller Number may adjourn from day to day, and may be authorized to compel the Attendance of absent Members, in such Manner, and under such Penalties as each House may provide.

Each House may determine the Rules of its Proceedings, punish its Members for disorderly Behaviour, and, with the Concurrence of two thirds, expel a Member.

Each House shall keep a Journal of its Proceedings, and from time to time publish the same, excepting such Parts as may in

their Judgment require Secrecy; and the Yeas and Nays of the Members of either House on any question shall, at the Desire of one fifth of those Present, be entered on the Journal.

Neither House, during the Session of Congress, shall, without the Consent of the other, adjourn for more than three days, nor to any other Place than that in which the two Houses shall be sitting.

Section. 6. The Senators and Representatives shall receive a Compensation for their Services, to be ascertained by Law, and paid out of the Treasury of the United States. They shall in all Cases, except Treason, Felony and Breach of the Peace, be privileged from Arrest during their Attendance at the Session of their respective Houses, and in going to and returning from the same; and for any Speech or Debate in either House, they shall not be questioned in any other Place.

No Senator or Representative shall, during the Time for which he was elected, be appointed to any civil Office under the Authority of the United States, which shall have been created, or the Emoluments whereof shall have been encreased during such time; and no Person holding any Office under the United States, shall be a Member of either House during his Continuance in Office.

Section. 7. All Bills for raising Revenue shall originate in the House of Representatives; but the Senate may propose or concur with Amendments as on other Bills.

Every Bill which shall have passed the House of Representatives and the Senate, shall, before it become a Law, be presented to the President of the United States; If he approve he shall sign it, but if not he shall return it, with his Objections to that House in which it shall have originated, who shall enter the Objections at large on their Journal, and proceed to reconsider it. If after such Reconsideration two thirds of that House shall agree to pass the Bill, it shall be sent, together with the Objections, to the other House, by which it shall likewise be reconsidered, and if approved by two thirds of that House, it shall become a Law. But in all such Cases the Votes of both Houses shall be determined by yeas and Nays, and the Names of the Persons voting for and against the Bill

shall be entered on the Journal of each House respectively. If any Bill shall not be returned by the President within ten Days (Sundays excepted) after it shall have been presented to him, the Same shall be a Law, in like Manner as if he had signed it, unless the Congress by their Adjournment prevent its Return, in which Case it shall not be a Law.

Every Order, Resolution, or Vote to which the Concurrence of the Senate and House of Representatives may be necessary (except on a question of Adjournment) shall be presented to the President of the United States; and before the Same shall take Effect, shall be approved by him, or being disapproved by him, shall be repassed by two thirds of the Senate and House of Representatives, according to the Rules and Limitations prescribed in the Case of a Bill.

Section. 8. The Congress shall have Power To lay and collect Taxes, Duties, Imposts and Excises, to pay the Debts and Provide for the common Defence and general Welfare of the United States; but all Duties, Imposts and Excises shall be uniform throughout the United States;

To borrow Money on the credit of the United States;

To regulate Commerce with foreign Nations, and among the several States, and with the Indian Tribes;

To establish an uniform Rule of Naturalization, and uniform Laws on the subject of Bankruptcies throughout the United States;

To coin Money, regulate the Value thereof, and of foreign Coin, and fix the Standard of Weights and Measures;

To provide for the Punishment of counterfeiting the Securities and current Coin of the United States;

To establish Post Offices and post Roads;

To promote the Progress of Science and useful Arts, by securing for limited Time to Authors and Inventors the exclusive Right to their respective Writings and Discoveries;

To constitute Tribunals inferior to the supreme Court;

To define and punish Piracies and Felonies committed on the high Seas, and Offences against the Law of Nations;

To declare War, grant Letters of Marque and Reprisal, and make Rules concerning Captures on Land and Water;

To raise and support Armies, but no Appropriation of Money to that Use shall be for a longer Term than two Years;

To provide and maintain a Navy;

To make Rules for the Government and Regulation of the land and naval Forces;

To provide for calling forth the Militia to execute the Laws of the Union, suppress Insurrections and repel Invasions;

To provide for organizing, arming, and disciplining, the Militia, and for governing such Part of them as may be employed in the Service of the United States, reserving to the States respectively, the Appointment of the Officers, and the Authority of training the Militia according to the discipline prescribed by Congress;

To exercise exclusive Legislation in all Cases whatsoever, over such District (not exceeding ten Miles square) as may, by Cession of Particular States, and the Acceptance of Congress, become the Seat of the Government of the United States, and to exercise like Authority over all Places purchased by the Consent of the Legislature of the State in which the Same shall be, for the Erection of Forts, Magazines, Arsenals, dock-Yards, and other needful Buildings;—And

To make all Laws which shall be necessary and proper for carrying into Execution the foregoing Powers, and all other Powers vested by this Constitution in the Government of the United States, or in any Department or Officer thereof.

Section. 9. The Migration or Importation of such Persons as any of the States now existing shall think proper to admit, shall not be prohibited by the Congress prior to the Year one thousand eight hundred and eight, but a Tax or duty may be imposed on such Importation, not exceeding ten dollars for each Person.

The Privilege of the Writ of Habeas Corpus shall not be suspended, unless when in Cases of Rebellion or Invasion the public Safety may require it.

No Bill of Attainder or ex post facto Law shall be passed.

No Capitation, or other direct, Tax shall be laid, unless in Proportion to the Census or Enumeration herein before directed to be taken.

No Tax or Duty shall be laid on Articles exported from any State.

No Preference shall be given by any Regulation of Commerce or Revenue to the Ports of one State over those of another: nor shall Vessels bound to, or from, one State, be obliged to enter, clear, or pay Duties in another.

No Money shall be drawn from the Treasury, but in Consequence of Appropriations made by Law; and a regular Statement and Account of the Receipts and Expenditures of all public Money shall be published from time to time.

No Title of Nobility shall be granted by the United States: And no Person holding any Office of Profit or Trust under them, shall, without the Consent of the Congress, accept of any present, Emolument, Office, or Title, of any kind whatever, from any King, Prince, or foreign State.

Section. 10. No State shall enter into any Treaty, Alliance, or Confederation; grant Letters of Marque and Reprisal; coin Money; emit Bills of Credit; make any Thing but gold and silver Coin a Tender in Payment of Debts; pass any Bill of Attainder, ex post facto Law, or Law impairing the Obligation of Contracts, or grant any Title of Nobility.

No State shall, without the Consent of ⟨the⟩ Congress, lay any Imposts or Duties on Imports or Exports, except what may be absolutely necessary for executing it's inspection Laws: and the net Produce of all Duties and Imposts, laid by any State on Imports or Exports, shall be for the Use of the Treasury of the United States; and all such Laws shall be subject to the Revision and Controul of ⟨the⟩ Congress.

No State shall, without the Consent of Congress, lay any Duty of Tonnage, keep Troops, or Ships of War in time of Peace, enter into any Agreement or Compact with another State, or with a foreign Power, or engage in War, unless actually invaded, or in such imminent Danger as will not admit of delay.

Article. II.

Section. 1. The executive Power shall be vested in a President of the United States of America. He shall hold his Office during the Term of four Years, and, together with

the Vice President, chosen for the same Term, be elected, as follows

Each State shall appoint, in such Manner as the Legislature thereof may direct, a Number of Electors, equal to the whole Number of Senators and Representatives to which the State may be entitled in the Congress: but no Senator or Representative, or Person holding an Office of Trust or Profit under the United States, shall be appointed an Elector.

The Electors shall meet in their respective States, and vote by Ballot for two Persons, of whom one at least shall not be an Inhabitant of the same State with themselves. And they shall make a List of all the Persons voted for, and of the Number of Votes for each; which List they shall sign and certify, and transmit sealed to the Seat of the Government of the United States, directed to the President of the Senate. The President of the Senate shall, in the Presence of the Senate and House of Representatives, open all the Certificates, and the Votes shall then be counted. The Person having the greatest Number of Votes shall be the President, if such Number be a Majority of the whole Number of Electors appointed; and if there be more than one who have such Majority, and have an equal Number of Votes, then the House of Representatives shall immediately chuse by Ballot one of them for President; and if no Person have a Majority, then from the five highest on the List the said House shall in like Manner chuse the President. But in chusing the President, the Votes shall be taken by States, the Representation from each State having one Vote; A quorum for this Purpose shall consist of a Member or Members from two thirds of the States, and a Majority of all the States shall be necessary to a Choice. In every Case, after the Choice of the President, the Person having the greatest Number of Votes of the Electors shall be the Vice President. But if there should remain two or more who have equal Votes, the Senate shall chuse from them by Ballot the Vice President.

The Congress may determine the Time of chusing the Electors, and the Day on which they shall give their Votes; which Day shall be the same throughout the United States.

No Person except a natural born Citizen, or a Citizen of the United States, at the time of the Adoption of this Constitution, shall be eligible to the Office of President; neither shall any Person be eligible to that Office who shall not have attained to the Age of thirty five Years, and been fourteen Years a Resident within the United States.

In Case of the Removal of the President from Office, or of his Death, Resignation, or Inability to discharge the Powers and Duties of the said Office, the Same shall devolve on the Vice President, and the Congress may by Law provide for the Case of Removal, Death, Resignation or Inability, both of the President and Vice President, declaring what Officer shall then act as President, and such Officer shall act accordingly, until the Disability be removed, or a President shall be elected.

The President shall, at stated Times, receive for his Services, a Compensation, which shall neither be encreased nor diminished during the Period for which he shall have been elected, and he shall not receive within that Period any other Emolument from the United States, or any of them.

Before he enter on the Execution of his Office, he shall take the following Oath or Affirmation: — "I do solemnly swear (or affirm) that I will faithfully execute the Office of President of the United States, and will to the best of my Ability, preserve, protect and defend the Constitution of the United States."

Section. 2. The President shall be Commander in Chief of the Army and Navy of the United States, and of the Militia of the several States, when called into the actual Service of the United States; he may require the Opinion, in writing, of the principal Officer in each of the executive Departments, upon any Subject relating to the Duties of their respective Offices, and he shall have Power to grant Reprieves and Pardons for Offences against the United States, except in Cases of Impeachment.

He shall have Power, by and with the Advice and Consent of the Senate, to make Treaties, provided two thirds of the Senators present concur; and he shall nominate, and by and

with the Advice and Consent of the Senate, shall appoint Ambassadors, other public Ministers and Consuls, Judges of the supreme Court, and all other Officers of the United States, whose Appointments are not herein otherwise provided for, and which shall be established by Law: but the Congress may by Law vest the Appointment of such inferior Officers, as they think proper, in the President alone, in the Courts of Law, or in the Heads of Departments.

The President shall have Power to fill up all Vacancies that may happen during the Recess of the Senate, by granting Commissions which shall expire at the End of their next Session.

Section. 3. He shall from time to time give to the Congress Information of the State of the Union, and recommend to their consideration such Measures as he shall judge necessary and expedient; he may, on extraordinary Occasions, convene both Houses, or either of them, and in Case of Disagreement between them, with Respect to the Time of Adjournment, he may adjourn them to such Time as he shall think proper; he shall receive Ambassadors and other public Ministers; he shall take Care that the Laws be faithfully executed, and shall Commission all the Officers of the United States.

Section. 4. The President, Vice President and all civil Officers of the United States, shall be removed from Office on Impeachment for, and conviction of, Treason, Bribery, or other high Crimes and Misdemeanors.

Article III.

Section. 1. The judicial Power of the United States, shall be vested in one supreme Court, and in such inferior Courts as the Congress may from time to time ordain and establish. The Judges, both of the supreme and inferior Courts, shall hold their Offices during good Behaviour, and shall, at stated Times, receive for their Services, a Compensation, which shall not be diminished during their Continuance in Office.

Section. 2. The judicial Power shall extend to all Cases, in

Law and Equity, arising under this Constitution, the Laws of the United States, and Treaties made, or which shall be made, under their Authority; — to all Cases affecting Ambassadors, other public Ministers and Consuls; — to all Cases of admiralty and maritime Jurisdiction; — to Controversies to which the United States shall be a Party; — to Controversies between two or more States; — between a State and Citizens of another State; — between Citizens of different States, — between Citizens of the same State claiming Lands under Grants of different States, and between a State, or the Citizens thereof, and foreign States, Citizens or Subjects.

In all Cases affecting Ambassadors, other public Ministers and Consuls, and those in which a State shall be Party, the supreme Court shall have original Jurisdiction. In all the other Cases before mentioned, the supreme Court shall have appellate Jurisdiction, both as to Law and Fact, with such Exceptions, and under such Regulations as the Congress shall make.

The Trial of all Crimes, except in Cases of Impeachment, shall be by Jury; and such Trial shall be held in the State where the said Crimes shall have been committed; but when not committed within any State, the Trial shall be at such Place or Places as the Congress may by Law have directed.

Section. 3. Treason against the United States, shall consist only in levying War against them, or in adhering to their Enemies, giving them Aid and Comfort. No Person shall be convicted of Treason unless on the Testimony of two Witnesses to the same overt Act, or on Confession in open Court.

The Congress shall have Power to declare the Punishment of Treason, but no Attainder of Treason shall work Corruption of Blood, or Forfeiture except during the Life of the Person attainted.

Article. IV.

Section. 1. Full Faith and Credit shall be given in each State to the public Acts, Records, and judicial Proceedings of every other State. And the Congress may by general Laws prescribe the Manner in which such Acts, Records and Proceedings shall be proved, and the Effect thereof.

Section. 2. The Citizens of each State shall be entitled to all Privileges and Immunities of Citizens in the several States.

A Person charged in any State with Treason, Felony, or other Crime, who shall flee from Justice, and be found in another State, shall on Demand of the executive Authority of the State from which he fled, be delivered up, to be removed to the State having Jurisdiction of the Crime.

No Person held to Service or Labour in one State, under the Laws thereof, escaping into another, shall, in Consequence of any Law or Regulation therein, be discharged from such Service or Labour, but shall be delivered up on Claim of the Party to whom such Service or Labour may be due.

Section. 3. New States may be admitted by the Congress into this Union; but no new State shall be formed or erected within the Jurisdiction of any other State; nor any State be formed by the Junction of two or more States, or Parts of States, without the Consent of the Legislatures of the States concerned as well as of the Congress.

The Congress shall have Power to dispose of and make all needful Rules and Regulations respecting the Territory or other Property belonging to the United States; and nothing in this Constitution shall be so construed as to Prejudice any Claims of the United States, or of any particular State.

Section. 4. The United States shall guarantee to every State in this Union a Republican Form of Government, and shall protect each of them against Invasion; and on Application of the Legislature, or of the Executive (when the Legislature cannot be convened) against domestic Violence.

Article. V.

The Congress, whenever two thirds of both Houses shall deem it necessary, shall propose Amendments to this Constitution, or, on the Application of the Legislatures of two thirds of the several States, shall call a Convention for proposing Amendments, which, in either Case, shall be valid to all Intents and Purposes, as Part of this Constitution, when ratified by the Legislatures of three fourths of the several

States, or by Conventions in three fourths thereof, as the one or the other Mode of Ratification may be proposed by the Congress; Provided that no Amendment which may be made prior to the Year One thousand eight hundred and eight shall in any Manner affect the first and fourth Clauses in the Ninth Section of the first Article; and that no State, without its Consent, shall be deprived of it's equal Suffrage in the Senate.

Article. VI.

All Debts contracted and Engagements entered into, before the Adoption of this Constitution, shall be as valid against the United States under this Constitution, as under the Confederation.

This Constitution, and the Laws of the United States which shall be made in Pursuance thereof; and all Treaties made, or which shall be made, under the Authority of the United States, shall be the supreme Law of the Land; and the Judges in every State shall be bound thereby, any Thing in the Constitution or Laws of any State to the Contrary notwithstanding.

The Senators and Representatives before mentioned, and the Members of the several State Legislatures, and all executive and judicial Officers, both of the United States and of the several States, shall be bound by Oath or Affirmation, to support this Constitution; but no religious Test shall ever be required as a Qualification to any Office or public Trust under the United States.

Article. VII.

The Ratification of the Conventions of nine States, shall be sufficient for the Establishment of this Constitution between the States so ratifying the Same.

⟨The Word, "the ", being interlined between the seventh and eighth Lines of the first Page, the Word "Thirty" being partly written on an Erazure in the fifteenth Line of the first Page. The Words "is tried" being interlined between the thirty second and thirty third Lines of the first Page and the

Done in Convention by the Unanimous Consent of the States present the Seventeenth Day of September in the Year of our Lord one thousand seven hun-

THE CONSTITUTION

Word "the" being interlined between the forty third and forty fourth Lines of the second Page.〉

dred and Eighty seven and of the Independance of the United States of America the Twelfth In witness whereof We have hereunto subscribed our Names,

Attest William Jackson Secretary

Go. Washington — Presidt. and deputy from Virginia.

New Hampshire	John Langdon Nicholas Gilman
Massachusetts	Nathaniel Gorham Rufus King
Connecticut	Wm: Saml. Johnson Roger Sherman
New York . .	.Alexander Hamilton
New Jersey	Wil: Livingston David Brearley. Wm. Paterson. Jona: Dayton
Pensylvania	B Franklin Thomas Mifflin Robt Morris Geo. Clymer Thos. FitzSimons Jared Ingersoll James Wilson Gouv Morris
Delaware	Geo: Read Gunning Bedford jun John Dickinson Richard Bassett Jaco: Broom
Maryland	James McHenry Dan of St Thos. Jenifer Danl. Carroll.
Virginia	John Blair — James Madison Jr.

THE CONSTITUTION

North Carolina	Wm. Blount Richd. Dobbs Spaight. Hu Williamson
South Carolina	J. Rutledge Charles Cotesworth Pinckney Charles Pinckney Pierce Butler.
Georgia	William Few Abr Baldwin

In Convention Monday September 17th. 1787

Present

The States of

New Hampshire, Massachusetts, Connecticut, Mr. Hamilton from New York, New Jersey, Pennsylvania, Delaware, Maryland, Virginia, North Carolina, South Carolina and Georgia.

Resolved,

That the preceding Constitution be laid before the United States in Congress assembled, and that it is the Opinion of this Convention, that it should afterwards be submitted to a Convention of Delegates, chosen in each State by the People thereof, under the Recommendation of its Legislature, for their Assent and Ratification; and that each Convention assenting to, and ratifying the Same, should give Notice thereof to the United States in Congress assembled.

Resolved, That it is the Opinion of this Convention, that as soon as the Conventions of nine States shall have ratified this Constitution, the United States in Congress assembled should fix a Day on which Electors should be appointed by the States which shall have ratified the same, and a Day on which the Electors should assemble to vote for the President, and the Time and place for commencing Proceedings under this Constitution. That after such Publication the Electors should be appointed, and the Senators and Representatives elected: That the Electors should meet on the Day fixed for the Elec-

tion of the President, and should transmit their votes certified signed, sealed and directed, as the Constitution requires, to the Secretary of the United States in Congress assembled, that the Senators and Representatives should convene at the Time and Place asigned; that the Senators should appoint a President of the Senate, for the sole Purpose of receiving, opening and counting the Votes for President; and, that after he shall be chosen, the Congress, together with the President, should, without Delay, proceed to execute this Constitution.

By the Unanimous Order of the Convention

Go: Washington Presidt.

W. Jackson Secretary

[Letter to Congress]

In Convention, September 17, 1787.

Sir,

WE have now the honor to submit to the consideration of the United States in Congress assembled, that Constitution which has appeared to us the most adviseable.

The friends of our country have long seen and desired, that the power of making war, peace and treaties, that of levying money and regulating commerce, and the correspondent executive and judicial authorities should be fully and effectually vested in the general government of the Union: but the impropriety of delegating such extensive trust to one body of men is evident — Hence results the necessity of a different organization.

It is obviously impracticable in the fœderal government of these States, to secure all rights of independent sovereignty to each, and yet provide for the interest and safety of all — Individuals entering into society, must give up a share of liberty to preserve the rest. The magnitude of the sacrifice must depend as well on situation and circumstance, as on the object to be obtained. It is at all times difficult to draw with precision the line between those rights which must be surrendered, and those which may be reserved; and on the present occasion this difficulty was encreased by a difference among the

several States as to their situation, extent, habits, and particular interests.

In all our deliberations on this subject we kept steadily in our view, that which appears to us the greatest interest of every true American, the consolidation of our Union, in which is involved our prosperity, felicity, safety, perhaps our national existence. This important consideration, seriously and deeply impressed on our minds, led each State in the Convention to be less rigid on points of inferior magnitude, than might have been otherwise expected; and thus the Constitution, which we now present, is the result of a spirit of amity, and of that mutual deference and concession which the peculiarity of our political situation rendered indispensable.

That it will meet the full and entire approbation of every State is not perhaps to be expected; but each will doubtless consider, that had her interest alone been consulted, the consequences might have been particularly disagreeable or injurious to others; that it is liable to as few exceptions as could reasonably have been expected, we hope and believe; that it may promote the lasting welfare of that country so dear to us all, and secure her freedom and happiness, is our most ardent wish.

With great respect,

We have the honor to be.

SIR,

Your EXCELLENCY'S most

Obedient and humble Servants,

GEORGE WASHINGTON, PRESIDENT.

By unanimous Order of the CONVENTION.

HIS EXCELLENCY

The President of Congress.

[Subsequent amendments to the Constitution are printed in Volume IV.]